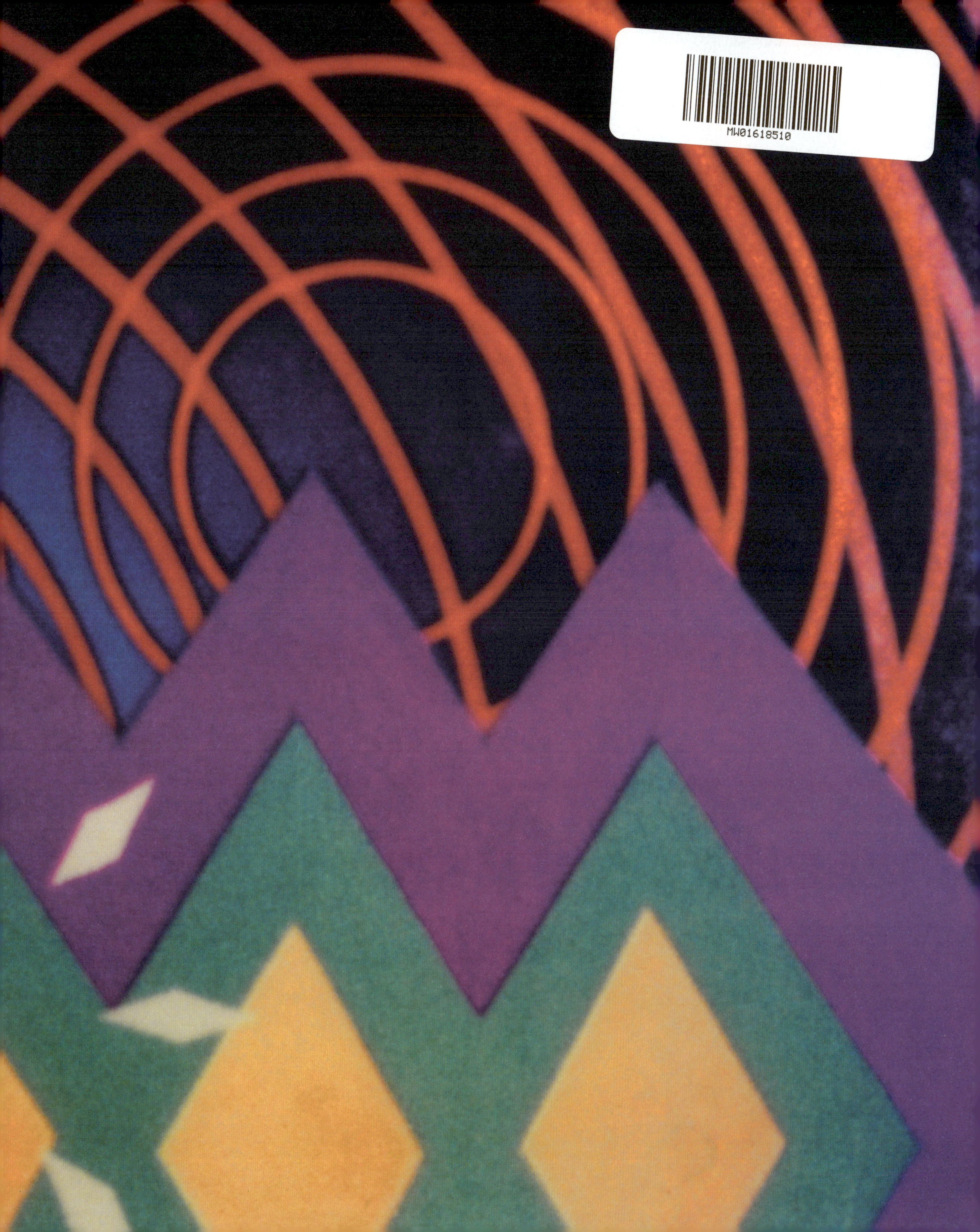

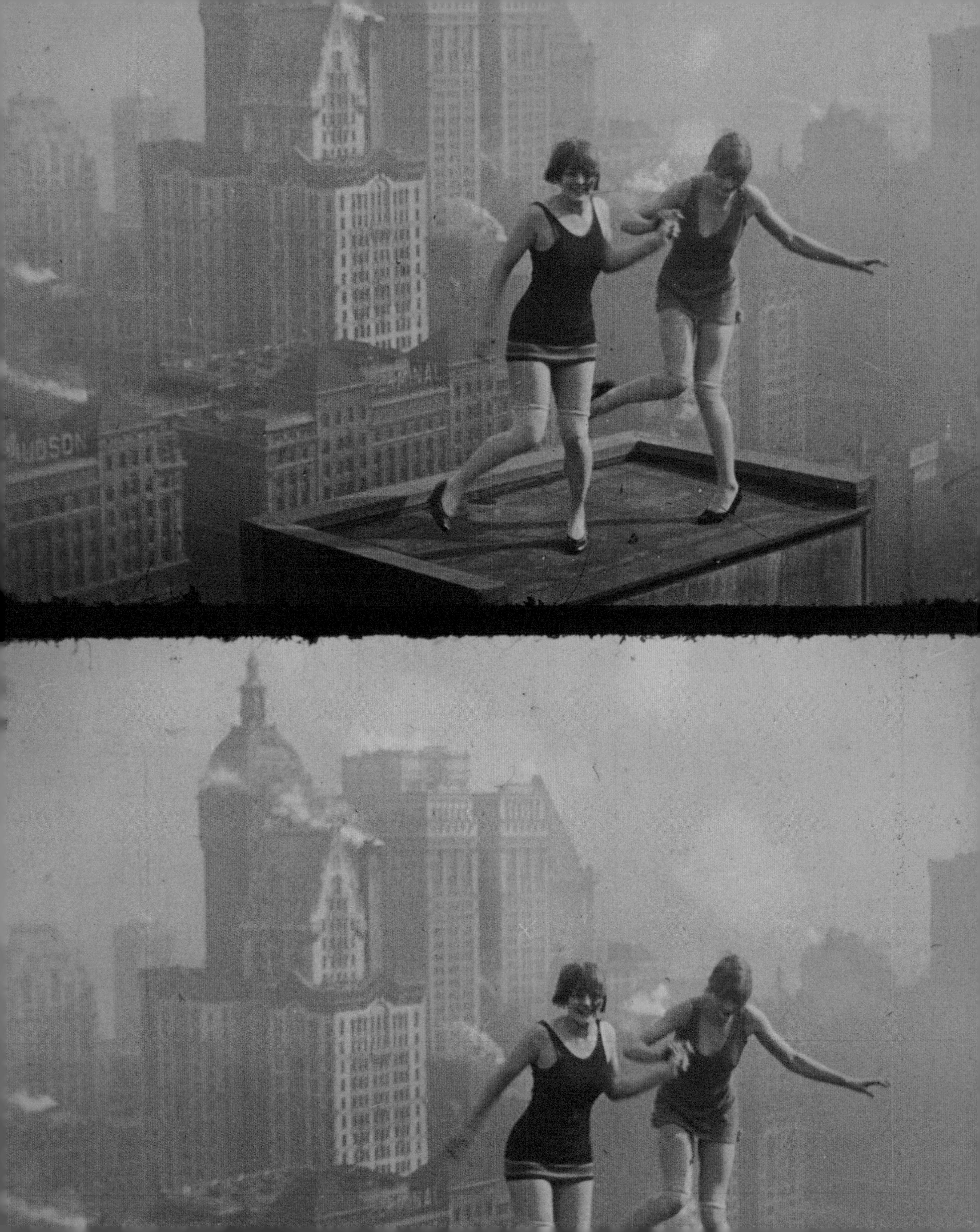

COLOR IN MOTION

CHROMATIC EXPLORATIONS OF CINEMA

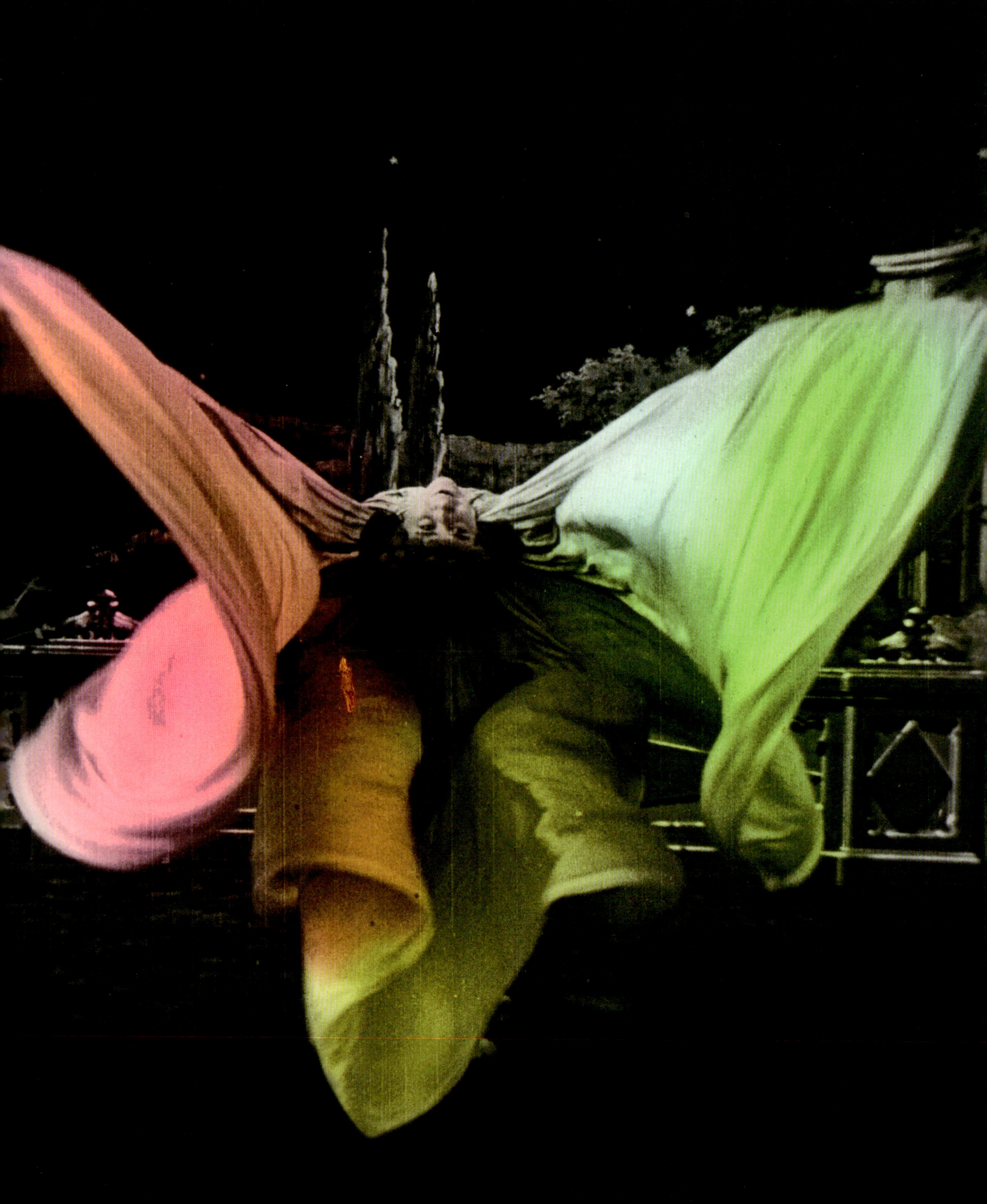

COLOR IN MOTION

CHROMATIC EXPLORATIONS OF CINEMA

EDITED BY
JESSICA NIEBEL
AND SOPHIA SERRANO

WITH CONTRIBUTIONS BY
BARBARA FLUECKIGER, ALEXANDRA JAMES SALICHS,
RANJANI MAZUMDAR, SARAH STREET,
KIRSTEN MOANA THOMPSON, AND JOSHUA YUMIBE

ACADEMY MUSEUM OF MOTION PICTURES, LOS ANGELES
DELMONICO BOOKS • D.A.P., NEW YORK

CONTENTS

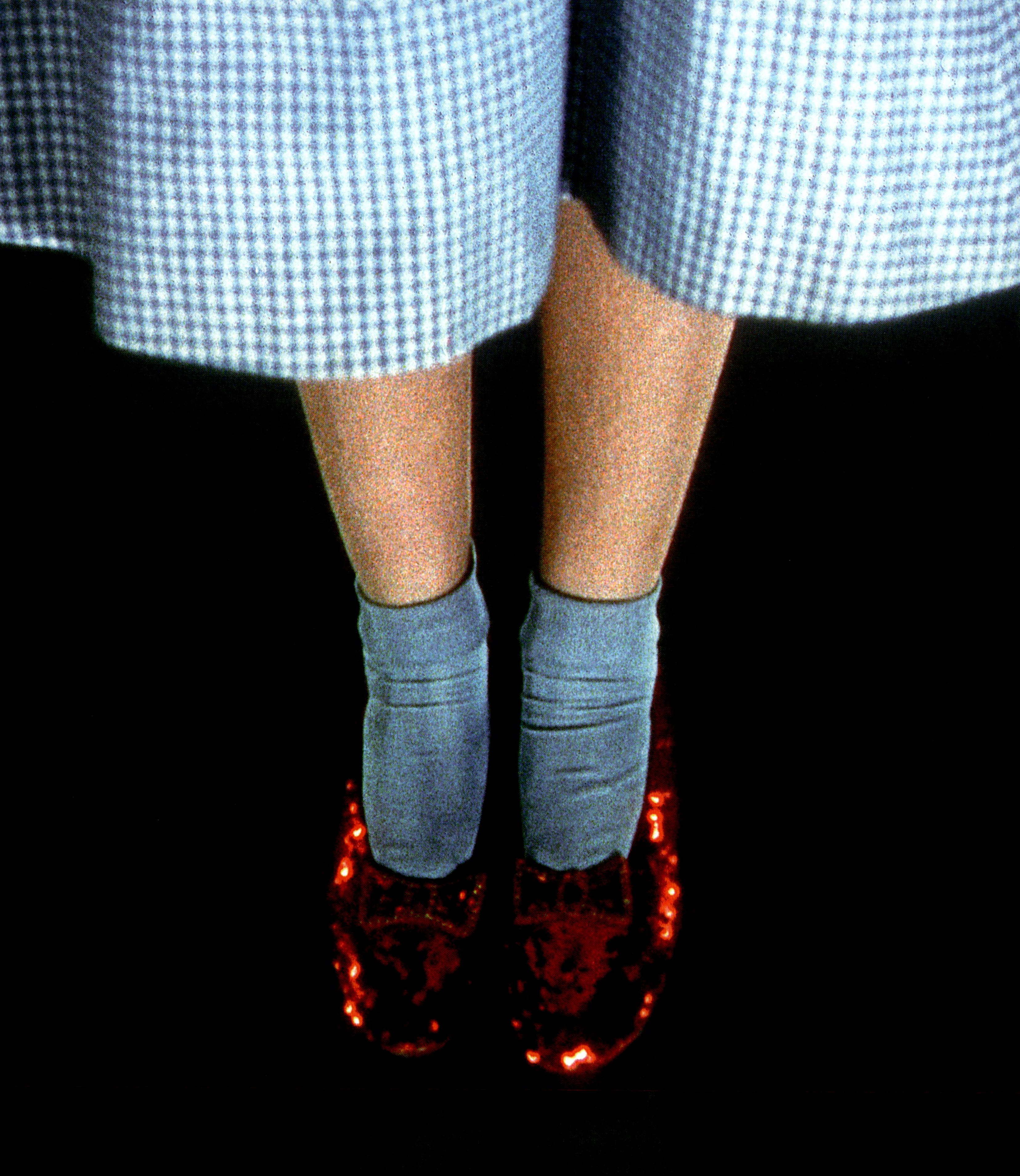

the earliest hand-painted films to Technicolor and today's digital colorization. Many people don't realize that, as early as the 1890s, much of silent cinema was in color—though sadly the dyes on tinted and toned prints have faded over decades. They also may not know that women were the main workforce behind the hand-painted techniques that first produced these effects, a tradition that continued as the practice evolved. Cinematic color works as a narrative device, a psychological phenomenon, and a means of artistic experimentation. It can be characterized as both an abstract and emotional sensation while simultaneously being the tangible result of dyes, chemicals, and other technological interventions. The results onscreen may often go unnoticed as effortless and natural aspects of the film image. However, a behind-the-scenes look at what constitutes color in cinema reveals a tremendous amount of labor, expertise, and technical detail.

The Wizard of Oz (USA, 1939, dir. Victor Fleming)

Color in Motion looks at the contributions of countless technicians and artists, especially their drive to produce colors in the name of expanding the cinematic experience. When we celebrate a famous color film such as *The Wizard of Oz* (USA, 1939), we acknowledge color director Natalie Kalmus, a critical figure in Technicolor's takeover of Hollywood and the developer of color palettes for countless classic-era movies. In looking at color innovations in iconic films including *Vertigo* (USA, 1958) and *2001: A Space Odyssey* (USA/UK, 1968), we highlight the contributions of artists and digital effects inventors such as James and John Whitney. When thinking about the standard practice of color calibration, we consider the many nameless "leader ladies" whose images were used by technicians to ensure uniformity in film exposure—a practice that favored white skin and fostered racial biases on film materials. Additionally, the scope of this project is global, as we highlight the history of color technologies, both in Los Angeles and around the world. There is no one singular history to color in film, but instead a myriad of moments that contributed to the uneven and idiosyncratic evolution of the practice.

I want to thank Senior Exhibitions Curator Jessica Niebel and her project team—Assistant Curator Sophia Serrano, Curatorial Assistant Manouchka Kelly Labouba, and Research Assistant Alexandra James Salichs—for their vision and dedication to capturing the historical nuances, technological facets, and aesthetic beauty of this underexplored topic. Academy CEO Bill Kramer and Chief Operating Officer Brendan Connell, Jr., supported us in making this an institution-wide effort. Academy Museum Chief Audience Officer Amy Homma helped expand this project's scope across our museum's many departments. I must also acknowledge the members of the Academy Museum Board of Trustees, led by Chair Ted Sarandos and Vice Chair Miky Lee, as well as Dominic Ng and Patricia Bellinger Balzer, co-Chairs of the Collections and Exhibitions Committee, for their commitment to sharing the many stories of cinema in our galleries and beyond.

Immersive, exciting, and unexpected, *Color in Motion* uncovers over a century of histories, both known and unfamiliar. This effort could only be realized with the generous collaboration of other institutions around the world, among them La Cinémathèque Française, Paris; the George Eastman Museum, Rochester, NY; the Center for Visual Music, Los Angeles; the American Society of Cinematographers Museum, Los Angeles; the Collection of Motion Picture Costume Design, Los Angeles; the Museum of Popular Culture, Seattle; Walt Disney Animation Studios, Burbank; the National Museum of American History, Washington, DC; and our own Academy Film Archive and Margaret

Herrick Library. I would especially like to acknowledge the international film archives that allowed us to produce new scans of rare film prints so our audiences can experience colors from the silent era as authentically as possible: Eye Filmmuseum, Amsterdam; Lichtspiel/Kinemathek Bern, Switzerland; Bundesarchiv-Filmarchiv, Berlin; and the Library of Congress, Washington, DC.

Color in Motion would not have been possible without the Getty Foundation, and I extend my deepest thanks to Director Joan Weinstein, Senior Program Officer Heather MacDonald, and Getty Trust President and Chief Executive Officer Katherine E. Fleming. We are so thankful to be part of this monumental PST ART initiative across Southern California. In addition to enabling us to further explore our own institutional assets and ambitions, it has given us a platform to connect and enter into dialogue with so many other institutions, artists, and specialists about critical issues our communities need to solve together. Our thanks also go to the Los Angeles County Board of Supervisors and the Los Angeles County Department of Arts and Culture, led by Director Kristin Sakoda. With that, I encourage you all to experience cinematic color in a brand-new light.

Jacqueline Stewart

Director and President

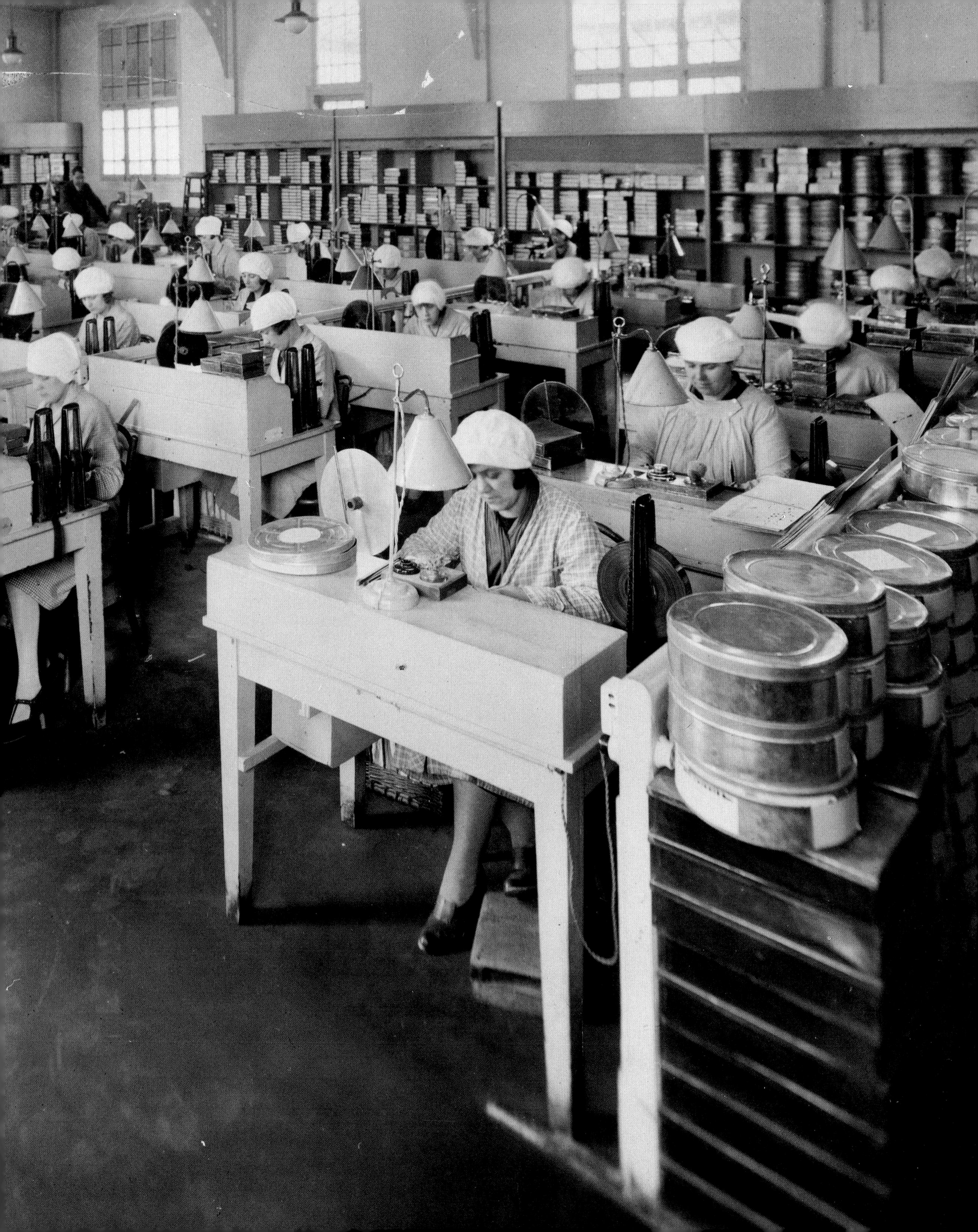

JESSICA NIEBEL

Color is a captivating yet complex phenomenon. My fascination with it, particularly in the context of film, began to deepen around 2015. As I delved into the subject, I didn't find much literature on it and so engaged with film historians and neurobiologists who specialized in the field. It quickly became evident that color—the way we perceive it and how filmmakers employ it as a narrative tool—constituted a challenging subject for an exhibition. When the Getty Foundation issued a call for exhibition proposals for their new PST ART cycle, *Art & Science Collide*, I saw the perfect opportunity to dive into this subject further. I was particularly interested in exploring the history of film colors and the overlooked role of women in this narrative. Simultaneously, I couldn't ignore the fascinating impact of colors on the human psyche and their capacity to evoke moods and sensations.

Thus, I found myself embarking on a journey with fellow team members Sophia Serrano, Alexandra James Salichs, and Manouchka Kelly Labouba into the intricate world of cinematic colors. It was important to us to approach the exhibition and this accompanying catalogue from three distinct angles—technological, artistic, and experiential—spanning cinema's origins to the present day. It must be emphasized that, while color was an important part of filmmaking from the medium's inception at the end of the 1800s, the development of color technologies, at least those that were commercially sensible, was challenging, long,

Workers in film assembly room at Pathé Studios, Vincennes, France, undated

and complex. It was driven forward by entrepreneurs and those filmmakers who desired to use color to add either realism or fantastical expression to their works. As technologies developed and filmmakers expanded the use of color as a tool for narrative or mood, the breadth of its impact on viewers widened. Whether tapping into the spectacular, psychological, or sensory, color became an integral part of the cinematic experience. As curators, we aspired to offer visitors not only conscious learning opportunities and visual beauty but also emotional connection through an engagement of the senses. Like color itself, we aimed to address both the rational and the irrational, crafting an exhibition that is entertaining and meaningful, with the hope that our catalogue will achieve a similar effect.

But first, before setting off on our journey, we had to ask: What is color? Color exists as either light or pigment, but as everyone perceives color subjectively, how can we define common ground when we speak about it? A conversation with experts Charles Poynton, Andrew Stockman, and Laurens Orij for this publication attempts to demystify color and shed light on the principles of human color perception and its translation into the technical production of colors in film, particularly through digital technologies.

With that knowledge in mind, we went back to the beginning of cinema to take a closer look at the fascination with the new medium. Still photography had been around for over half a century when, at the end of the 1800s, the Lumière brothers began introducing moving images to audiences all around the world. Now it was possible to photographically capture people in their movements. Motion became a sensation, and adding to the sensation was the idea of color. While early film still had to rely on the paints and dyes that were applied to the film stock through hand painting, stenciling, tinting, or toning, color nevertheless enhanced the motion presented on the big screen.

We chose to open with an early hand-colored film of the Serpentine Dance, a form of modern dance first developed by Loïe Fuller at the end of the nineteenth century. This dance was popularized in early film, a testament to its success in showcasing a new form of expression while amplifying the spectacle of colors set in motion. The serpentine dancer leads the way to the exhibition's first gallery, "Color and Motion," which features a large projection and costume displays, bringing together filmic dance scenes from the United States to India and highlighting the expressiveness and dynamism of colors in motion. The connection between physical movement, flowing textiles, femininity, and color is something I take a closer look at in my essay in this volume.

Before visitors enter "Color and Motion," however, they encounter dance scenes from the first commercially released three-strip Technicolor film, the animated Silly Symphony *Flowers and Trees* (USA, 1932). As Kirsten Moana Thompson discusses in her essay on American animation in color, Walt Disney had long been on the lookout for a convincing technology that would make his productions chromatic, thus adding expressivity and entertainment to his films. He found it in the Technicolor IV process, which he started to implement after a demonstration by Herbert and Natalie Kalmus in 1932. Although the switch to color was expensive and brought with it great changes to the production process, Disney felt it was well worth the risk. History would prove him right. After successfully using the Technicolor IV process for short films, Disney applied it to their production of *Snow White and the Seven Dwarfs* (USA, 1937) to become the first feature-length animated film to employ Technicolor's dye-transfer process to produce an actual color print. (Lotte Reiniger had used color tinting for her silhouette animation *The Adventures of Prince Achmed* [*Die Abenteuer des Prinzen Achmed*, Germany, 1926].)

The "Technologies and Spectacles" gallery then offers visitors an opportunity to delve into the materiality of film and historical color technologies such as Technicolor, stenciling, and Kinemacolor. These are but a few of the countless color technologies that were developed over time. Barbara Flueckiger illuminates this history in her comprehensive essay in this volume, and we are also pleased to include an excerpt from her Timeline of Historical Film Colors, a website that has earned international scholarly acclaim. Two popular early methods of applying color to film, tinting and toning, evolved to dominate the film industry throughout the 1920s. A monochrome film installation in the exhibition immerses visitors in the vibrant colors of films from the silent era. It is represented here by a selection of film frames illustrating the otherworldly allure of this imagery and its potent visual expression. Although the practice of dyeing film stock has disappeared, the bold monochromatic aesthetic is embraced by many contemporary filmmakers and endures into the digital age.

Learning more about color technologies not only furthers our understanding of its scientific and artistic qualities but also points to color as a signifier of cultural expression and social definition. In her text for this catalogue, Ranjani Mazumdar explores art direction in Bombay cinema following the introduction of Eastmancolor to India in the 1960s, emphasizing how the placement of other media forms, such as the black-and-white photograph, in colorful interior designs created dialogues touching upon issues ranging from social class to the country's position in the world.

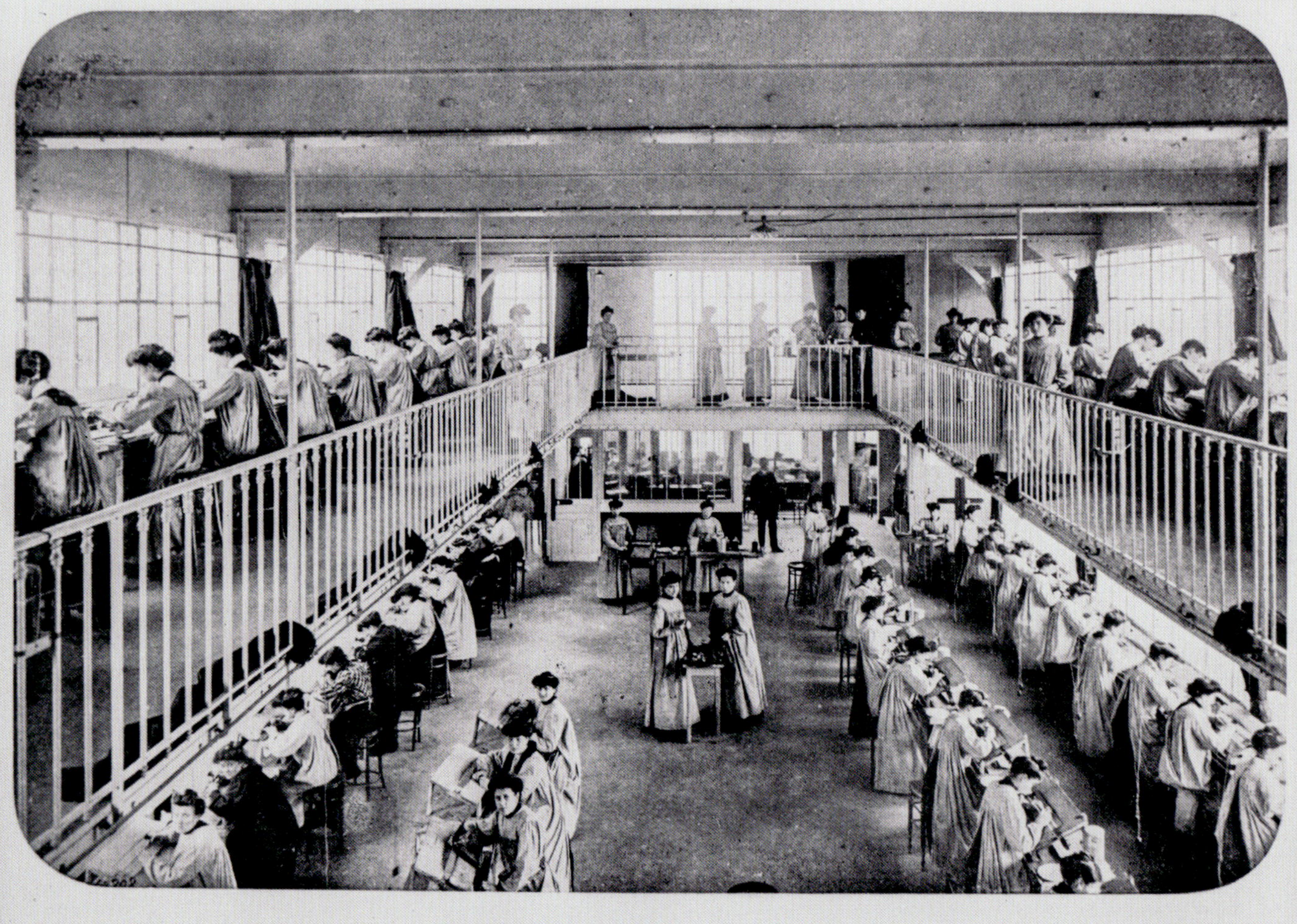

Color film laboratory at Pathé Studios, 1912

Some will be surprised to discover the significant role women played in the production of film colors and technologies, from Pathé's color room to Disney's Inking & Painting department and key figures such as Technicolor's Natalie Kalmus. Sarah Street's essay elaborates on women's contributions to the history and development of film colors that have often been overlooked. Just as the "leader ladies" ensured color accuracy at the beginning of each film reel, Sophia Serrano's conversation with members of the Chicago Film Society and their collaborators deepens our understanding of how films were calibrated to white women's skin tones, sparking questions about gender and race in this widespread practice. Expanding on the portrayal of people of color in film, Joshua Yumibe examines the challenges of accurately depicting Blackness with conventional color technologies and film stocks, revealing colonial contexts and inherent biases.

Considerations of the best film stock for a specific project's needs as well as availability and affordability impacted the color design of film productions until the digital age. In addition, hundreds of conscious choices on which colors to use in front of the camera had to be made by filmmakers interested in using color as a narrative tool

Organized by the colors of the spectrum, the exhibition's "Color as Character" gallery explores how filmmakers harness color as a potent cinematic device. Not only directors and cinematographers but also production, set, and costume designers, not to mention animators, employ colors to drive a film's narrative, convey meaning, shape characters, evoke moods, depict states of mind, and establish time and location. Notable instances of this, from Alfred Hitchcock's use of green in *Vertigo* (USA, 1958) to the yellow "Mexican filter" deployed in *Traffic* (USA, 2000) and the abundance of pink to define and challenge female sexuality and gender roles in *But I'm a Cheerleader* (USA, 1999), are examined in the color case studies within this book.

In contrast to narrative film, experimental works have envisioned color as a fundamental element of cinematic expression. The "Experimentation" gallery of the exhibition offers a rare opportunity to view full-length examples, highlighting their handcrafted artistry, vision, and creativity. Liberated from realism and the confines of storytelling, experimental films represent the purest exploration at the intersection of form, movement, sound, and color. In her essay, Sophia Serrano dives into this realm, exploring the close relationship between experimental artists and their techniques, some of which were adopted on a broader scale by major movie industries. Such films as Oskar Fischinger's *Circles* (*Kreise*, Germany, 1933–34), Len Lye's *Rainbow Dance* (UK, 1936), and Mary Ellen Bute's *Color Rhapsodie* (USA, 1948) captivate with their colorful imagination, polychromatic diversity, and innovative form. Rhythmically, colorful shapes dance across the screen, having freed themselves from the confines of the physical world and the human body.

While *Color in Motion* is an exhibition about color in film, it's also conceived as an emotional and sensory experience, designed to entertain, educate, and inspire. At the end of the exhibition, we return to the idea of dancing; three interactive experiences in the "Color Arcade" invite visitors to move their own bodies to activate colors in various ways, bringing full circle the idea of a direct connection between physical movement and film colors. These interactives are integrated into a futuristic gallery design that includes a projection of, among other clips, Stanley Kubrick's iconic Star Gate sequence from *2001: A Space Odyssey* (USA/UK, 1968), propelling us to another reality. It is our hope that this accompanying catalogue (which features an image from this sequence on its back cover) reflects the exhibition's kaleidoscopic experience, adding valuable insights and deepening the understanding of cinema's chromatic explorations while also celebrating the complex, captivating, and exuberant world of cinematic colors.

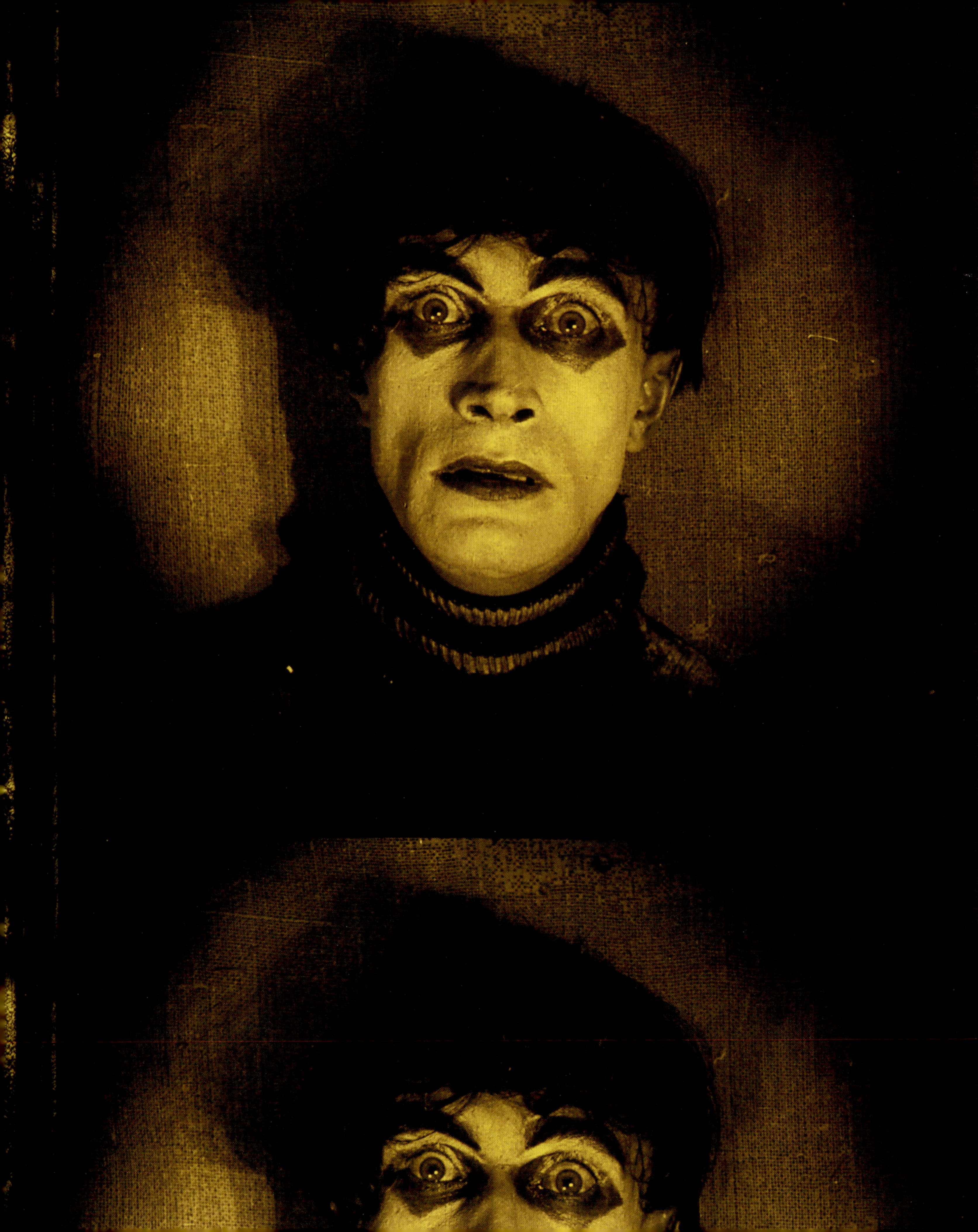

MONOCHROME FILM COLORS

Color has been applied to filmstrips since the earliest days of filmmaking. The practice of tinting films began as early as 1896; by the 1920s, an estimated 80 to 90 percent of all films were at least partially dyed. Often paired with toning, a chemical process that replaces the silver in the film's emulsion with a specific color, its results were stunning: monochrome images vibrant with color. While some associations were common, such as blue for nighttime, each film—and, at times, even each print—had an individual color scheme to support its narrative and to create mood. These colors faded over time, presenting a challenge for today's film restorers.

The following pages present new multispectral scans of original silent-era film prints archived at the Eye Filmmuseum, Amsterdam; Lichtspiel/Kinemathek Bern, Switzerland; and the Library of Congress, Washington, DC. The color of each film has been meticulously reconstructed by film historian Barbara Flueckiger and her Scan2Screen team. Rich with color and mesmerizing aesthetic appeal, the images give us a sense of how these films looked when they were first released.

The Cabinet of Dr. Caligari (*Das Cabinet des Dr. Caligari*, Germany, 1920, dir. Robert Wiene)

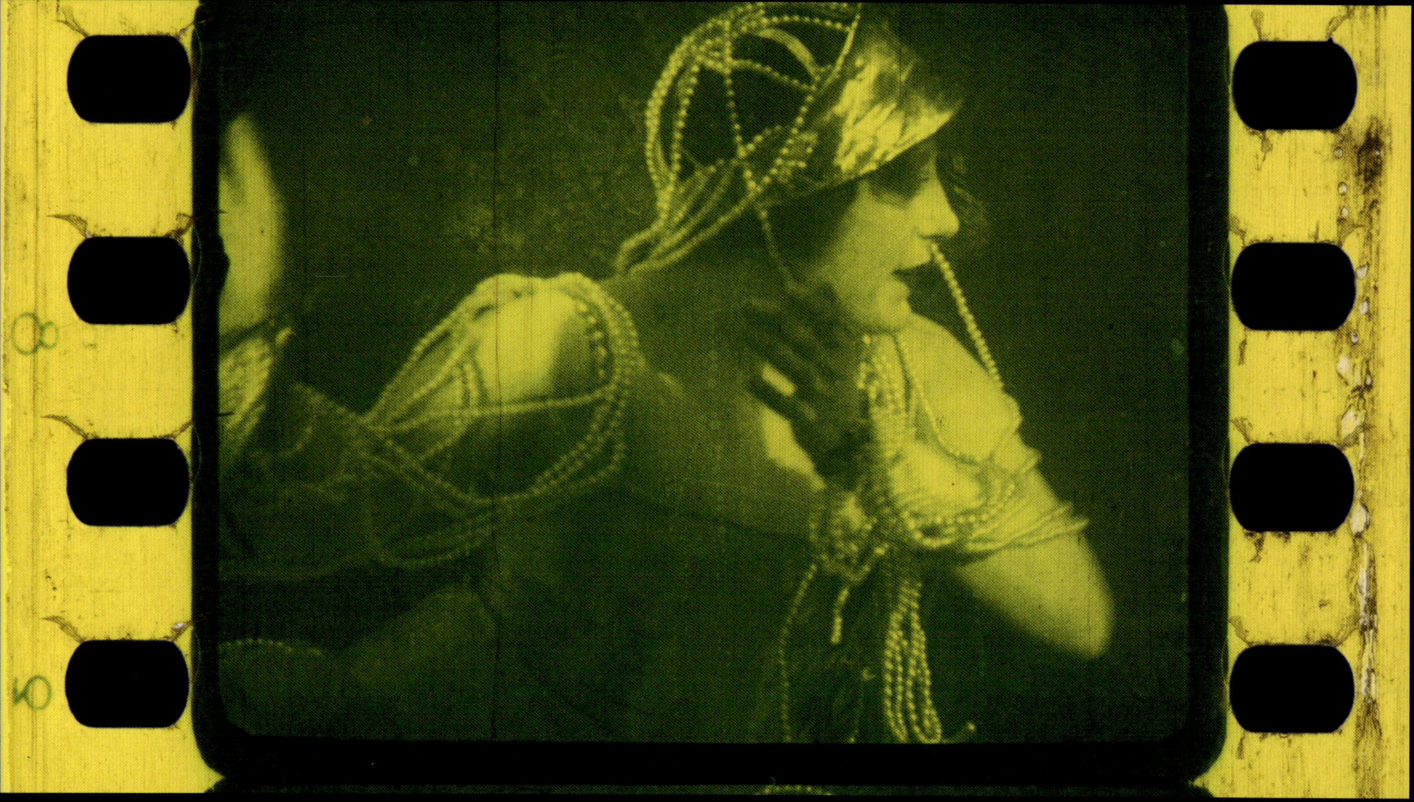

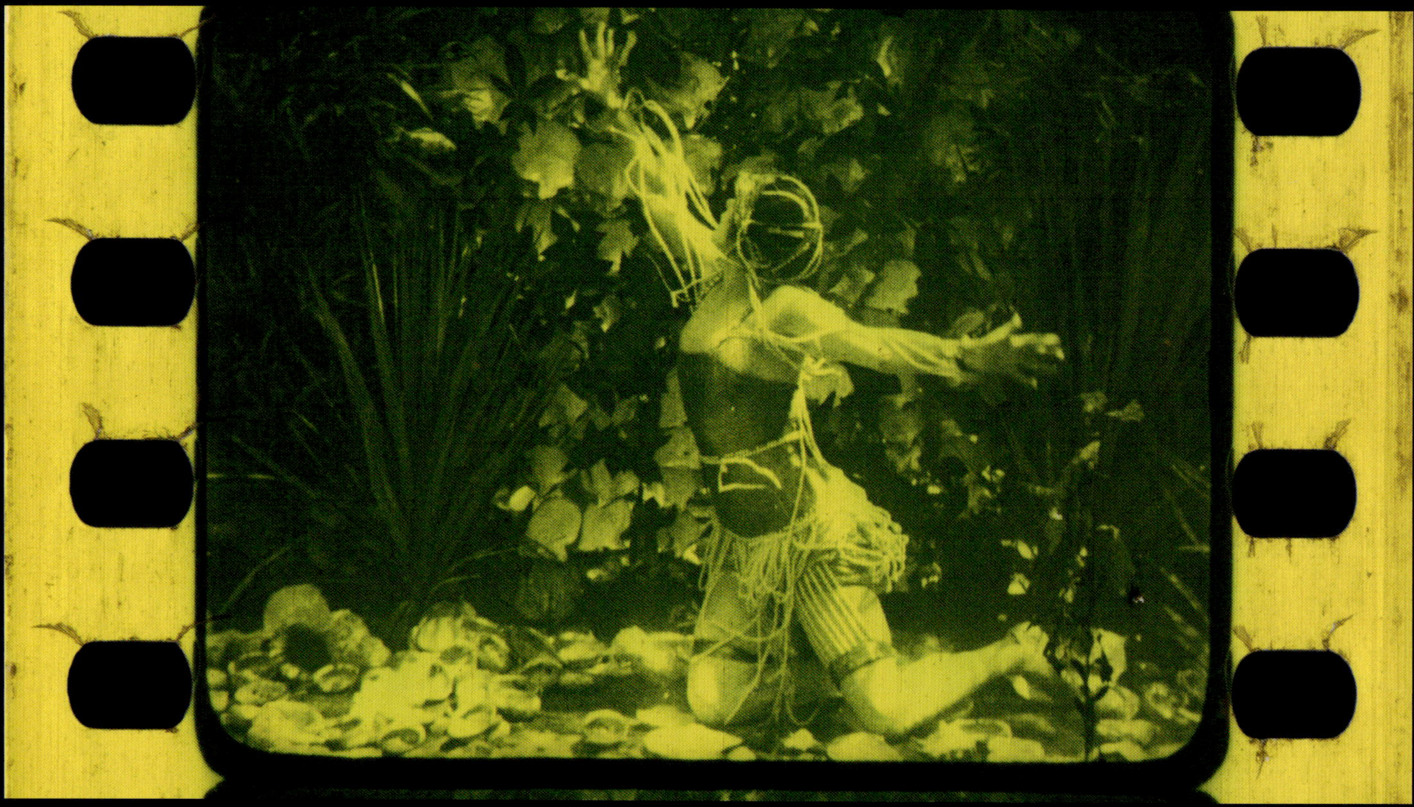

Venus of the South Seas (New Zealand, 1924, dir. James R. Sullivan)

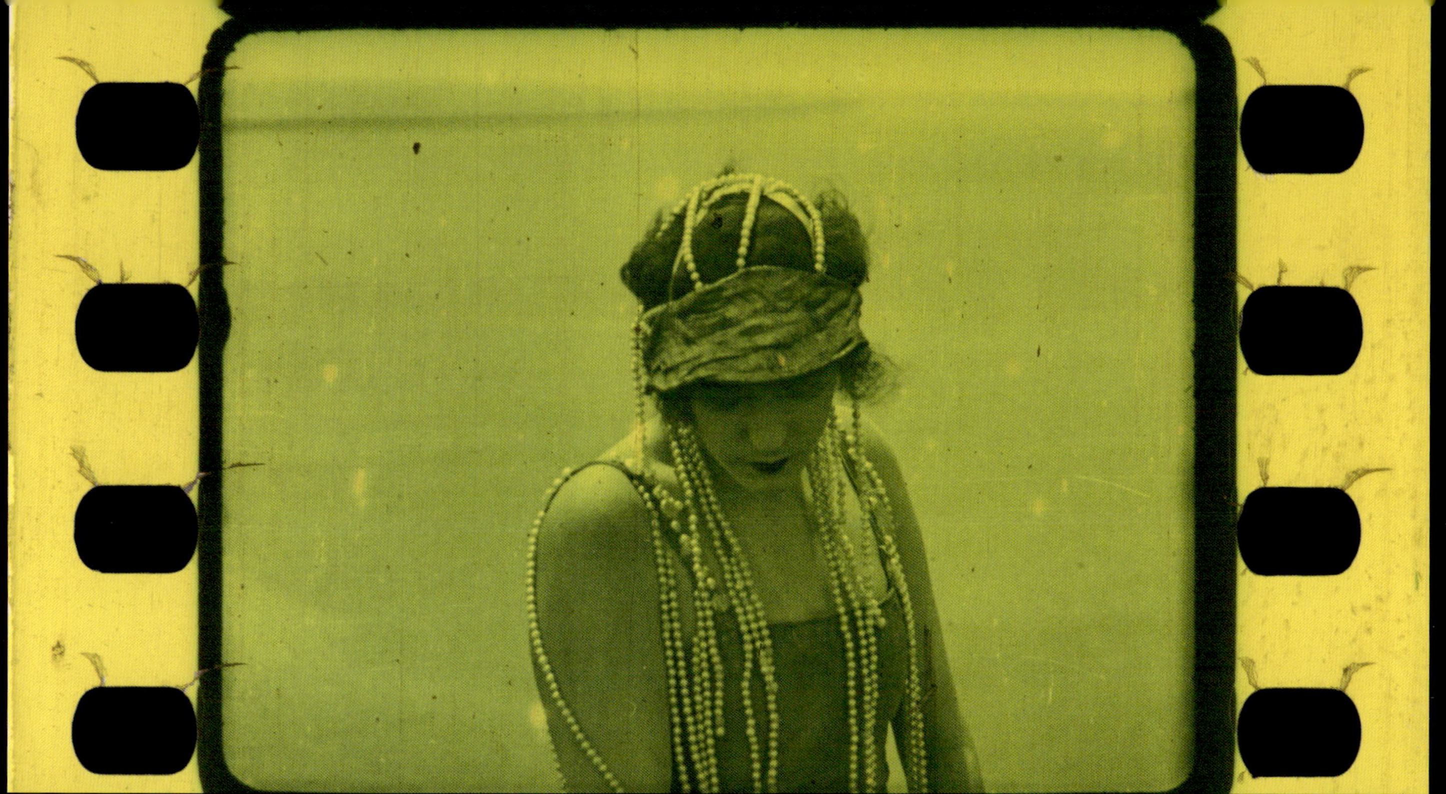

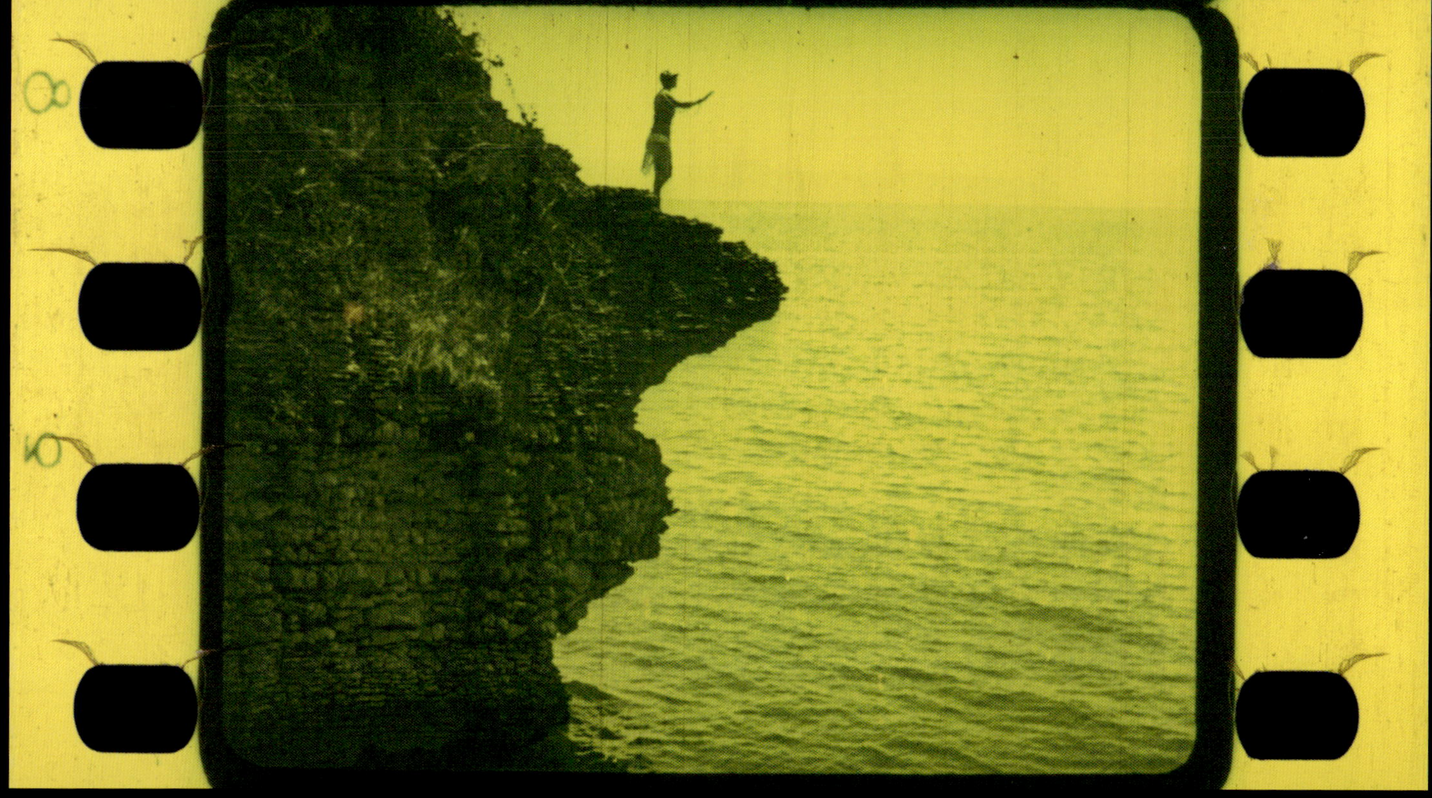

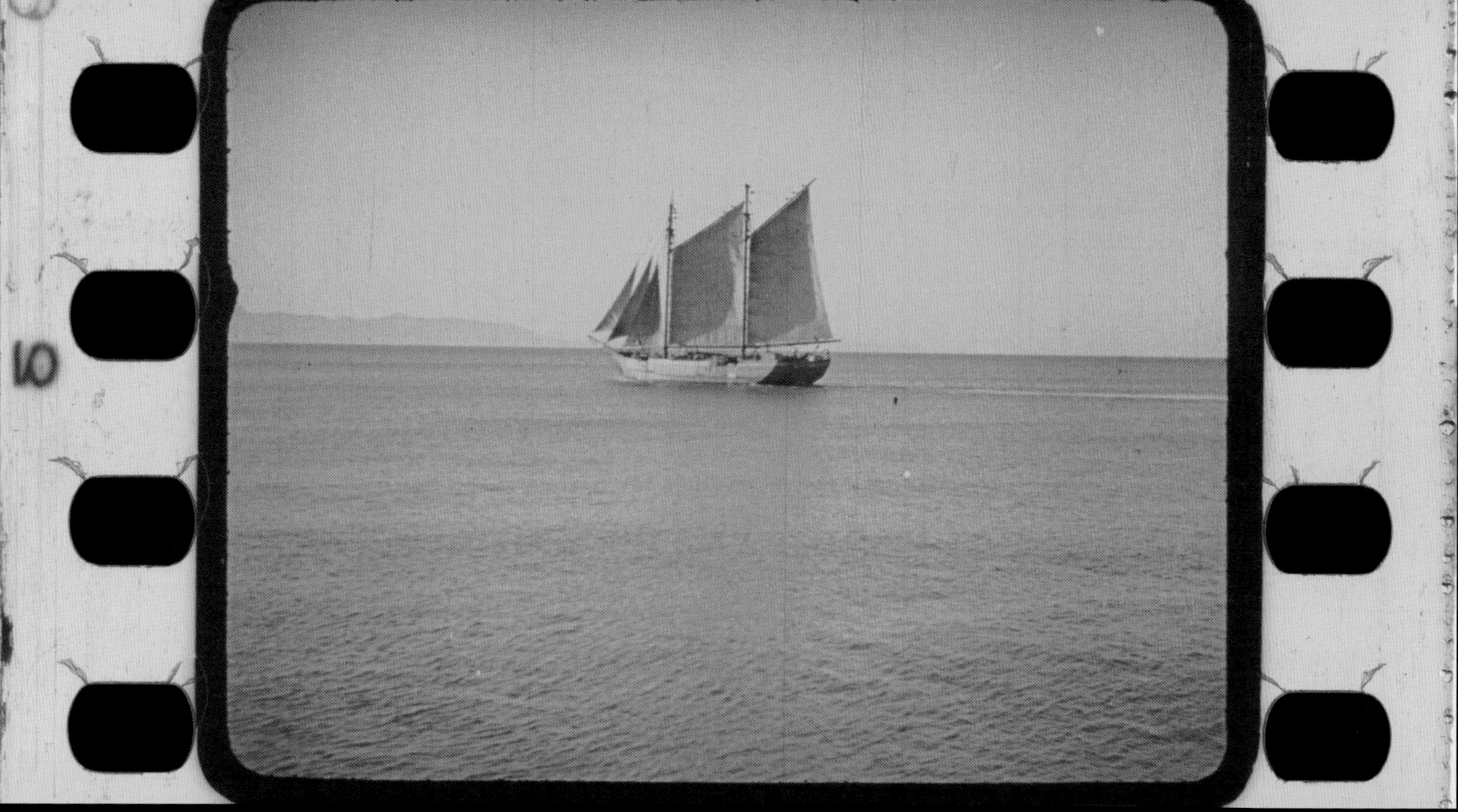

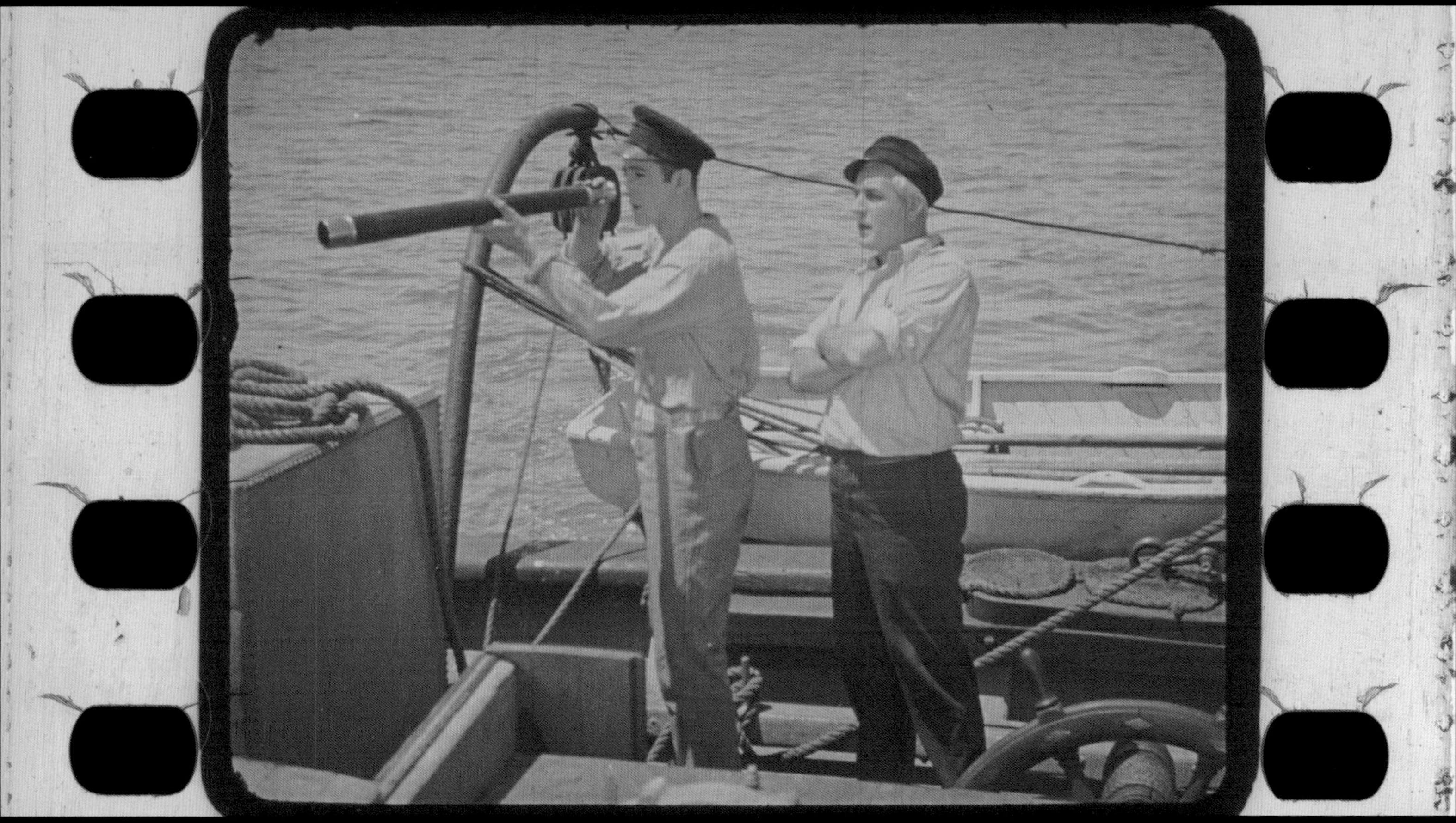

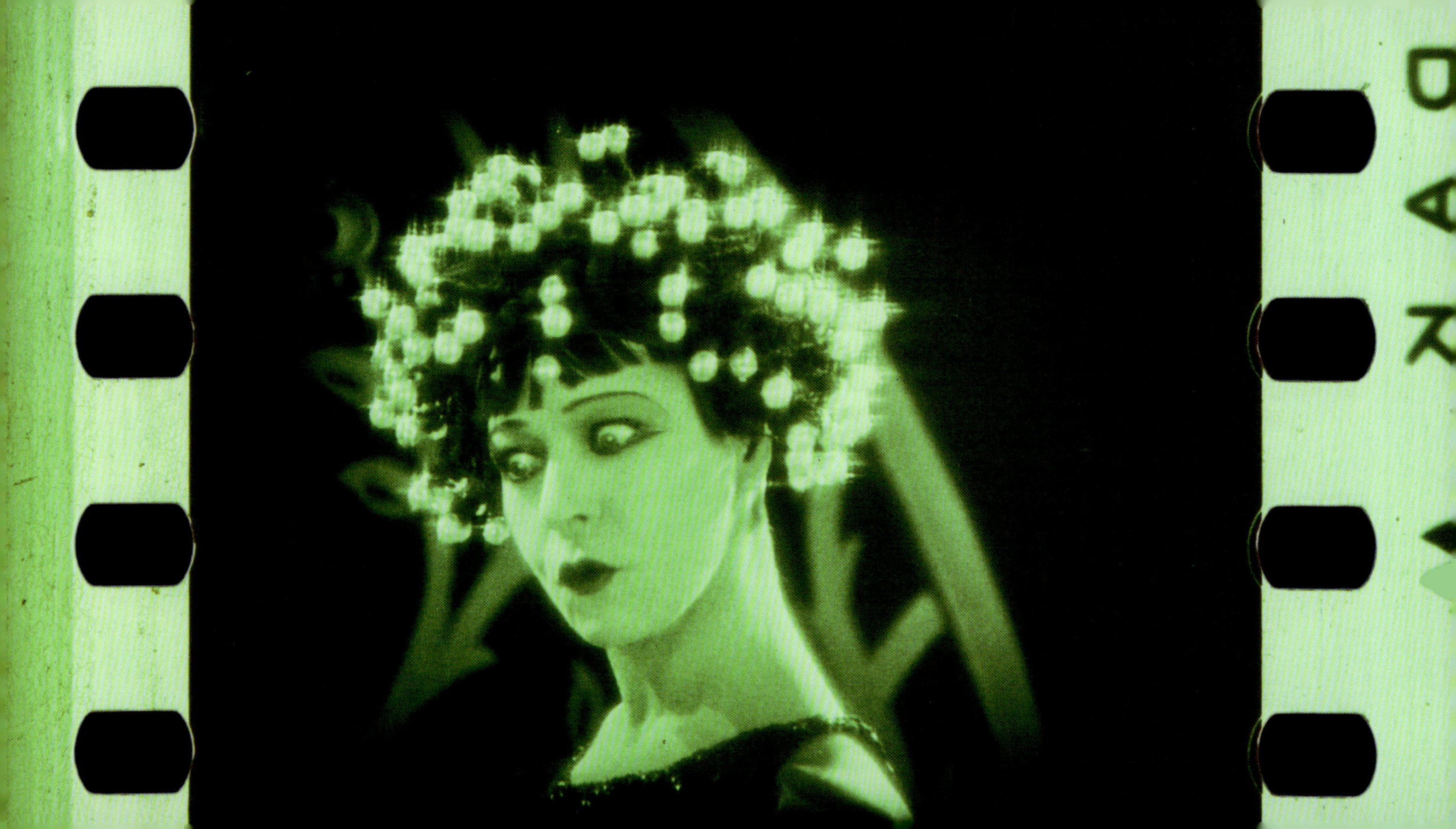

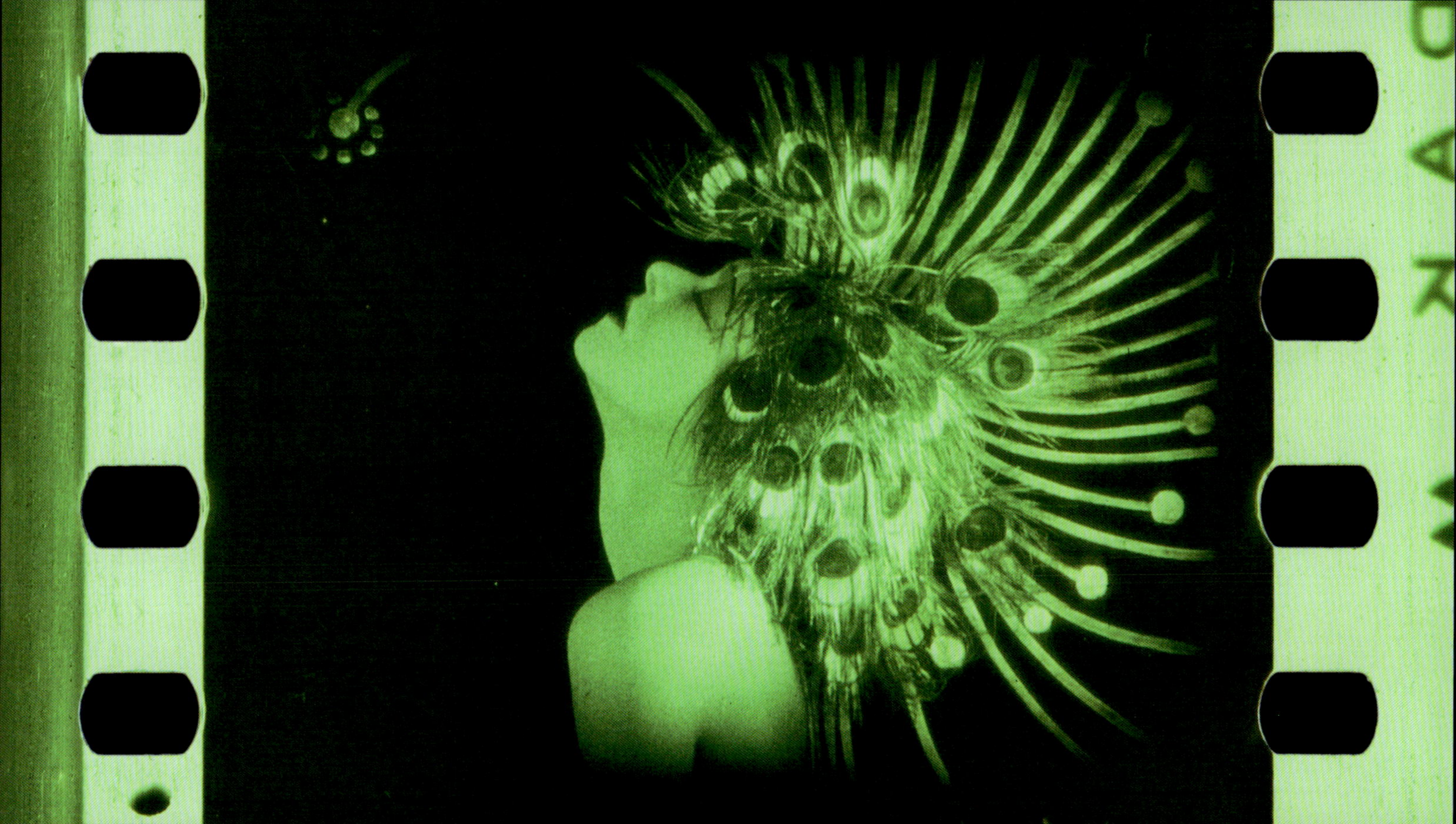

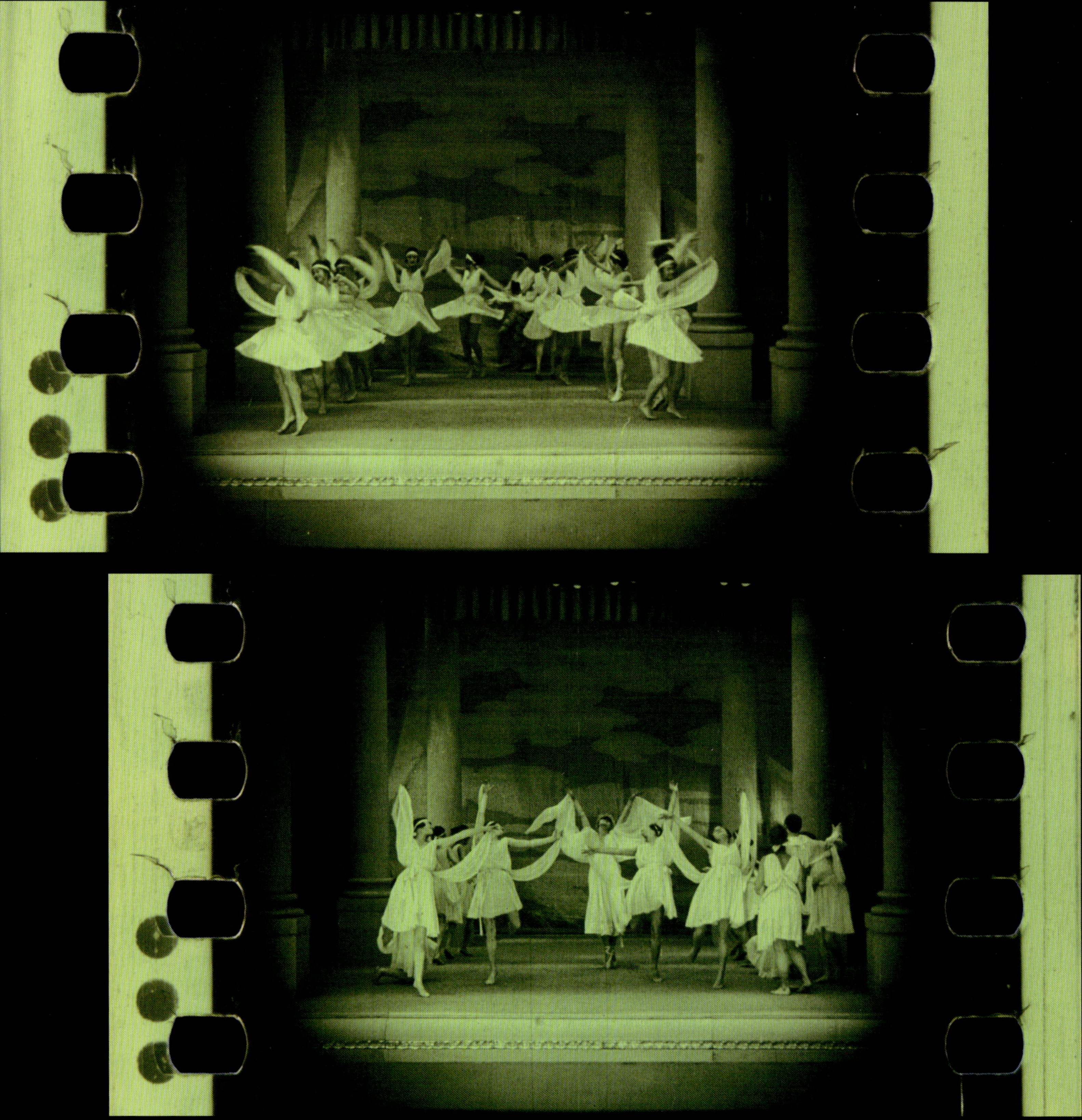

The Shadow of Gaby Leed (*Der Schatten der Gaby Leed*, Germany, 1921, dir. Carl Boese)

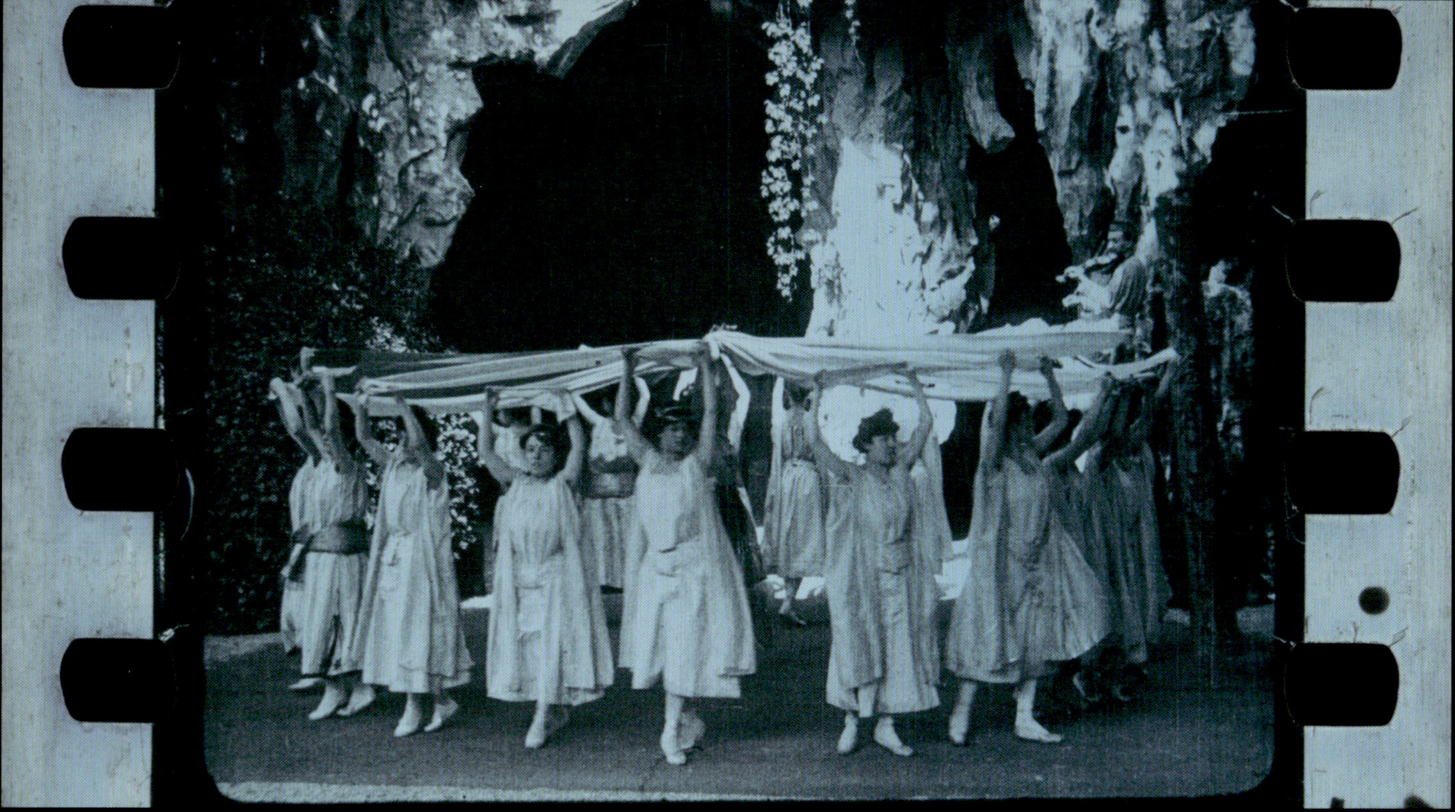

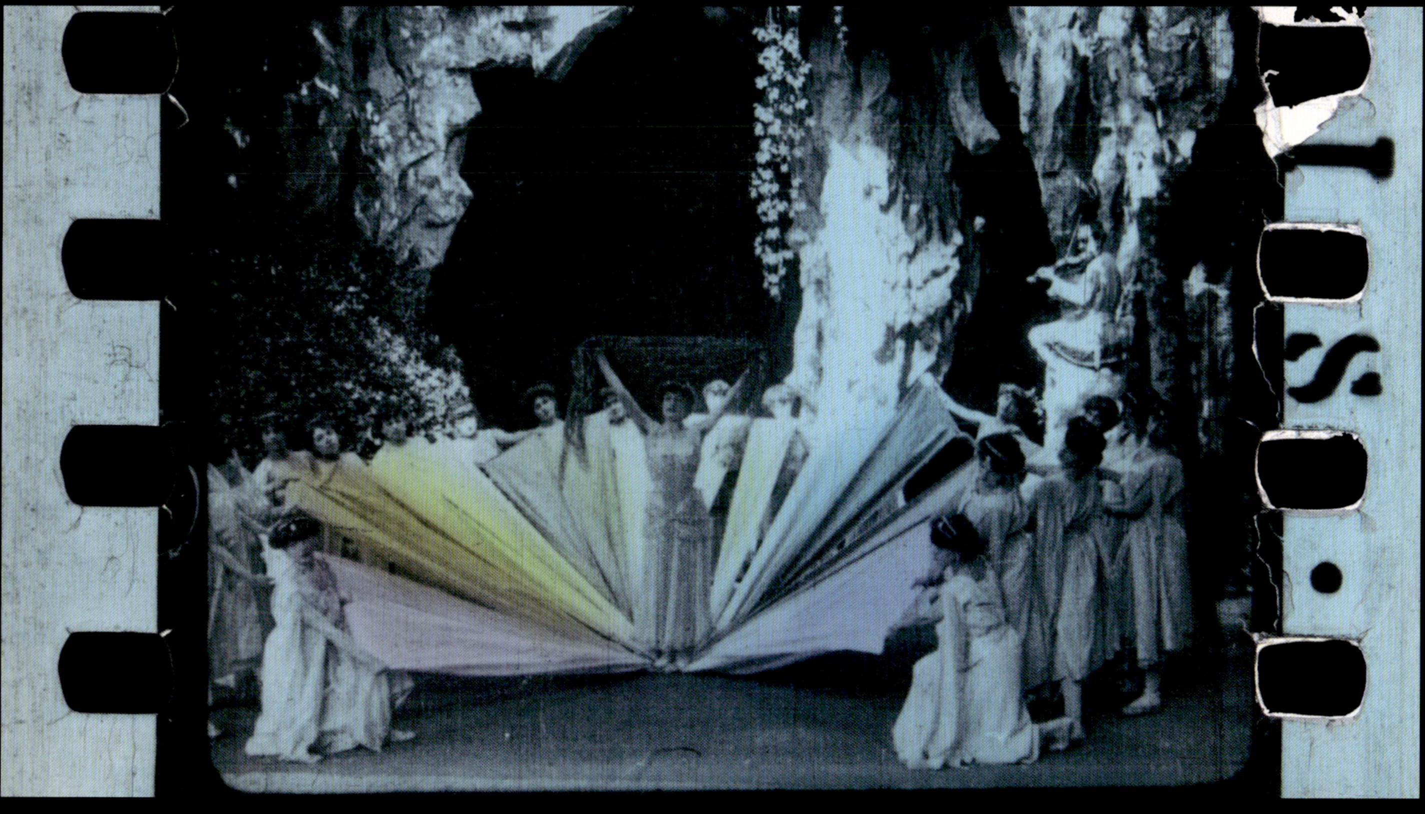

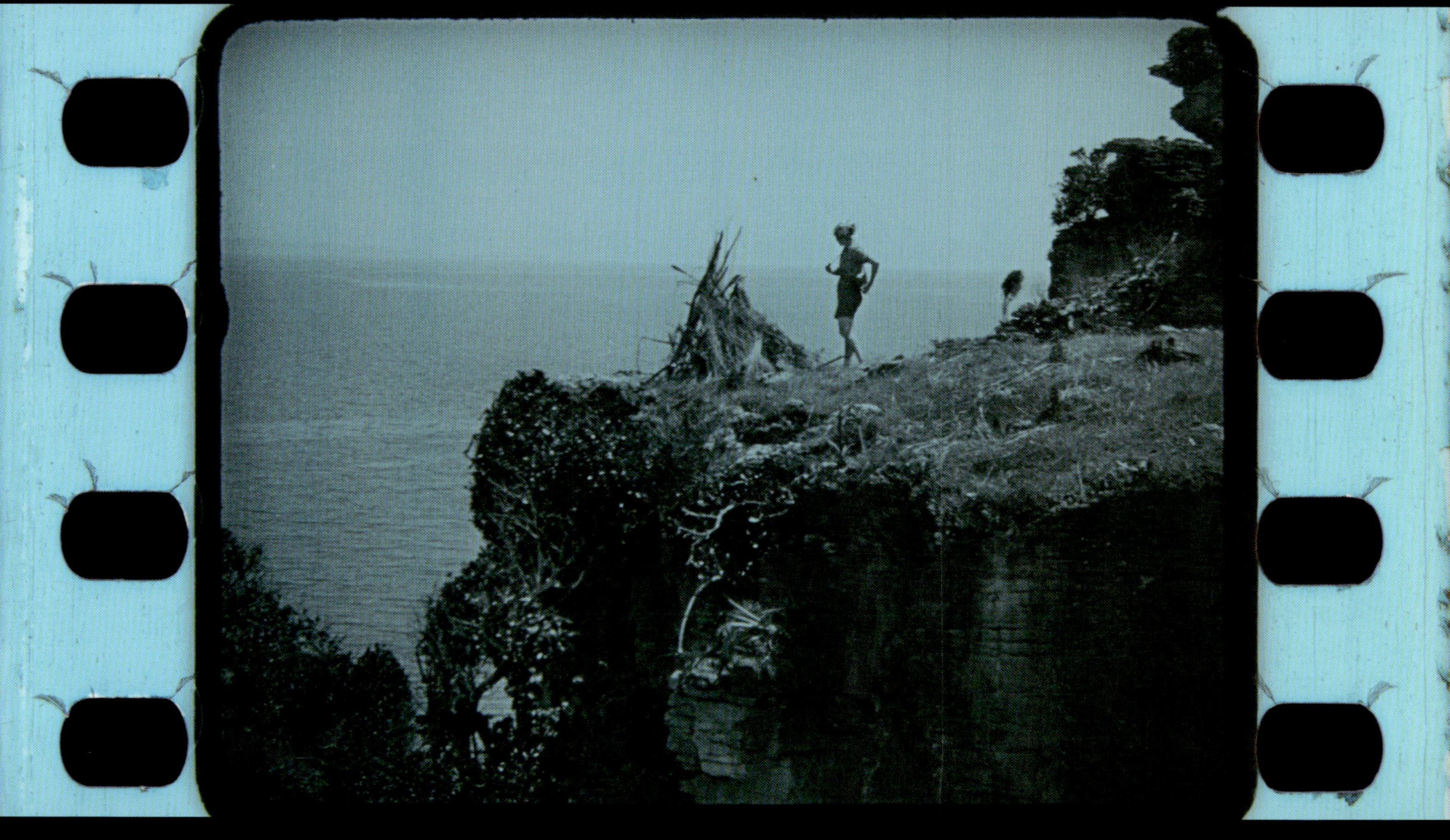

Venus of the South Seas (New Zealand, 1924, dir. James R. Sullivan)

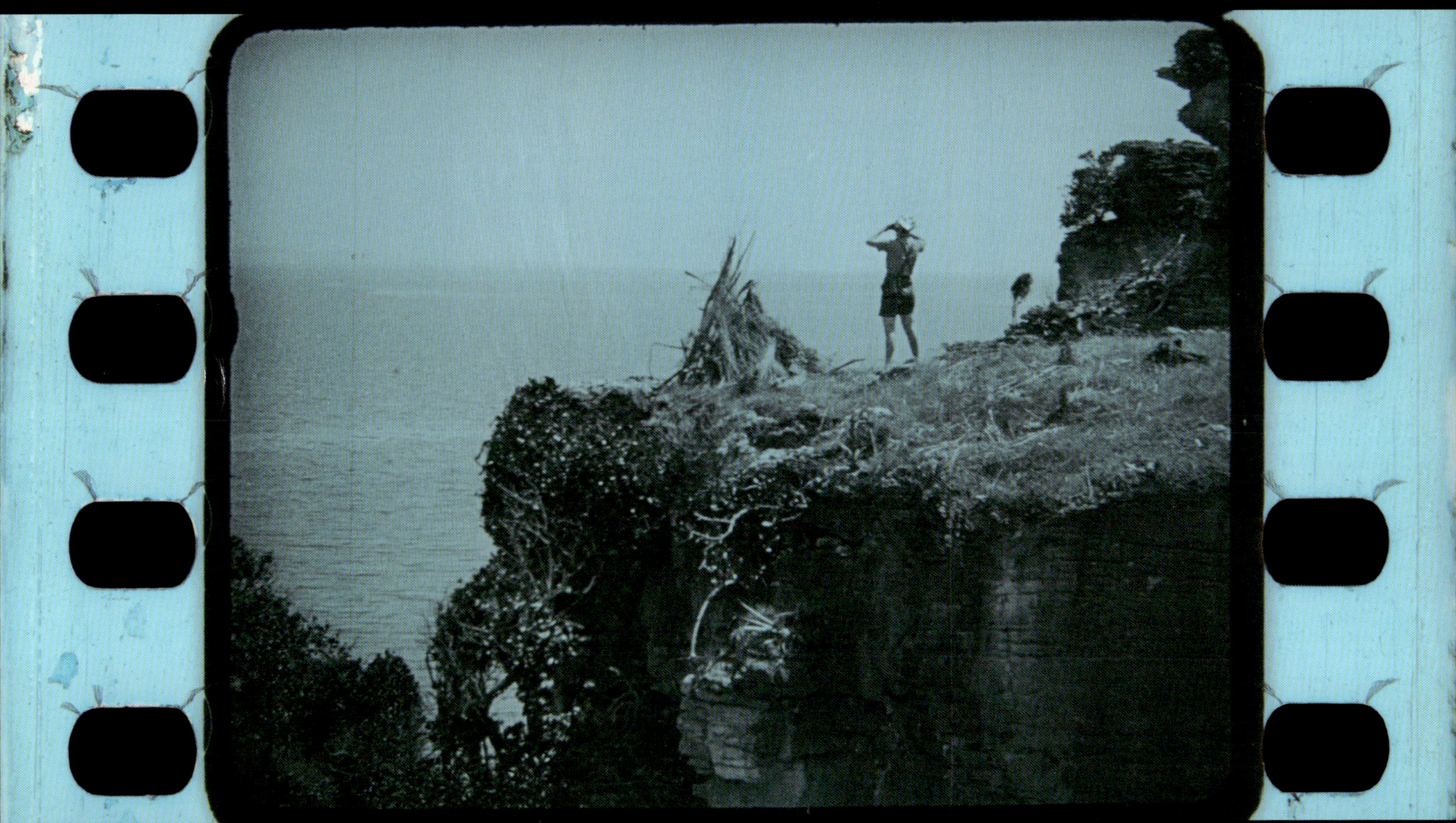

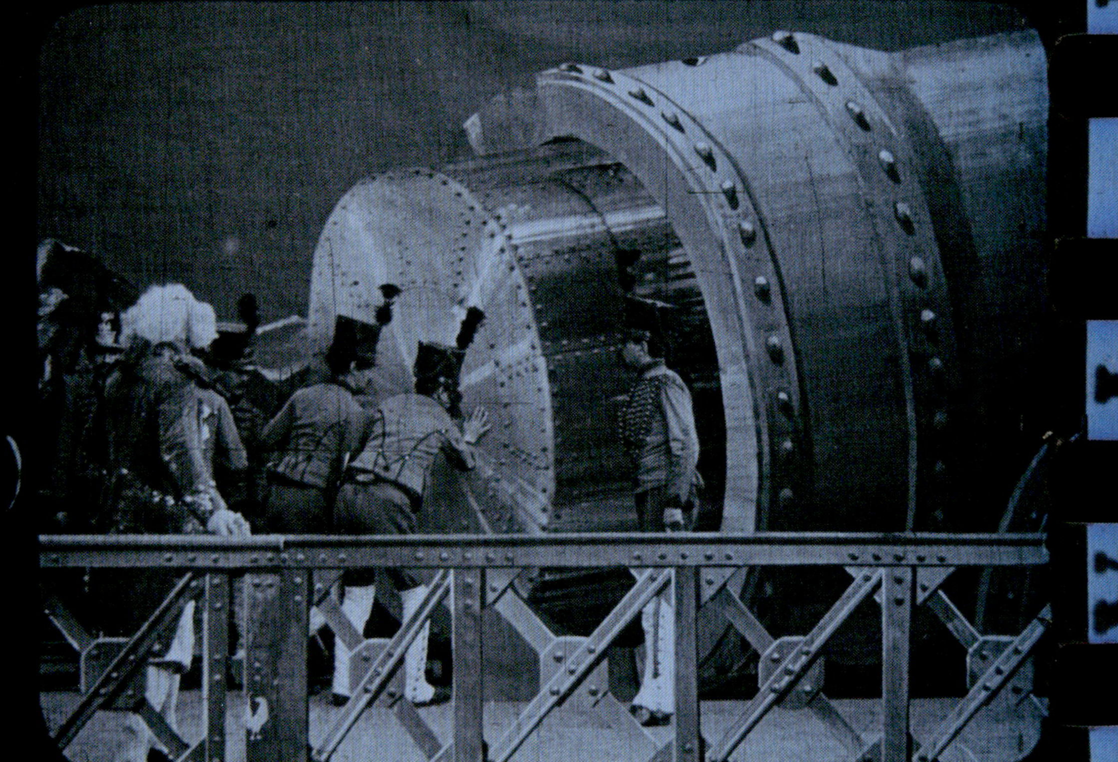

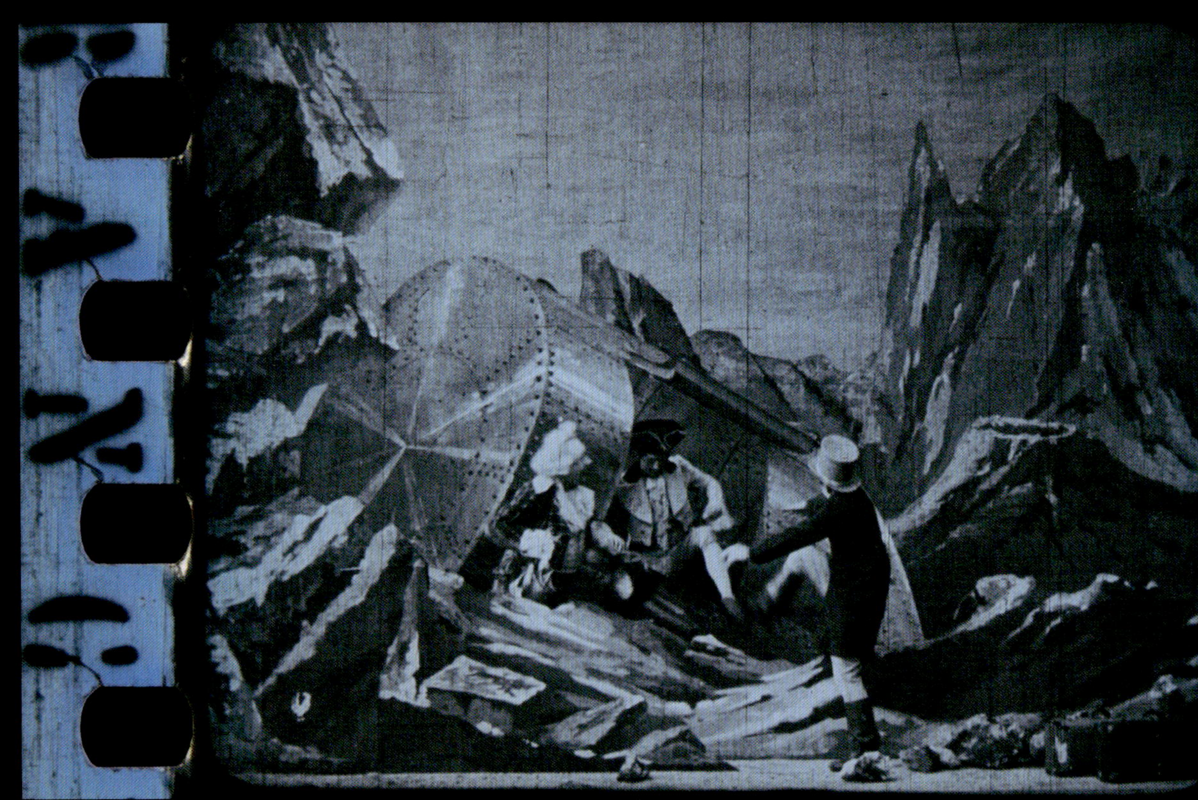

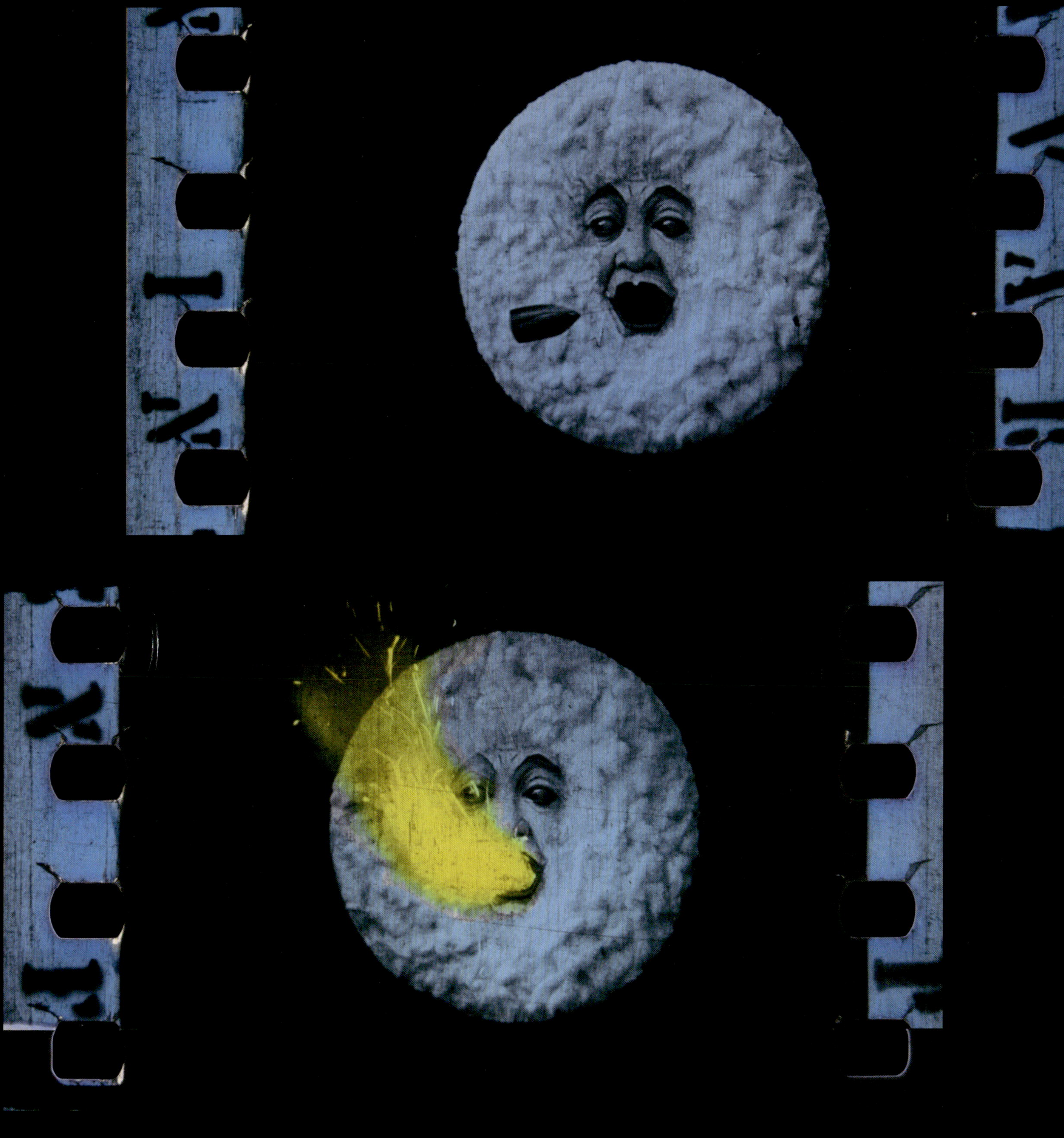

Excursion to the Moon (*Excursion dans la lune*, France, 1908, dir. Segundo de Chomón)

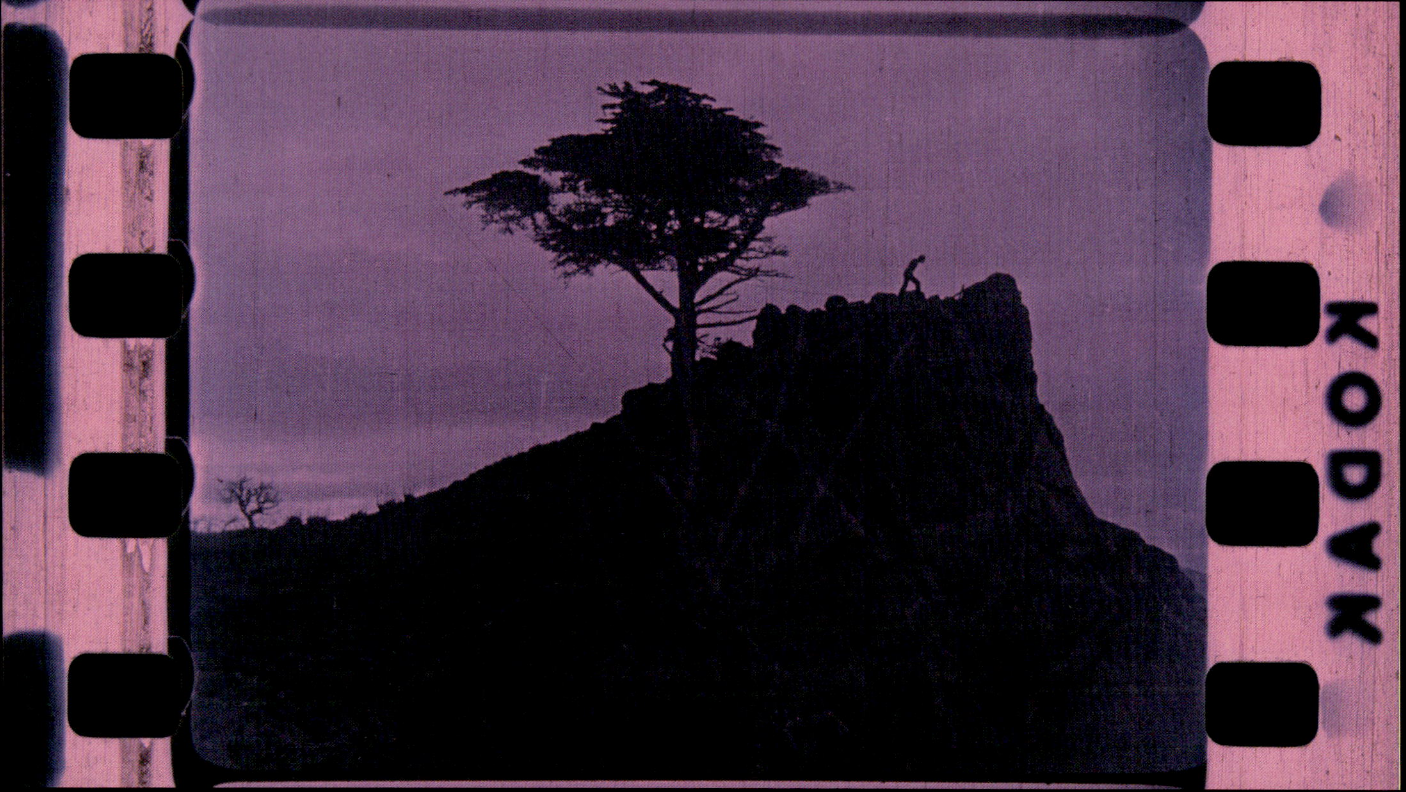

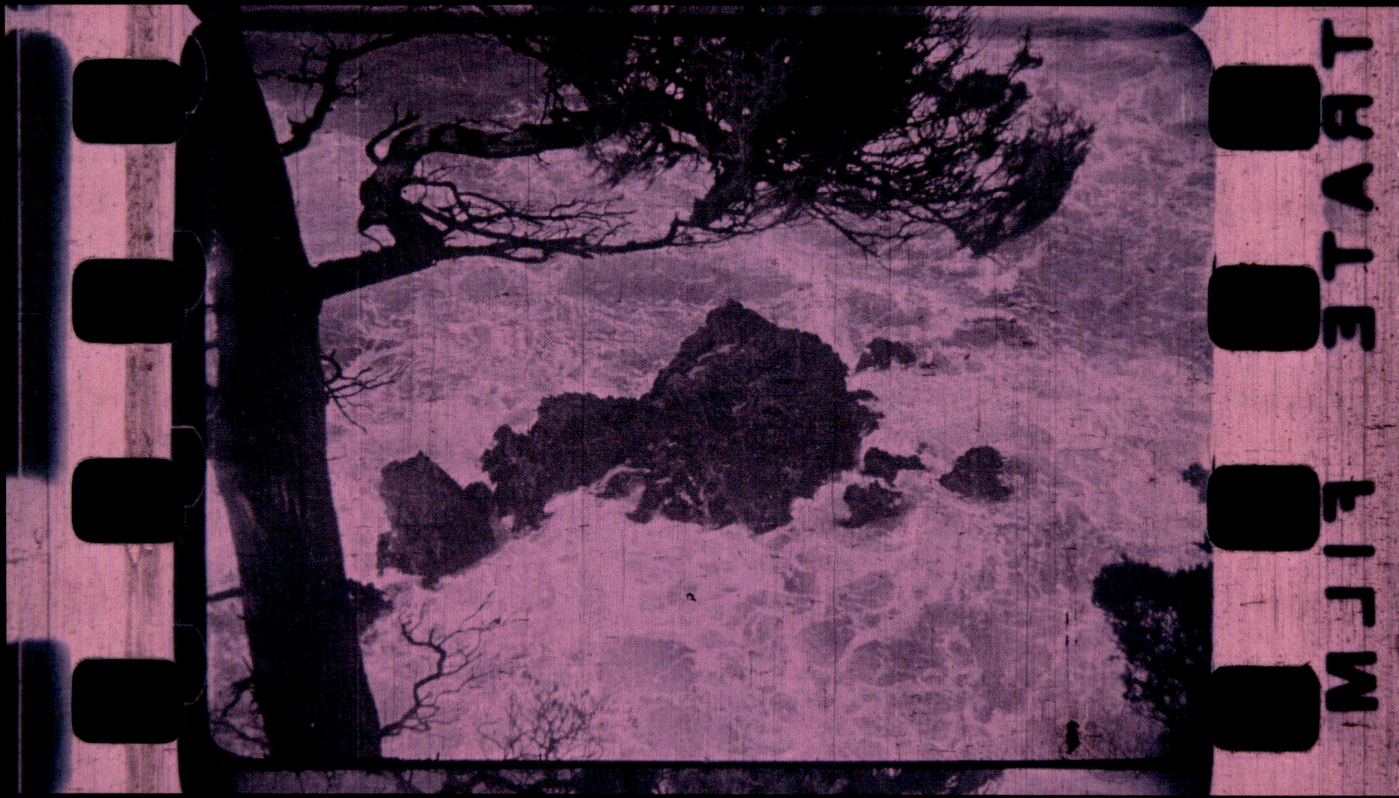

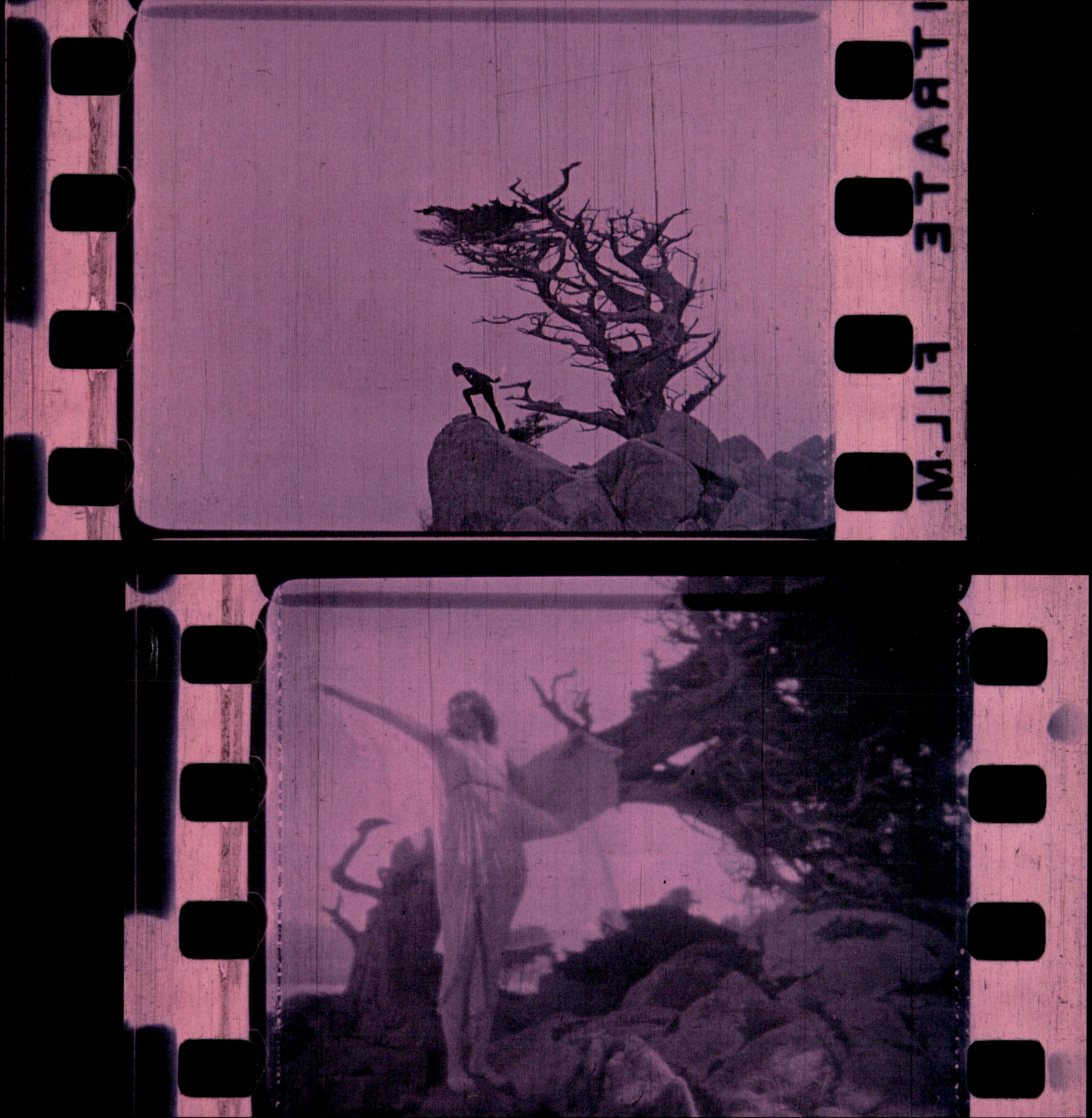

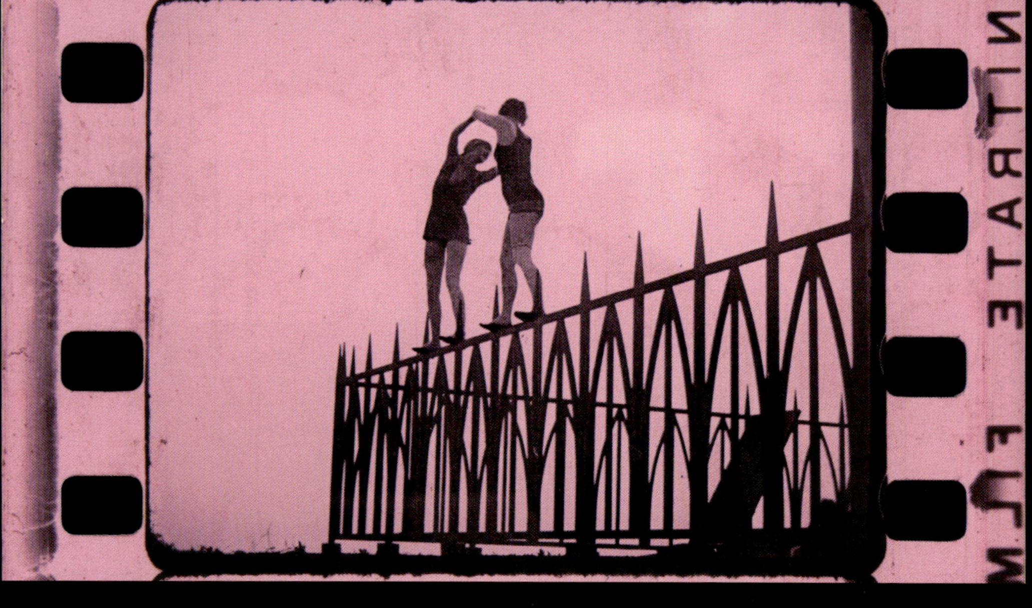
NITRATE FILM

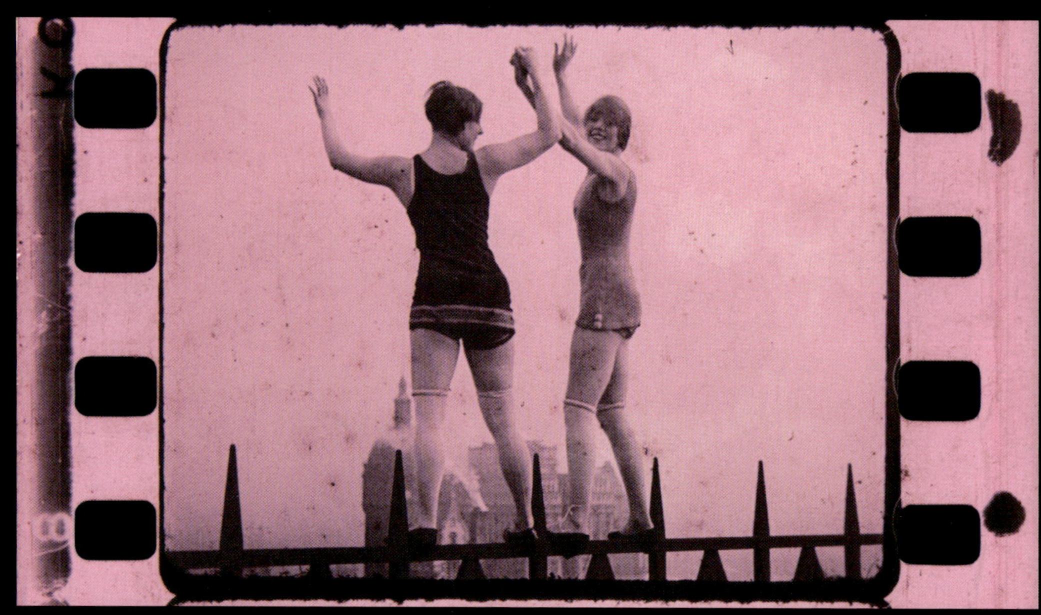

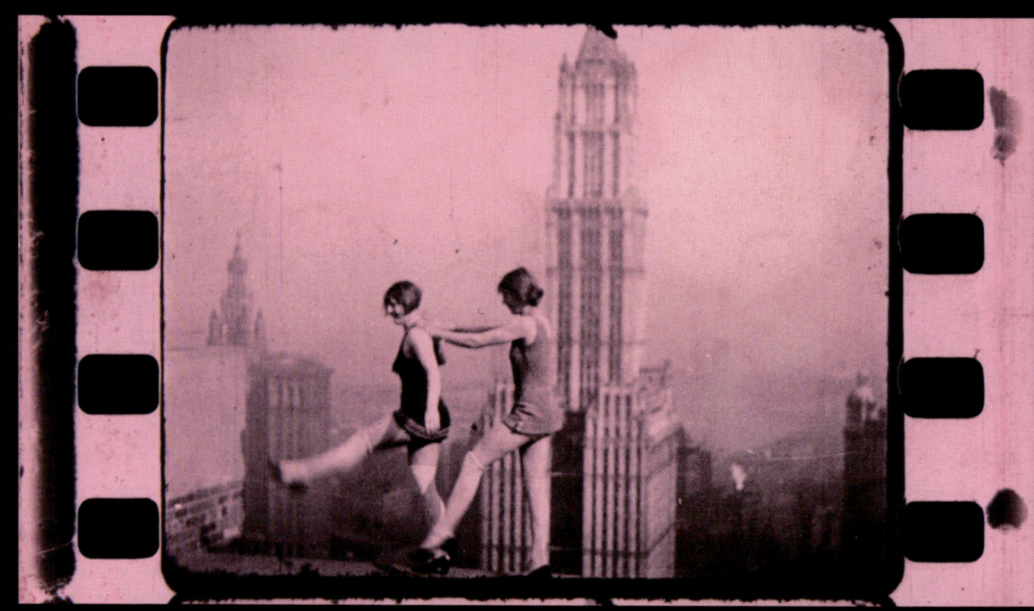

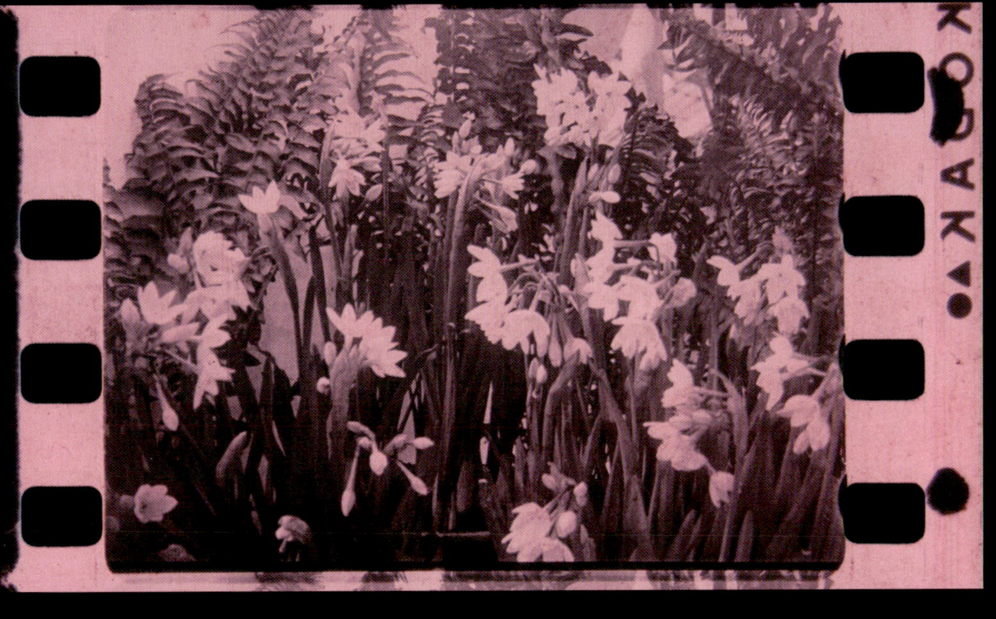

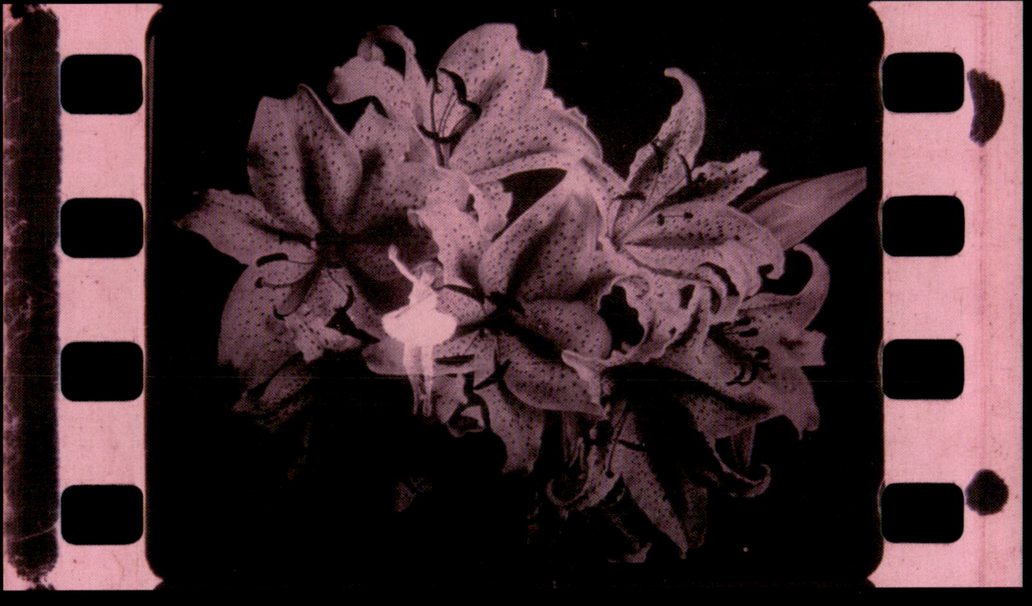

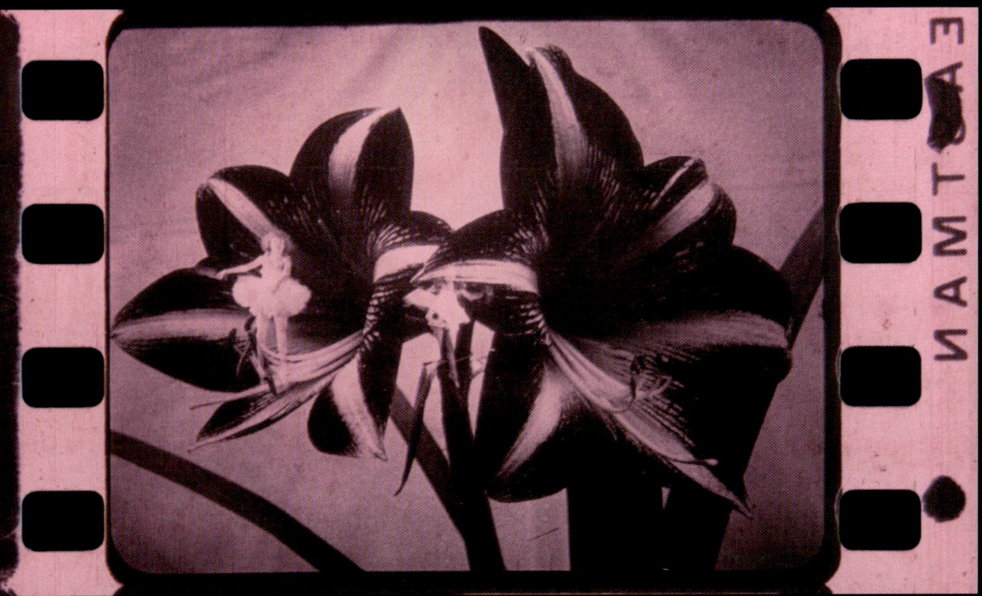

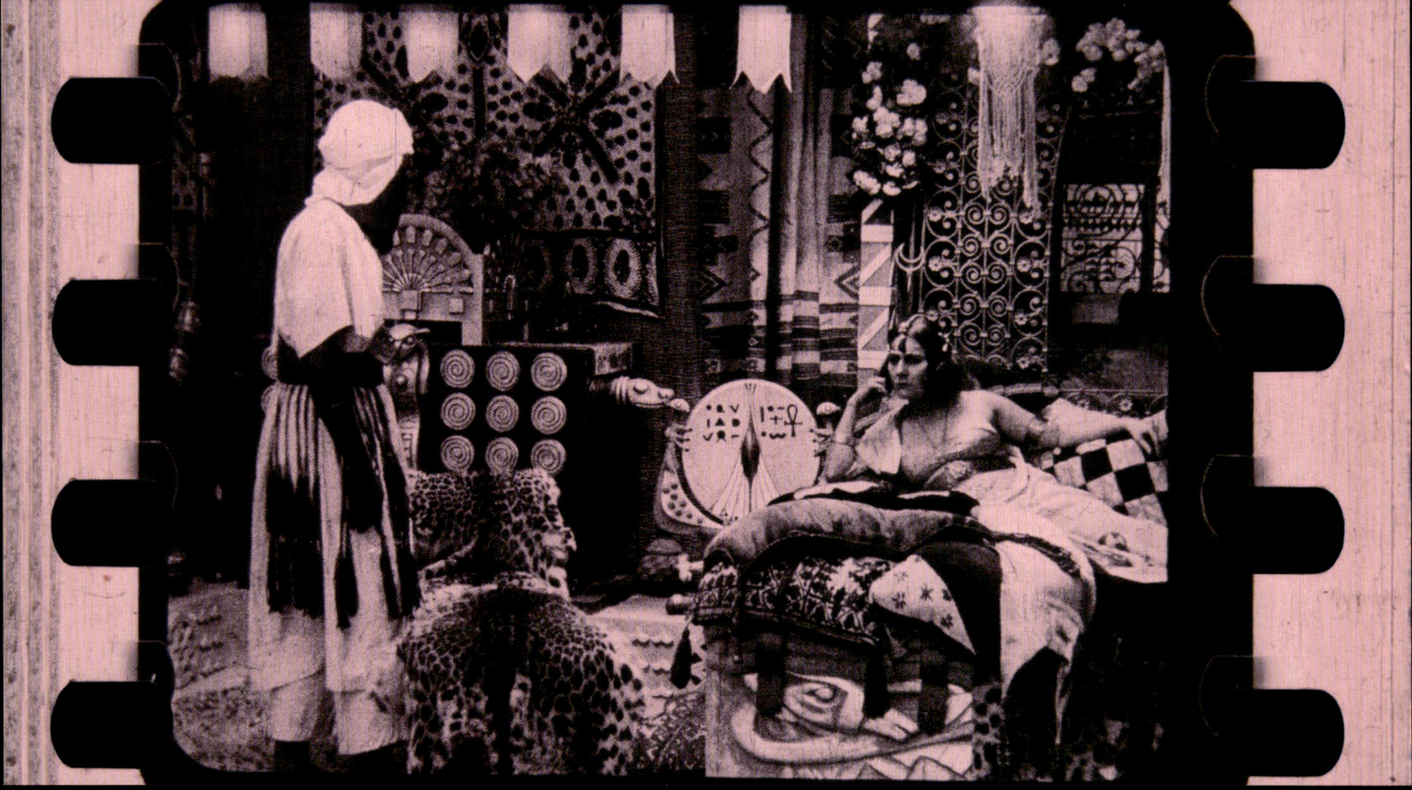

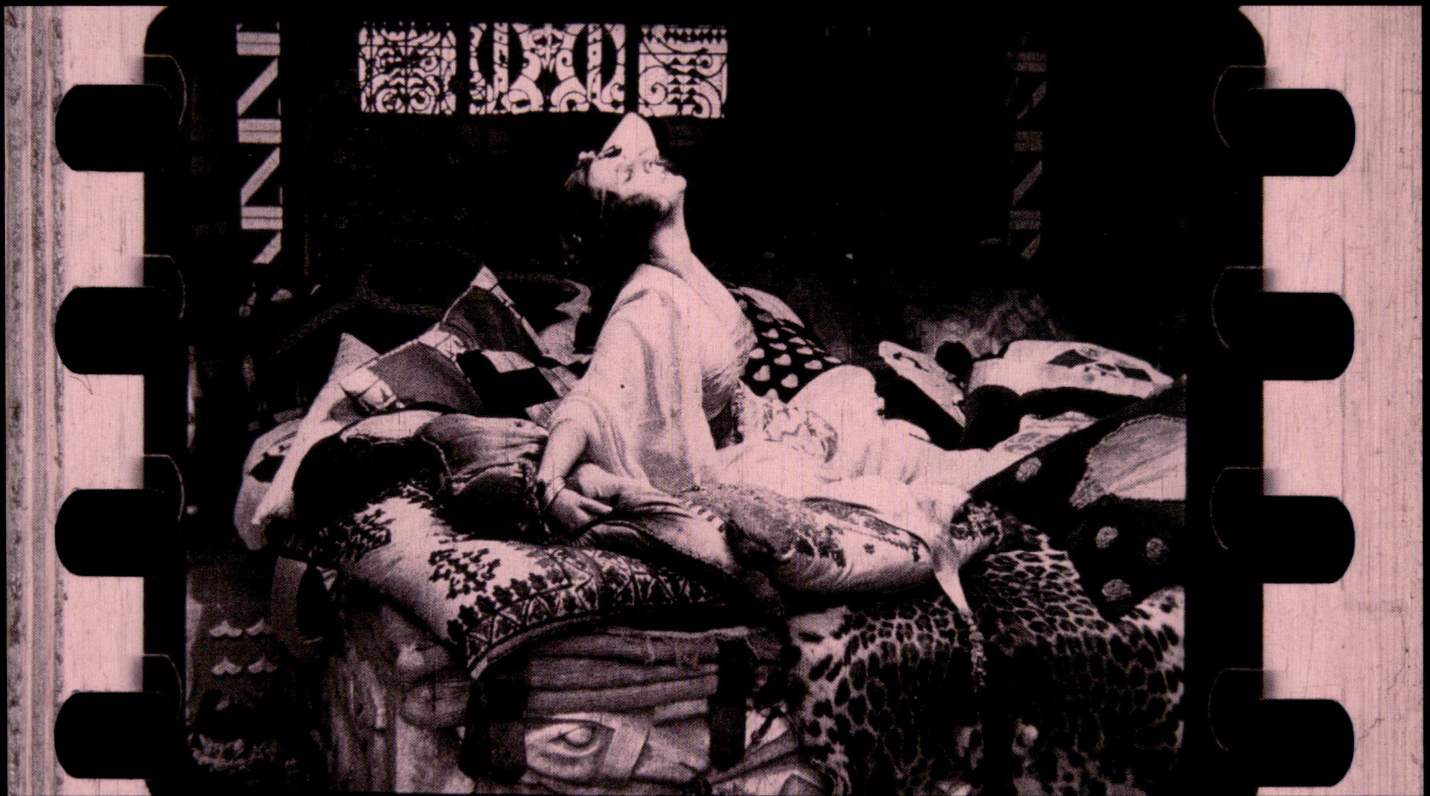

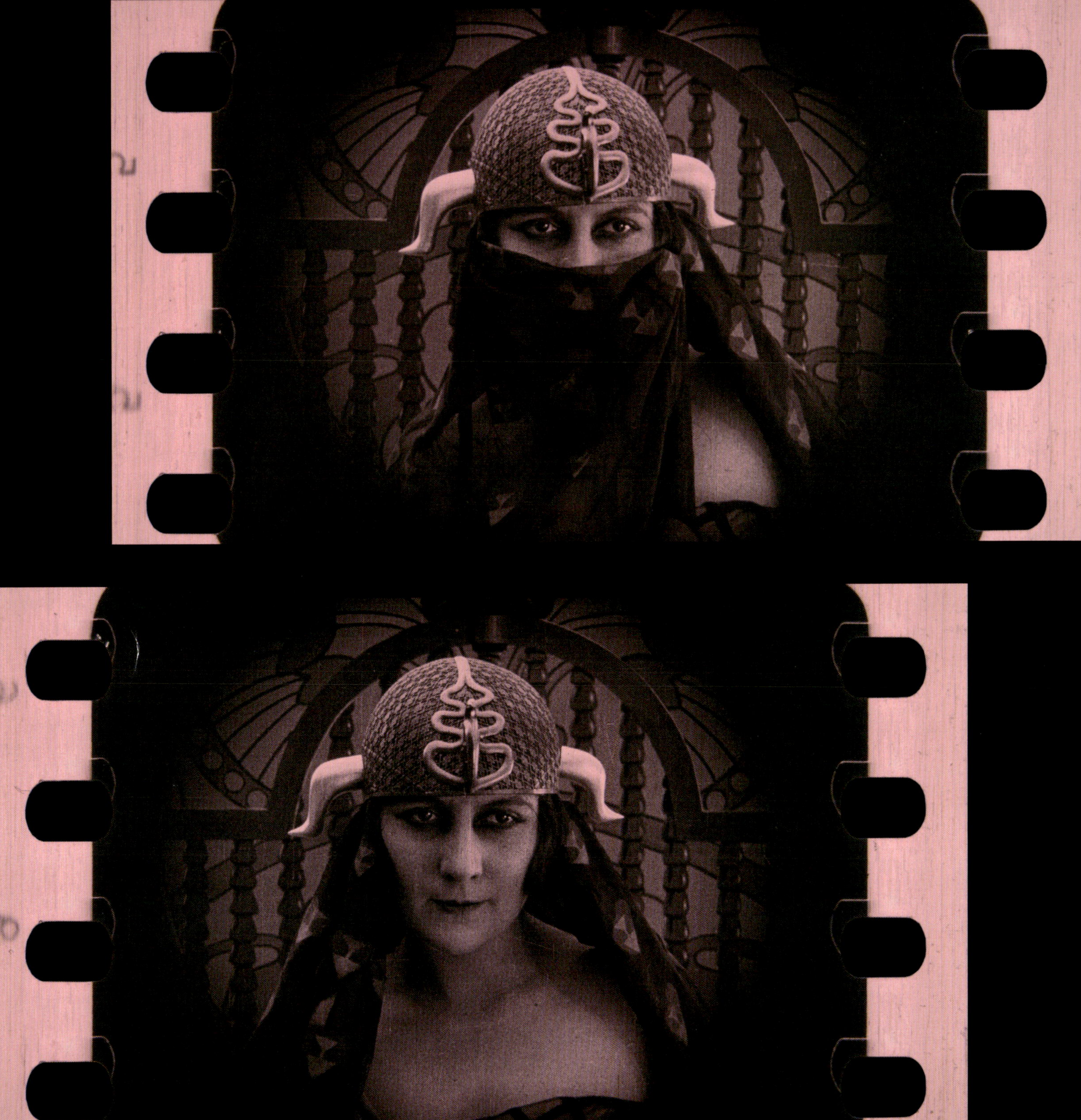

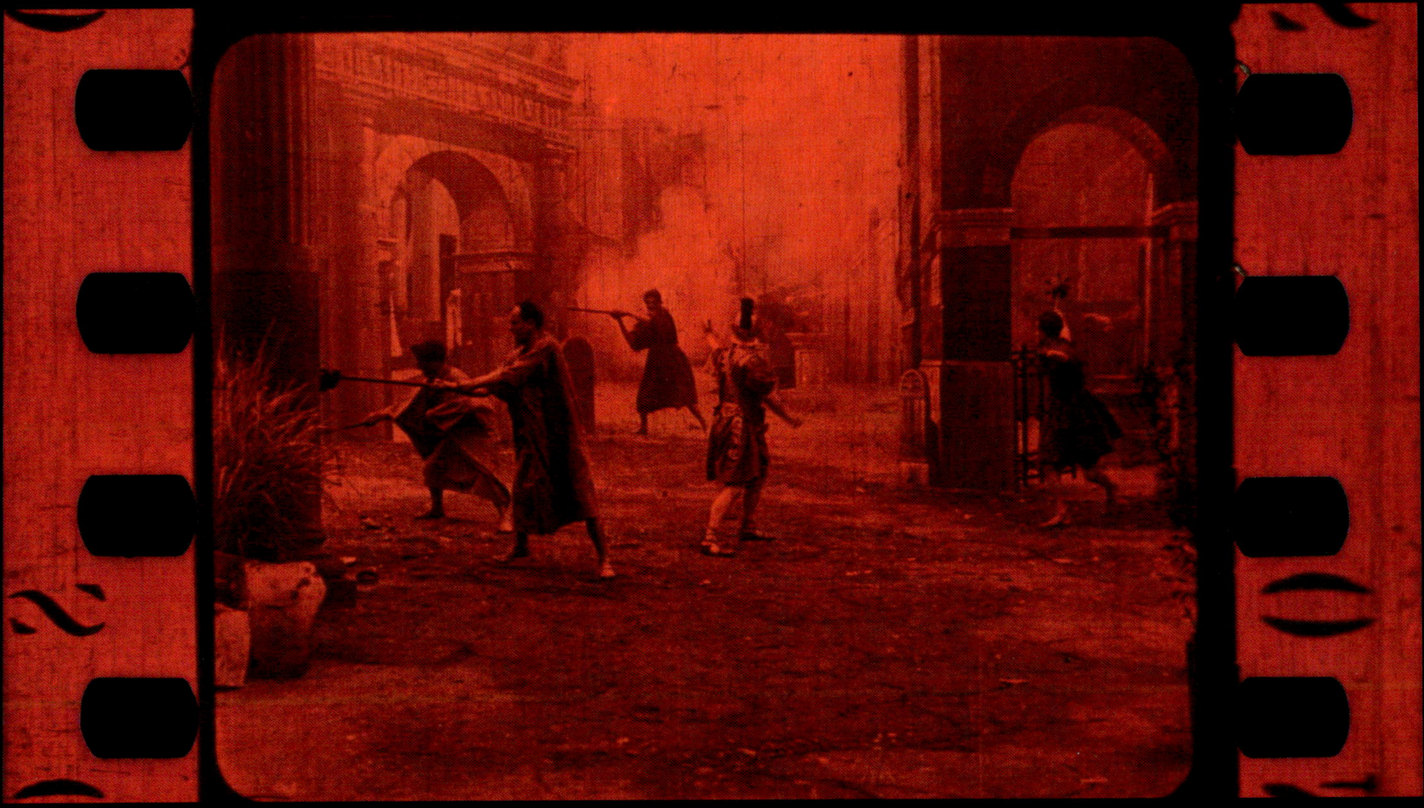

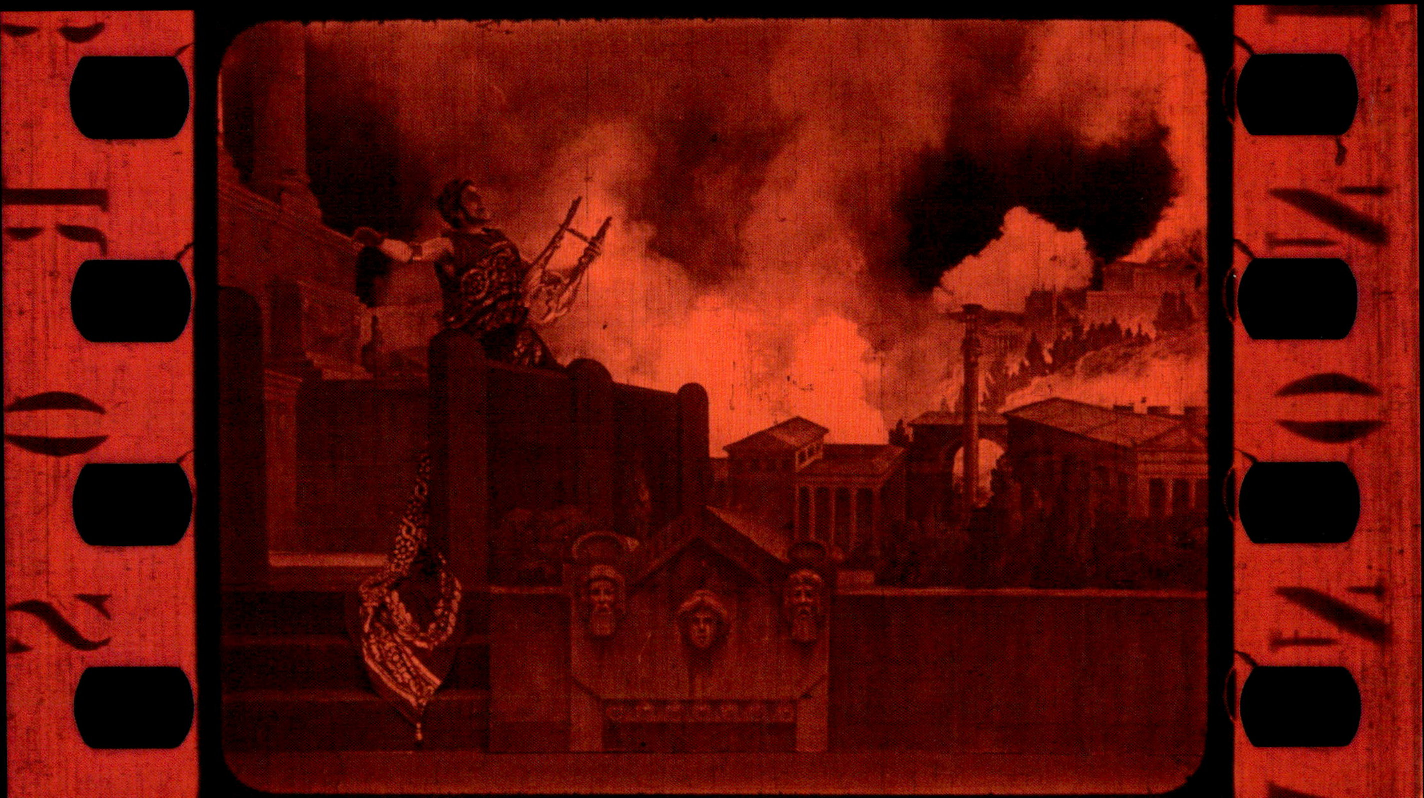

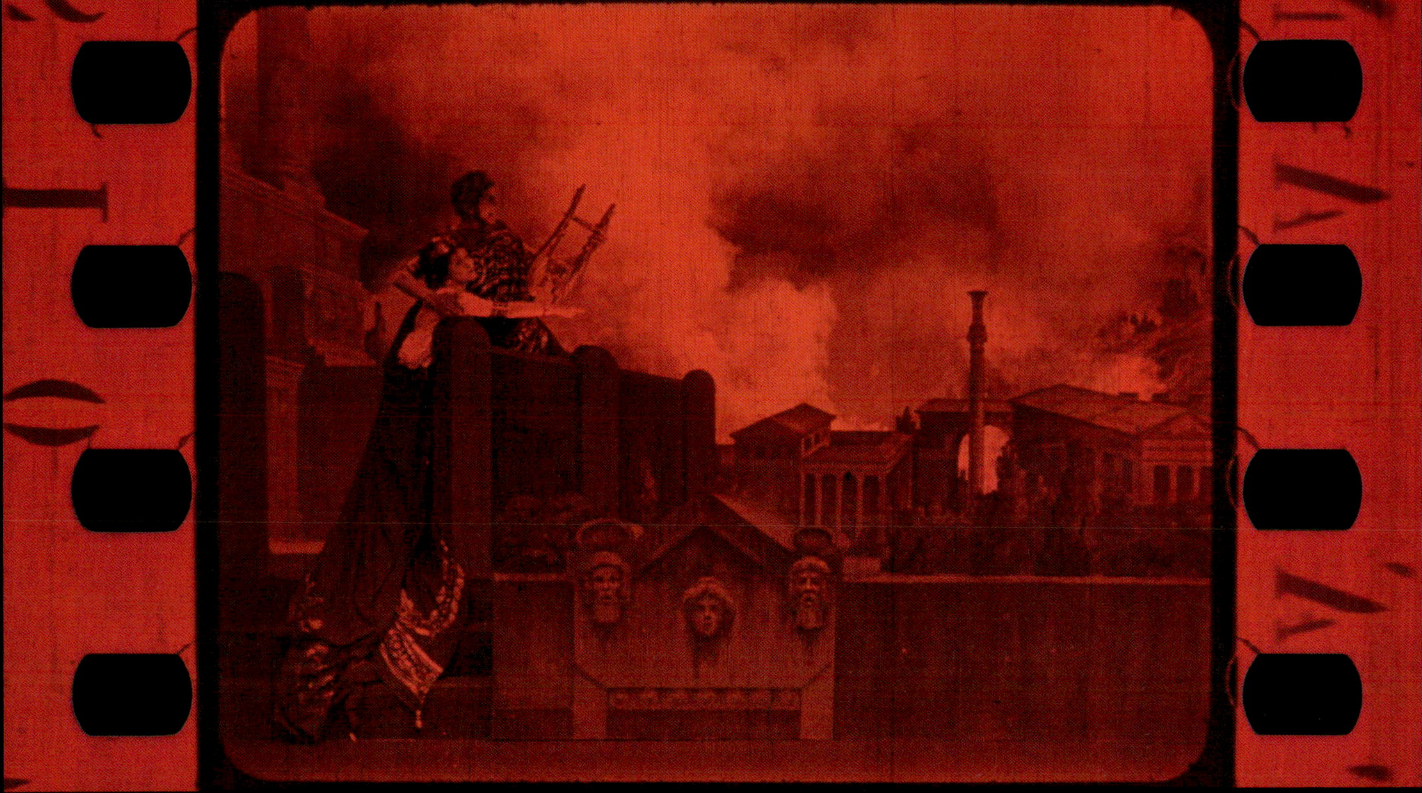

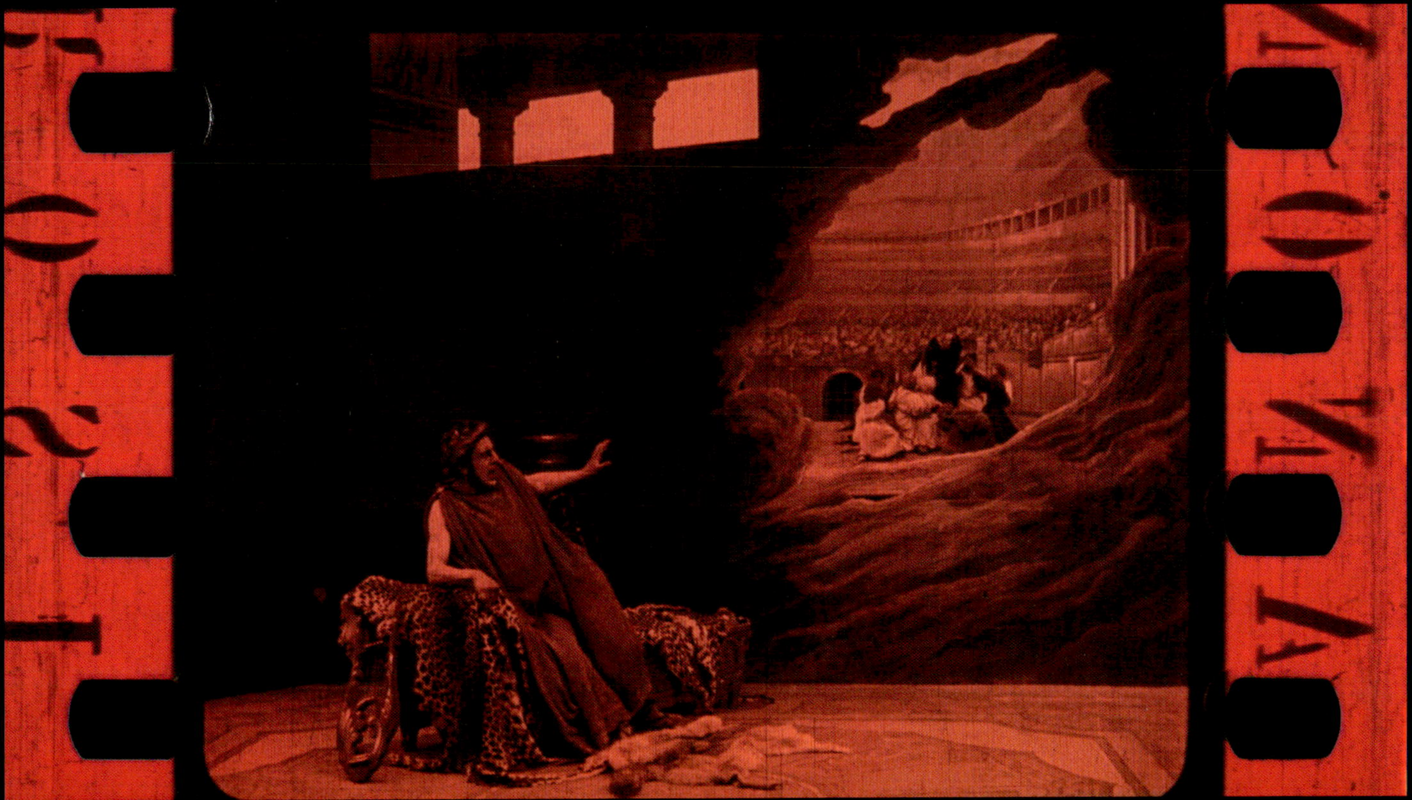

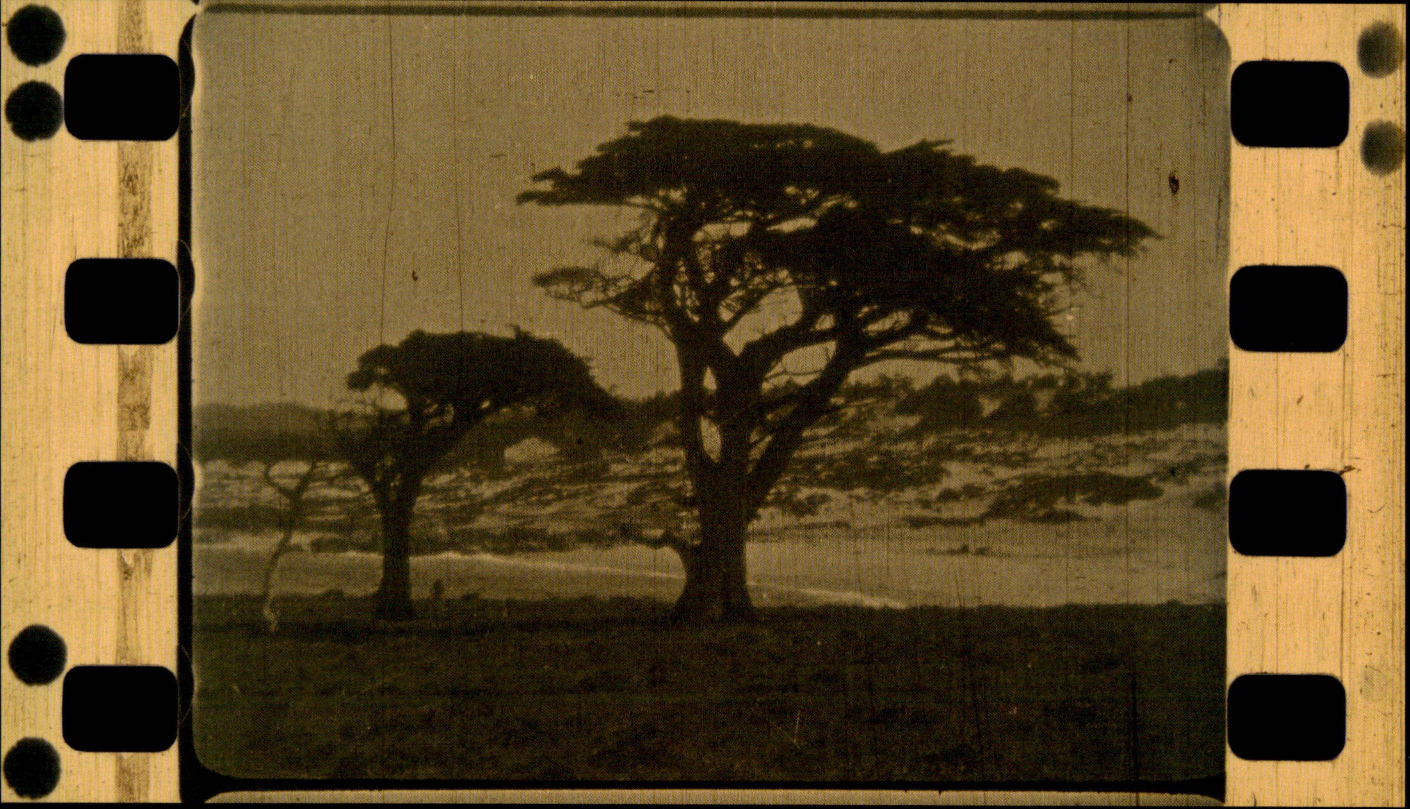

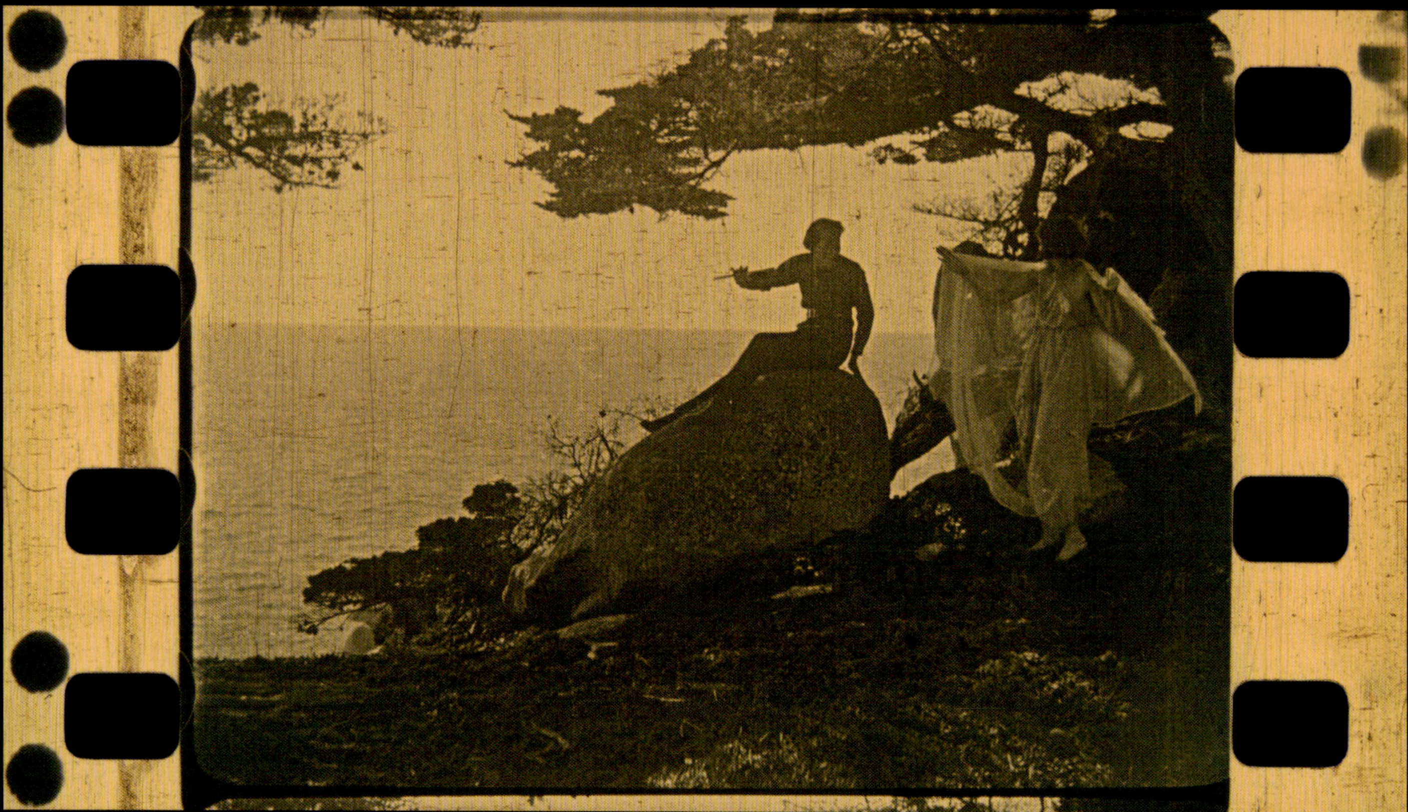

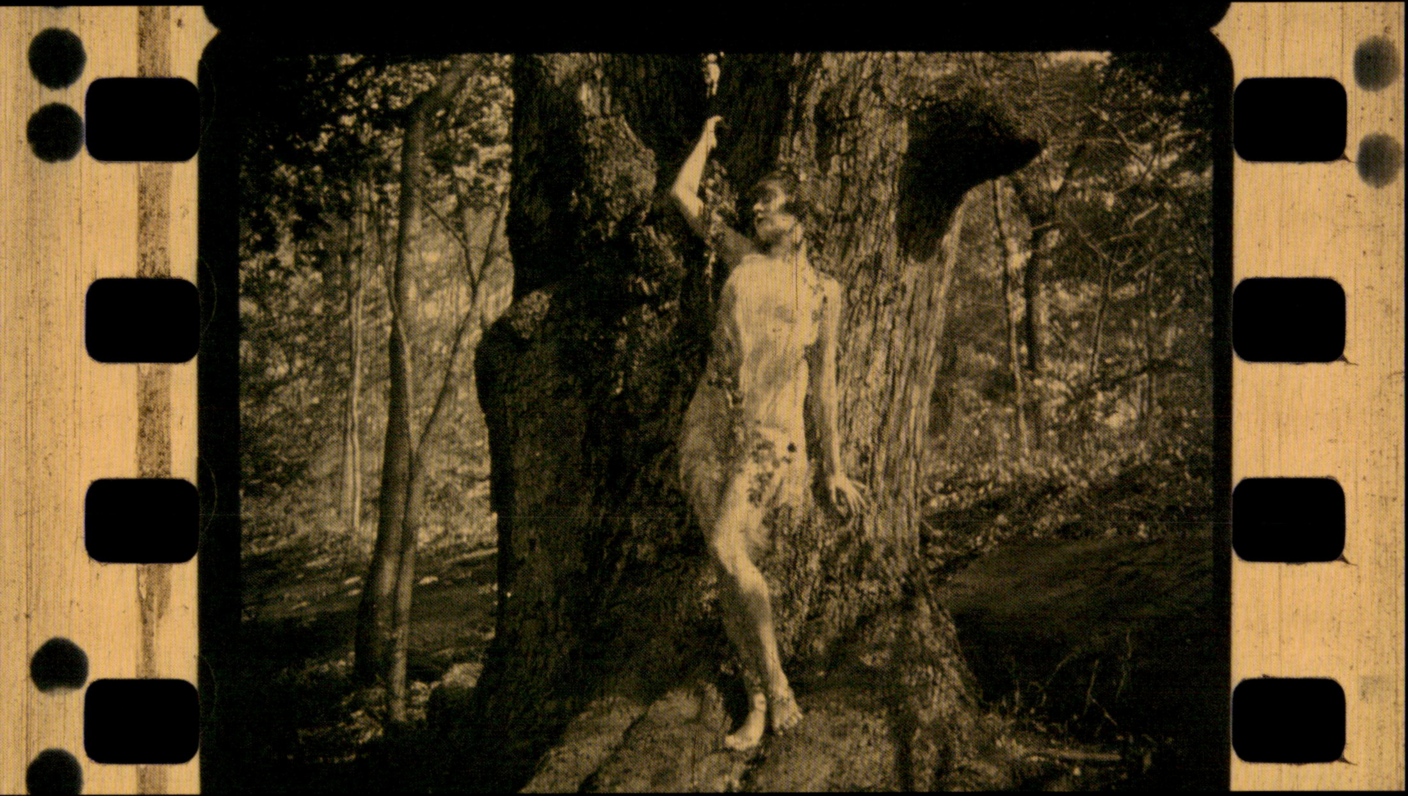

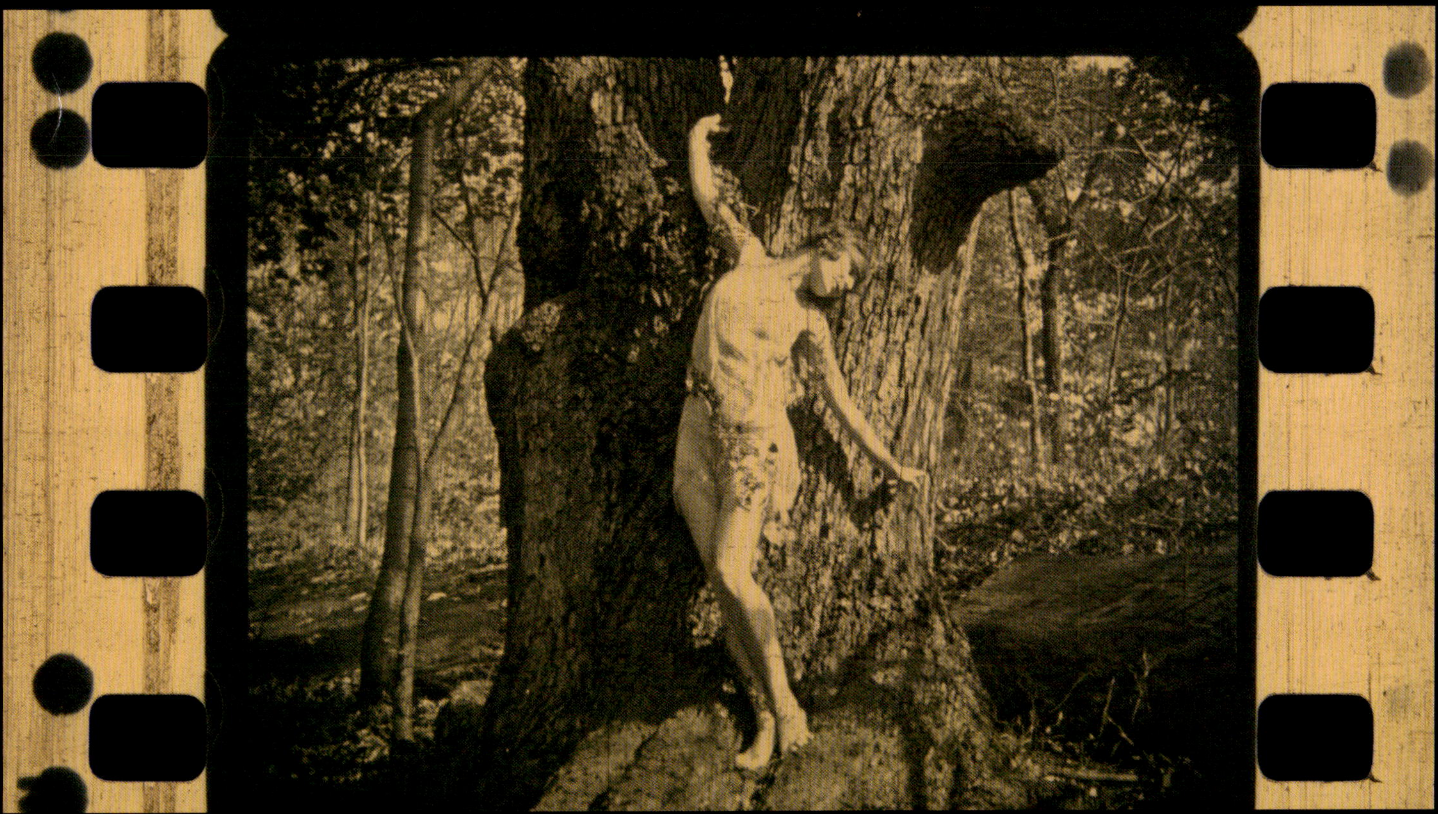

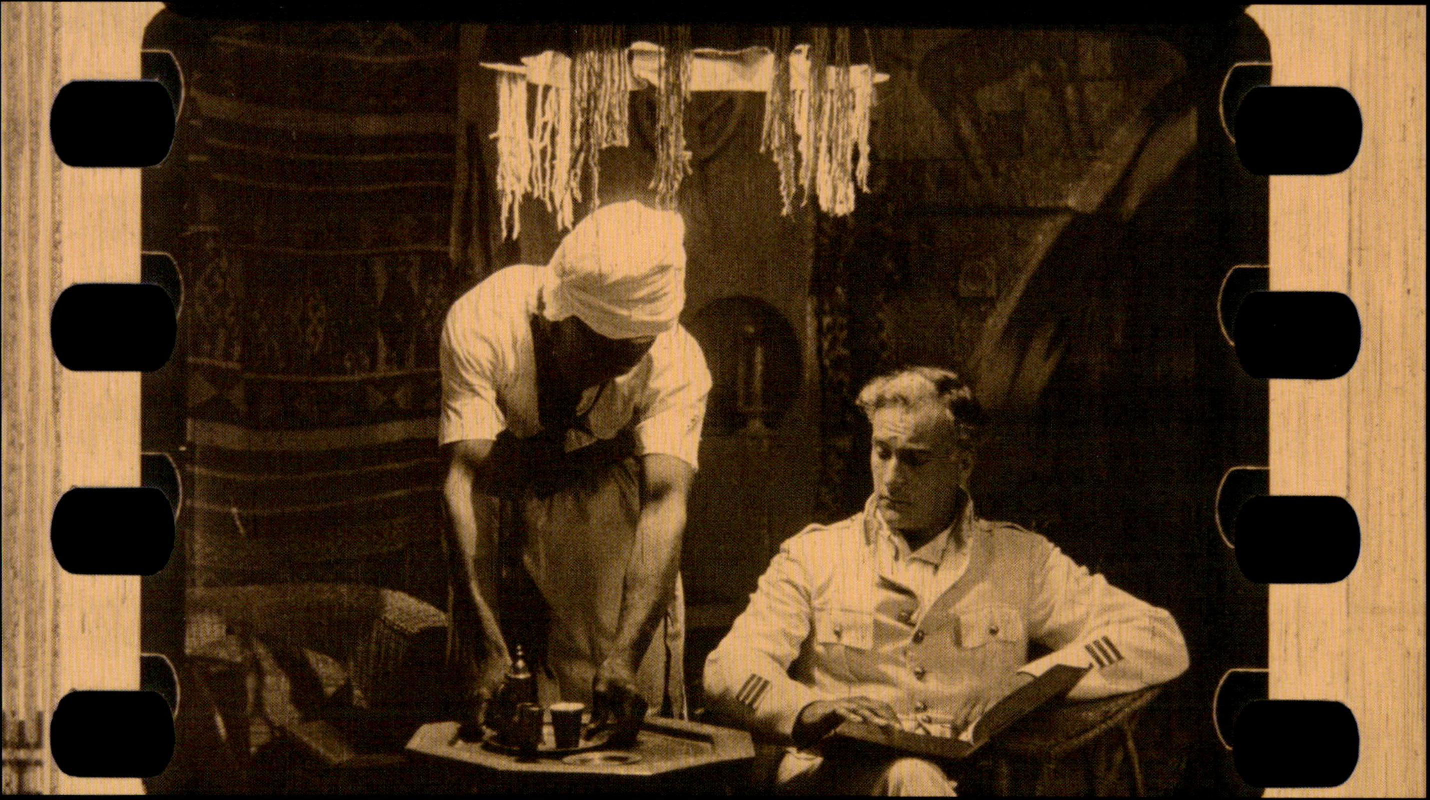

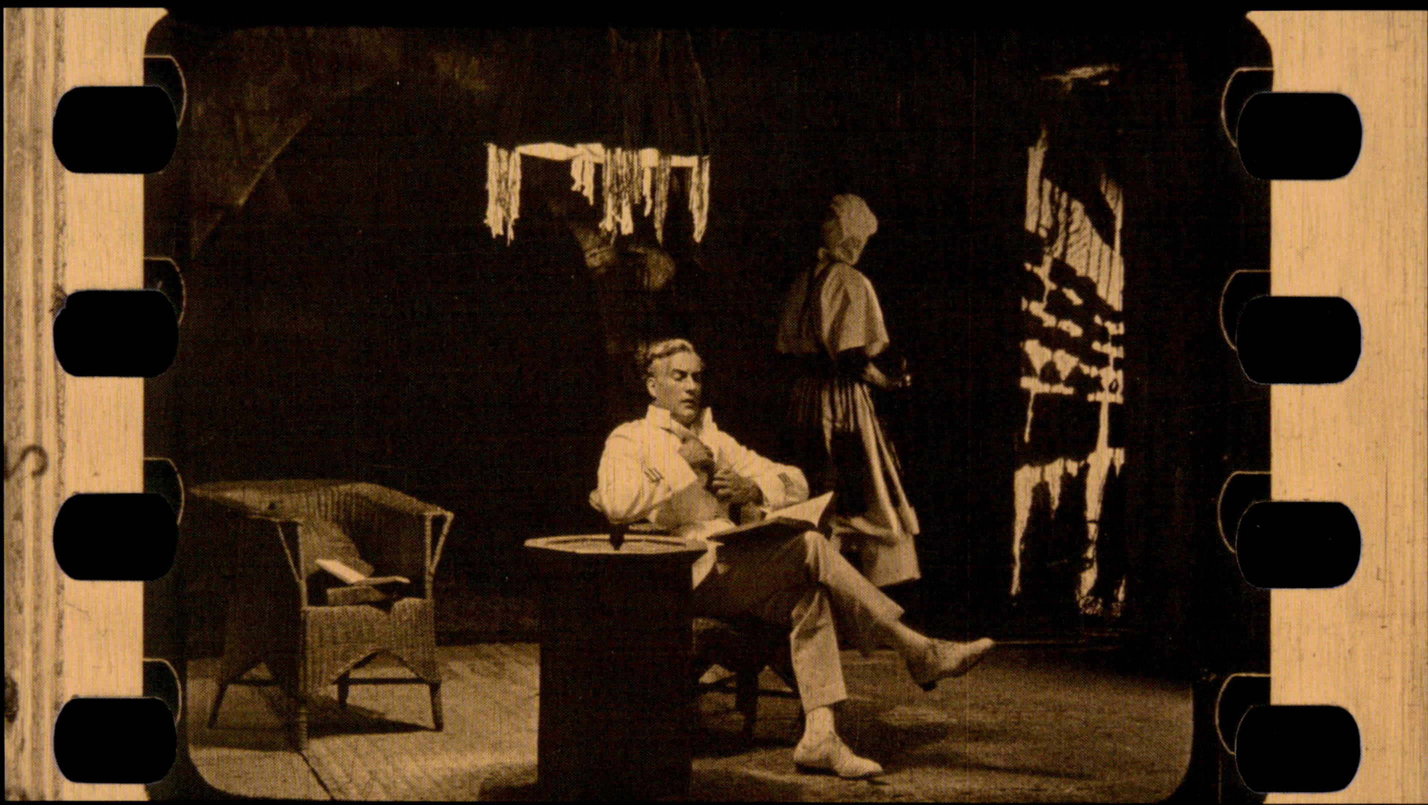

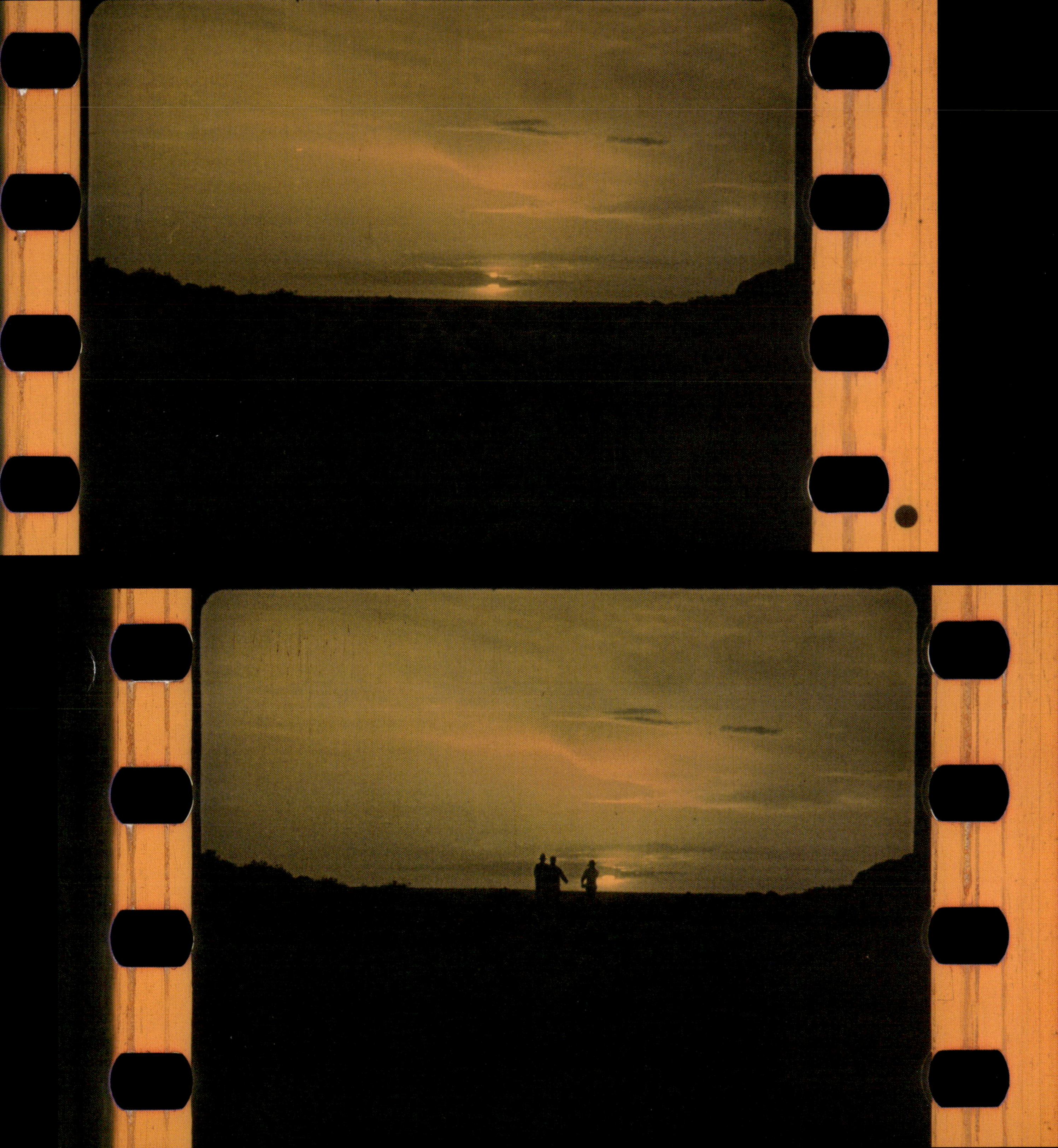

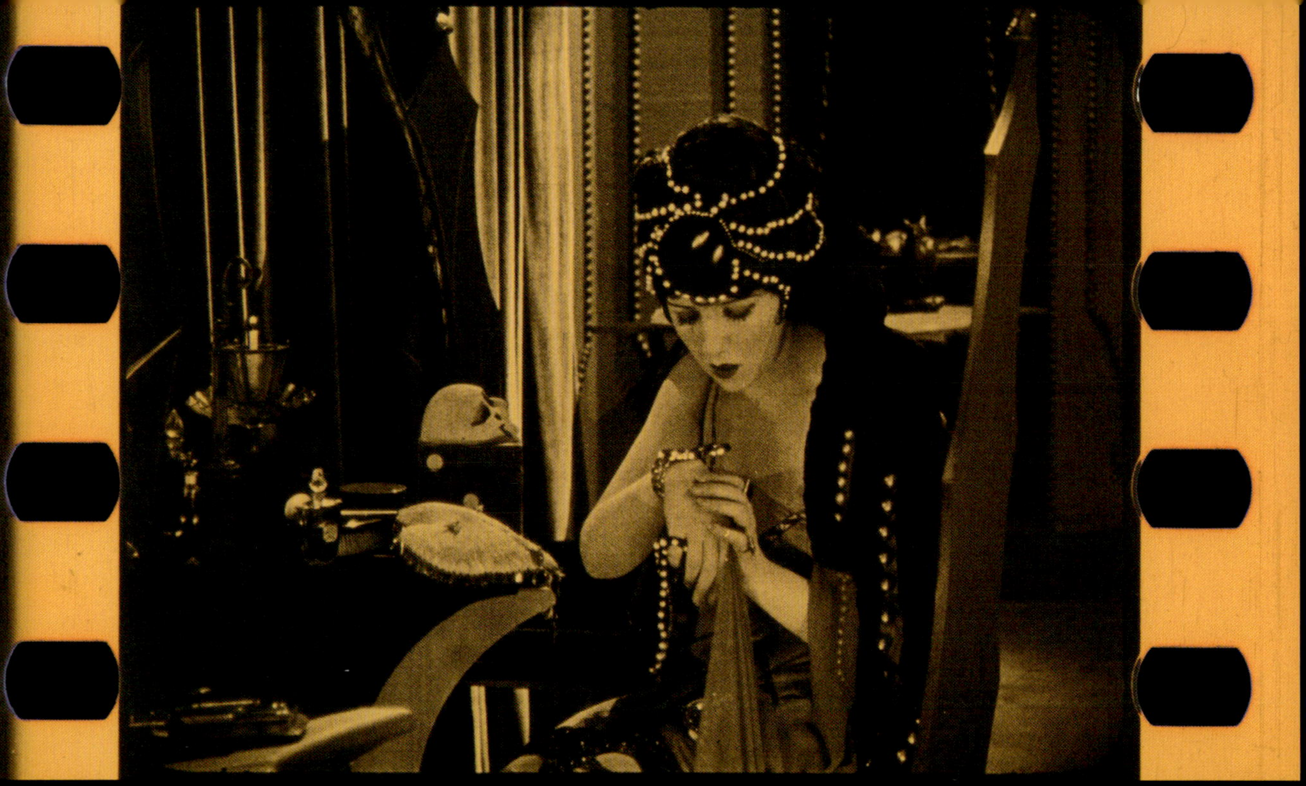

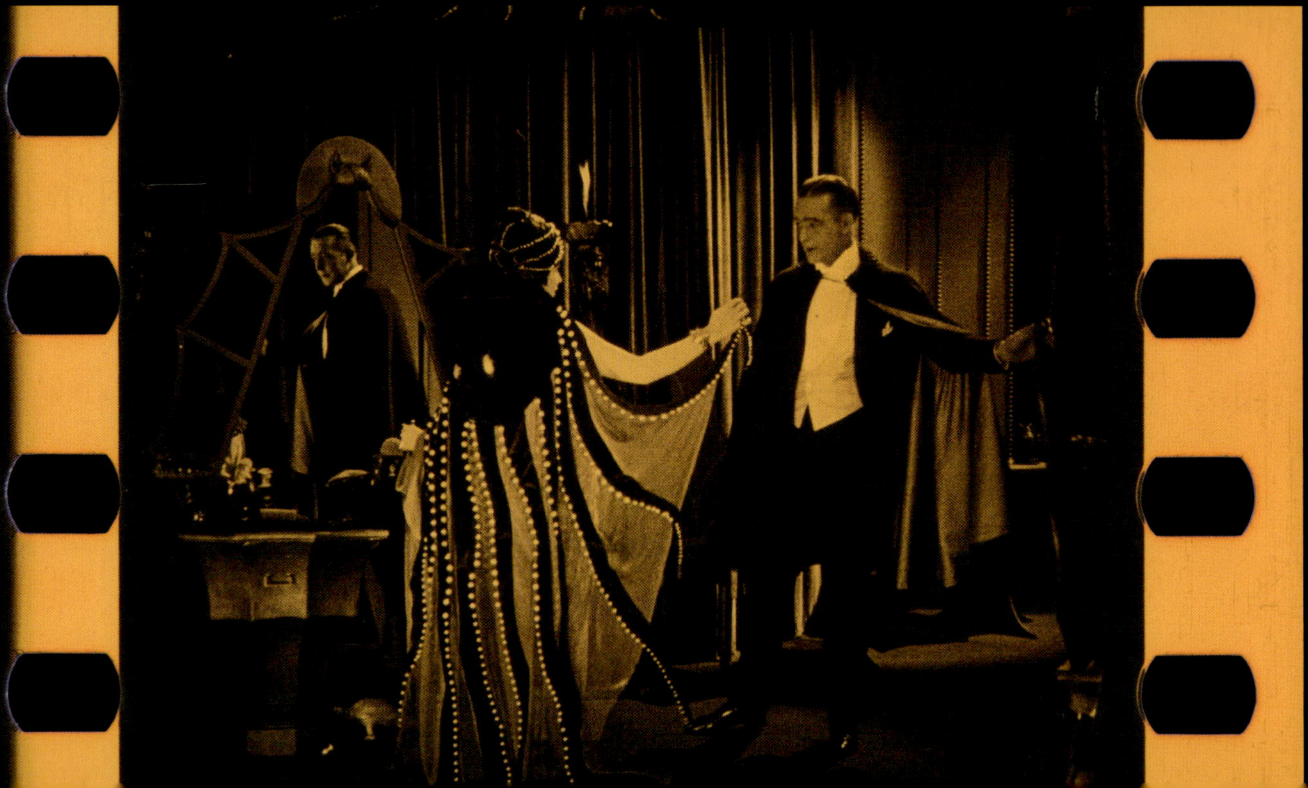

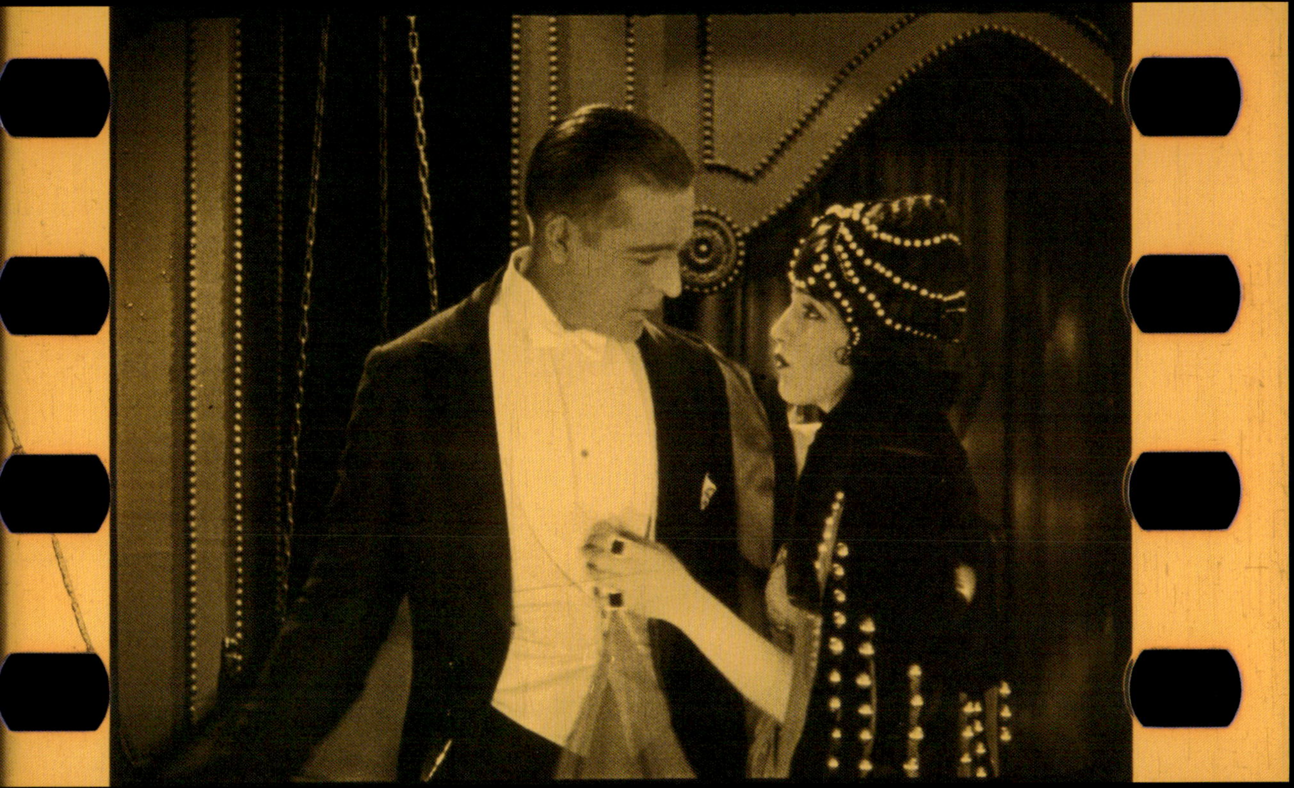

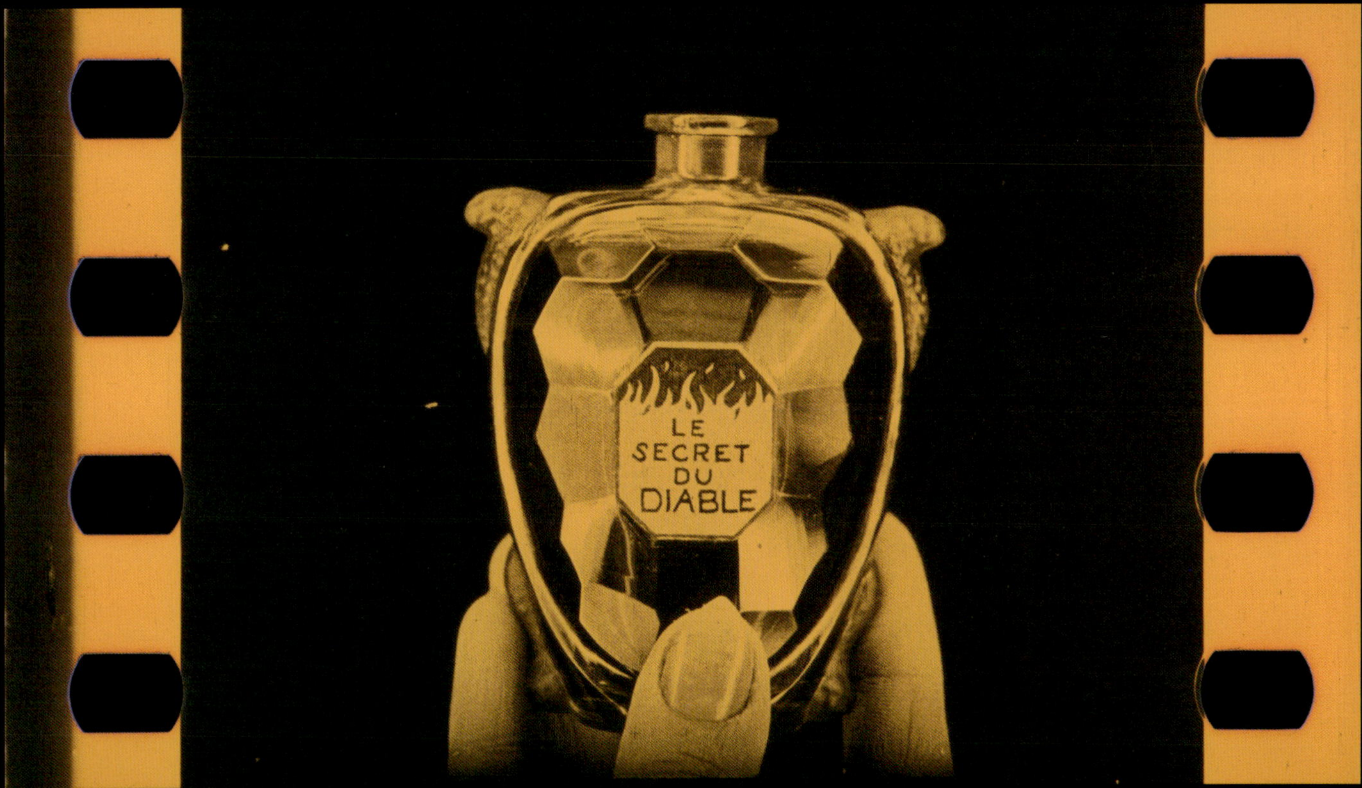

LE
SECRET
DU
DIABLE

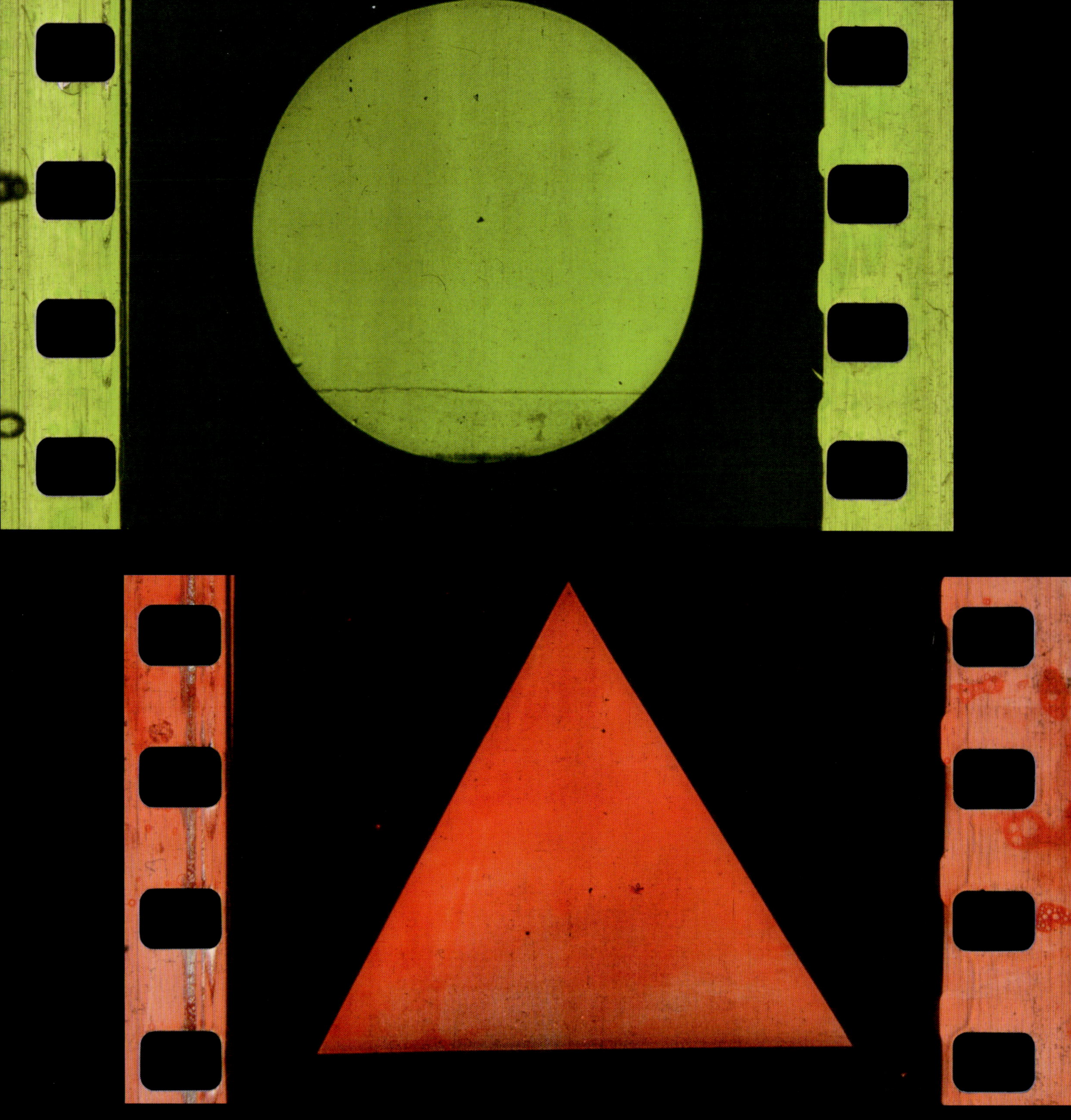

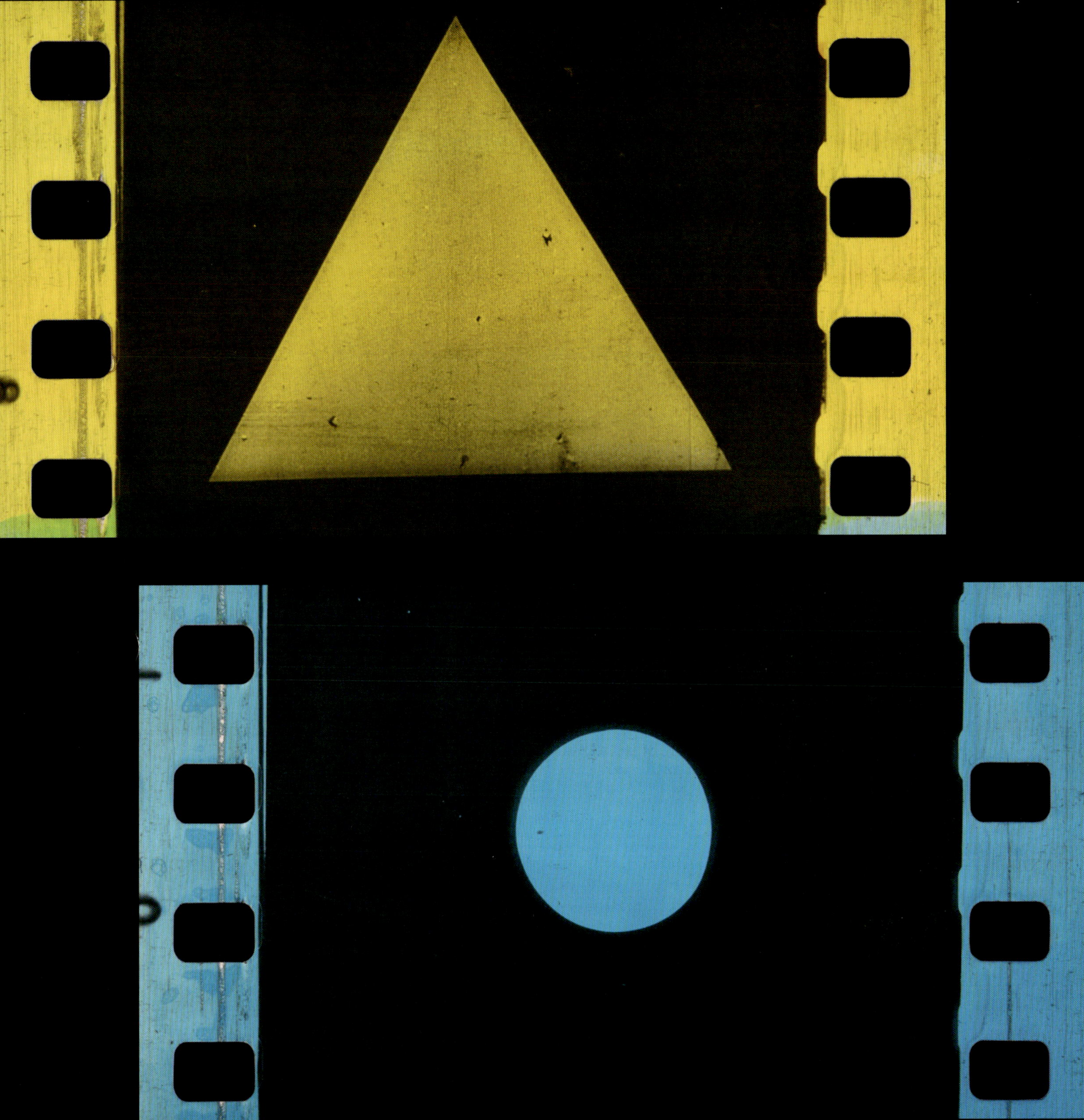

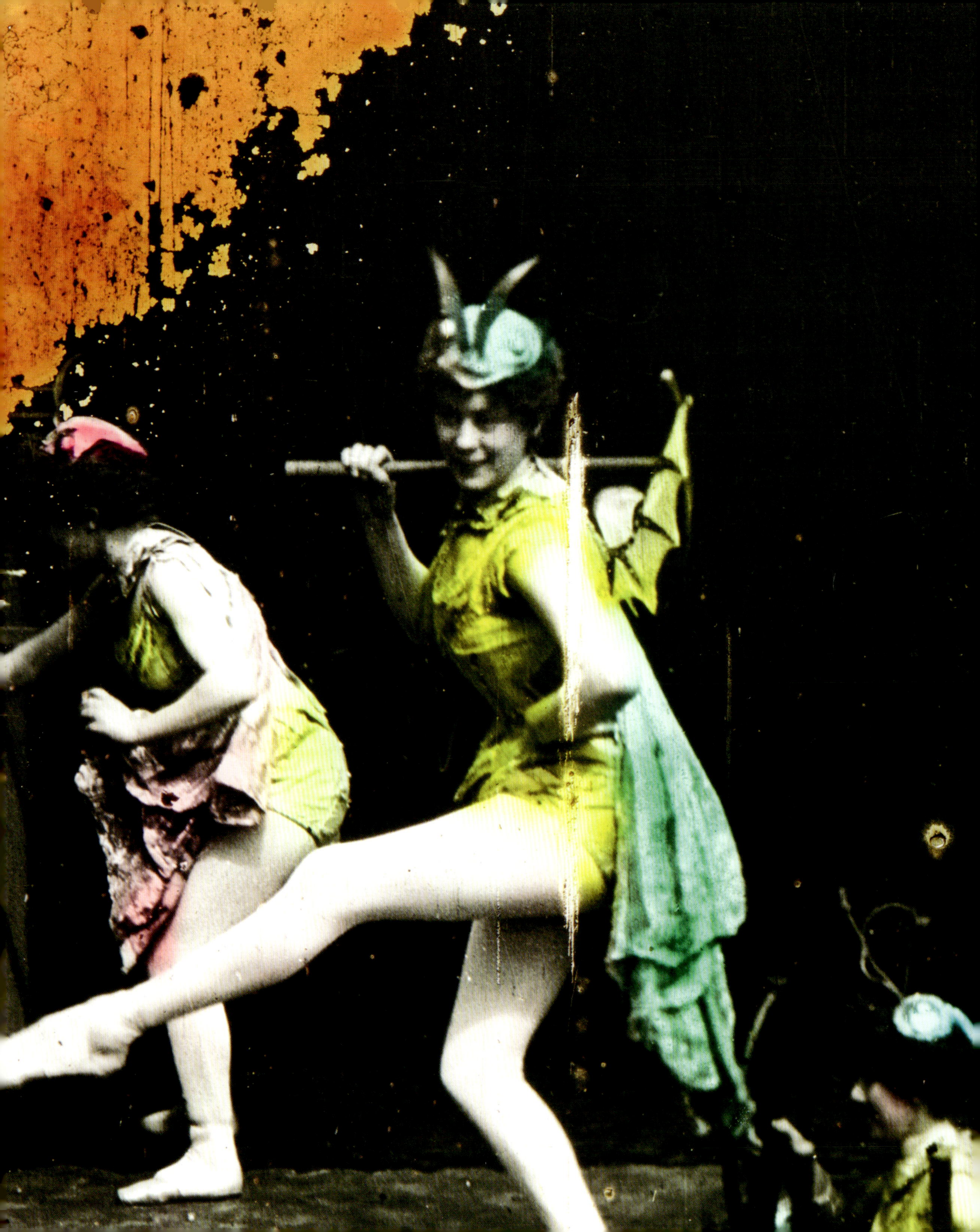

BARBARA FLUECKIGER

THE MATERIALITY AND TECHNOLOGY OF FILM COLORS

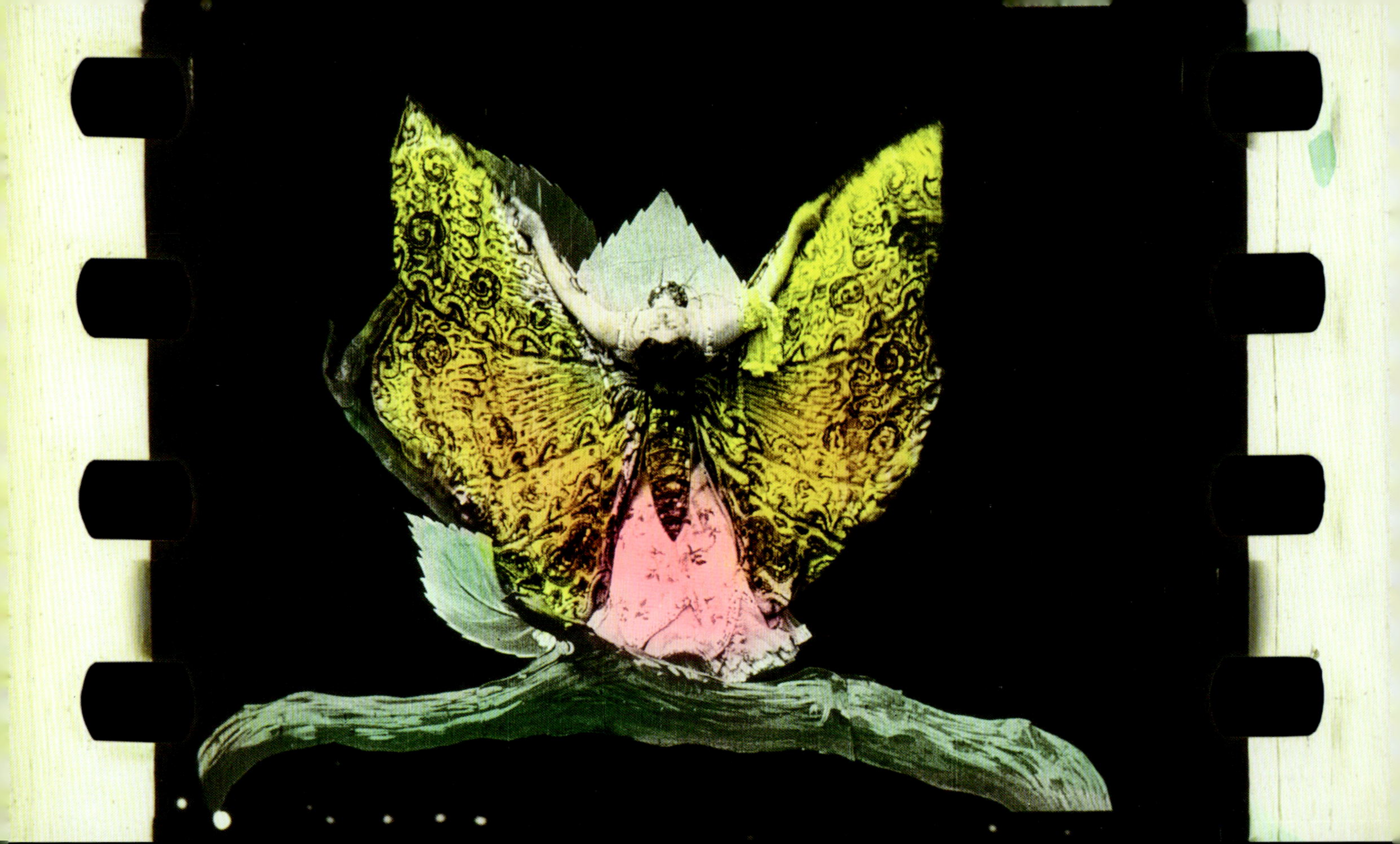

CLOCKWISE FROM TOP: Hand-painted frame from *The Butterfly's Metamorphosis* (*Les Métamorphoses du papillon*, France, 1904, dir. Gaston Velle); toned frame from *L'Atlantide* (France, 1921, dir. Jacques Feyder); and tinted frame from *Malombra* (Italy, 1917, dir. Carmine Gallone)

PAGE 46: *La Biche au bois* (France, 1896, dir. Georges Demeny)

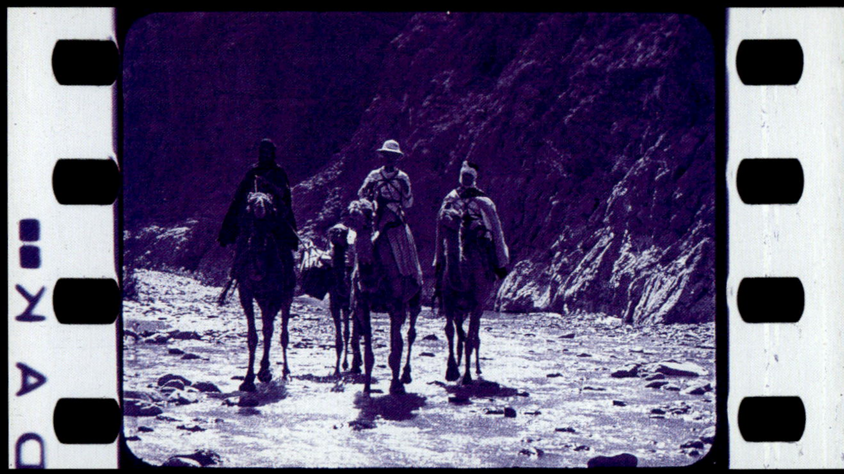

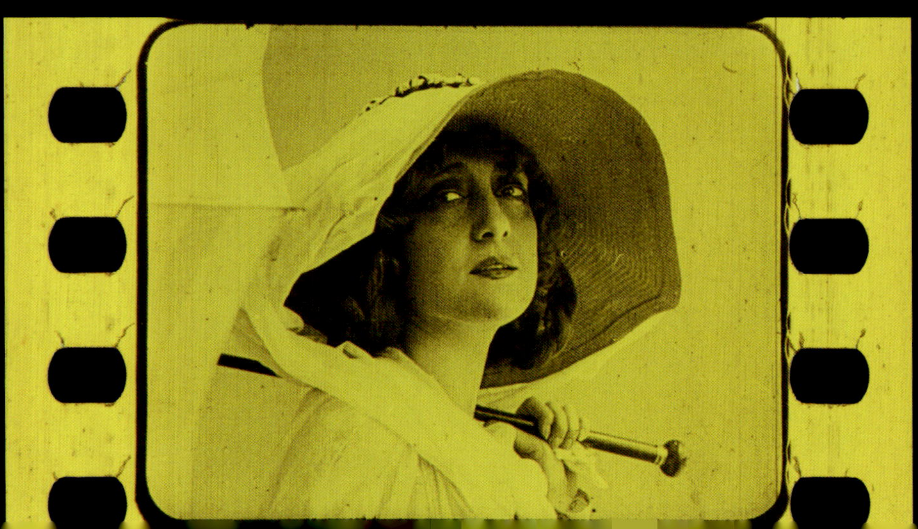

In the cinema, colored beams of light projected onto the screen form what we see. For the general audience, the filmstrip remains hidden, running through a projector in a booth or encased in cans sitting on archive shelves. And with digital means of circulation—DVDs, Blu-ray discs, video streaming on smartphones, computer or tablet displays—the physicality of film has receded even further from the public's perception. To understand color film and its properties and technical principles requires a close look at the material foundations of its appearance and aesthetics.

Each filmstrip is materially composed of several layers. A carrier consisting of a synthetic material—nitrocellulose, acetate, or polyester—provides the sturdy but flexible base. One or more emulsion layers of gelatin are embedded with silver grains and/or pigments or dyes that form the images on screen by filtering the rays of light emanating from the projector. Over more than one hundred years of film history, a wealth of ingenious approaches to capture and render colors has been developed, reflecting the historical quest for a convincing technical solution. Each of them bears a physical imprint in the film stock or the mechanical setup in the cinema, and each has produced incredibly attractive and beautiful film elements in its own right. Their material traces testify to each individual film's history, with far-reaching consequences for their restoration and digitization. This text will provide insights into key concepts and technologies of color film. It will show not only how difficult it was to depict the world in color in motion pictures but also how the technical solutions were a central foundation for the evolution of film style and aesthetics, as shown in photographs of historical film stocks.[1]

APPLIED COLORS

From the earliest years after the invention of film, there were attempts to bring color to the screen. Based on concepts developed in still photography and used in magic lantern slides, colors were applied to black-and-white prints of a film to enrich them with color. Single colors were added by submerging segments of film in dye baths (tinting) or by replacing the silver grains with dyes or pigments (toning).[2] Tinted films can easily be identified by the presence of dye in the filmstrip's perforated edges, while toned films have a clear border. In the case of hand-colored films, colorists applied dyes with tiny brushes. Stencil coloring mechanized this process, allowing dye to be applied through hand-cut stencils to each frame of film.[3] Hand- and stencil-colored films not only were incredibly beautiful and decorative but achieved a heightened impression of reality in travelogues and nature films as well.[4] While most hand- or stencil-colored films until about the mid-1910s featured tableaux—frontally staged in depth for a single camera, inspired by the experience from the stage—the camera became increasingly mobile and spatial arrangements more varied through montage and lighting starting in the 1910s and especially the 1920s.

For films tinted or toned with one or two colors, the attribution of hues was not as regulated and semantically charged as one would expect. Night scenes were often blue but could be tinted green or purple. Red for fires was likely the most consistent color coding of the era. Pinks or dusky roses used to denote female environments were also quite widespread, as was amber to indicate interior lights. Instead of searching for fixed or symbolic meanings, it can be more productive to analyze an individual film's color scheme with a focus on its internal narrative, temporal, and spatial structure.[5] Although color attributions were documented in production notes or written along the edges of the black-and-white camera negative, more often than not it is unclear who made the decisions for a tinted or toned film's color scheme.

As a result, various copies of the same film could display different color schemes, possibly informed by the cultural preferences of their local audiences, a hypothesis that has not been confirmed yet. But the variation reveals precious information when we deal with restorations or digitizations today. The material traces of a film's elements tell its history of production, circulation, and handling. Or, as film historian Paolo Cherchi Usai wrote, "Film is a multiple object."[6] Only when we analyze and compare as many sources as possible can we make learned decisions that guide a restoration today. *The Cabinet of Dr. Caligari* (*Das Cabinet des Dr. Caligari*, Germany, 1920) is a prime example in this regard, with five differently tinted and toned film prints surviving from the period. The 2015 restoration under the guidance of Anke Wilkening of the Friedrich Wilhelm Murnau Foundation necessitated a detailed photographic documentation and physical analysis of these historical prints to reconstruct the genealogy, as no original German print from the time survives.[7]

A variety of the earliest hand-colored films showcase dance scenes. *La biche au bois* (France, 1896), *Les Parisiennes* (USA, 1897), and short films featuring serpentine dances performed by Loïe Fuller or Annabelle Whitford Moore, produced in France and the United States as early as 1895, are among the most intriguing and famous examples.[8] Broad brushstrokes enhance the black-and-white image with colors that move like the colored light beams on the theatrical stage. The labor-intensive process of painstakingly coloring eighteen frames per second with six or eight hues each, work performed by women stationed at benches in a factory setting, paid off in ostentatious visual pleasure for audiences.

Stencil coloring enabled more precise application of dyes, from foregrounding individual characters to ever smaller details of fabrics, sequins, shine, and embroidery. Intense, more saturated dyes were deployed in early films as an element of attraction—often connected to spectacular displays of exotic worlds and expressive of the colonial gaze popular at the turn of the century. Selected dyes became more toned down and translucent over time, with a tendency toward pastel shades or earth tones. Fashion films from the late 1910s and 1920s made use of stencil coloring for the display of the latest trends in consumer culture.[9]

MIMETIC COLORS

Tinting, toning, and hand and stencil color application are autonomous processes: they are detached from the scene in front of the camera and added only after the development of the final black-and-white positive, which does not contain any trace of the original hues present during the shooting of a film, be it in a studio or at an exterior location. From the earliest days of film, however, ideas were developed for physical—optical and/or mechanical—techniques to capture the colors of a scene into a true color record, either embedded in the film or re-created optically in the cinema. Apart from the theoretical ideation of a convincing color process, there were also practical, economic, and, not least, political factors that shaped the development of mimetic film colors. Therefore, the history of color film has been speckled with a host of unsuccessful attempts and failures. Retrospectively, it seems quite obvious which paths turned out to be dead ends. But often core ideas from one technical approach migrated to a new one. As film historian John Belton once said, every color film is in essence a black-and-white film with color attached to it.[10]

A broad range of these technological ideas date back to developments in color photography. In 1861 James Clerk Maxwell demonstrated how the superimposition of three black-and-white records, taken and projected through three colored filters, re-created the color impression according to physiological principles of human vision. In 1869 both Louis Ducos du Hauron and Charles Cros wrote extended papers about various techniques for the ideation of color photography. However, it was much more demanding to translate these ideas onto motion pictures. Not only does film require a huge number of single frames—eighteen to twenty-four frames per second—but it also calls for their enlargement in motion onto a large screen, thereby exposing even the smallest inaccuracies. Misalignment results in either flickering, by exposing the deviations from frame to frame, or color fringes on the edges of figures and objects.

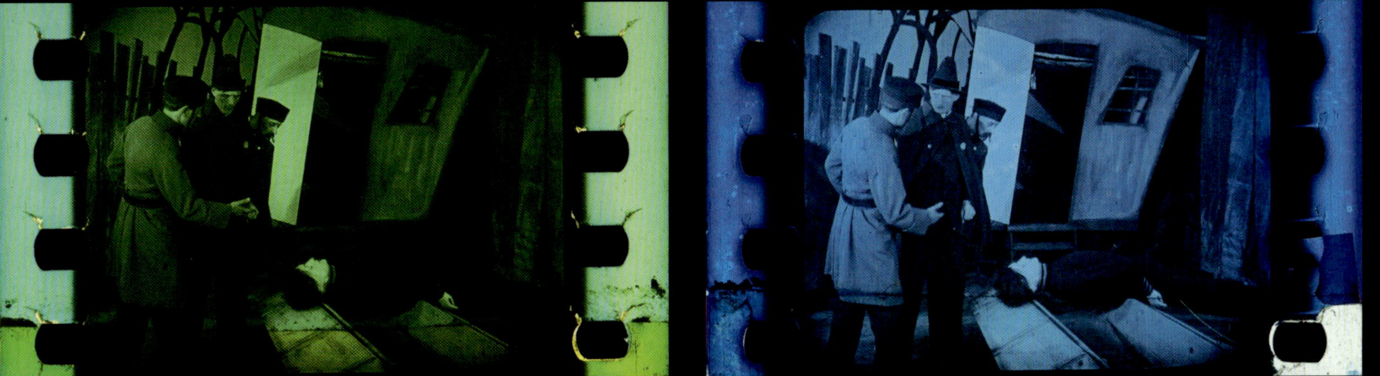

ABOVE: Tinted frames from different prints of *The Cabinet of Dr. Caligari* (*Das Cabinet des Dr. Caligari*, Germany, 1920, dir. Robert Wiene)

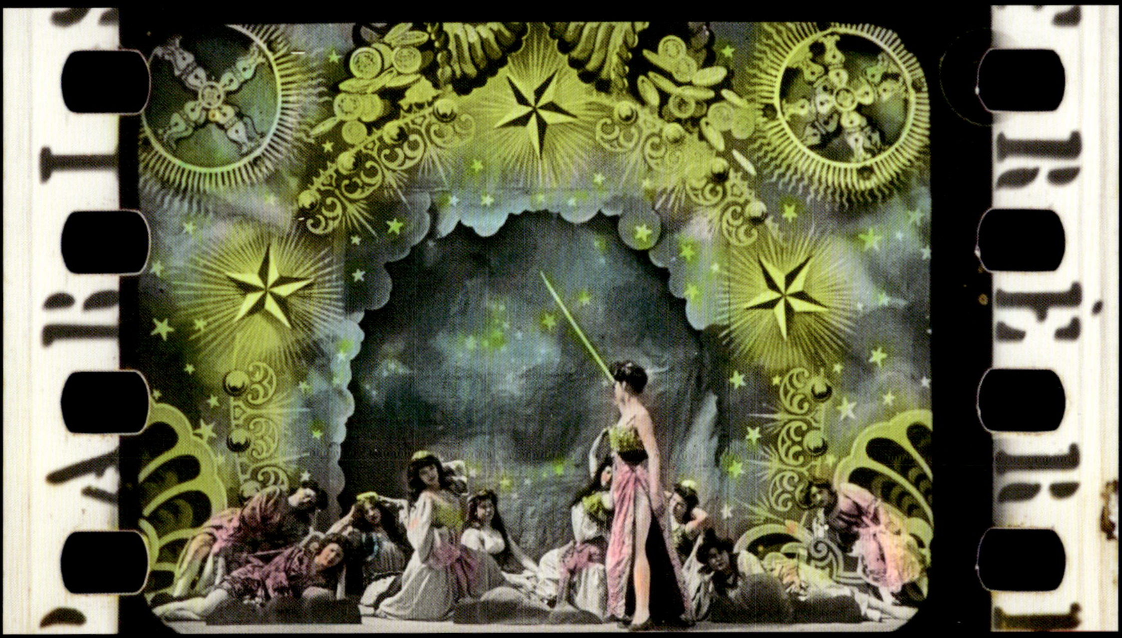

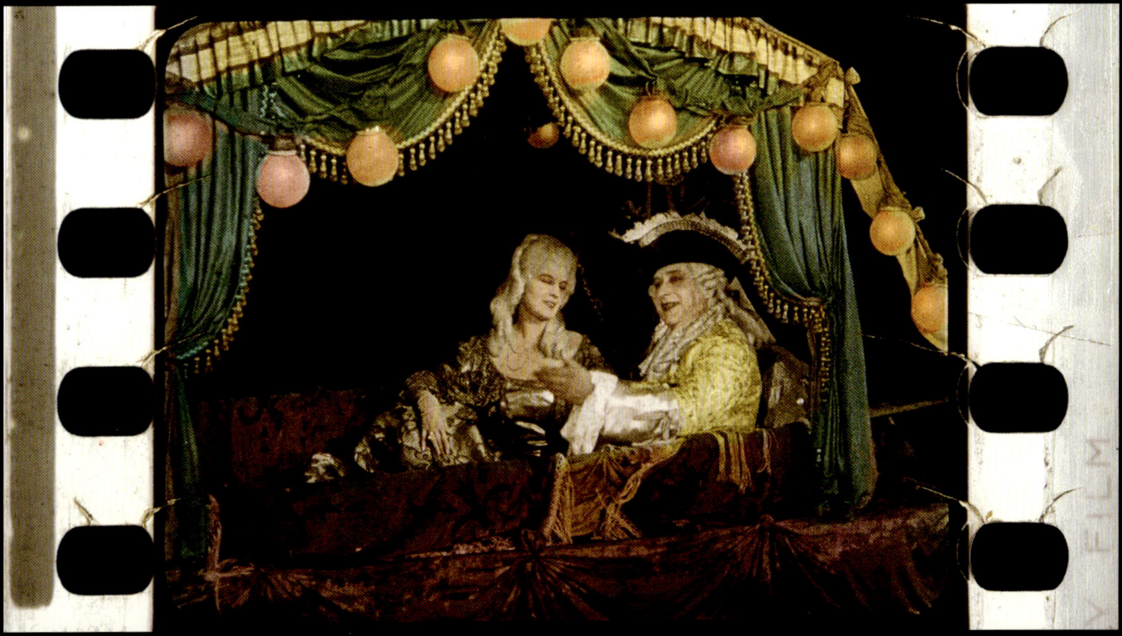

CENTER: Stencil coloring in *Ali Baba and the Forty Thieves* (*Ali Baba et les quarante voleurs*, France, 1902, dir. Ferdinand Zecca)

BOTTOM: Stencil coloring in *Casanova* (France, 1927, dir. Alexandre Volkoff)

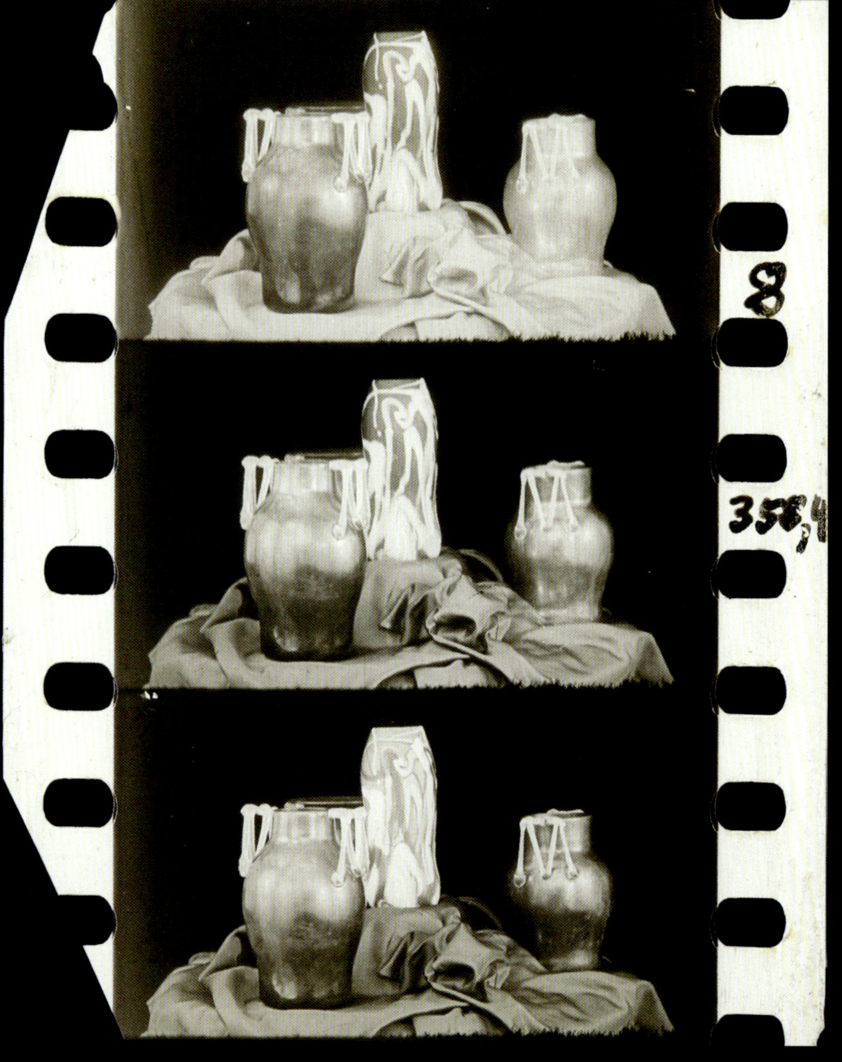

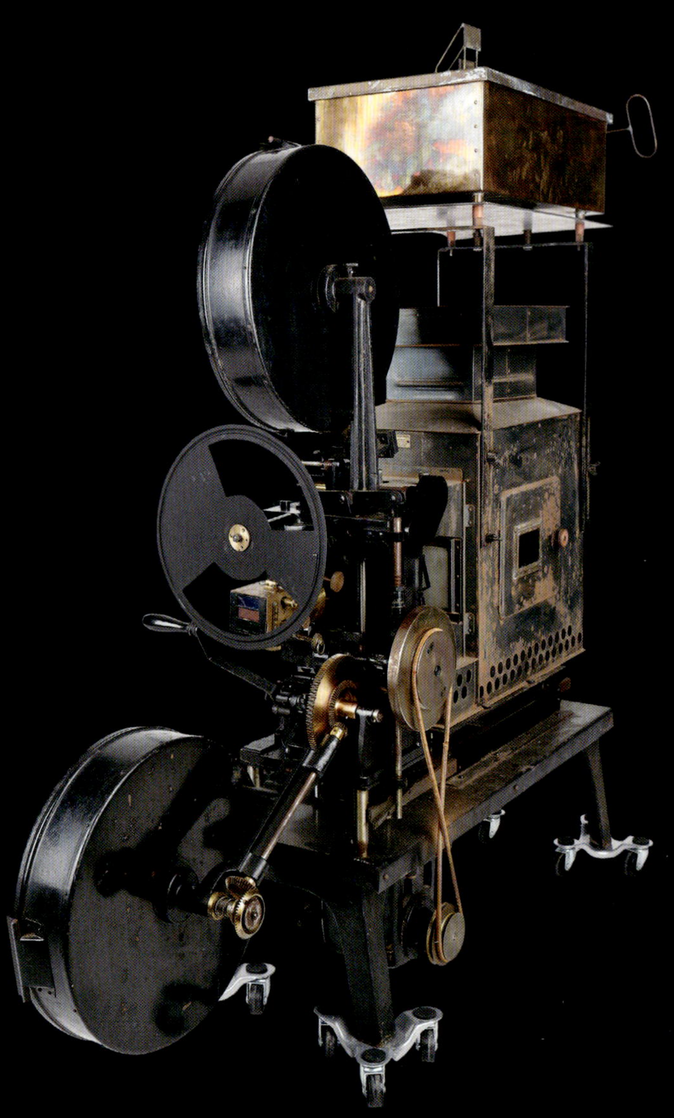

TOP: Gaumont Chronochrome sample, ca. 1910

RIGHT: Gaumont Chronochrome 35mm three-color projector, ca. 1912

Maxwell's initial idea laid the groundwork for countless variations. Additive processes like the one he presented in 1861 relied on an admixture of colored illumination. Applying this principle to film technology, color filters were used in spinning wheels, beam splitters, and camera lenses or embedded into the film stock in the form of translucent grains or line screens. A spinning wheel with red, green, and blue filters was patented as early as 1897 by German inventor Hermann Isensee. His idea laid the foundation for a long period of innovation in film colors produced by temporal synthesis, with different colored images projected in rapid succession to create a composite color impression for spectators. These included the Lee and Turner process from 1899 and the most successful early invention, Kinemacolor, introduced in 1908 by George Albert Smith and Charles Urban.[11] Urban was a clever businessperson who advocated color film for its enhanced reality effect.

Despite the essential capability of the system to record three color components, such a technical setup proved to be too demanding mechanically because it would have necessitated a frame rate three times higher than the usual standard. A host of articles were published at the time that lauded Kinemacolor's vivid impression of color, but digital reconstructions have since revealed that its two additive colors of red and green yielded a limited color spectrum, the temporal gap between the alternately recorded red and green records produced grotesque color fringing, and the flickering effect of the alternating projection was considerable. Kinemacolor's greatest success was *The Delhi Durbar: With Our King and Queen through India* (UK, 1912). As film historian Sarah Street summarized, "As such it represented the apotheosis of British imperialism preserved 'for all time,' as *The Bioscope* put it, by Kinemacolor, 'the modern Elixir of Life.'"[12] However, by 1914 Kinemacolor lost a lawsuit to competitors. Though initially brought "on the grounds of prior use of the two-color process by Friese-Greene and others, its resolution was effected by the determination that Smith's two-color process was unpatentable."[13] As Gorham Kindem rightly observes, the legal defeat was just one factor in Kinemacolor's failure, in addition to aesthetic, economic, and technological concerns.[14]

Kinemacolor's success and demise provides a textbook example of factors that influence a technical innovation's adoption and distribution, most importantly discursive practices and negotiations of power, as convincingly argued by Noemi Daugaard and Josephine Diecke in their publications.[15] There are also practical considerations, not least a technology's compliance with existing technical infrastructure on location and in cinemas. Kinemacolor not only required a double frame rate—resulting in double the amount of film stock needed—but also necessitated special cameras and additional equipment for cinema projectors.

Beam splitters and multiple lenses, both of which split the incoming rays of light, were core elements of a next wave of innovations in the field of color cinematography. In contrast to temporal synthesis, in which the colors appear in rapid sequence, spatial synthesis processes captured two or three records simultaneously through filters. Again, the degree of optical precision required to deliver correct alignment on screen was almost unsurmountable, thus these processes caused distortions and color fringing as well. However, spatial synthesis eliminated flickering and did not necessarily require higher frame rates.

Gaumont's Chronochrome process, introduced in 1912, combined three records taken through filters and separate lenses on the filmstrip.[16] Thanks to the three components provided by red, green, and blue filters, its color range superseded earlier innovations such as two-color Kinemacolor. However, Chronochrome still required a special camera and additional installations for cinema projection.[17] Recent digital reconstructions of the process deliver flamboyant results but possibly do not render an accurate historical impression. Filters tend to lower brightness, which was a more critical issue in the 1910s, when projector illumination was dimmer and the reflective properties of cinema screens were not as developed; those screens were also likely yellowish due to smoke and pollution in theaters of the time. Beam splitters would remain at the core of various later innovations, most notably Technicolor, including the three-strip process that became the industry standard from the mid-1930s to the 1950s.

TWO-COLOR PROCESSES

Many two-color processes were invented from the mid-1910s until the 1930s. Their films contain two layers of emulsion, either on both sides of the filmstrip or, rarely, on the same side. Black-and-white separations were captured through a beam splitter, multiple lenses, or so-called bipack film, which exposed two strips of film at once, the two emulsion sides facing each other. First patented in 1912 by Arturo Hernandez-Mejia for his Colorgraph/Cinecolorgraph process, the principle was adopted by many subsequent innovations. A large spectrum of test materials has survived from this period, but only a very few were so developed or economically backed to allow the shooting of longer formats; the productions range from commercials and short documentaries to a few feature films. All of these processes required specially fitted cameras,

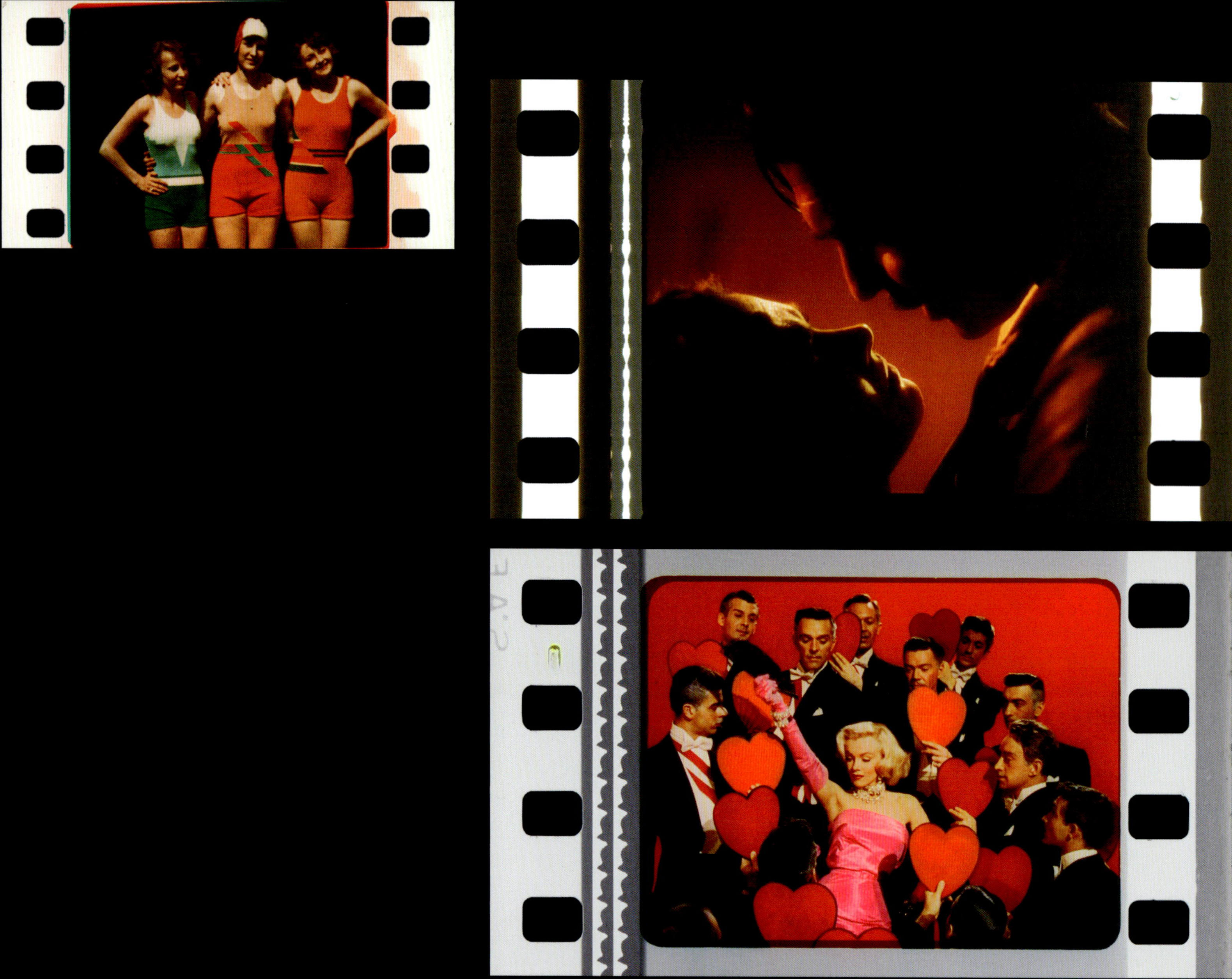

and their printing techniques were complex and error prone. The filters attached to the beam splitter reduced the level of illumination able to reach the film stock in the camera, thus requiring more light and longer exposure times, which in turn created high amounts of motion blur when the camera or the characters were moving.

Not only did the two-color components produce a limited range of the visible spectrum, but it was also difficult to balance these components in a convincing manner to meet spectators' historically and culturally informed expectations. Almost all test shots of the 1920s and 1930s showcased young white women in flattering illumination.[18] As their skin tones served as reference, most evident in the so-called leader ladies, a strongly gendered and racial bias was integrated into color film from the start.[19]

TECHNICOLOR I TO IV

Technicolor is likely the most famous brand for film color. Audiences today associate it with saturated, bright bursts of color in Hollywood films with stunning settings, lavish landscapes, dramatic sunsets, and beautiful stars in spectacular costumes, all of which culminated in *Gone with the Wind* (USA, 1939). Only recently has the not-so-successful prehistory of Technicolor's three-color dye-transfer Process IV gained more attention.[20] Little is known about the many failures and struggles of the company for almost twenty years before its breakthrough.

Technicolor had tested nearly the whole range of options to depict the world in front of the camera in color. The additive Process I, introduced in 1916, was an instant failure because it required a less than practical physical setup for both the camera and the projector; in fact, additive color had proved to be a dead end with Kinemacolor even before Technicolor adopted the principle. For Process II, Technicolor switched to a subtractive two-color process. In contrast to the double-coated film stocks mentioned above, it took two filmstrips, dyed orange-red and green, and cemented them together. This material condition led to excessive wear and tear in cinema projection, as the resulting film stock was too thick to pass neatly through the projector. The filmstrips also tended to warp in the heat generated by the carbon arc illumination used in projectors of the time.

The biggest shift toward a convincing solution occurred in 1927, when Technicolor took up the idea of dye-transfer printing, an idea first applied to still photography in the 1870s. While technical history has often been written as a chronicle of men, cherry-picked "geniuses" who came up with groundbreaking ideas, a closer look reveals that the foundations for these ideas had been circulating earlier. Daniel Frost Comstock, Herbert Kalmus, and W. Burton Westcott's Technicolor is a prime example. Chromolithography, a printing process employed earlier in magic lantern slides and the first to be applied to film, was used to produce short animated film loops for children's play projectors during the first decades of the twentieth century. The Handschiegl process, introduced in 1916, used dye-transfer printing but in an applied process that can be likened to stencil coloring, as the color was added manually to a printing matrix that absorbed the dyes to be transferred onto the film prints—an expensive and laborious process.

In contrast, Technicolor's dye-transfer process was a photographic and mimetic one. The printing templates were produced directly from black-and-white separations captured through colored filters attached to the beam splitter in special cameras: originally two, for the two-color Technicolor Process III, and then three for the three-color Process IV. In a tanning process, the parts of the image that contained silver grains hardened; the soft parts, those that didn't contain silver, were then washed off with warm water to create the printing matrices. Subsequently, these were imbued with dyes in the three primary colors (cyan, magenta, and yellow) and slowly transferred onto a print containing the frame's edge and, after the introduction of sound, the soundtrack as a silver image. Thus, Technicolor dye-transfer prints have highly idiomatic material properties that enable easy identification of the process today. Also, the dyes have proven to be stable. Due to their low viscosity—necessary to prevent the dyes from diffusing into neighboring areas, which would have diminished detail and sharpness—the colors appear dense and somewhat opaque, with a dark glow that would come to be identified as the Technicolor look.

By the end of the 1920s Technicolor III was in vogue. A number of musicals were produced after Great Events, a series of twelve short films produced by Technicolor with MGM to showcase the potential of the process. However, as mentioned above, various factors made the translation of technical principles from color photography to film complicated and demanding, as became evident with Technicolor's dye-transfer processes. These processes required not only double or triple the amount of camera negative but also special cameras and cinematographers trained in their handling. The arbitrary assignment of dyes to the black-and-white records brought about unusual shifts in hues, white and bright areas had to be avoided, and the film stocks necessitated high

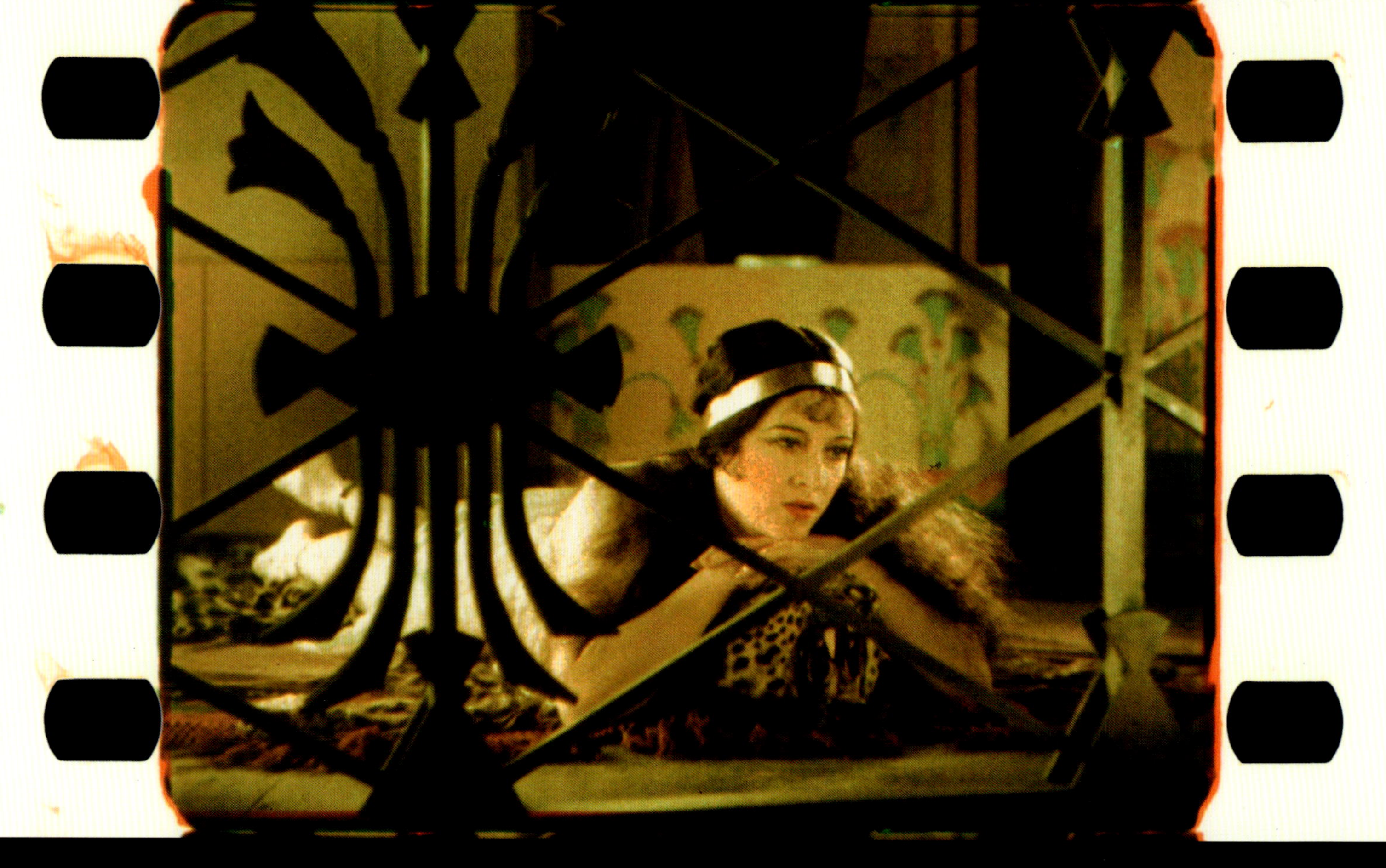

Frame from the Technicolor III film *Cleopatra* (USA, 1928, dir. R. William Neill)

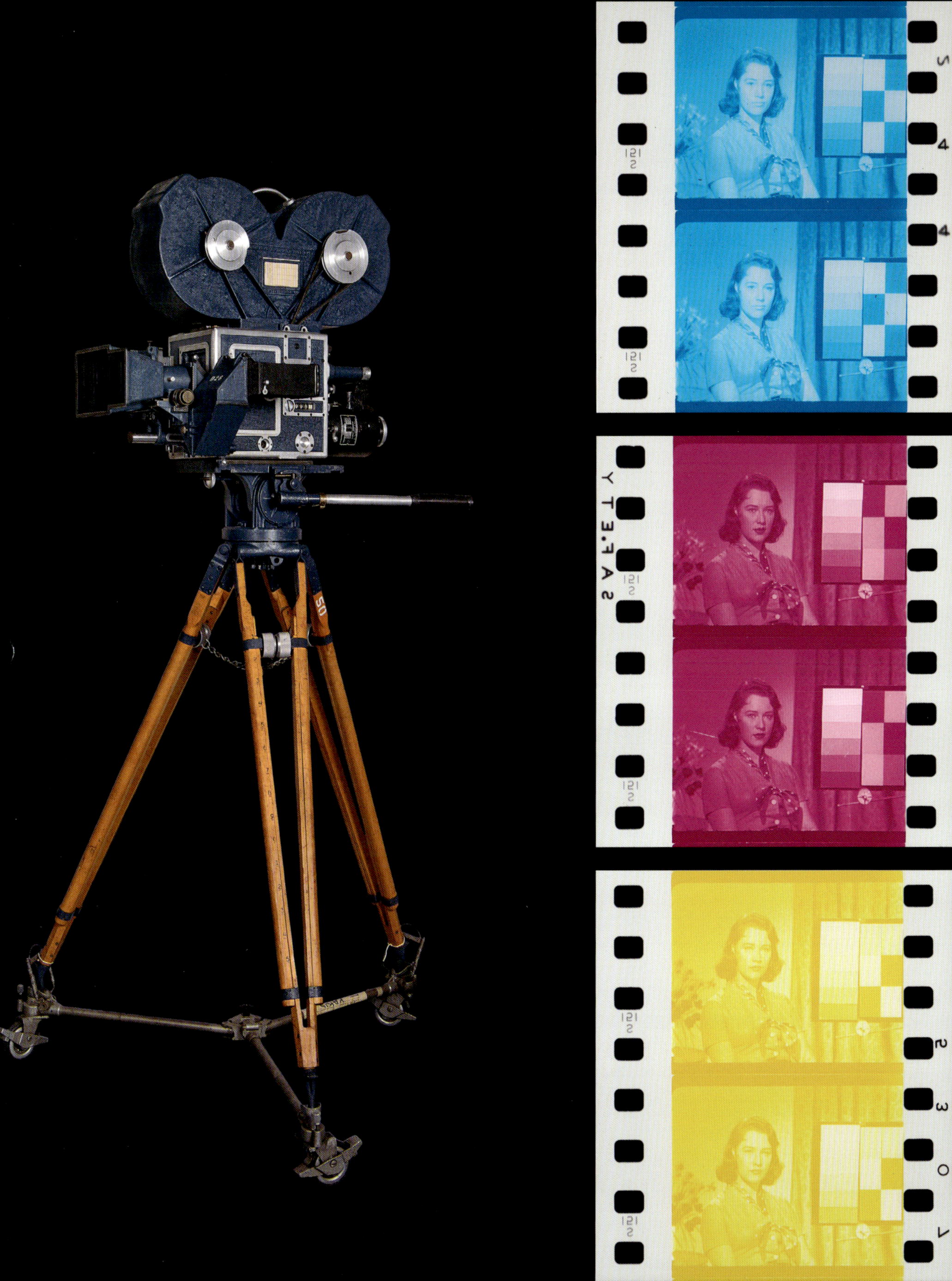

levels of illumination. Finally, and not least, was the most demanding part of the dye-transfer technology: an exacting registration of the records in the printing process to avoid color fringes.[21]

The Technicolor company tackled these weaknesses with a comprehensive service chain, starting with the Color Advisory Service led by Natalie Kalmus, to guarantee that color choices made for costume and set design were in line with the processes' color range and limitations while also "tasteful" according to a normative set of rules laid out by Kalmus and applied by her team.[22] Technicolor cameras, cinematographers, and operators had to be rented from the company; Technicolor also took care of developing the film stocks and handling the dye-transfer process in its own laboratories. Despite all the drawbacks and the excessive costs, Process IV became associated with high-quality film colors and films—not least because only the most financially robust productions were able to cover the bill.

CHROMOLYTIC AND CHROMOGENIC FILMS: GASPARCOLOR, AGFACOLOR, AND EASTMANCOLOR

While the dye-transfer process was intrinsically mechanical, with the most demanding parts being the alignment of the color records and the printing process, chromolytic and chromogenic films shifted that complexity to the chemical domain. From early in the twentieth century, ideas emerged to embed the dyes in layers within the emulsion. Two complementary principles can be discerned in these types of color processes. Chromolytic processes destroy the dyes relative to the concentration of exposed silver salts. Chromogenic processes, on the other hand, develop the dyes coupled to the silver halides in the emulsion layers. Initially, both routes proved to be prohibitively demanding; thus it took several decades for the development of practical applications.

Gasparcolor, invented by Béla Gaspar in Germany and utilizing a chromolytic process, was available for production starting in 1933. Like Technicolor, it necessitated the capturing of three black-and-white separations either with a beam-splitter camera or sequentially through filters. Consequently, most Gasparcolor motion pictures were animation films, many of which were abstract experimental works following the European avant-garde movements of the 1920s. Notable experimental filmmakers Oskar Fischinger and Len Lye, for example, used the Gasparcolor process to yield bright, saturated colors that remain stable and stunning to this day. Gasparcolor might even have won the race for a convincing color film process were it not actively sidestepped and ultimately blocked by competitor IG Farbenindustrie during the Third Reich in Germany.[23]

In the era before World War II, Germany's scientific research and industry led the world in the domain of chemistry. Starting at the end of the 1930s, Agfacolor, the first chromogenic film stock, was also first to offer a negative–positive process, in which the camera captured an inverse negative that could then be mass printed on positive stock for cinema screenings. During the Nazi era, German propaganda minister Joseph Goebbels thus pushed the development of Agfacolor as an instrument to showcase Germany's superiority. Compared to Gasparcolor, however, the Agfacolor process proved to have striking nonlinearities in its rendition of colors. Resulting colors appeared pale and mostly pastel, reds tended to be a tomato hue with an orange cast, and greens were dark and muddy. Long term, it also turned out that, as with all chromogenic film stocks, the dyes were unstable, resulting in faded prints with strong magenta-to-red casts due to the decay of the cyan dyes over time. After World War II, Agfa's patents were taken over by the Allies, thus enabling global adoption of the chromogenic principle for color film and the negative–positive technology necessary for mass distribution.

As a result, from the late 1940s onward a huge range of chromogenic color processes emerged in Middle and Eastern Europe, the Soviet Union, the United States, India, and Japan, with Eastmancolor becoming the most widespread.[24] Eastmancolor differed from Agfacolor in the chemical composition of the dye couplers and the corresponding development process, which proved to be more efficient. While such chromogenic processes did not require any additional equipment during shooting and projection, their complexity was outsourced to the chemically and mechanically demanding production of the film stocks and to the equally challenging development of the films at the lab.[25] Initially, Eastmancolor's rendition of colors appeared quite underwhelming in comparison to those of Technicolor. But the formula, distribution of the dye clouds in the emulsion, speed of the film, and grain size and texture were continually redeveloped to meet the aesthetic requirements of filmmakers and cinematographers. In contrast to Technicolor, Eastmancolor and other rival brands of chromogenic films did not insist on a corporate structure to control every step, from the shooting to the final film print including the color design. Thus a wide variety of styles emerged, allowing more individualized and independent filmmaking to blossom, from the French Nouvelle Vague in the late 1950s to 1960s and the New Hollywood in the 1960s and 1970s to a new emergence of auteurs in Russia, India, Japan, and China.

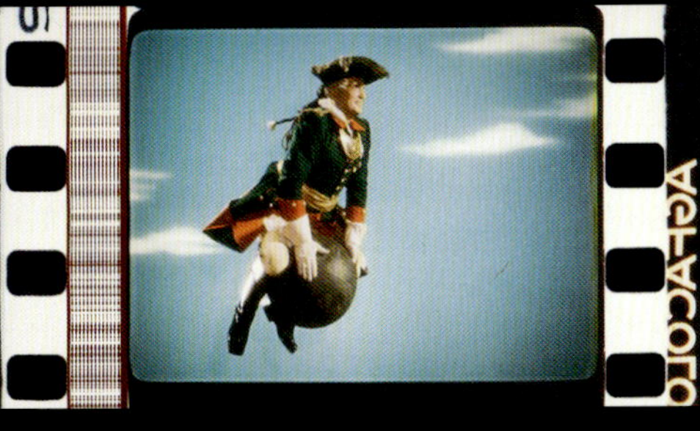

Frame from the Agfacolor film *Münchhausen* (Germany, 1943, dir. Josef von Báky)

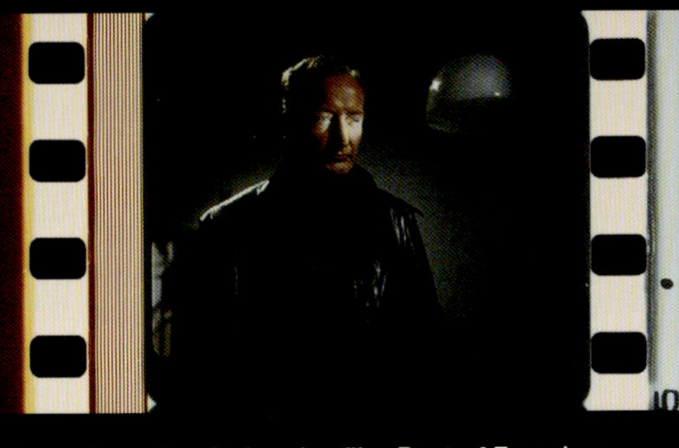

Frame from the Agfacolor film *Port of Freedom* (*Die Grosse Freiheit Nr. 7*, Germany, 1944, dir. Helmut Käutner)

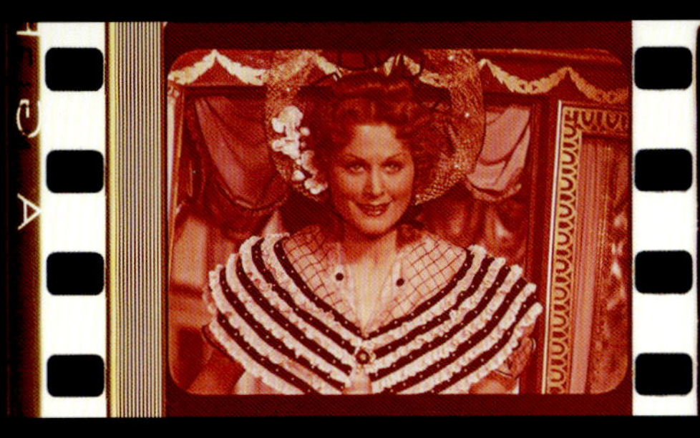

Frame from the Agfacolor film *Women Are Better Diplomats* (*Frauen sind doch bessere Diplomaten*, Germany, 1941, dir. Georg Jacoby)

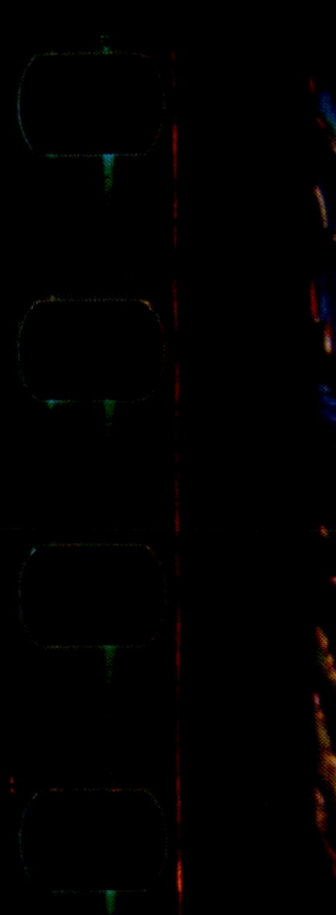
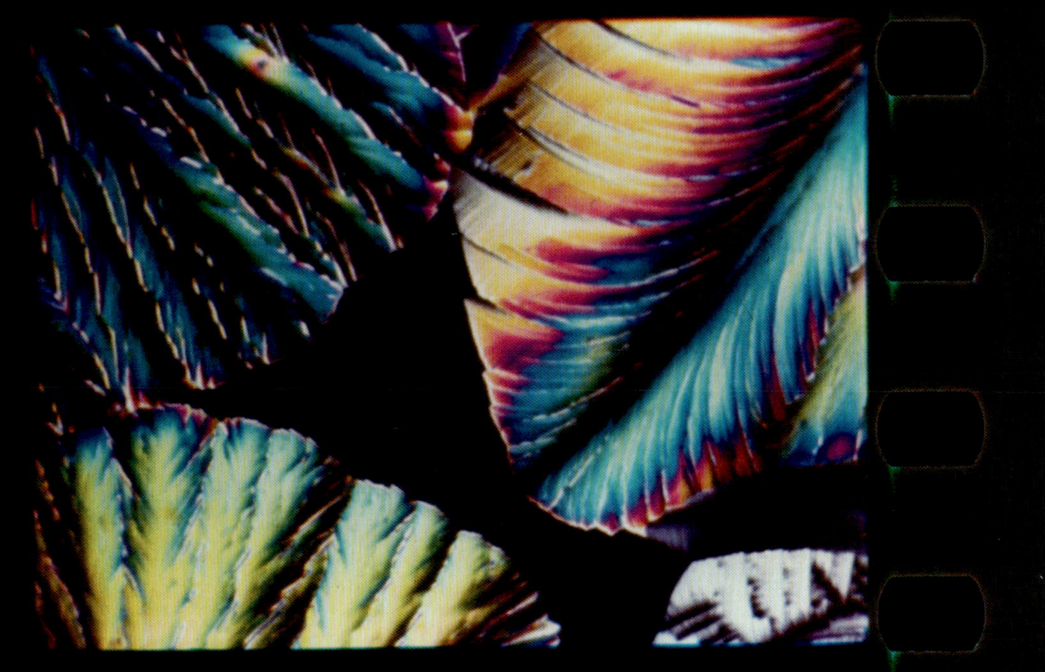

Frame from the Gasparcolor film *From the Realm of the Crystals* (*Uit het rijk der kristallen*, The Netherlands, 1927, dir. J. C. Mol)

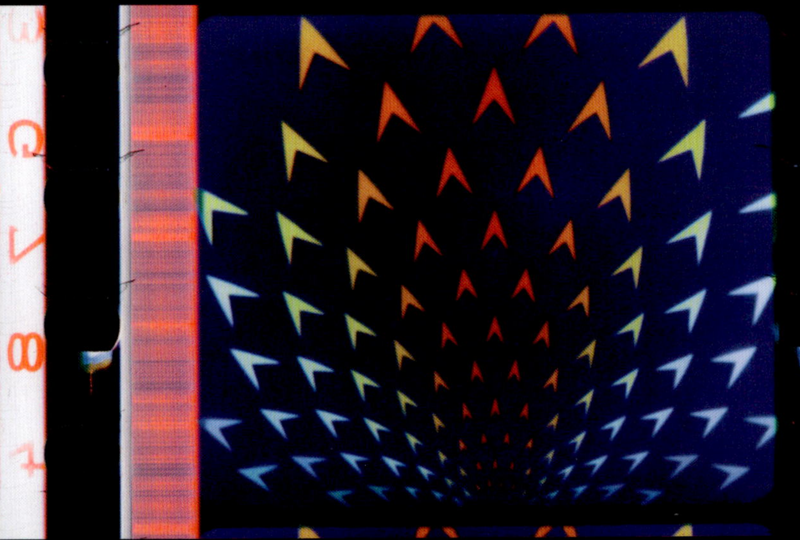

Frame from the Gasparcolor film *Dance of the Colors* (*Tanz der Farben*, Germany, 1939, dir. Hans Fischinger)

The transnational diffusion and circulation of ideas and concepts were important factors technically, economically, and stylistically.[26]

However, in the early 1980s Martin Scorsese sounded the alarm over the instability and decay of the dyes in chromogenic film stocks, raising public awareness of how color fading was destroying film heritage. A large number of chromogenic films from the 1940s to the 1980s have lost their aesthetic characteristics, fading into reddish and magenta hues. "How can we sit back and allow a classic film, *2001: A Space Odyssey*, to fade to magenta?," Scorsese wrote. "Far worse, can we continue to live with the problem and design our films around it as George Lucas, by his own admission, has done with *Star Wars*, a film color-designed to appear faded?"[27]

TRANSLATING FILM HERITAGE INTO THE DIGITAL DOMAIN

With the turn to digital technologies in cinema projection and distribution, including widespread circulation on DVDs, Blu-ray discs, and streaming platforms starting in the early 2000s, it has become necessary to digitize historical films in order to keep them accessible. Conceptually, aesthetically, and technically, there is a huge gap between analog and digital motion pictures. Since 2012 I have worked on developing an online database, the Timeline of Historical Film Colors (filmcolors.org), to provide a comprehensive resource for the technology, aesthetics, and restoration of color films. The database provides historical and technical information about color film technology because understanding the physical characteristics of analog film stocks—including their material composition and the spectral properties of the color components involved—is key not only to identifying color film stock but also to finding the best ways to capture and translate it into the binary codes defined by digital formats for restoration and digitization.

A physical inspection of film elements in archives is a critical place to start. Color components appear either in edge markings or in scratches, especially around splices. Thus measurements and photographs of splices, among many other details, are integrated into the Timeline. The perforation area also contains crucial information about the color process, possibly the year of production and other analog metadata. It should be a core requirement for photographic documentation to capture the full film width, but this is oddly not a standard practice for film scanning. It is therefore close to impossible to identify a film color process based on a digitized element. Surface properties, such as reflection in raking light, that play a central role in the identification of color film stocks also often go undocumented in current digitization workflows.

The materiality of digital elements is polyform. Data can be stored on a large range of media; binary data could even be engraved into stone. Thus, the material properties of the data container are detached from the aesthetic appearance of the medium. Consequently, storage media undergo dynamic changes and new standards evolve constantly. In contrast to the relative stability of analog film materials—35mm film has been the standard for more than a century—digital formats and techniques can become obsolete within short time spans, which is problematic for the long-term storage of films and videos. More awareness and better technical solutions are needed to safeguard the wealth of our beautiful film heritage in color and access to the stunning richness of our cinematic past.

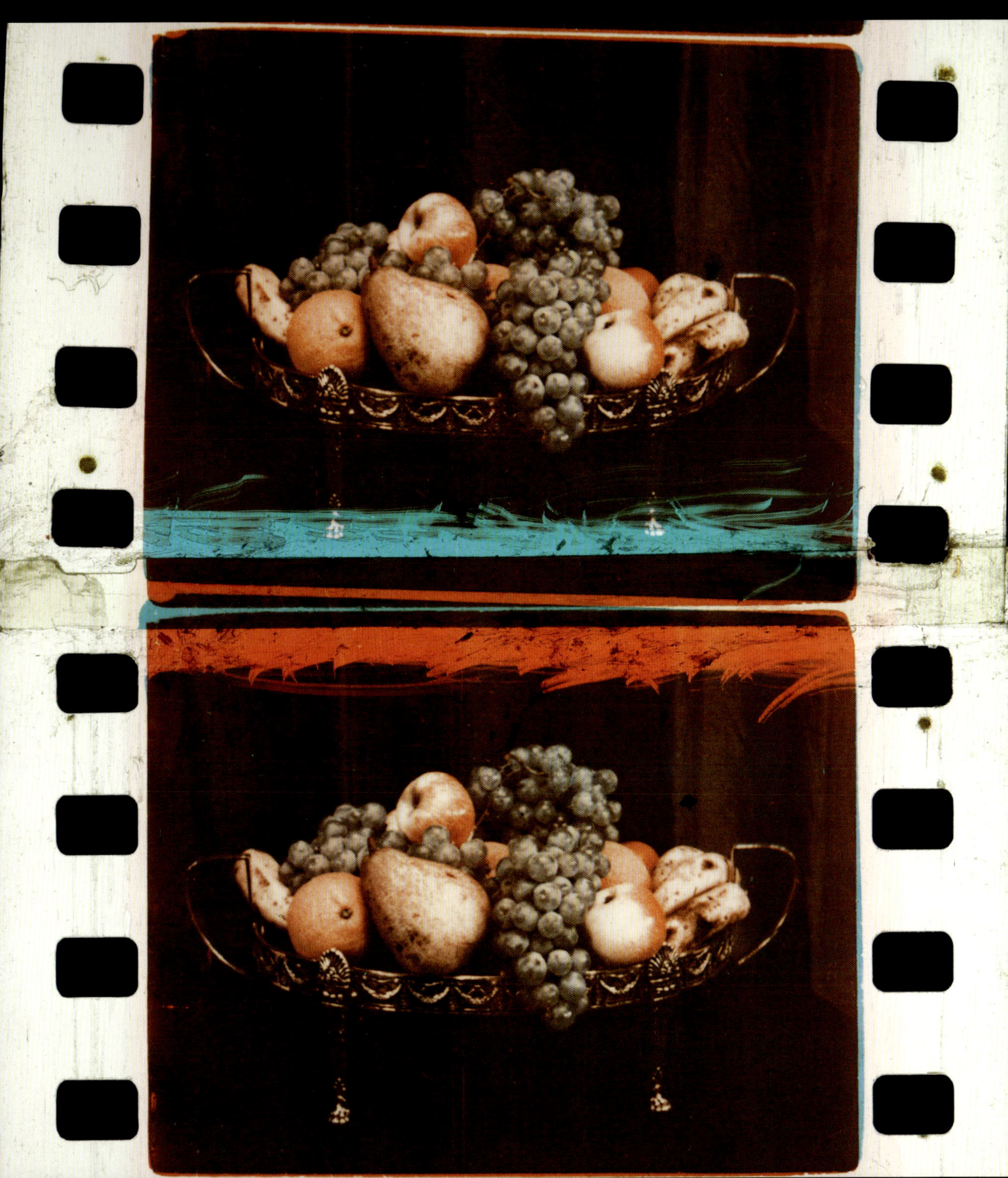

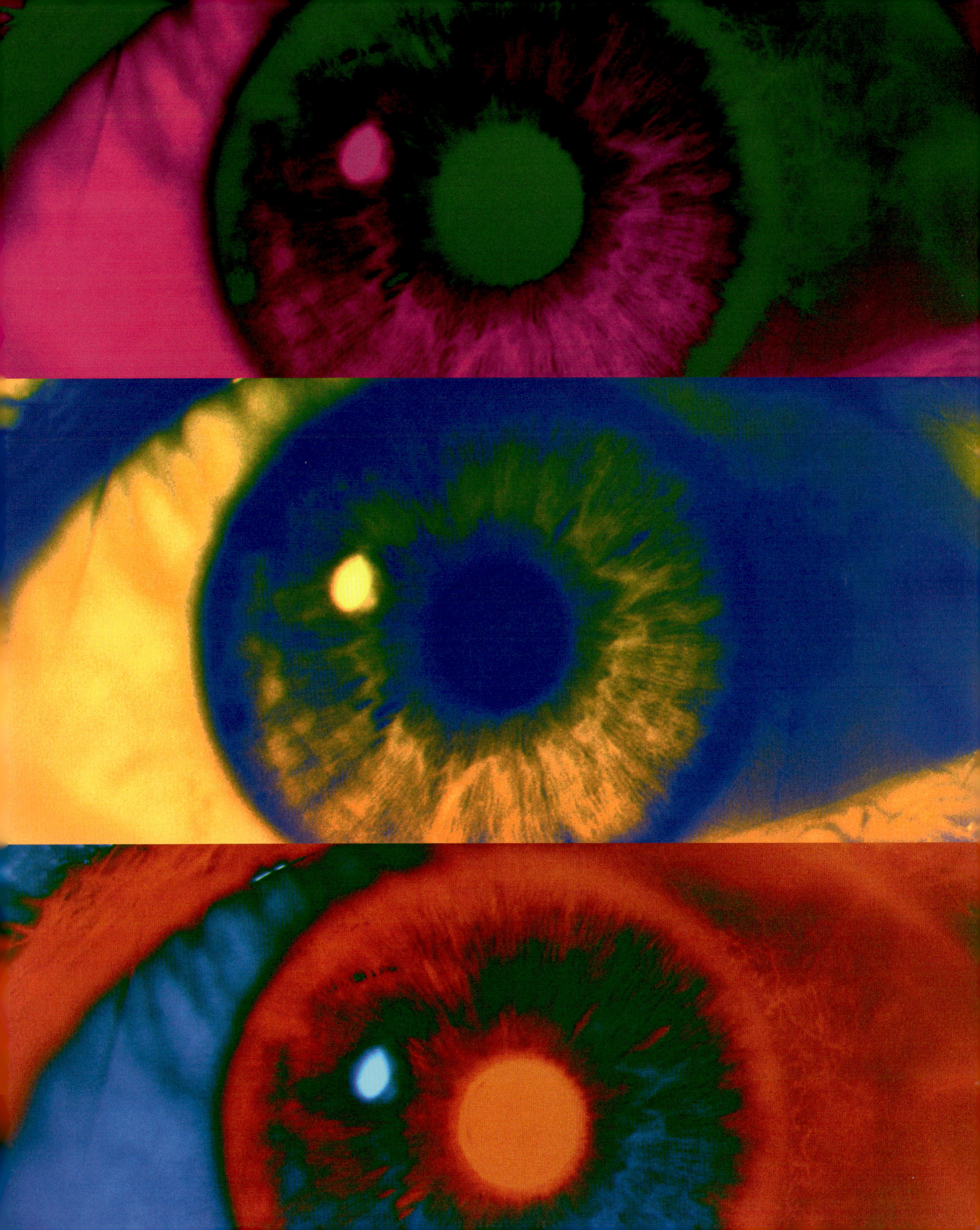

SOPHIA SERRANO

THE SCIENCE OF COLOR

The science behind our perception of color is a fascinating and complex combination of physical, biological, and emotional mechanisms. To understand color in cinema, it is also important to understand color as an experiential phenomenon. This conversation brought together three color experts—Charles Poynton, an independent researcher and color scientist based in Toronto; Andrew Stockman, a professor at University College London; and Laurens Orij, a colorist for feature films and commercials based in Amsterdam—to help illuminate the fundamentals at play when we see color on screen. Our conversation, on June 26, 2023, has been edited and condensed for clarity.

SOPHIA SERRANO: I'd like to start by asking each of you to give a brief definition of color. How would you describe it?

ANDREW STOCKMAN: Although color seems to be a property of physical objects in the real world, it is very much a biological or psychological interpretation of the spectral properties of those objects based on the wavelengths they reflect or emit. The brain, through a patchwork of light sensors in the retina, processes the information and then assigns colors to those objects. It usually works well, but the colors we see are limited, and those assigned by the brain sometimes disagree with the colors that would be expected based on the spectral properties of the light reaching the eye.

CHARLES POYNTON: The question you're asking is a difficult one. My take on it, to summarize Andrew and almost in the words of Isaac Newton: color is in the brain. Color is the cognitive result of the distribution of wavelengths of light that form an image on the retina.

LAURENS ORIJ: Well, we can't be saying the same thing three times, so I'll come at it from a different angle. I would say that color is a fundamental element of visual language and expression—something that filmmakers use to evoke specific responses from audiences and to convey emotions and to do a lot of other things.

AS: The color of an object very much depends on the context in which that object appears. You've probably all seen the dress illusion that went viral on the internet, right?

SS: The striped dress that people were seeing as either white and gold or blue and black?

AS: Yes. It's an example of how things that are physically the same can look very different, in terms of color appearance, to different people.

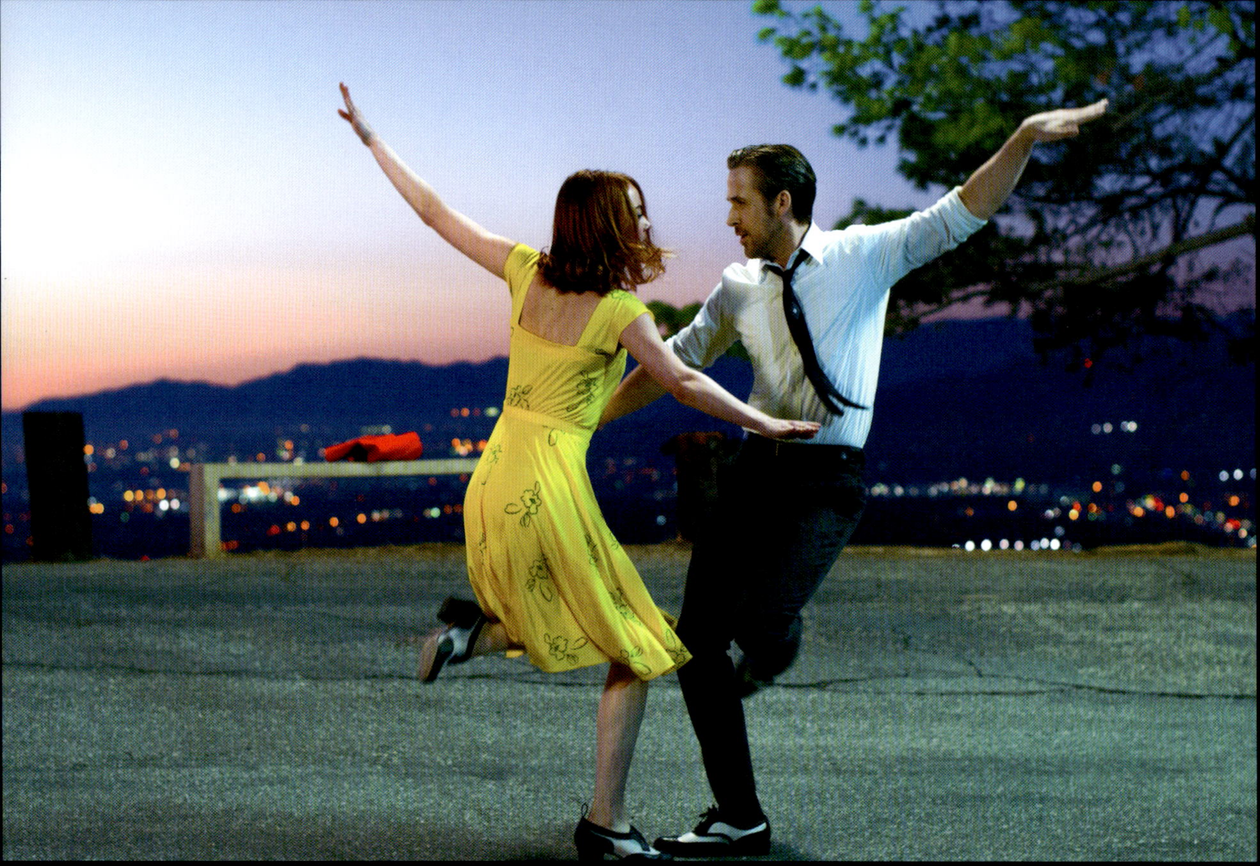

La La Land (USA, 2016, dir. Damien Chazelle)

PAGE 62: Images from *2001: A Space Odyssey* (USA/UK, 1968, dir. Stanley Kubrick)

SPECTRAL (RAINBOW) AND EXTRA-SPECTRAL COLORS

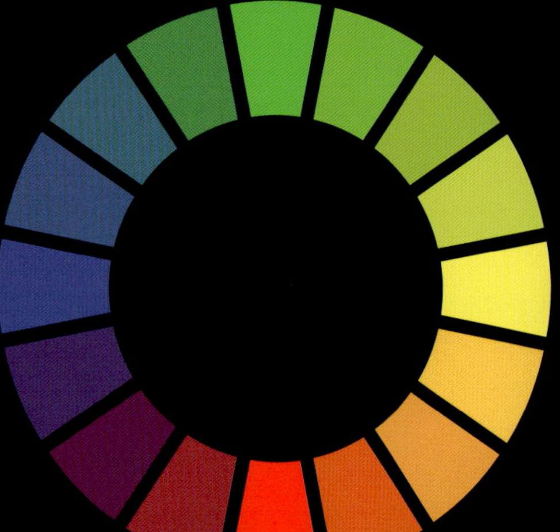

COLOR OPPONENCY

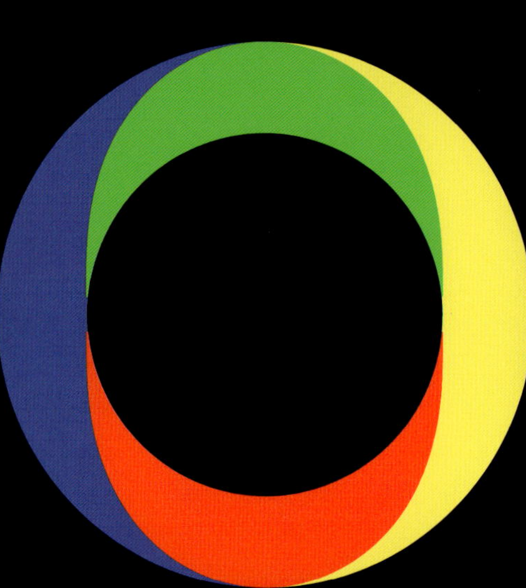

SS: Andrew, could you elaborate on the actual way that humans perceive color on a biological level?

AS: Color perception depends on a series of processing stages from the eye to the brain. The back of the retina has a layer of photosensitive cells, called rods and cones, that are excited by light. Color processing begins at the cones, of which there are three types, sensitive to long [L-], middle [M-], or short [S-] wavelength lights. The relative levels of excitation in these cones is the initial "trichromatic" color code that is processed by the brain. The colors that you eventually perceive depend on activities that begin in the retina even before the information travels via the optic nerve to the brain. Color processing in the retina transforms cone signals into "color-opponent" code, whereby redness is opposed to greenness, and blueness is opposed to yellowness. The brain eventually transforms this opponent code into categories of color such as red, green, blue, and yellow.

An object's color depends on both the illuminating and reflected light. The brain tries to disambiguate the color of the illumination from the spectral reflectance of the object, so that we can arrive at the true color.

CP: What you're suggesting is very much the source of the dress illusion. You can read it two different ways, depending on what your perceptual machinery fills in, and what it decides is the illumination. There are two interpretations.

AS: Yes. The brain changes the perceived color of the object based on how it interprets the color of the light source. Another factor affecting color perception is the surrounding color. Something surrounded by red light appears greener, while something surrounded by green light appears redder. This is known as color contrast, and filmmakers and artists take advantage of it all the time.

SS: What would be an example of this from film?

AS: I think of *La La Land* [USA, 2016] as one where saturated complementary colors are juxtaposed to enhance each other.

SS: Over the span of your lifetime, as you go from childhood to adulthood, does your ability to see color fluctuate? Is it something that evolves, or is it a constant that's just ingrained biologically from an early point?

AS: Your ability to see some color deteriorates with age. The lens, for example, becomes denser. Nevertheless, some brain mechanisms seem to balance the colors that we see so that color perception is fairly stable. A good example of the system becoming unbalanced is cataract removal, when the lens suddenly becomes transparent. Colors look quite different at first, but eventually the system rebalances and colors look normal again.

SS: In comparison, how does a camera capture color, if we were to contrast the systems?

AS: I'll respond regarding the human bit and then leave it to Charles and Laurens. The human array of light-sensitive cones on the back of the retina is very tightly packed in the center of vision but becomes quite sparse at the periphery. You can see that for yourself: if you look directly at an object you can see fine details, but if you look at the same object away from the center of vision the details disappear. A camera has a fairly uniform and high density across the sensor array, so things can be seen in good detail not just in the center but also away from the center.

CP: Andrew is hinting at how eye movements impact the perception of a scene. Your eyeball is constantly moving around the scene to pick up details, many times per second. However, those eye movements are usually unconscious. I would say there is quite a marked difference between the eye and a camera, in particular the three L-M-S cone sensors in the eye that Andrew mentioned earlier. There are a lot of engineering considerations behind which wavelengths and distributions a camera uses, and so there can be quite a difference between the way people see colors and the way the camera "sees" them. Consequently, there are a host of technical problems that various people along the movie-making chain, especially colorists, learn to deal with. Sometimes those effects are compensated for by lighting, for example, or by altering the color of costumes so that color is picked up as intended by the camera.

AS: One thing about the eye is that the lens is very poor compared to that of a camera. The red and green sensors in the eye are very close together in wavelength, but in a camera, they're much farther apart. So, you get a better color signal in that sense with a camera than you do with the human eye.

LO: To illustrate what Andrew and Charles are talking about, and why you need eye movements: if you stretch out your hand you can see your thumbnail in high detail, but everything surrounding it is out of focus. Eye movements are necessary to see the details of everything around us.

AS: Most of the brain is dedicated to processing visual signals from the central area of vision. Part of that is due to the limited capacity of the optic nerve from the eye to the brain. We have to process and compress information before sending it to the brain, but you don't have that same limitation in a camera.

CP: This topic is interesting not only for filmmakers but for photographers and to some extent graphic artists. You'll hear artists and designers talk about "leading the eye," the idea being that—in composition or even visual storytelling, in the case of a movie—you can direct the eye to a high-detail area, wherever you want it to go. That ends up being an important aspect in the art of moviemaking and even photography.

AS: One more thing: the blue S-cone sensors in the retina are sparse and primarily signal color, not spatial detail. Unlike a camera, where the blue image is in good focus thanks to multi-component lenses, blue or violet images are very much out of focus in the back of the eye.

LO: The retina registers color with three different sensors, whereas the camera can either split the light and use three sensors or use one sensor that only registers light, but with a mosaic of filters on top that allows it to register different colors. Actually I should say different types of light, but they result in what we would call colors.

SS: Everyone has had the experience of taking a picture of something so beautiful in person, but the photographic result is washed out or the colors don't look right. Laurens, applying this to your work in color grading, can you talk a little bit about your process of translating that real-world perception of colors to the screen?

LO: Absolutely. I like the way you introduced the question because that's exactly what happens. You see something beautiful—say, a beautiful sunset—and you try to take a picture but it does not at all represent what you're trying to capture. If you think about the camera and the eye, the biggest difference is that your eyes are connected directly to your brain, and a camera sensor is not. With cameras there's always something in between: a display. And all displays have shortcomings, but maybe it's better to say they all have different qualities. In order to create an image that represents a scene the way your eyes see it, you need to alter the image taking into account the properties of the display.

For example, a picture of a sunset in a newspaper is never going to look the same as a real sunset. But that also opens up possibilities. Artists work within the limitations of different mediums and come up with creative solutions to convey the same emotions that scenes carry in the real world. Part of the color grading process is indeed overcoming those limitations. In calibrating, you have the tools to adjust for shortcomings, but you can also emphasize certain elements of a scene by altering palettes or images.

SS: Following up on Charles's point about color as a tool to subtly drive the narrative and direct the audience's attention, Laurens, when you're given a scene, what is your general process? Do you identify the driving narrative force and focus on color and then build from there? I'm curious about how you start.

LO: I would say there is a visual hierarchy that's a part of the process of grading. If you look at an image, what is the first thing you see? Do you want the character to be the focus? You can direct the viewer's gaze to support the narrative, but that's also something the cinematographer does when he is shaping the light. Colors are also able to convey emotions. If I want a warm or a cold feeling, I can push related colors in the scene. You can create palettes that are in harmony or create contrasts in palettes that might be disturbing. The look of the film can support the narrative.

SS: Could you discuss the difference in color between film stock versus digital? How do the processes differ?

LO: That topic is on a lot of people's minds, not only filmmakers and cinematographers, and the debate has widened a bit. Both digital sensors and film stock have unique characteristics. With film stock, there's a chemical process that captures light. With a digital sensor, light intensities are converted to electrical signals and digitized. Film is an organic process as it's based on chemistry. Digital can be much more consistent. But the biggest difference when it comes to cinematography is that film is a consumable, meaning you need to buy rolls and rolls of it to make a movie. You could have a preference for one product over another, and you could choose a film stock based on its color and other qualities.

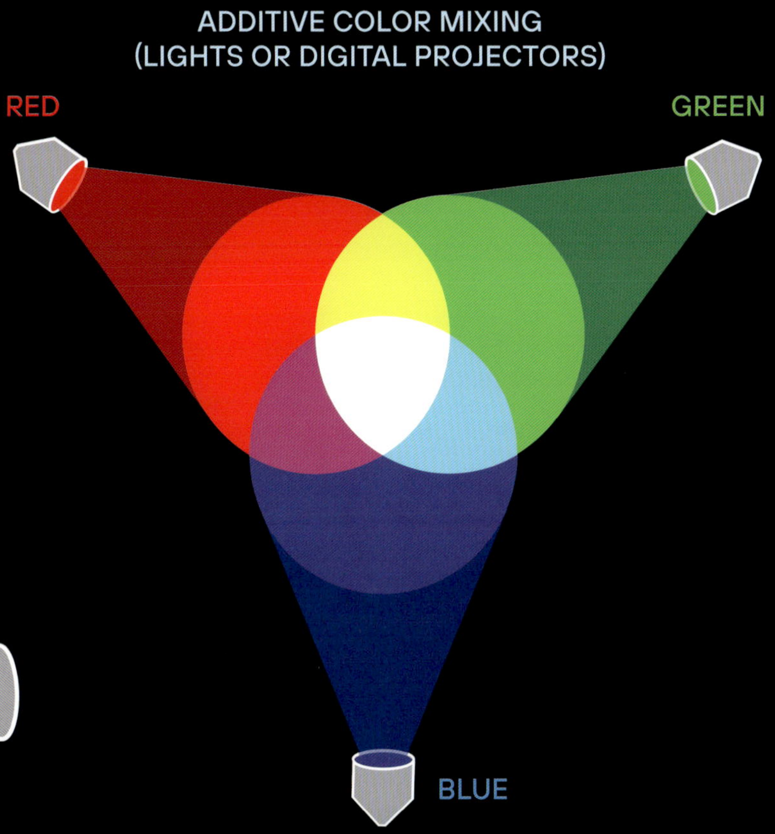

CONE SENSOR SPECTRAL SENSITIVITIES

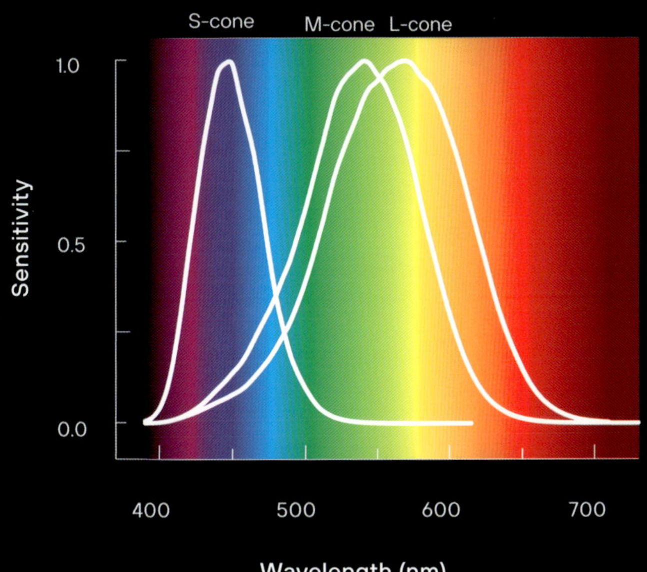

ADDITIVE COLOR MIXING (LIGHTS OR DIGITAL PROJECTORS)

RED
GREEN
BLUE

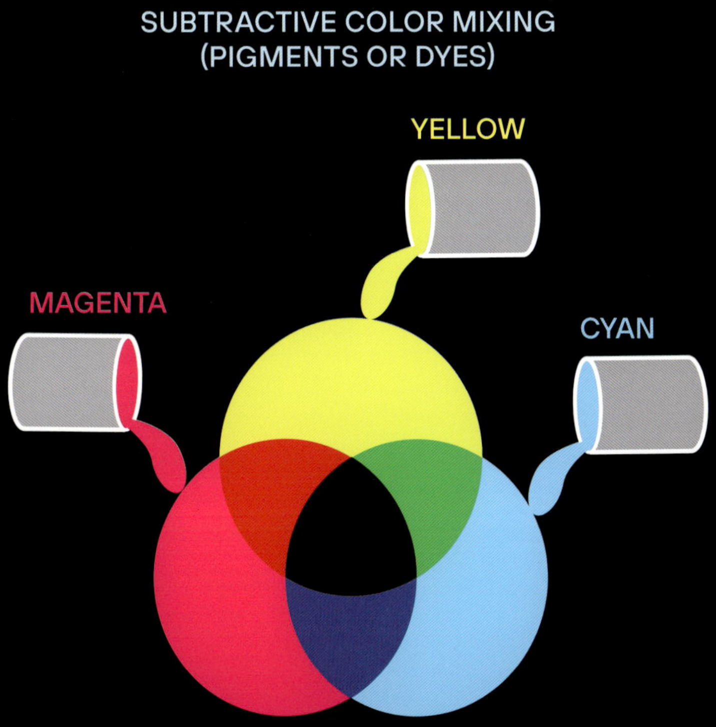

SUBTRACTIVE COLOR MIXING (PIGMENTS OR DYES)

YELLOW
MAGENTA
CYAN

Illustrations by Andrew Stockman

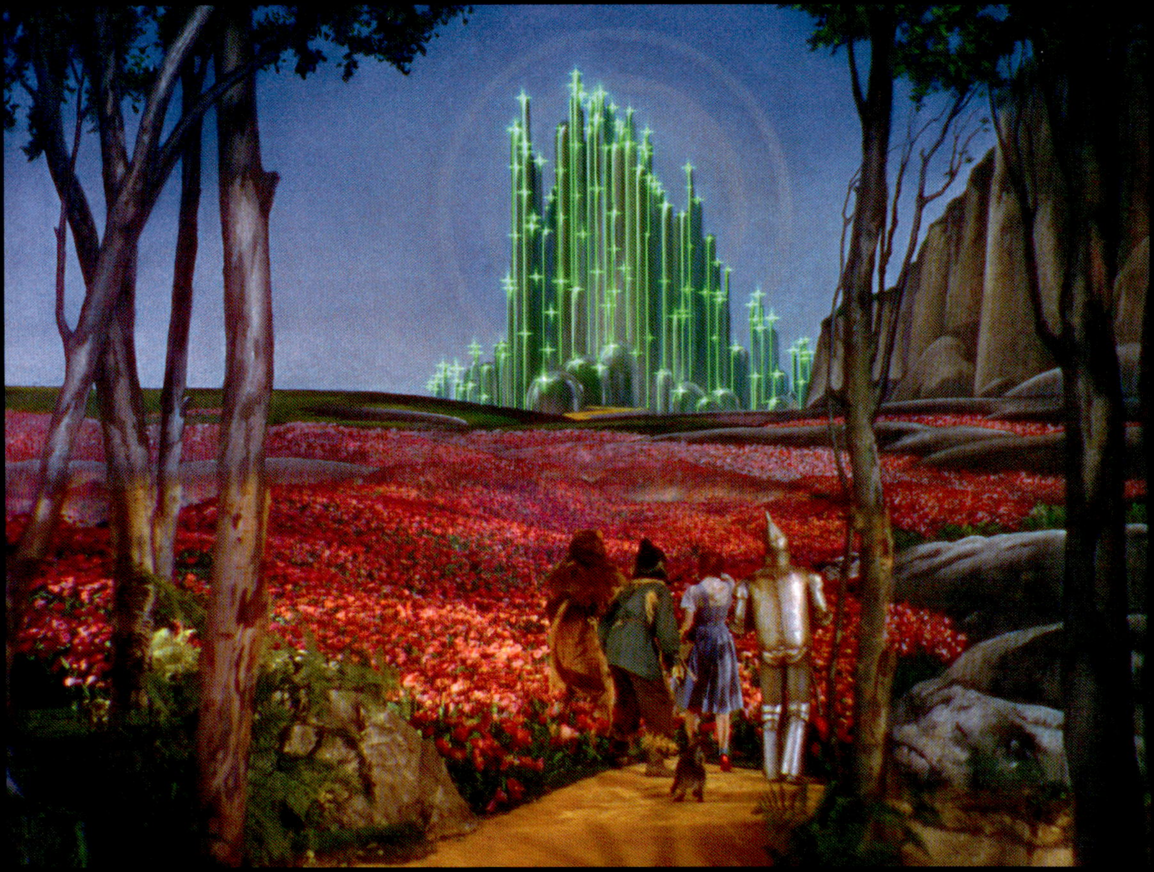

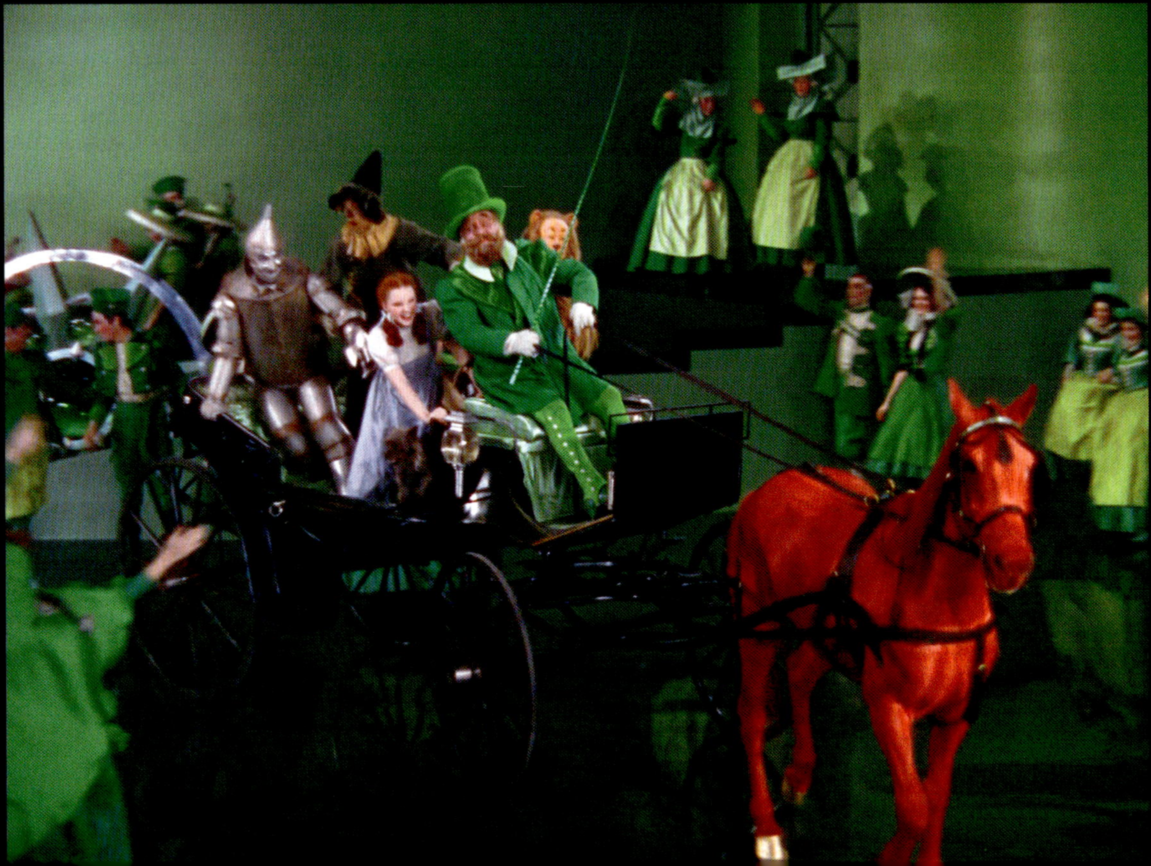

If you think about what that once meant, when a film came out in theaters, possibly thousands of film prints had to be made; that's a lot of film to be manufactured. So, film was a big business at its height. Up to sixty thousand people were working at Kodak, and some of the world's best-known color scientists had jobs there. If you compare that to a leading digital cinema camera manufacturer, maybe there is a team of around one hundred people working on that camera and less than a handful of them are responsible for color. The cost of getting a print in theaters, just in film stock alone, was many times the cost of a full digital cinema camera. The market for film was so large that it allowed for the creation of products that were really tailored for what motion pictures needed. I think that with digital cinema, most of what's possible is thanks to technologies that have been borrowed from other markets.

SS: Charles, I want to get your thoughts about this and the introduction to digital as someone who supervises the color aspects of a film.

CP: Making a movie is a very long process requiring a number of steps. There was a time when digital was introduced in the middle of the chain, in post-production, still keeping film as the medium for distribution and presentation. But those days are now largely gone, and the few movies acquired today on film invariably go into a digital pipeline and have a digital, or a predominantly digital, release.

To answer your question about how digital affects the overall process of moviemaking, I'll riff on what Laurens said. Historically in color movies, Technicolor was dominant from the 1930s to late 1940s. Kodak reigned from the late 1940s until the mid-1990s. In both eras, there was basically one system designer for the whole film industry. The rapid shift to digital completely eroded what was essentially a monopoly. Fuji and Agfa were also present and making important contributions, but the whole ecosystem shifted from a single system designer, Kodak, to a dozen or two prominent manufacturers of digital cameras, displays, and post-production software. And that meant that the system design was now fragmented, happening in many places around the world. Each company had its own approach, so the post-production facilities—and even directors of photography and colorists and digital imaging technicians—could no longer rely on a two-hundred-page document from Kodak to tell them everything they needed to know. This forced a wide variety of ways of doing, and that's both the good news and the bad news. The good is that it allows for diversity. The bad is that it has become difficult to achieve the kind of consistency that was present during the monopoly years.

AS: We recently saw a technical print of *The Wizard of Oz* [USA, 1939] and some of those colors, like the scarlets and green-cyan, you simply don't see in digital cinema. Why is that?

CP: It's a little bit like the viral dress. If you were to measure those colors, you would find that they are available in digital cinema. However, presented in the context of *The Wizard of Oz*, the entire composition of color makes visual things happen that we're not used to today.

SS: Thinking a little bit about digital color and accessibility, does digital color offer new accessibility for people with conditions such as color blindness?

AS: Well, you can remap reds, oranges, yellows, and greens so that people can have a more enhanced color experience, but the enhancements are limited. For true dichromats—that's people, generally men, who are missing either the L- or M-cones—all you can do is adjust to the intensities of colors in the red-green range so that they can be better distinguished by their intensity differences.

CP: This has relevance to the design of user interfaces and information displays. But to me any developments in that arena for entertainment seem unlikely. What we always do in making movies or TV shows is produce a color sensation that's roughly comparable to what the real world would produce. We might make a fictional other world, but it's always rooted in the way that we see things on planet Earth. A viewer with a color vision deficiency would interpret colors the same way that they would interpret those colors in real life.

SS: One of the interesting things that we were looking at with Technicolor is this idea of calibration and the standard or process. Even in the early days of Technicolor, there was a lot of discussion about whether color should reflect real life or go for something vivid and fantastical.

CP: That touches exactly on Laurens's point about giving filmmakers the ability to create a visual world that is not necessarily the one we live in. Calibration to me, even though I do it fairly routinely, is always at the bottom of the stack of important things to do. The art is always at the top, there's the craft in the middle, and then there's the science forming what we hope is a stable foundation at the bottom. But that doesn't say that we're trying to mimic reality, just that we want the pipeline to be repeatable.

SS: To build off of this, is it safe to say that movies have become more colorful with digital technologies, as in the number of colors that we can see on screen?

LO: It largely depends on your focus. In relation to the early discussions that were happening at Technicolor and in the movies, people were unsure if color movies would ever become the standard. They didn't know if there was a place for color movies because color was so distracting—some reviews of early color films lament that you're only looking at the color of the flowers and not paying attention to the actors. If I recall correctly, one of the goals of Technicolor was to create a harmonious color palette that wouldn't distract or disturb the viewer, because it was such a big shift from black and white. I would like to think the exact use of color is a creative and cultural decision, less a technology-driven decision.

CP: It's a totally interesting and provocative question, Sophia, and it verges on philosophical discussion, but we do have a few practical reference points. You can draw analogies from audio mixing. With pop music of, let's say, forty years ago, there were a lot of dynamics in the levels of sound found within a song—this has been well documented by musicologists. But in today's songs, everything is basically at the same volume from beginning to end. I certainly feel that something has been lost by the failure to use the variation that's available in the medium.

It's an artistic decision on the part of the director, the cinematographer, and even the colorist how much of the color spectrum to use. In terms of television, all you need to do is tune in to a sports channel to see vibrant colors all over the screen all the time. That is the visual color equivalent to that loss of dynamic sound in popular music—it's a flattening. We could say there is more colorfulness available now, but a light touch is needed to use that range in a manner suitable for telling stories. When you see vibrant colors all the time, like you do on the sports channels, those are often not the strongest stories.

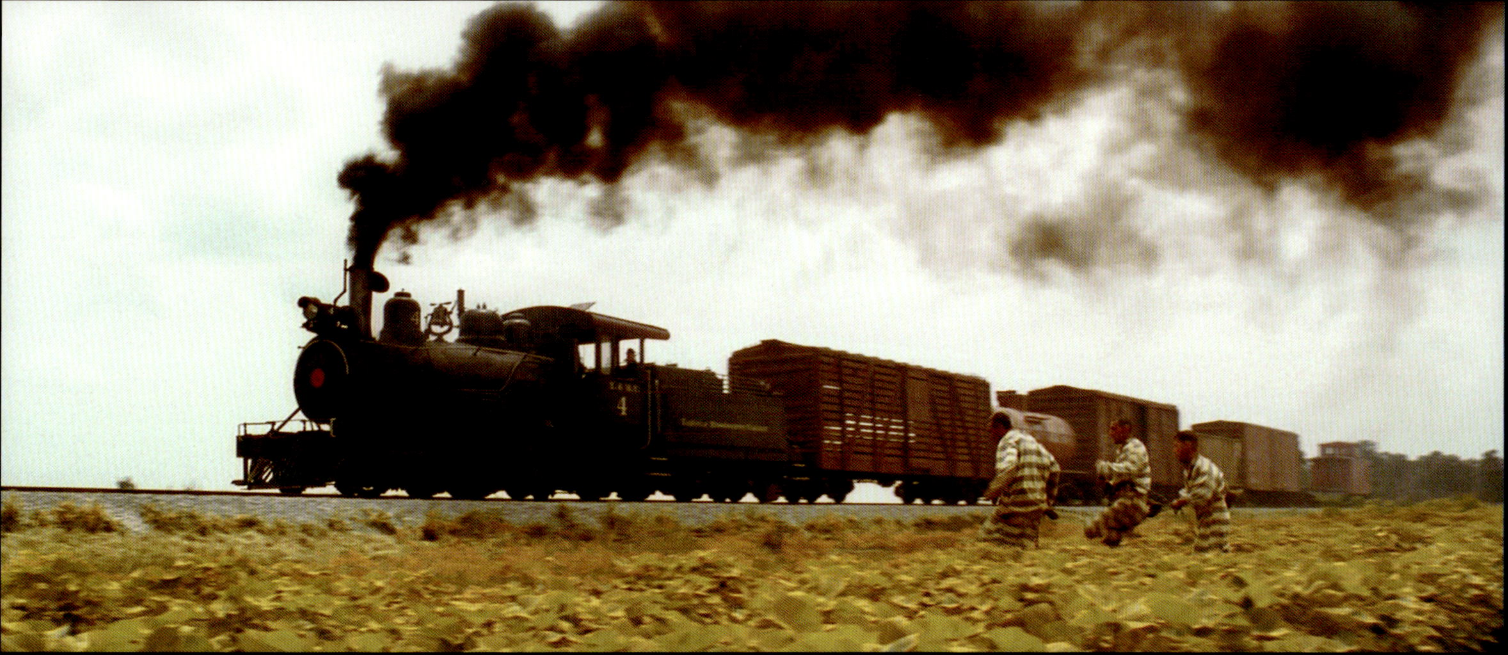

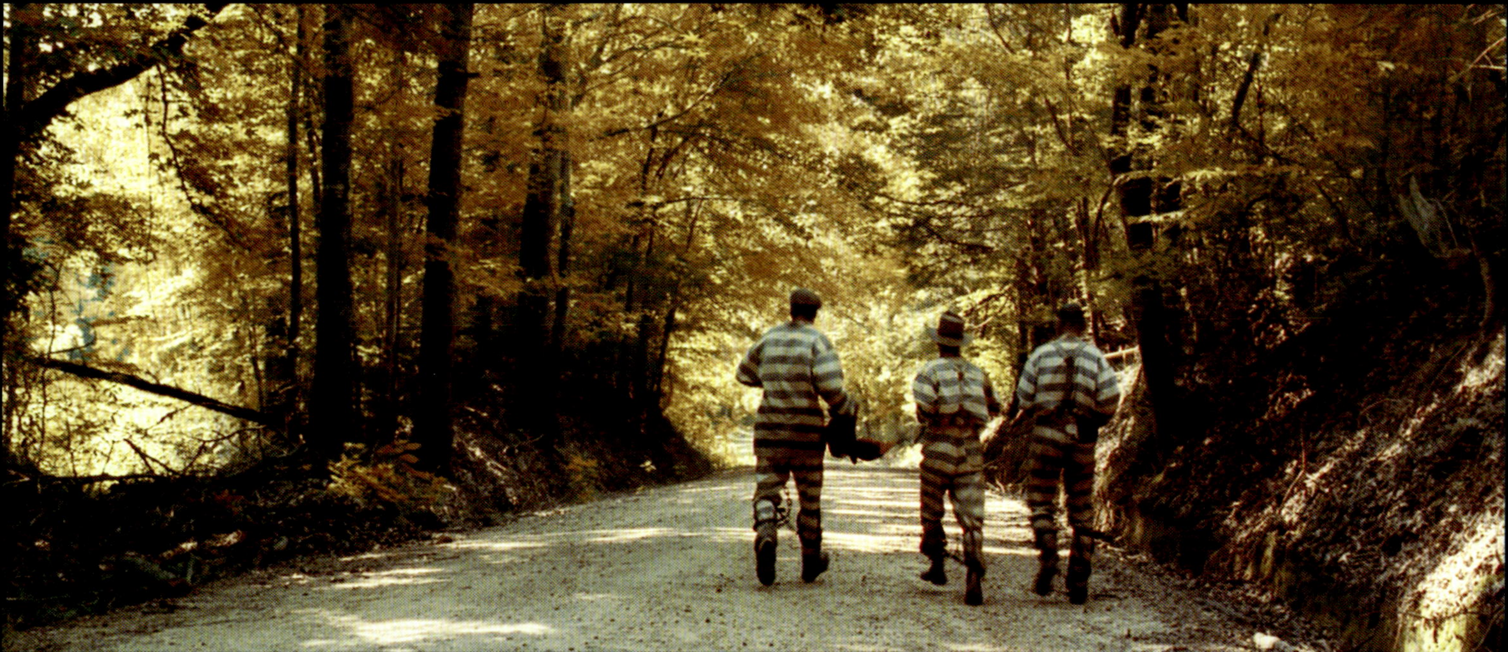

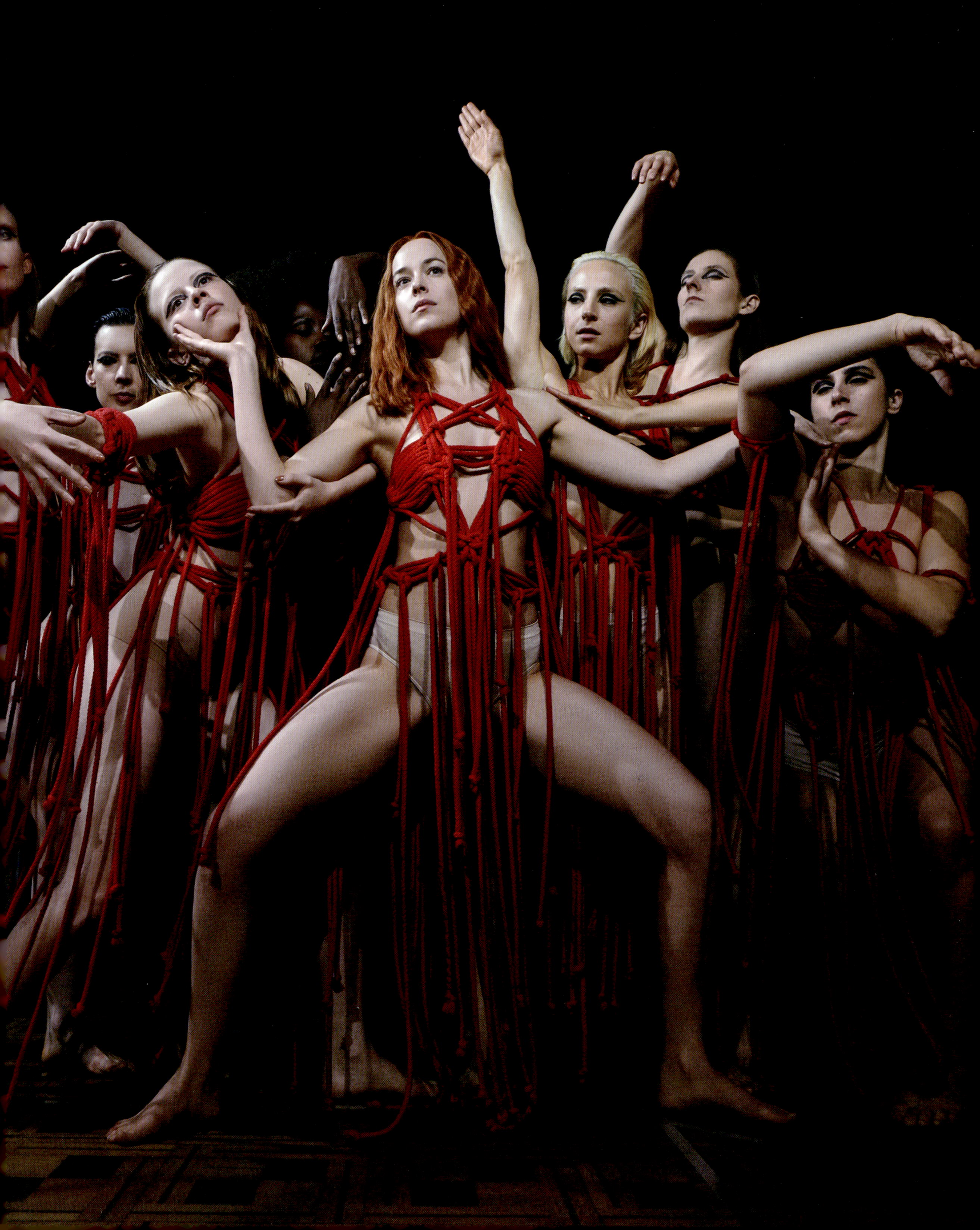

JESSICA NIEBEL

CHOREO-GRAPHING COLOR

THE CAPTIVATING DANCE OF COLOR AND MOTION IN CINEMA

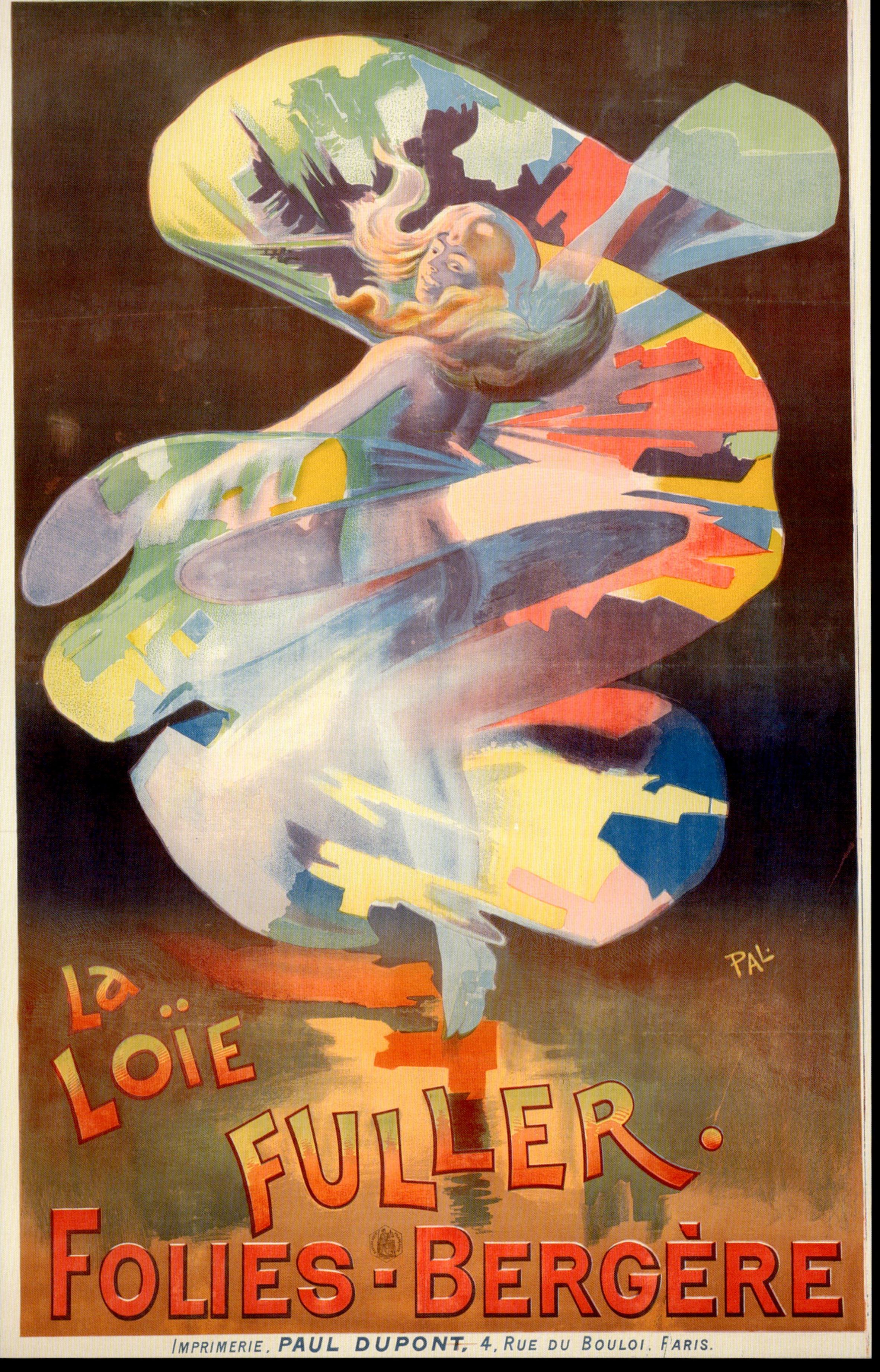

Pal (Jean de Paleologu), *Loïe Fuller*, ca. 1894, lithograph, 48 × 33 inches

PAGE 72: *Suspiria* (USA/Italy, 2018, dir. Luca Guadagnino), producti

When the new medium of film conquered the world at the turn of the last century, the public was captivated by its ability to capture motion. Recording people in movement seemed to offer a taste of immortality. However, the first commercial short films shot by the Lumière brothers—whose *operateurs* (cameramen/projectionists) captured scenes of everyday life all around the world—lacked a crucial element to achieve complete realism: color. Filmmakers, inventors, and technicians were eager to introduce color to this young art form, thereby aligning it with other visual media that had successfully presented color for centuries. Glass slides had been used in magic lantern projections starting in the 1700s, and Émile Reynaud's more recent animated moving picture system known as the Théâtre Optique (Optical Theater) was patented in 1888; both employed applied colors painted by hand to harness the potential of color as a narrative tool or simply to dazzle audiences with vivid visuals.[1] Naturally, the same technique was applied in the early days of filmmaking. Notably, Georges Méliès employed color not as a superficial layer added for mere effect or to enhance the realism of his imagery. On the contrary, he integrated color as an essential means of expressing his fantastical visions through film. From 1897 to 1912, the majority of his films were meticulously colored by the studio of the mother-daughter duo Élisabeth and Berthe Thuillier to infuse his wondrous creations with the enchantment of color.

Whether it was used to enhance realism or conjure fantasy, from the beginning of the new medium color was intricately interwoven with motion. In cinema's history, the symbiotic relationship between color and motion emerges as a captivating thread, interwoven with the creative genius of filmmakers and the laborious dedication of artists behind the scenes. No other form of early film expressed this more significantly than the spectacle of colors and motion in dance film. American dancer Loïe Fuller, who had originally invented the Serpentine Dance for the stage, experimented with ways of adapting it for the moving image. The dance—an interplay of a single female performer's costume, its flowing and voluminous skirt manipulated by the dancer, with multi-colored lighting effects—was hugely successful with audiences and inspired a whole series of dancers, including Broadway dancer Annabelle Whitford Moore (who performed in *Annabelle Serpentine Dance* for an 1895 Edison Studios production), to work Fuller's style into their repertoire. Fuller, who found artistic recognition after moving to Paris, regularly dancing with the Folies Bergère and operating her own dance company and school, also experimented with new lighting and color technologies in the lab she ran with her partner, Gab Sorère. They developed new color gels, fluorescent paints, and visual effects to enhance Fuller's stage performances. The Serpentine Dance became a staple of early film, the colored lighting replaced by hand-tinted colors; what audiences saw

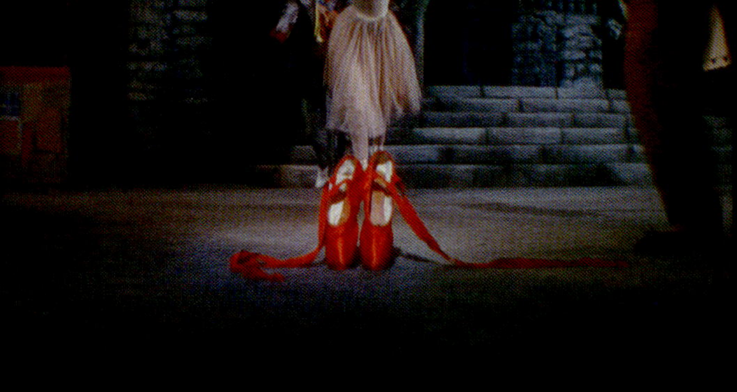

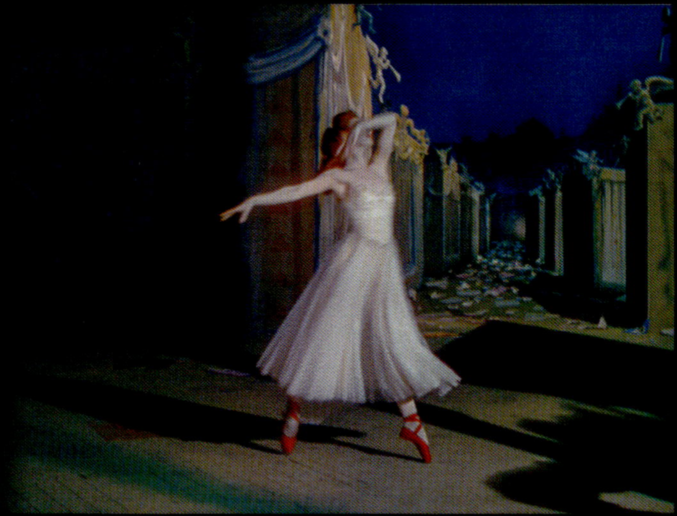

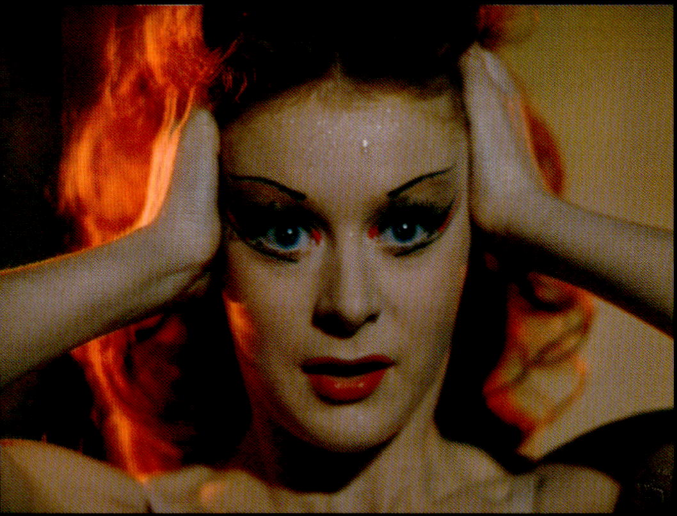

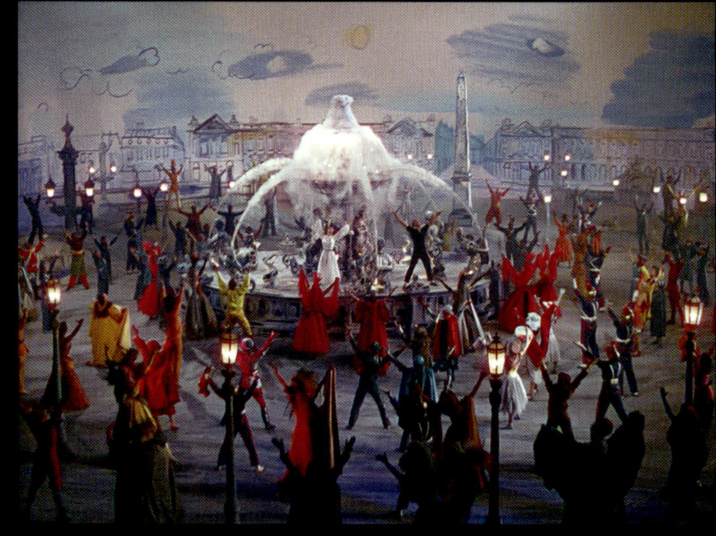

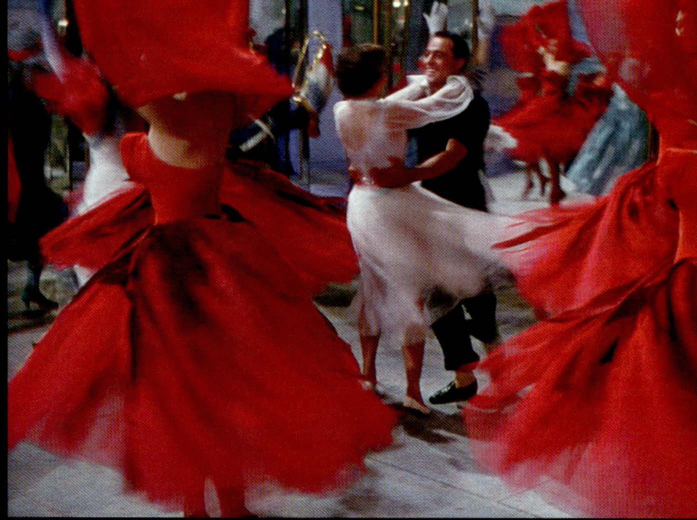

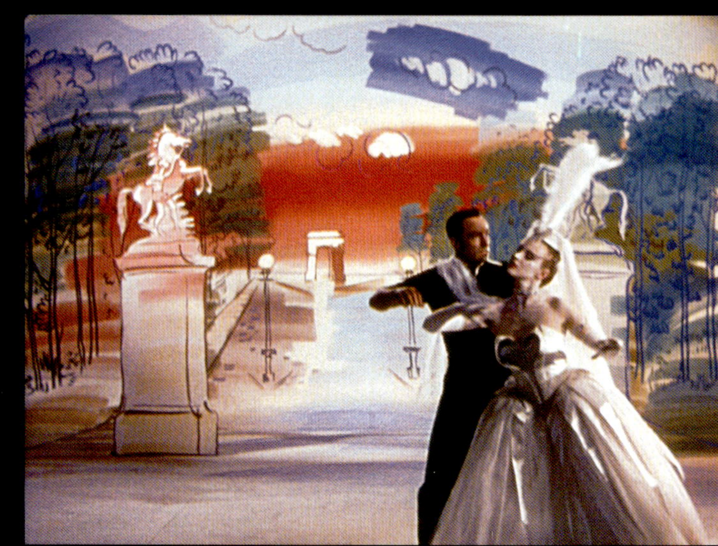

ABOVE: *The Red Shoes* (UK, 1948, dirs. Michael Powell and Emeric Pressburger)

on screen was a free form of female dance, expressed through a combination of textile and color movement.

Color and dance, often in conjunction with textiles, remained a popular subject throughout many film histories across the globe. Dance films and musicals celebrate the human body in motion and convey emotions that transcend the limitations of speech. However, there's also an element of danger inherent in dance—a subtle yet ever-present possibility that a dancer might become lost in a tumultuous sea of emotion, and a meticulously choreographed dance might take on a life of its own or transform into something wild and unpredictable. In some cases, it might even erupt to a degree where the dancer becomes a vessel for an uncontrollable and greater power. A parallel sense of fear about erupting emotions and loss of control has long surrounded the concept of color. Given that color, as either light or pigment, is a phenomenon that is subjectively perceived, and variably so given different conditions, how can it be trusted? When color is set into motion before our eyes, it can rapidly evolve into a hallucinatory and ecstatic experience that spirals beyond our control. The likelihood that chaos might disrupt the established order becomes even more pronounced when the two come together. Such a combination multiplies the risk of losing oneself and the potential to disrupt or challenge societal norms. This convergence can lead to a cascade of consequences including excess, indulgence, decadence, and, ultimately, even death. This phenomenon has found depiction in a great variety of films—although I will discuss only a select few instances—yet what stands out is the frequency with which this kind of excess affects the female dancer.

Could this prevalence be attributed to the perception that women are particularly susceptible to these dangers as they were traditionally seen as having less self-control and discipline? Or could it be indicative of man's (the film director/cinematographer/viewer) fear of losing dominion over woman (the dancer/actress)? What remains unequivocal is that the era of modern dance ushered in a fresh and liberating avenue for self-expression, affording (primarily women) performers a sense of ownership over their own bodies. Some, like Fuller, even managed to establish their own enterprises and achieve financial autonomy. In the context of color and female expression, dance then becomes either a means of personal liberation or an obsession that can lead to (self-) destruction. This dichotomy underscores the profound power that dance and color wield in filmic narratives of empowerment and excess.

Beyond the dance film, these dynamics also manifest in other genres, such as musicals, horror films, and even martial arts movies. A prime illustration can be found in Michael Powell and Emeric Pressburger's classic *The Red Shoes* (UK, 1948). In a thirteen-minute dance sequence titled "The Ballet of the Red Shoes," Vicky Page (Moira Shearer) dances the role of a ballerina capable of delivering an exceptional performance only when donning a magical pair of crimson ballet shoes. However, this comes with a dire trade-off: the moment she removes the shoes, she must die. The ballet's commencement sees her tempted by a wicked shoemaker into wearing the shoes, immediately transforming her dance into perfection with a near-dreamlike quality. Yet, her moments of triumph and elation are inevitably followed by terror and the looming specter of death. As she moves from one scenario to the next, her once-pristine white dress, which brightly contrasted with her red shoes, becomes dirtier and tattered as her dance evolves into a fantastical spectacle, interwoven with increasingly maniacal music and action that signal the impending cost she must pay. This shifting of realities, or perhaps consciousness, finds visual representation in the set design itself. Painted components spring to life, blurring the boundary between reality and illusion, while superimpositions and translucency in both the filming and the dance's stage design amplify the ballet's hallucinatory ambiance. This hypnotic performance culminates with the ballerina collapsing from sheer exhaustion, desperately pleading for her shoes to be removed—an act that promptly seals her fate with death.

Similar techniques are employed in Vincente Minnelli's 1951 film *An American in Paris*. The film reaches its zenith with the seventeen-minute "An American in Paris Ballet," with music composed by George Gershwin. This sequence serves as the film's climactic conclusion, centered around the painter Jerry (Gene Kelly) as he delves into a dream that encapsulates his pursuit, discovery, and subsequent loss of his love interest, Lise (Leslie Caron). The dream takes the form of a ballet and starts with Jerry staring into and then finding himself within his black-and-white drawing of the Champs-Élysées. He stoops to pick up a red rose, upon which the scene bursts into life as color infuses it, creating a portal to his fantasies. Progressing through various locales, Jerry's dance leads him to encounter Lise in diverse Parisian settings and roles, only to lose her repeatedly. As the dream's intensity heightens, his dance swings between the elation of their reunions and the crushing realization that it's all an illusory construct—instilling fear that his quest for her may never end. Set against opulent and ever-shifting backdrops, the dream weaves through nightmarish elements—including seductresses in red keeping him from a white-robed Lise and uniformed men pursuing him—enriched by intricate costume designs and elaborate choreography that crescendos into a whirlwind dance set against mirrors toward the end of the ballet. Colors meld and intertwine, amplifying the dramatic undertones of Jerry's fixation on Lise and the dynamic of his dream. The ballet ends after the once-alive, fantastical drawing drains of its color and Jerry once again finds the red rose, whereupon the screen fades to black and returns him to conscious reality, back to staring into the drawing. Color, often linked to dreams, nightmares, and the subconscious, takes on heightened prominence, vibrancy, and chaos within cinematic moments like these.

While many commonalities can be found between the ballet sequences in *The Red Shoes* and *An American in Paris*—exertion, obsession, danger, all of which are conveyed through the allure of color—there is one striking difference in the narratives of the two films. Vicky must die in the end, but Jerry will ultimately be united with Lise. A third outcome is presented in *West Side Story* (USA, 1961), directed by Jerome Robbins and Robert Wise—a film adaptation of the Broadway musical about a gang rivalry between young Puerto Rican immigrants and white teenagers in a New York neighborhood and the forbidden love between Maria (Natalie Wood) and Tony (Richard Beymer). The narrative begins with Maria as she prepares for her first dance, aspiring to become a "lady of American society." She voices discontent with her white dress, perceiving it as childish, and yearns for it to be dyed red. After donning the dress and beginning to twirl, an enthralling interplay of fabric and color emerges that visually transitions into a shot of the dance. Inside a vibrantly red hall, a frenzy of dancers moves to the latest music until the host endeavors to establish order by trying to start a "get-together dance" intended to mix the youths. The experiment falters as the dancers opt to remain within their ethnic groups, and the ensuing dance morphs from a celebration of self-expression through movement into a competitive and confrontational dance duel, echoing the rivalry between the (Puerto Rican) Sharks and the (white) Jets. Amid the intensifying turmoil and the kaleidoscope of dancers and vivid hues, Maria and Tony, a former member of the Jets, share a glance across the room and the world fades away, everything but the two figures at first blurring and then darkening. In an instant they fall deeply in love, a reality unto themselves, untethered from time and external influences. The moment soon passes, however, returning to the ballroom where the rivalry persists; in the end it leads to Tony being shot and dying in Maria's arms, her dress red in the end.

It's intriguing how these films especially employ the colors white and red to underscore contrasting themes: childhood versus adulthood, sexual purity versus maturity, the dynamics between female seduction and male desire, and even life and death. This interplay of colors, and the associations they evoke, is a potent cinematic device in its own right, able to construct meaning and evoke moods. Extending beyond musicals and dance films, the white-red contrast features prominently in dramas such as Ingmar Bergman's period piece *Cries and Whispers* (Sweden, 1972), which examines themes such as suffering, illness, and looming death and was shot in the red interior of a Swedish family home. (Its female protagonists clad in white and surrounded by red, it has come to epitomize the striking and loaded use of the white/red contrast in film.) Horror films, as well, exploit the contrast between the pristine white of certain surfaces, like textiles or snow, and red blood. A vivid illustration of this is the iconic scene in Brian de Palma's *Carrie* (USA, 1976), where a cascade of pig's blood drenches Carrie at the prom. Indeed, color possesses the ability to shock, and it is noteworthy how often it is coupled with dance, whether as a form of joyful self-expression or as a terror imposed by other entities.

In his 2018 adaptation of Dario Argento's 1977 film *Suspiria*, Luca Guadagnino employs dance in combination with color to usher in the forces of witchcraft over the young—in this version, exclusively female—students at a prestigious dance academy. While Argento's film features a generally more intense and vibrant color palette, Guadagnino opts for red costumes against the girls' pale skin in the dance performance "Volk." Friends Susie (Dakota Johnson) and Sara (Mia Goth) both take part in this piece, but the latter, who has just uncovered the school's affiliation with a coven of witches capable of mentally and physically manipulating, harming, and even killing its students, joins the performance belatedly. The choreography and rhythmic, heavy breathing of the dancers combine with the starkness of their revealing crimson costumes against bare skin to create an atmosphere wherein the dancers appear simultaneously exposed, vulnerable, and empowered in their state of rapture. In a close-up shot of the two girls, it becomes evident that Sara's brown eyes have changed to blue, while Susie's have changed from blue to brown. This transformation is unsettling as reality is undermined, and colors, once perceived as steadfast, can be utterly unreliable. Forces beyond the girls' control are at play, interfering with their bodies and movements.

While the dancers' bodies in *Suspiria* become a vessel for powers outside of their control, martial arts films offer an extreme, almost otherworldly self-control. Through meticulous choreography and artistry, these films conjure a realm where physical feats transcend earthly limitations and colors accentuate the emotional and visual intensity of each

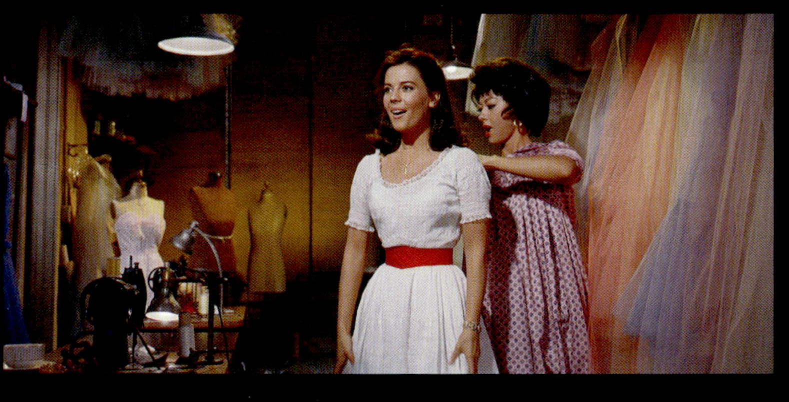

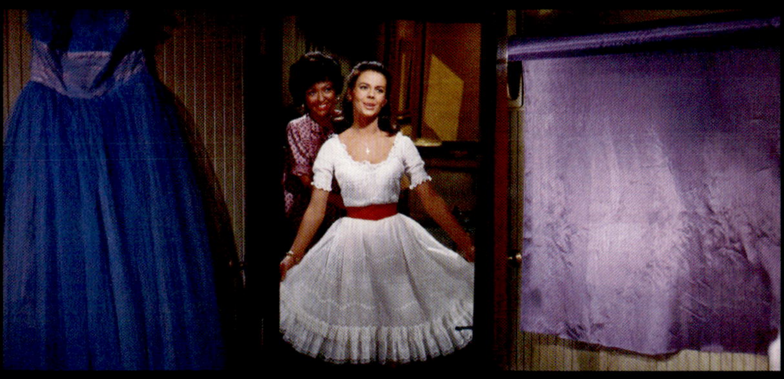

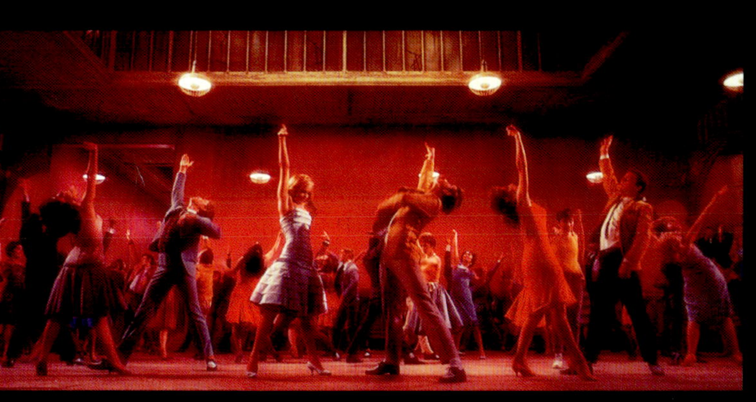

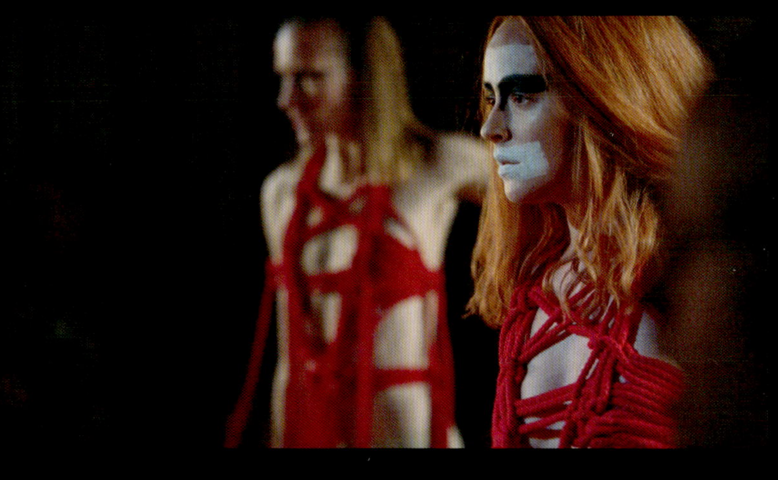

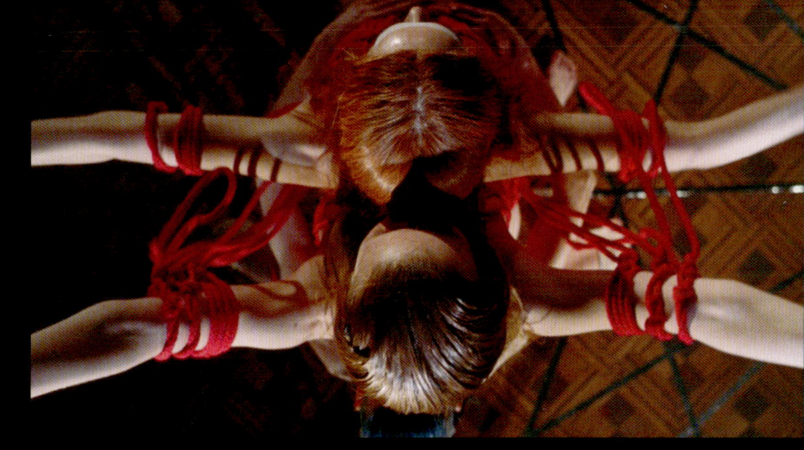

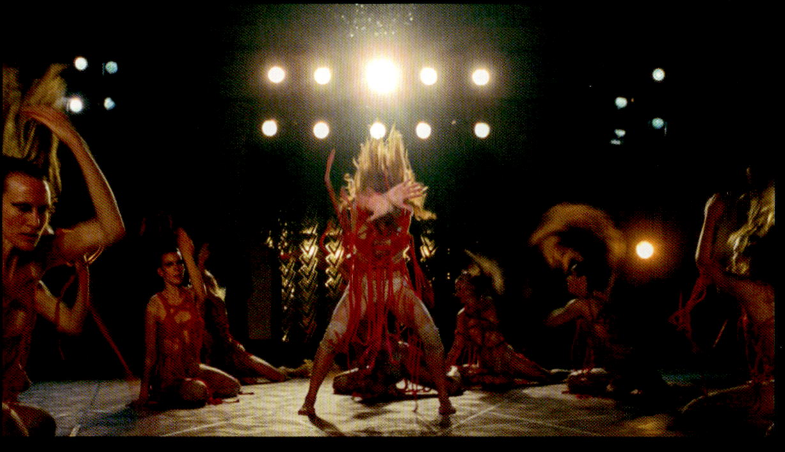

TOP: *West Side Story* (USA, 1961, dirs. Jerome Robbins and Robert Wise)

RIGHT: *Suspiria* (USA/Italy, 2018, dir. Luca Guadagnino)

sequence. While their fighting abilities appear almost supernatural, Flying Snow (Maggie Cheung) and Moon (Zhang Ziyi) possess complete mastery over their bodies in Zhang Yimou's 2002 martial arts film *Hero*. The apprentice, Moon, confronts the seasoned warrior, Flying Snow, within a forest of yellow leaves, driven by a deep-seated anger to avenge her master's death. Initially unfazed, Flying Snow reluctantly engages in a sword duel with Moon—a confrontation choreographed much like a dance, albeit one that defies the laws of physics. Adorned in red costumes that stand out against the yellow forest backdrop, their flowing attire expands and obscures their physical forms, recalling the Serpentine Dance from the early days of cinema. Highly stylized in its color scheme, dynamic movements, and cinematography, this sequence takes on an ethereal quality, wherein beauty, danger, and suffering intertwine. Eventually, Flying Snow inflicts a wound upon Moon, resulting in a solitary drop of blood falling from her sword, staining the yellow forest red. In this act, the forest itself becomes drenched in the hue, symbolizing the bloodshed and turmoil wrought by their clash.

From Méliès's early cinematic wonderworks to the brilliance of Technicolor and into the digital era, color has ceaselessly danced across the screen, breathing life into stories and emotions. Dance and moving colors became a vessel for liberation and transcendence, a gateway to euphoria or, at times, a descent into chaos. As colors swirled and bodies moved, filmmakers painted stories of empowerment and vulnerability, control and chaos, life and death. The mastery of color and dance intertwined to create a language that defied convention, offering glimpses into the human psyche and the boundless depths of color as cinematic expression. In the end, the convergence of color and motion on screen remains an ever-evolving dance, a symphony of emotions, narratives, and sensations that extends an invitation to the audience to step beyond the ordinary and explore the infinite realm of cinematic possibilities.

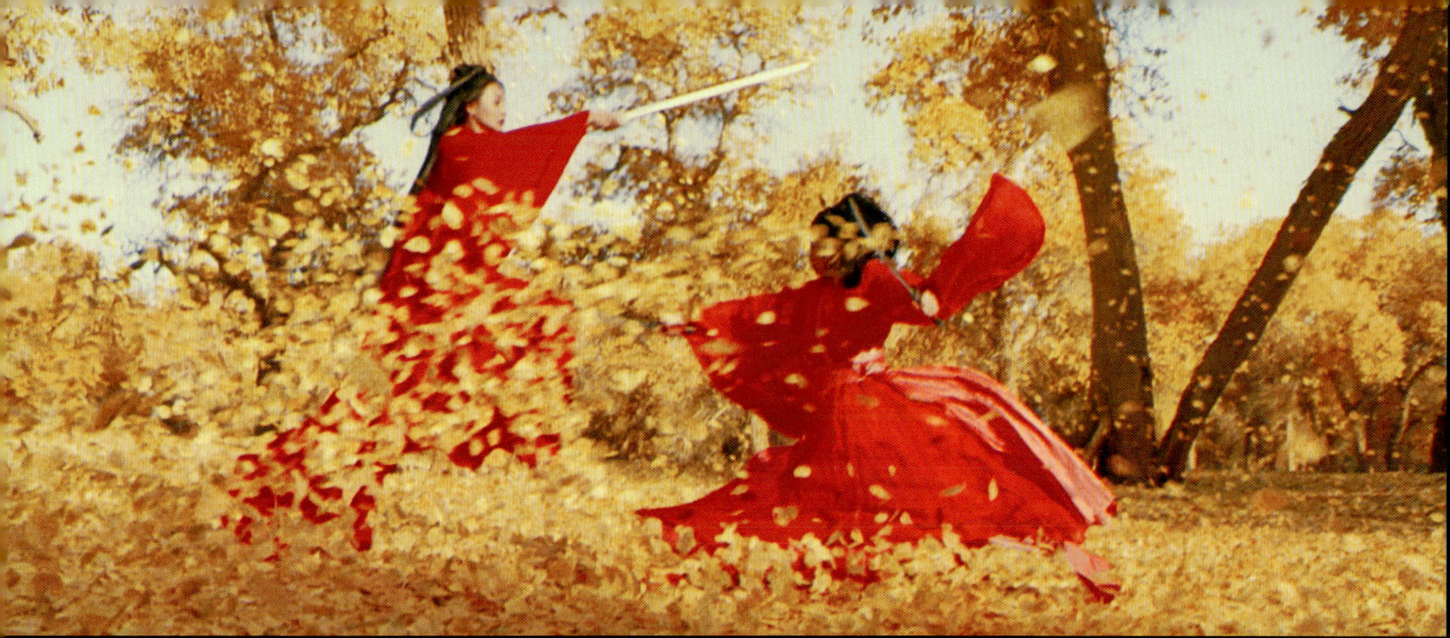

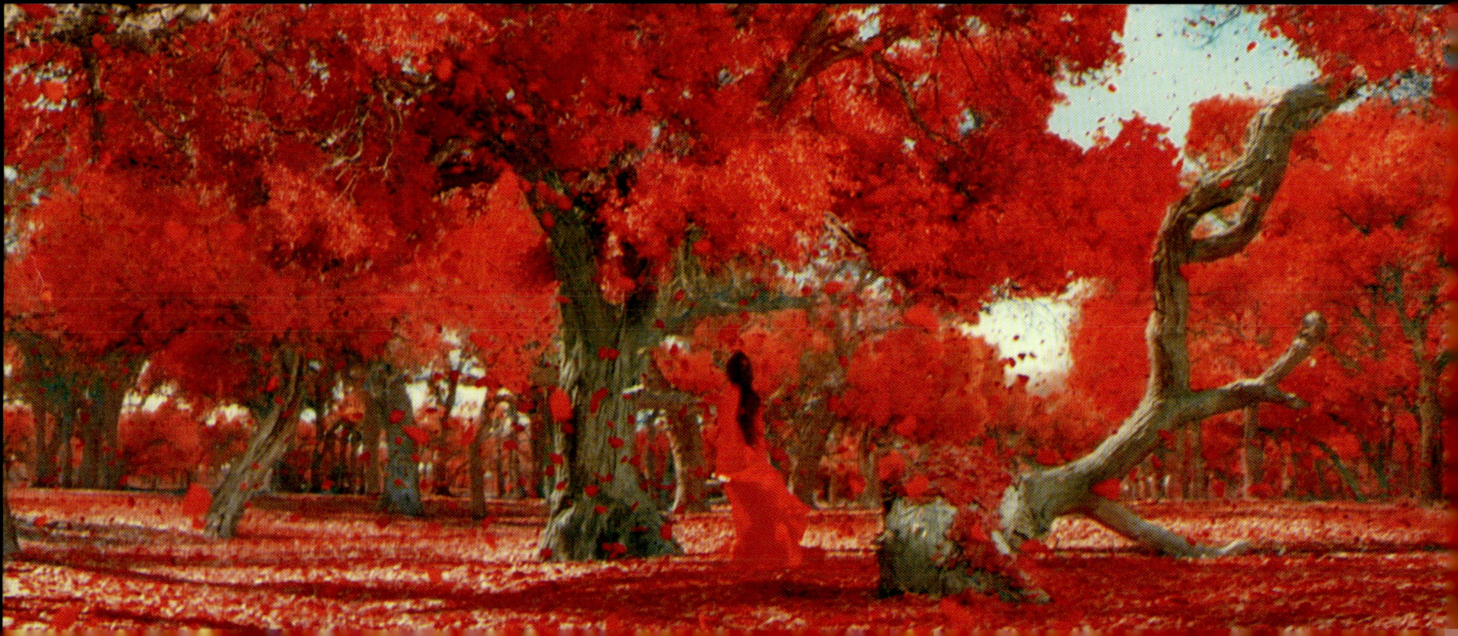

RED

AND

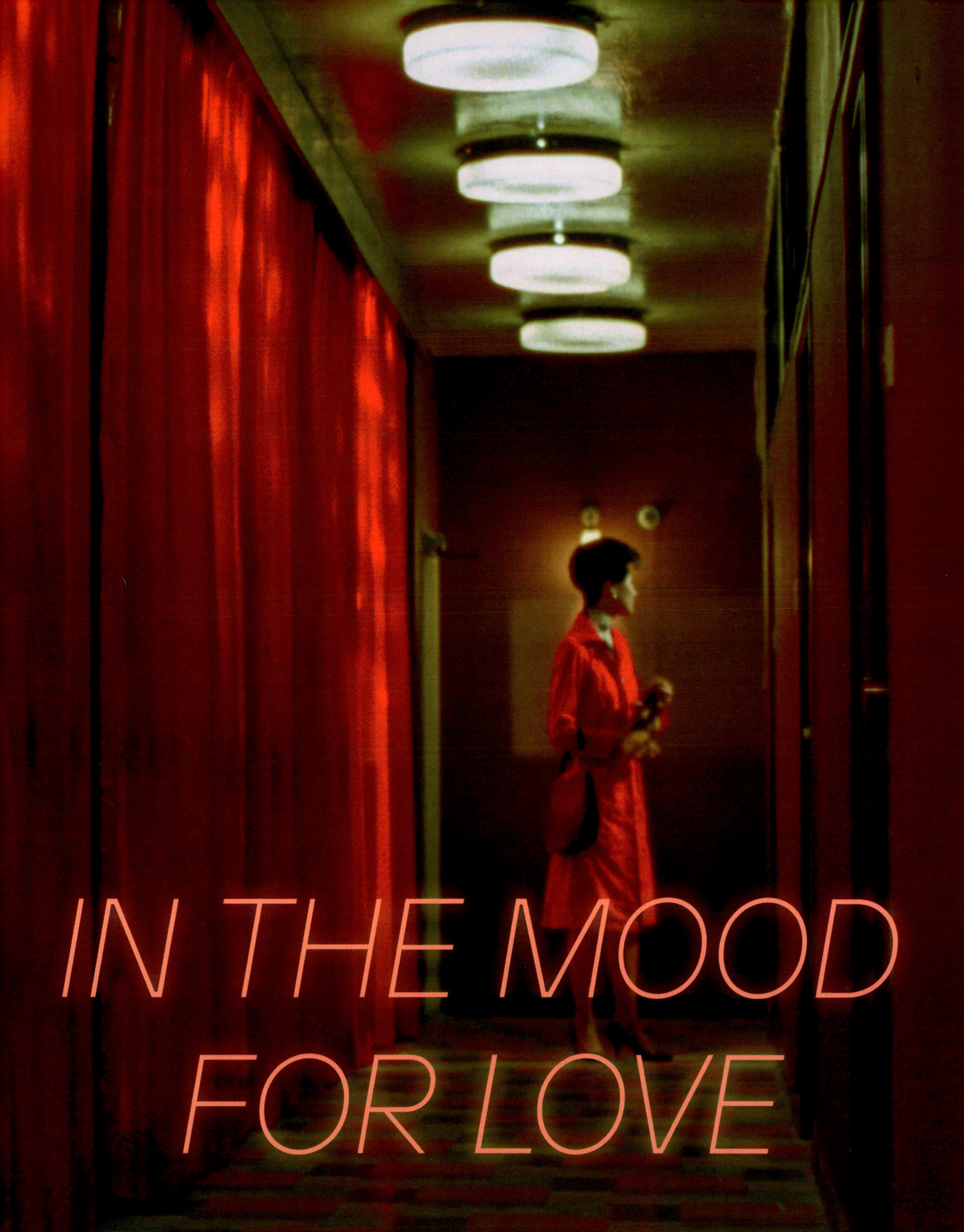
IN THE MOOD
FOR LOVE

The opening titles of Wong Kar Wai's film *In the Mood for Love* (*Huayang Nianhua*, Hong Kong, China/France, 2000) immediately command attention, their bold white type contrasting with a vibrant red background. Set in 1962 Hong Kong, the story follows Mrs. Chan (Maggie Cheung) and Mr. Chow (Tony Leung), who become neighbors after moving into adjacent apartments as subletters. Through the use of warm, saturated tones in a brown-yellow palette, the film effectively portrays their introverted loneliness and the absence of their respective spouses. As the film progresses, they gradually realize that their partners are having an affair with each other. This affair, as well as their growing feelings for each other, can be traced throughout the film by Wong's utilization of the color red.

The significance of the color deepens when Mrs. Chan and Mr. Chow first go out to dinner and later return to the same restaurant, pondering how their partners' affair began. A somewhat subdued red envelops the pair in the restaurant's leather booths and carpeting. This is contrasted by the green of the plates and lighting, reflecting the betrayal they both feel. Red becomes more prominent when Mrs. Chan and Mr. Chow learn that their partners have gone on a trip together. They visit a hotel in their pursuit of understanding the sexual aspect of the affair. Wong skillfully cuts to the hotel's long, empty hallway lined with red curtains and illuminated by white lights—an alluring corridor that exerts a magnetic pull. The corridor's red-white contrast is repeatedly employed, its intensity changing to reflect the evolving emotions between the characters. Eventually, Mrs. Chan and Mr. Chow are shown in a close-up shot, suffused in an orange-red glow. Here, the color of seduction and desire represents both their partners' adultery and the growing eroticism and mutual sexual attraction.

In a pivotal scene a little over halfway into the movie, Mr. Chow walks down the red-curtained hallway. This time the ceiling lights, previously white (typically associated with purity and innocence), are red, bathing the corridor crimson and illuminating his act of opening a door. He calls Mrs. Chan at work, and she, clad in a bright red coat, rushes to meet him. The otherwise slow rhythm and sensual tone of the film shifts dramatically. Mrs. Chan frantically navigates the building, accompanied by accelerated editing that heightens the sense of frenzy, chaos, and confusion. Red is used to intensify the feeling of unstoppable lust, with the corridor acting as an irresistible path of desire. However, the same red soon becomes associated with a sense of guilt when she leaves his room, her red coat blending with the hallway. When he tells her, "I didn't think you'd come," she responds, "We won't be like them," and walks away.

Following this crucial scene, the two characters spend more time together, working on his martial arts story and relishing each other's company. As they realize their burgeoning love, Mr. Chow honorably decides to leave for Singapore. He invites her to the hotel room one last time, but she refuses. He switches off the light and departs the room, leaving it in darkness. Wong presents Mr. Chow once more in the hallway, motionless and frozen, as the camera retreats. He then cuts to Mrs. Chan in a green dress sitting in a room, shedding tears. An additional shot of the hallway, this time with the red curtains exposed to more white light, representing the candor of daylight, imparts a sense of realism and reduces the stylized, enchanted mood. (Later, she leaves a trace of red lipstick on a white cigarette butt during a clandestine visit to his Singaporean room.) However, red, the color that once enveloped and surrounded them and represented the force of their attraction, fades in prominence.

Only in the end credits, where white characters, significantly smaller than before, appear on a red background, does the color regain dominance; its return serves as a poignant reminder of the lingering impact of their affair and the indelible mark left by their forbidden love. Wong Kar Wai's masterful use of color not only accentuates the emotional depth of the narrative but also mirrors the intricate complexities of human relationships and the transient nature of intense connections. **—JESSICA NIEBEL**

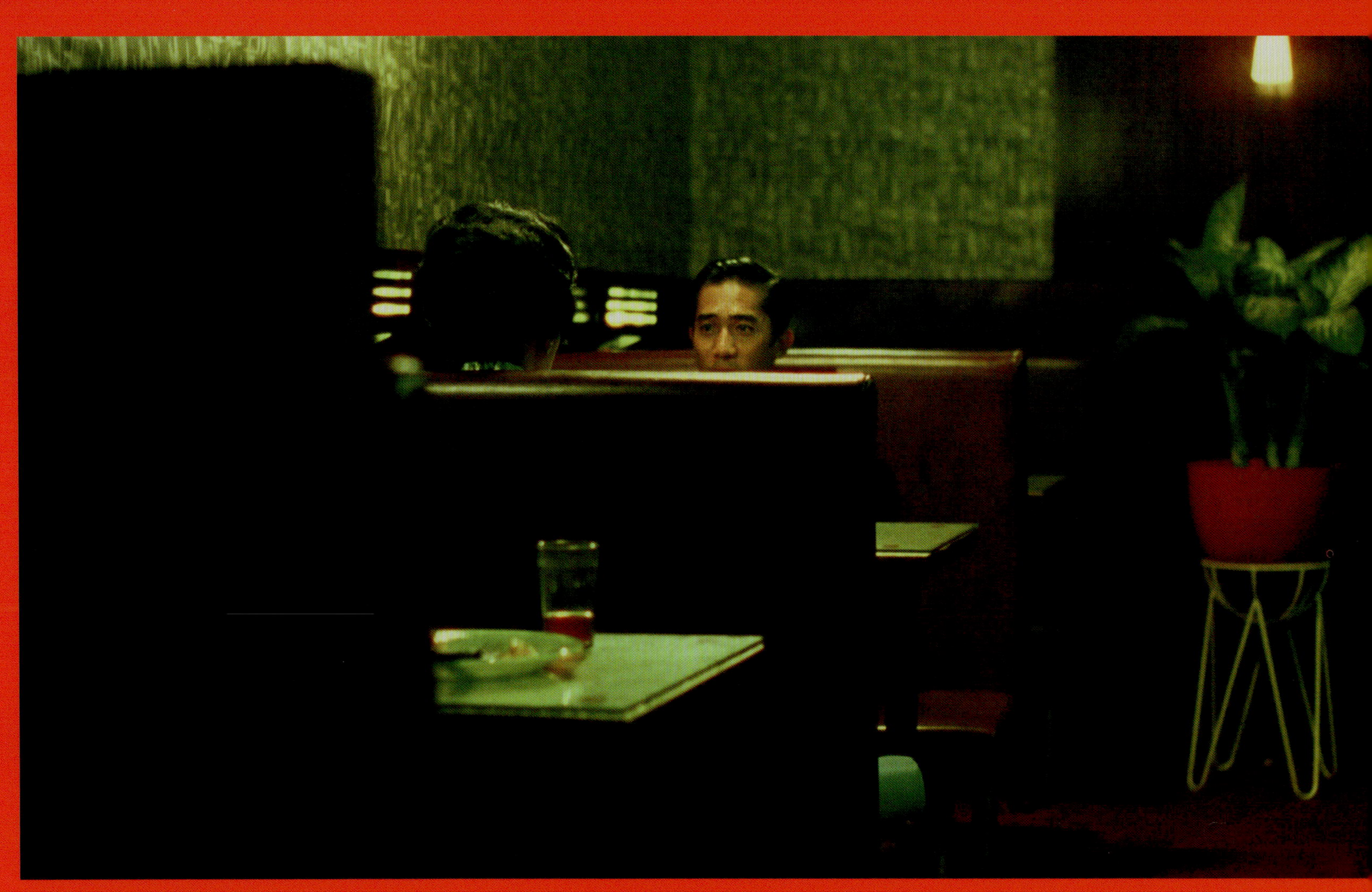

In the Mood for Love (*Huayang Nianhua*, Hong Kong, China/France, 2000, dir. Wong Kar Wai)

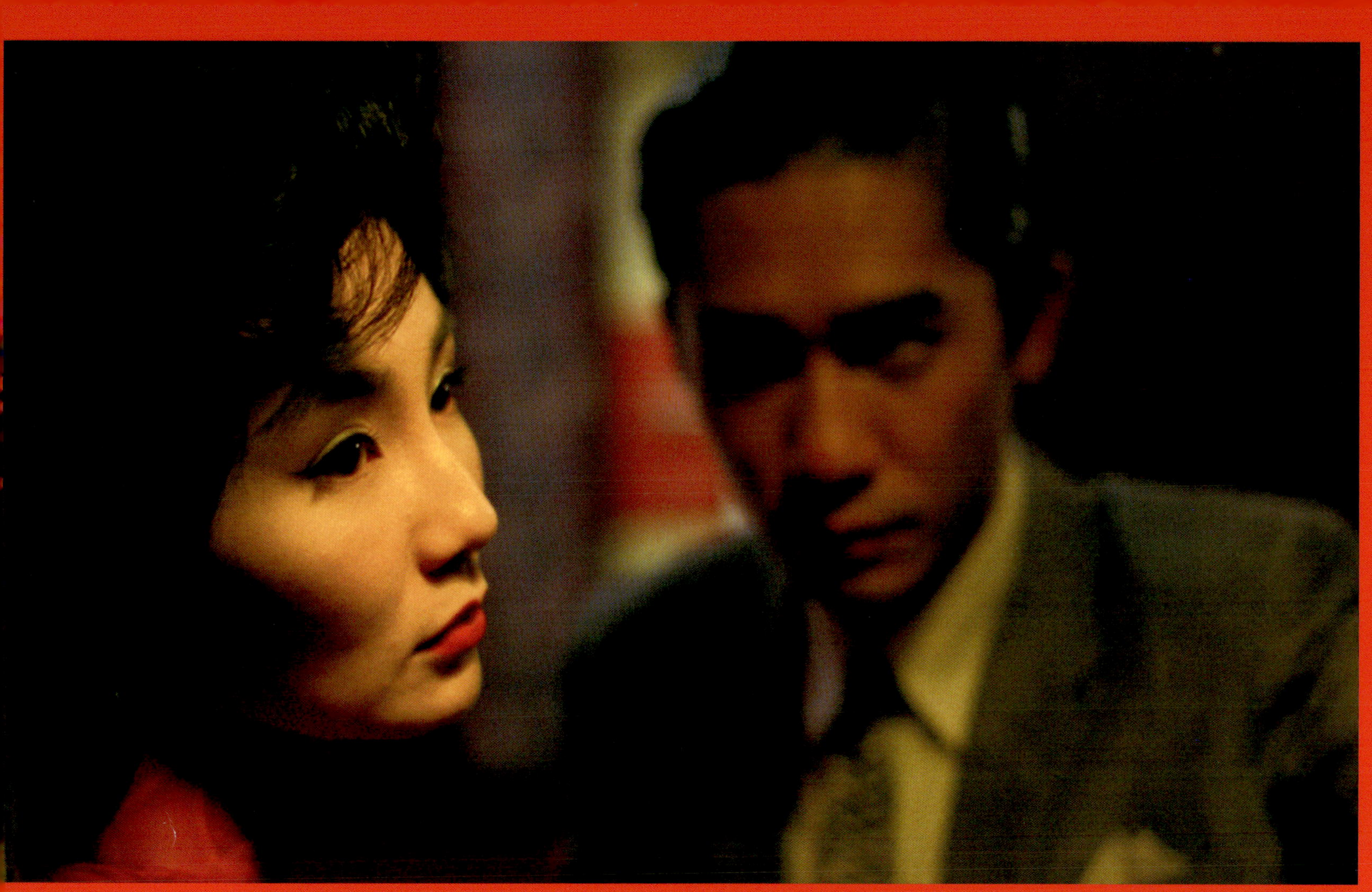

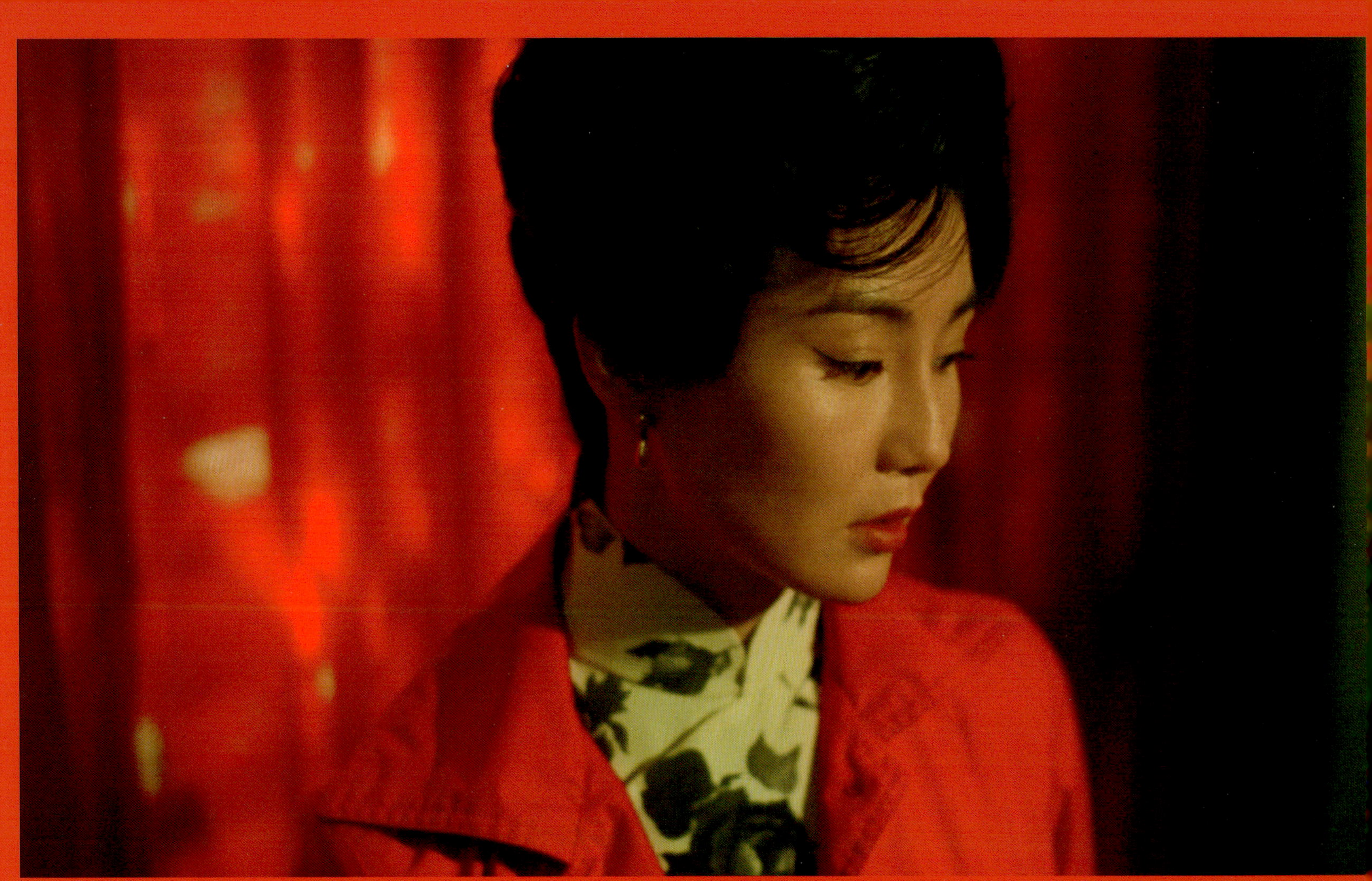

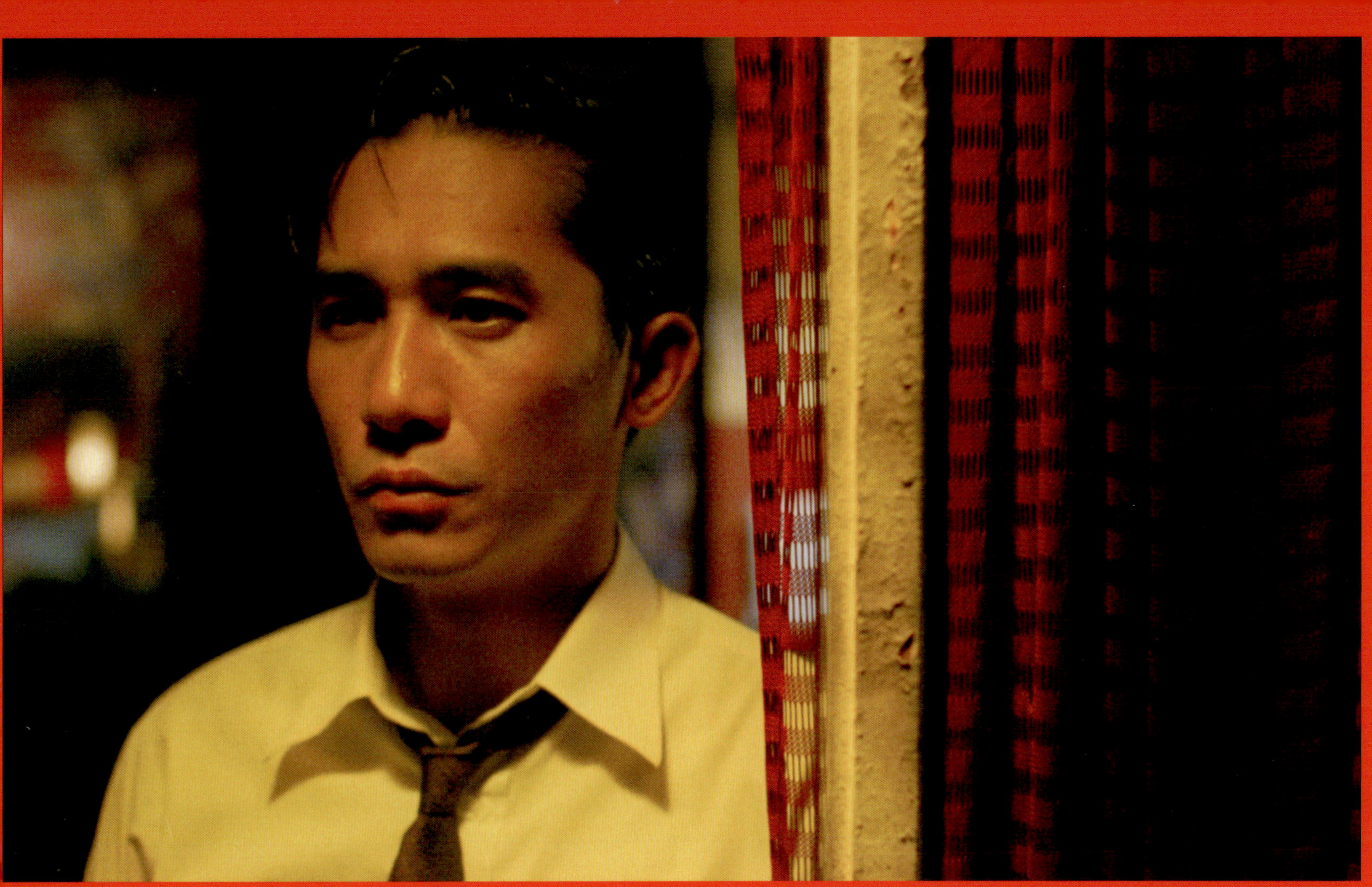

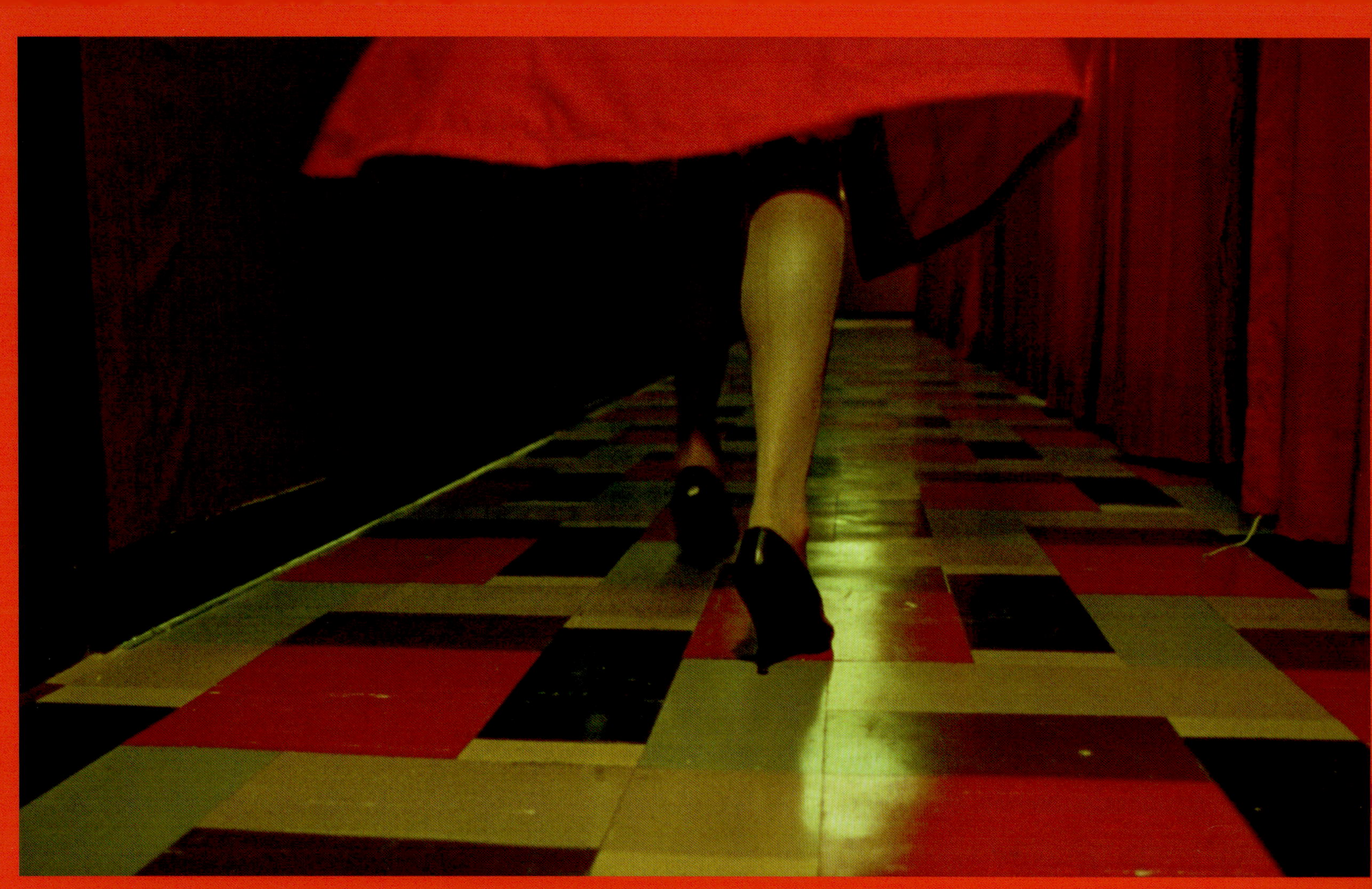

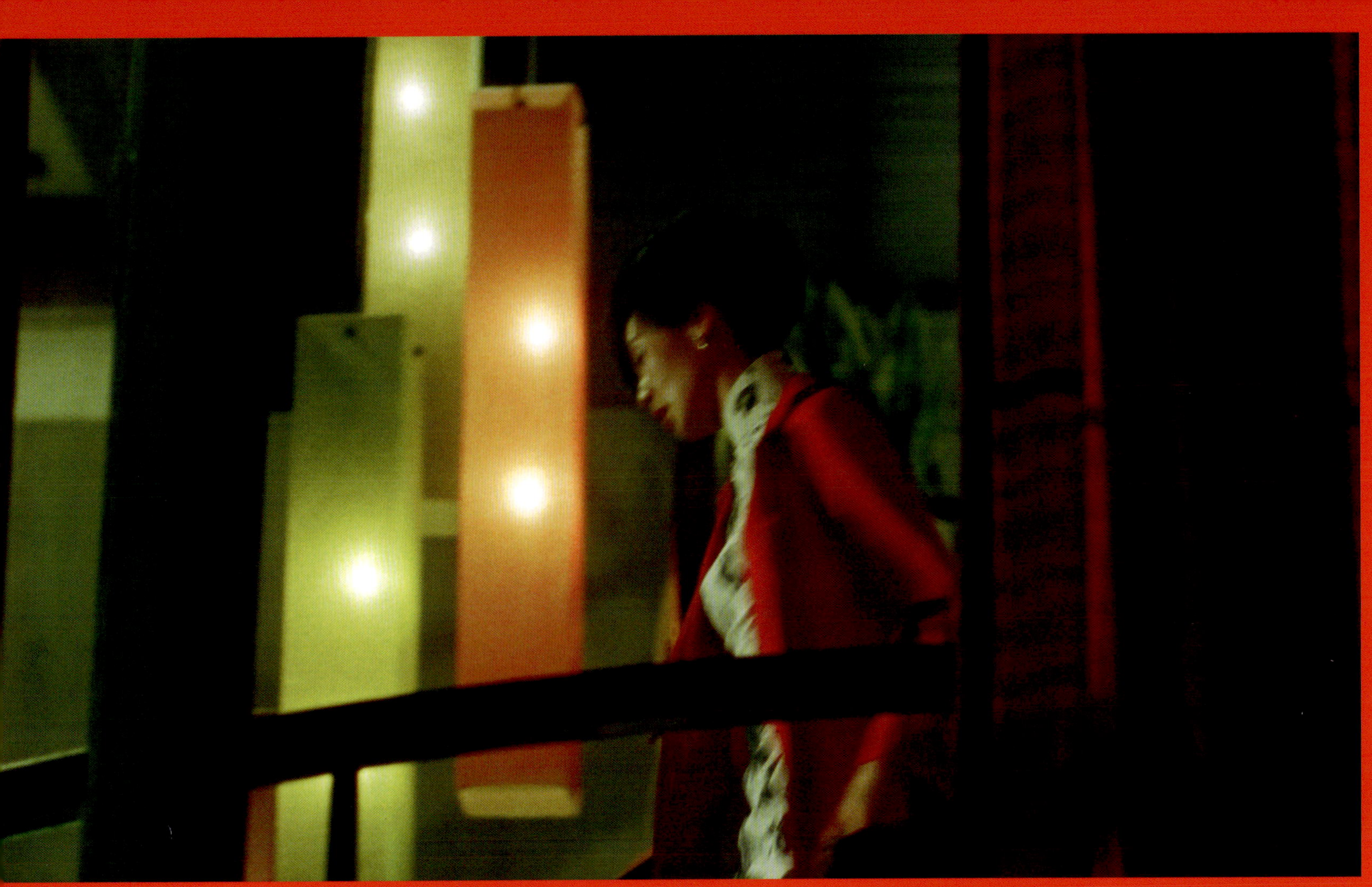

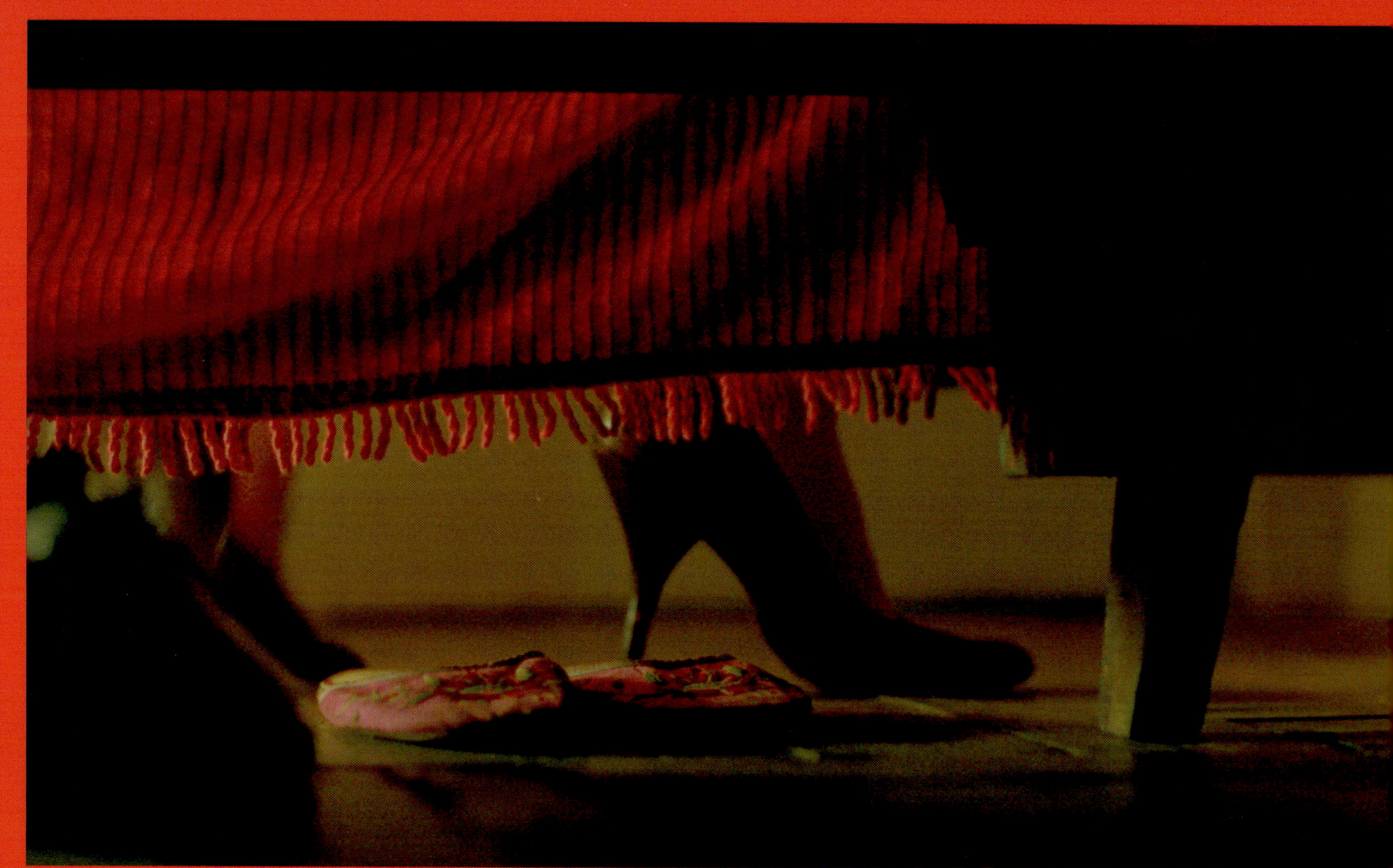

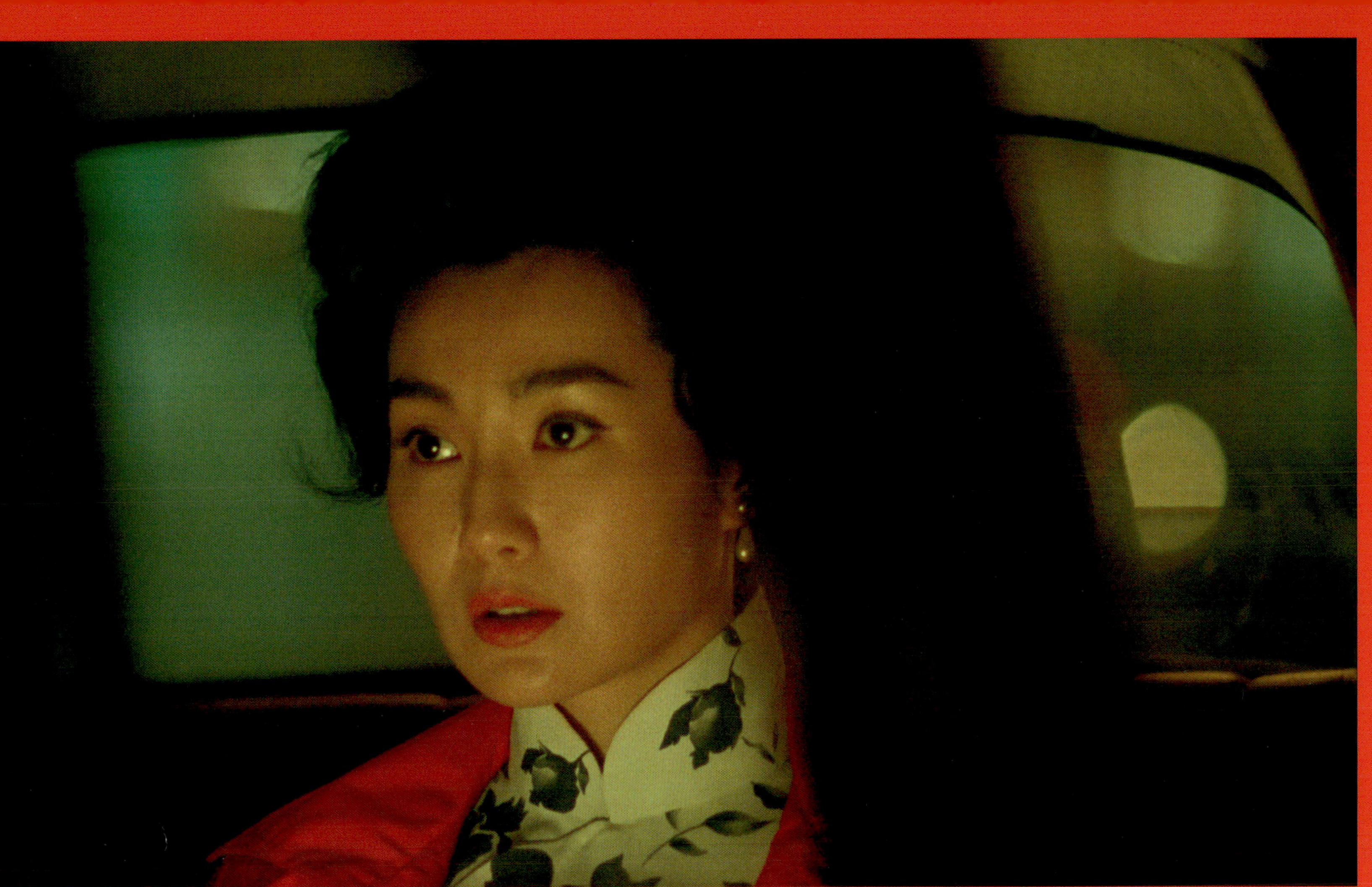

ORANGE

AND

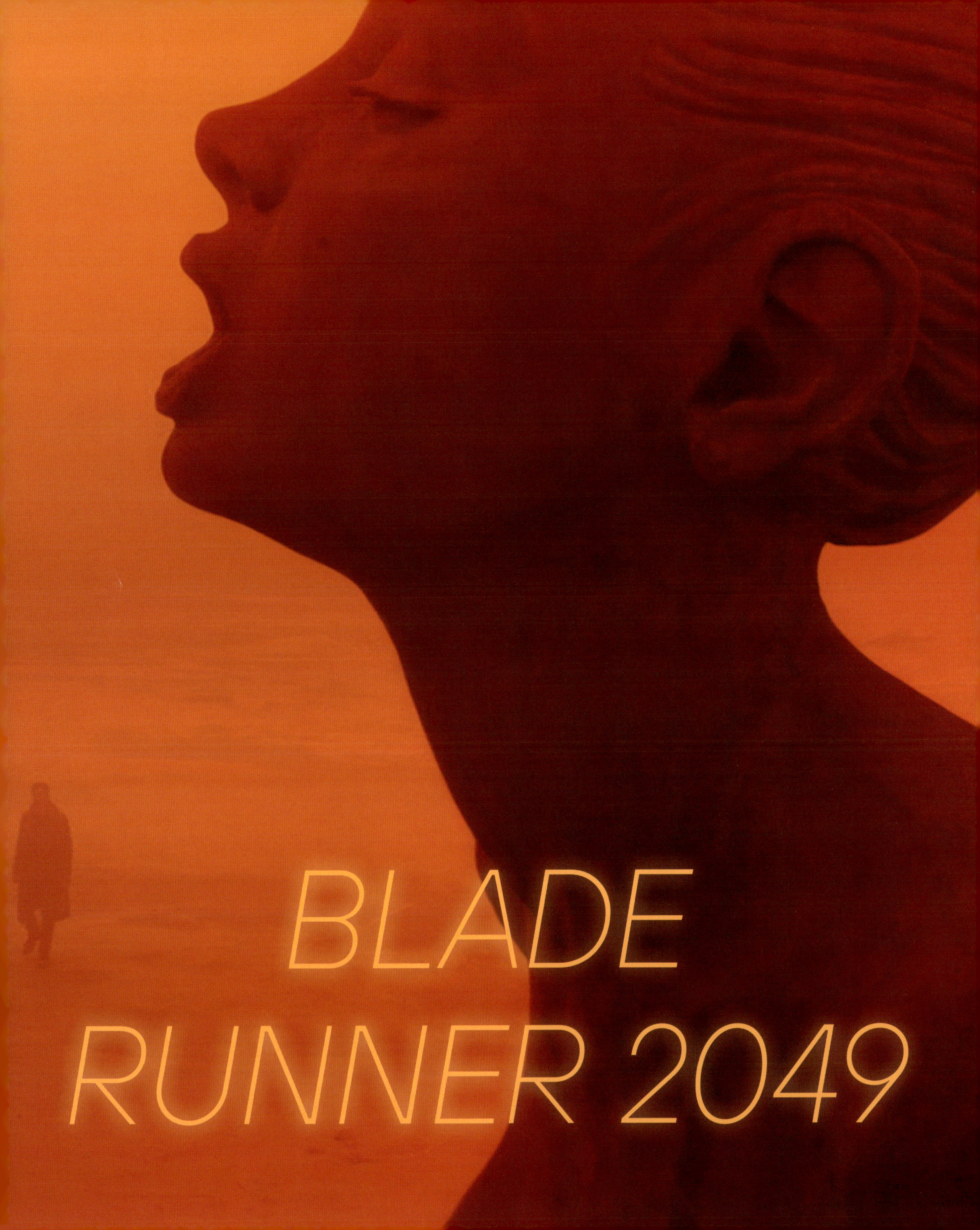

BLADE RUNNER 2049

In a foundational scene in Denis Villeneuve's *Blade Runner 2049* (USA, 2017), illuminated by the soft orange glow of birthday candles, Dr. Ana Stelline (Carla Juri) explains to police officer K (Ryan Gosling) that the average person misunderstands memories because they are supposed to be as accurate as possible and filled with details. In fact, she explains, "anything real should be a mess." K already knows at this point in the film that this statement by Dr. Stelline, who designs memories for replicants (or bioengineered humans), is true. Deciphering what is real and what is not is at the heart of K's mission—and a larger theme of the film—as he tries to track down the child of a replicant. While the philosophical dilemma posed in the film is clear through the plot, acting, and direction, it is orange that punctuates the importance of memory in the film.

Orange follows K throughout the film, and the color's connection to memory is established in the viewer's first encounter with it, when K notices an orange flower at the base of a dead tree. The tree marks the grave of a replicant, Rachael (Sean Young), who once gave birth—something thought impossible. Believing that this development could spark a war between humans and replicants, K is tasked by his superior, Lieutenant Joshi (Robin Wright), with killing the child. As a "blade runner" (an officer tasked with "retiring," or killing, rogue replicants), K begins his work of tracking the child down by digging through memories. Orange punctuates these scenes in a range of hues from warm glow to harsh glare in an otherwise strikingly dark and severe environment. The flower, a speck highly contrasted against a black ground, serves as a visual cue that memories will lead K to the answer.

After K finds the flower, the first sweeping use of orange is in a scene at the archives of the Wallace Corporation, which took over the manufacturing of replicants. The vast server room emanates an almost regal orange-gold tone, reinforcing for the viewer its importance as a memory keeper, one of the few places left in this world that contains data from the past. K is looking for information regarding Rachael, but because she existed before the Blackout—a worldwide event that wiped almost all computer data and subsequently much of the past—there is little record of her. In fact, the only memory found, in a seldom-visited wing of the archive, is one of Rachael's, of a tender moment between her and former blade runner Rick Deckard when they first met and their love affair was born.

However, nostalgia does not always present tender moments, as we observe in K's recollection of a childhood memory. Prompted by his superior, K recalls hiding a precious wooden horse in an unused furnace to prevent bullies from taking it. What starts as hints in K's memory of his gray apartment—an orange bowl and an orange book—grows into an intense fire, as young K stares at the burning furnace. This reflection, one he previously shrugged off due to its presumably implanted nature, becomes a crucial point that has K questioning the nature of his existence. A memory of something as benign as a small orange bowl grows into a roaring fire that demands to be seen and investigated. This memory isn't comforting—it details how K is bullied—yet its importance is undisputed. K must relive this memory to continue his search for the missing child.

At the climax of the film, in which K hopes to find the child's whereabouts, orange grows from a glow to a fire to a highly saturated, overwhelming presence. Seeking confirmation of his suspicion that he is in fact Rachael's child, K interrogates Deckard in his window-lined apartment, the thick orange-yellow fog outside suffusing the interior, its intensity perhaps hinting at the importance of this scene. Deckard, now living in the apocalyptic ruins of a once-majestic Las Vegas, recalls his relationship with Rachael, who died in childbirth, and his child, whom he gave up and protected by scrambling their identity with another replicant. Thus, the color is simultaneously comforting, eliciting memories of his love for Rachael and his child, and unforgiving—renewing thoughts of Rachael's death, the abandonment of his child, and hiding in a barren desert to escape death.

Many other moments in *Blade Runner 2049* are punctuated with orange to remind the viewer about memories, but even the few examples described here show how the color offers a powerful presence that could not be evoked through dialogue or narrative. Just as memories can be friendly and nostalgic or aggressive and harsh, orange—depending on its hue or intensity—can simultaneously provide comfort and conflict. Like memories, orange can be messy, which is what makes it so poignant. —**ALEXANDRA JAMES SALICHS**

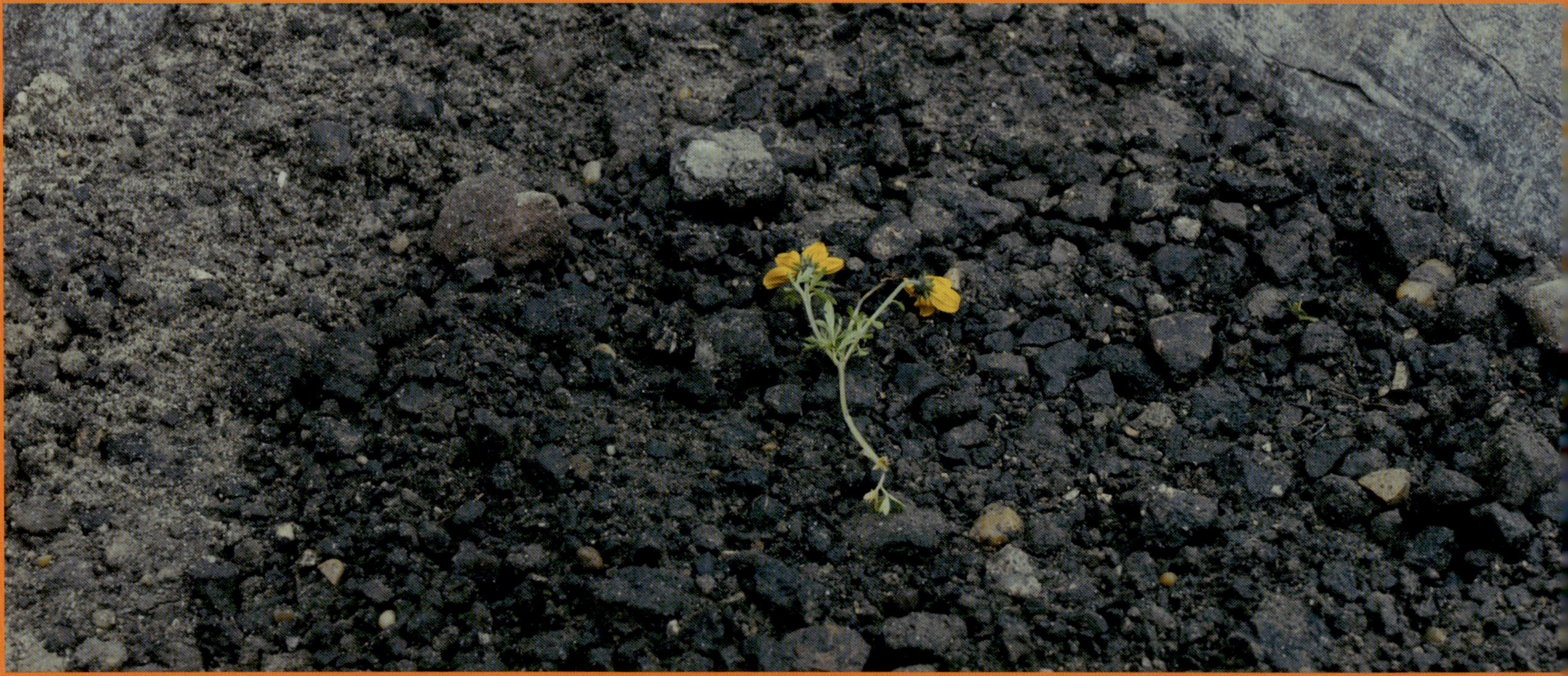

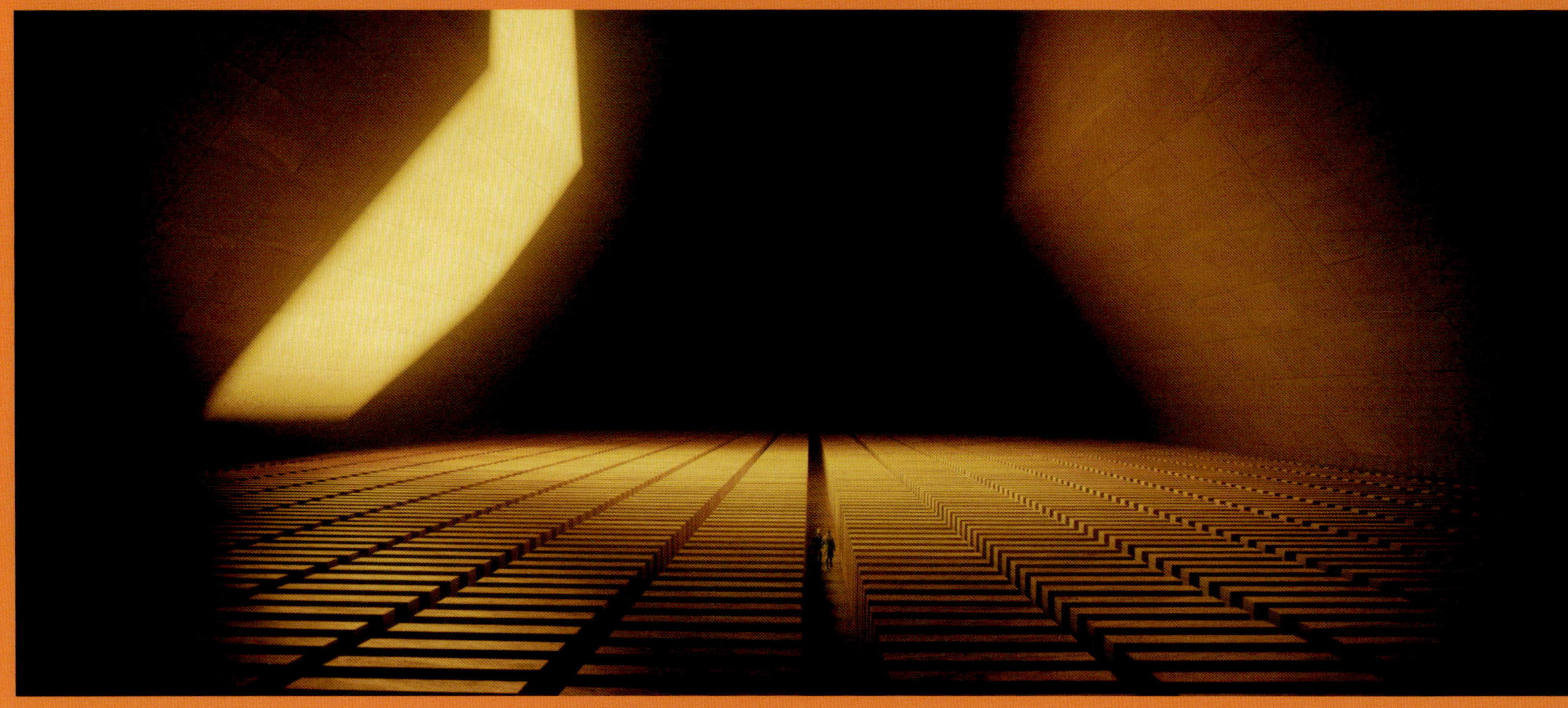

Blade Runner 2049 (USA, 2017, dir. Denis Villeneuve)

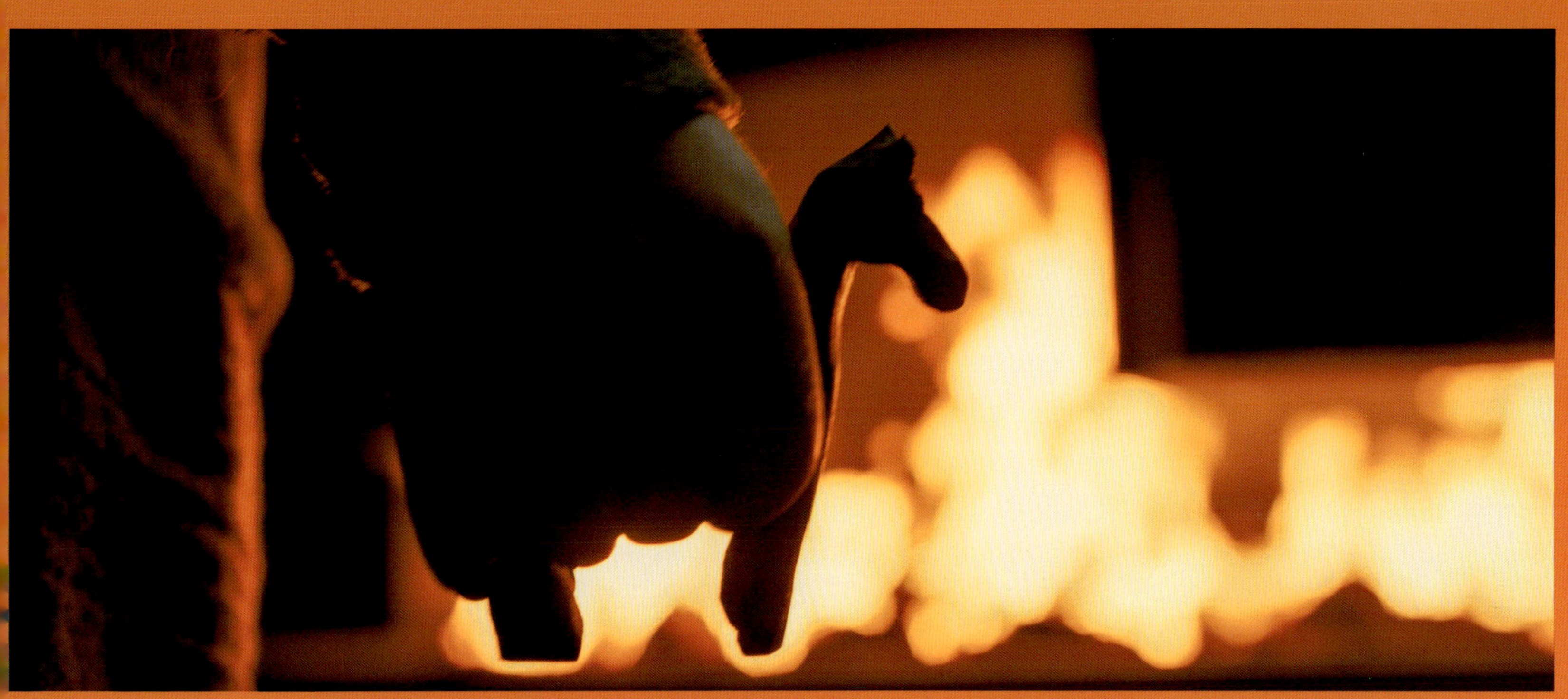

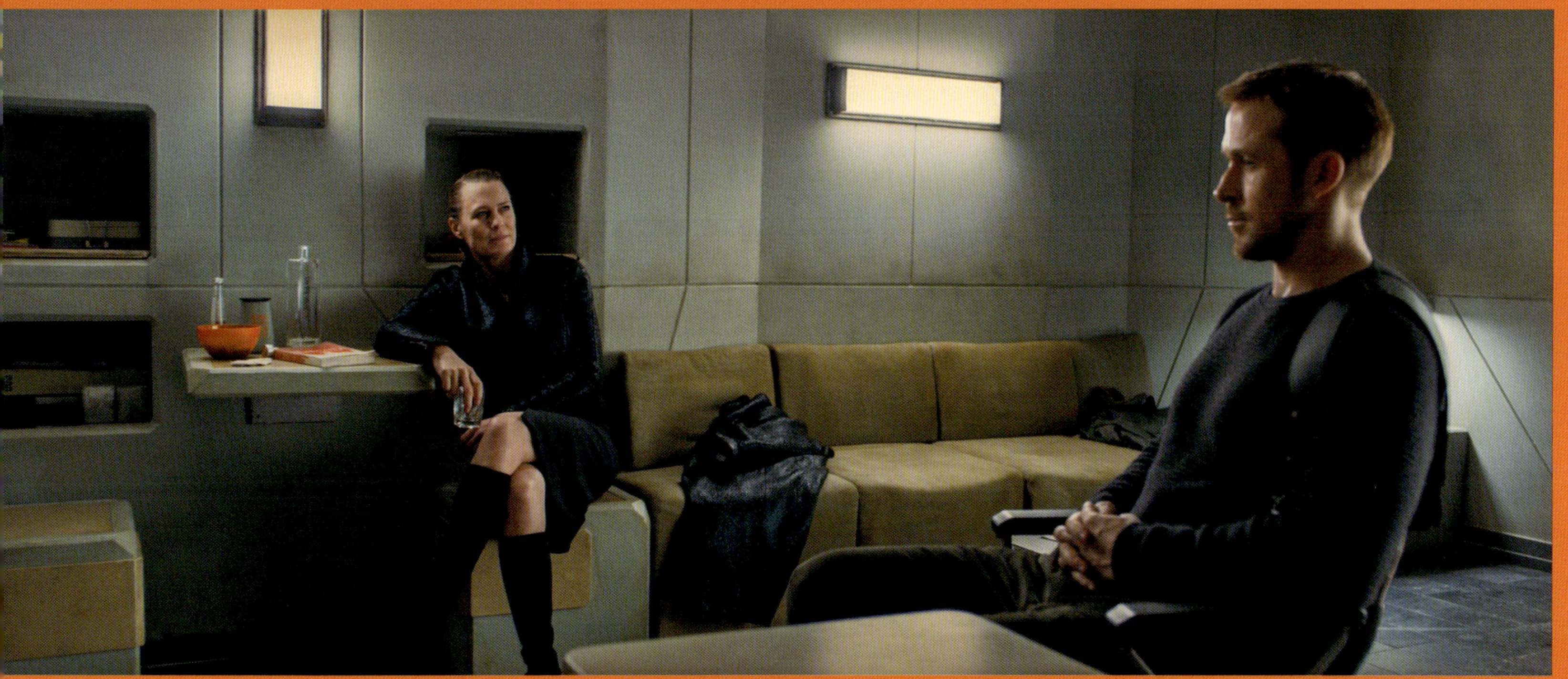

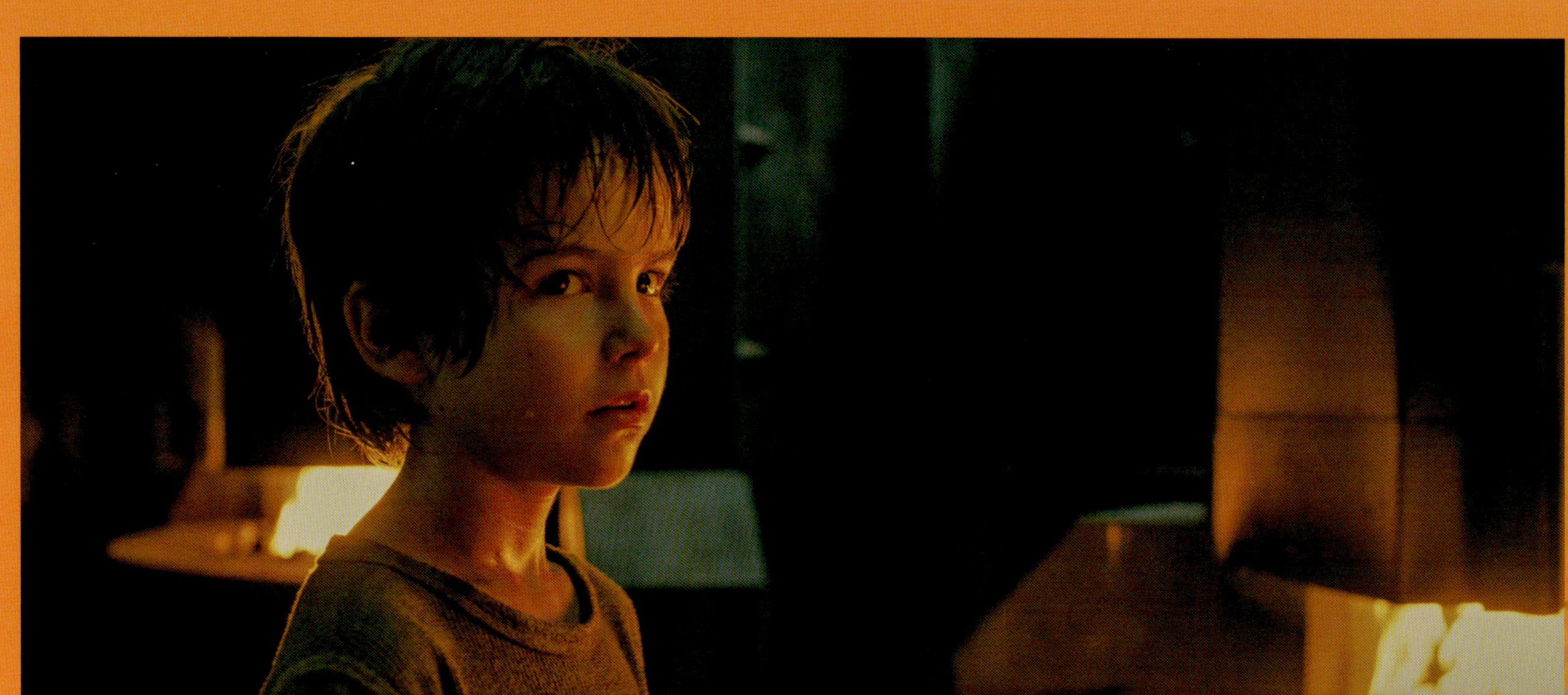

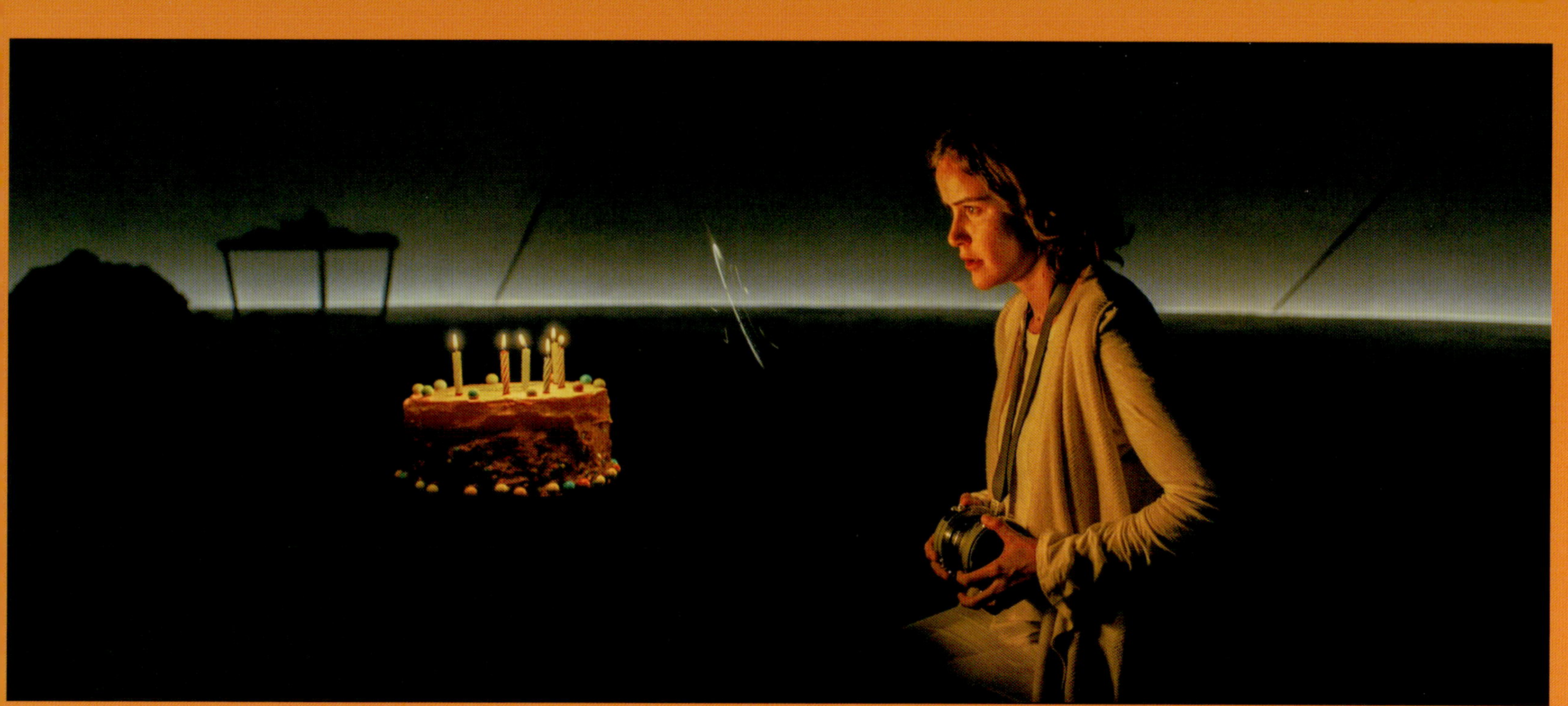

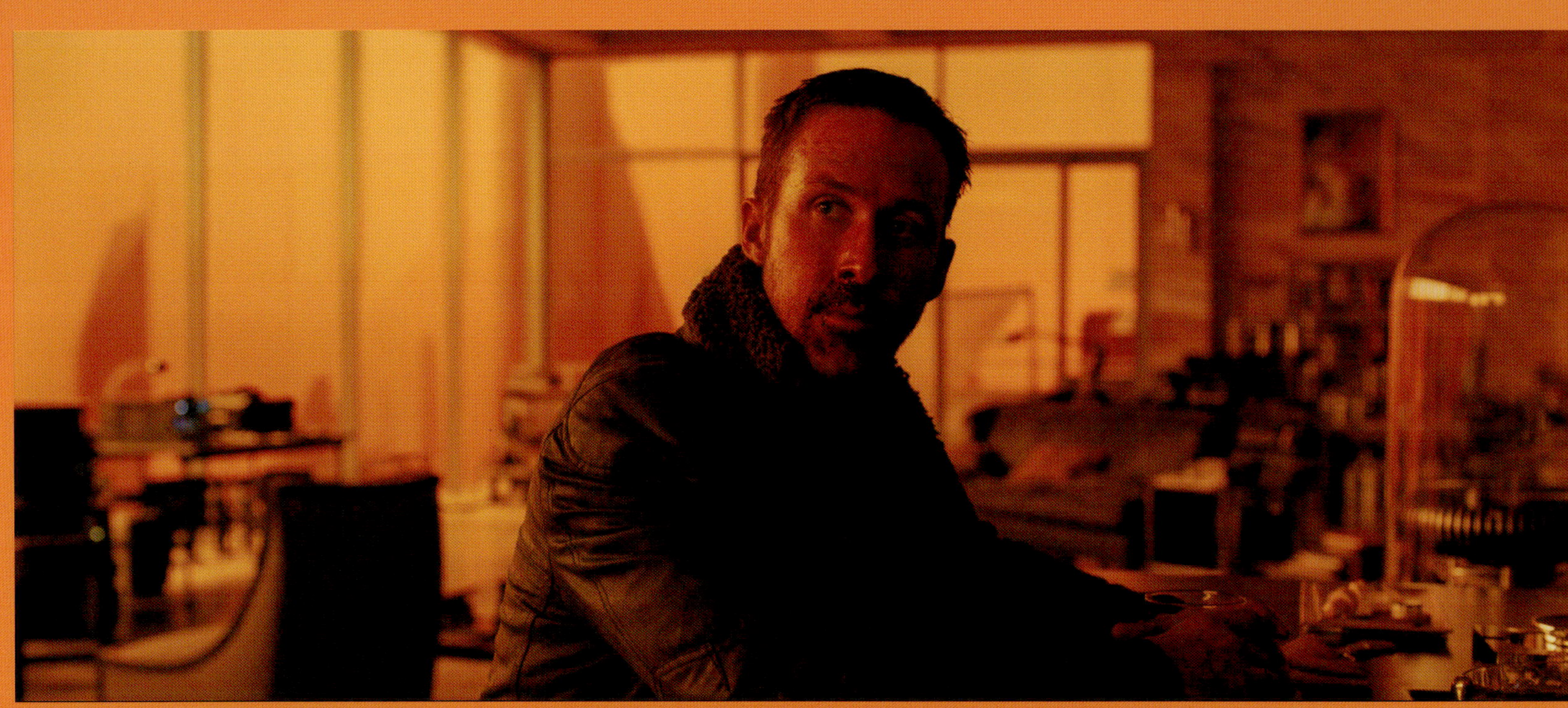

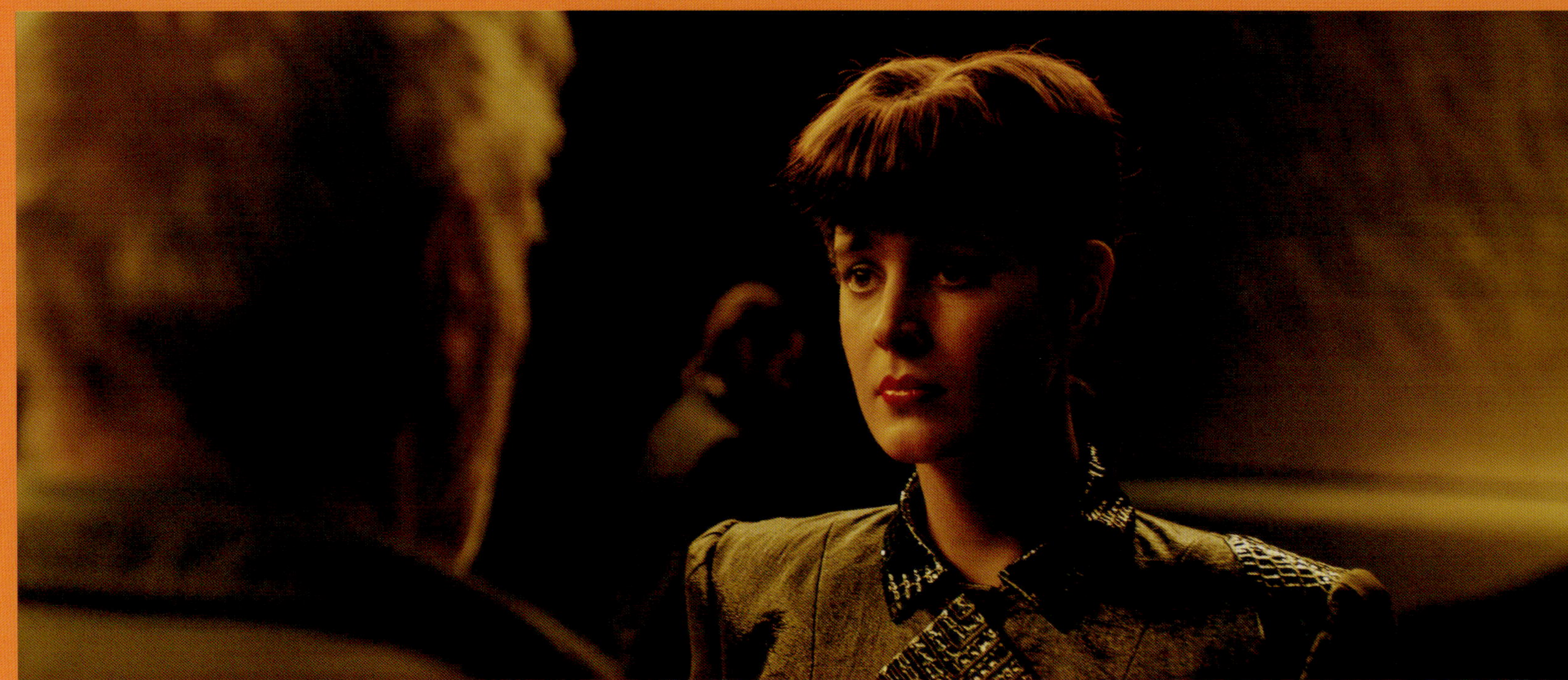

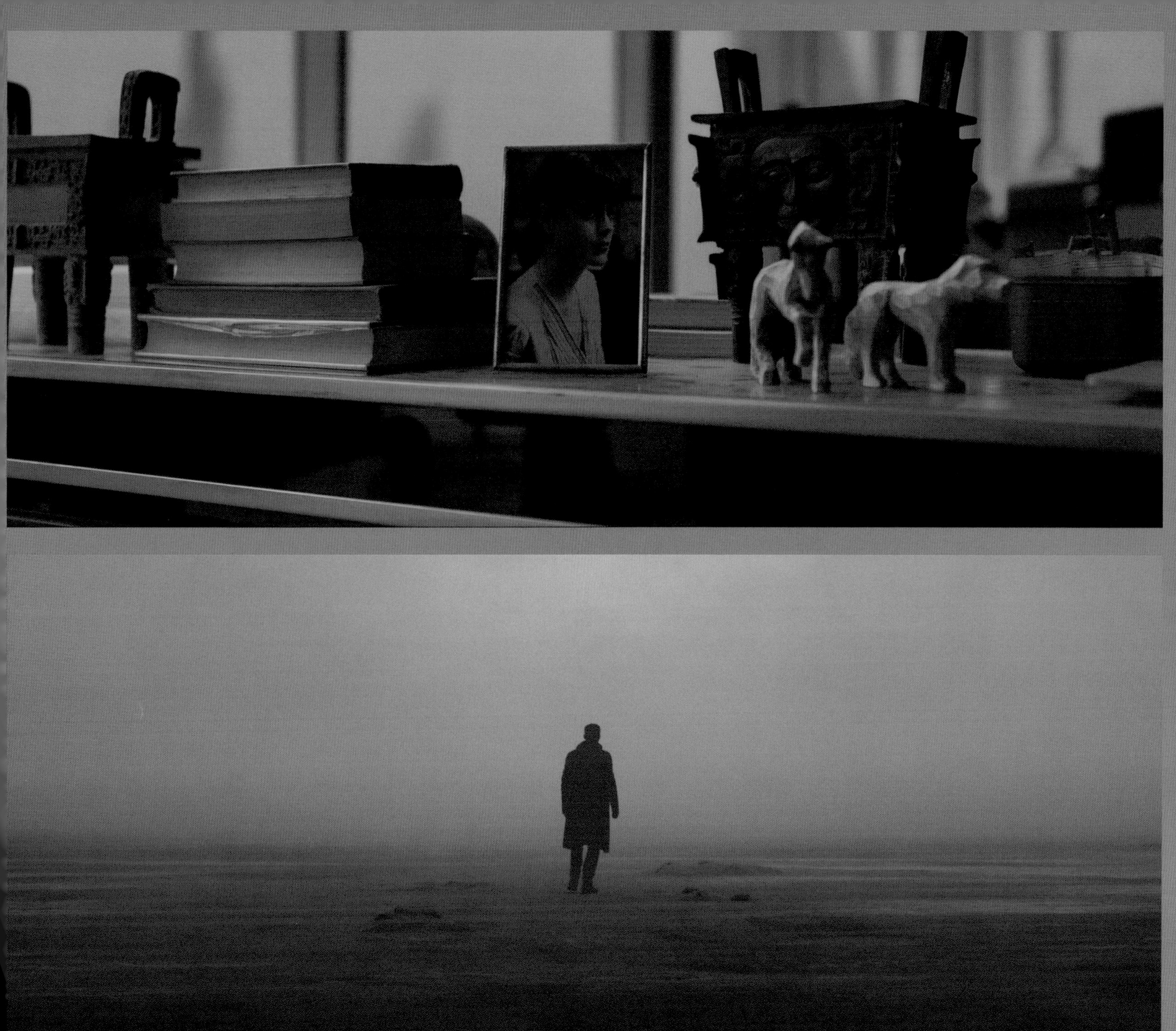

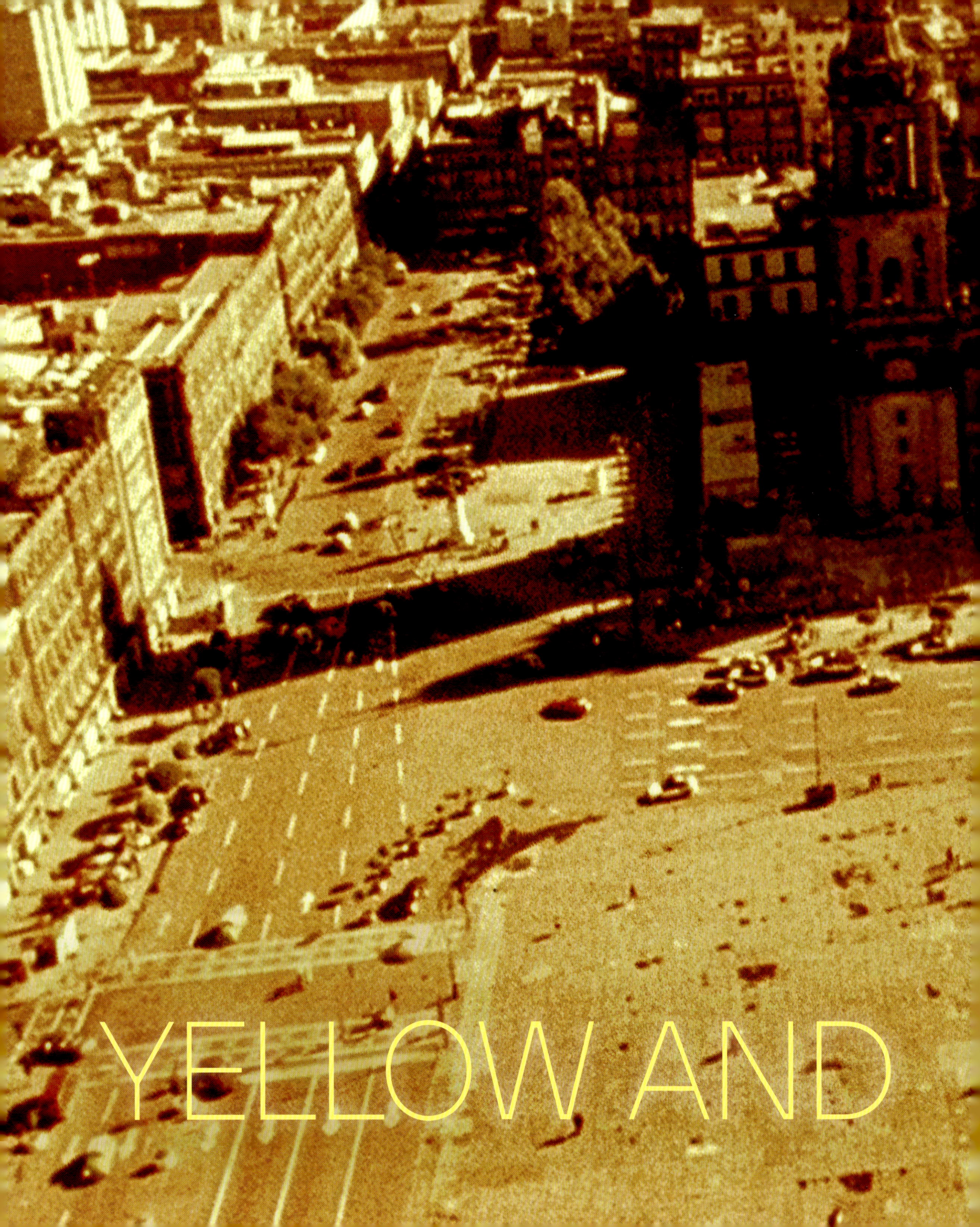
YELLOW AND

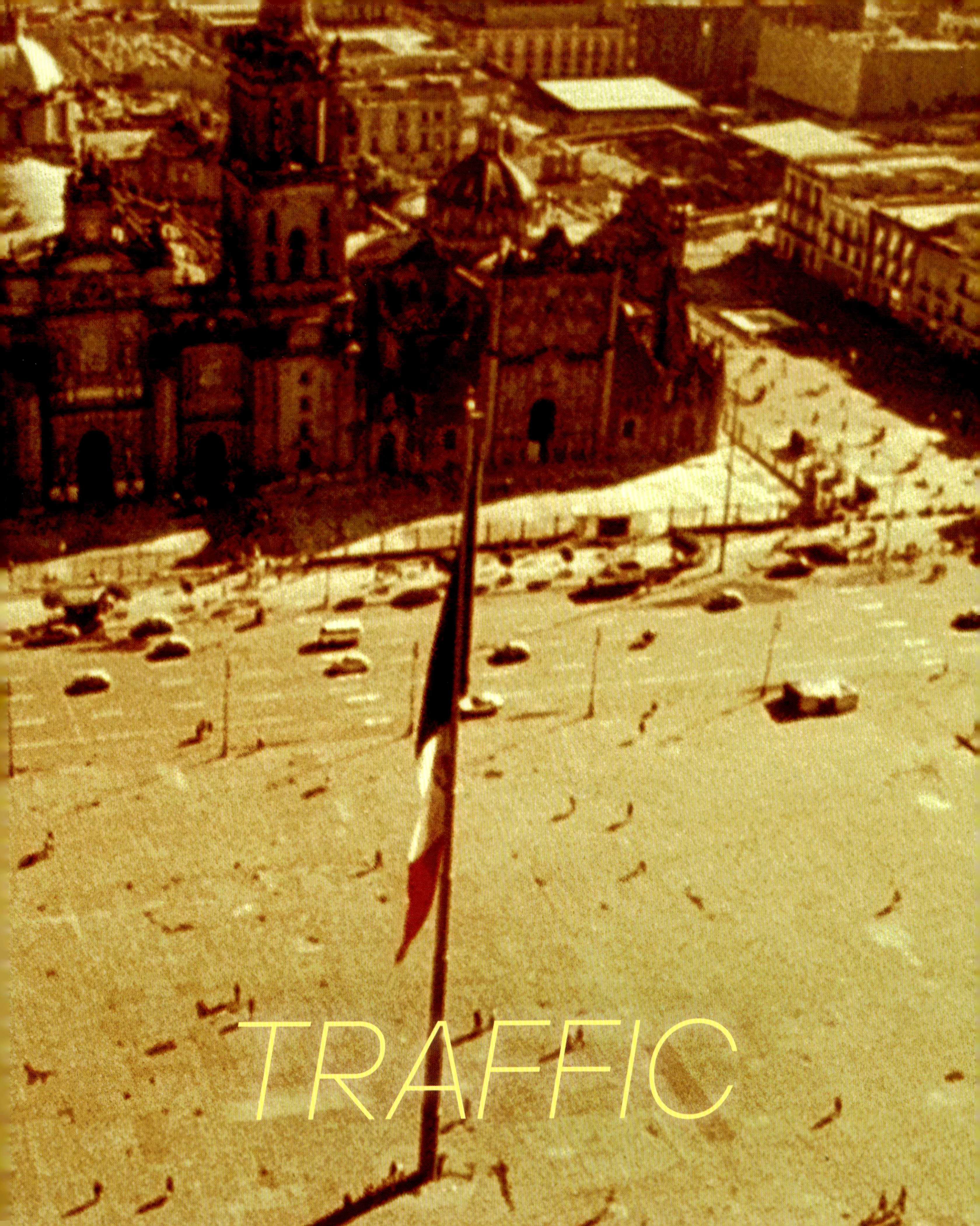
TRAFFIC

Steven Soderbergh's *Traffic* (USA, 2000), a crime thriller that follows the illegal drug trade, earned praise not only for its direction, editing, and acting—receiving Oscar wins in all three categories—but also for its use of color. Soderbergh wanted to help the audience keep track of the numerous locations and storylines involving politicians, drug users, cartels, and law enforcement by designating a specific color palette for each location: a saturated blue for the East Coast, a grainy sepia tobacco yellow for Mexico, and a diffused white for San Diego.[1] However, the choice of yellow for Mexico ended up sparking a trope colloquially called the "Mexico filter" and raising questions about utilizing this color to depict an international country.

Initially used to describe the look of films or television shows that take place in Mexico, the Mexico filter has since expanded to suggest countries in Southeast Asia or Africa and mainly any locale outside the United States. The term was first identified in 2001 by *The Christian Science Monitor*, which interviewed Mexicans about their thoughts on *Traffic*. Dulce Maria Sauri, then-president of Mexico's Institutional Revolutionary Party, emphasized that *Traffic*'s monochromatic palette depicts the country as "sepia, old, and shadowy."[2] Jorge Bustamante, then-director of Colegio de la Frontera Norte, a think tank that focuses on border issues, commented that *Traffic* "doesn't come right out and say, 'Mexico is the enemy of the US,' but that is the portrayal," implying that the yellow filter symbolizes an antagonistic lens.[3] The article didn't attract much attention at the time; however, a decade later the conversation arose again with such films and television shows as *Breaking Bad* (2008–13), *Sicario* (USA, 2015), and *Extraction* (USA, 2020).

While many conversations around the Mexico filter trace its use to Soderbergh's *Traffic*, the practice of the color representing gritty, dangerous, and impoverished locations dates to the beginnings of film itself. In the early days of cinema, there was a debate between the merits of natural and unnatural color; the former sought to replicate the world that the human eye perceives in real life, while the latter featured arbitrary colors to suit a film's individual narrative needs.[4] For example, in the silent film *Snow White* (USA, 1916), a pink-purple color was used for a dungeon scene in which the queen and the witch brew a poison. This at first seems like a curious choice, since amber was traditionally used to evoke interior lighting. However, deviating from the traditional interior tint was a choice made by the director to emphasize the magical and sinister nature of the scene.

Filmmakers of the silent era chose tints or tones that best suited their creative needs, whether to represent feelings, locations, or time of day or to highlight the scenery, even if it meant sacrificing an element of fidelity. Soon enough, dyes would be named for these messages or usages. For example, the "nocturne" dye, described as a "deep violet-blue," would be used for a nighttime scene, and yellow (or "sunshine") would be used to depict daytime or heat.[5] Early Westerns such as *Wagon Tracks* (USA, 1919) and adventure films set in the desert like *L'Atlantide* (France, 1921) utilized yellows to suggest dry conditions or emphasize the hot sun.

Because color films were dyed at the direction of each individual director, there is no one way to utilize colors. However, it turns out yellow has a long history of depicting Mexico. As early as 1917 with *The Woman God Forgot*, a romance film that takes place during the Aztec Empire, yellow was used not only to signal daytime but also to emphasize the empire's wealth. This use of yellow extends beyond the silent era and its tradition of unnatural color. The Western musical *Under a Texas Moon* (USA, 1930) utilized Technicolor III to show a yellow-tinged Mexican Texas. Technicolor III was one of many technologies that attempted to capture natural color, but because the process used only red and green filters, it could not capture yellows well; the additional step of running the film through a yellow tanning developer was meant to fix the deficiency.[6] Just as they did with *Traffic* seventy years later, Mexicans found *Under a Texas Moon* offensive.[7] The movie's premiere was picketed by local Latino activists due to its ugly stereotypes of Mexicans (and the already cliché use of saturated yellow); it turns out that even natural color technologies could utilize yellow to promote the idea of Mexico, accurate or not.[8]

The history of yellow and its correlation with Mexico is one that long predates *Traffic*, even though there isn't just one interpretation of the color. *The Woman God Forgot* and *Under a Texas Moon* use yellow to connect with the location itself. While there did not seem to be any underlying commentary initially, the continued use of the color for Mexico eventually solidified an association between yellow and the harmful stereotypes Hollywood promoted. *Traffic* is neither the first nor the last to employ yellow in the way that it did, but the film is vital in the popular culture's understanding of the Mexico filter and serves as a jumping-off point in understanding Hollywood's fraught record of Mexican representation. **—ALEXANDRA JAMES SALICHS**

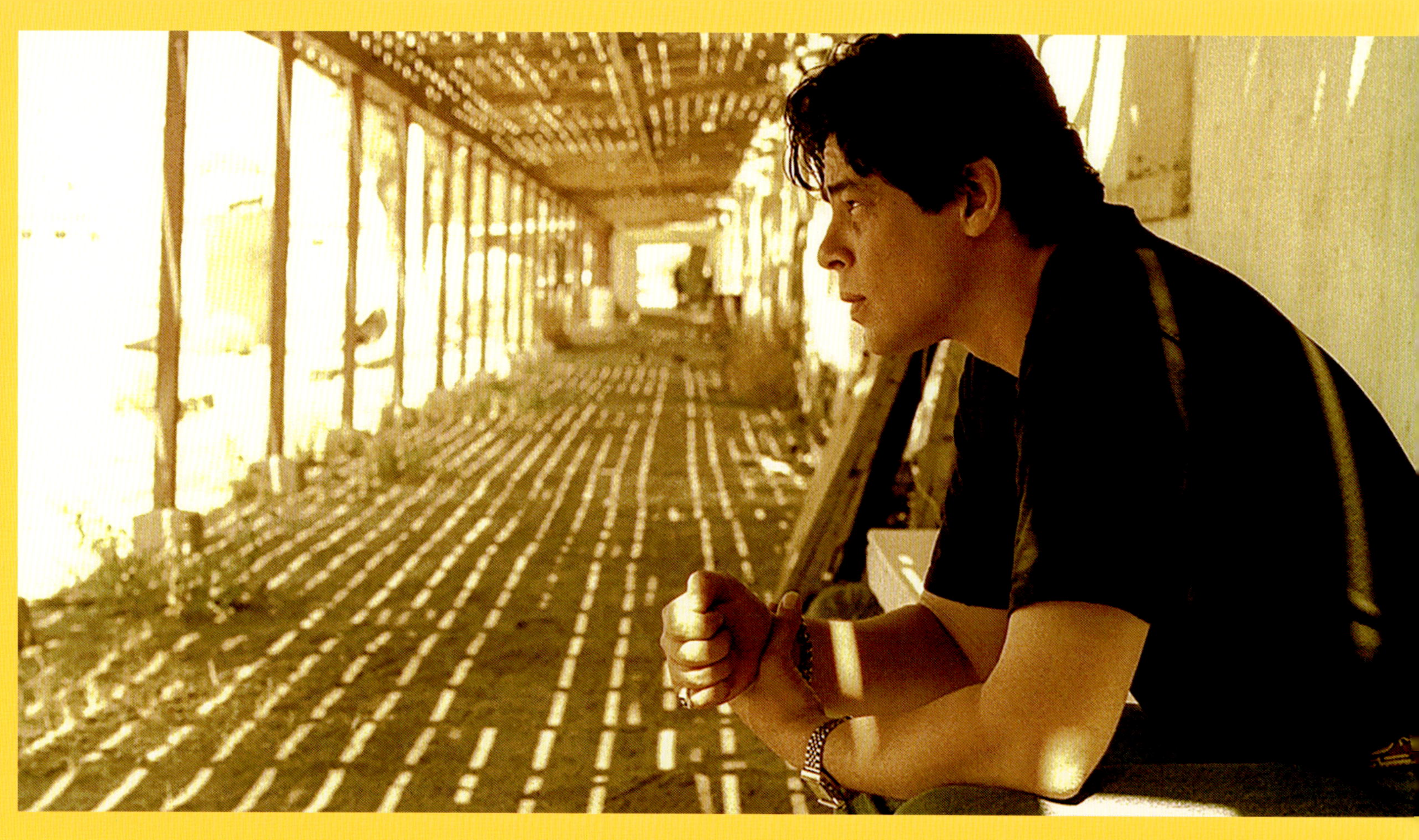

Traffic (USA, 2000, dir. Steven Soderbergh)

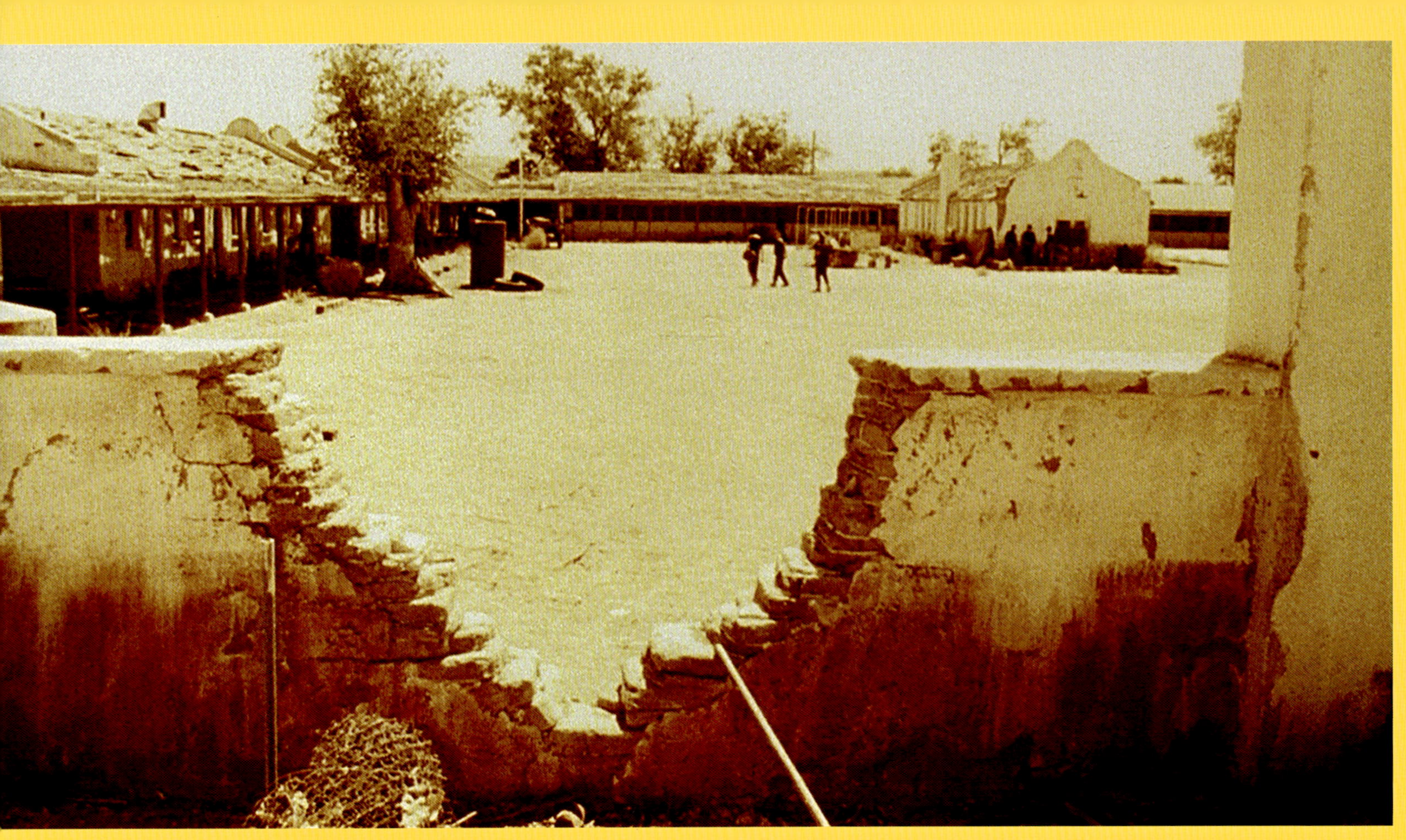

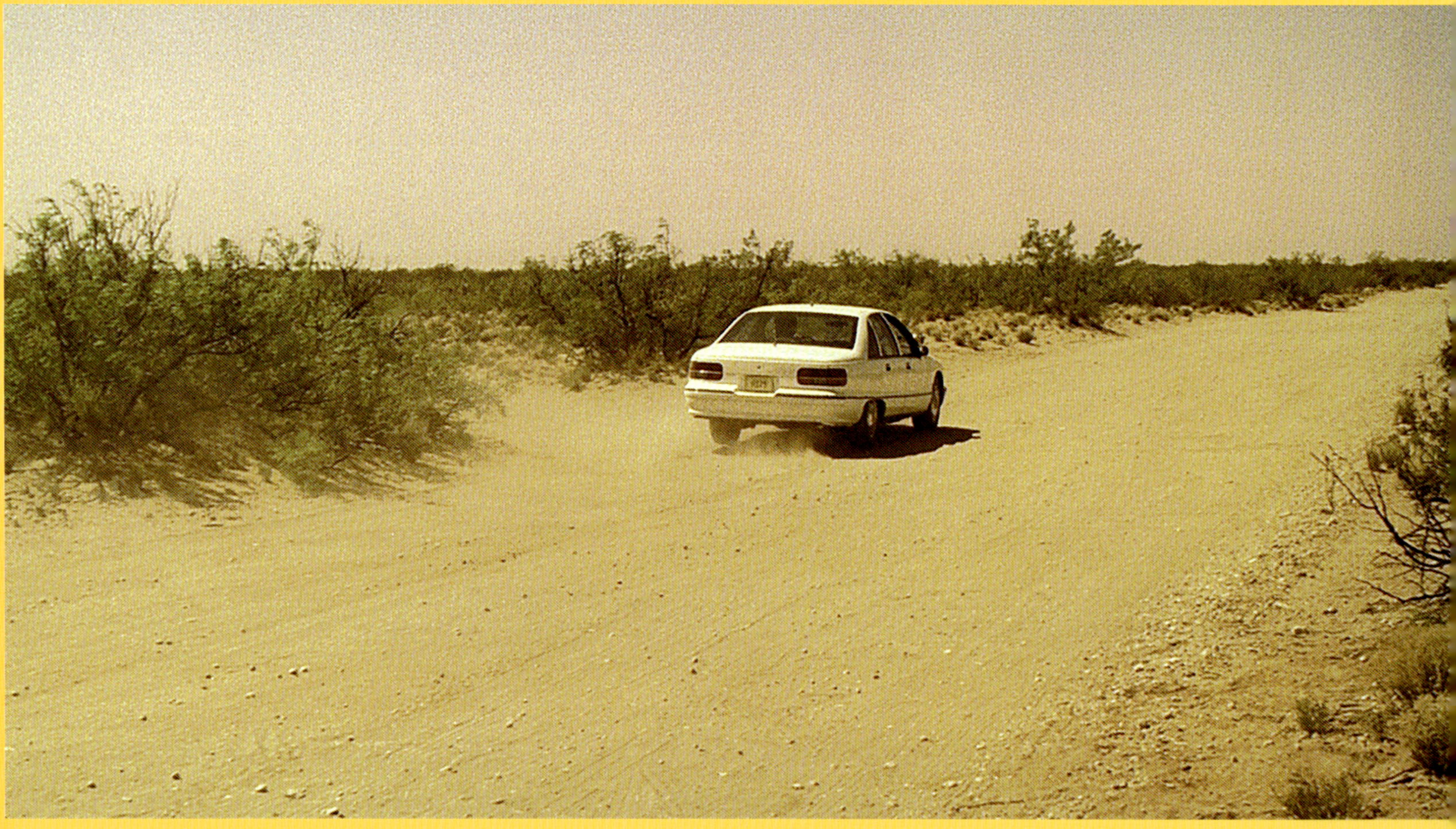

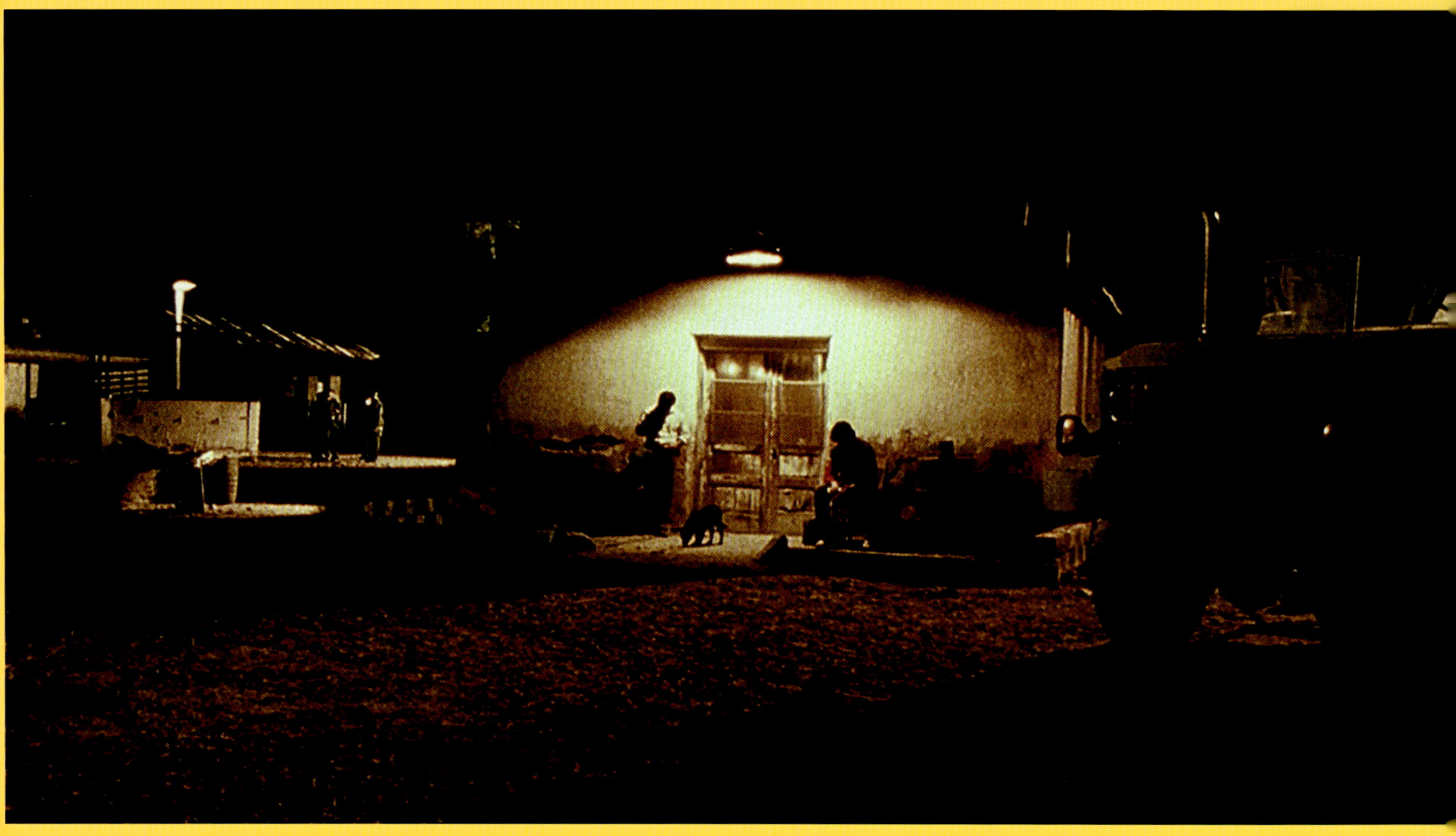

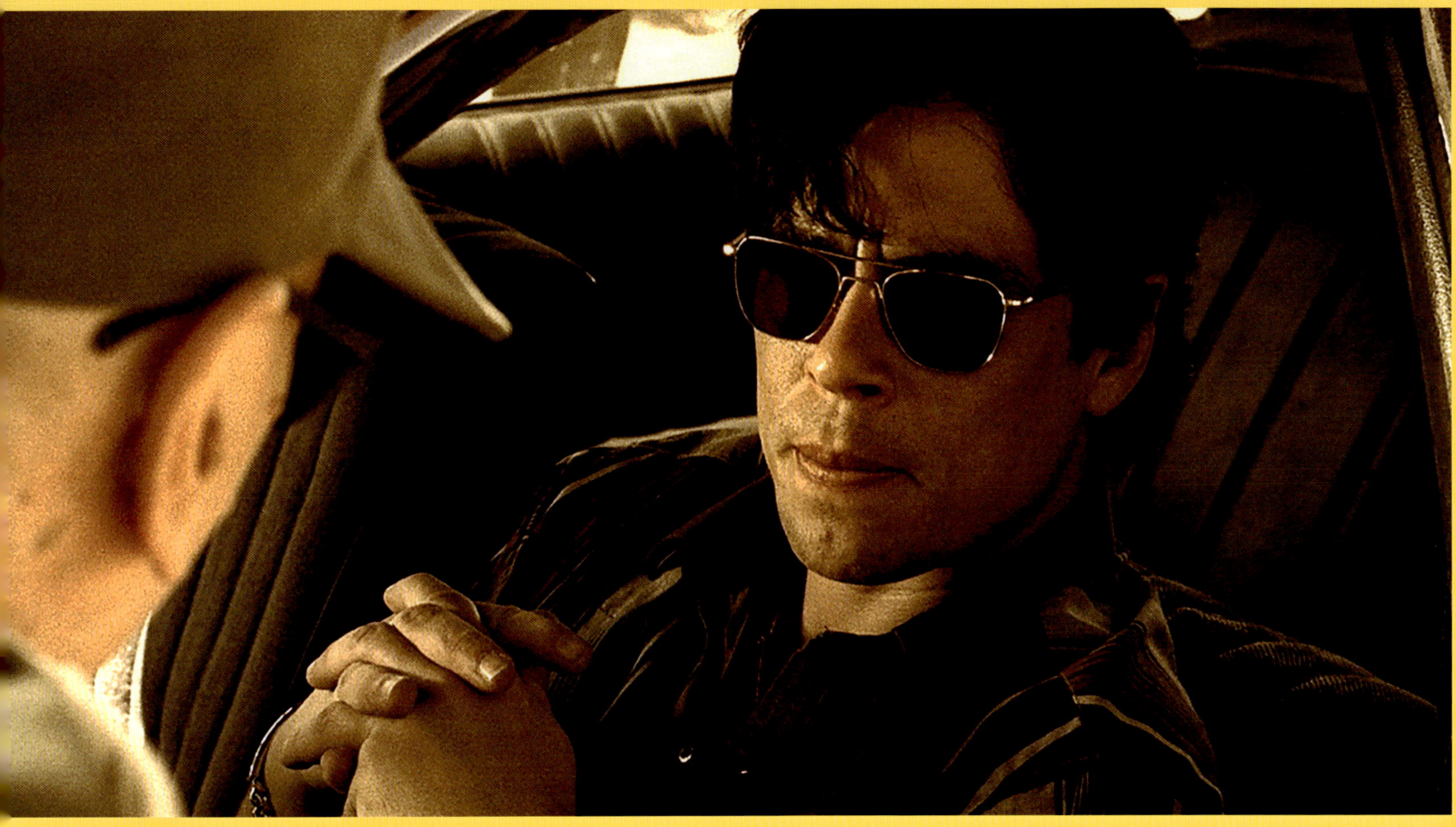

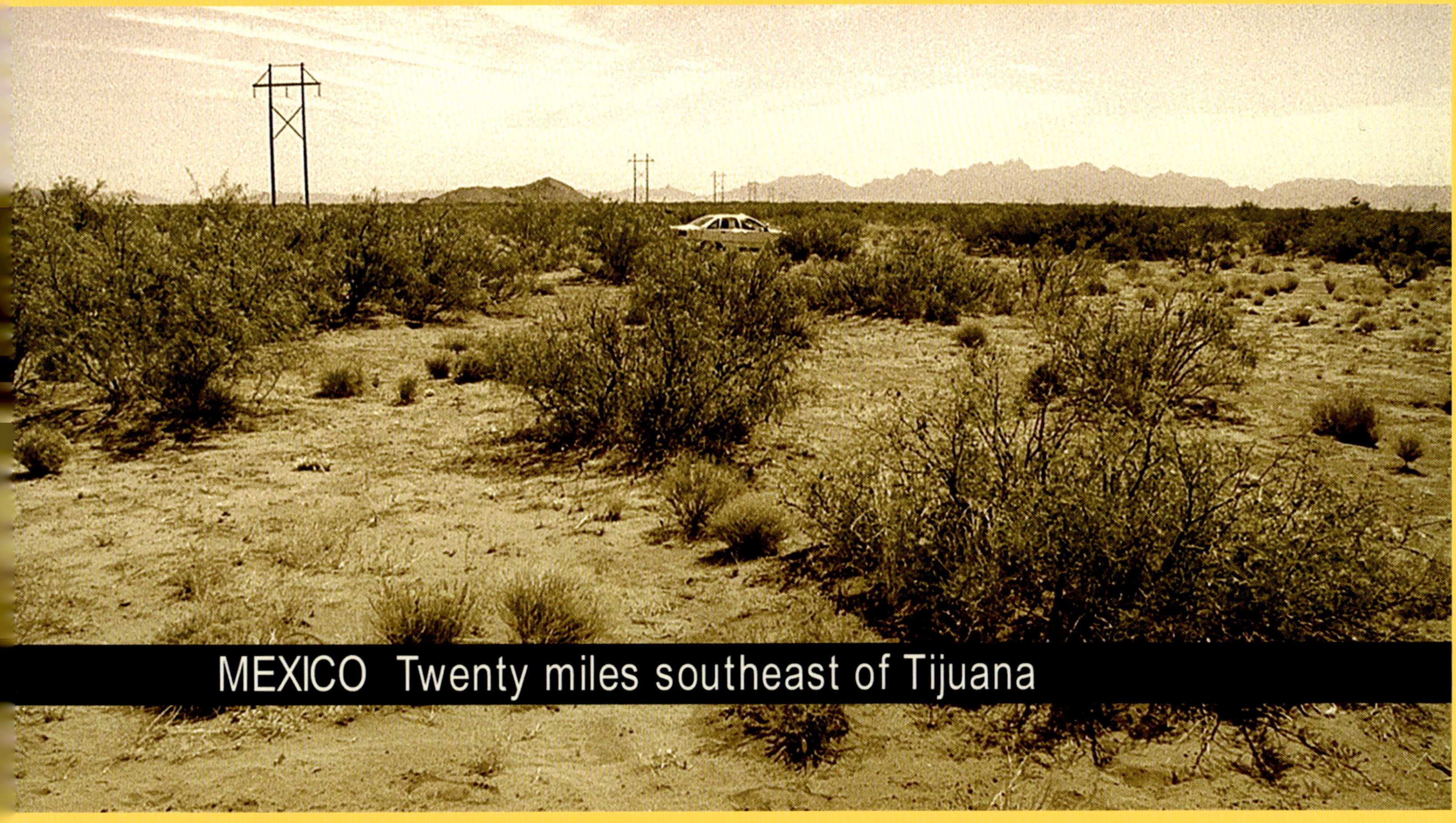

MEXICO Twenty miles southeast of Tijuana

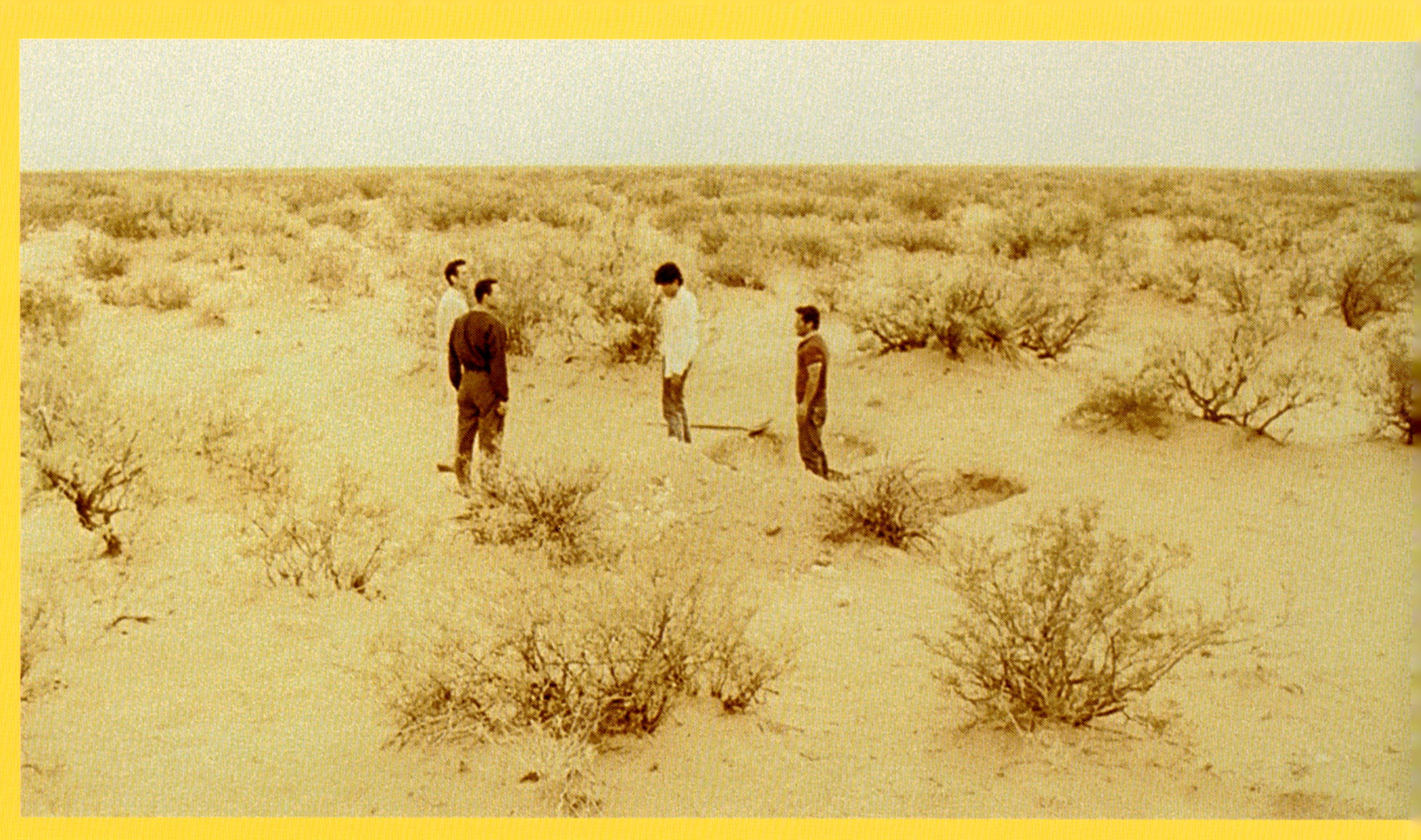

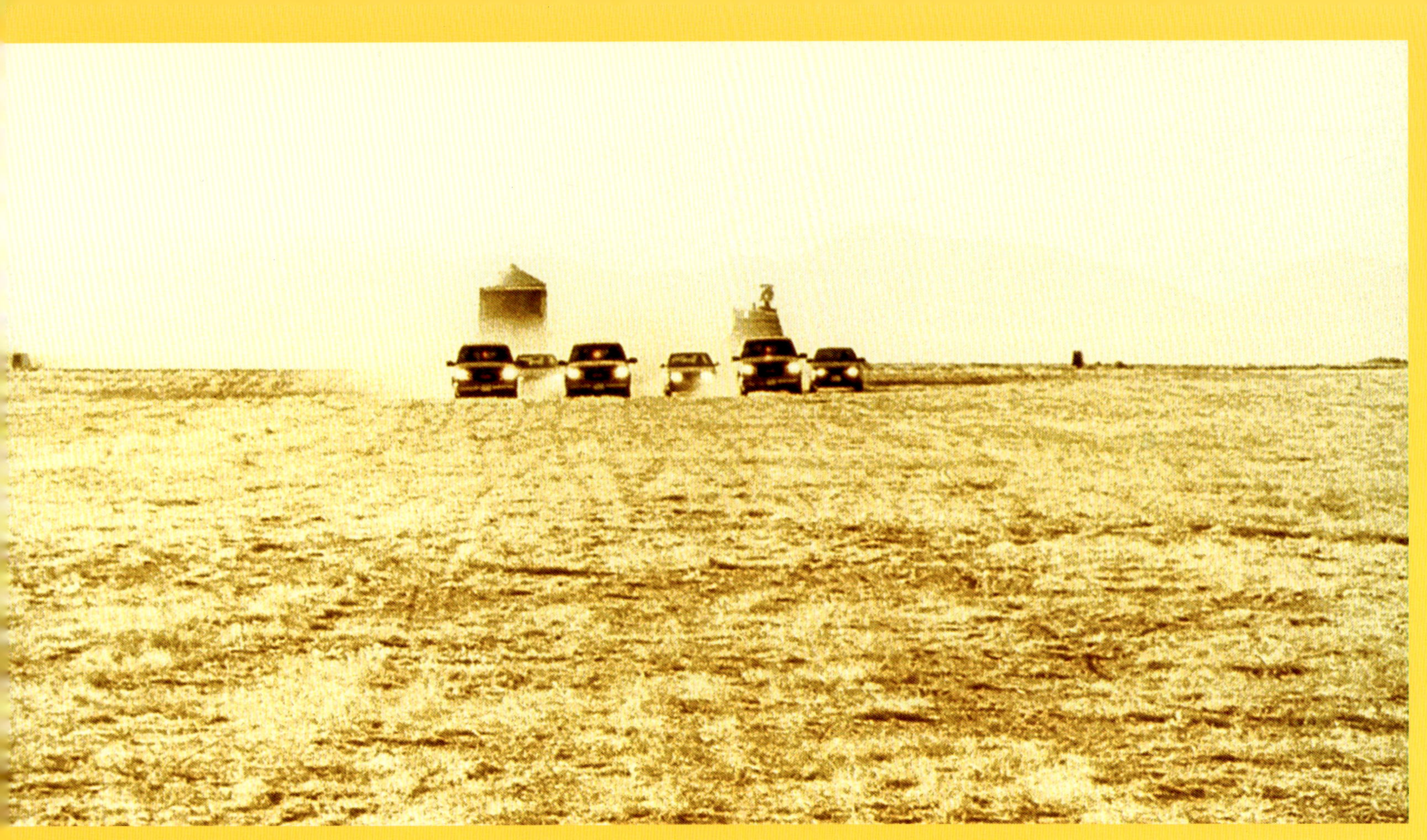

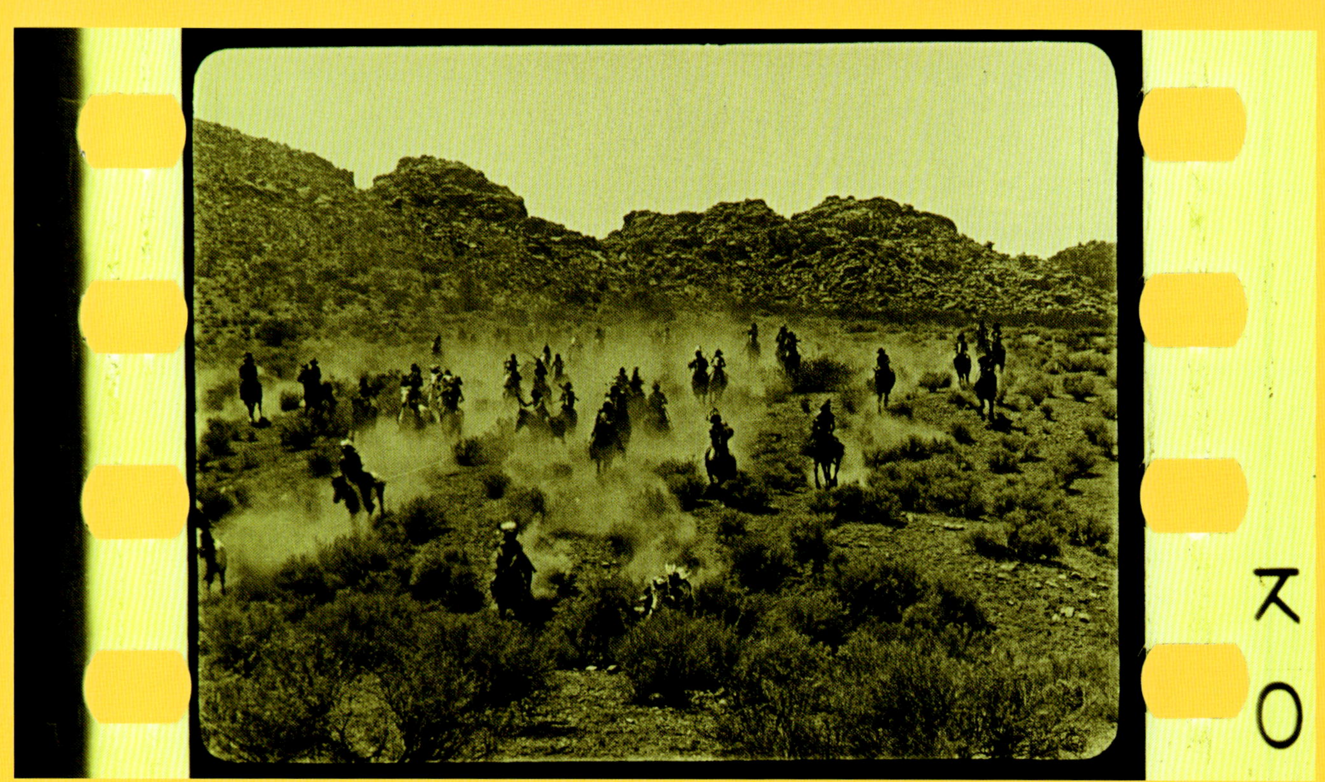

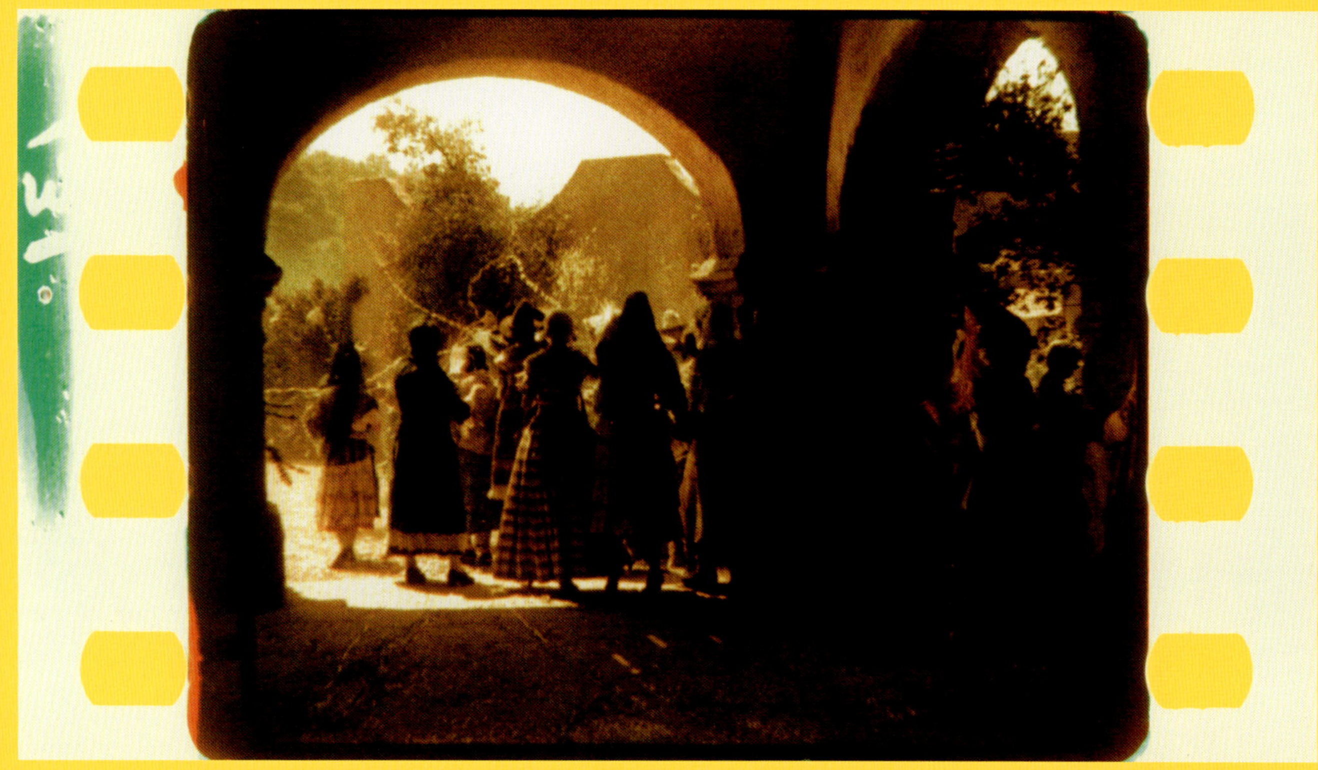

TOP: *Wagon Tracks* (USA, 1919, dir. Lambert Hillyer)

BOTTOM: *Under a Texas Moon* (USA, 1930, dir. Michael Curtiz)

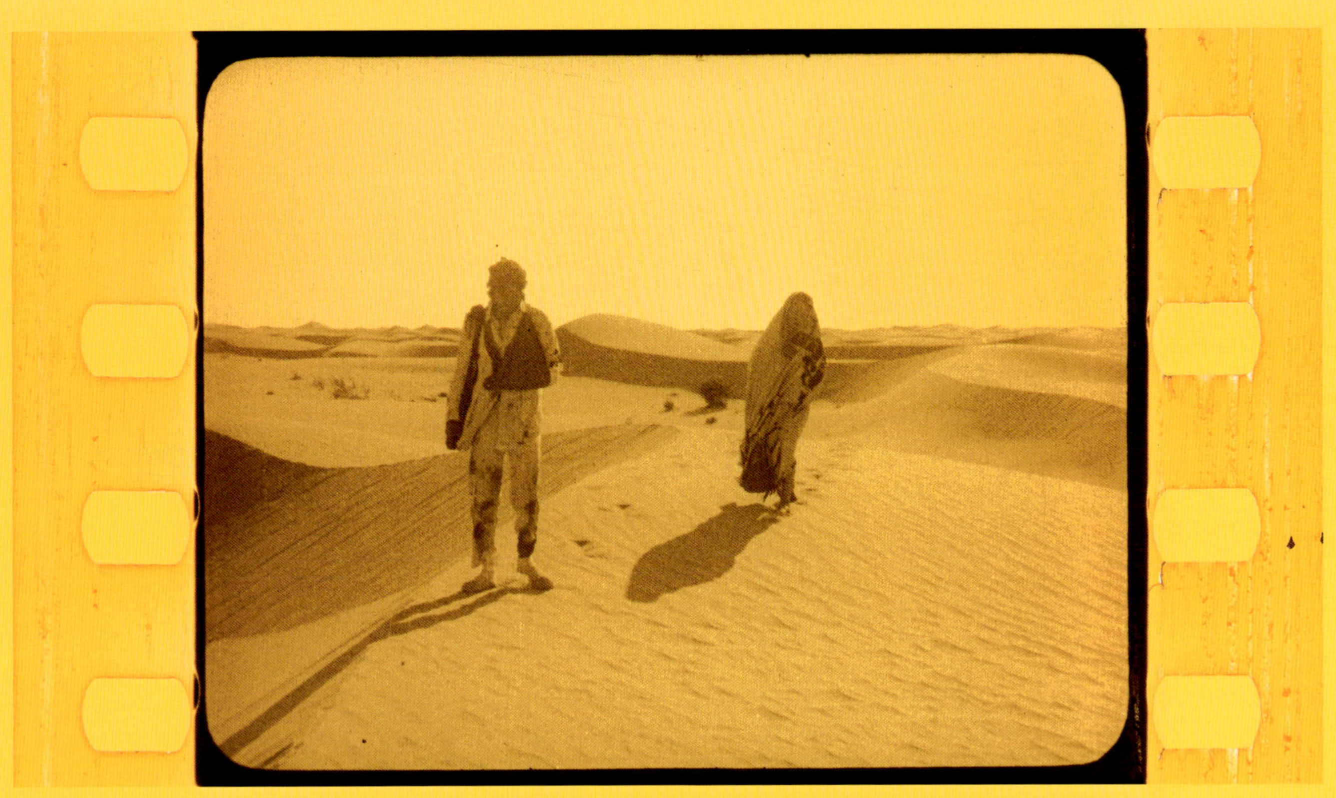

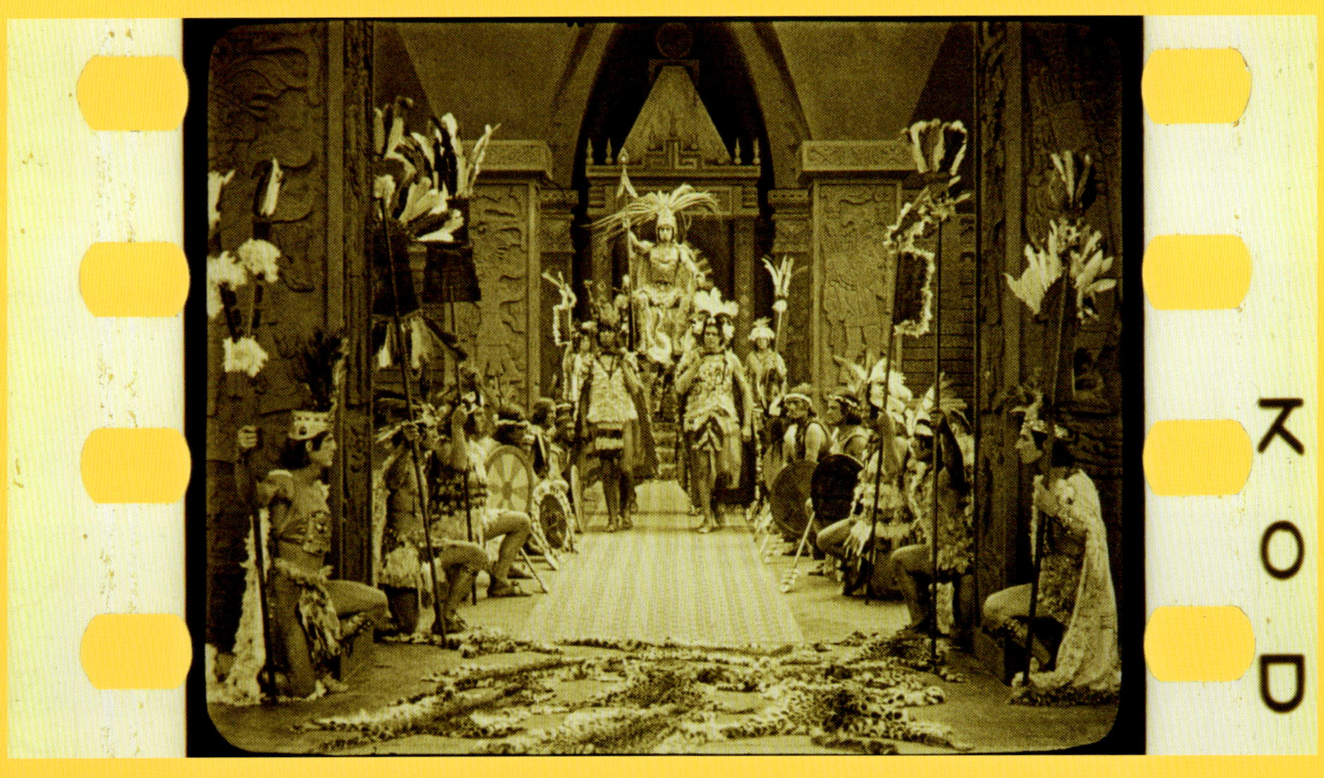

TOP: *L'Atlantide* (France, 1921, dir. Jacques Feyder)

BOTTOM: *The Woman God Forgot* (USA, 1917, dir. Cecil B. DeMille)

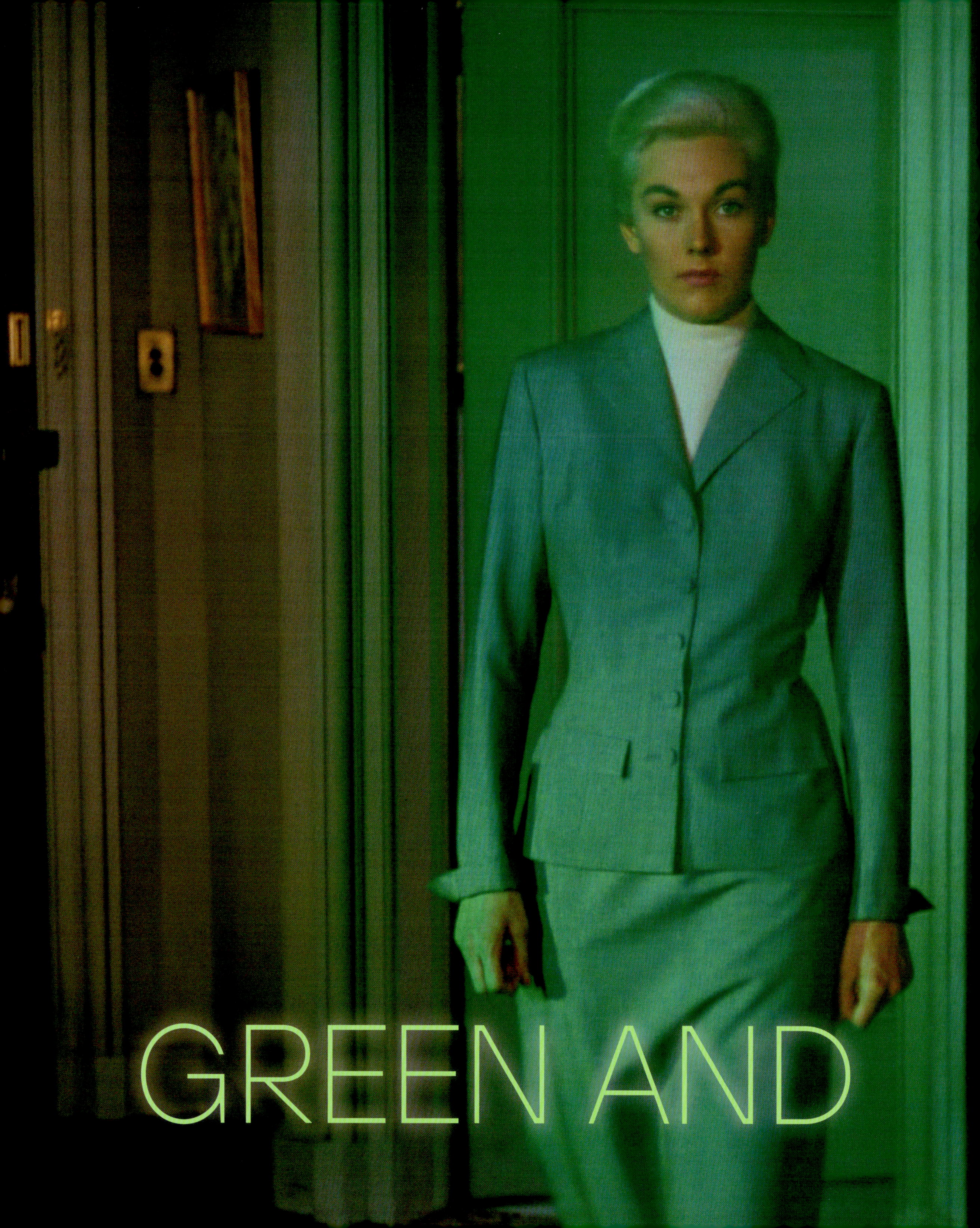

GREEN AND

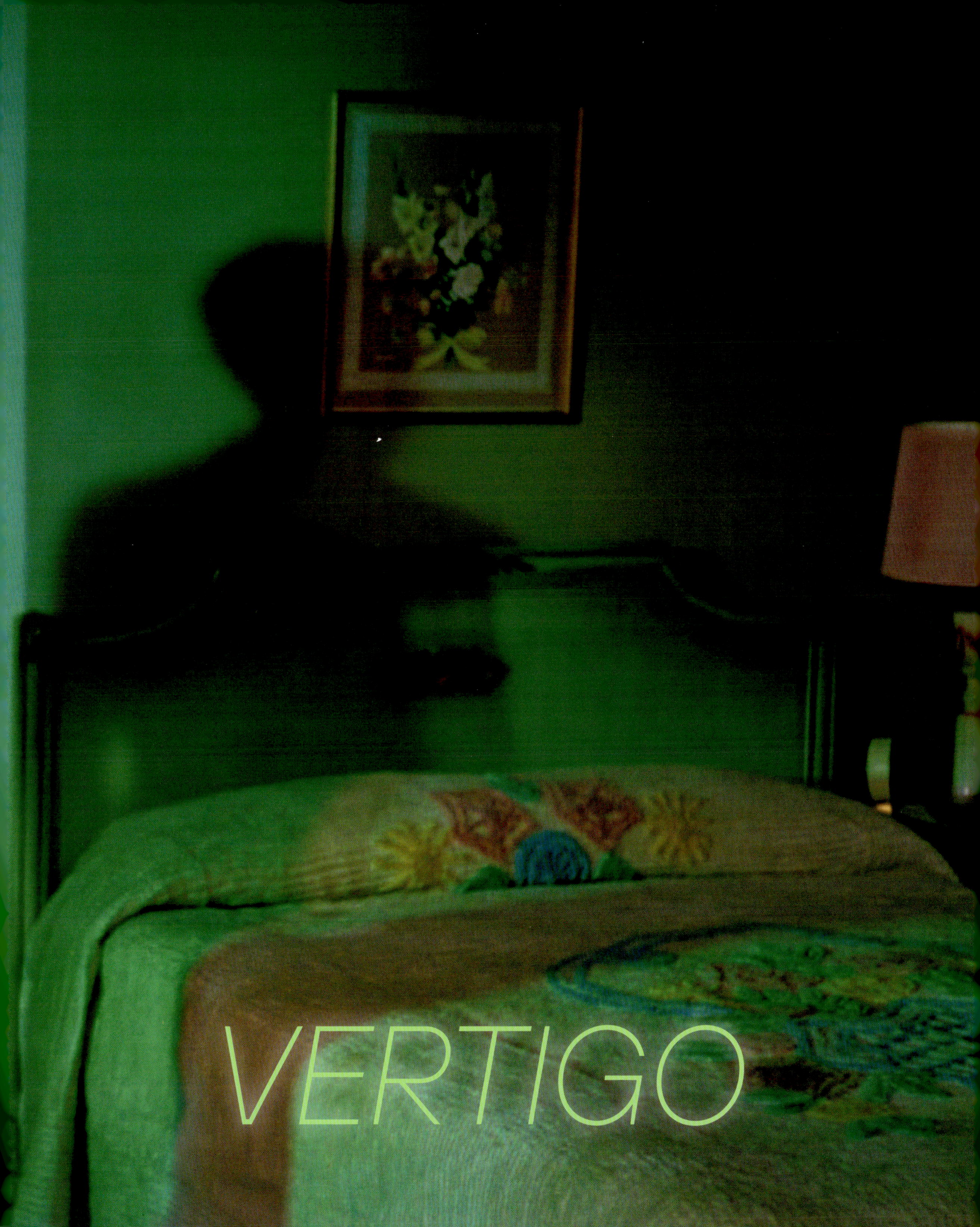
VERTIGO

SCOTTIE: What are you thinking?

MADELEINE: Of all the people who were born and died while the trees went on living.

SCOTTIE: Their true name is *Sequoia sempervirens*—always green, ever living.

Vertigo (USA, 1958) marks Alfred Hitchcock's eighth film in color and features one of his most notable and provocative Technicolor palettes. As early as 1937, Hitchcock had voiced support for color use in film:

> I am whole-heartedly in favor of color films. . . . Color will give me the chance to portray what I want to portray most—lack of color. . . . How can I show the drabness of a slum street compared with the glory of a lovely landscape when I must photograph them both in tones of grey? . . . But although I'm all for color, it must help the script—never conquer it.[1]

Beginning with *Rope* (USA, 1948), Hitchcock's use of color—or lack thereof, as in *Psycho* (USA, 1960)—plays an important role in enriching the complexity of his narratives and underscoring their themes. Perhaps one of the most memorable examples is his employment of green in *Vertigo*. The film's animated opening credits feature the iconic spiraling and spinning motif designed by Saul Bass in an array of vivid colors including red, purple, blue, and green. However, these are quickly contrasted by the more neutral palettes of the opening scenes: the ill-fated chase by policeman Scottie (James Stewart), dominated by dark grays and blues, and his subsequent interaction with his confidante and ex-fiancée, Midge (Barbara Bel Geddes), dominated by browns, beiges, and yellows. However, the film shifts when Scottie, now a private investigator, is hired by his old acquaintance Gavin Elster (Tom Helmore) to follow his wife, Madeleine (Kim Novak), whom he believes is possessed by the spirit of an ancestor; the sets for Elster's office and Ernie's Restaurant, where Scottie begins his investigation, are infused with red. Of notable contrast in the restaurant scene is the green-trimmed wrap of Madeleine, which introduces an intriguing and recurring dynamic between red and green in the film.

Green enhances the narrative themes on multiple levels. On the most superficial plane, it signifies mystery, intrigue, and Scottie's increasing infatuation with Madeleine. On another, it underscores the recurrent idea of eternal life and reincarnation associated with Madeleine. For example, it suffuses the environment when Scottie and Madeleine venture to Muir Woods together, where Madeleine reflects on her own mortality. As Scottie points out, the scientific name of the redwoods, *Sequoia sempervirens*, means "always green, ever living." The trees' green and stoic stillness represents a constant that goes beyond the brief dealings of Madeleine and Scottie, which she reflects on through mapping the life of her haunting ancestor, Carlotta Valdes, on the cross section of a displayed tree. She muses, "Somewhere in here I was born—and there I died. It was only a moment for you. You took no notice." This use of green as a signifier of immortality is echoed in the costumes (expertly designed by costume designer Edith Head) and car of Madeleine. Scottie's story is also tinged with green in key moments; it appears in scenes demonstrating his escalating romantic obsession but also in his quest to redeem the death of a colleague (from the incident that opens the film, which revealed Scottie's vertigo) by saving Madeleine's life.

The failure to save Madeleine from a fall induced by Carlotta's spirit (or at least his perceived failure) sends Scottie into a catatonic state requiring hospital care. However, it is clear the issue is unresolved for him. After leaving the hospital he sees Madeleine's green car (a momentary red herring), only to find out Gavin sold it to a neighbor. Most significantly, when Scottie sees a brunette look-alike of Madeleine's, Judy Barton (Kim Novak), on the street, she is wearing an all-green ensemble. (We later learn that Judy was hired by Gavin to impersonate Madeleine in an elaborate murder scheme.) While the color connects Judy to Madeleine and symbolizes the rebirth and reincarnation of Scottie's obsession, the costumes were very purposely designed by Head to distinguish the two characters' personas. The costuming for Madeleine is rigid, formal, and intentionally uncomfortable to underline Judy's impersonation, whereas Judy's own attire echoes her more modern and comfortable nature. During interactions with Scottie, Judy is often pictured via mirror reflections, emphasizing her duplicitous nature. When Judy goes on her first dinner date with Scottie, she deliberately chooses a bright purple silk slip that strongly contrasts the typically gray or black structured clothes of Madeleine in the hopes of starting the romance anew. She quickly realizes this is a false hope, as Scottie finds signs of Madeleine in other diners, and, upon returning to her room at the Empire Hotel, the building's neon sign casts a green glow that quickly subsumes Judy back into Scottie's ethereal nostalgia for Madeleine.

For the last act of the film, the use of green, often still in contrast to red, provides a driving visual pulse as Scottie finally unravels the murderous plot. After transforming Judy into Madeleine and ultimately catching Judy in her lies, Scottie finds himself losing Madeleine/Judy yet again with her accidental (but this time real) fall from a tower. As Hitchcock suggested in his early thoughts on color, green emphasizes the narrative themes, tying in Scottie's romanticized obsession not just with Madeleine but also with his own agency. His desire to be in control and to save the day (and the girl) is ultimately his downfall.[2] As the film closes on Scottie's revelation that his dreaded fate has repeated itself, the color palette leading up to this moment enforces and foreshadows the futility, and ultimate doom, of Scottie's condition.

—SOPHIA SERRANO

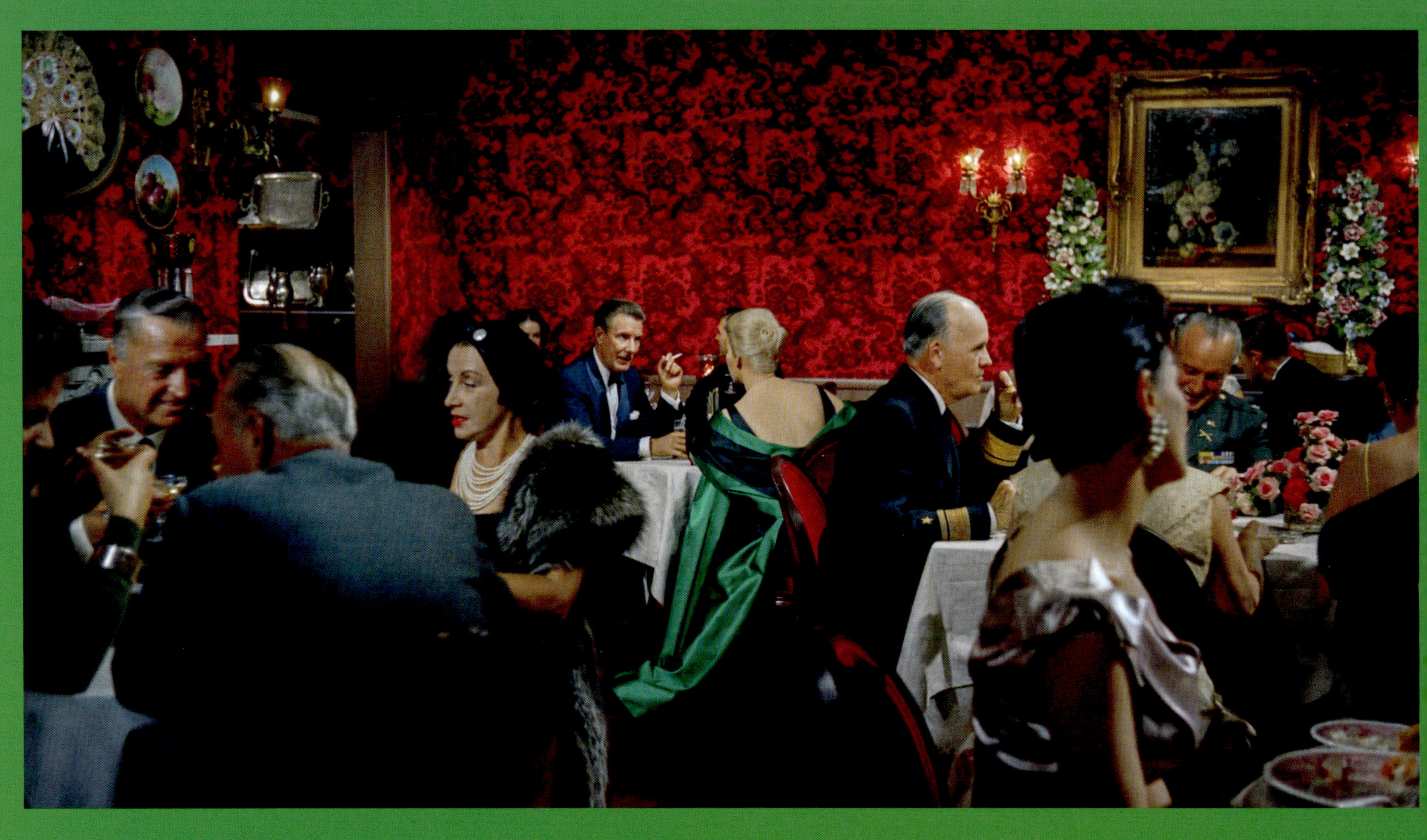

Vertigo (USA, 1958, dir. Alfred Hitchcock)

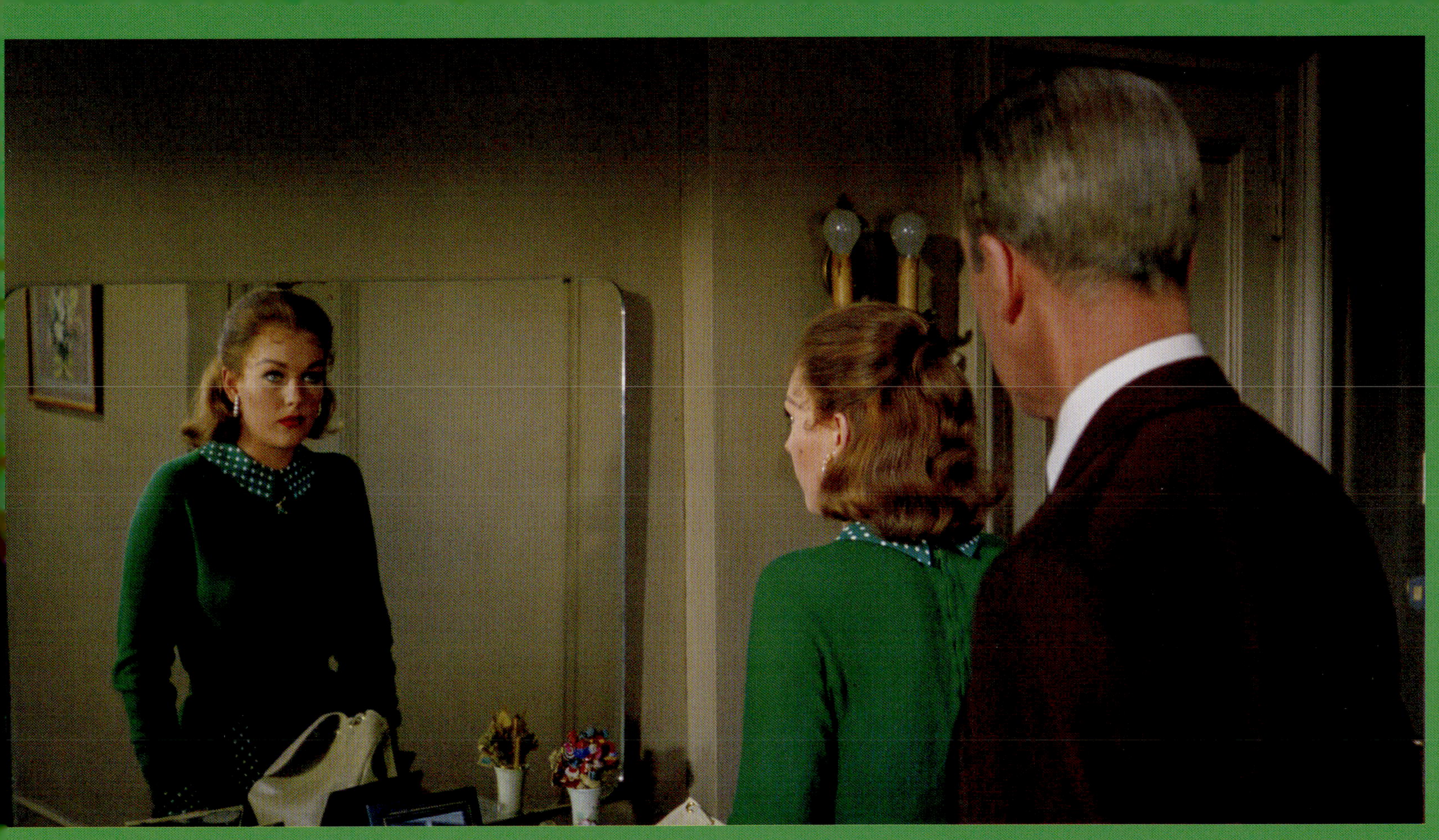

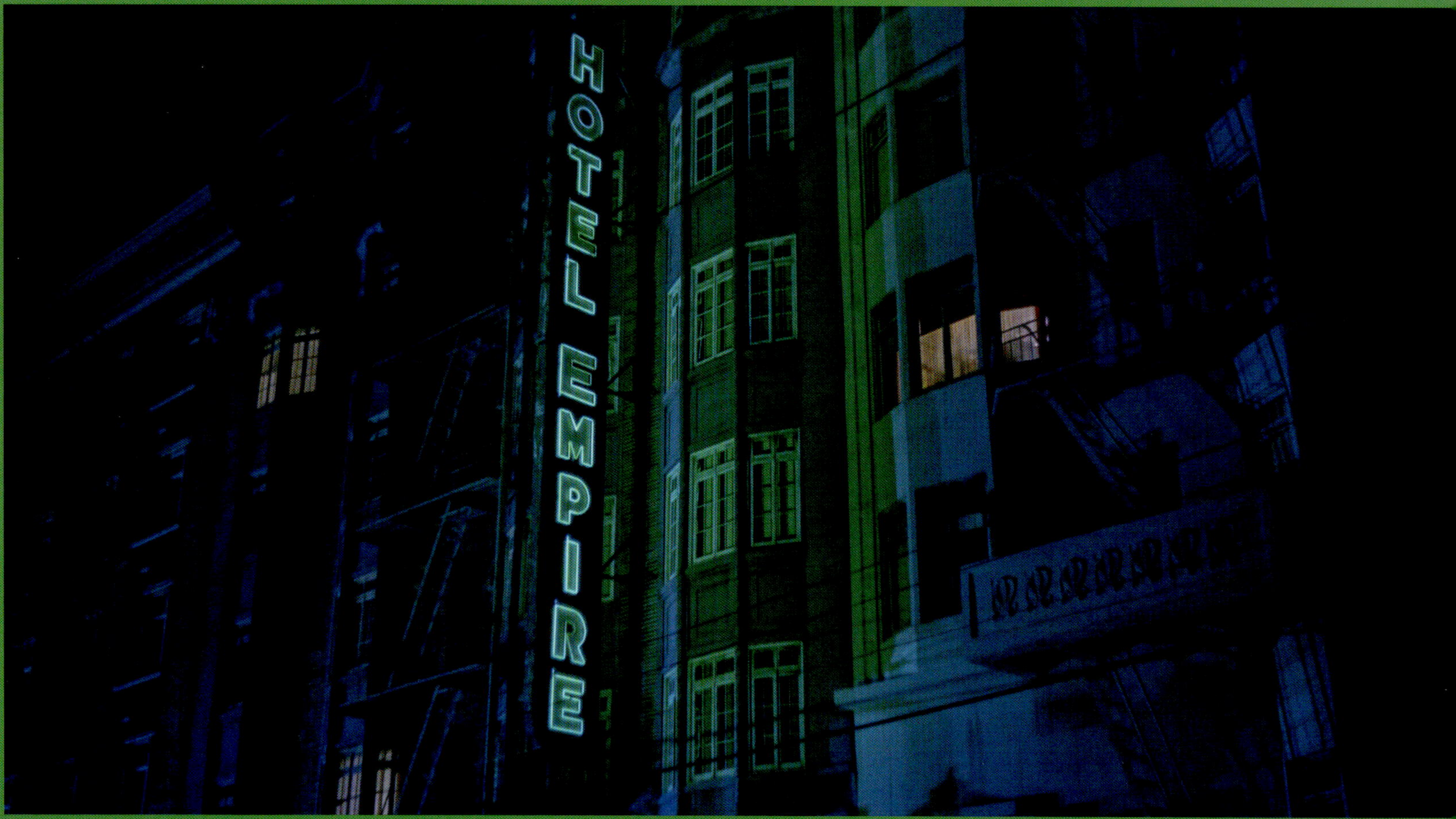

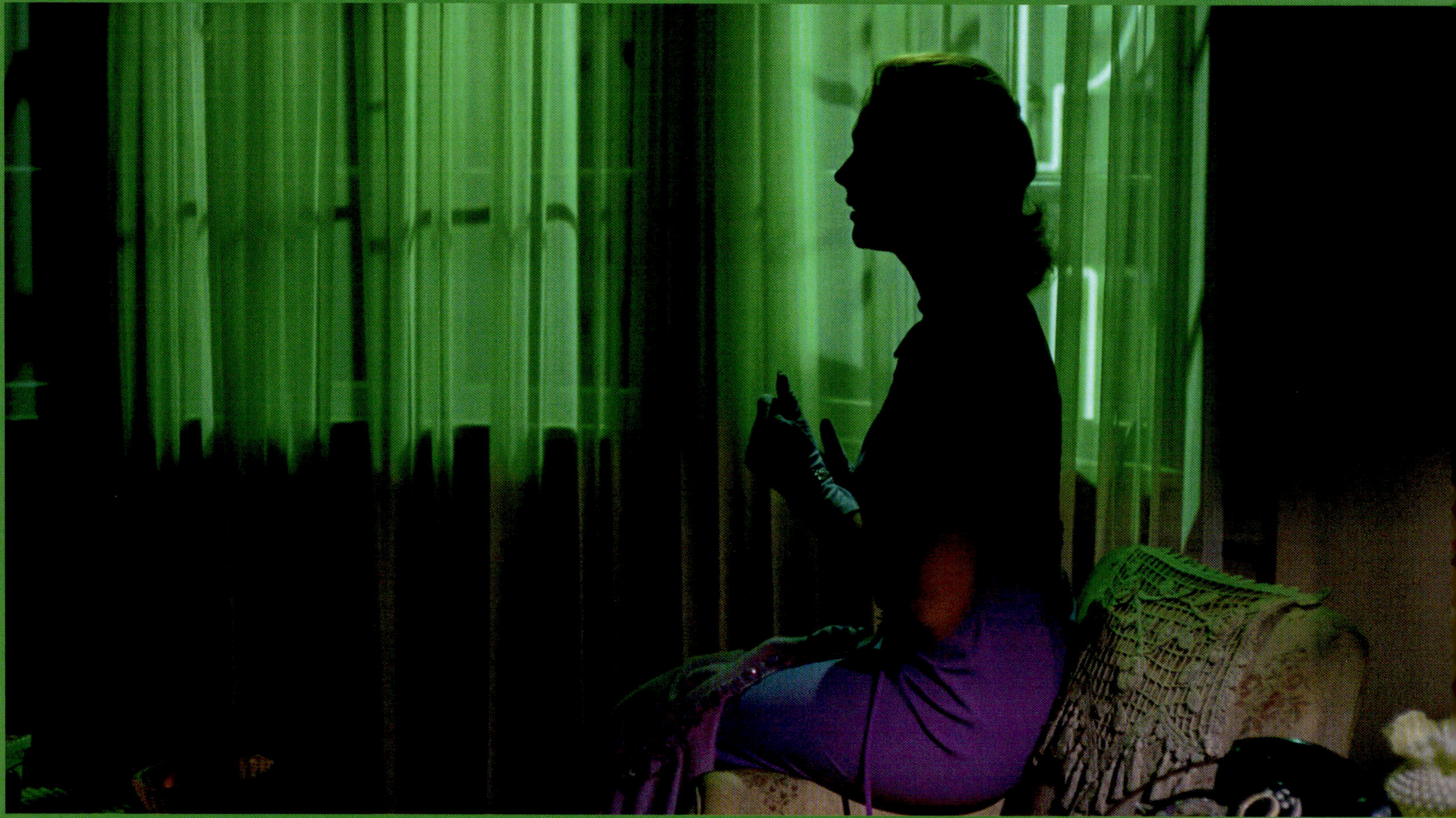

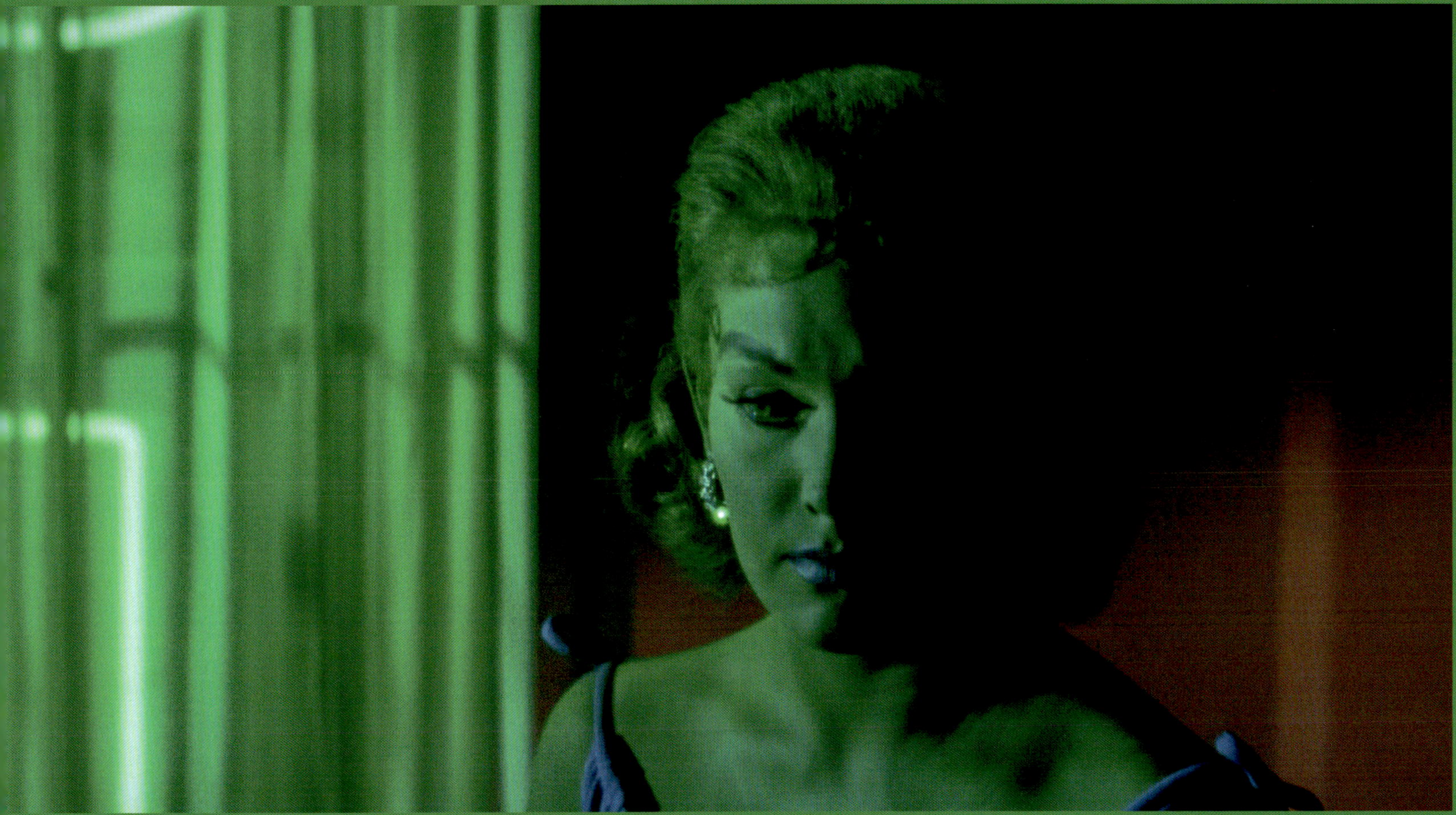

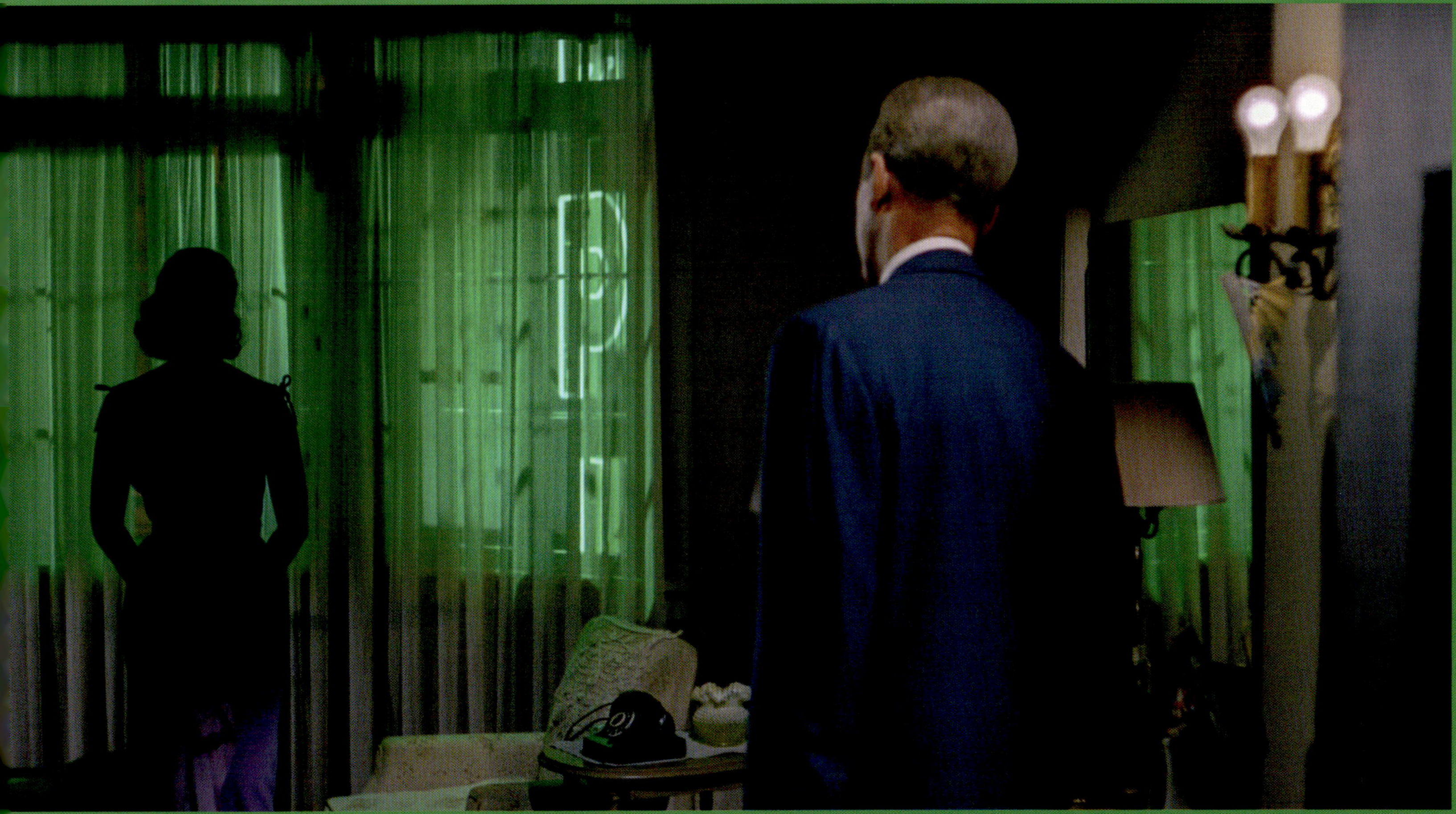

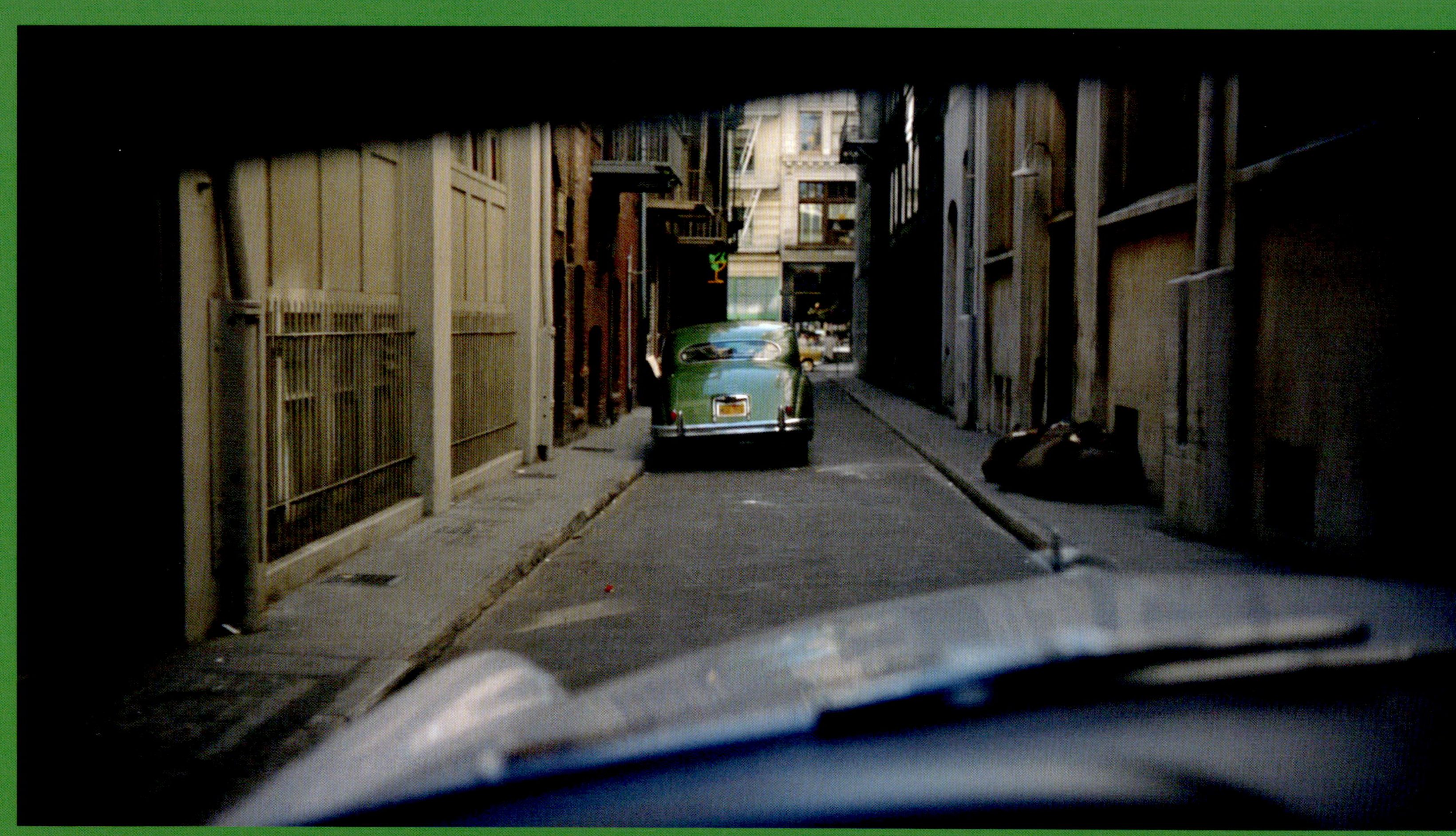

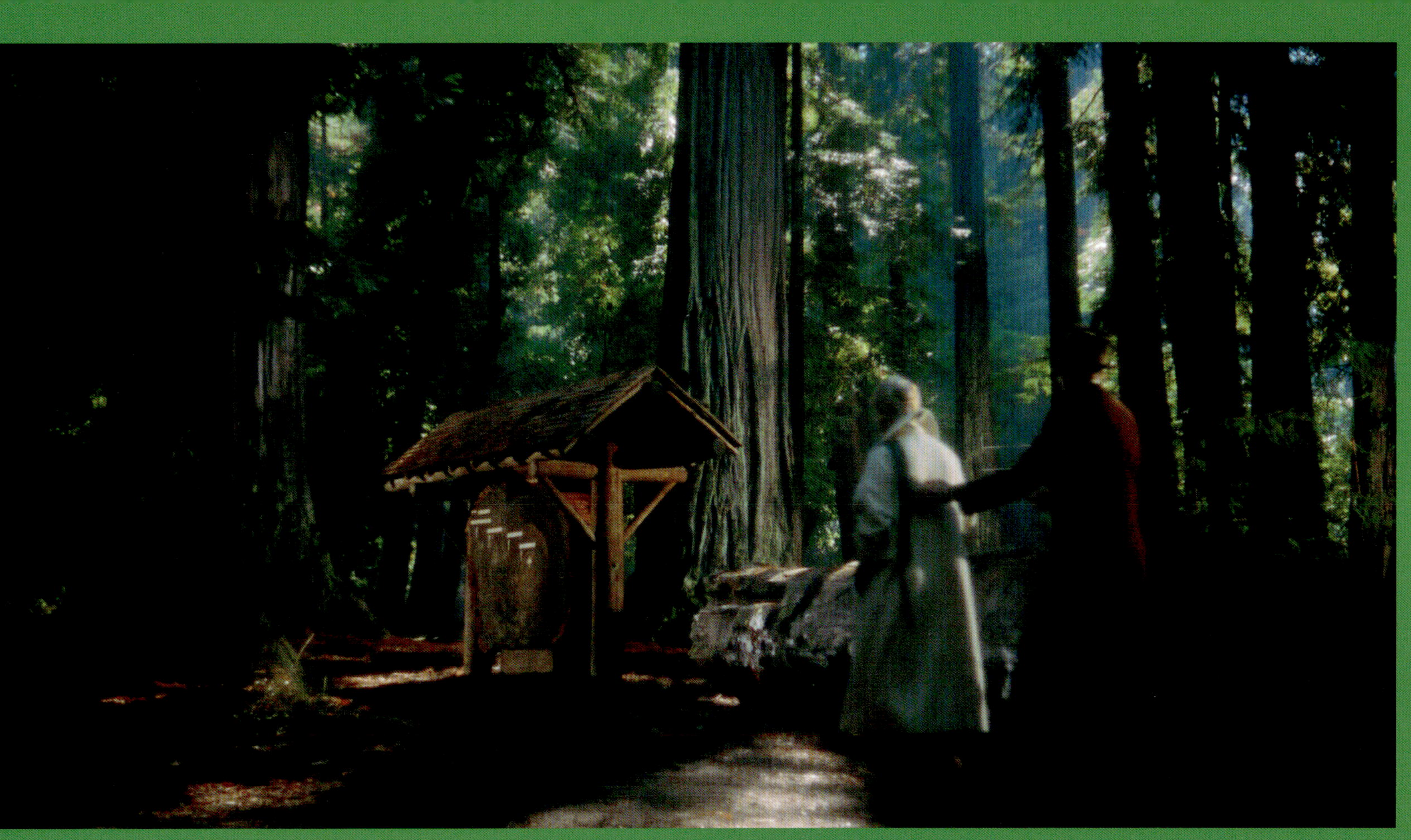

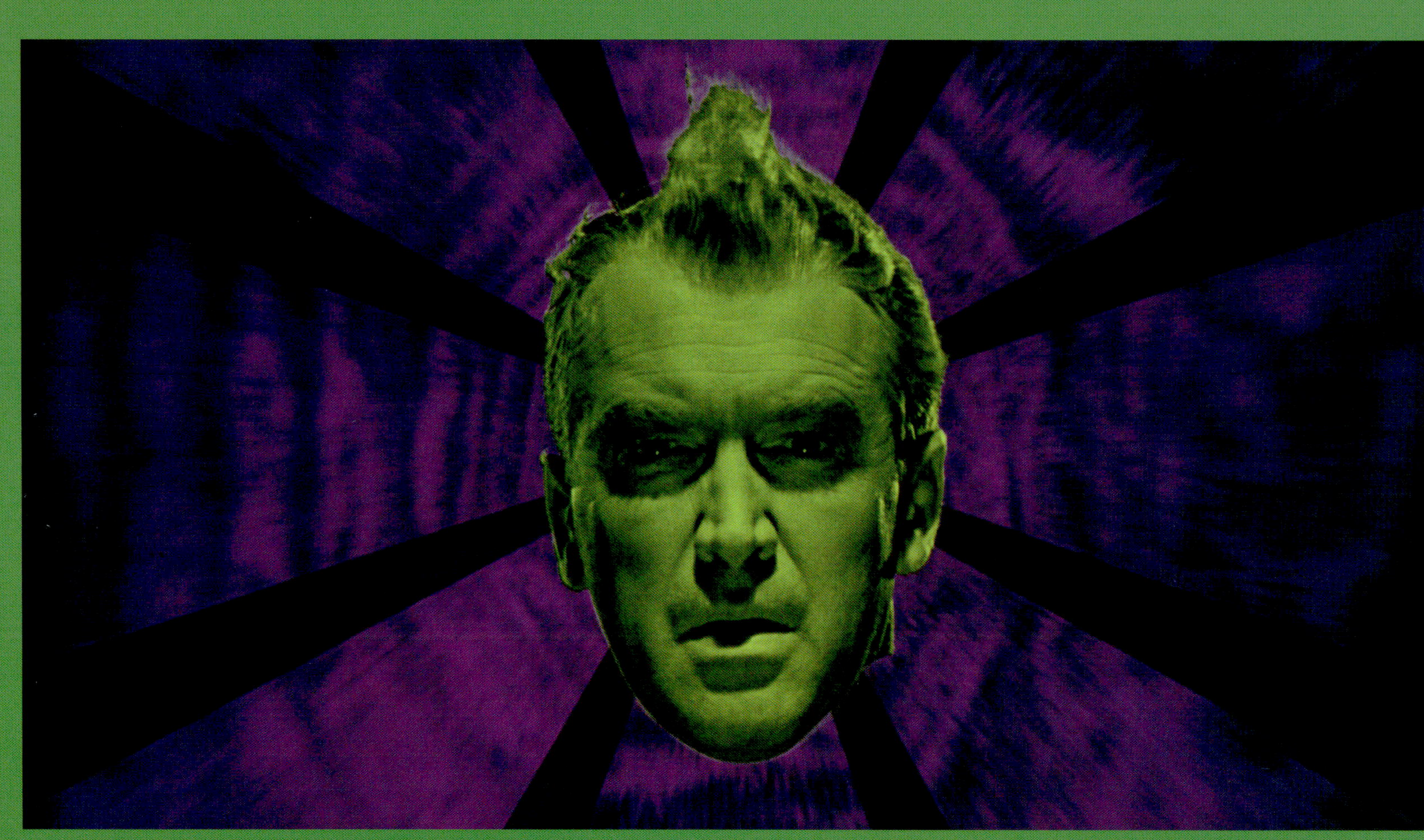

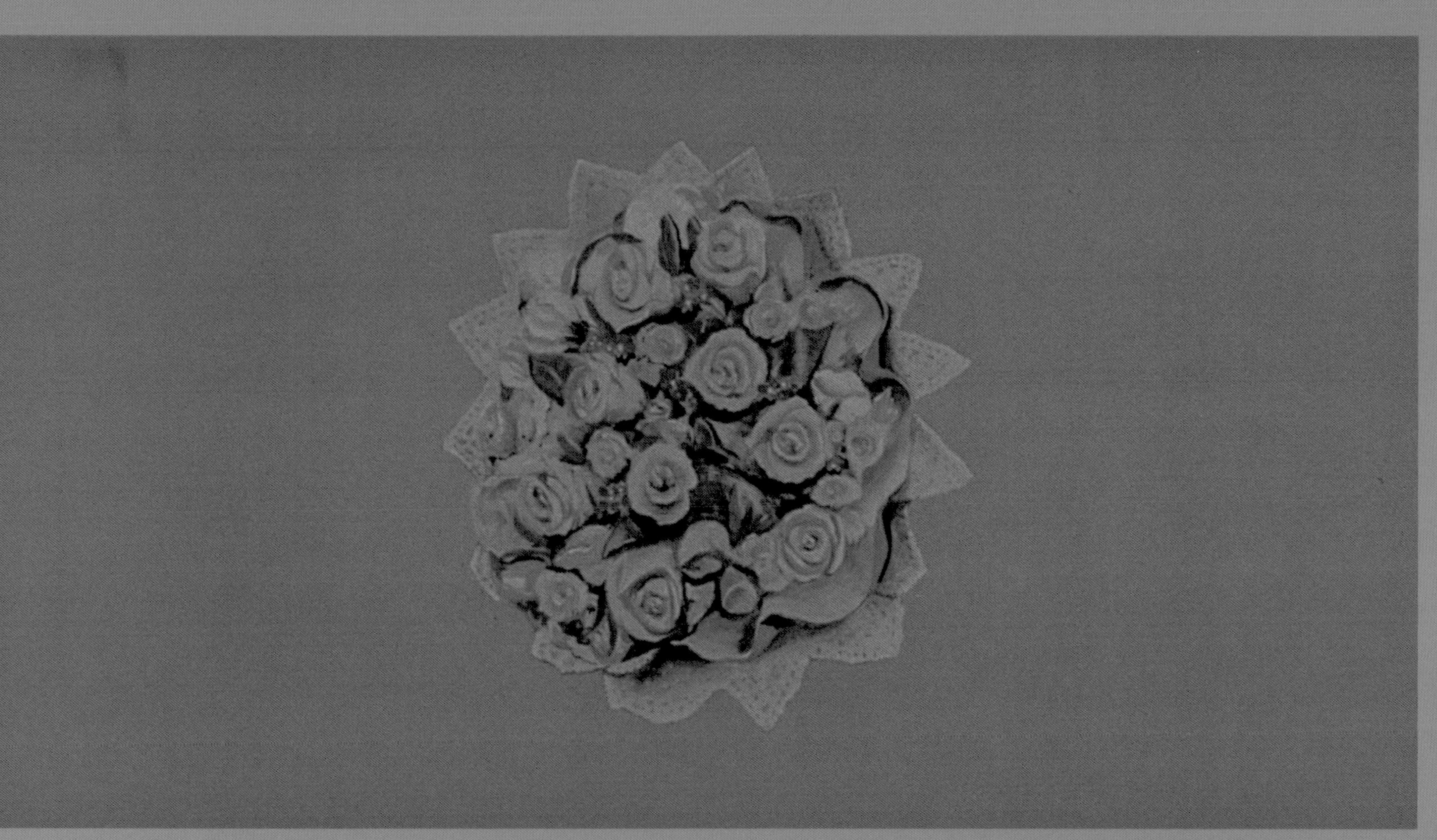

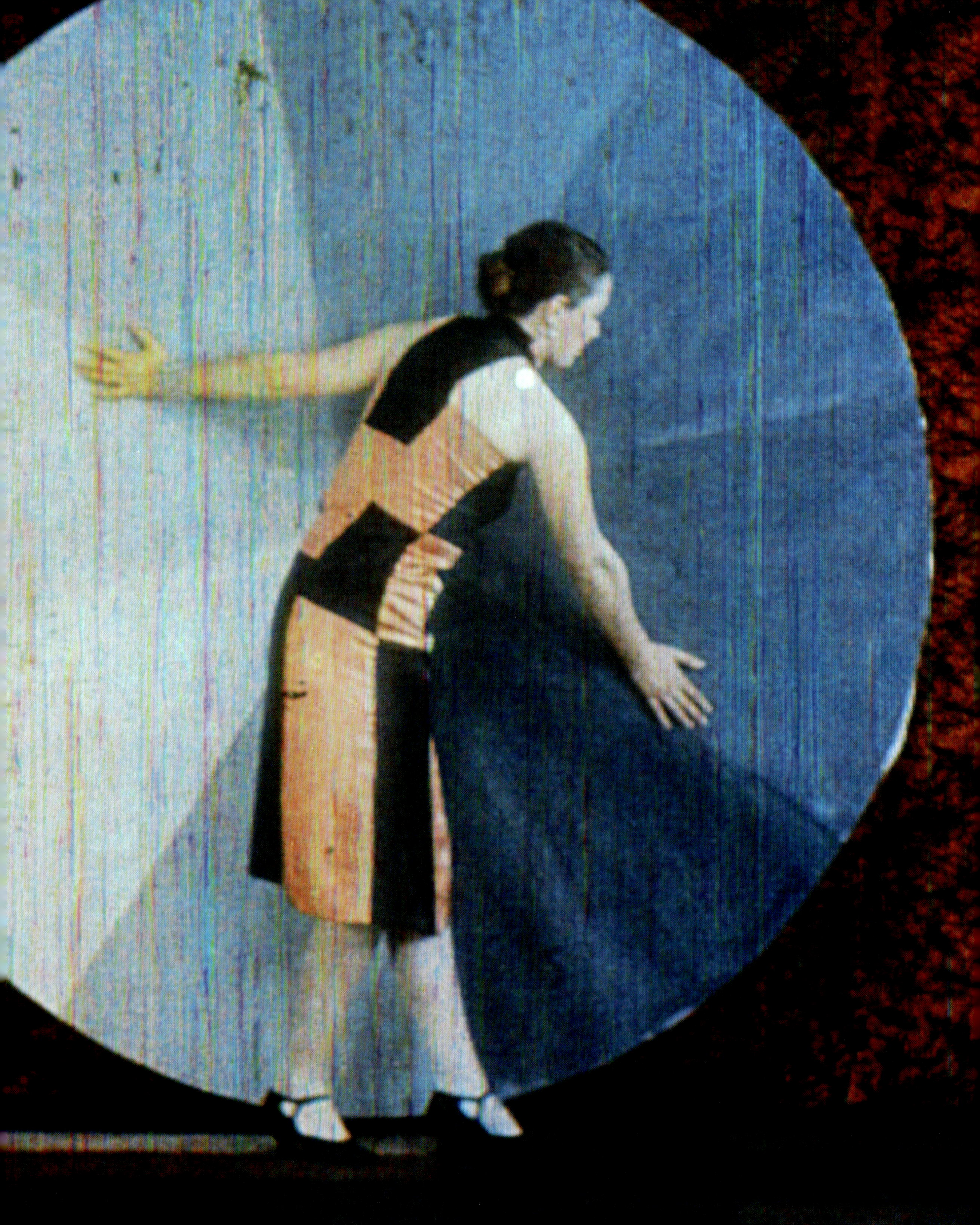

SARAH STREET

WOMEN AND COLOR TECHNOLOGIES

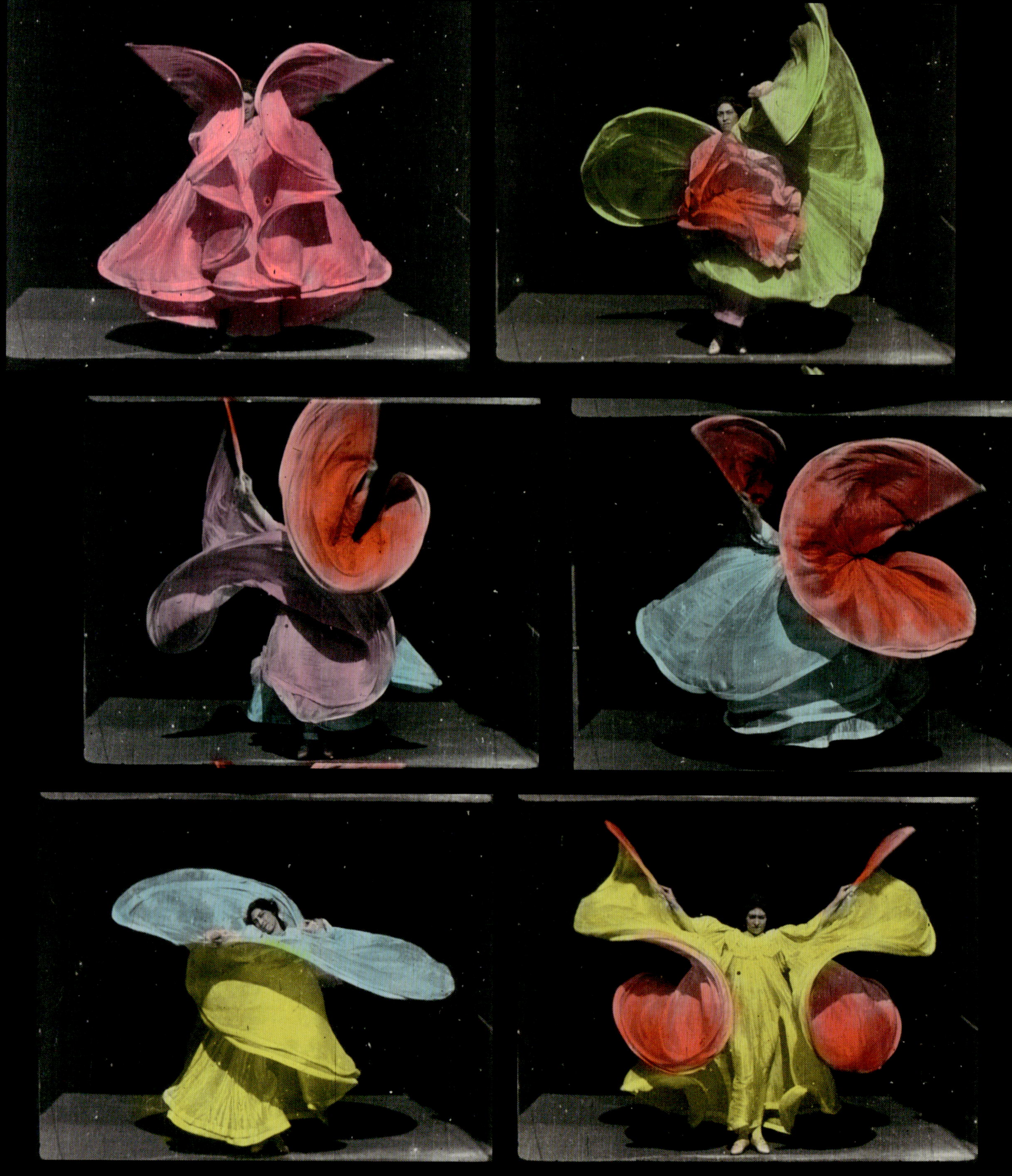

The Serpentine Dance (USA, ca. 1894, dir. William Kennedy Dickson)

Women's involvement in the development of color technologies for film was notable from the silent era onward. This is perhaps not surprising, since a recurrent theme in cultural history has been to conceptualize color as a "female province" associated with notions of femininity and superficiality that were not always positive or appreciative. This idea, particularly expressed by sixteenth-century Renaissance art critics, was also articulated in later periods by philosophers and other cultural commentators.[1] Some scientists have, however, identified women as having acute color perception.[2] Picking up on such trains of thought, film companies were keen to exploit the idea that women were naturally predisposed to appreciate color, employing them as colorists and stencil cutters for silent films and later as color consultants in the Technicolor era. This trend intensified in the 1920s, when color was popularized by advertising theorists and commercial organizations targeting female consumers of fashion, home decor, and products. The vibrant colors of fashion newsreels and "women's genres" such as melodramas and musicals were also aimed at female consumers and audiences. This essay foregrounds key contributions made by women through silent cinema's exquisite hand-colored and stenciled frames, films advertising sumptuous fashions, the glorious attractions of Technicolor, and animated films that experimented with color and motion.

Color was an important attraction of the first motion pictures produced in the 1890s, a trend that expanded during subsequent years of the silent era. The ability of new color technologies to render colors both accurately and attractively often determined their success or failure. For the first colored films, much depended on the skill with which color dyes were applied by hand to each frame. Women with experience coloring lantern slides and postcards were employed to color early films.[3] In these industries, women's labor was relatively cheap for highly repetitive work that required precision and dexterity.[4]

Hand coloring provided a visually striking means of embellishing films featuring female dancers as a means of accentuating female spectacle and eroticism. Indeed, colored dance films "constituted the first color-specific genre in film."[5] *Annabelle Serpentine Dance [#2]* (USA, 1895) captured the full spectacle of Annabelle Whitford Moore's expansive physical movements and the iridescent colors of her costume's billowing, swirling fabrics as she danced. Filmed by the Edison Company, this iconic display of color spectacle and femininity expressed a kinetic symbiosis between color, costume, and vaudeville's effervescent spirit. Inventor Thomas Edison was keen to color dance films as a means of capturing the spectacle of the popular stage shows on which they were based. These featured colored lights projected on the dancer as she raised her arms to reveal voluminous fabrics that resembled a fluttering butterfly's wings. Other themes for early hand-colored films, such as

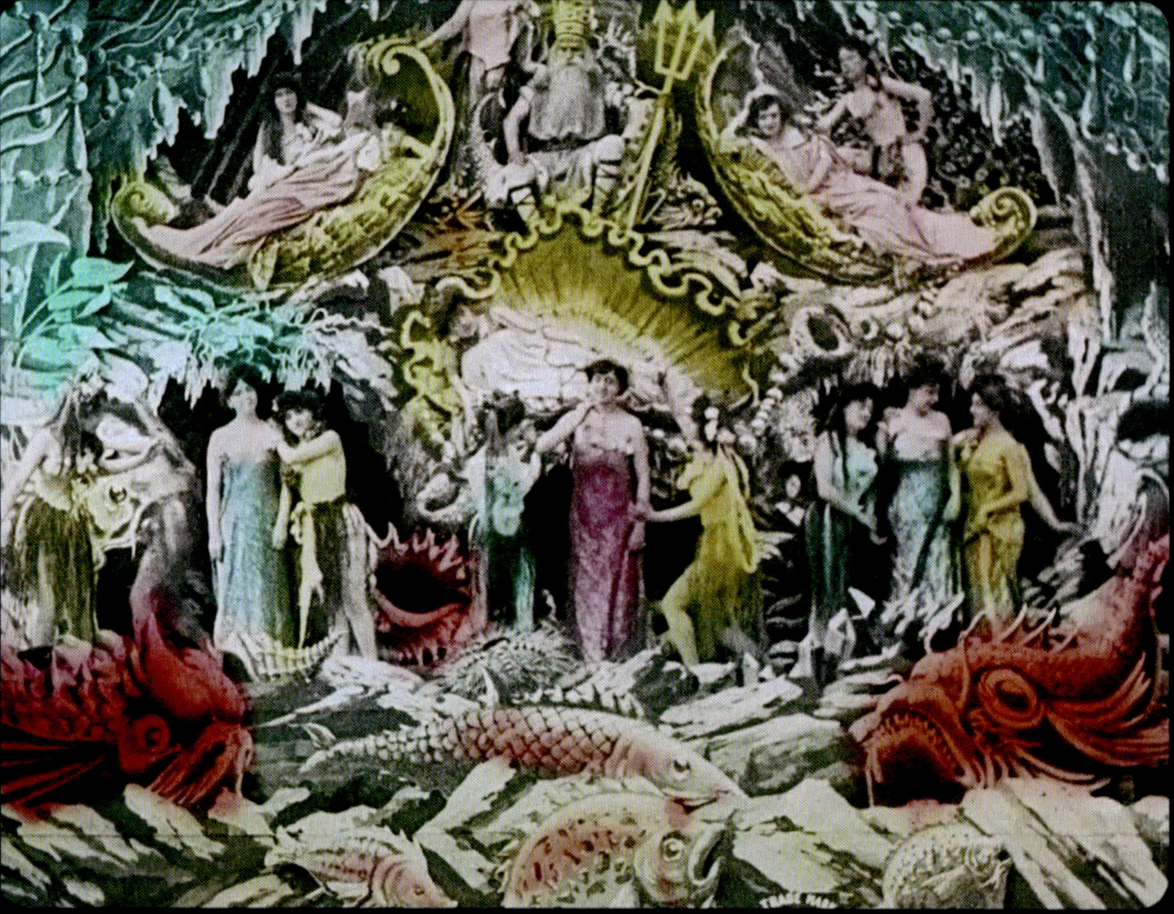

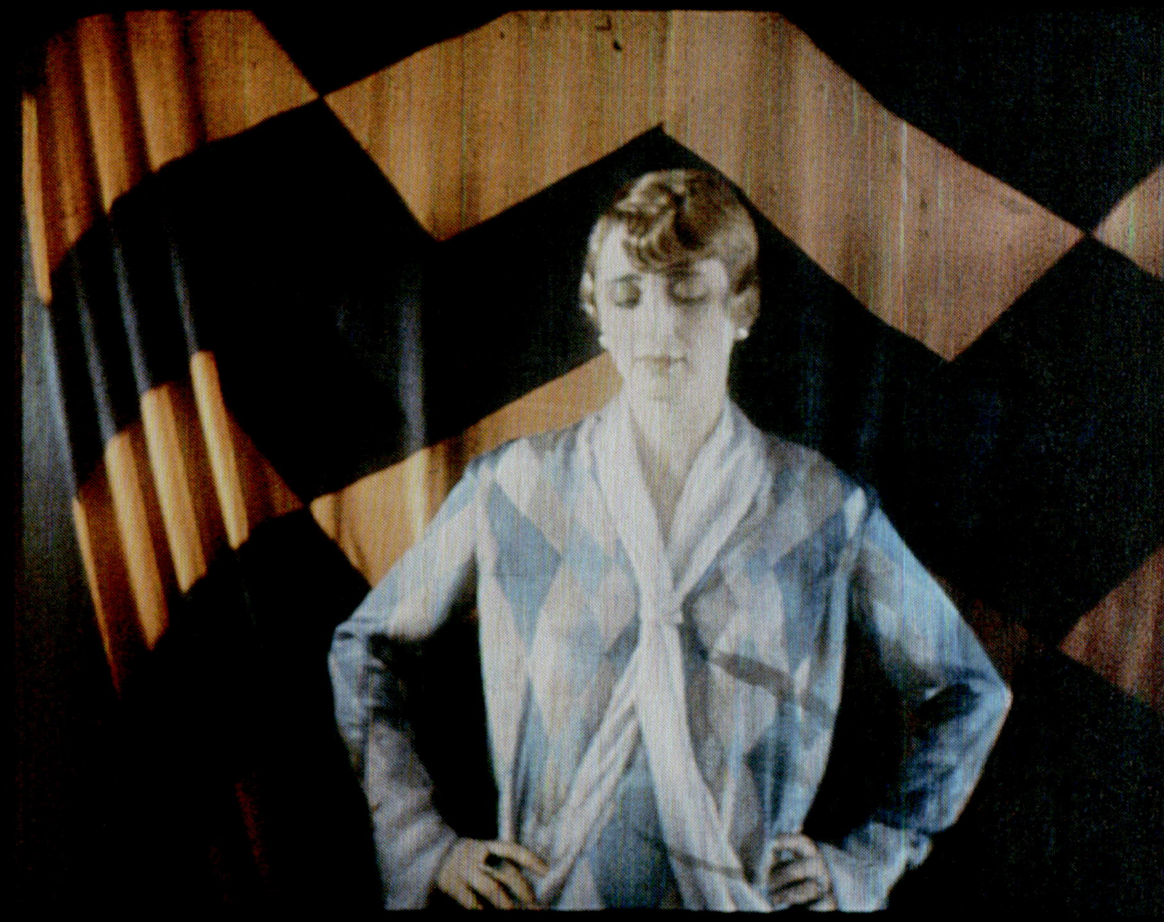

TOP: *The Kingdom of the Fairies* (*Le Royaume des fées*, France, 1903, dir. Georges Méliès)

BOTTOM: *L'Élégance* (France, 1926, dir. Sonia Delaunay)

those produced in France by Auguste and Louis Lumière and exhibited internationally, include celebrations of natural phenomena, vignettes of everyday life, and scenes based on historical events.[6]

As film production expanded, hand coloring was outsourced to specialist companies, such as when Georges Méliès and Pathé Frères contracted the Thuillier workshop in Paris from 1897 to 1912. The studio had been established by coloring expert Élisabeth Thuillier, who worked there with her daughter, Berthe. Berthe recalled selecting and sampling the colors that a workforce of 250 female colorists then applied according to her instructions. More than twenty colorists were employed on a typical film, each worker applying a single color.[7] The colors in films such as *The Kingdom of the Fairies* (*Le Royaume des fées*, France, 1903), with its vivid depiction of sea creatures and elaborate decor for the princess's bedroom, are spectacular for their richness. As in other Méliès films, the beautifully painted colors capture the vibrant chromatic sensibility of the fairy tale's fantasy world.

When the demand for color films increased, methods more suited to mass production were developed. At first stenciling was carried out as a manual process, most notably by Pathé. Several prints, corresponding with the number of different colors featured, were made of a film. The areas to be colored in each print were marked out and cut with scalpels, a laborious task undertaken by a typically female workforce. Each cutout print was then laid over the final projection print and color applied in turn, producing very precisely demarked colors. To expand production, mechanical stenciling, known as Pathécolor, was introduced from 1906. Machines cut the stencils and applied the dyes to the composite prints. Modifications of this system, such as connecting the stencil cutter to a tracing stylus, enabled the operators to produce even more precisely applied colors. The process was, however, labor intensive and required expertise.[8] The women undertaking this specialized work were well paid, as recalled by Germaine Berger, who worked as a colorist at Pathé. Her skill at drawing and experience in color application made her and other women colorists valued employees, although working conditions were strictly regulated "and did not encourage chattering or socializing."[9]

Stenciling was particularly effective for trick and fairy films, which were popular genres in the first decade of silent cinema.[10] Stenciling was also used for the Pathé-Revue fashion newsreels aimed at female consumers in the 1920s, in which the stenciling celebrated the chromatic vibrancy of clothes, furniture, flowers, accessories, and settings. It accentuated the contrasting hues of silken textures and other fabrics, highlighting details such as shimmering, sequined gowns and showcasing luxury footwear. The precision of the stenciling meant that color contrasts were emphasized as well as differences between the work of haute couture designers. Even though the items were not affordable for most consumers, the newsreels promoted a culture that was "color conscious" and informed about new fashion trends.[11]

The symbiosis between color and fashion films is also demonstrated by the work of French artist and designer Sonia Delaunay. Her film *L'Élégance* (France, 1926) featured models wearing clothes patterned with Delaunay's characteristic geometric shapes and zigzags in bold contrasting colors; in the background were draped fabrics of the same patterns to reveal a total design. The film, screened to accompany a lecture delivered by Delaunay in January 1927 at the Sorbonne in Paris, was the first public demonstration of the French three-color additive lenticular Keller-Dorian process.[12] Delaunay knew the son of the process's inventor, Rodolphe Berthon, so it is likely that this connection encouraged a filmic experiment featuring highly distinctive costumes to demonstrate the accuracy with which the process rendered vibrant colors.

Similar tie-ins were encouraged in the United States by high-profile commercial institutions such as the Textile Color Card Association (TCCA), founded in 1915. Two key strategies were developed by the TCCA to assist the business community in the exploitation of new chromatic initiatives: forecasting color trends and the provision of color consultancy services. The TCCA's color expert and public advocate of its work was Margaret Hayden Rorke, the most influential color forecaster of the 1920s and 1930s. She saw the TCCA's role as crucial for influencing new seasonal trends and spreading knowledge about the impact of colors on psychology and commerce. The TCCA produced the Standard Color Card of America with 110 basic shades. Swatches of the colors were produced to inform manufacturers about appropriate colors for hosiery, shoes and leather, woolens, and other goods. In addition, forecast cards, designed to anticipate new seasonal accents in a small group of colors, offered greater variation than the standard card. As the TCCA always had to be one step ahead of trends, it changed color names for textiles and materials so that the products available on the market would appear to be different from season to season, even if they looked similar. Rorke traveled extensively to Europe, where her views on color forecasting were exploited, particularly by businesses and manufacturers.

Technicolor's short-film series *Fashion News* directly advertised the latest colors publicized in TCCA's seasonal cards. In one, film actress Corliss Palmer is seen wearing a striking "wavecrest green" hat, as described in the intertitle. The TCCA's card for spring 1929 includes "wavecrest," confirming that the films directly referenced the latest forecasting trends. In this way the development of color technologies was closely related to targeting women as consumers, while Rorke's color expertise enabled her to occupy a highly influential position at a time when senior roles in commercial organizations were rarely occupied by women.

Probably the most well-known woman associated with color film was Natalie Kalmus of Technicolor. While she is credited as color consultant on most Technicolor films from the late 1920s to the 1950s, less is known about what her role involved or how she contributed to the company's success. She was married to Herbert Kalmus, who cofounded Technicolor in 1915, and was employed by the company until 1948. Even though they divorced in 1921, Natalie worked amicably alongside Herbert during the key years of Technicolor's development.[13]

The job of color consultant at Technicolor was established for Kalmus toward the end of the 1920s. Color control was a vital part of the company's monopolistic practices, which restricted use of the process to films shot with special cameras that could only be leased from Technicolor. The company's unique imbibition processing methods and the Color Advisory Service were also part of the package.[14] Drawing on ideas of "color consciousness," which were being popularized in the 1920s, Natalie published an article with that title as part of a branding exercise by Technicolor in 1935 that became a seminal statement of the process's aesthetic norms.[15] It was guided by the idea that color must be used selectively and grounded in notions of harmony, accents, and complements that drew loosely on art history. Far from encouraging Technicolor to be garish, Natalie warned against the use of nonnaturalistic "super abundance." She also reiterated established cultural associations between "cool" and "warm" colors, as well as how colors indicated personality. After reading film scripts, she and other consultants issued charts advising how Technicolor should be used for each production. The intention was for these to operate like a musical score, supporting a film's dominant moods or emotional trajectory. The Advisory Service consulted on colors for sets and costumes in addition to testing fabrics and color combinations. Samples of materials and colors from previous Technicolor films were provided to assist with planning a film's color scheme.

While documentation on the charts and their application is scarce, occasionally there is a record of their deployment, such as for Tim Whelan's *The Divorce of Lady X* (UK, 1938). Natalie's charts were photographed and sent to the UK with a memo advising how the company should work with them in advance of her arrival to supervise the production. The memo described the process: "Included with the print there is a set of the colored cards of which the charts were composed. Each one is numbered to correspond with its number on the chart, and the formula for mixing each color is written on the back of each card and on a separate list as well. By reconstructing the charts and comparing them with the projected print a general idea of the process of translation can be gained."[16]

The importance of this system of aesthetic control and standardization went hand in hand with the idea that Technicolor was a highly specialized process requiring not only bespoke technical equipment but also detailed, careful application. At times this caused conflict with production companies and, in particular, technicians, who saw the restrictions as limiting and interfering. There are many examples of Technicolor objecting to new, untried approaches, such as those attempted by cinematographer Ossie Morris for films that were later celebrated for their experimental Technicolor, including *Moulin Rouge* (UK, 1952).[17] Some cinematographers disparaged Natalie's work by claiming she knew little about the technology; they even criticized her appearance, and her taste in clothes and hats was typified as gaudy.[18] Such criticism was often inflected with personal remarks that probably would not have been the case had she been male.

Natalie worked productively with color consultant Joan Bridge on many British films. In the 1930s Bridge had worked with Dufaycolor, a three-color additive process that was used for several British films at a time when it was not clear that Technicolor would dominate the market. Dufaycolor was generally known for its soft pastel look, as demonstrated in *Making Fashion* (UK, 1938), a short fashion film directed by Humphrey Jennings to showcase fashion designer Norman Hartnell's spring collection. This expertise put Bridge in a good position to advise and work alongside Natalie when she came to the UK in the late 1930s. In the 1940s, when Natalie's visits were less frequent, Bridge became the main color consultant on most British Technicolor films, many of which were admired for their quality in terms of applying selective color "restraint" that was often referred to as a "British School of Technicolor."[19] Her experience with Dufaycolor influenced a subtle approach to color design. She worked as an associate color controller, often with Natalie, on many important Technicolor films including David Lean's *Blithe Spirit* (UK, 1945) and Michael Powell and Emeric Pressburger's *A Matter*

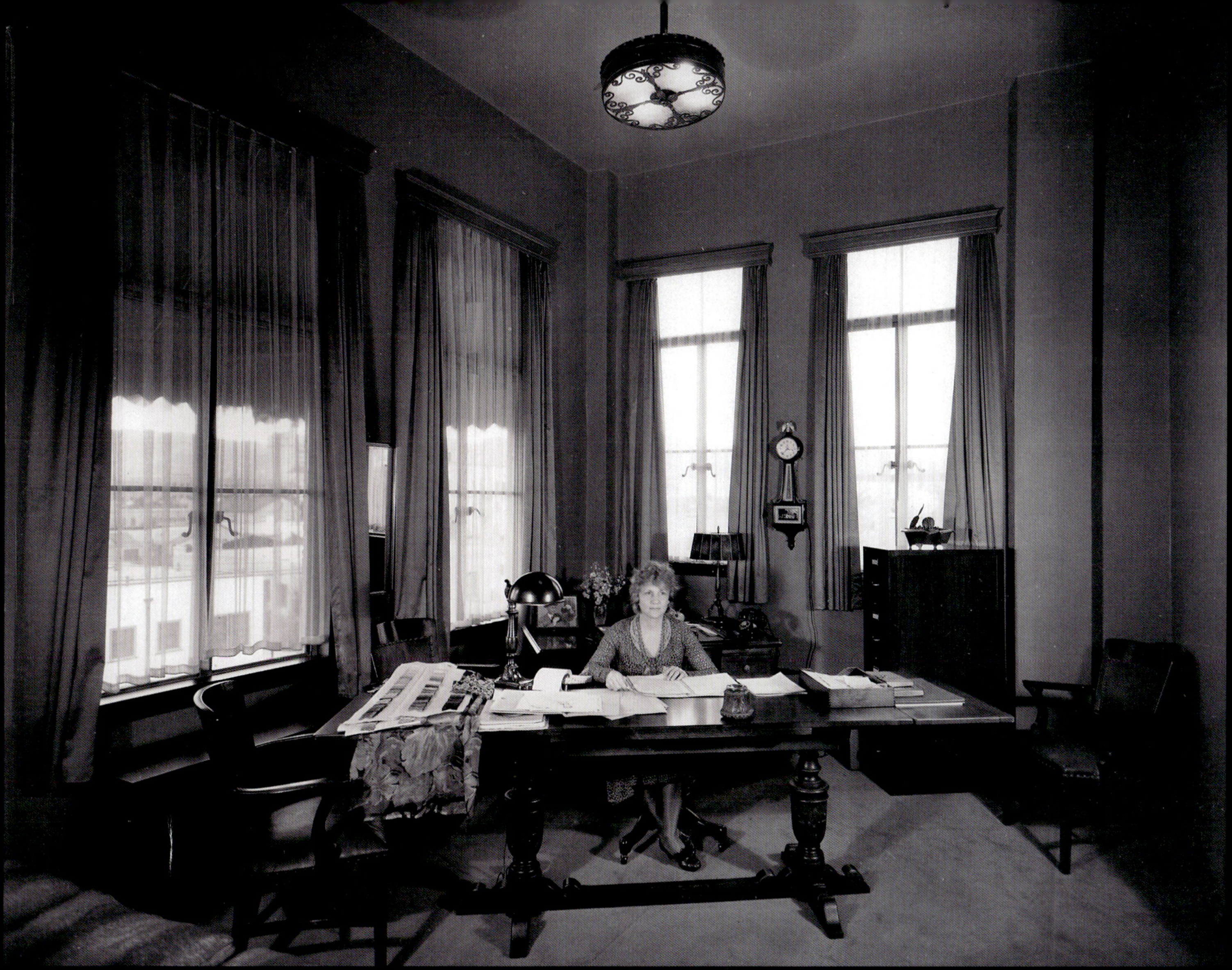

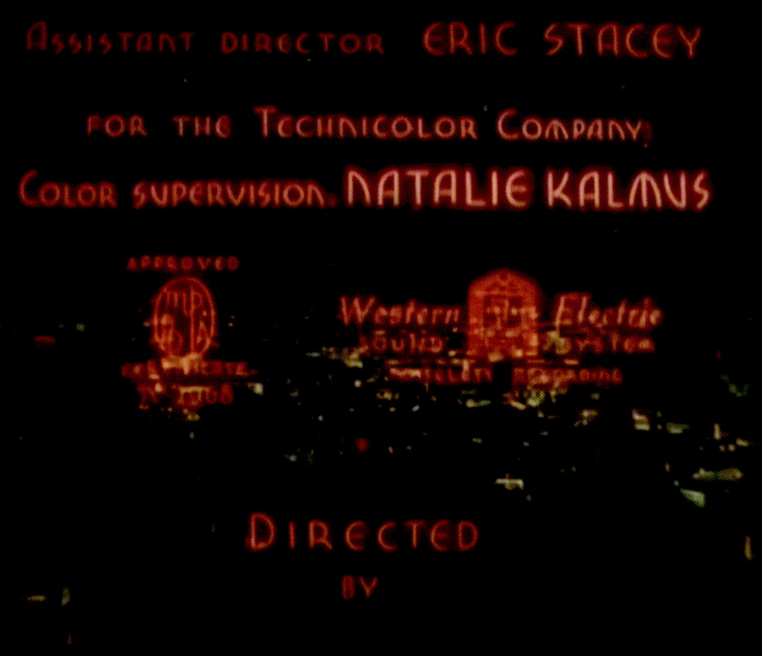

TOP: Natalie Kalmus at her desk, 1920s

RIGHT: Credits from the Technicolor film *A Star Is Born* (USA, 1937, dir. William A. Wellman)

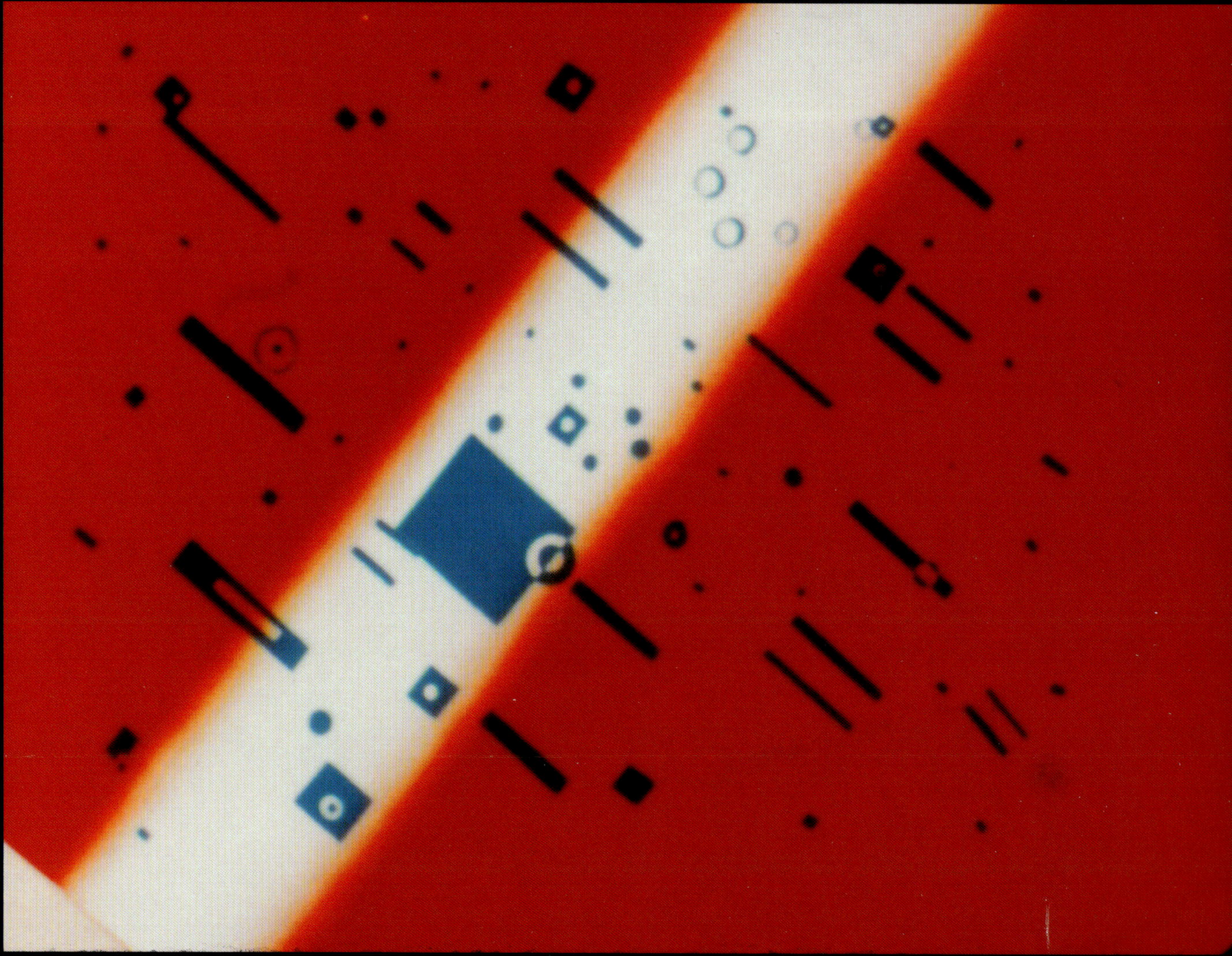

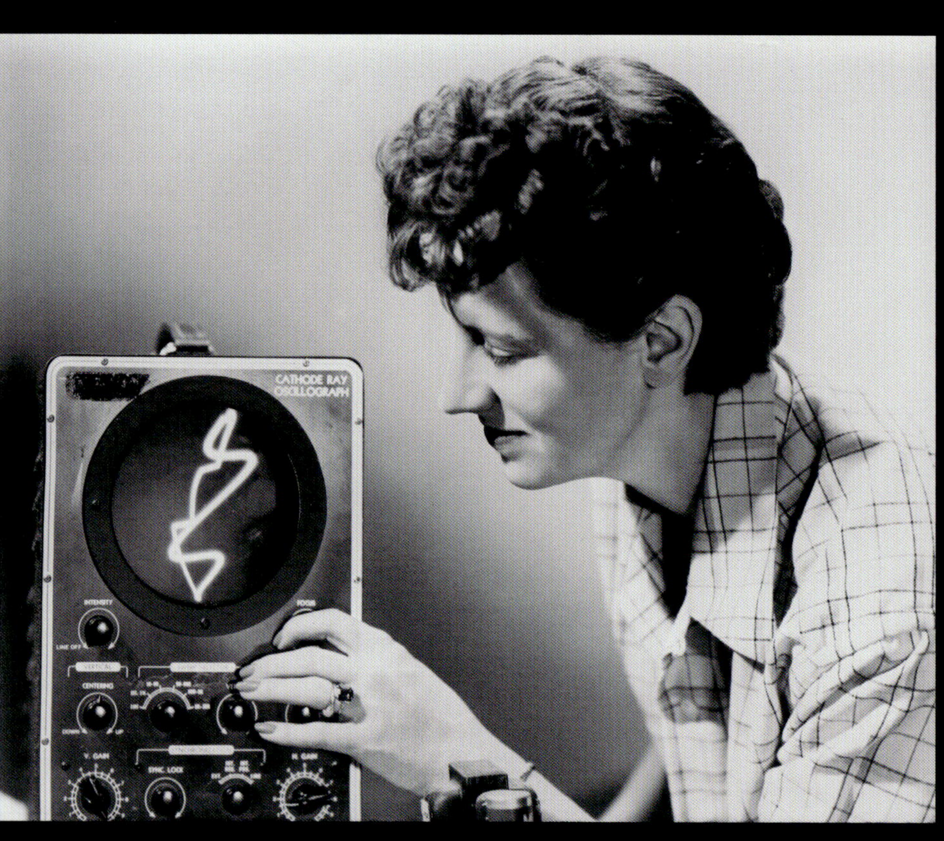

TOP: *Tarantella* (USA, 1940, dir. Mary Ellen Bute)

of Life and Death (UK, 1946), *Black Narcissus* (UK, 1947), and *The Red Shoes* (UK, 1948). Cinematographers tended to respect Bridge more than Natalie, whose reputation for "interference" was resented in part because she was identified with an American corporation at a time when British films struggled to compete with Hollywood.[20]

Natalie's work both branding and celebrating Technicolor was invaluable. When interviewed for her color advice in many women's and fan magazines, her prominent role in the company was often a talking point. Technicolor was astute to take advantage of her public profile, on one occasion putting her name on an article written by a male colleague. She gave radio interviews, and there are examples of her advice being taken up commercially by department stores.[21] In this way she played a key role in popularizing the idea of color consultancy and in making Technicolor a household name. Even though one article described Herbert as the "Techni" of the company and Natalie as the "color," this binarism tends to play down the complexity of her work as well as the extent to which it was an essential part of both applying and disseminating knowledge about the process.[22]

Women have also been significant in the development of color in experimental film. Although the individuals discussed below are not as well known as their male counterparts, their work explored color's impact on the senses and, in particular, color's relationship to music. Mary Hallock Greenewalt's Sarabet color organ, for example, used light displays and a color console as a means of enhancing musical appreciation. Her color organs were installed in theaters in the 1920s in Philadelphia, New York, and Washington, DC. She also experimented with hand-painting film to create a "score" that guided the performer.[23] Her work can be compared with that of more celebrated inventors of color organs such as Thomas Wilfred, who drew on her patents in his own work.[24] Color organs were influential in the development of experimental film color because they similarly explored the combined sensual impact of "mobile color" and music.[25]

In the field of animation, Mary Ellen Bute, in New York, was also fascinated by the interplay of light and color, color organs, and the idea of "visual music." She specialized in stage lighting when she was at Yale University in the mid-1920s, and she was in contact with and influenced by Wilfred. Working in the tradition of Absolute Film typified by abstract animators Walter Ruttmann, Hans Richter, and Viking Eggeling in Weimar Germany, Bute's work was preoccupied with motion "as a form of unfettered expressive potential."[26] From the 1930s to the 1950s she completed fourteen short abstract films, ten of which are in color. These were often shown before feature films at theaters such as Radio City Music Hall. Influenced by painter Paul Cézanne's conception of color as resonating with the modulations, tones, and scales of music, Bute's use of color freed it from the burdens of literal representation and naturalism. She was also inspired by Wassily Kandinsky's paintings, which explored relations between shapes, colors, and music.

Bute's film *Tarantella* (USA, 1940) incorporated an unused sequence from her film *Spook Sport* (USA, 1939), which was animated by Norman McLaren. *Tarantella* aimed to integrate mobile color and sound developed from a series of rhythms that she worked out arithmetically with composer Edwin Gerschefski. In this enterprise, as film scholar Kristian Moen suggests, Bute was "most concerned with creating powerful affects and sensations by combining these aesthetic elements."[27] This kind of multimedia experience deployed color as intense stimulation for both the intellect and emotions. As a kinetic abstract film, *Tarantella* indeed delivers a series of rapid, pulsating images using reds, blues, and black and white, as well as undulating shades of pink that accompany the music. An early intertitle informs us of the context: "A rapid Neapolitan dance in triplets; so called because it was popularly thought to be a remedy for the supposed poisonous bite of the tarantula." The film's combination of deeply saturated colors, jagged lines, and shapes that appear intermittently communicates the sensation of stinging perhaps being countered ("a remedy") by dancing, primary colors. The playful interaction between the various shapes and contrasting colors also appeals directly to the senses.

Bute experimented with color in subsequent films including *Abstronic* (USA, 1952), for which she used an electronic cathode-ray oscilloscope combined with conventional animation techniques to generate a "seeing sound" experience for music composed by Aaron Copland and Don Gillis. Full of the energetic movement of geometric shapes and squiggling lines, this film places colors relationally so that a sense of depth is created in the image. In a few frames this is emphasized by centripetal force drawing the eye to the center of the frame as a horizon is indicated and by a train track disappearing into the distance. The overlaying of color with rapidly moving lines is inspired by and in time with the rhythm of the music. This creates sensations of effervescence and exuberance as saturated colors jockey for the viewer's attention. In films such as *Mood Contrasts* (USA, 1953), one of her major oscilloscope works, Bute further experimented with color. Bute's films were widely exhibited in the United States, giving her an unusually broad public profile for an experimental animator.[28]

In Scotland, animator Margaret Tait was also fascinated by correspondences between color, movement, and music, as demonstrated in experimental works by leading figures associated with the Absolute Film movement.[29] Her technique involved painting aniline dyes frame by frame for *Calypso* (UK, 1955), a film in which vibrant colors animate figures that dance in syncopation with a Cuban soundtrack. Influenced by artist Len Lye, Tait was distinctive for applying the medical dyes she was familiar with from her former career as a doctor prior to becoming an animator and poet.[30] More commonly used as stains in biological laboratories, these dyes rendered particularly deep, saturated colors. Although her work was not well known at the time, her films and influence have since been recognized for their striking chromatic qualities.[31] Like Bute's films, Tait used loops, shapes, and colors to deliver an assault on the senses, as well as drawings that appeared to respond to the music. *Colour Poems* (UK, 1974) combined live-action footage with painting and scratching on 16mm film. The past (the Spanish Civil War), recollected through a poem, is combined with contemporary footage of the Orkney archipelago (where Tait was born and lived for much of her life) to suggest uncanny resonances between timeframes. Tait's film *Aerial* (UK, 1974) resonates with coloring techniques used in the silent era, with its footage of changing seasons shifting from tinted frames to normal color stock: the heritage of color film becomes a self-referential aesthetic technique.

Other filmmakers have drawn on hand-coloring and tinting traditions in experimental practice. Canadian artist Joyce Wieland played with different tints of textile dyes on discarded documentary footage in the short film *Hand Tinting* (Canada, 1967) to suggest the vulnerabilities of a group of young women. In *Sanctus* (USA, 1990), Barbara Hammer rephotographed and colorized moving X-rays to dramatize skeletal forms in extraordinary ways. The film also features scratching and hand painting, set to music by composer Neil Rolnick. Experimental animator Jodi Mack uses discarded objects such as holographic wrapping paper, stained glass, and fabrics to explore color and texture in works such as *Glistening Thrills* (USA, 2013).

These women are connected by their imaginative and highly original approaches to the techniques of more established male filmmakers working in visual music and experimental animation. Such artistry and inventiveness exemplify how color continues to inspire women as past practices inform and energize new works. These serve as fitting examples to end this survey of the many ways in which women were, and continue to be, key innovators in the development of moving, color films.

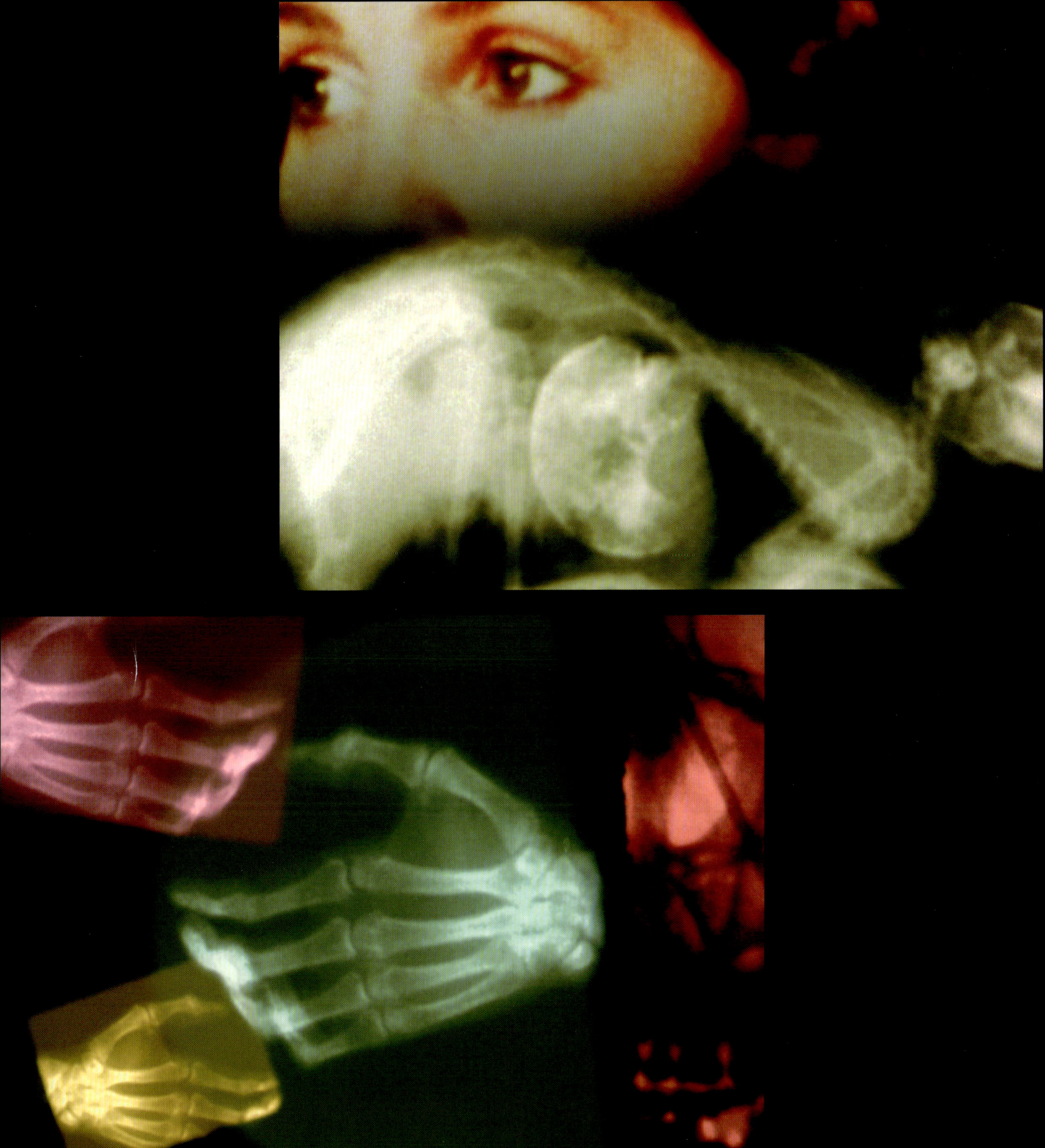

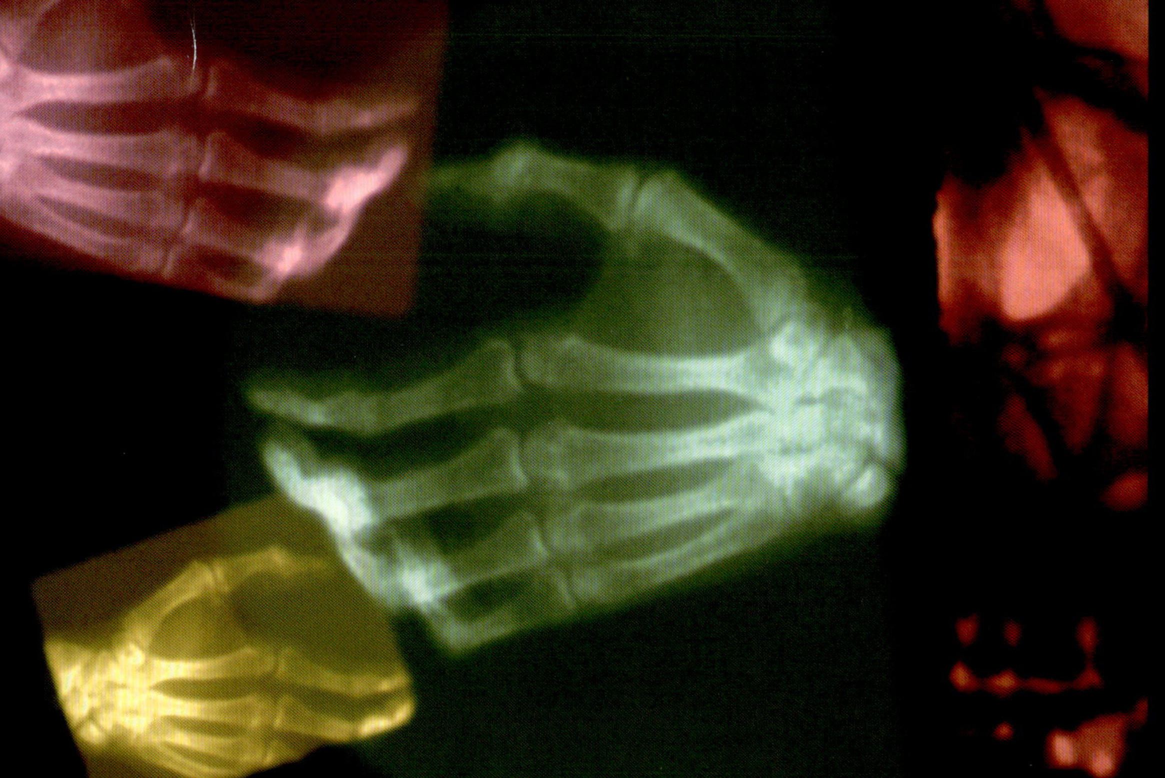

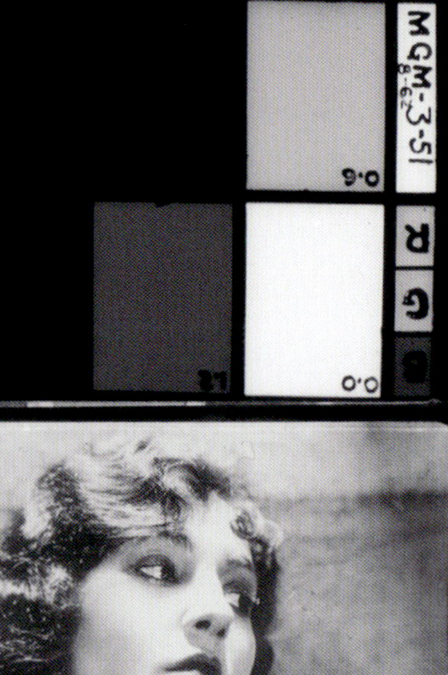

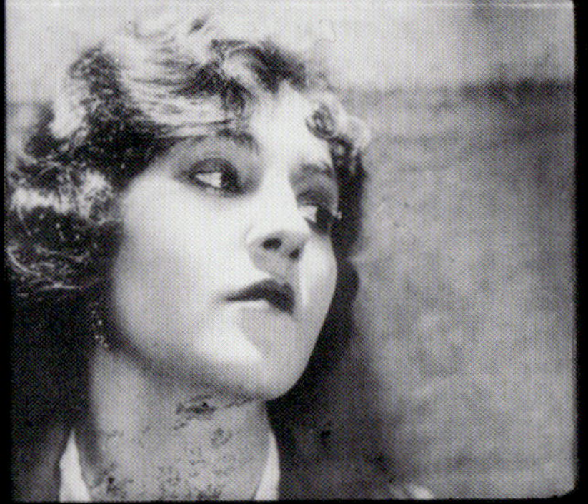

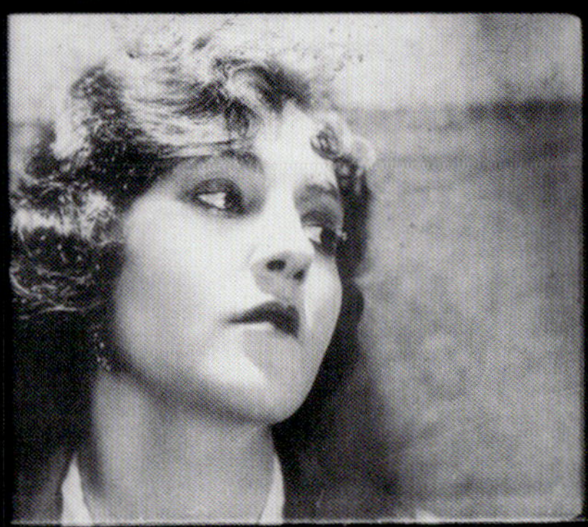

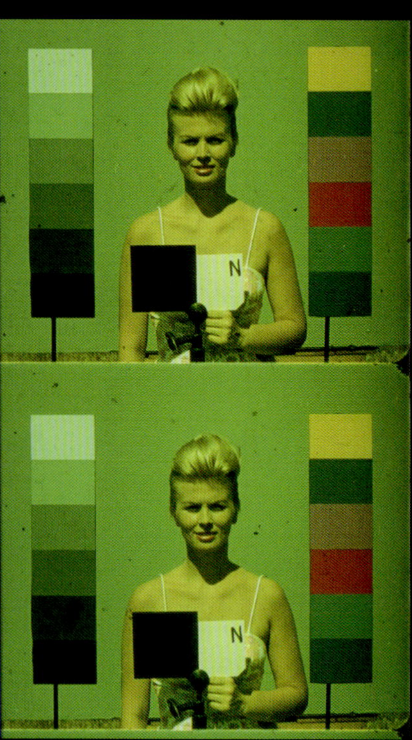

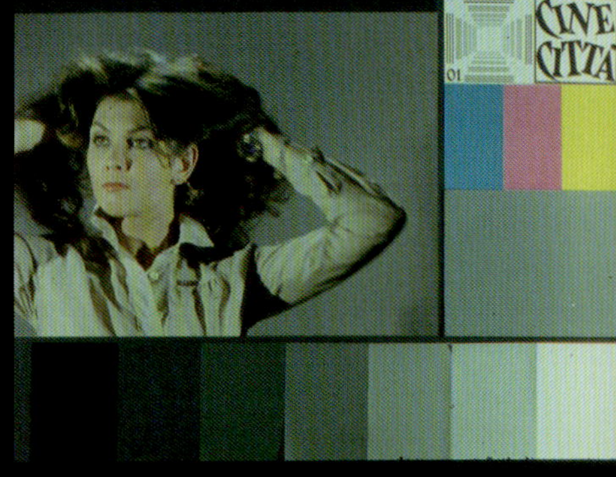

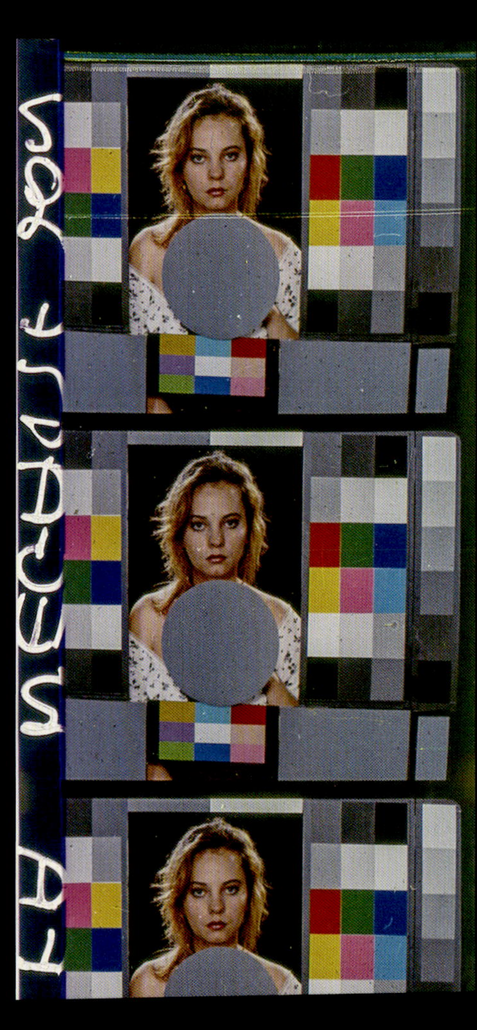

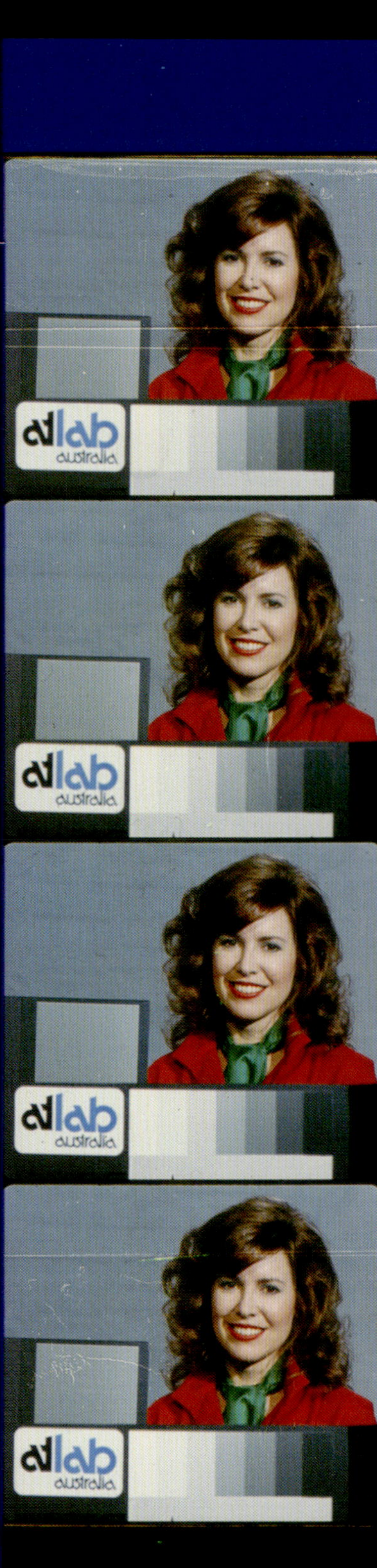

Leader lady images, 1930s–present, submitted to the Chicago Film Society's Leader Ladies Project

SOPHIA SERRANO

LEADER LADIES

REFRAMING A CALIBRATION PRACTICE

"Leader ladies" are little known but integral aspects of motion picture history that have a large impact on the colors we see ultimately on screen. To highlight and explore this practice, Sophia Serrano spoke with motion picture preservation specialist Ivy Donnell, author and film scholar Genevieve Yue, and Chicago Film Society members Rebecca Lyon, Rebecca Hall, and Kyle Westphal, whose Leader Ladies Project has compiled and shared a wide array of these fascinating film ephemera since 2011. This conversation, on June 27, 2023, has been edited and condensed for clarity.

SOPHIA SERRANO: Just to start off, what are leader ladies?

REBECCA LYON: I can start, speaking from the perspective of a projectionist. They're essentially a color calibration tool that's used in the photochemical processing and printing of analog film. Exhibition prints will often still have maybe four or five frames of a leader lady on the countdown of a film, which is something the audience doesn't see. But as a projectionist you see them on almost every film print, especially if you work anywhere that runs films from all eras.

REBECCA HALL: I think it might be helpful for me to describe what a single frame of leader lady looks like. Just imagine a frame with a woman, usually from the shoulders up, and somewhere in the frame is a line of color bars that serve as a template. And sometimes it might be sneaky—the "color bar" might just be something like a flower of each color, but you can still tell it's a leader lady because of how it's using color and where it comes up in the front matter of a film reel.

IVY DONNELL: I'd be happy to break it down from a lab perspective. It is a very purposeful image. Usually, the leader lady portraits are very well lit so you can see details and hair, and she's usually wearing a bright shirt and holding black, white, and gray patches or a color chart. The portrait of the woman is essentially a visual confirmation that you have your settings right. If her hair is too dark or her skin is green, you did something wrong. It's a quality-control mechanism for the lab.

In more modern versions, instead of the women holding a grayscale card, there's a digitally added LAD [Laboratory Aim Density] patch, which is 18 percent gray. It's supposed to be the midpoint between minimum and maximum possible camera exposure. Technicians use a densitometer—a device that measures the optical density, or darkness, of film—on the LAD patch to get a numerical reading that tells them if they're close to the target Kodak specifies for a particular film stock. That's a little more scientific.

GENEVIEVE YUE: I can add to that a bit, in terms of the history of the China Girl, which is another name these are known by. This practice began in the mid-1920s, roughly around the time when the densitometer was invented and developed in Kodak research laboratories. You'll see mentions and uses of leader ladies, China Girls, China Dolls; many different names pop up in the technical literature. Every time there's a technological advance, like the addition of sound or color, one falls back to the uses of the China Girl in conjunction with these other instruments for tightening up quality control.

SS: You mentioned that it starts roughly in the 1920s. How has the practice shifted over time? Can you talk a little bit about contemporary practice for digital processes?

GY: I can start with the LAD system, which came about in 1976 and was extremely interesting because that little gray patch was effectively all that was needed, technologically, to do that same work that the China Girl image is supposed to do. But the image remains as part of the vernacular of the practice. Even as we have shifted to digital processes for most motion picture imagery, anytime there's a chemical process involved you might find vestiges of a China Girl. I've seen also versions of what's called a DLAD or digital LAD frame, printer calibration charts, monitor calibration charts. These are all descendants of the China Girl.

Again, the portrait of a conventionally attractive woman dressed in brightly colored clothing or adorned with fruit or whatever flowers and these standard reference colors somewhere in the image survive into digital practices—not necessarily in the same way they appeared in film, but it's a remarkably persistent facet of digital imaging.

RL: Before Kodak developed the LAD system, film labs were making their own images for calibration, so there was a very wide variety of images made by different designers and labs. But after the introduction of the LAD images, smaller film labs could purchase the negatives directly from Kodak and no longer needed to make their own. Which was too bad, because a lot of the smaller labs were creating the weirdest, most beautiful ones.

Kodak has many LAD images featuring different women but the design is essentially the same for all of them. These are the most common ones you see, but the older leader ladies are still very much out there because when you make a newer print of, let's say, a title from the 1950s, the original leader lady might still be on whatever source material you're using.

SS: So even old Leader Lady examples are still useful today?

ID: We still use them at the National Archives and Records Administration [NARA]. Aside from the film preservation work that we do, we digitize films for reference purposes, and even the really old leader ladies that were added on decades ago are still very useful to us, especially if they're printed in and they have the same color fading as the rest of the roll. With the capture and color correction software that we use, we can calibrate the leader lady to look nice and then everything else looks great. There's a tool that we use where you need to select something in the image that's supposed to be gray. So, we just pick that gray card that she's holding 99 percent of the time, and it turns out great. I just love that it was added decades ago but is still very useful today.

RH: Every time I've visited a film lab, I notice little strips of leader ladies taped to the wall or displayed in a way that suggests they were used for something recently.

GY: I'd like to add something about the uniqueness of leader ladies. When you're a viewer of a film print in an audience, you have the chance to see the China Girl pass by if the projectionist doesn't change the reels over in time or shows more of the leader. I've definitely been in screenings where you see it and it signals this other existence of the print, like a back end to its material history. And I think that's really lovely about the leader ladies. Every once in a while you'll see one, and it's like spotting an animal in the wild.

ID: And because it's a motion picture that's been cut up, you only get a small section of the lady and don't know which snippet you're going to get. So sometimes she's laughing or blinking or smiling or looking bored.

KYLE WESTPHAL: I would add that when you're encountering a leader lady, when you're winding through a print, it's not isolated. It's part of the leader. You're also seeing writing by the lab to identify what roll it is, what the title is, what cut it is. Those things also flash on screen. I think we really need a new vocabulary for talking about them because there's been this shift in the last few years to talking about films as moving images or time-based media, not as film.

But what the leader ladies suggest is something different. They don't really exist in time in the way that the rest of a film print does. They aren't made as part of the production—they often predate the production—so they're part of the film but exist outside of it. They're not legible as "moving images," but

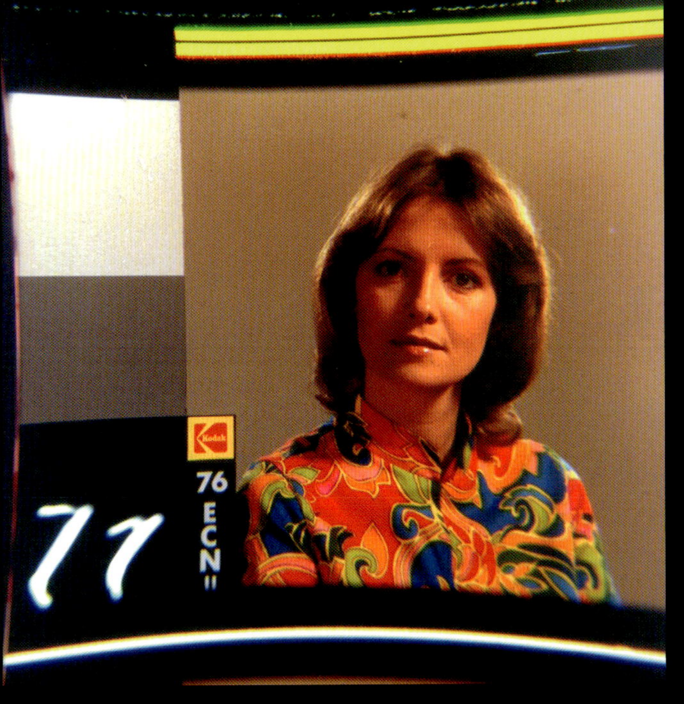
Kodak
76
ECN
77
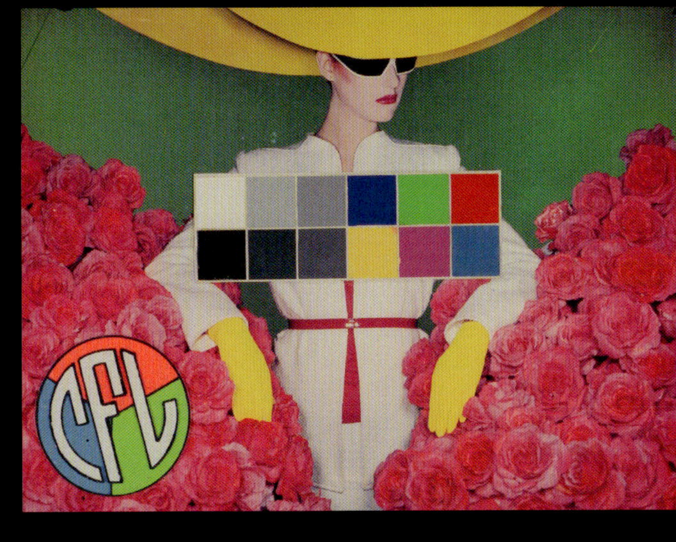
CFL
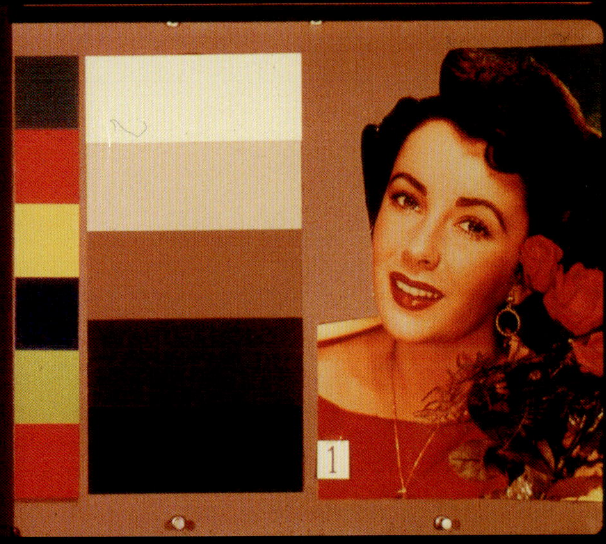
1
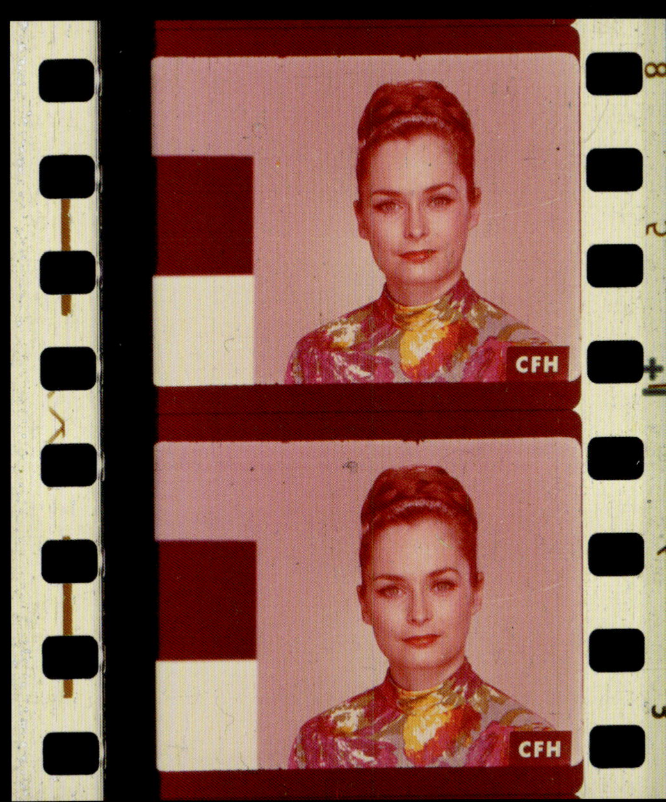
CFH
CFH

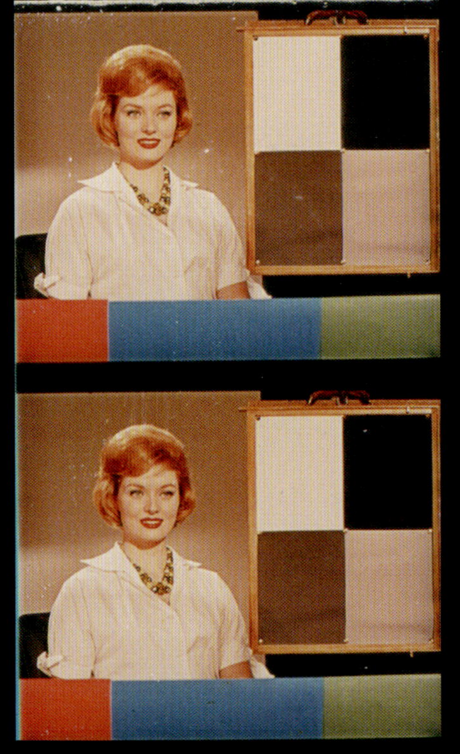

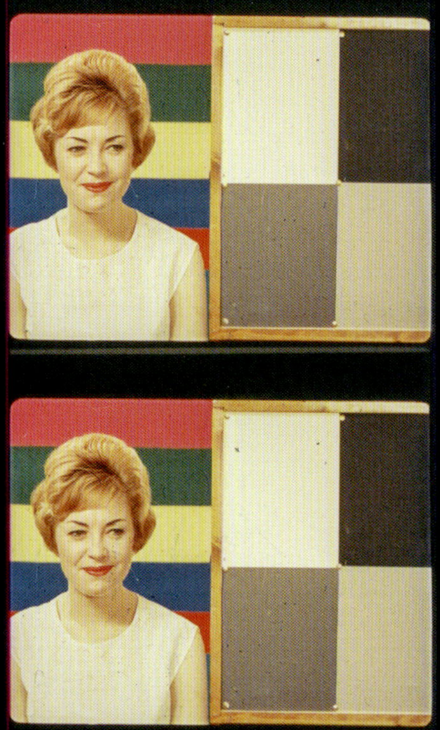

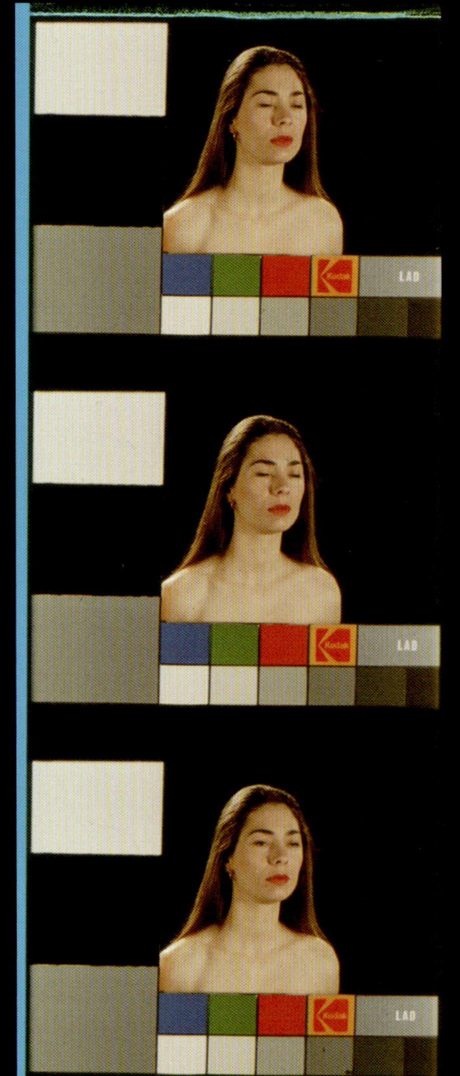

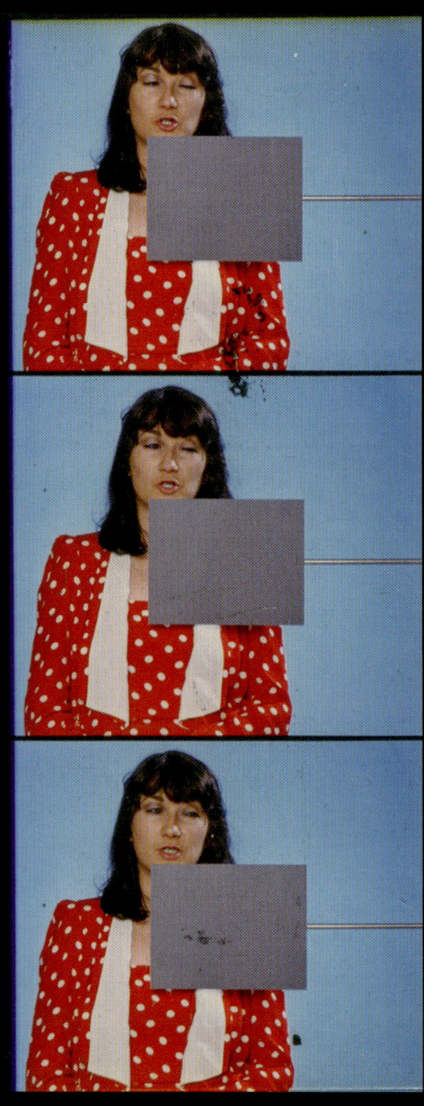

Leader lady images, 1930s–present, submitted to the Chicago Film Society's Leader Ladies Project

only as a static filmstrip, as an object. This is one reason why, when they're taken out of context in the Leader Ladies Project, they have a whole life of their own beyond the film.

RH: I think this is also why it is so spooky to see them blink. You have the feeling that they're not really supposed to be in motion, but they actually are a lot of the time.

RL: They have a presence in experimental film also, especially with filmmakers who are concerned with film as a physical object or the filmmaking process, and in films with found footage. So, even if you don't work behind the scenes, they might be visible to you in avant-garde or experimental films.

GY: In popular film too. The end credits to Tarantino's *Death Proof* [USA, 2007] is entirely a sequence of leader ladies, for example.

SS: As we're talking about the women, can you explain who they were? How did one become a leader lady?

RL: We spoke about a decade ago by email with a woman named Val Scott, who was "the BKSTS Girl" [British Kinematograph, Sound and Television Society, now International Moving Image Society]. Her image is, I would say, almost as prevalent as the Kodak LAD and was used in television and motion picture work. Kyle did a short interview with her almost a decade ago.

So, Val gets a job at a television studio and while working there, one of the producers asks her and another girl to take some photographs, they have no idea what for. Val says, "Out of the three of us, I was chosen to be filmed for the BKSTS 1 and 2. This entailed me sitting still for about three hours facing the camera. I was no actress. I worked in the drawing office. I was given a check for 10 pounds for each sitting, 16mm and 35mm. It was very low key. I was told that the frames would be used up and down the country for color correctness. [...] I left the job in 1971 and pretty much forgot about it. Then in 1983, I took my boys to see *Superman*: *The Movie*, and in the background of Lex Luthor's cave was the BKSTS Girl. Several years later, frames were used in a Woolworths ad on television. I had no idea the frames were used almost worldwide. In retrospect, it's a shame I did not get royalties."

Her image was used countless times from that one shoot. A lot of these women were models, and it was just another job for them. But some of them were people who worked in the film labs, which to me is a little bit more interesting because they're from a labor pool that's less seen or thought about.

GY: I had a chance to speak to Lili Young, who was the model for DuArt Labs. They captured her image in the late 1960s, and she was a girlfriend at the time of one of the brothers who owned the company, later his wife. It's very similar to what Rebecca described. One afternoon they brought her in, and she just had to sit there for a while. When I interviewed her, she was a little confused: "Why are you asking me about this one very momentary thing that I did?" It didn't seem very consequential because she wasn't part of the lab herself. She said, "It was not a very exciting thing to do, just sit and be very still, expressionless. They just wanted my flesh tone. It was like being in a long still shot, forever."

I also spoke to a woman named Ulli at Cineric in New York, and she worked in the lab and happened to be their model as well. I asked her if it was weird to work with her own image all the time as a technician, and she had just disregarded it. She did tell me that a client had come in and noticed that she was the China Girl and thought that was amusing. She had sort of detached from that experience in an interesting way.

ID: I found one example, a [US] Navy-produced film, where the leader lady appears to be wearing a Navy uniform. We know that some government agencies and military branches had their own labs. So that's a unique example where everything was produced under one house. She probably worked there and they asked her to sit for it. Other agencies like the United States Department of Agriculture also had their own labs for a while. I have my eye out for certain record groups at NARA that we know had their own production and lab in the same house. I want to see if there are other leader ladies who don't look like hired models or the same faces you see over and over.

RL: The Leader Ladies Project definitely has several images of women who are obviously wearing lab coats, especially for small gauge. We've received several from 16mm films, for example, that must be of somebody on their break doing some extra work for the film lab.

GY: There were also instances where, especially as the practice became more formalized at Kodak, models were hired through agencies. I tried to figure out what agencies and who these people were in the 1970s and '80s in and around their headquarters in Rochester, New York. My understanding is that when it became a bit more professionalized, they hired professional models, which tracks with the standardization of the practice.

KW: There is this fascinating question about how leader ladies relate to broader currents of film history and film style. What's interesting to me is that when you look back over the decades, there is a correspondence, especially in some of the more iconic ones, between the predominant style in which films were shot and the way some of the leader ladies were shot. There are high-key leader ladies in the 1940s that look like images out of a film noir, for example. The fact that the style in the film is carrying over onto the lab side is this whole other question of how much things were going back and forth between professional cinematographers and lab people, and how much they saw this work as all being part of the same thing.

GY: There's an image of a woman wearing a red cheongsam outfit, with her hair pulled back by a blue headband. I've seen this same woman in test strips used at Kodak for the first Kodachrome in the 1930s. I believe her name is Shirley. I was told that Shirley was the name of [Kodachrome creators] Leopold Mannes and Leopold Godowsky's secretary, and they were calling these "Shirleys." That's one of the little rabbit holes that I've been trying to track down. Is this Shirley, and does this image actually come from the 1930s?

RL: I was floored to find out it was that old. I assumed it was from the 1970s just based on the way it looked.

ID: I found it on an Air Force film way later than the '30s. I want to say more like the 1950s. Obviously it just kept getting reused over and over.

GY: It's deceptive because it's in color.

RL: Yeah, that woman is really interesting because she appears in multiple outfits.

SS: The term China Girl has been used a number of times here. Genevieve, your book *Girl Head: Feminism and Film Materiality* [2020] explores this origin and history—why were they called that and what is the significance of it?

GY: It's funny because the subjects were almost always white, at least in the American film industry context. Apocryphally, Bob Smith at DuArt, who was trained in the Navy lab, said he had seen an Asian woman posed as a China Girl in the 1940s, but I have yet to find that. Certainly there are many orientalized descriptors—in hairstyle, in dress—potentially in the connotation of China with porcelain, a certain kind of material, but also an ideal image of whiteness or fairness. It may just be one of those cases where there is not necessarily any kind of origin but a cluster of signifiers of Asianness associated with a kind of stereotypically submissive femininity.

KW: Rebecca, when you started this project, you had a choice, and you didn't call it the China Girls Project.

RH: I wish I could remember more of my early thinking about this because it was such a long time ago that we started it. But definitely I remember feeling uncomfortable with the ambiguity of where that term came from.

RL: China Girl isn't the only term for the images, but you hear it a lot. There are some other names for them, like Lady Wedge and Girl Head, which Genevieve used as the title for her book.

SS: Can you tell us a little bit about the Chicago Film Society and the Leader Ladies Project, Rebecca? When did it start and how has it evolved?

RL: Both started in 2011. The Chicago Film Society [CFS] was cofounded by Rebecca Hall, Kyle, and our colleague Julian Antos. That period of time was very important for people working in analog film because it's when digital cinema essentially took over. There was a lot of uncertainty surrounding our jobs and this medium that we all loved so much. The Leader Ladies Project and similar projects were started as a way—though we may not have been thinking of this at the time—to build a record of practices related to analog film, to make sure that they were documented and shared.

KW: Rebecca [Hall] and I were working as projectionists when CFS started—she was at the Gene Siskel Film Center and I was at the George Eastman House in Rochester, New York. Leader Ladies started with us just sending pictures back and forth when we saw things as we were projecting. We started posting them online, and other archivists, projectionists, and lab people started sending us unsolicited shots, and so the collection grew.

RH: I had been thinking a lot about all of the behind-the-scenes work, the work that I and everyone else in film history had been doing, in the context of the industry changing technologically in this way. It's funny because it wouldn't have even been possible to share images online that way too much earlier than when we started, during social media's

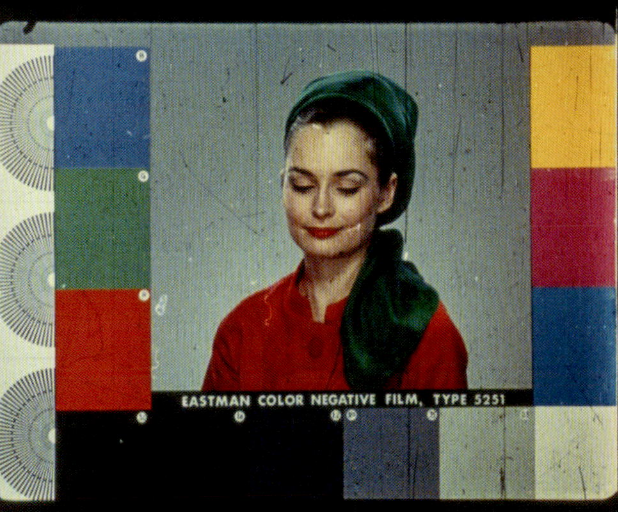
EASTMAN COLOR NEGATIVE FILM, TYPE 5251

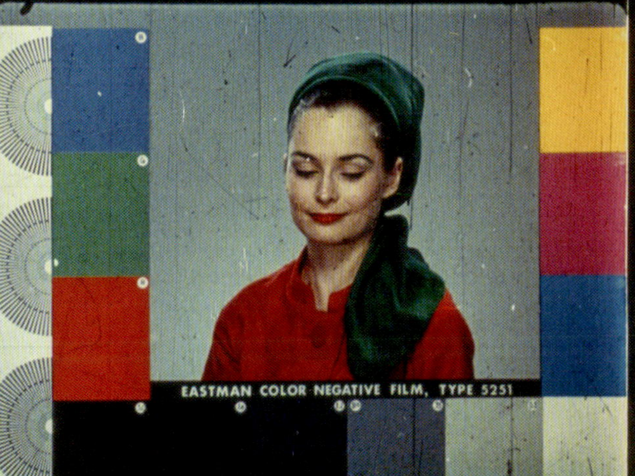
EASTMAN COLOR NEGATIVE FILM, TYPE 5251

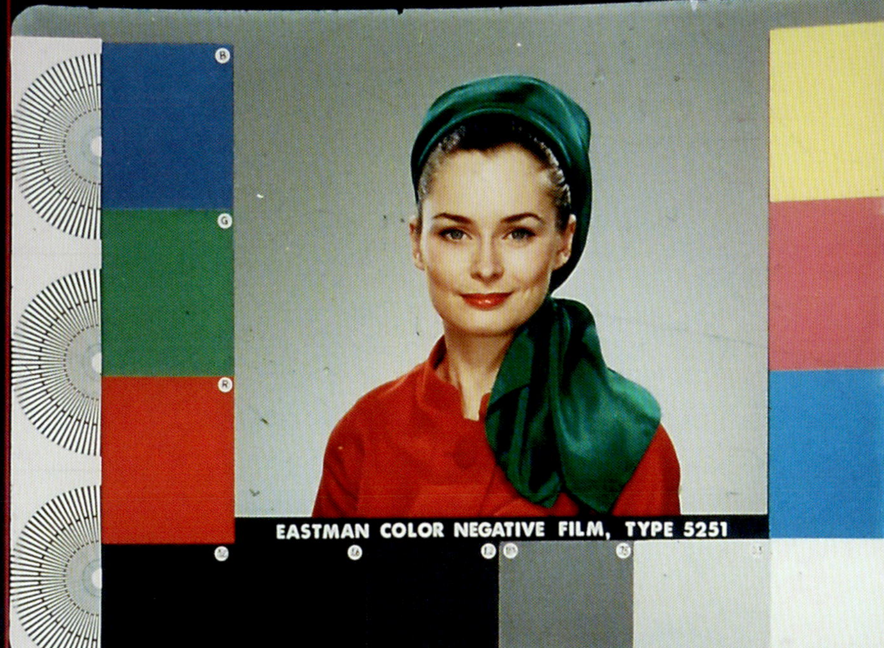
B
G
R
EASTMAN COLOR NEGATIVE FILM, TYPE 5251

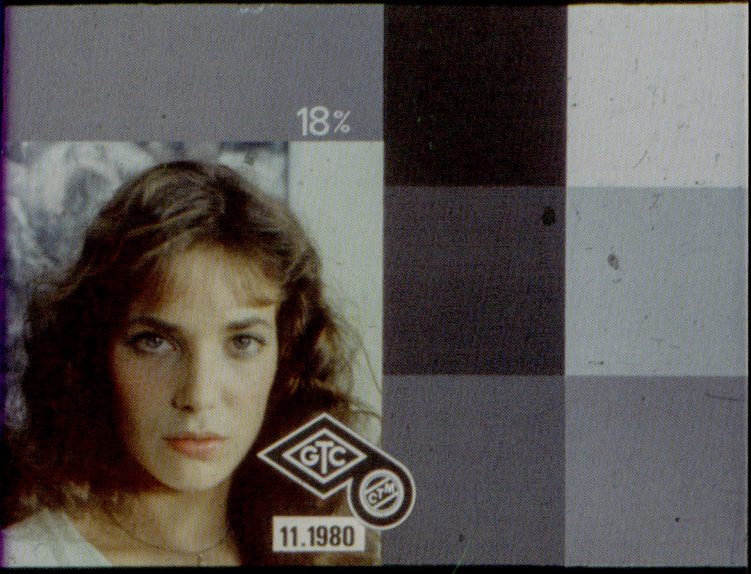
18%
GTC
11.1980

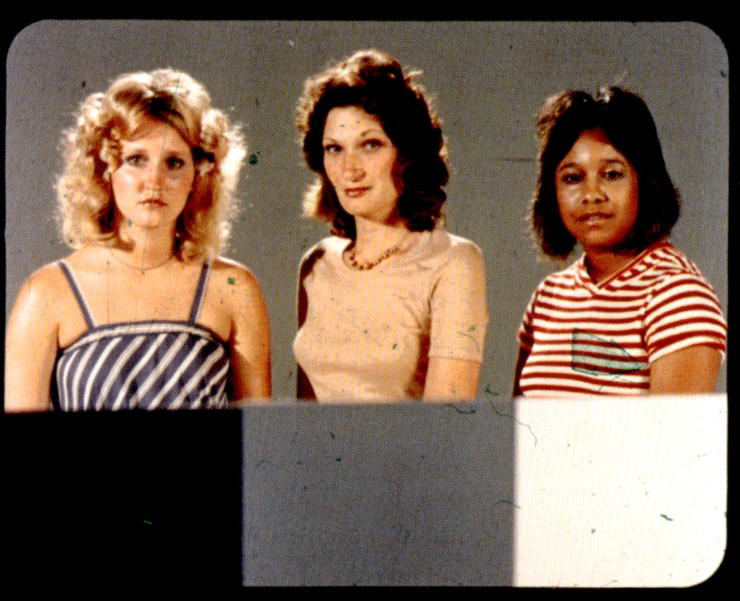

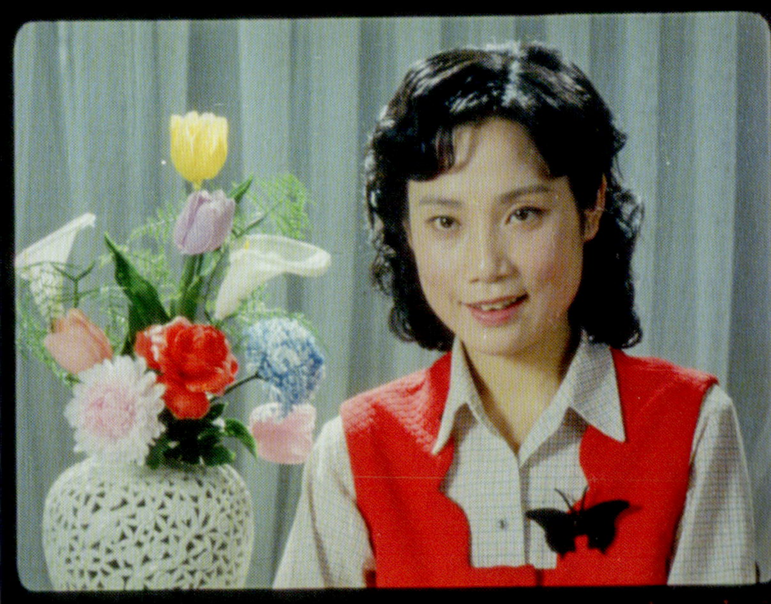

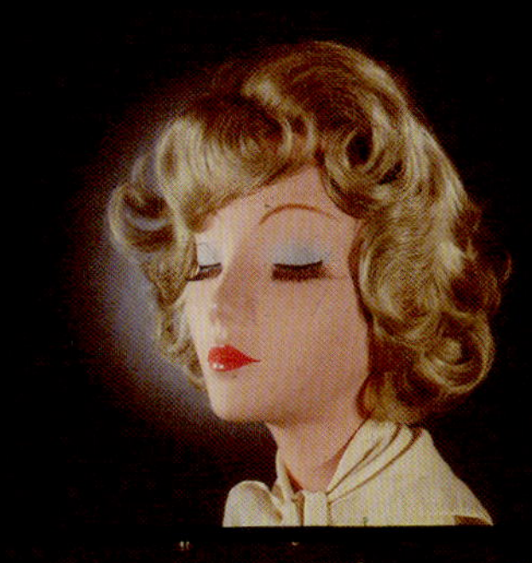

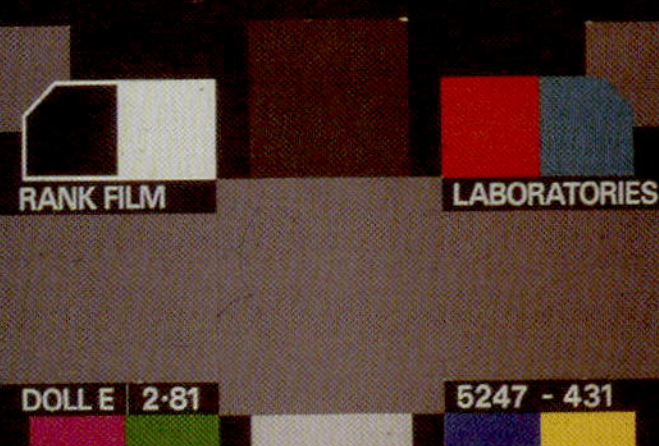
RANK FILM
LABORATORIES
DOLL E
2·81
5247 - 431

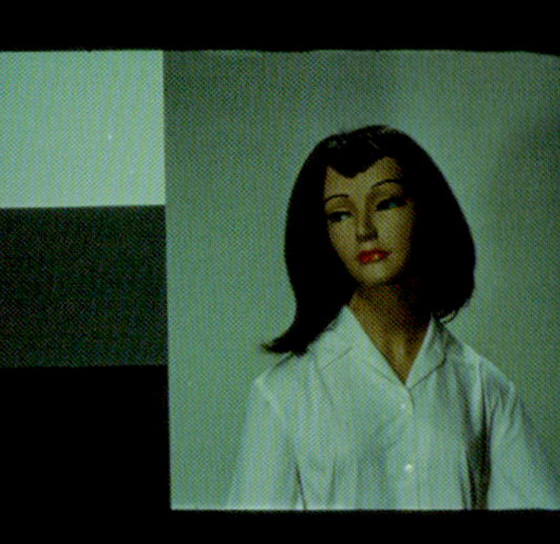

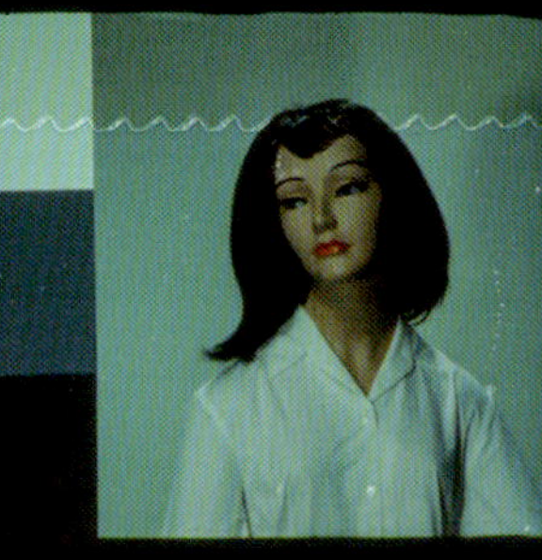

golden age. It wasn't clear to me when we started the project how much variety there was out there. And it was a total mystery whether we would learn anything about them at that time.

SS: Ivy, when did you start contributing to the project?

ID: I started working at Colorlab in Rockville, Maryland, in 2012, just after the Leader Ladies Project started. I don't remember exactly when I became aware of it. But for a long time, all the leader ladies I was seeing at the lab were already part of the project's collection. Once I got to the National Archives, I started seeing more unique examples and sending those in.

RH: I should also say that I ran out of steam at a certain point. Rebecca Lyon has been responsible for the project for much longer than I ever was.

SS: Rebecca Lyon, how has the project evolved in your time there?

RL: As the project grew—we now have over seven hundred images—most of the work was in getting the backlog posted to our website. A few years ago, we made a database to keep track of our collection images as well as the submissions we receive. I try to record things like which film they were spotted on, who sent it, even the film stock or print year. Now about once a month somebody sends me a new one, and I talk to them a little bit and put the image on the website. I'm loath to say anything nice about social media, but our Instagram account opened the door to analog film workers with images to share. It has been a wonderful way to connect with people working in film all over the world.

SS: As I understand it, it's not always a woman in front of the camera. What are some other odd alternatives you've seen?

ID: Occasionally at Colorlab we would make what I would call a novelty LAD. The head of the company once used a picture of his dog as a test image. Every now and then we would make a LAD for fun and take it to conferences. I can totally imagine other labs doing the same thing throughout time.

RH: There's a mascot aspect to them sometimes.

RL: FotoKem, a lab in Los Angeles, has one with an iguana. When you get a 70mm print from them, there's always an iguana on the countdown. There's another lab in Los Angeles that uses a static image of a chimp wearing a Hawaiian shirt.

SS: When you're looking at international examples, does the practice vary based on the location? Can you see one and identify the country of origin, or are they more universal?

RL: We've received them from all over the place. Certain labs do have a distinct look. GTC in France has a very specific aesthetic which I love; the models are very "too cool for school." But other than that, they're more similar than different, really. We've received several from Asia where there's a vase of flowers or a plant next to the woman, and some from Eastern Europe where instead of a person, it's a mannequin or doll. Every country seems to have their own unique way of making them, while still following the standard that Ivy described earlier.

KW: Beyond any kind of variation in national or lab practice, there are still a lot of mysteries, right? Sometimes we look and they're not images that were made for calibration—maybe they're frames cut out of a print that were then used by the lab as calibration images. There are some of Elizabeth Taylor that turn up on prints now and then. So, there are still a lot of questions about the process and where these all came from.

SS: In recent years there's been discussion about film calibration being specific to white skin. We talked about this a little bit already, but is there now more diversity and less voyeurism in leader lady images? Has the industry come up with alternatives to sidestep this problematic aspect of calibration?

RL: I'm not sure about the dates, but I think in the 1980s and '90s you do start to see images where, for example, there are three women of various skin colors.

RH: My perception is that as time goes on, they become less diverse in every sense because the LAD and the digital LAD—Kodak's images—became standard toward the 1990s. Those images feature white women who look like professional models. When I was working on the Leader Ladies Project more intensely, I almost resented them because they were crowding out all the interesting variety I would see while working with older prints. There are examples like the one with the three women here and there, but I don't think it was a progression toward anything. It's almost like chance. I'd love to know who made that image and what they were thinking.

Another thing I want to bring up in the context of talking about skin is the fact that the women in these images are not always wearing a lot of clothes. Some of them are dressed normally, but there's a whole category where you can't even see if they're wearing a shirt. And that's another dimension that is unsettling. In my mind it's related to women's labor and work [and how] that is less valued in the industry.

GY: There's a bit of a pinup girl quality to it.

RH: Yes. Or more that she worked there, and they were *treating* her like a pinup girl. The whole combination was sort of odd but also very fascinating to me when I was collecting the images.

KW: The whole Leader Lady Project has a broader purpose of reclamation. When you think of the history of these images and the places where they were seen, it's no secret that film labs and projection booths were very male spaces where pin-ups would've been unremarkable. It was also unremarkable for projectionists to snip out frames, not of leader ladies but of scenes they thought were hot. The number of times we've gone to booths or met collectors who have personal pinup collections from prints again suggests it was a whole different era—both in terms of respecting the bodily autonomy of women and respecting the physical integrity of film prints. I think that part of the point of the project is to reclaim that history and dig into layers that were not previously discussed.

GY: This idea that a sexualized image of a woman could be attached to any film regardless of the content—it could be a children's film or a cartoon—I find really interesting because a vestige of that culture is literally attached on the print even if you don't necessarily see it.

ID: At the National Archives, we work with a lot of military and government films. Sometimes we'll be working on a stack of films that need to be inspected or digitized for a researcher and that lady might be the only woman we see on screen all day.

KW: As Ivy and Genevieve pointed out earlier, the only thing that is supposed to matter in the LAD is the gray patch that the densitometer reads. It's not supposed to be human-eye readable. So, everything we're talking about and find interesting, all of these variants, is vestigial to the purpose in a modern lab. The practice continues even though there is no technological need for there to be a human subject at all. And so, I find the leader ladies moving. I find them to be about the camraderie of lab people carrying forward a tradition from the earliest days of their profession, for reasons as much mystical and aesthetic as scientific.

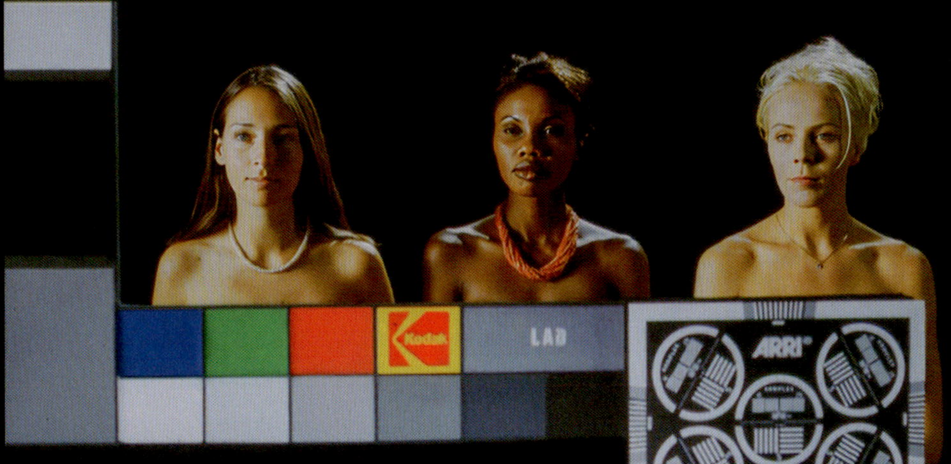

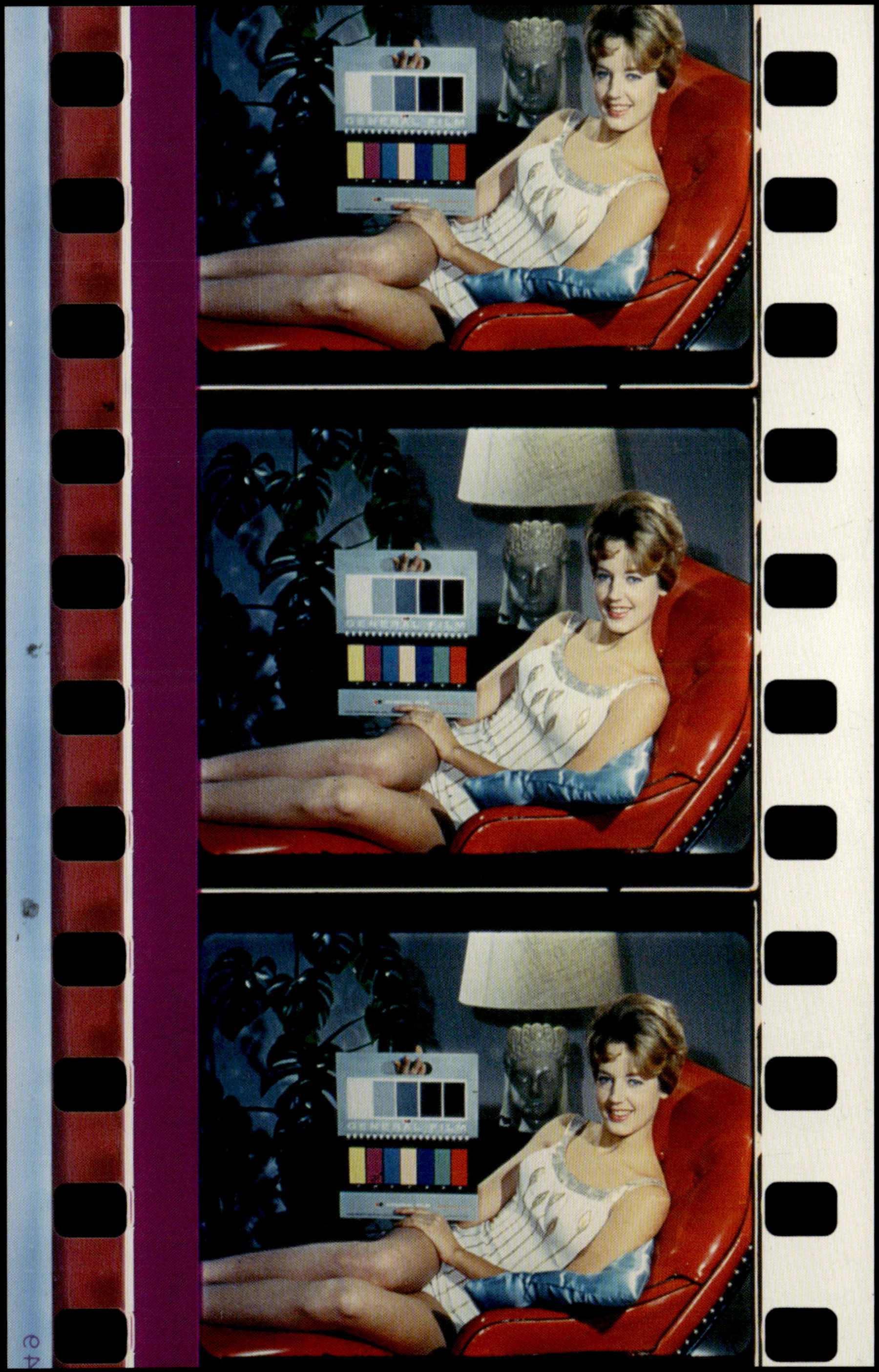

Leader lady images, 1930s–present, submitted to the Chicago Film Society's Leader Ladies Project

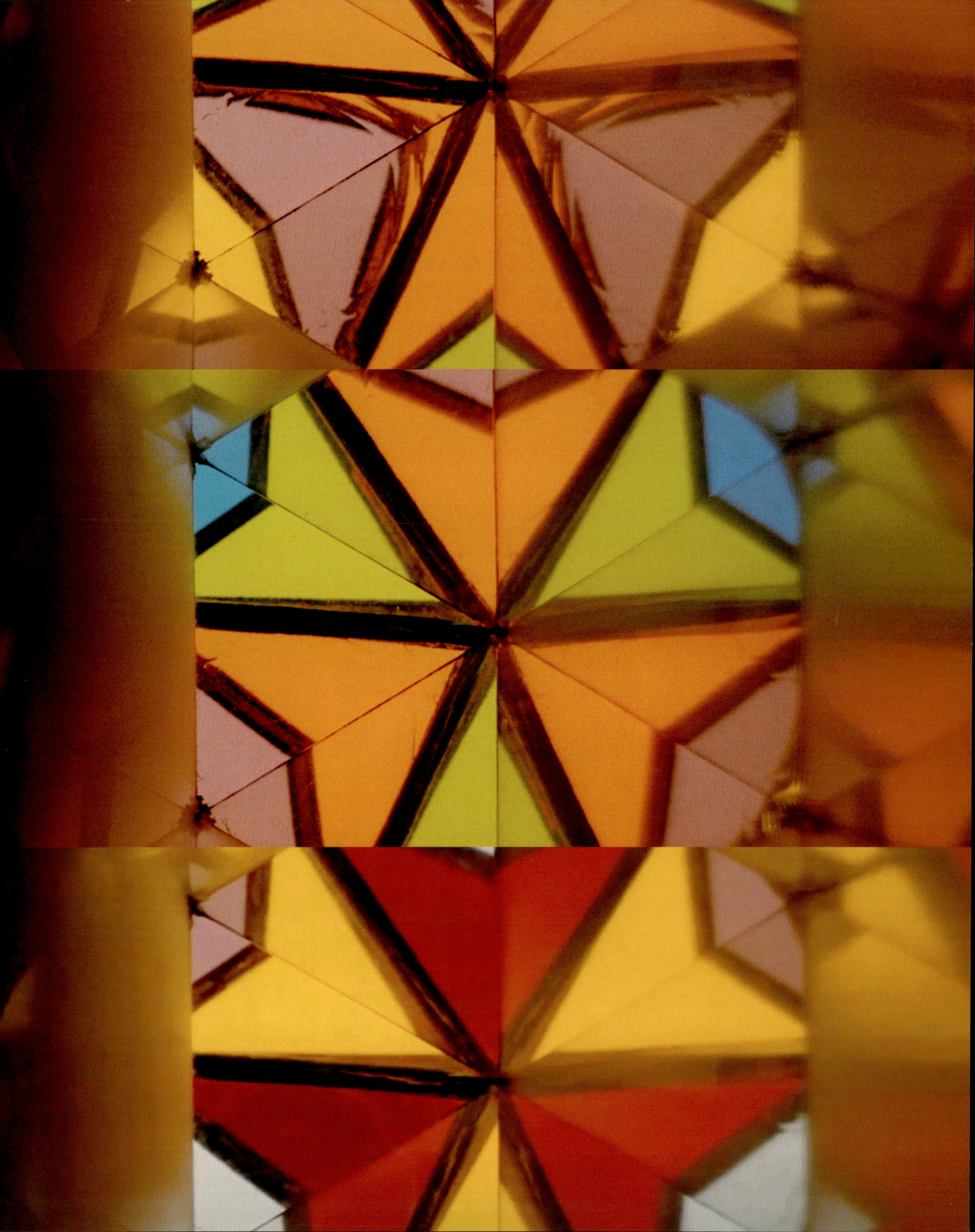

CHROMATIC BLACKNESS

COLOR, RACE, AND THE MOVING IMAGE

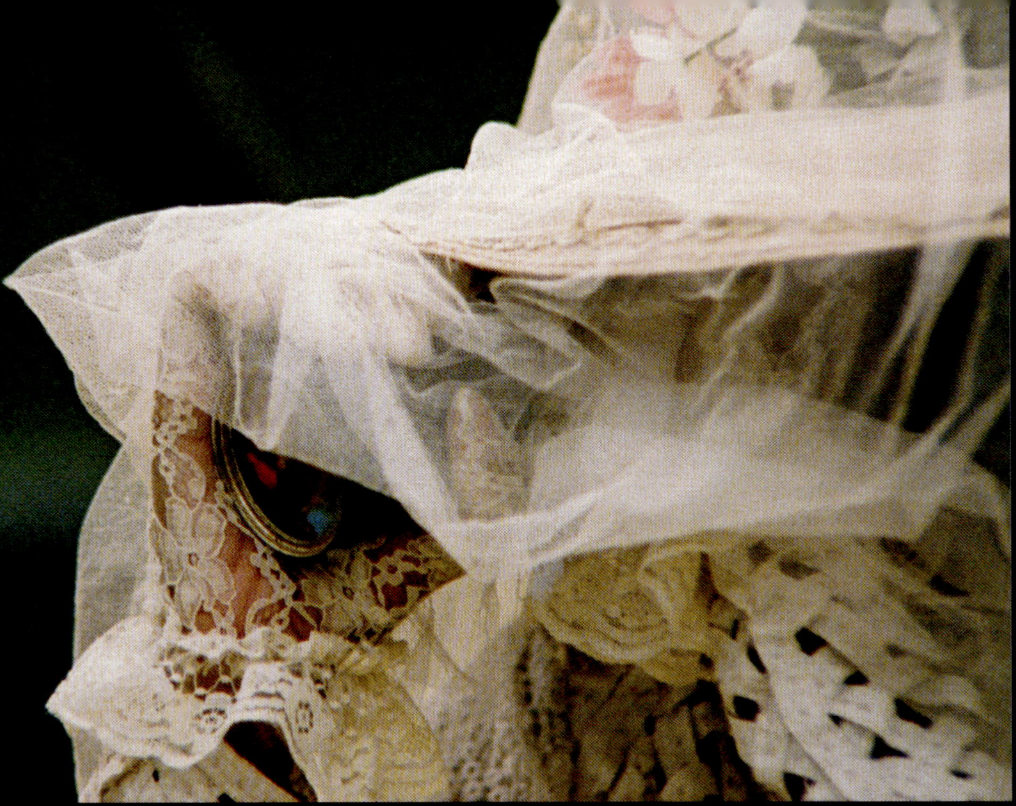

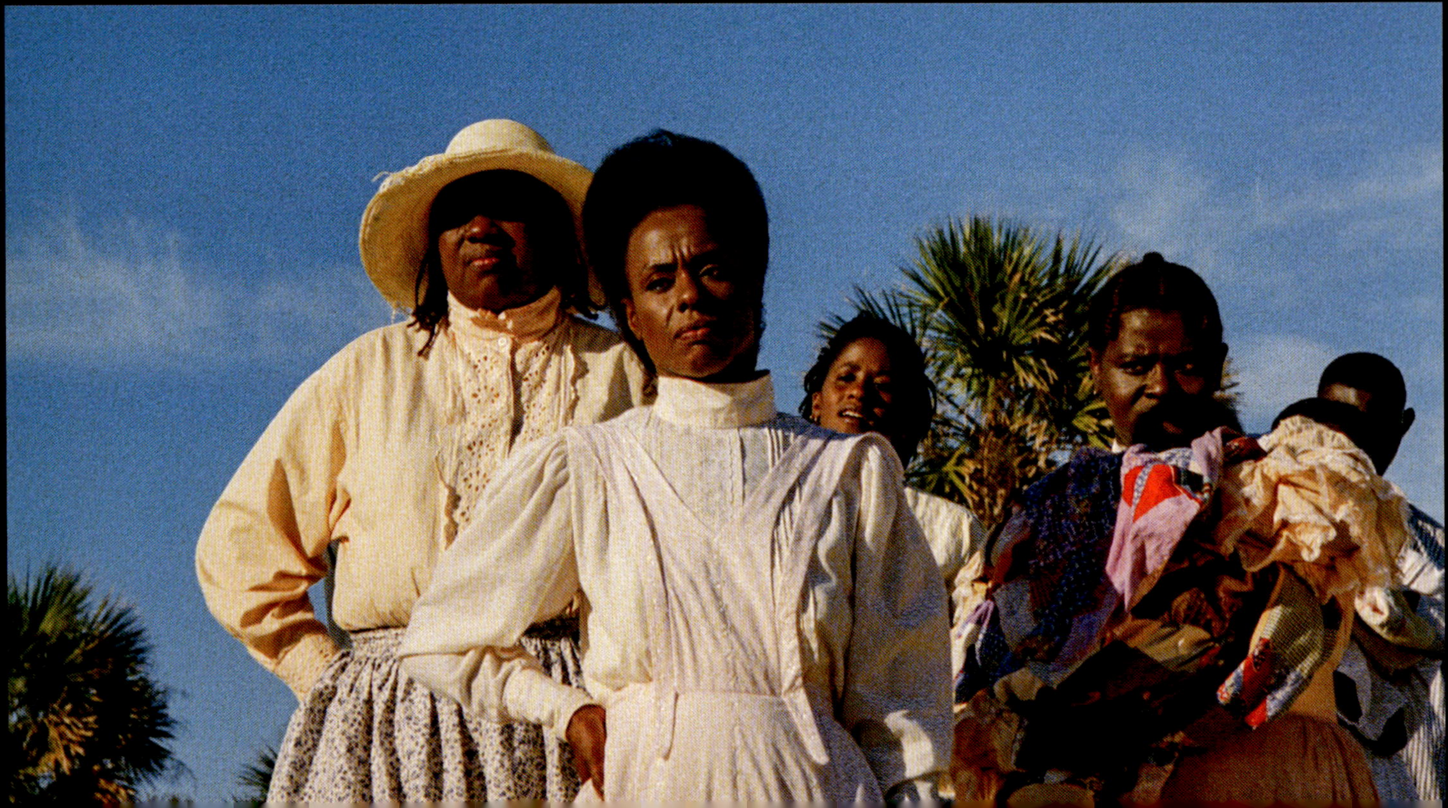

A kaleidoscopic image fills the screen, shifting in hues of reds, oranges, greens, and blues, before cutting to a near-monochromatic image of a woman, Yellow Mary Peazant, framed in close-up and veiled in soft white against a black background. She holds the kaleidoscope to her hidden eye and slowly rotates its end cap. A voice-over from one of her companions explains the kaleidoscope's etymology: "*kalos*, beautiful; *eidos*, form; *skopein*, to view." Such is *Daughters of the Dust*, Julie Dash's revelatory and chromatically rich film from 1991. Famous for its depiction of a matriarchal family, the Peazants—Gullah plantation descendants of enslaved West Africans on the Sea Islands off the coast of Georgia in the early 1900s—the film recounts their final day at Ibo Landing as they gather and prepare to move to the mainland.

These two shots, nine minutes in, draw attention to the importance of color in *Daughters of the Dust*. The abstract wonder of the kaleidoscope is motivated by the ensuing chiaroscuro, black-and-white framing of Yellow Mary holding it. It is a secret world of color that the optical device conjures, just as Dash and her cinematographer, Arthur Jafa, along with their remarkable collaborators, bring this hidden world of color to the cinematic screen. The cinema, like the kaleidoscope, is a device of prismatic wonder.

Yet, the sensuous hues in *Daughters of the Dust* are laden with deeply ambivalent histories, just as color technologies, kaleidoscopes, and the cinema are anything but transparent. Their sedimented histories require decolonization: an unpacking of their colonial and anti-Black pasts as well as aesthetic and political reconfiguration. While color dazzles throughout the film—from these shots to the resplendent naturalistic hues of the Gullah landscape to the folk art that abounds on the walls and property of the mise-en-scène—it is also a haunting, scarring substance for the Peazants. The primary crop the family tended when enslaved was indigo, and its blue dye still stains the hands of Nana Peazant, the matriarch of the family. Indigo was a colonial commodity intricately entwined with chattel slavery. In the seventeenth and eighteenth centuries, it was transplanted from India and Africa to the New World, facilitating the rise of the plantation economy.[1] Enslaved West Africans brought their expertise in cultivating and processing indigo to the colonies, turning the crop into the most lucrative of colonial exports. It was even used as currency in the transatlantic slave trade, where processed indigo could be exchanged directly as payment. Due to the heavy metals used in its processing, the colorant was also toxic to handle. This material history of indigo is famously foregrounded in *Daughters of the Dust* when, halfway through, the film flashes back to the Peazants' ancestors processing it on the plantation, stirring boiling vats of dye, coloring fabric, and shaping the dyestuff into molds. Like Nana, their hands are stained blue. As Dash has recounted, the recurrence of blue on various objects throughout the film

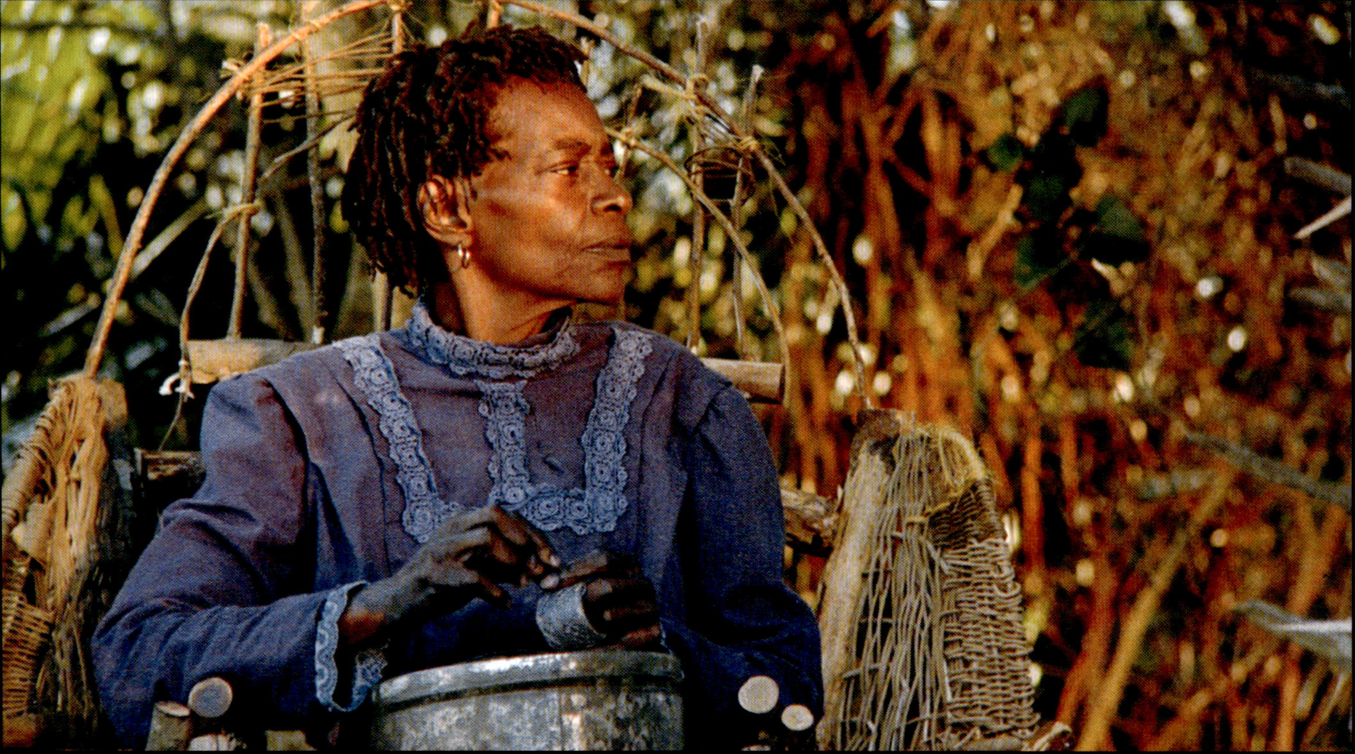

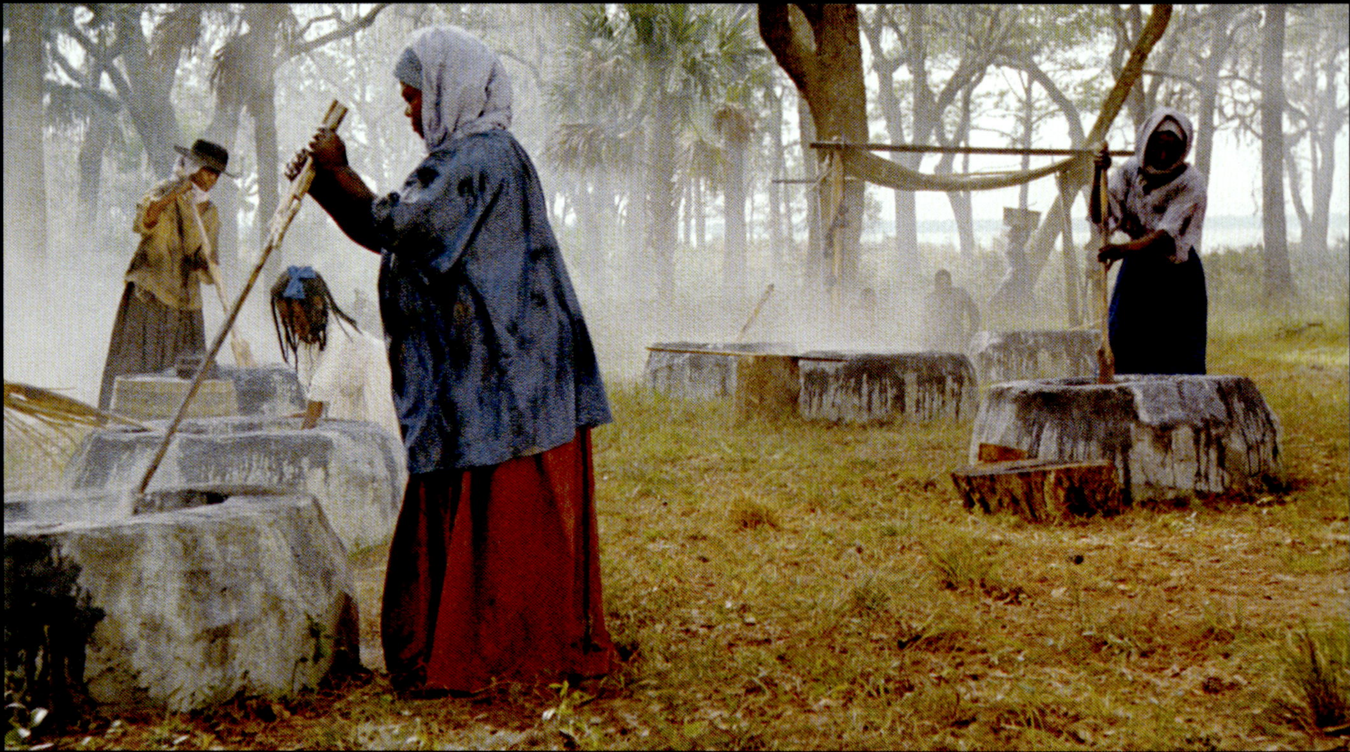

"is my way of signifying slavery, as opposed to whipmarks or scars, images which have lost their power. Processing the indigo plant was an African practice that became poisonous when transferred to the new world. The colour is a trace like a scar."[2]

If the materiality of color in *Daughters of the Dust* has a racialized history, so, too, does the technology of color cinema. Dash and Jafa initially filmed on Agfa-Gevaert negative but, due to budgetary constraints, made release prints on Kodak Eastmancolor stock without properly color grading for the transition, which in part led to a murkiness in the colors. The problem also went beyond poor analog grading to the very stocks themselves: as Dash contends, Agfa-Gevaert reproduces Black skin tones better, as it "reads warm in the shadow areas. Kodak film stock is blue/green in shadows. It reads black people as shadows, so they look blue or green."[3] It was only with the 2K digital restoration by the Cohen Media Group in 2016 that this was corrected. Overseen by archivist Tim Lanza, who worked closely with Dash and Jafa, the restoration used an original internegative (a duplicate negative created to produce release prints) and, through a digital intermediate process, was able to enhance the vibrancy of the hues as Dash and Jafa originally intended, allowing the new prints to capture "the variety of African-American skin tones."[4]

As *Daughters of the Dust* illuminates, color is one of the most complex and expansive materials to grapple with. In the moving image, color can both structure "a beautiful form to view" and expose its inherent ambivalences. Through its kaleidoscopic hues, *Daughters of the Dust* serves as an entry point for exploring the intersections of color and race in cinema, specifically related to the chromatic nature of Blackness on screen.

"BLACK IS FULLY CHROMATIC"

Dash provides several ways for understanding the technical relationship between color and race. Historically, the tonal sensitivities of film have not often been calibrated for non-white skin tones. Further, the material dyestuffs and corresponding aesthetics of color have deeply embedded colonial roots—indigo being the most well known, but colonial colorants like cochineal red and Indian yellow also saturated the Global North. Dash is far from alone in these critiques. As John Akomfrah, British artist and cofounder of the Black Audio Film Collective, has recounted:

> a long-running discussion in black film circles firstly about the inherent "biases" of most film stocks and secondly on the way in which film processing laboratories, set up to process these stocks, worked with a "correct exposure truth" which increasingly worked against appropriate black skin tones.... what film stocks should we use for black skin? Out of the primary hues which formed the base of most film stocks, should we choose the one characterized by the red (Kodak), the blue (Fuji), or the brown (Agfa)?[5]

Additionally, Larry Clark, another director like Dash central to the L.A. Rebellion film movement, carried out detailed film stock tests for skin tone sensitivity in the 1970s, when he was a student at UCLA. Using Kodak, Fuji, and Ilford stocks, he filmed three African American test models (including Dash) of varying complexions under different lighting situations with each of the stocks. He found at the time that Fuji "had better shadow detail," which "really showed people of color more flattering[ly]" because it drew out the depths of their skin tone better.[6] As he, Akomfrah, and Dash make clear, the particular tonal sensitivities of film stocks are only a partial aspect of accurate racial reproduction; it also requires calibrating lighting, costuming, and the mise-en-scène, in addition to careful lab work.[7] Scholars such as James Snead, Brian Winston, and Richard Dyer undertook key studies of the color sensitivities and racial biases of the filmic apparatus in their seminal works of the 1980s and 1990s, and, building on these studies, Lorna Roth has been researching the cultural intersections of color balance and racism across a variety of media.[8]

As these examples suggest, in examining color it is necessary to interrogate the racial horizon of color technology to, as Kirsty Sinclair Dootson has incisively put it, "recognise the intimate connections between the politics of colour-as-hue and the politics of colour-as-race."[9] Throughout its history, color has always been a technology of race that organizes and structures power. For instance, the spiritual and formal purity of classical statuary was celebrated in the Renaissance and Enlightenment, elevating the assumed whiteness of these marbles while ignoring their faded colors to mythologize a Eurocentric racial hierarchy.[10] Color also exemplifies the interconnection of Enlightenment rationality with colonial expansion. Just as colonial networks led to the growth of the colorant industry through the rise of plantation labor, particularly with indigo crops in the New World, Enlightenment writings on aesthetics pressed increasingly for strict control over the allures of color.[11] For thinkers from Goethe to Kant to Charles Blanc, preference for vivid color was a hallmark of the colonized, of the so-called primitive cultures who were easily swayed by bright, vulgar colors—the very colorants being extracted through colonial labor and chattel slavery. To control color allows for the promotion of rationality over sensuality, of genteel taste cultures, and of the domination of colonized people of color.

But the anti-Indigenous and anti-Black racism inherent to this aesthetic paradigm is only a partial history of color, a subject that has always been multivalent. Even as particular technologies, hues, and practices are embedded with racial biases, with effort they can be reworked and decolonized. Take, for instance, the paintings of Kerry James Marshall, works renowned for their dynamic and lustrous imaging of Black figures and of Blackness. The skin tones of his subjects are deep black, appearing absolute in their depth. Yet these blacks are not monotone in hue: they are saturated with color. Marshall mixes his black pigments with various colors to provide dimensionality and range, yet without diluting or lightening the blacks through the addition of white. Marshall has noted of these mixtures that "the black is fully chromatic."[12] Marshall was also the production designer for *Daughters of the Dust*, and there are shared aesthetic and political concerns among Marshall, Dash, and Jafa in deploying color to depict the immense range, complexity, and beauty of Blackness in their works. Indeed, they encapsulate the diverse aesthetic labor of many Black artists and filmmakers who liberate color across an expansive range of media.

MOVING COLORS

Such reconfigurations of color intersect with a broader question raised by Akomfrah regarding the future of the moving image: "How do you literally re-align the skin of film with the skin of the diasporic subject?"[13] Dee Rees's *Pariah* (USA, 2011), Barry Jenkins's *Moonlight* (USA, 2016), and Mati Diop's *Atlantics* (*Atlantique*, France/Senegal/Belgium, 2019) are three recent films that have dynamized the possibilities of color design and aesthetics. Each is an award-winning exemplar of contemporary Black cinema, of global art cinema, and to varying degrees of queer cinema (implicitly with *Atlantics*, as Rosalind Galt argues regarding the mutability of gender and desire imagined in the film), and their color designs exemplify these modes.[14] *Pariah* and *Moonlight* are explicitly queer coming-of-age stories following the struggles of Alike in Brooklyn and Chiron in Miami, respectively, as they confront homophobia from family and peers. *Atlantics* is set in Dakar and centers on Ada, a young woman whose lover, Souleiman, drowns at sea while en route to Europe to seek work. He returns as a djinn, or more specifically a Senegalese *faru rab* (lover spirit), to be with her. *Pariah* was filmed on Kodak 35mm negatives, while *Moonlight* and *Atlantics* were filmed digitally, and each went through extensive color grading that dynamized their final look. Indeed, color design serves as an aesthetic fulcrum for the cultural and political work of each film. Their final shots will be my focus here, both for concision and because closing images often bear such narrative and aesthetic weight. All three films end with their main character in medium close-up, staring thoughtfully off screen or into the camera. These parallel looks are, at a basic level, reflexive, summative moments for the viewer to consider both what has unfolded and what may come next. These moments are also lush with color.

The concluding sequence of *Pariah* is crosscut through a complex layering of shots and sound bridges: Alike's fraught parting with her mother, who refuses to accept her sexuality; her reading an emotional final poem in class, her words providing a diegetic voice-over across the intercut sequence; her father packing up her room and driving her to the bus station, where she says her goodbyes; her boarding the bus; and the final framing of her in her seat. As she watches the city pass by through the window, she wipes away a tear. This is crosscut back to the classroom as she finishes the poem, before returning to the final shot on the bus, which holds on Alike for a forty-second-long take. A subtle smile flashes across her face, as the light dramatically shifts across the duration of the shot: seemingly filmed at the golden hour, the light streams intermittently into the bus, creating a dappled play of light and shadow across Alike's face that dynamizes her skin tones, from overexposed to deep shadow to radiant and glowing. In the final moments, an abstract wash of colors superimposes over the frame, light lavender followed by streaks of in-camera lens flare that intermittently wash out the image in a range of pastels and white, illuminating her new beginning, just as the film cuts to its end credits.[15]

Rees and cinematographer Bradford Young collaborated with colorist Joe Gawler, working then at Deluxe Laboratories, on the digital intermediate to achieve this range of hues. The vibrant yet subtle play of colors in the scene is central to the overall working of the film. Further, Rees and Young are well aware of the technical and aesthetic difficulties that people of color face when working with technologies of color. Young has spoken incisively about the racial biases of moving-image technology. In response to a question about the remarkable ways in which they lit and photographed Black skin tones in the film, Young notes that he and Rees "come from a long tradition of Black people who have been very aware of why it is important to have a certain acumen and a certain rigor

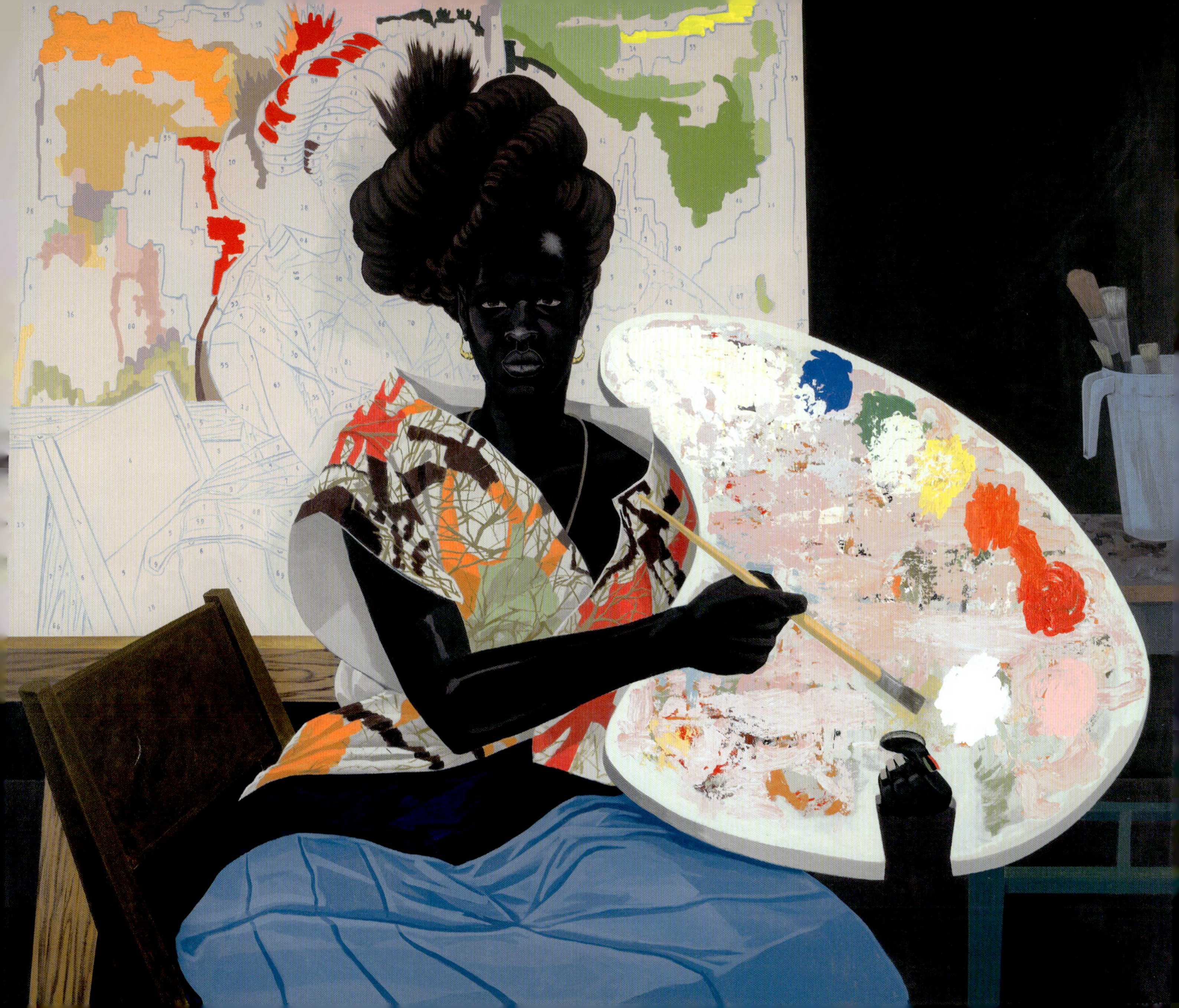

when it comes to photographing Black people." While film stocks have improved, "All of these pieces of technology have a bias. Some of them have intentional biases; some of them have unintentional biases, but whatever it is, it never worked out for Black people. So we knew we had to get within the bias to figure out our sweet spot."[16] This meant calibrating *Pariah*'s mise-en-scène tightly, carefully balancing the lighting, costuming, and setting values to enhance a variety of Black skin tones, as well as collaborating closely on the digital intermediate process. Far from static, color's "sweet spot" in the film shifts dynamically across scenes—from deeply saturated queer club scenes to the resplendent concluding shot—and this variability illuminates the characters' diverse skin tones in a multitude of ways. The rigor and acumen demonstrated by Young and Rees through this color work provides one realignment of the skin on film.

With the closing shot of *Moonlight*, the film cuts back from the intimate embrace of the adult Chiron and his childhood friend Kevin, after just reuniting, to Chiron as a boy at the beach at night. The flashback recalls an earlier scene in which Chiron's mentor, Juan, taught him to swim. As with *Pariah*, *Moonlight*'s final shot is a concluding long take: a twenty-second zoom from medium long shot to medium close-up that centers Chiron. He initially stares out to the ocean with his back to the camera, and as the zoom comes to an end, he turns to look into the camera. Blueness saturates the mise-en-scène, conveying darkness and literalizing the title of Tarell Alvin McCraney's unfinished play from which the film was adapted, *In Moonlight Black Boys Look Blue*.

Blue in the film's final shot both evokes the sadness that inhabits Chiron's character, as he grapples with his sexuality as well as homophobic abuse, and saturates the lush blackness of his skin. Indeed, blue is the key color of the film, and Jenkins and cinematographer James Laxton worked with digital colorist Alex Bickel at Color Collective to add blues into the blacks of the film without lightening them. *Moonlight* is divided into three chapters to mark different ages of Chiron's life. To visualize this, Bickel used digital LUTs (short for "look up tables," which are presets for color grading) during post-production to emulate a distinct color stock for each section, that gave each a particular feel and texture. The film opens with Chiron as a young boy in Fujicolor, providing a warmer glow to the childhood scenes. When Chiron is a teenager, it shifts to the greenish-blue hues of Agfacolor. And for the final chapter, with Chiron as a young man, it changes to Kodak, which is vibrant and less "restrained," adding more "pop and shine" to the image, as Bickel explains. He further adjusted each LUT to better reproduce Black skin tones.[17] As is evident in the final shot, this emphasis on capturing the diverse vitality of Black skin resonates with Kerry James Marshall's color palette. Indeed, Jenkins has discussed their overlapping interests in color:

> I love his thoughts and work for his use of blackness and the black form while keeping white pigmentation out of his black colors. Now, I had not read Kerry James Marshall's ideas about blackness and color before I made *Moonlight*. But reading him I saw a lot about the approach we took and how we treated black skin in this film. When you're on a Hollywood set, or any movie set, the makeup person has powder and they powder you down so you don't reflect light. You can't be shiny. You can't be moist. Fuck that ... because my memory of this place I grew up in is of shiny, moist, basically revitalizing and replenishing and alive skin.[18]

Skin that is black and glistening, undiluted, yet also refracting color in the moist humidity of the mise-en-scène: to be blue, or not, to be Black and queer in one's chromatic skin is what is posed, and meticulously dialed-in digitally, when Chiron turns to look the viewer in the eye.

With *Atlantics*, Ada seemingly looks directly into the camera in the final shot for a sustained eight-second-long take. Through the closing montage, it becomes apparent that the image is in fact structured through a mirror. In the previous shot—after waking and dressing in the beachside club where she had reunited the night before with Souleiman, as a faru rab spirit possessing the body of another man—she turns to look into a mirrored wall behind her. Thus, the gaze of her direct address is to herself as much as it is to the viewer. A subtly warm, tungsten-yellow hue suffuses the image, a color temperature that is used for most of the daytime scenes in the film, which contrasts with the deep blues and electric greens that dominate the film's night scenes. Diop worked with cinematographer Claire Mathon and colorist Gilles Granier of Le Labo, in Paris, to construct this contrasting color scheme: the warm daylight scenes were filmed with a RED Dragon camera, whereas the nighttime scenes of blue and green were filmed with a more sensitive Panasonic Cinema VariCam, known for its lowlight capabilities.[19]

The split hues for day and night are important for the nightclub and its mirrors. In the night, blue infuses the mise-en-scène, while streaming LED club lights radiate green patterns throughout the space. As Galt notes, the green lights convey the supernatural world of the film: they "render cinematically

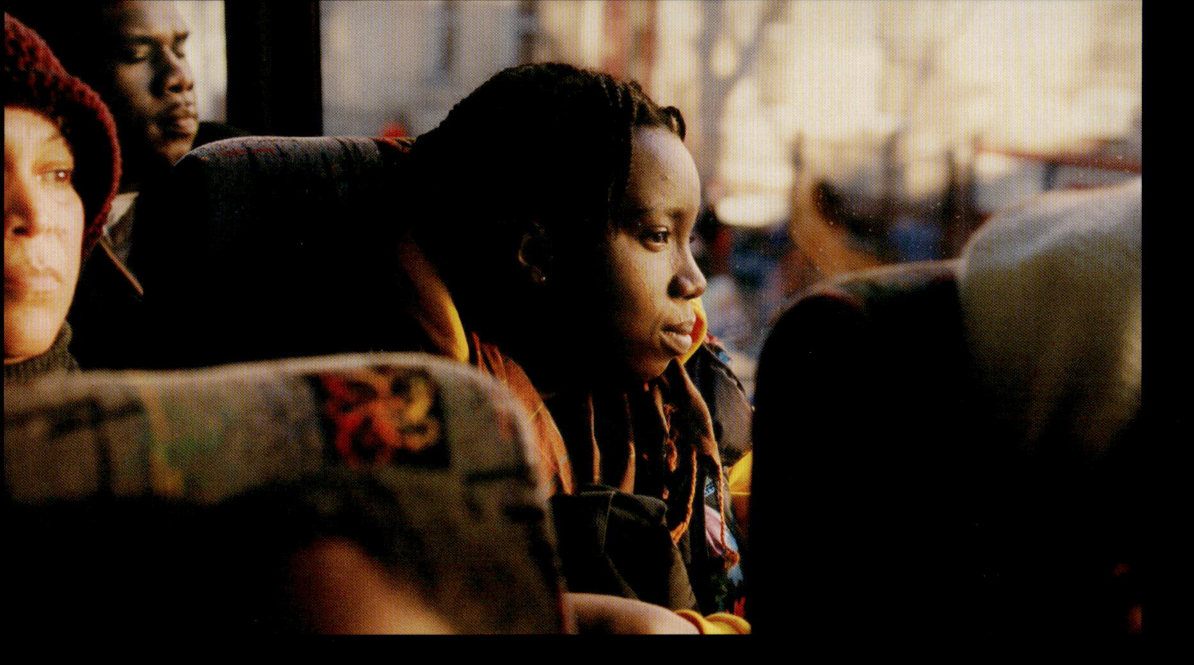

TOP: *Pariah* (USA, 2011, dir. Dee Rees)

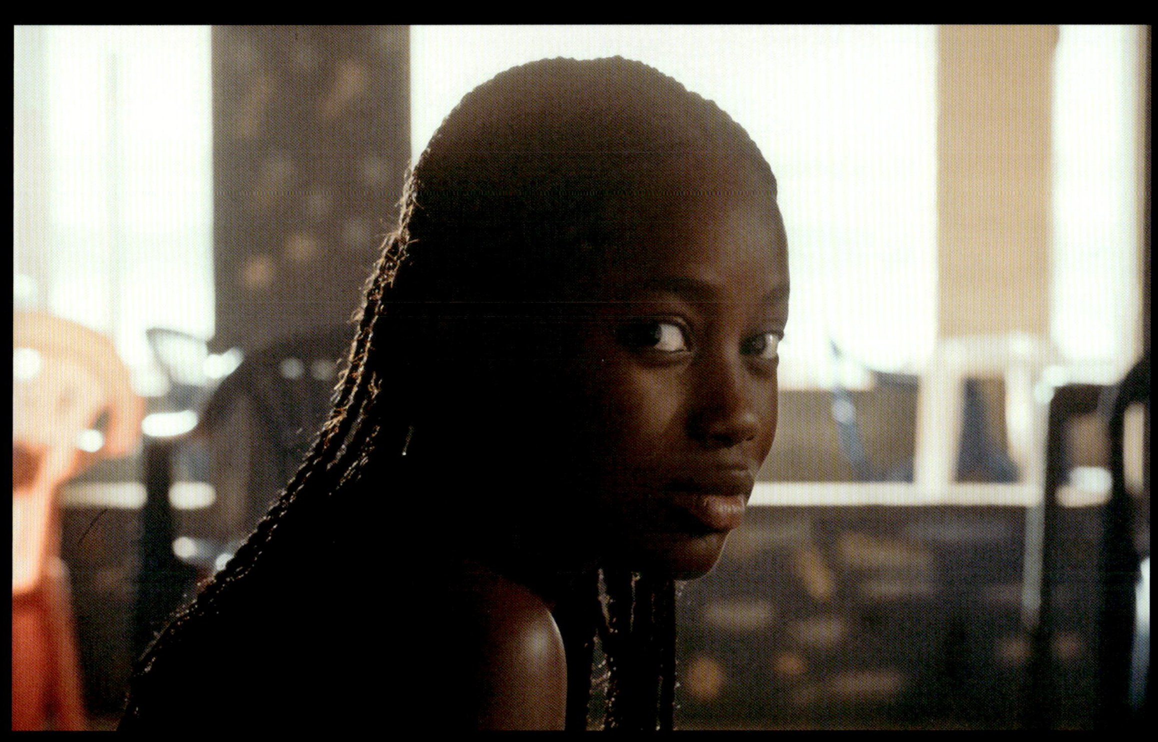

CENTER: *Atlantics* (*Atlantique*, France/Senegal/Belgium, 2019, dir. Mati Diop)

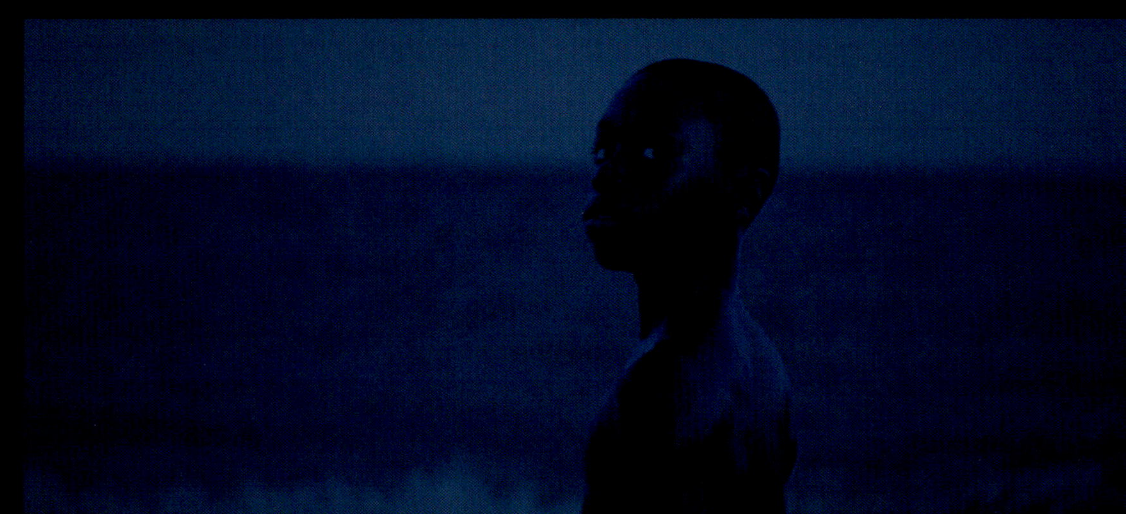

BOTTOM: *Moonlight* (USA, 2016 dir. Barry Jenkins)

what is written on the body in the forms of haunting."[20] She refers to the physical possessions that take place at night: Souleiman inhabiting the body of another. In the radiant dance hall, one can see Ada and the other man embrace when filmed directly, but against the mirror, with green lights shimmering across their bodies, one sees the reflected image of Souleiman closely embracing her. This doubling of bodies evokes for the postcolonial subject the beloved, ghostly presence of loss, rooted in the Black trauma of transatlantic crossings both past and recent, while also beckoning to new possibilities.

In the morning, Souleiman is gone, and in the final shot, we find Ada staring into the mirrored camera in shallow focus with low-key lighting. She is lit primarily by the warm morning light streaming in from the windows behind her that overlook the ocean, the sound of waves filling the sonic background. As in the previous examples, her complexion is radiant. She speaks over the closing montage in voice-over narration for the first and only time in the film: "Some memories are omens. Last night will stay with me, to remind me who I am ... [*cut to final shot*] and show me who I will become. Ada to whom the future belongs [*cut to black*]. I am Ada." This language of futurity, of coming of age and self-realization, speaks elegantly to the work of the film. Reflected in the morning warmth of the mirror, the past both infuses these colors but also does not restrain their potential future in the black slate of what is to come. Blackness in the final moment is not an absence but, rather, an assemblage that absorbs all colors and memories, opening them to the future.

These concluding examples each point to the intensive work that contemporary Black filmmakers are carrying out with color. Technically, aesthetically, and politically astute, they also point to a broader zone of inquiry regarding the history and ongoing exploration of chromatic Blackness. These engagements with color are of necessity ambivalent and critical, given the immense technical and cultural biases embedded into the material structure of color, but they are also saturated with possibility.

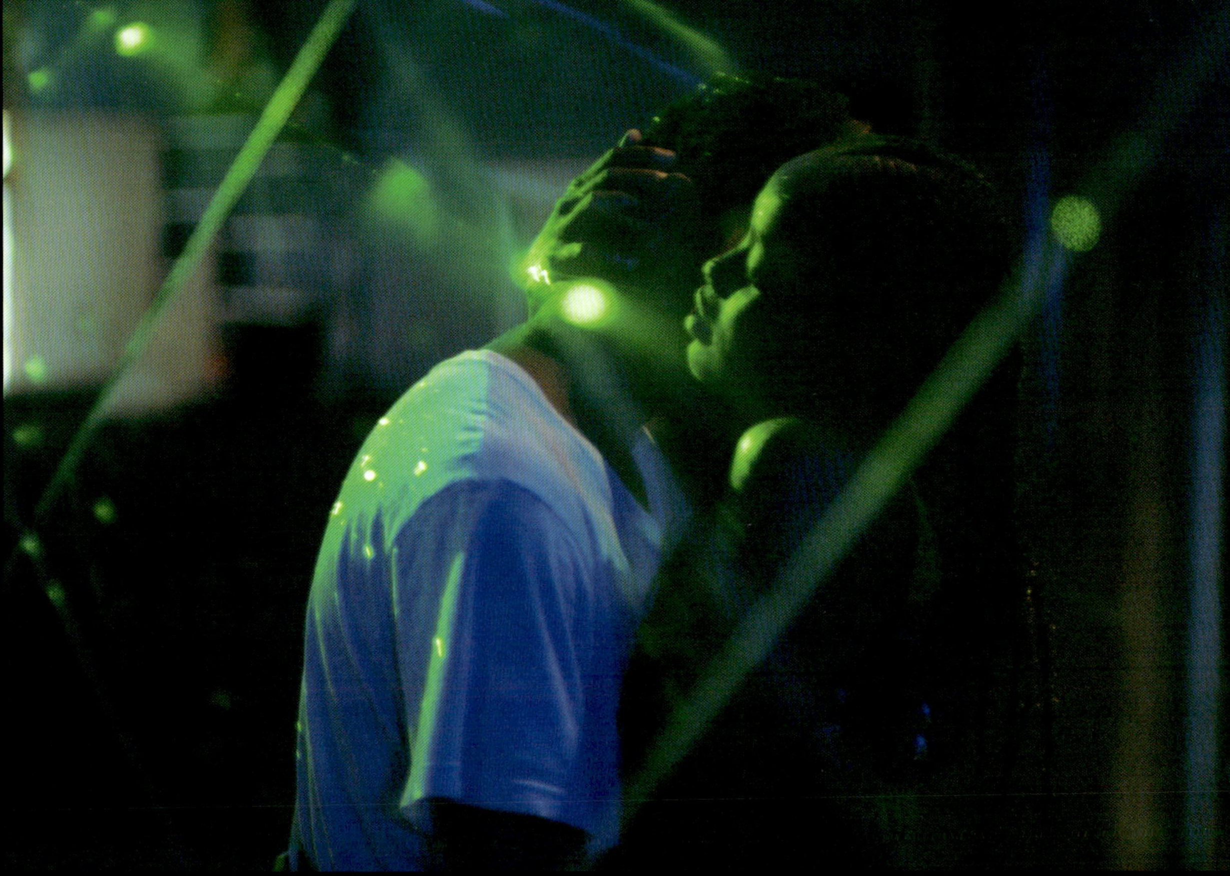

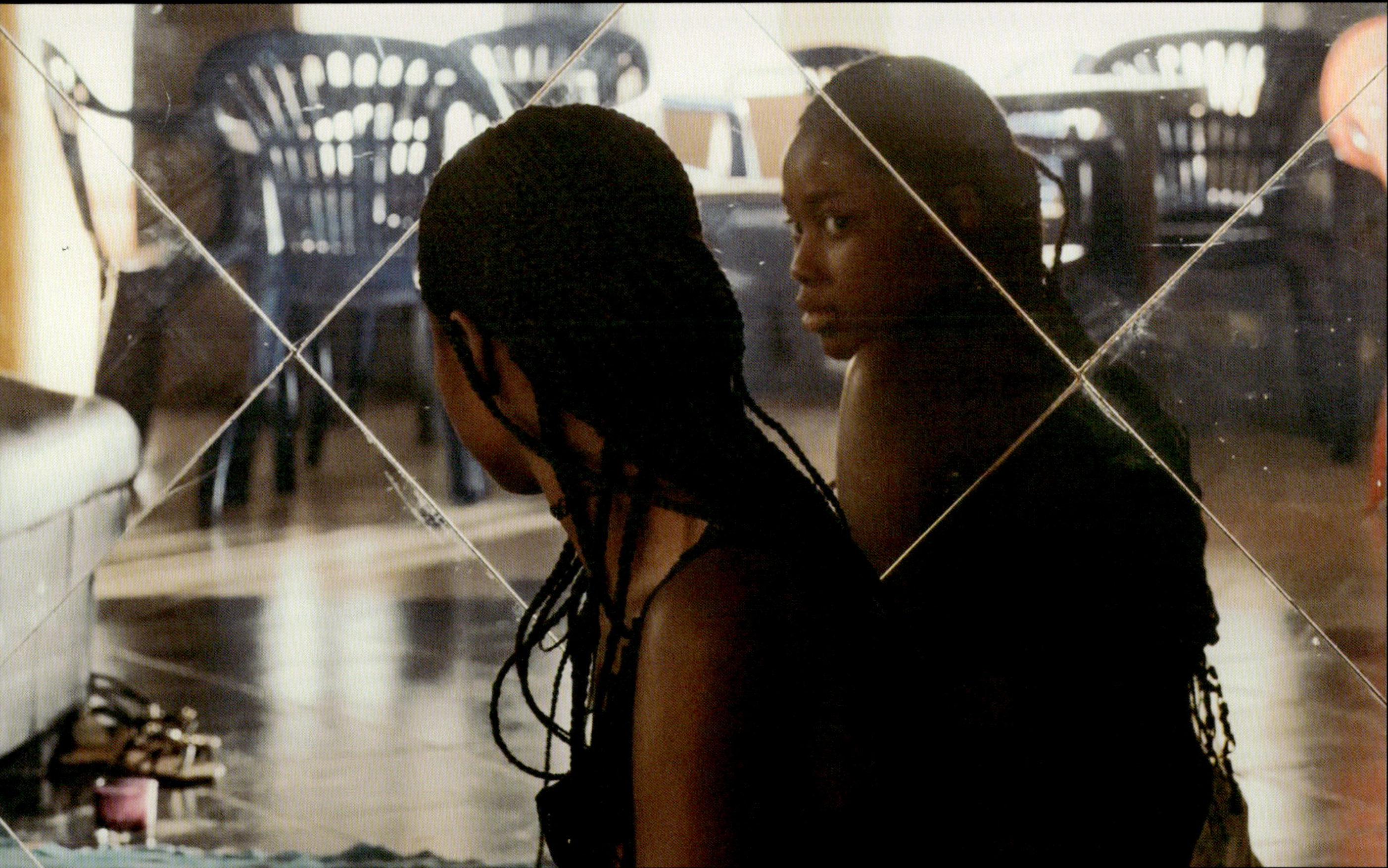

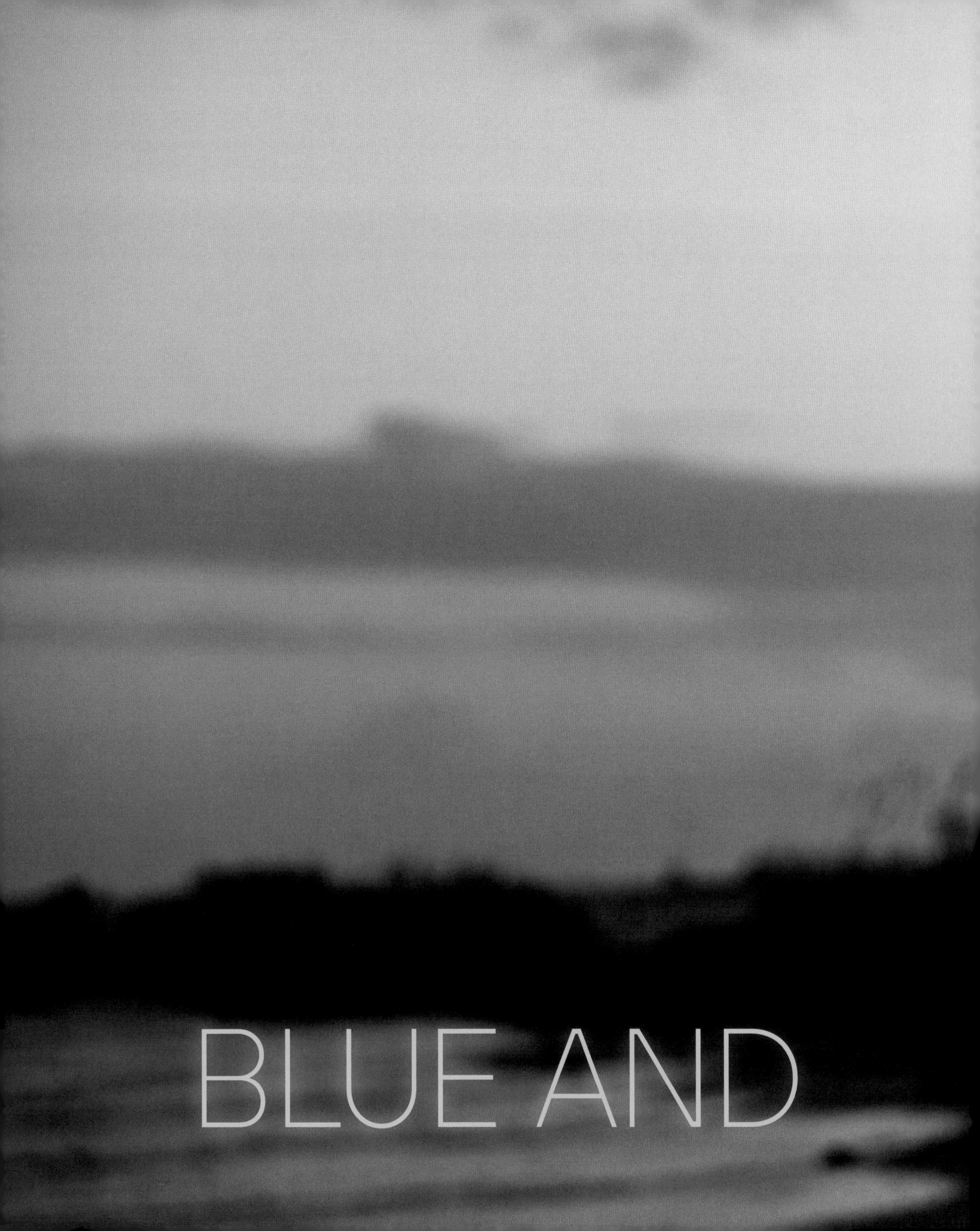

BLUE AND

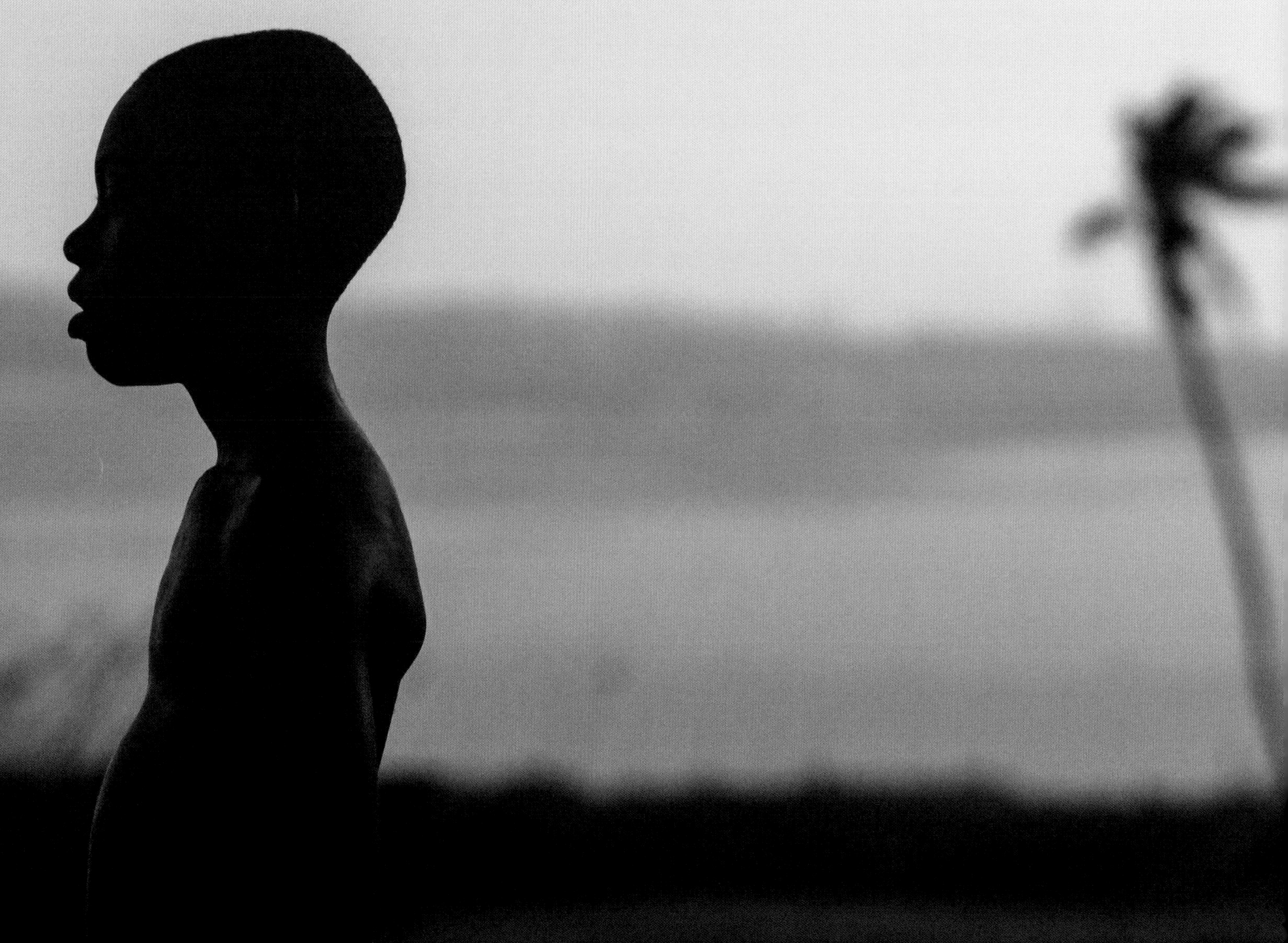

MOONLIGHT

Moonlight (USA, 2016) was a critical and commercial success celebrated for its poignant depiction of the life of Chiron, a young Black kid growing up in the Liberty City neighborhood of Miami. Based on a play by Tarell Alvin McCraney and directed by Barry Jenkins, Chiron's story is told in three chapters—childhood (in which he is played by Alex Hibbert), adolescence (Ashton Sanders), and early adulthood (Trevante Rhodes); each features different saturated colors and film stock aesthetics developed by cinematographer James Laxton and colorist Alex Bickel to both distinguish and connect the different sections.

Most prominent in Jenkins's color palette is blue, particularly as it is established in the first chapter, where seven-year-old Chiron (then known as Little) struggles to define his identity and sexuality as he copes with bullying from other kids and a neglectful and abusive mother, Paula (Naomie Harris). He finds some solace in his friendships with parental stand-ins Juan (Mahershala Ali) and Teresa (Janelle Monáe) and schoolmate Kevin (Jaden Piner). The section was shot to mimic the warm colors and detailed textures of Fujicolor film and is dominated by shades of blue: Juan's car, Little's backpack, his school's walls, his mother's nurse uniform, Liberty City's buildings, classmates' clothes, and the interior of Little's house all contribute to the dreamlike and at times monochromatic aesthetic. Blues saturate the world, pushing the imagery to underscore McCraney's original vision of Miami as a "beautiful nightmare."[1] To capture the sun-drenched, tropical feel of Florida, Laxton shot in high contrast, while Bickel approached his work "in three distinct steps: create a nice thick color by pulling information out of the mid-tones, add blue to the blacks, and tease out the highlights so there's white glint that's on top of the image."[2]

In early silent cinema, blue tinting and toning were often used to signify nighttime, but as palettes evolved with new color technologies, other associations became linked, including tranquility, isolation, introspection, and sadness. (Of course, "feeling blue" being synonymous with melancholy enforces this color psychology.) In *Moonlight*, blue has multiple levels of meaning that further the story's themes. The title of McCraney's play, *In Moonlight Black Boys Look Blue*, is employed as a line said by Juan in recounting a memory to Chiron as he teaches him to swim in the ocean. The sentiment has multiple meanings and interpretations, but most notably the film ends with a shot of young Chiron standing on the beach in the moonlight, the image entirely saturated in blue. His character is often associated with water, perhaps suggesting his fluid and evolving sense of self.

Being "blue" can also be read in a variety of different ways, and the color often appears in significant moments for Chiron. This emphasis in the first chapter of the movie associates blue with the vulnerability and rawness of childhood. However, contrasting reds increasingly appear in key scenes of emotional distress, for example as his mom continues to struggle with addiction, her blue nursing attire switching to red tank tops. In the second chapter the palette, which was given a greenish-blue hue to mimic Agfacolor film, drastically shifts, its costumes and set design consisting of yellows, reds, and oranges, further indicating the alienation experienced by Chiron during his adolescence as the bullying intensifies, Juan has passed away, and his mother's state continues to deteriorate. The third chapter uses a modified Kodak stock, continuing to feature high-contrast images but a more neutral color palette overall. An exception to this is in the reconnection between Kevin (André Holland) and Chiron (now known as Black); returning to Kevin's home after reuniting, Kevin changes into a bright blue shirt as their conversation revisits the past and their intimacy.

Many of the pivotal events in the film take place at night, particularly at the beach, in this sense furthering the motif of blue and nighttime as a setting of shedding one's veneer or being one's true self. In the third act, Chiron's exterior projection of being "hard" is challenged by Kevin, the scene ultimately ending with a contemplative embrace between the childhood friends as Chiron grapples with the past. In other words, "blue" reveals a true self, or at least an identity better defined by oneself and not one's surroundings. – **SOPHIA SERRANO**

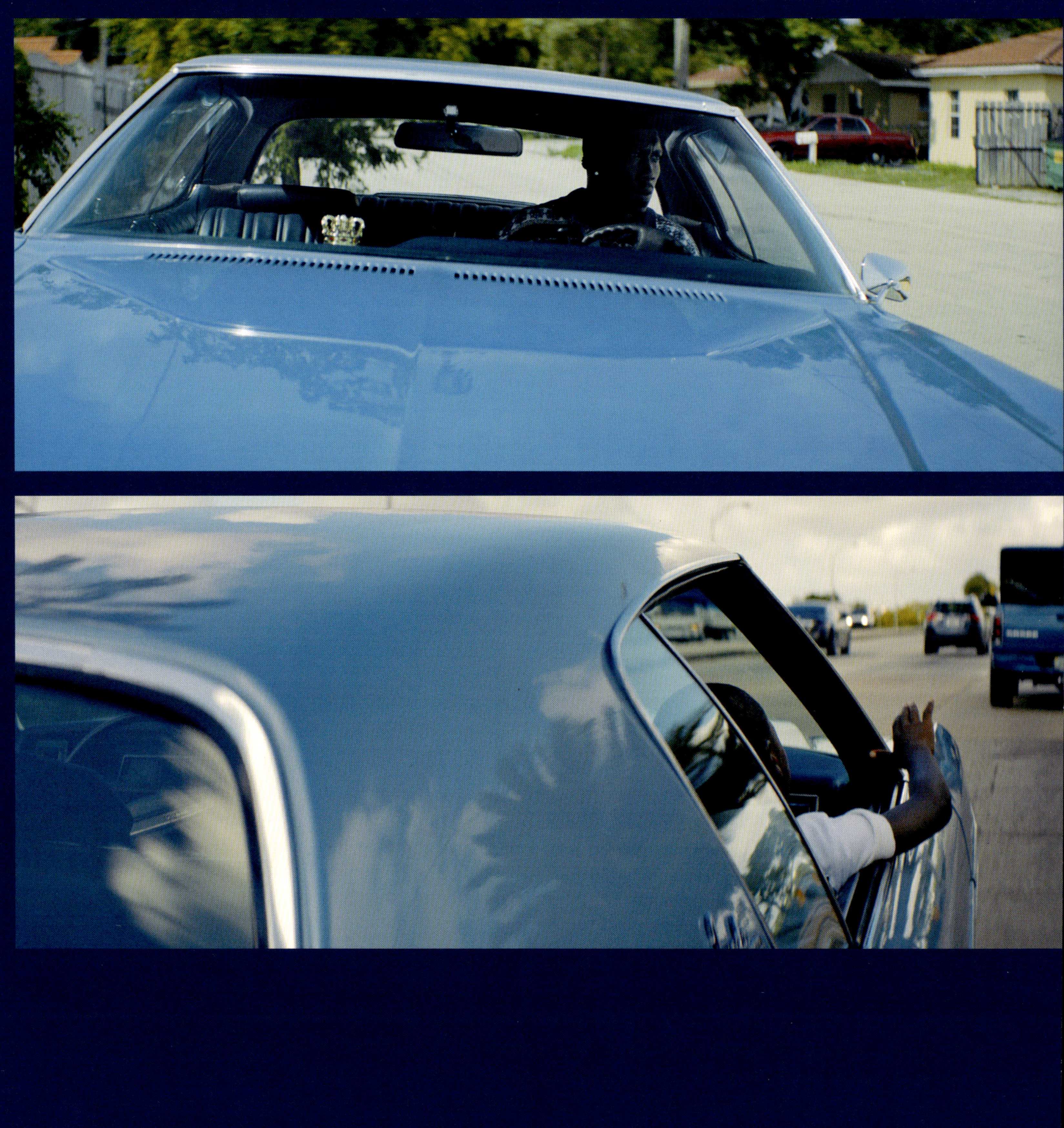

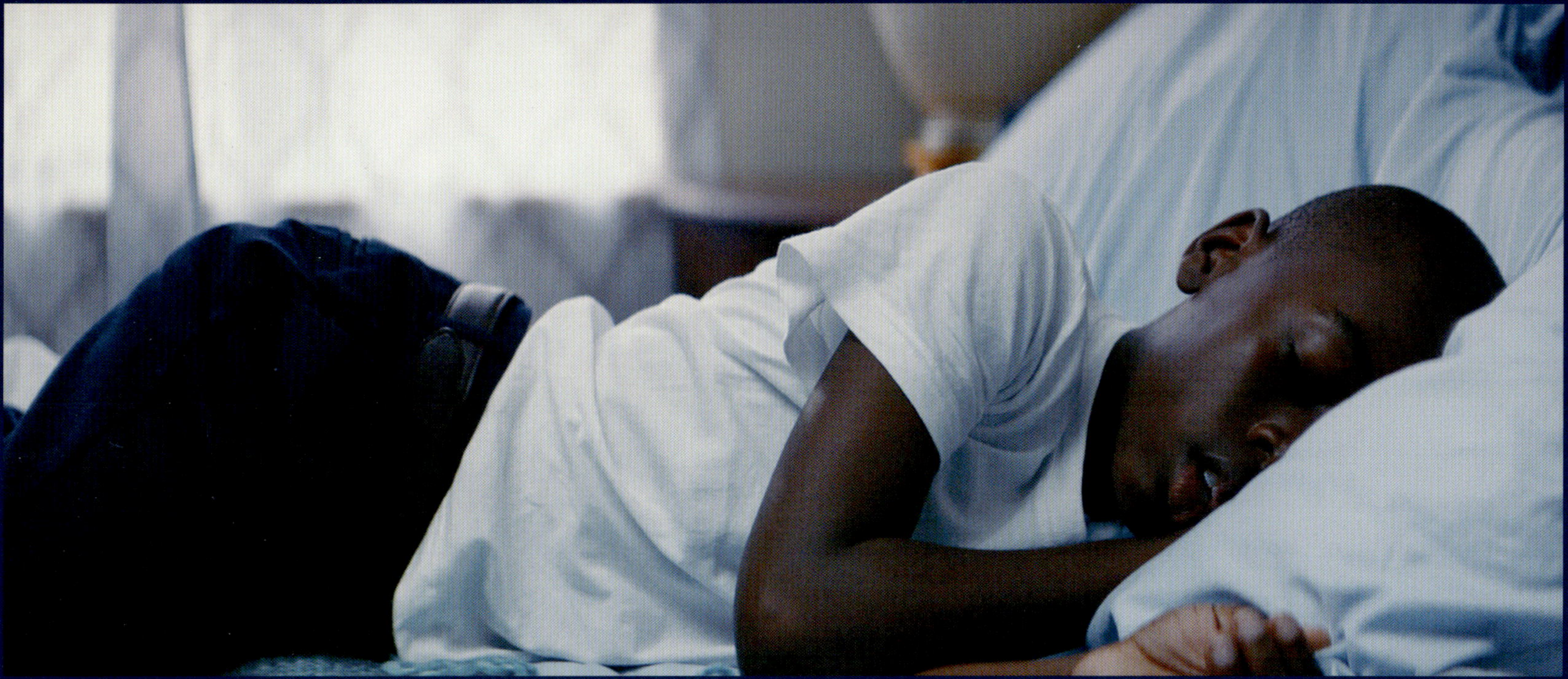

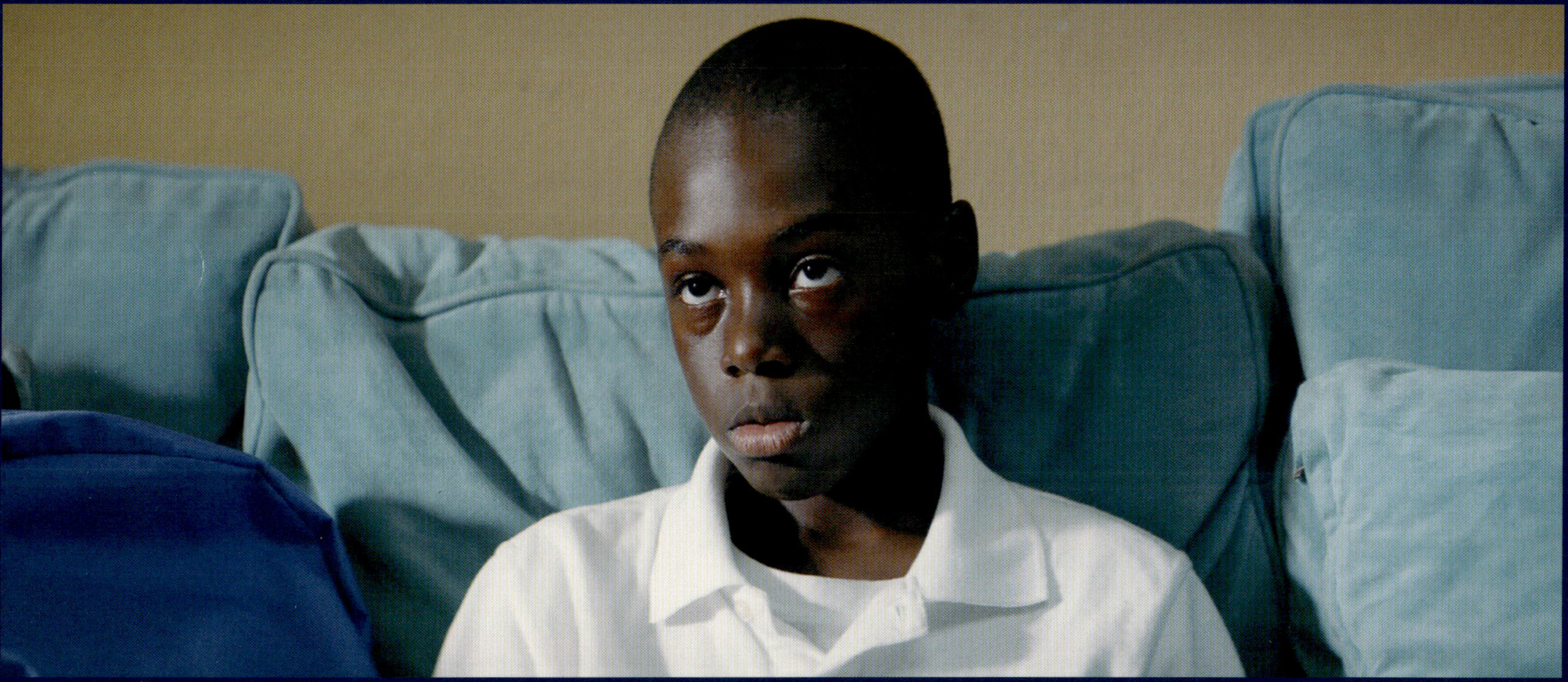

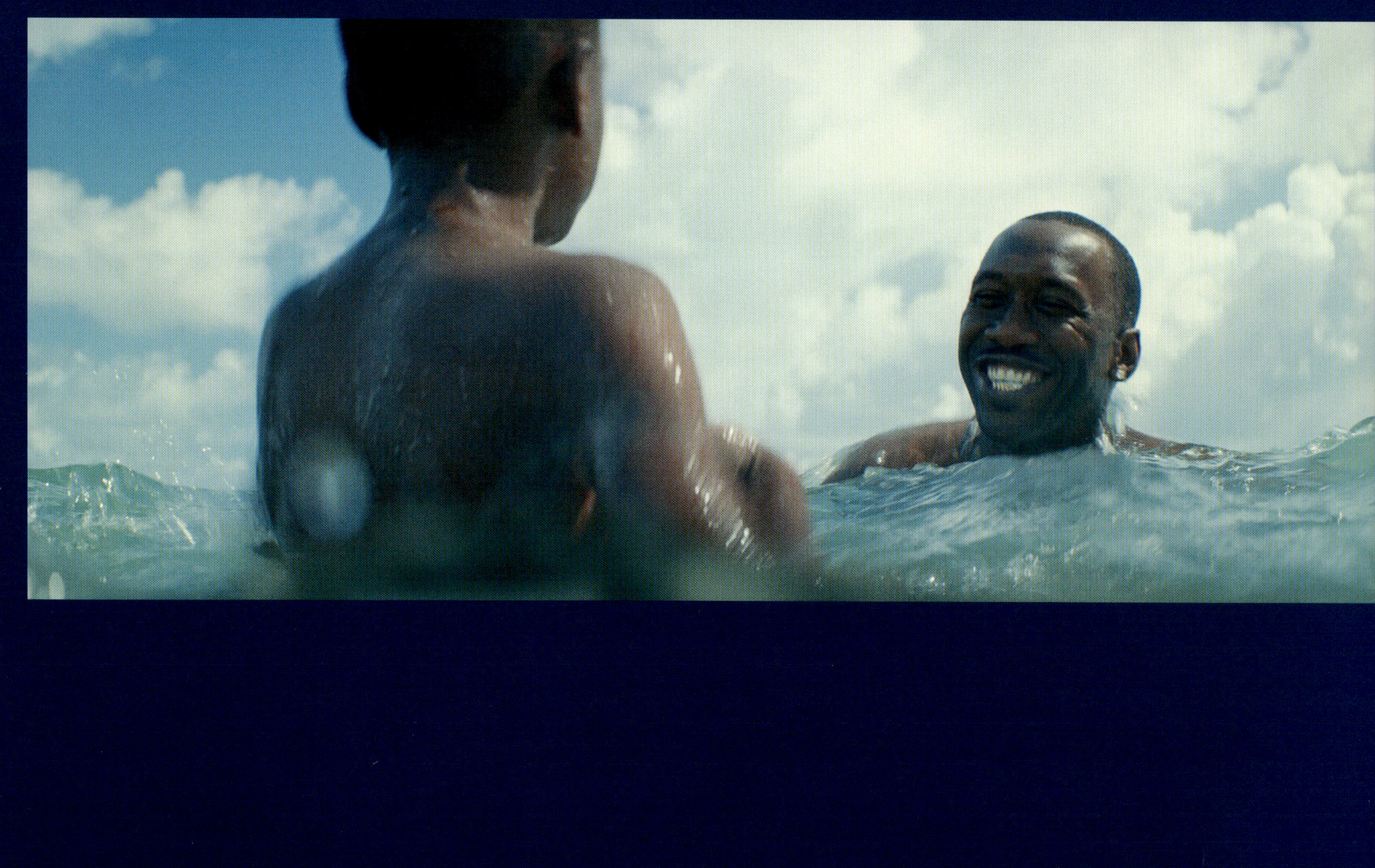

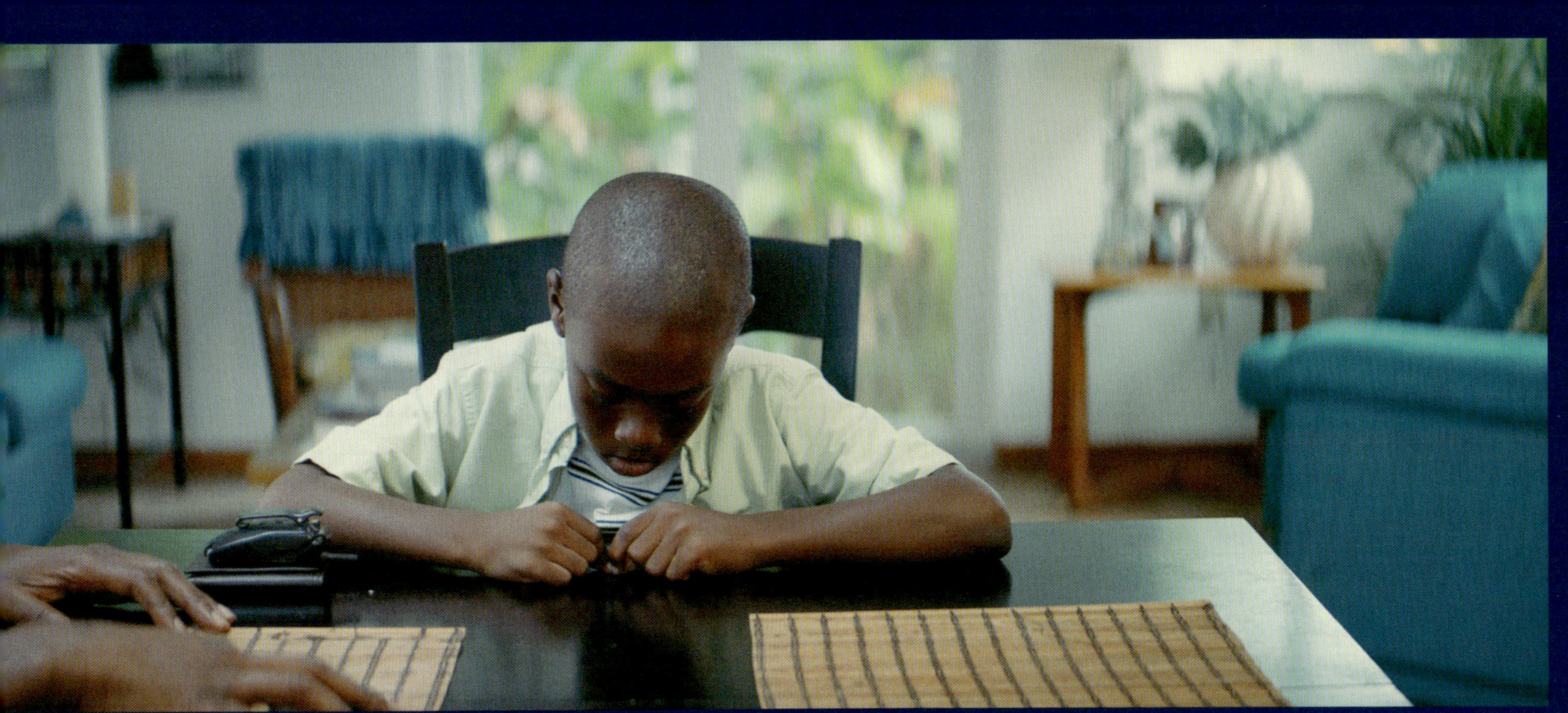

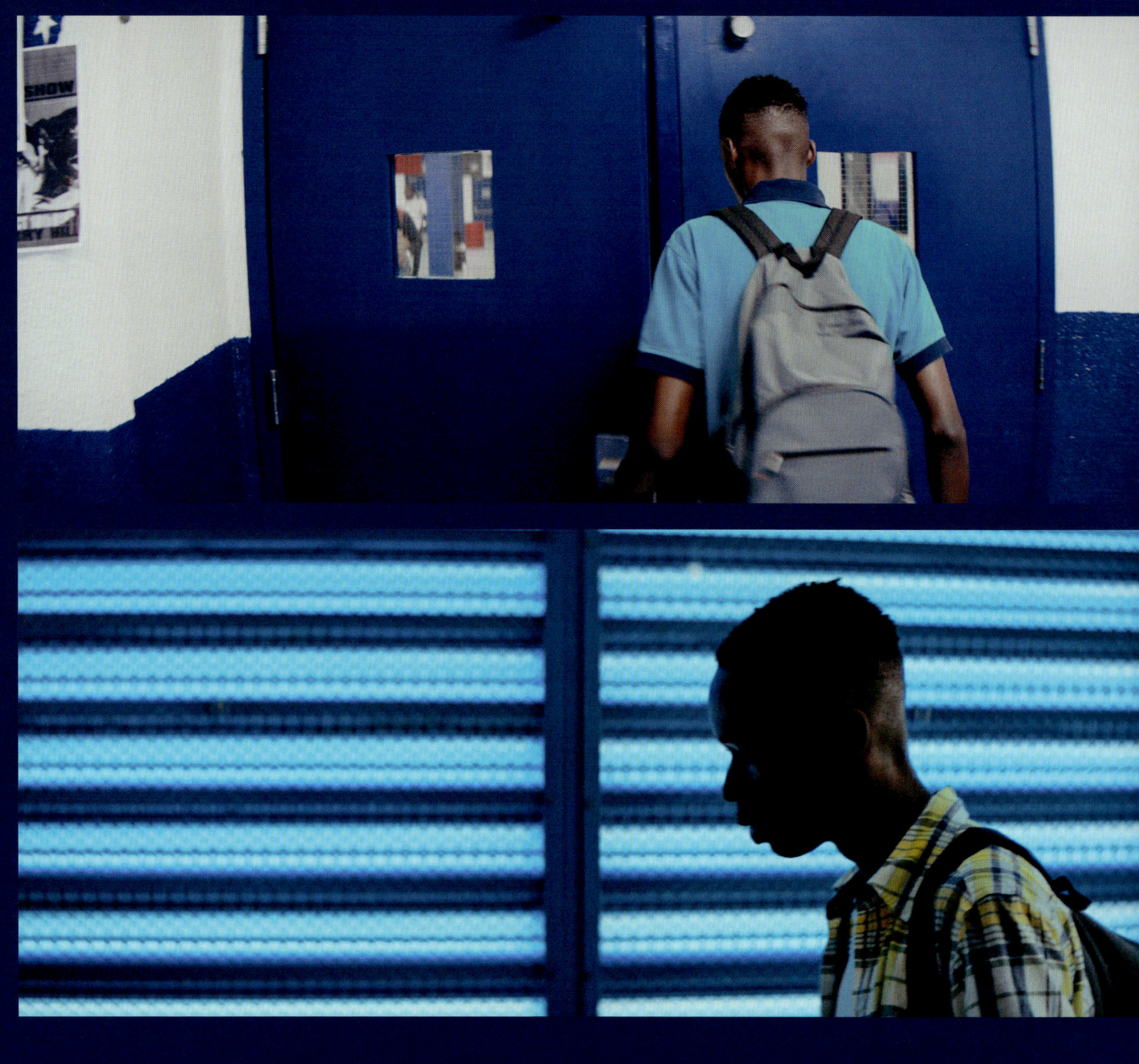
SHOW

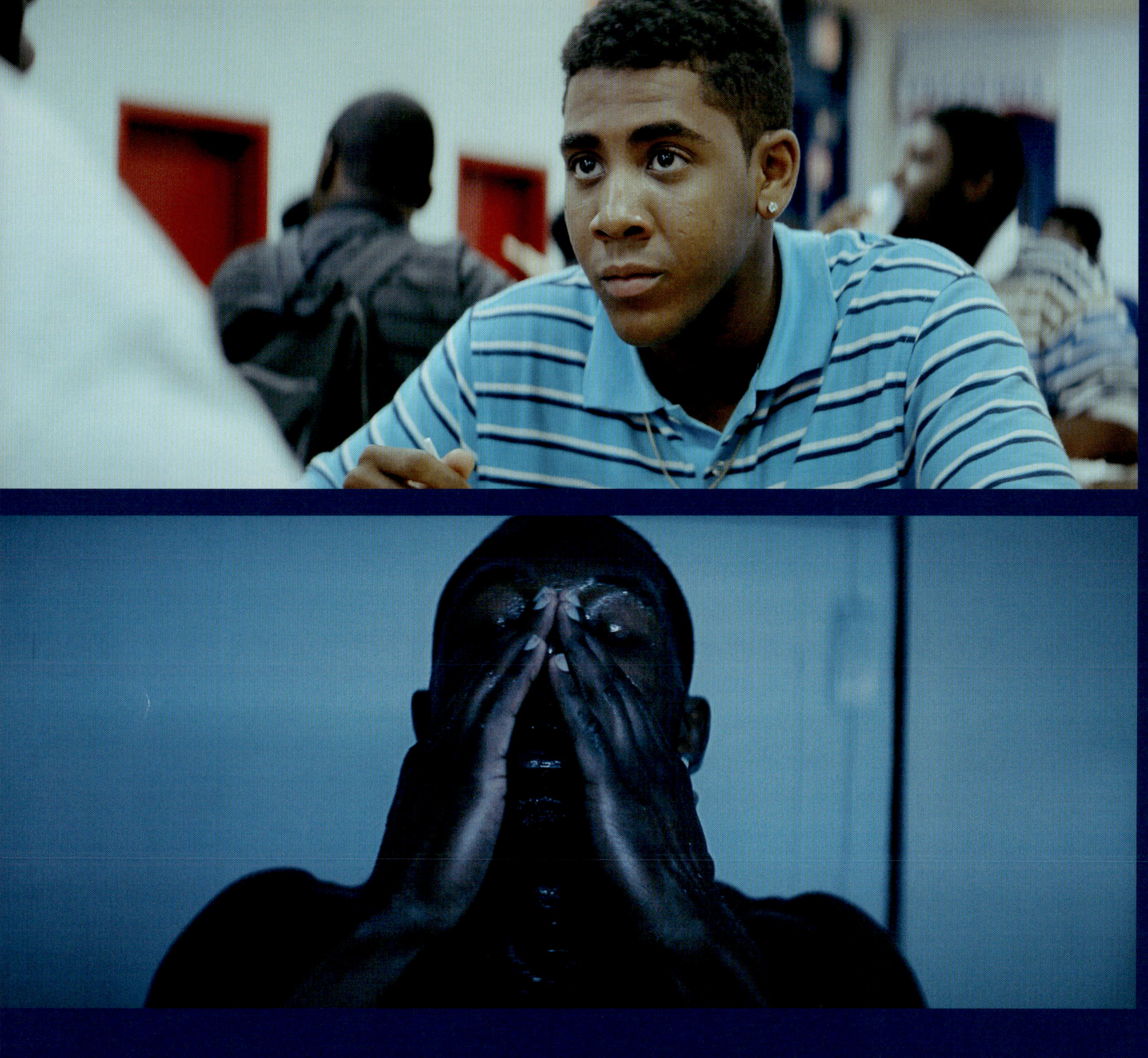

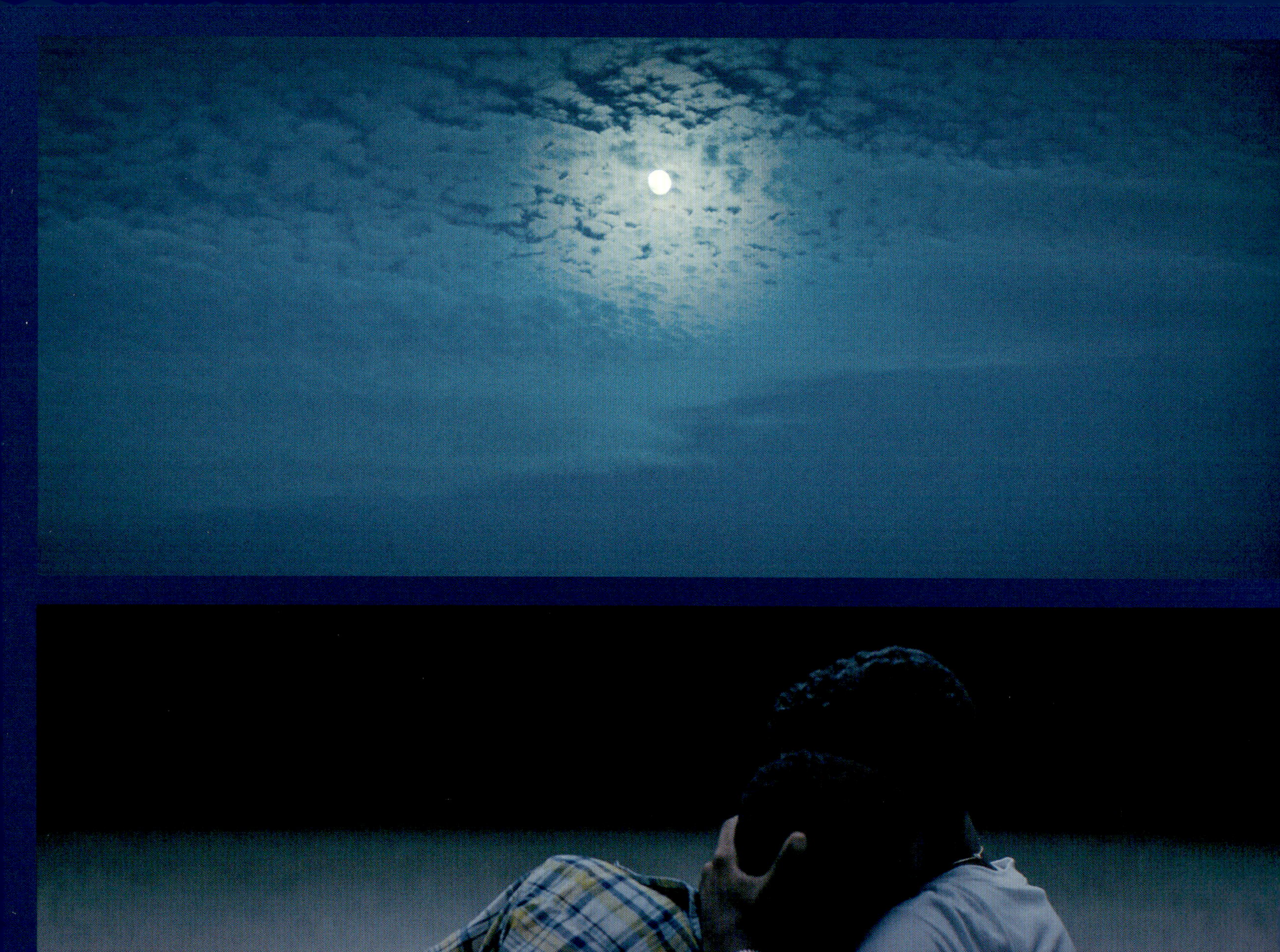

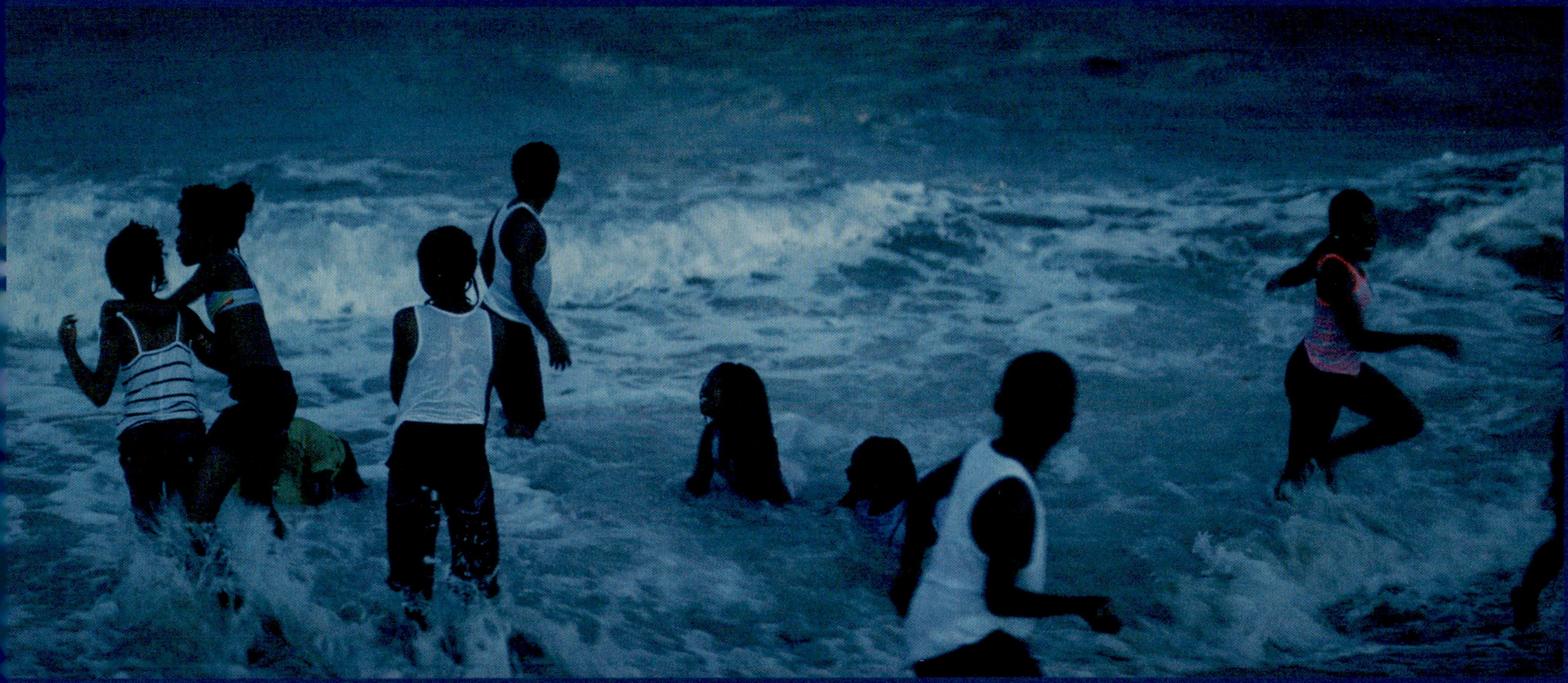

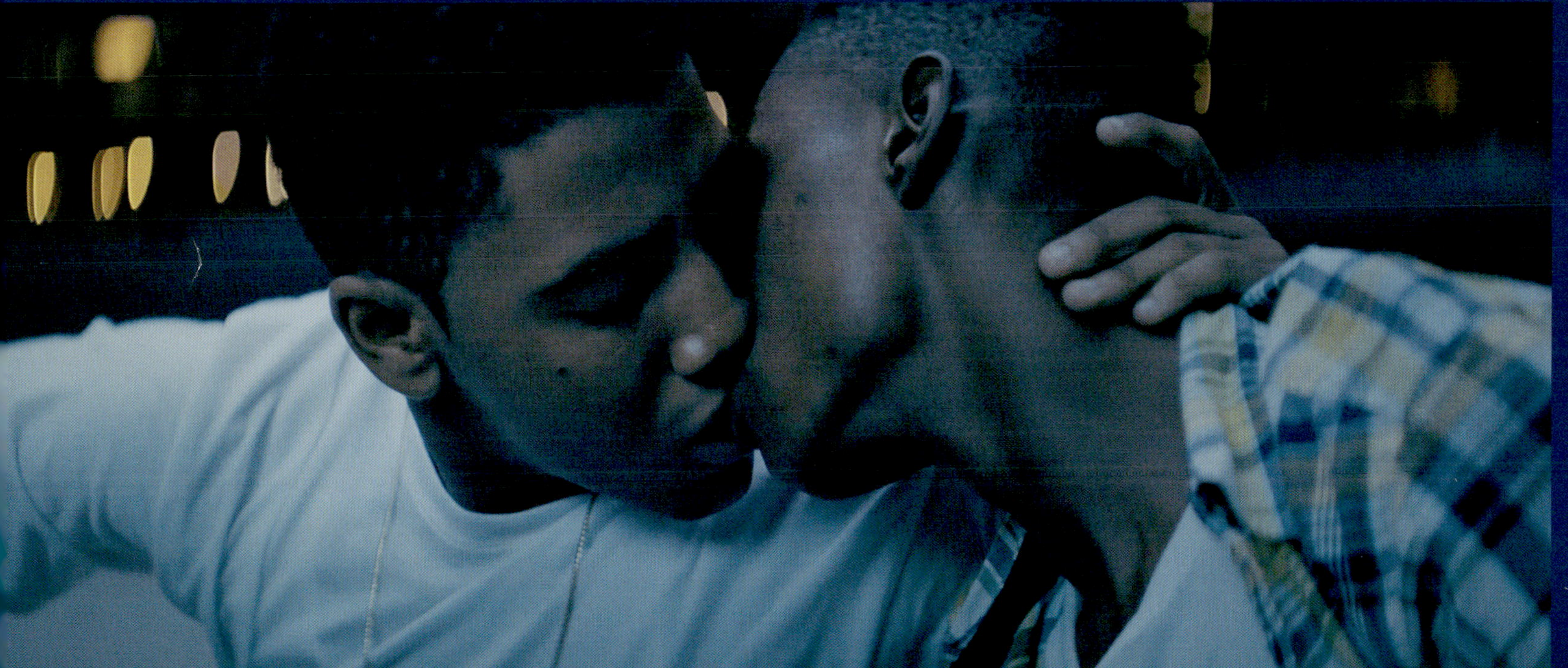

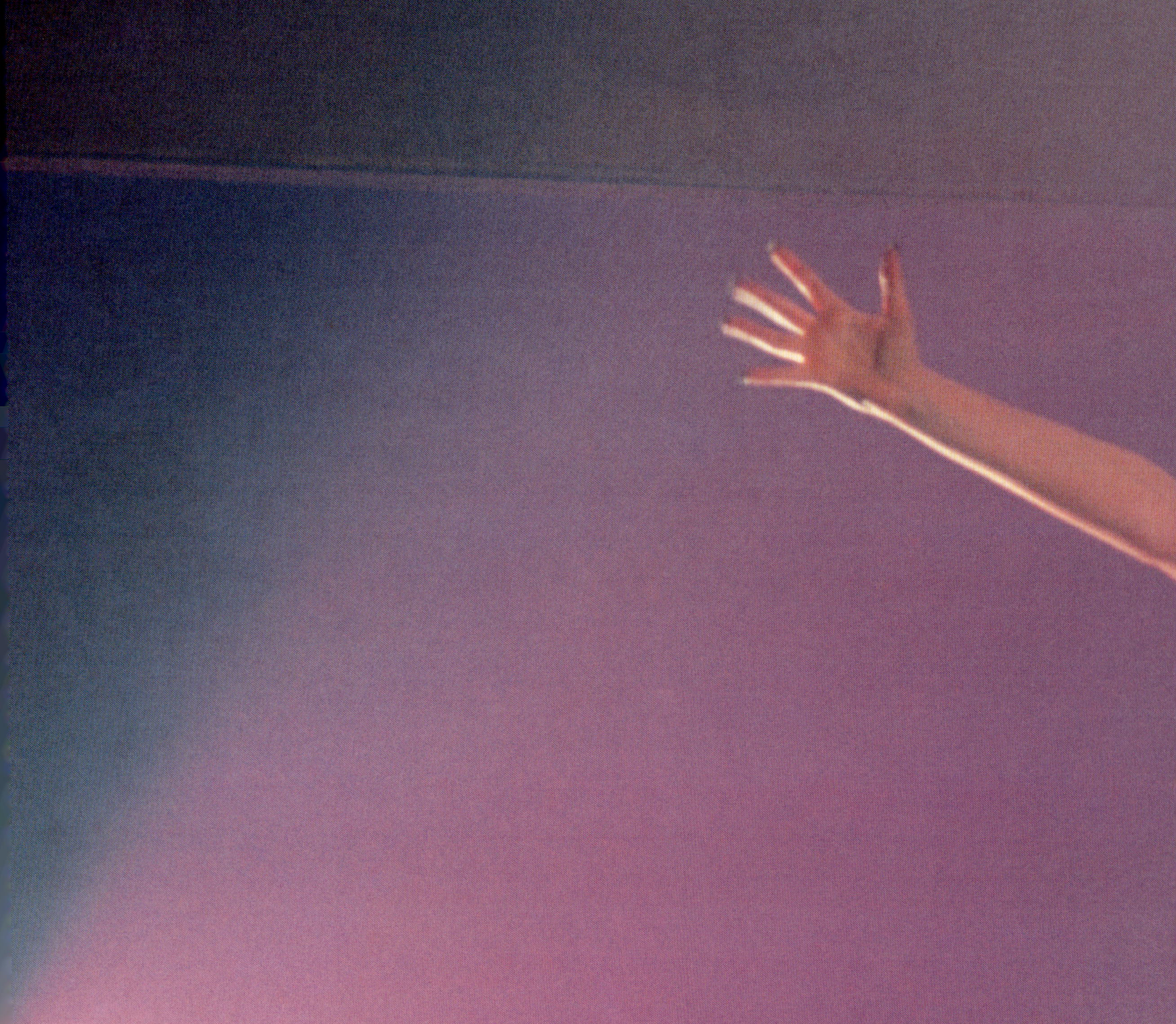

PURPLE AND

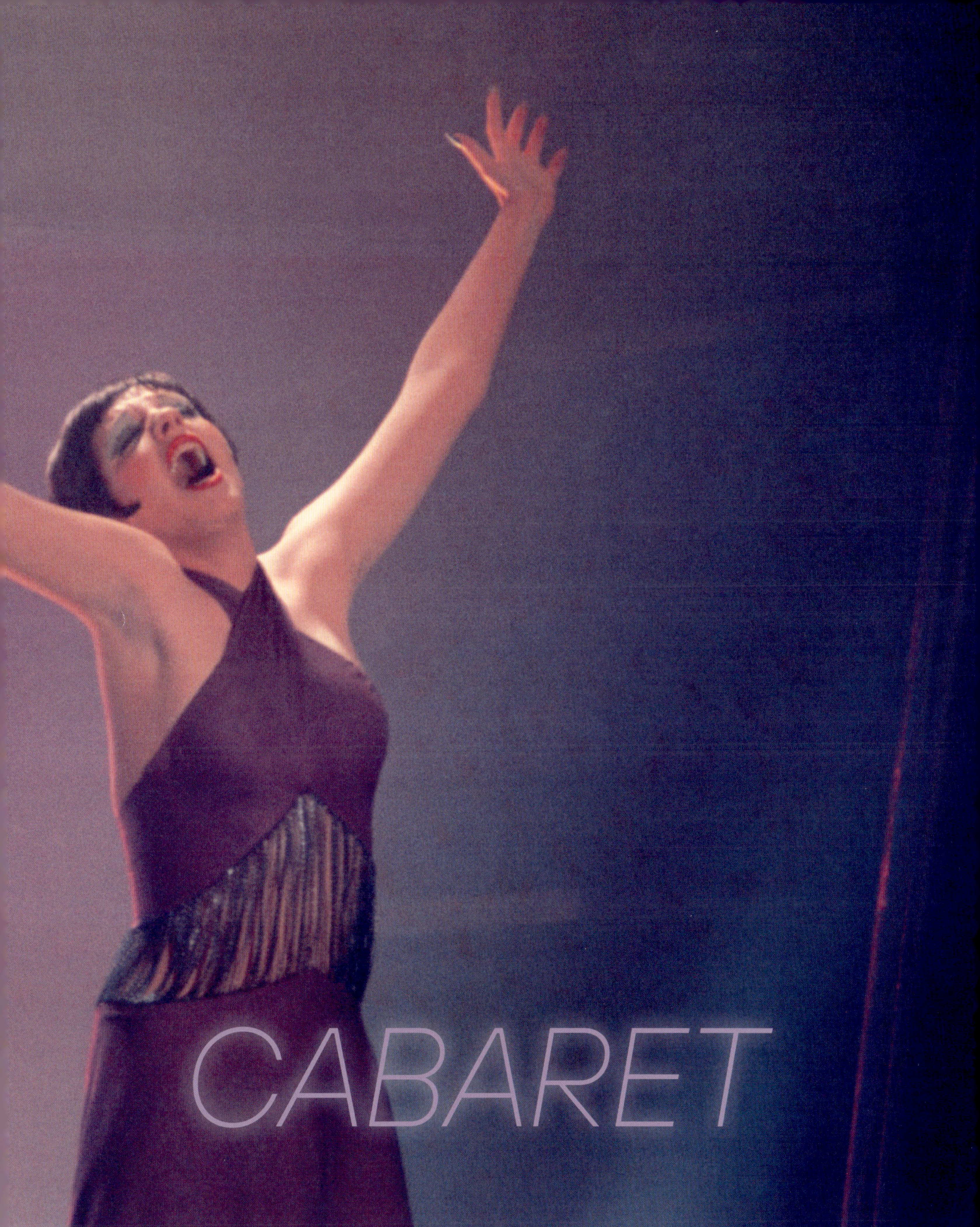
CABARET

Set against the hedonism of the Berlin cabaret scene amid sweeping societal changes in Weimar Germany, Bob Fosse's *Cabaret* (USA, 1972) follows the story of Sally Bowles (Liza Minnelli), a young American eager to shock and bored with traditional roles. A cabaret performer at the Kit Kat Klub who dreams of stardom, Sally wears purple throughout the film, especially during the moments where Fosse wants the viewer to understand her as decadent: cabaret acts, moments of seduction, and dreams of wealth.

Sally's fascination with decadence began with her creator, author Christopher Isherwood. Though not the screenwriter for *Cabaret*, Isherwood wrote the novel *Goodbye to Berlin* (1939), which served as the inspiration for the film and the 1966 Broadway musical. To aid in the film's production, Isherwood wrote multiple treatments with extensive notes, emphasizing that the "cabaret itself is absolutely amoral" and its significance is tied to "its madness [. . .], its sinister hypnotic flashing mind-blowing magic," a symbol of the decadence of 1930s Berlin and the looming threat of Nazi power.[1] As "this is where she belongs," Sally must exude the madness and magic of the cabaret. Minnelli took these notes to heart in her performance, providing a "decadent drawl" to complement the "enormous gap between the person and the performer," as Isherwood later reflected on Minnelli's rendition of Sally Bowles.[2] The film reproduced this gap with the casting of Minnelli, who won an Oscar for her performance as the amateur singer Sally Bowles.

Despite her apparent lack of talent, Sally dreams of being discovered at the cabaret and becoming a film star, a new version of royalty in the 1930s. In her quest to stand out and be noticed, she behaves outrageously to appear more opulent than she really is, which ultimately leads to her acceptance of a life forever within the walls of the Kit Kat Klub. However, that doesn't stop Sally from dreaming; she wears purple, a color often associated with regality, to reflect these fantasies.

Cabaret begins with the arrival of Brian Roberts (Michael York), a reserved English doctoral student who meets Sally when he moves into the boardinghouse where she lives. Greeting him in a purple floral silk robe, Sally comments, "Divine decadence," after Brian gives her a cigarette. This is humorously punctuated by Sally's tour for the new resident of the boardinghouse, her ornate robe standing out against the grays and browns and wood accents of the residence's sedate interior. Sally may act decadently, but she certainly does not live that way. However, Brian does not seem to mind; he is enchanted by Sally's fun-loving energy and apparent hedonism.

During Sally's first solo cabaret song in the movie, "Mein Herr," she dons a bowler hat with a purple band, purple sequined choker necklace, black halter vest, black shorts embellished with purple sequins, black stockings, and a black garter. Framed by blue and red lights—the primary colors that create purple—Sally sings about how she cannot be tied to one single man and makes it clear that she plans to be sexually independent and casual in her affairs. She glamorizes this liberation through romance and sex as stepping stones to a grand life free of mundane obligations and traditional relationships.

Her penchant for purple increases throughout the film, as she finds a way to incorporate the color into her wardrobe when romantic situations arise. Sally wears her purple silk robe when she attempts to seduce Brian. When the rich baron Maximilian von Heune (Helmut Griem) courts her and Brian with the promise of an African safari trip, Sally earnestly packs her bags while wearing her robe and a lilac scarf. Sally's dreams of a lavish and self-indulgent lifestyle, which the baron represents, are eventually dashed when he leaves her. They also cloud any chance of a future with Brian despite her fondness for him, a choice punctuated by her bright purple eyeshadow during their sentimental parting at the train station.

Ultimately, Sally can only feel truly decadent in the cabaret, fully enveloped in purple. In her ballad "Cabaret" near the end of the film, wearing a floor-length purple gown, she sings of a hedonistic lifestyle, one that rejects staying at home and embraces the cabaret. And while she is aware that this lifestyle will eventually cause an early death, she knows that life "isn't that long of a stay." As she sings the final notes, lights flash around her and envelop her in purple. As Isherwood noted in his treatment, the finale needs to highlight that the Kit Kat Klub is "pathetically second rate and trashy" and "Sally [is] a hopelessly poor performer." However, the cabaret's dirty, depraved setting does not matter to Sally; in the Kit Kat Klub she is queen, and therefore "[she] can't leave her way of life."

—ALEXANDRA JAMES SALICHS

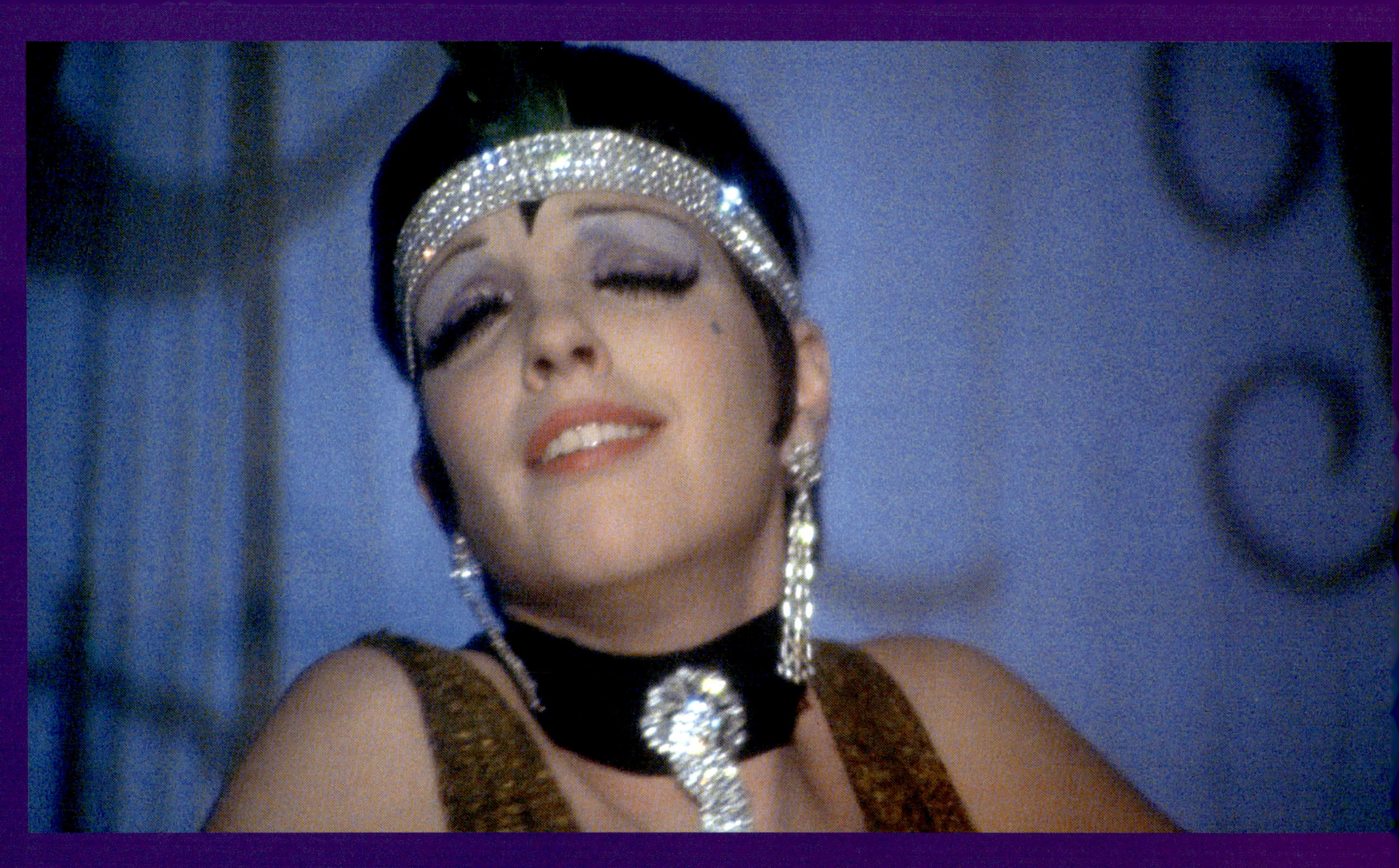

Cabaret (USA, 1972, dir. Bob Fosse)

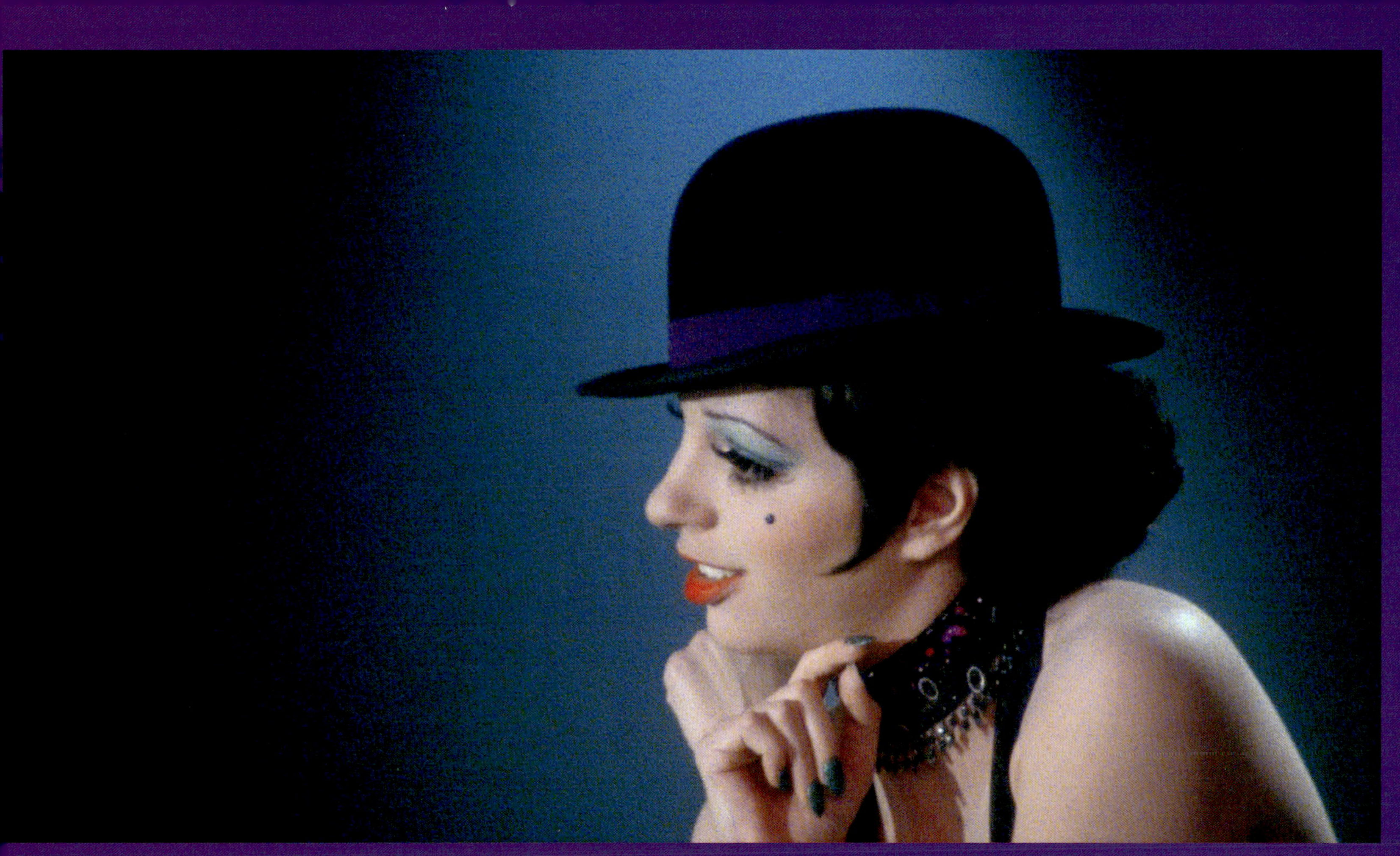

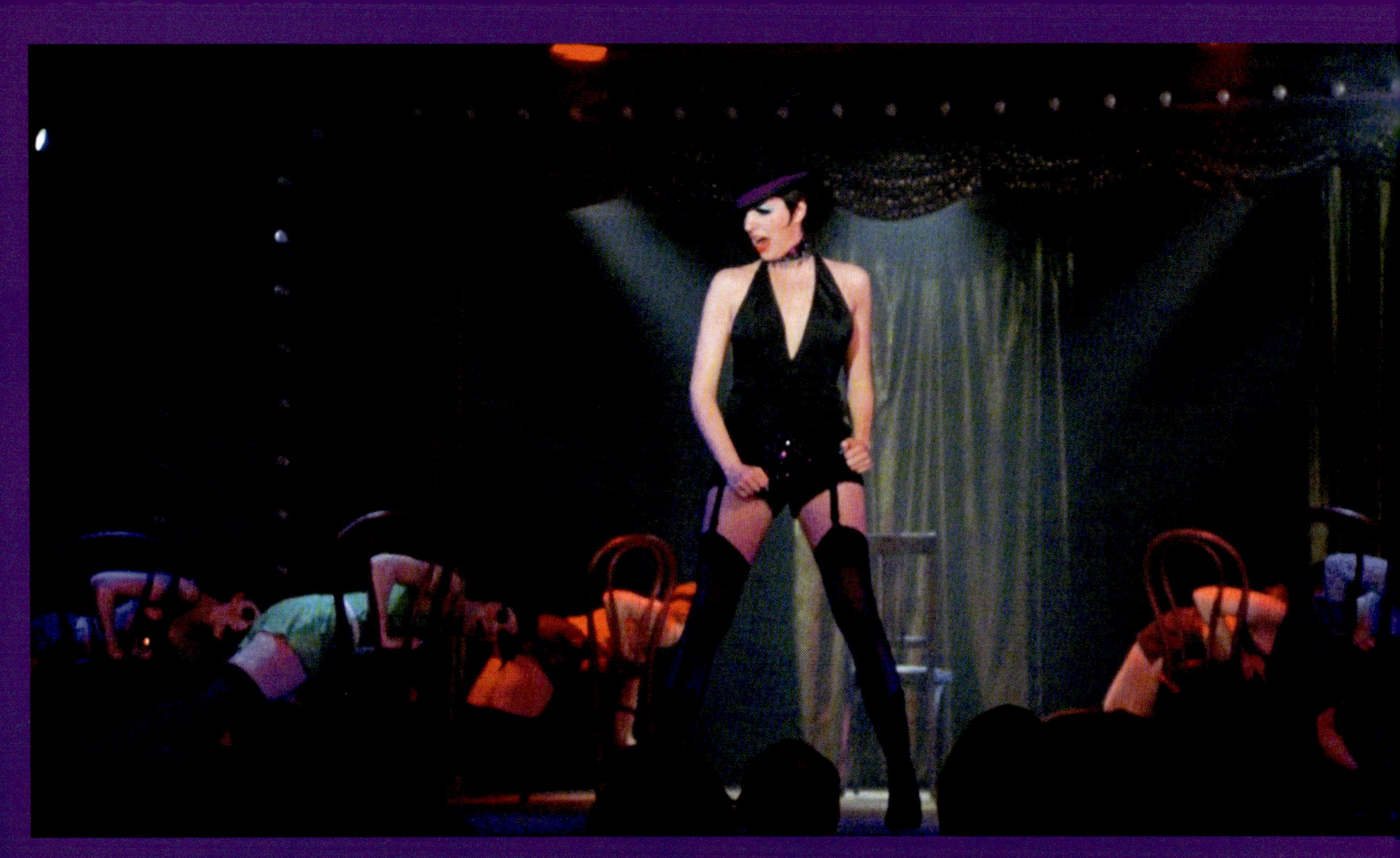

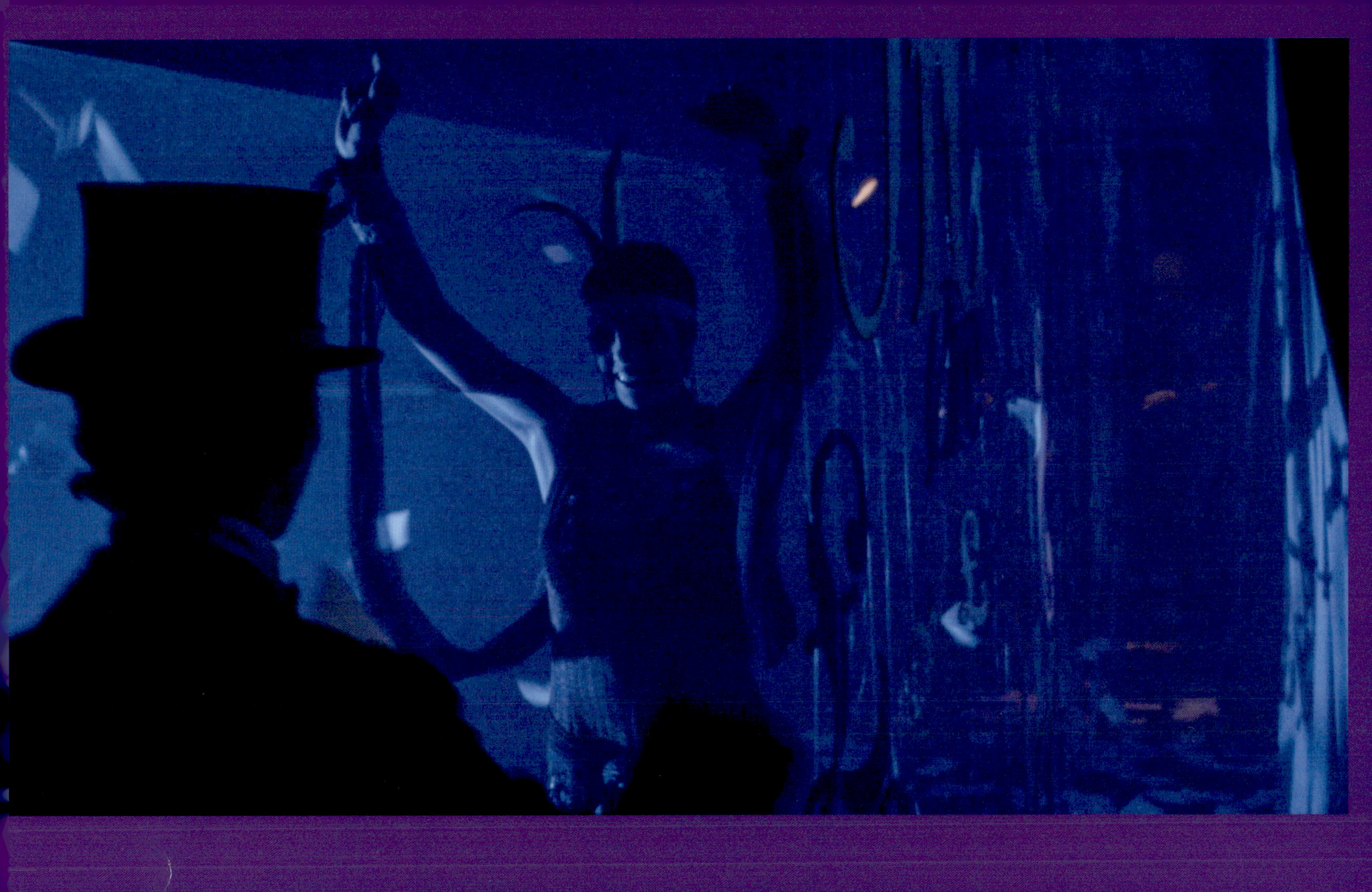

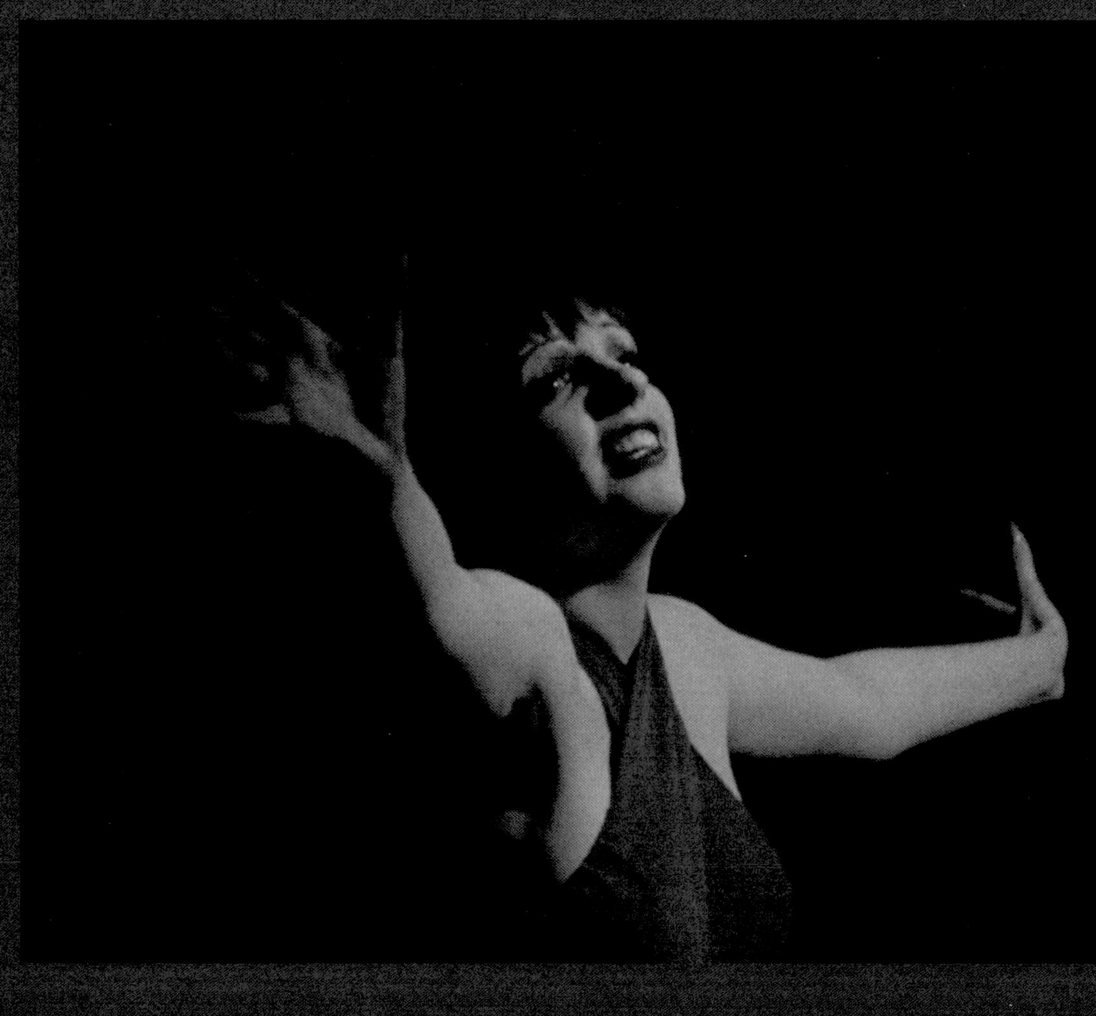

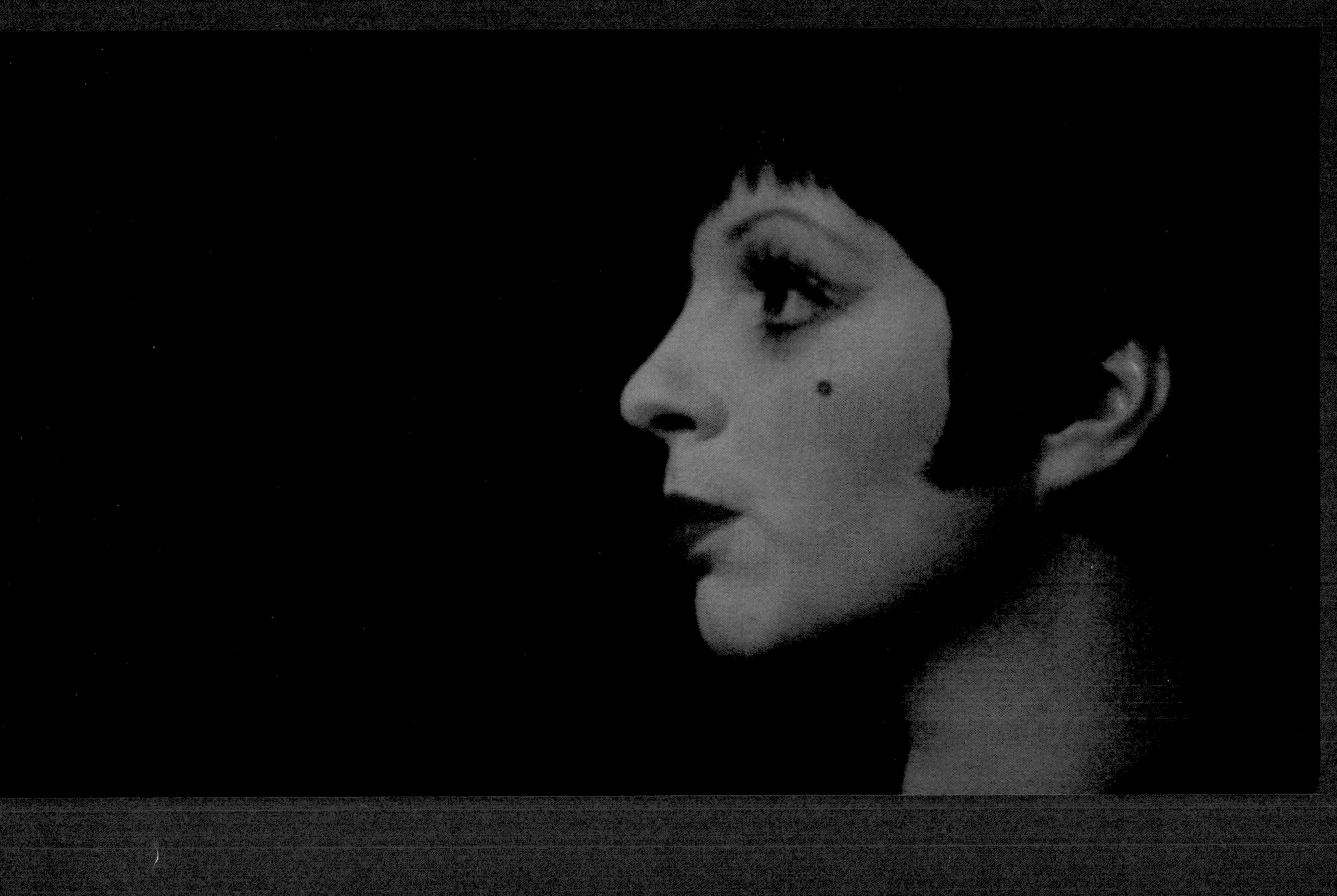

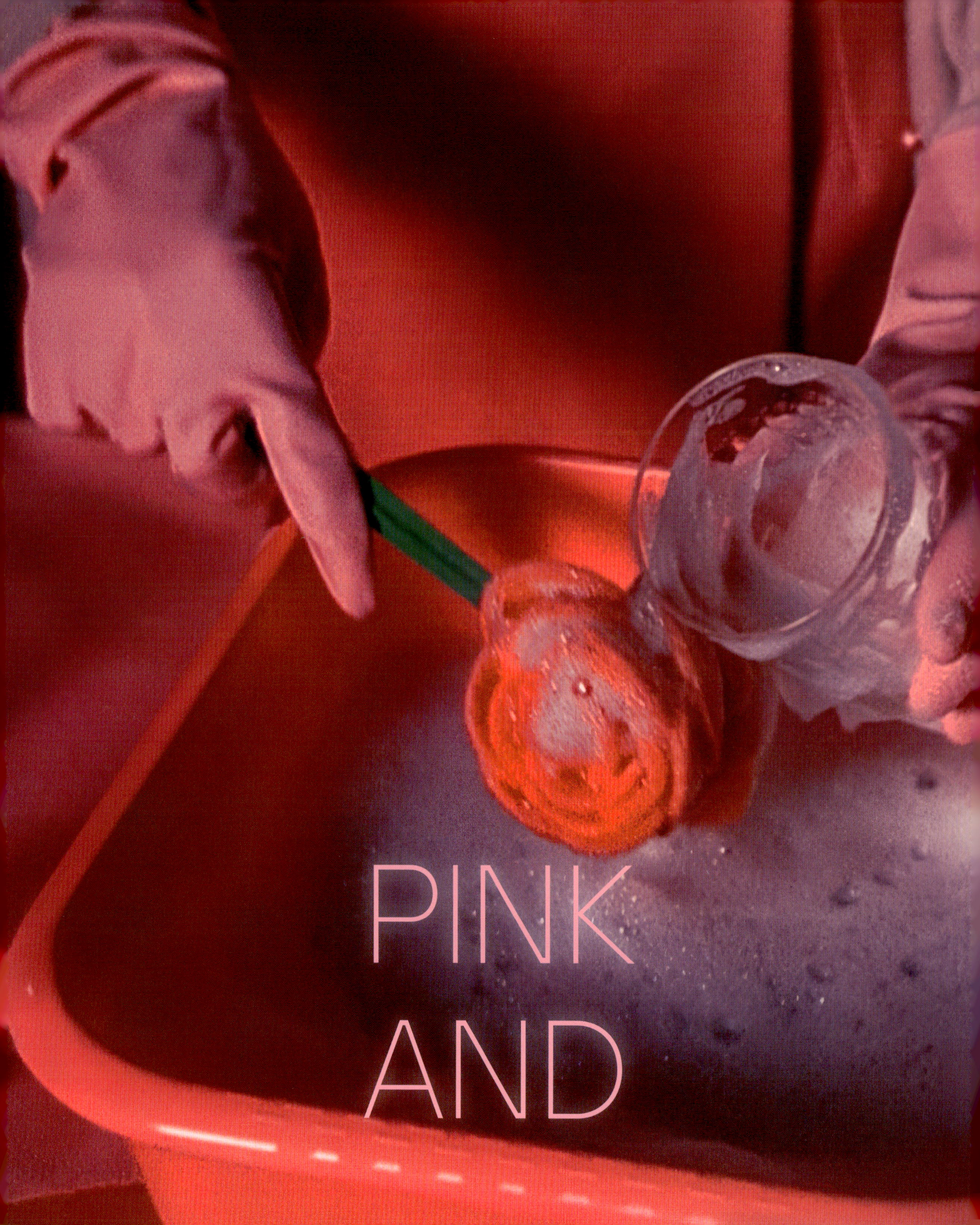
PINK
AND

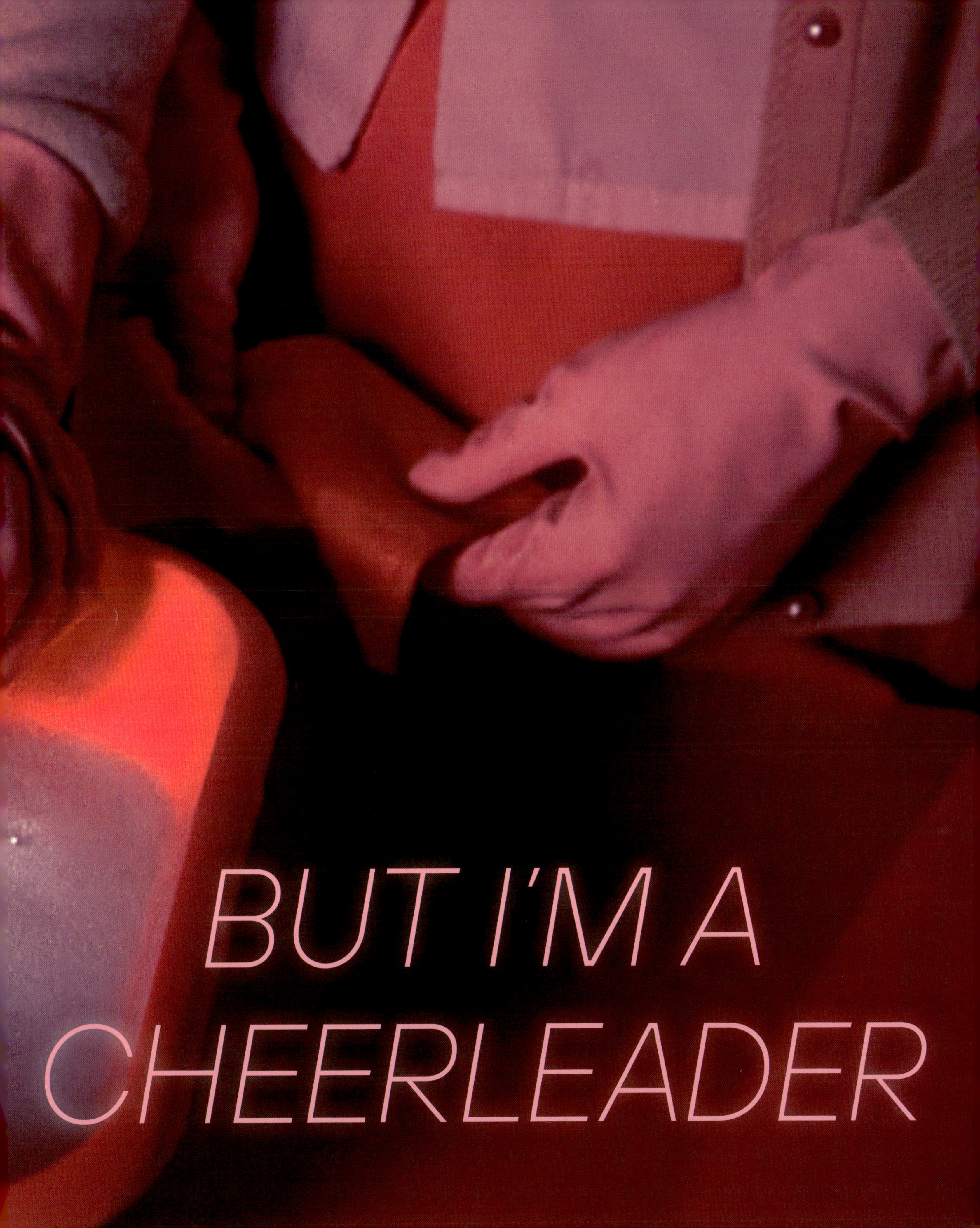
BUT I'M A
CHEERLEADER

Jamie Babbit's debut film, *But I'm a Cheerleader* (USA, 1999), revolves around Megan (Natasha Lyonne), a seventeen-year-old cheerleader who is suspected by her family and friends of being a lesbian, and her evolving relationship with Graham (Clea DuVall), whom she meets at the "reparative therapy" camp True Directions. Run by Mary J. Brown (Cathy Moriarty), the camp aims to convert teenagers, including Mary's own son, Rock, into heterosexuals. In her social satire, Babbit exposes and deconstructs outdated gender roles as well as homosexual stereotypes. She skillfully employs the colors most commonly associated with gender—pink and blue—to exaggerate clichés to the point where they become absurd.

Pink, historically associated with boys (due to its relation to the masculine color red) until it was linked to girls and femininity in the 1940s, plays a simple yet powerful role in the film. It represents a rigidly defined, one-dimensional gender role and is used as a conversion tool not only to turn lesbians into heterosexuals but also to force them into a prim and proper ideal out of the 1950s. The twelve-step program to "heal" the teenagers from their "homosexual addiction" includes steps like "rediscovering your gender identity" and "simulated sexual lifestyle," in which the girls learn about housework, marriage, heterosexual intercourse, and tending to newborns.

Pink is pervasive throughout the girls' experiences. The color floods the girls' shared bedroom, where Megan first meets Graham lying on a bed casually smoking a cigarette, openly displaying her resistance to conforming to the "feminine" environment created to convert her. Megan, a girlish teen who has had a boyfriend for two years, is still baffled about being sent to the camp and incredulous at the accusation of being a lesbian: "But I'm a cheerleader!" Gradually, she realizes that she might indeed be homosexual and, upon admitting her lesbianism, Megan earns her pink uniform. The girls' entire world is dominated by pink, from their bedrooms to their clothes and the household tools they use, while the boys are confined to a complementary blue universe.

However, instead of succumbing entirely to the pink void, the girls' personalities begin to shine through. Megan and Graham fall in love and eventually decide to run away together, fully embracing their identities and rejecting parental threats and societal pressures. They liberate themselves from the unfulfillable expectations placed upon them. Megan is a lesbian *and* a cheerleader. As the patients rebel against being molded into standardized roles, the pink-blue dichotomy breaks down, making way for the rainbow colors of LGBTQ pride.

Babbit introduces the rainbow colors in a scene at the dance club Cocksucker, to which the patients escape for a night of fun. Later, after being expelled from True Directions, Megan reunites with fellow patient Dolph at a gay couple's house, where he found refuge after his own expulsion for kissing another boy. He has exchanged his blue uniform for a rainbow-colored suit that blends in with the couple's multicolored house. In this chromatic environment, Megan learns a valuable lesson. Upon asking how to be a lesbian she is told, "There's not one way of being a lesbian. You just have to continue being who you are." As simple as it sounds, this message is a revelation to Megan, who only knows the one-dimensionality of her high-school existence and the conformist approach of True Directions. The camp's conversion strategy not only fails but in fact helps Megan learn about and accept her true self.

Pink, which initially appeared to be an overpowering therapeutic tool, turns out to be a shallow facade and a simple cover-up imposed on the girls rather than a catalyst for change. Babbit overstylizes her imagery with floods of pink and blue, undermining the heteronormative world of True Directions and exposing it as artificial and unnatural. One memorable scene shows Mary dressed primly in a pink suit, spraying pink plastic flowers with a pink spray can. At the end of the film, the graduates of True Directions are shown wearing plasticky pink dresses and blue suits. Exaggerated by the glossy texture of the costumes, the colors that were intended to establish gender and sexual conformity now render the idea of heteronormativity and conversion therapy farcical. This sets the stage for Megan's entrance in her orange cheerleading uniform. She has come for Graham, and the two escape together, setting off into a future full of promise. By exposing the gendering of pink and blue as random and dysfunctional social constructs, Babbit's film overcomes the notion of sexual normativity and instead celebrates the multifaceted, individualistic nature of lesbian and gay existence, representing it with all the colors of the rainbow. —**JESSICA NIEBEL**

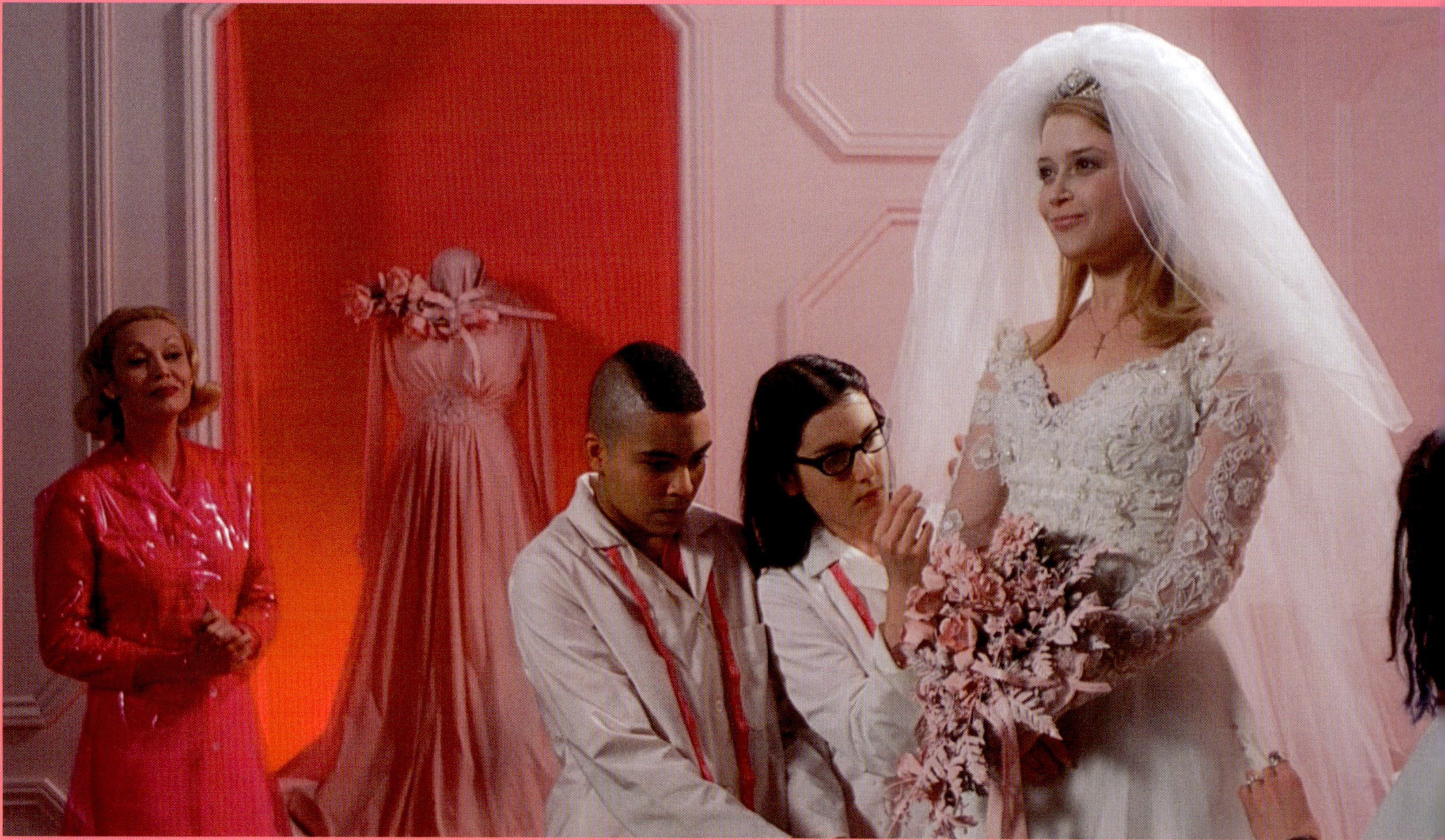

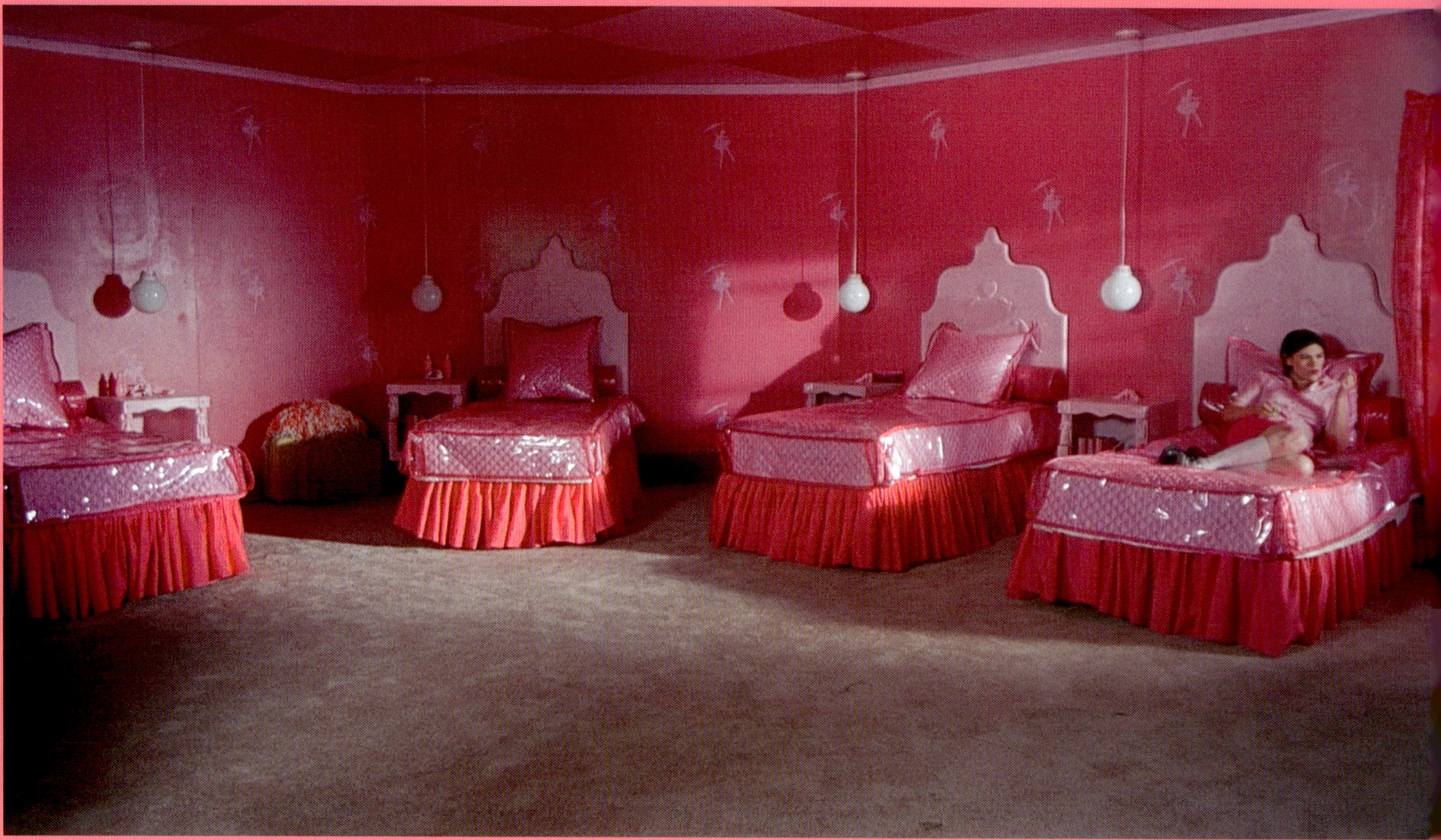

But I'm a Cheerleader (USA, 1999, dir. Jamie Babbit)

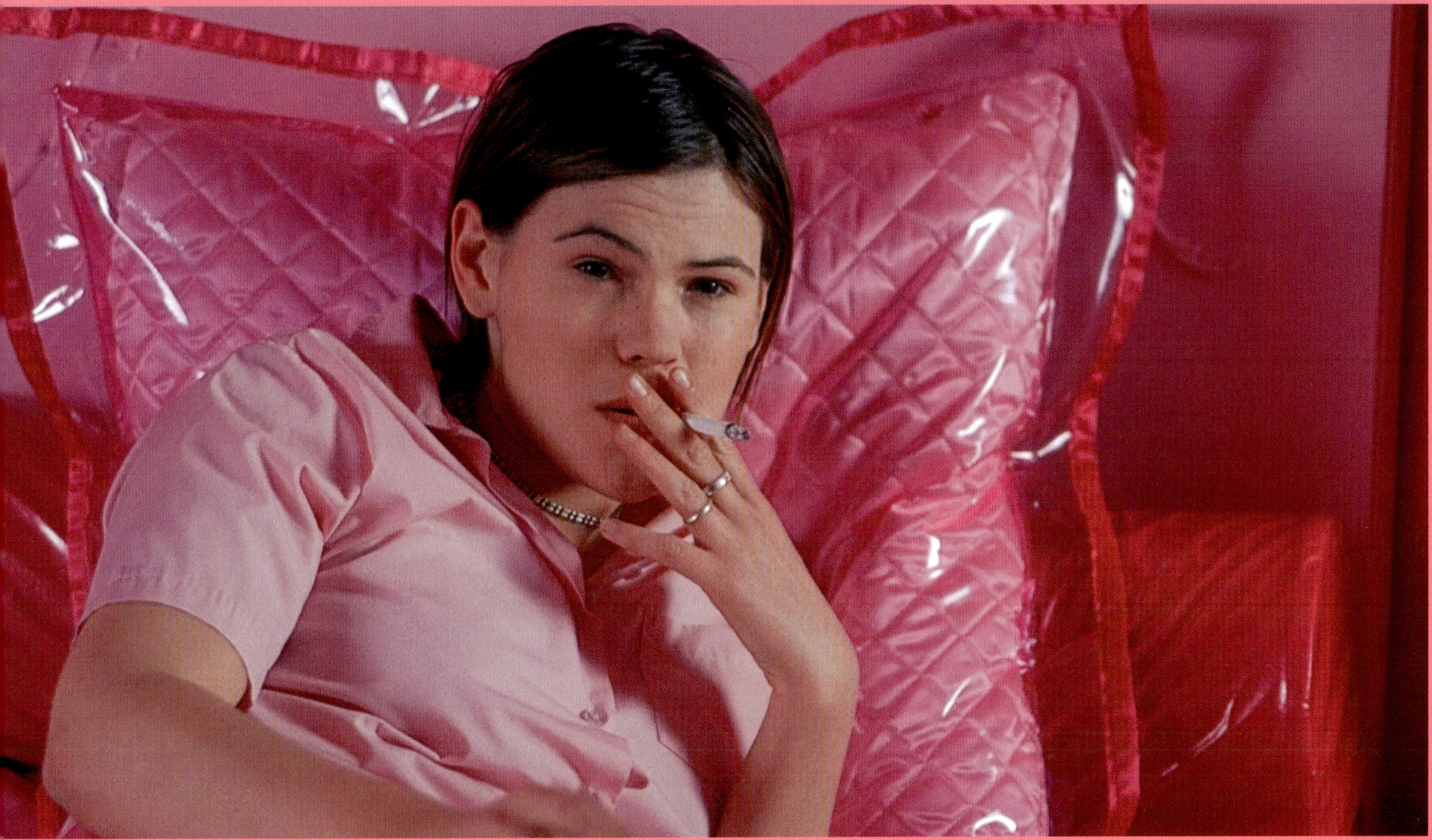

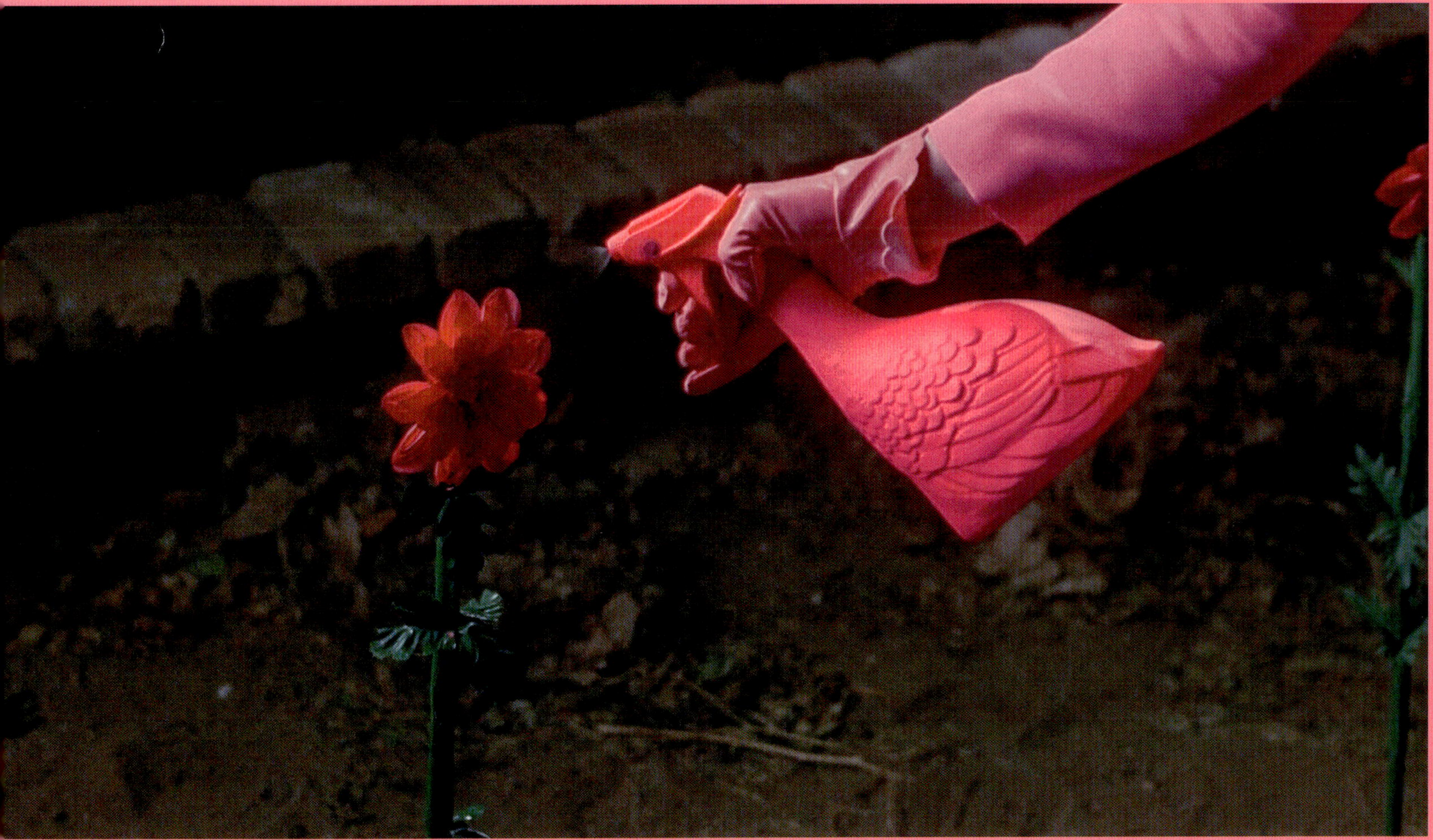

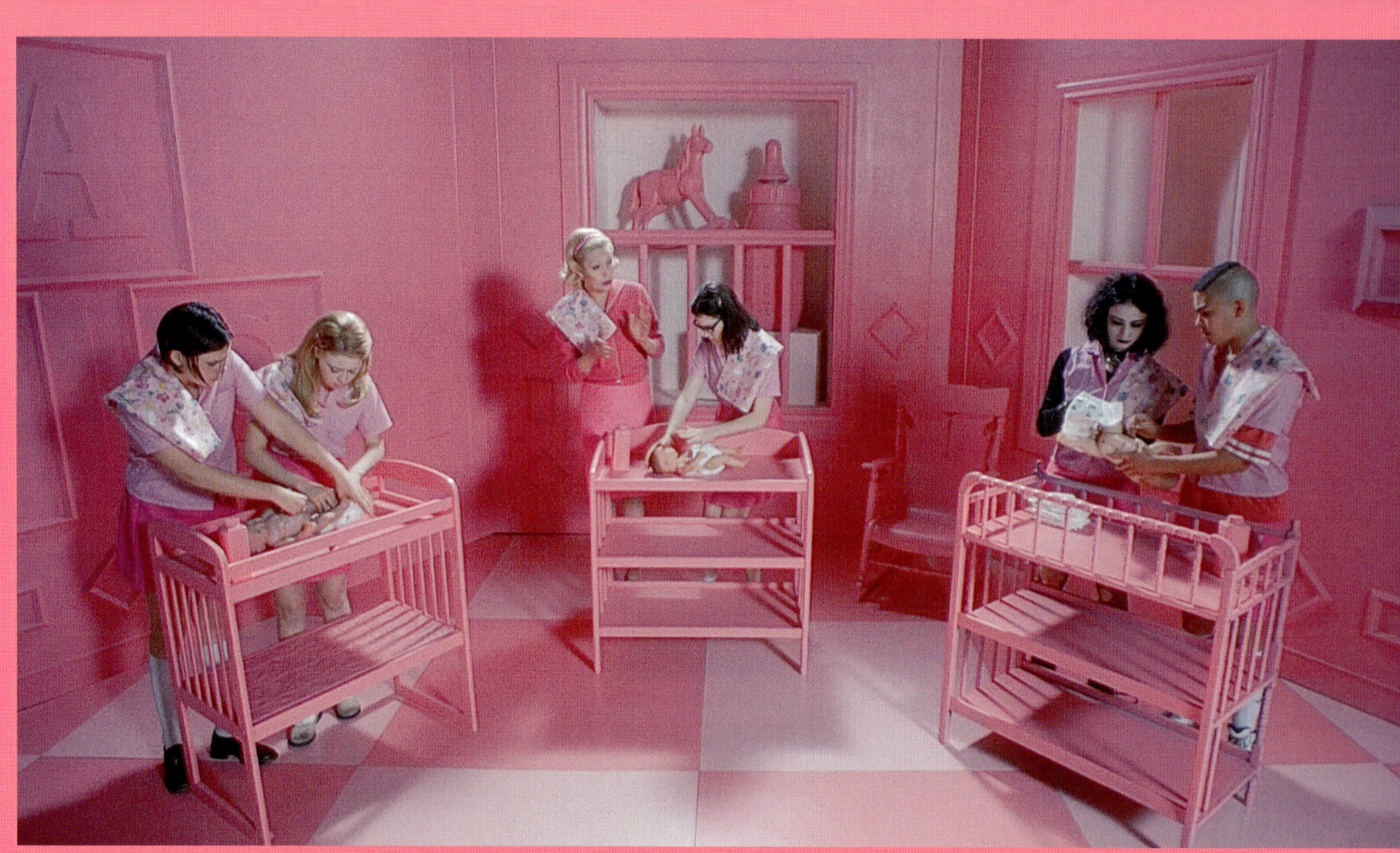

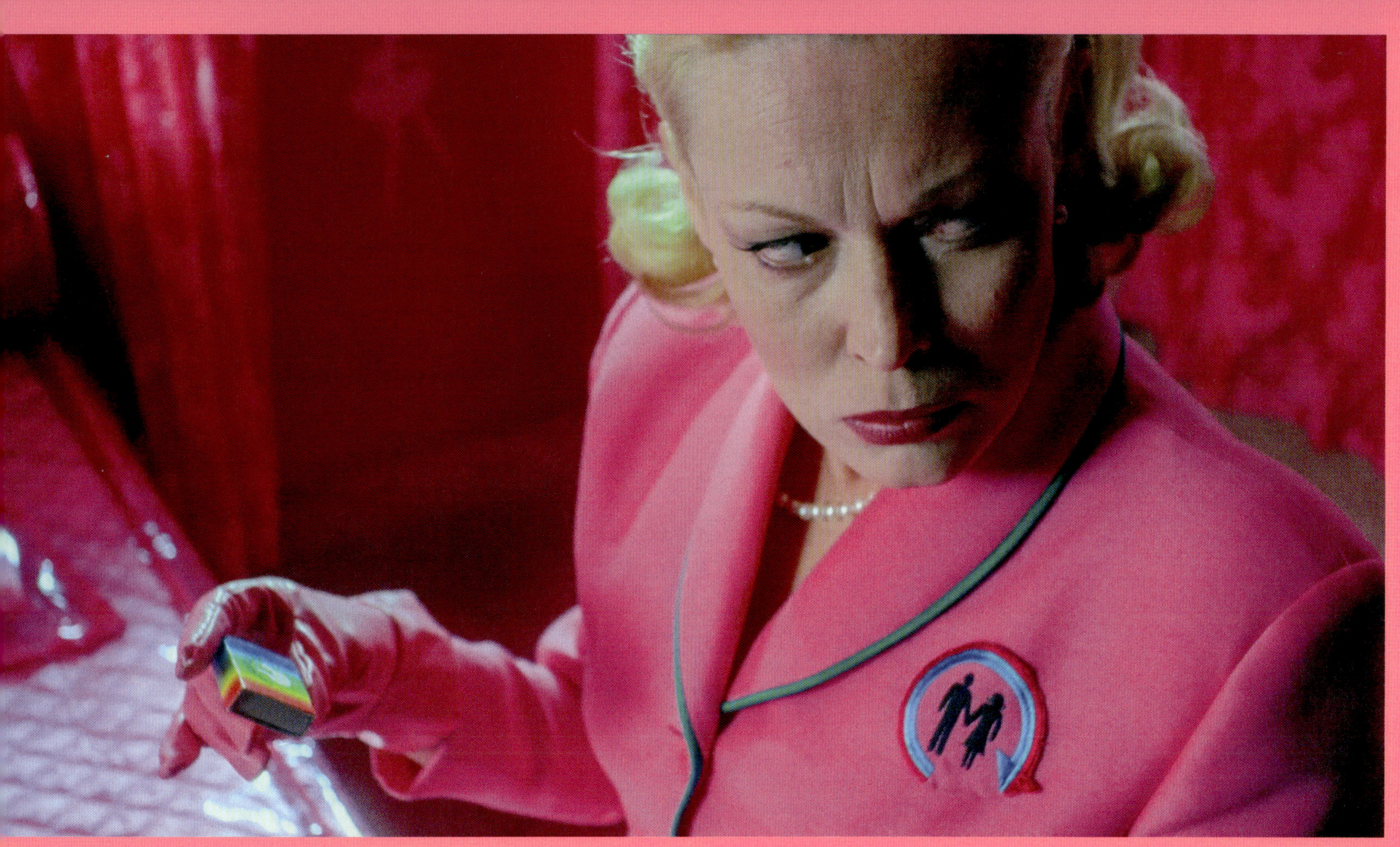

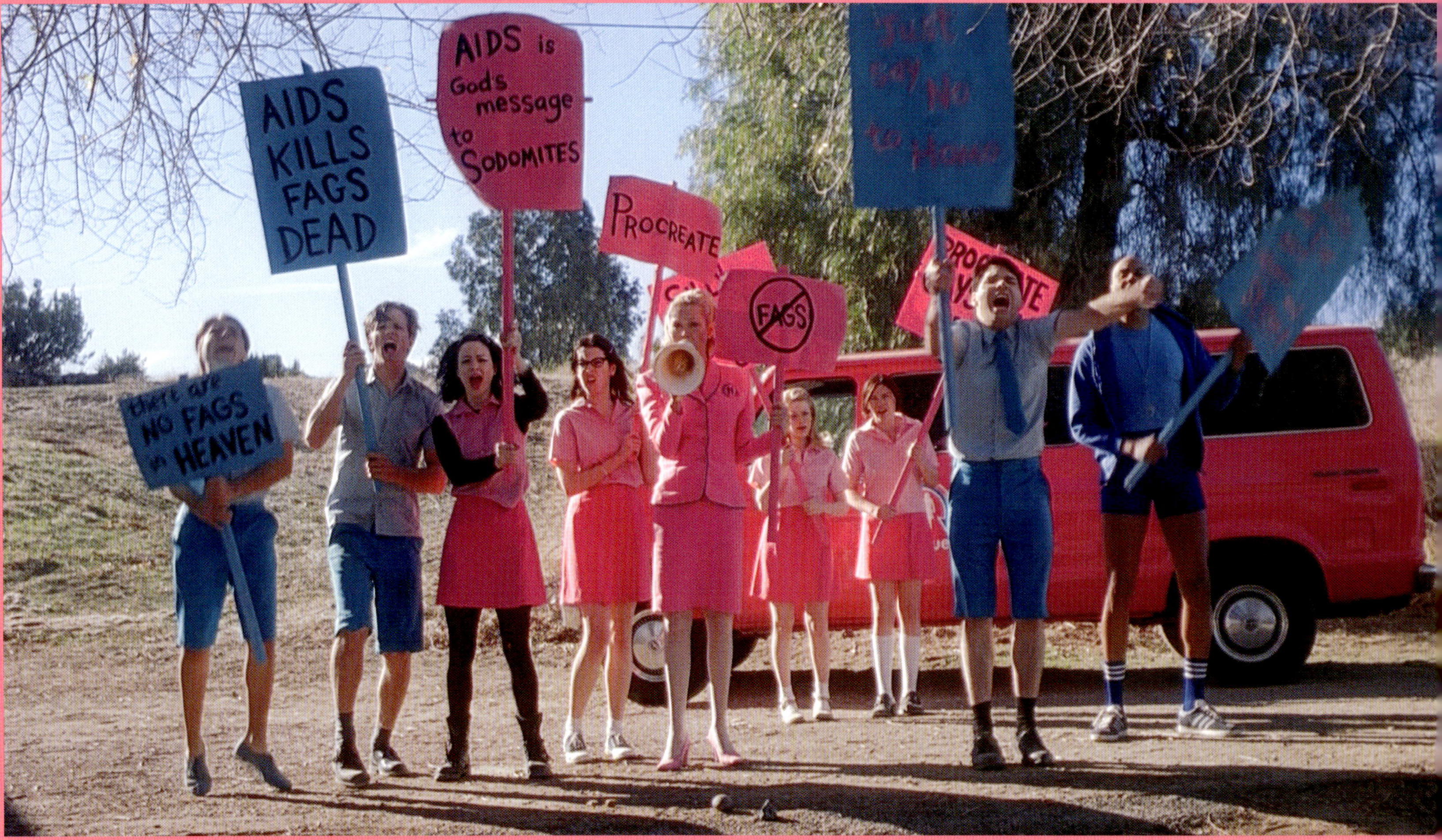

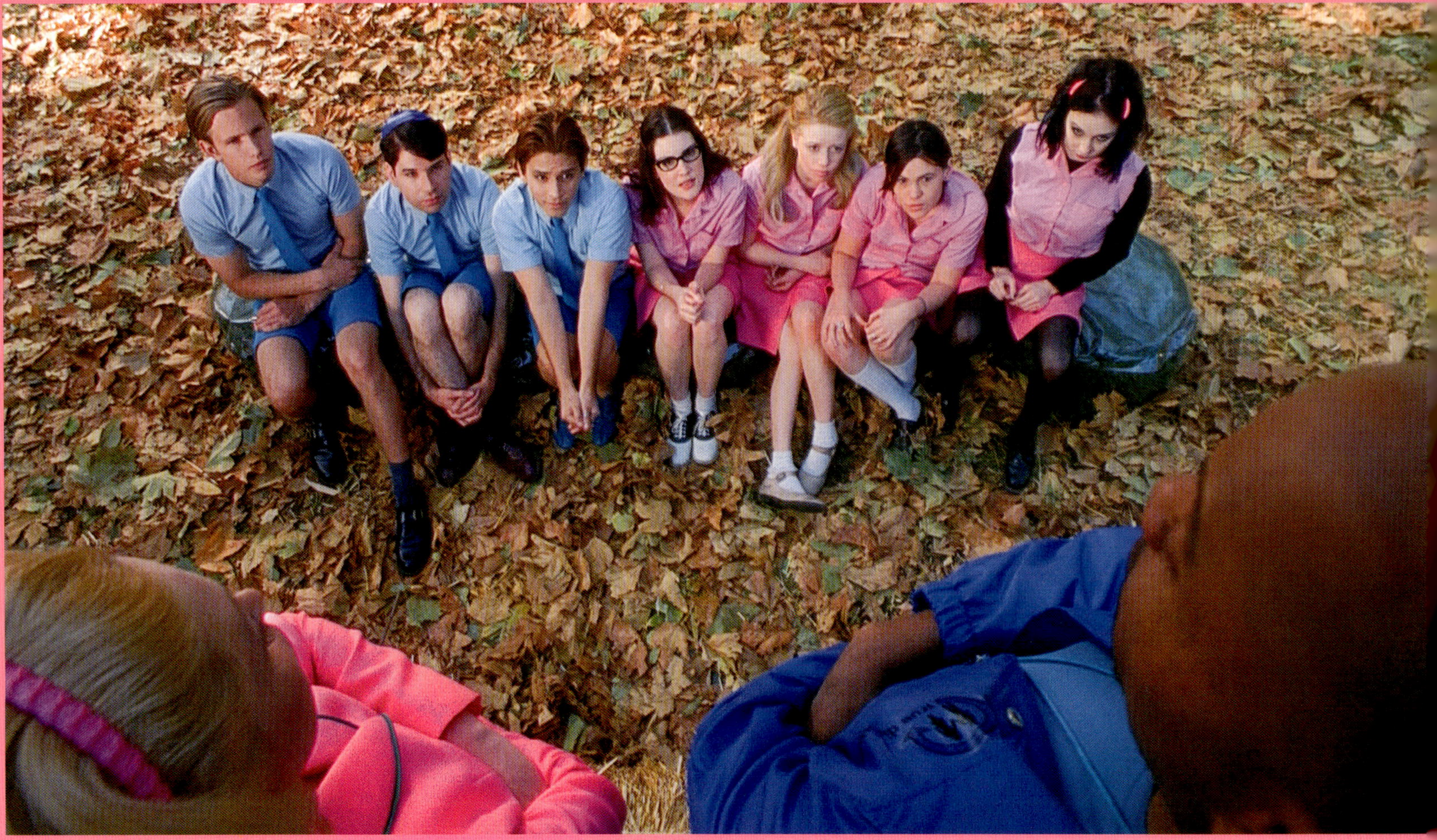

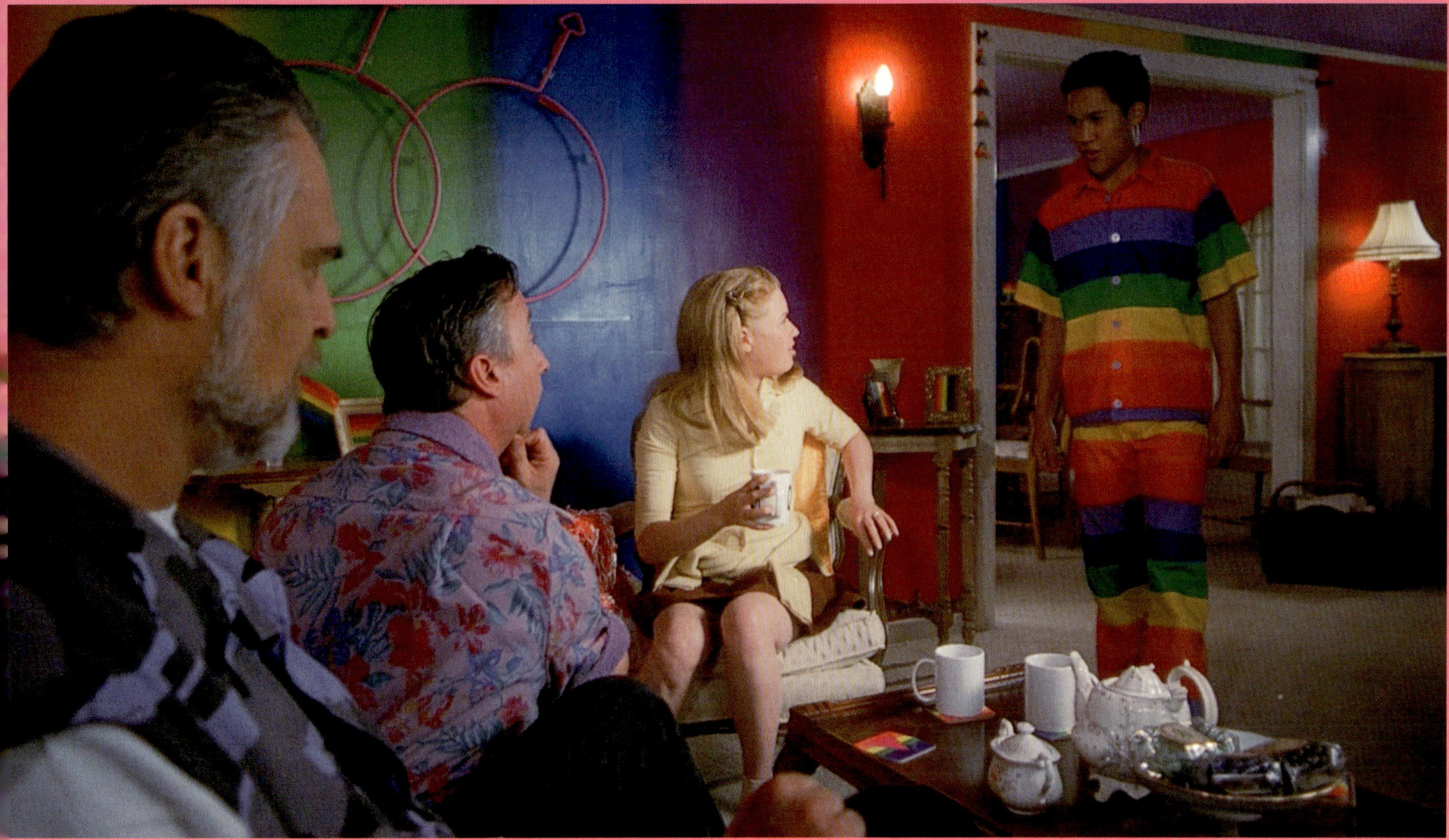

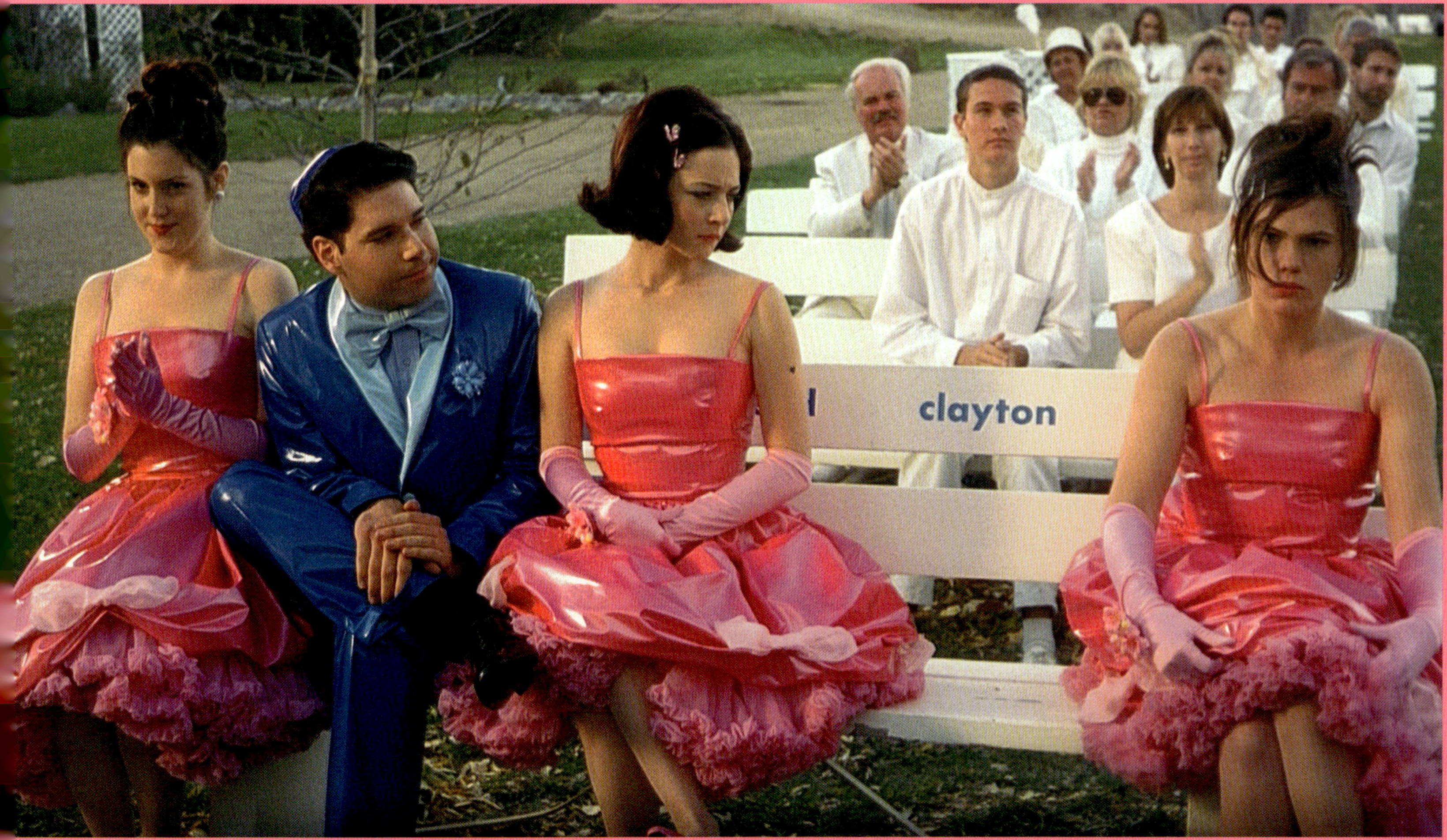

clayton

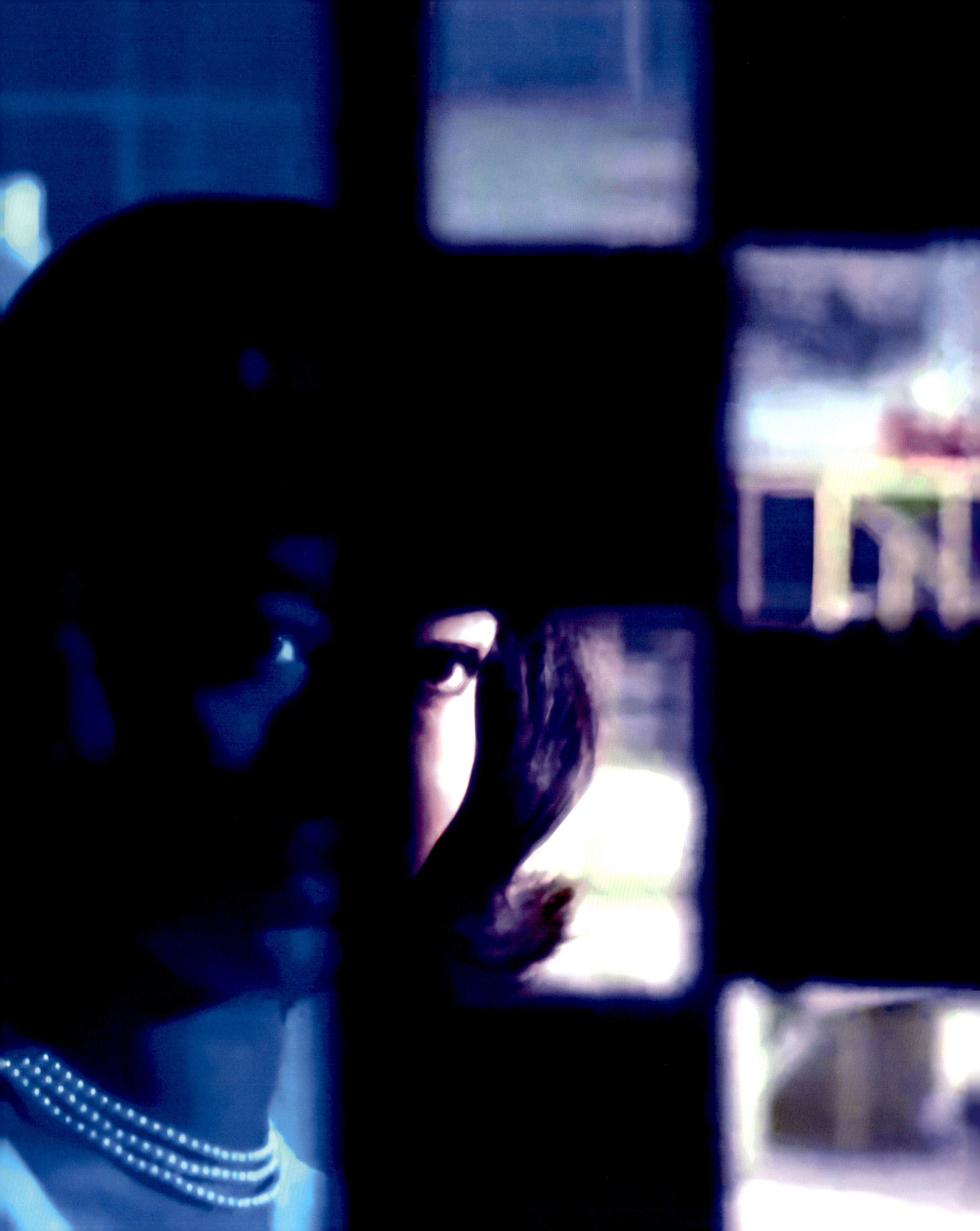

RANJANI MAZUMDAR

THE EASTMANCOLOR EFFECT

INTERMEDIAL DIALOGUES IN 1960s BOMBAY CINEMA

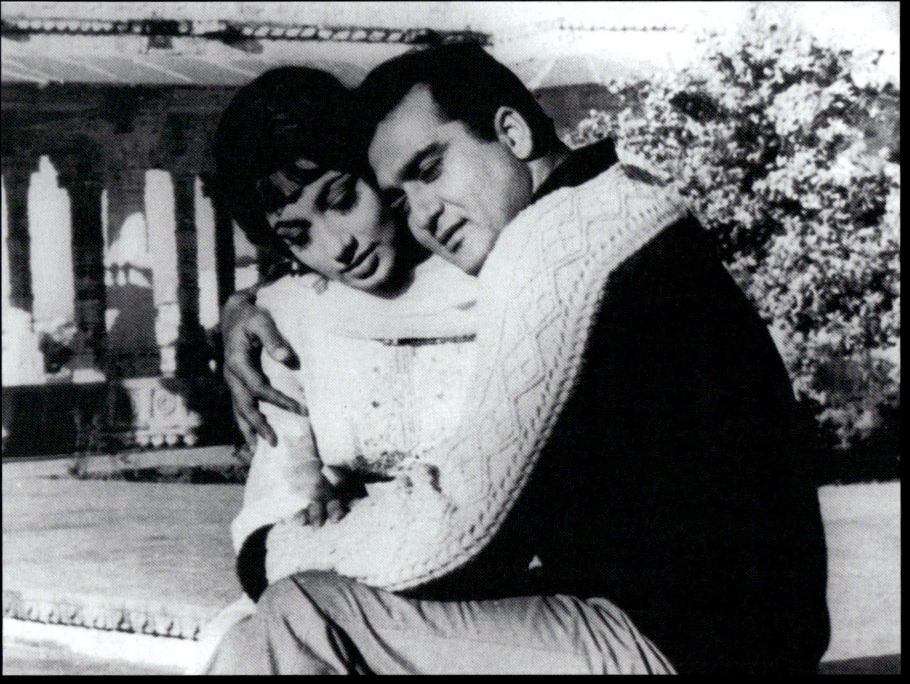

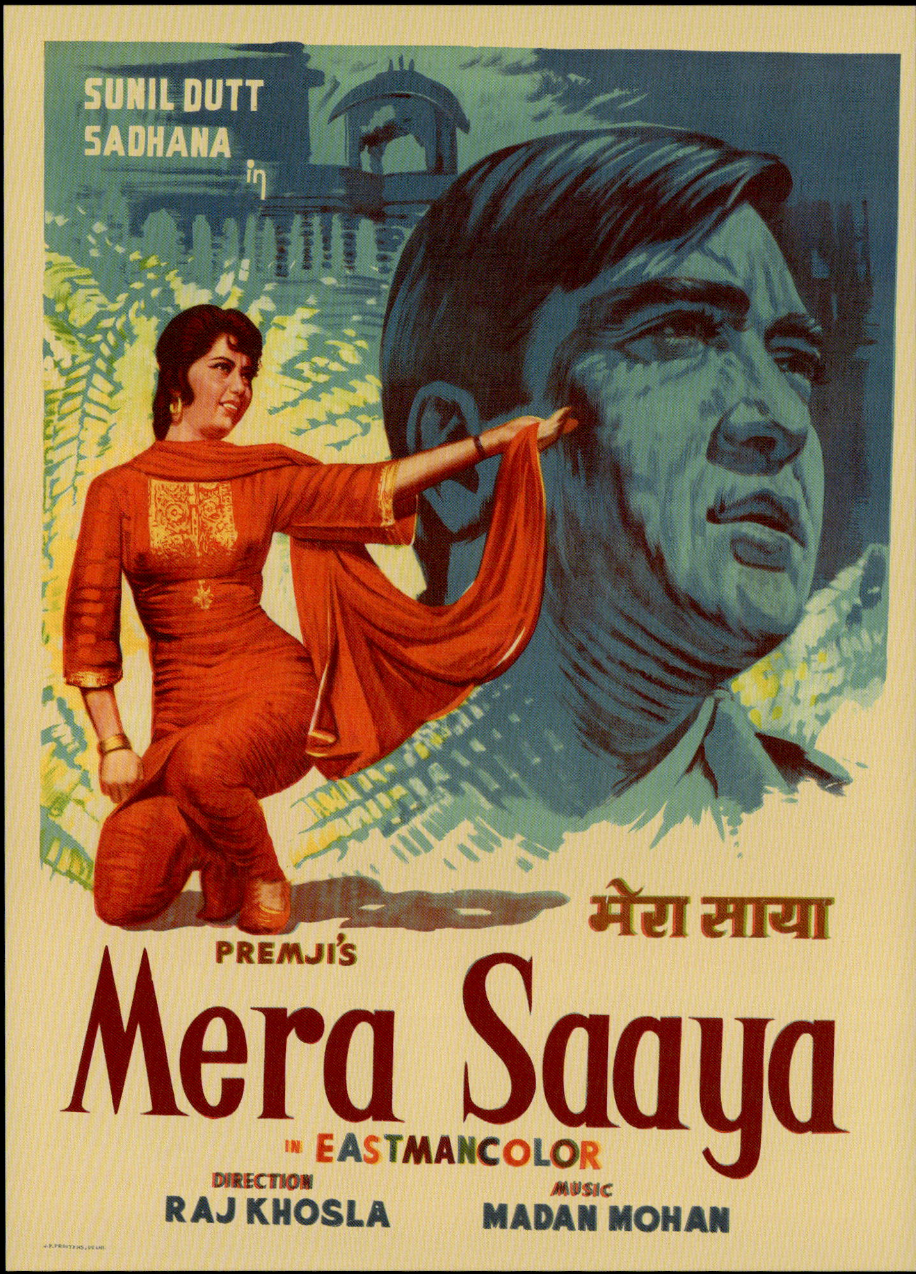

SUNIL DUTT
SADHANA
in

मेरा साया

PREMJI'S

Mera Saaya

IN EASTMANCOLOR

DIRECTION
RAJ KHOSLA

MUSIC
MADAN MOHAN

TOP: *Mera Saaya* (India, 1966, dir. Raj Khosla), production still

RIGHT: Theatrical poster for *Mera Saaya*

PAGE 196: *Anita* (India, 1967, dir. Raj Khosla)

Eastmancolor was introduced to the world in 1950. Its single-strip color process was less expensive and could be used with any camera and processing equipment, gradually displacing the more cumbersome Technicolor to become the preferred color film across the world. In India, however, the widespread impact of Eastmancolor was experienced during the 1960s, a decade of severe economic and political turmoil.[1] A major outcome of this economic crisis was a severe shortage of foreign exchange, which placed tremendous pressure on the import of goods. For the Bombay film industry, the crisis was directly experienced through government regulation over the movement of color film stock, as all negative and positive Eastmancolor stock had to be imported from the UK's Kodak facility.

The move to color was therefore slow and gradual, with many films managing to afford only one song sequence in color; *Mughal-e-Azam* and *Chaudhvin Ka Chand* (India, both 1960) are two examples. Despite the challenges, color was in the air, spreading initially through stills in printed advertisements and photo essays, highlighting a new form of interaction with the country's geographic terrain as well as its interior spaces. As in most parts of the world, set design after the widespread adoption of color film posed an interesting challenge for art directors. One of the significant interventions in the creation of the Bombay interior was the evocative constellation of other media, whether directly featuring photographs, paintings, and periodicals in the mise-en-scène or evoking them through equipment such as still cameras, musical instruments, radios, home-movie cameras, and more. The presence of these items extended beyond their function as objects of use, display, and decoration to incorporate a new kind of expressivity. In recent years, the term increasingly used to assess these connections across media forms is "intermediality," and with the arrival of every new media technology, cinema has expanded its intermedial connections.[2] While the presence of other media on screen was not new, the arrival of Eastmancolor caused a perceptual upheaval, leading to dynamic constructions of outdoor and indoor space. The creative use of multiple media in the conjuring of home interiors was one such spatial construction, and analyzing set decoration in a cluster of Bombay films from the 1960s can reveal the entanglements between social and cultural contexts and the dynamism unleashed by color.

One of the most prominent techniques used to highlight the arrival of color film was the integration of black-and-white photography into settings, whether as portraits, albums, decorative objects, or ghostly apparitions. In other words, with color the black-and-white photograph acquired a new sense of "pastness," most explicitly demonstrated in the interior spaces of Raj Khosla's *Mera Saaya* (India, 1966). When Geeta (Sadhna) dies suddenly of an illness, her husband, Rakesh (Sunil Dutt), is confronted by his wife's look-alike, who claims she is the real Geeta. The melancholic narrative of the film moves between a trial, where Geeta struggles to prove her identity, and Rakesh's grief, staged in the interior of his home through the innovative use of black-and-white photographs. There is a moment when Rakesh sees an album placed casually on the mantelpiece. He sits down to flip through the pages, which appear on screen in close-up. The film's well-known song, "Tu Jahan, Jahan Chalega, Mera Saaya Saath Hoga" (Wherever you go, my shadow will follow you), envelops the mise-en-scène with an air of sadness.

All of this—Geeta's death, the song, and the album, with its black-and-white recollections of Rakesh and Geeta's honeymoon and marriage—constitutes the film's opening, staged as an intermedial dialogue with photographic memory. When the album reaches a blank page, there is an abrupt switch to color and a discordant break in the soundtrack. The opening-title sequence is then introduced with the names of the lead actors. This is followed by the title of the film, with "in Eastmancolor" boldly announced below, each letter of "Eastmancolor" in a different color. This opening sequence allegorically alludes to the Bombay film industry's transition to color using the emotional force of death tied to memories stored in the family album. The album offers nostalgic comfort in the past for future generations. It is no accident that *Mera Saaya,* which means "my shadow," should invoke the family album—as both the repository of now-painful memories as well as a staging ground for the gradual disappearance of the black-and-white imagination associated with the history of cinema. Death in the film signifies a range of emotions, not necessarily linked only to a person's demise.

Khosla used song sequences to evoke Rakesh's majestic home, with the camera evocatively showcasing pillars and arches associated with the aristocracy of Udaipur. The haunting voice of the popular singer Lata Mangeshkar on the soundtrack lends a melancholic mood to the sense of loss conveyed by the lyrics. The interior appears like a shrine, with framed photographs adorning the walls, cabinets, and stone pedestals. In one scene, Rakesh leans close to Geeta's black-and-white portrait in the middle of a song. His face appears as a colored reflection peering back through the frame's glass pane overlaying the portrait. In the film's many photographic moments such as this, a monochromatic world is juxtaposed against one in color. The moments serve a dual purpose: they provide unusual potency to the story while also referencing the film industry's move to color. *Mera Saaya* uses the emotion of loss attached to death as an inevitability to showcase the black-and-white era, now on its way out, as a spectral presence.[3]

One strand of writings on the domestic interiors of the wealthy has usually conjured these spaces through a sense that is dependent on the careful negotiation of any threat of displacement. The persistent and felt experience of these threats makes one thing clear: the house is not truly a private space. As a result, we must reflect on the complicated relationship between public and private as well as the slipperiness of all property relations. In highly unequal and hierarchical countries like India, the carving of wealthy domestic interiors is meant to stage a form of spectacular value. In his book *Spectacle of Property* (2017), John David Rhodes shows that the house is one of the primary sites where intangible relations are made visible.[4] At one level, the interior displays aspirational notions of identity; at another, conflicting social interactions are rendered through psychic dislocations. In films such as Moni Bhattacharjee's *Jaal* (India, 1967) and A. Bhim Singh's *Aadmi* (India, 1968), color is used imaginatively to reinvigorate the expressive and performative charge of private property—a value that becomes twisted by forces beyond the control of the home.

Jaal is a thriller in which the disappearance of Sundar (Sujit Kumar) sets the stage for unusual events in interior spaces, where framed black-and-white images, palatial furnishings, and elegant apparel play important roles. Sundar is pronounced dead, causing distress for Sheela (Mala Sinha), who is his fiancée by arrangement. Sheela had never met Sundar, yet after her own father's death she goes to live with Sundar's aunt in a huge coastal house with a spiral staircase, enormous chandeliers, and labyrinthine passageways. Sundar's black-and-white photograph appears everywhere in the seaside house. We later learn that Sundar is a criminal who staged his own death in an elaborate scheme to torment Sheela, appearing either as a ghostly figure at night or through the constant rearrangement of his portrait on the wall to convey the sense of an invisible force. He had his eye on her property, and the bizarre events that occur inside the house are meant to induce Sheela's gothic spiral into madness. Sundar's omnipresence creates a horrific, unsettling ambience, with the sound of stormy nights, rain, and terrifying wind adding to the eerie effects.

Sheela's gradual transformation from a fashionable, lively woman to a screaming, hysterical, and traumatized persona is reminiscent of international gothic melodramas. We can also see traces of Alfred Hitchcock's experiments with color in the rendering of domestic interiors as oppressive, claustrophobic, and threatening.[5] In Hitchcock's *Rear Window* (USA, 1954), color is deployed to establish the distinctness of each of the apartments viewed by L. B. "Jeff" Jeffries (James Stewart)

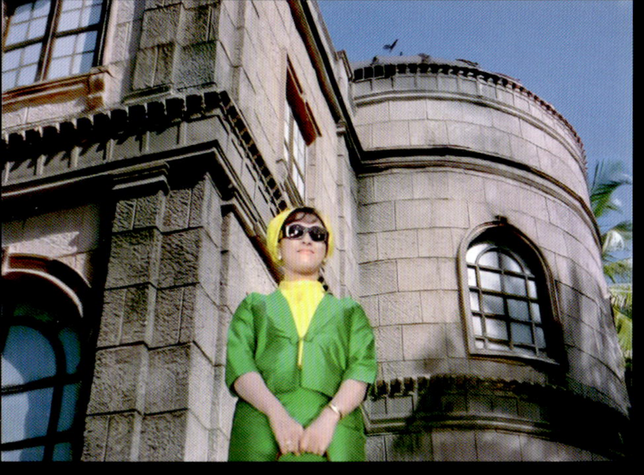

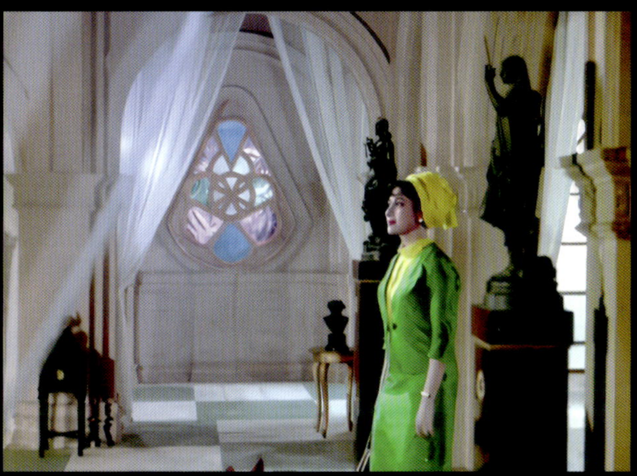

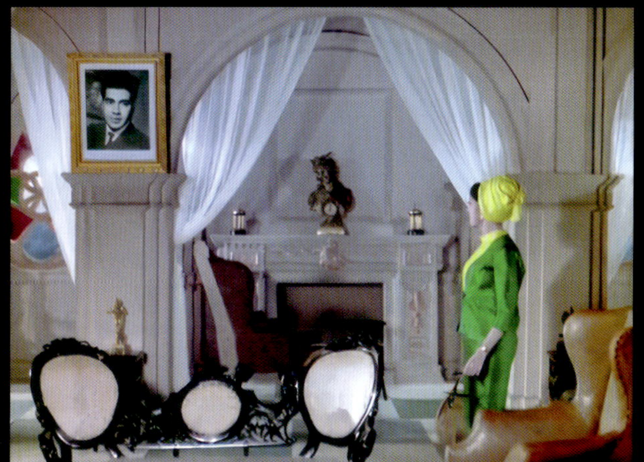

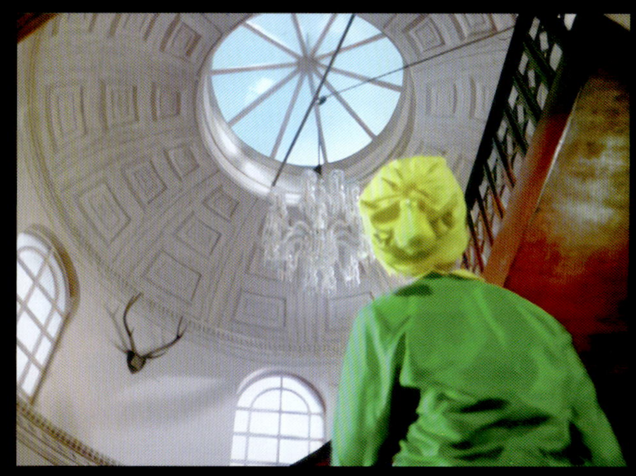

Jaal (India, 1967, dir. Moni Bhattacharjee)

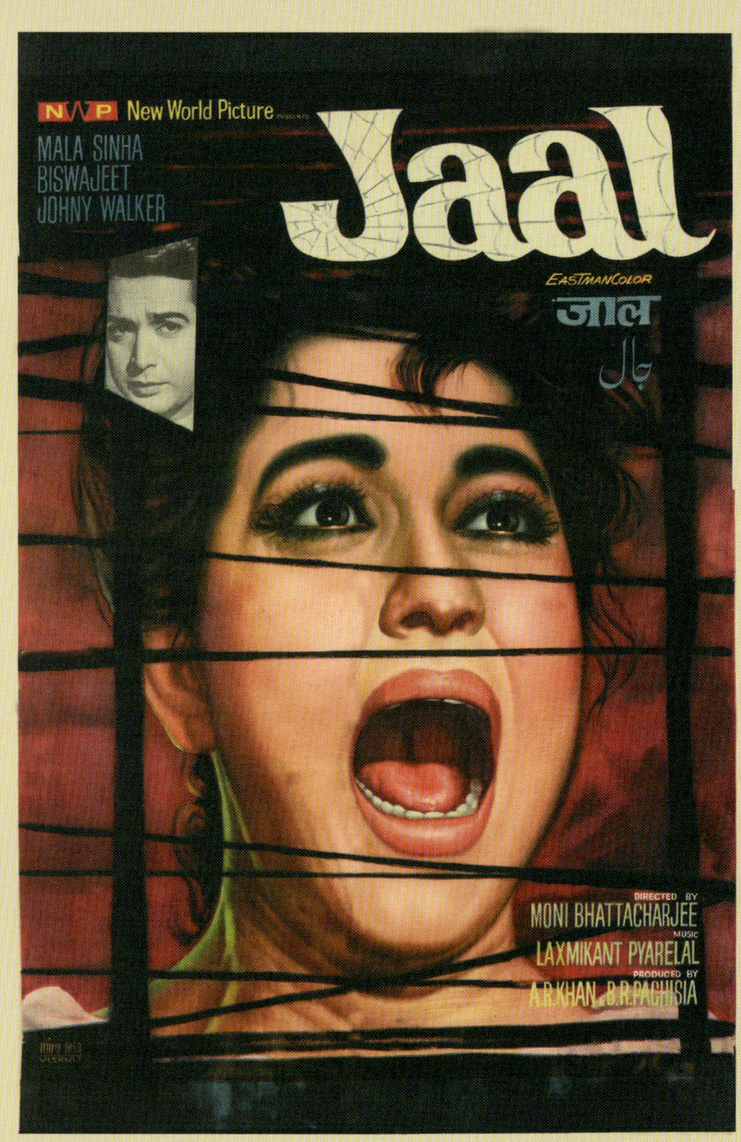

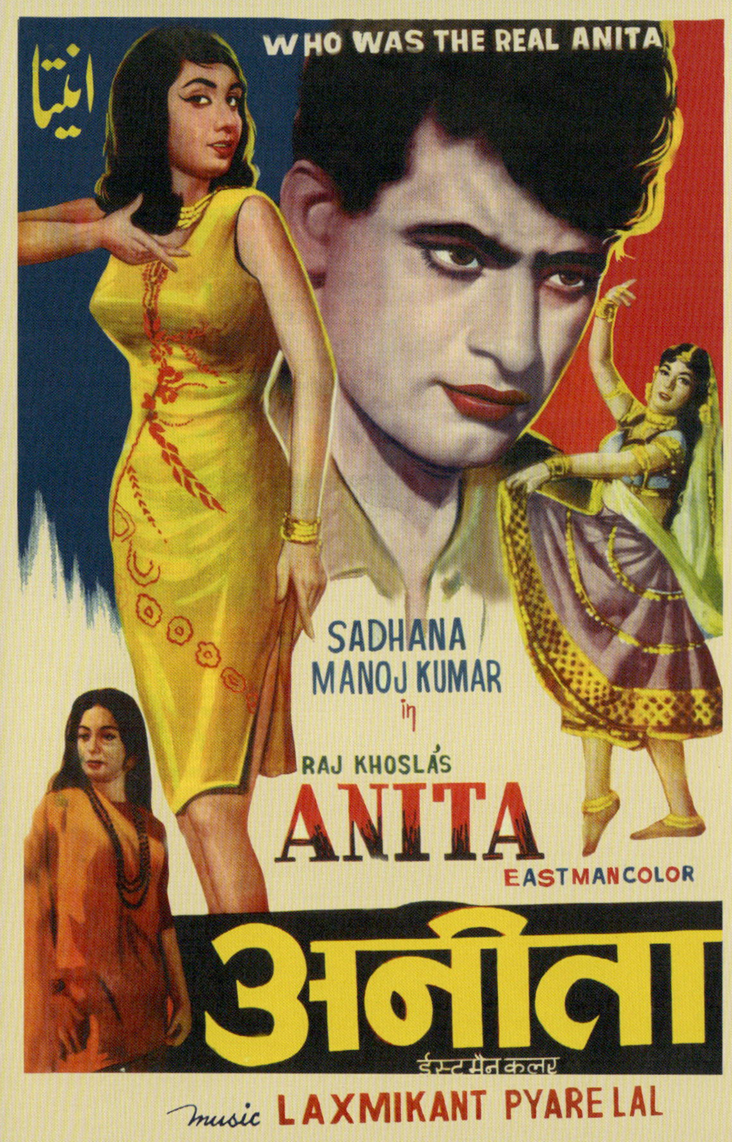

TOP: Theatrical poster for *Jaal* (India, 1967, dir. Moni Bhattacharjee)

across the courtyard. In the director's *Vertigo* (USA, 1958), green is used to provide a mysterious ambience to Judy's (Kim Novak) apartment. While light and color play a role in Hitchcock's atmospheric portrayal of the home as uncanny, the black-and-white photograph is used for an intermedial staging of lurking danger in *Jaal*.

Sheela moves between three distinct interiors. Her meticulously calibrated modernist residence in Bombay—with its art objects, wall decor, olive-green carpeting, textured walls, and glass partitions—identifies Sheela as a young woman accustomed to her freedom. Bombay cinema's use of color in the 1960s resulted in a visual push for new textures of value in the presentation of domestic interiors, where the home as a sensual and psychological setting could be enhanced. These architectural modes of expression were influenced by global aesthetic currents that were prevalent at the time and circulated widely through fashion and home decor magazines. In one scene, Sheela entertains friends at home in a casually fashionable outfit before sitting on a white cushioned bench against a textured white wall and reclining like a model to face the camera. The spectral presence of fashion spreads and home-interior magazines emerges through an intermedial dialogue with the film's mise-en-scène. Film and media scholar Giuliana Bruno has suggested that such moments foreground a surface condition or a tension that allows us to understand the materiality of the image. Materiality, for her, "is not a question of the materials themselves but rather concerns the substance of material relations."[6] In this moment from *Jaal*, it is color that triggers a dialogue between such magazines and cinema.

In addition to her Bombay apartment and the coastal house, Sheela encounters one more interior. This is the temporary apartment of Shankar (Biswajit); unbeknownst to her, he is a police inspector investigating Sundar's disappearance. Shankar is disguised as a gas station owner who also paints in his spare time. His frequent movements at home allow the camera to fully capture his apartment's very modern decor. Between these three architectural spaces, Sheela's experience with the palatial residence appears as an anomaly, where greed for property is staged as an intermedial performance of the ghostly that is ultimately resolved through investigation.

For *Aadmi*, celebrated art directors Sudhendu Roy and Desh Mukherjee designed a palatial home for the film's protagonist, Rajesh/Raja Sahib (Dilip Kumar), a wealthy industrialist. Inside this large residence, with its imposing staircase, chessboard floor, and muted lighting, Rajesh is frequently haunted by the childhood memory of murdering his friend Babu for frivolous reasons. This tragedy not only invades Rajesh's guilt-ridden nightmares but also is manifested as a black-and-white photograph of Babu in an album, which is kept secure in a gold-colored cabinet along with a doll named Meena. This cabinet is frequently presented as the source of terror for Rajesh and the link to his past and its psychological trauma; in one scene, Rajesh imagines Babu's voice laughing at his property and wealth. The past threatens to blur with Rajesh's present when he begins to suspect his wife, Meena (Waheeda Rehman), of infidelity. She married Rajesh to help her family's difficult financial situation despite her love for Shekhar (Manoj Kumar), a doctor and friend who is also indebted to Rajesh for financial support for his medical training.

Property as a social and cultural value pervades the film's mood; financial indebtedness merges with suspicion, psychological crisis, guilt, and personal redemption, all of which is largely staged through the atmosphere created inside the house. Roy and Mukherjee deployed surface color over fabric, objects, walls, glass panes, and pillars to create a heavily opulent interior. Within this display of wealth is the cabinet, where dark forces are stored. The film allows transgressions to hover in the narrative, but the family is sacrosanct, and all deviations are ironed out. Yet we see through the narrative an explicit play of tensions, and the black-and-white photograph in the album becomes the intermedial link between the trauma of the past and the crisis of the present. As in *Jaal*, property as a value is staged as precarious, but this time the threat lies within as a schizophrenic force.

Anita (India, 1967) is a suspense story that is part of Raj Khosla's female-led doppelgänger mysteries, following *Woh Kaun Thi?* (India, 1964) and *Mera Saaya*. Anita (Sadhana) is a fashionable young millionaire whose life spirals into crisis, forcing her to disappear. Unlike the traditional royal aesthetic of the home in *Mera Saaya*, Anita's home is modern and spacious, with large glass doors and windows. The flowing sheer curtains expressively capture the movement of air, lending a breezy and comforting ambience to the space. The film opens with an overhead shot of Anita in her bedroom, sprawled on her white carpet, surrounded by colorful women's magazines. Amid this cluster of colors, a male voice-over starts a romantic conversation with Anita, which then turns into a song in which the bedroom and its spacious form are captured from various angles. The voice belongs to Neeraj (Manoj Kumar), whose affair with Anita is supposed to be a secret.

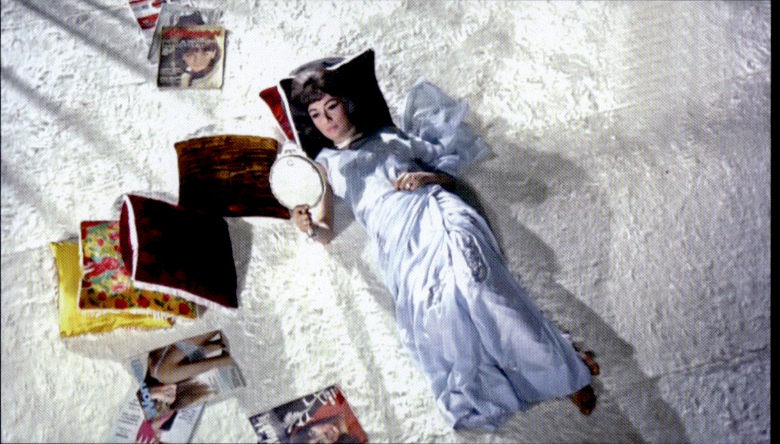

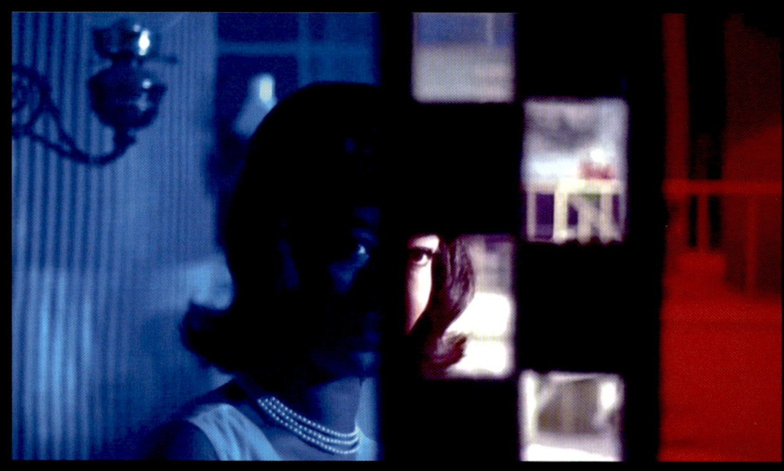

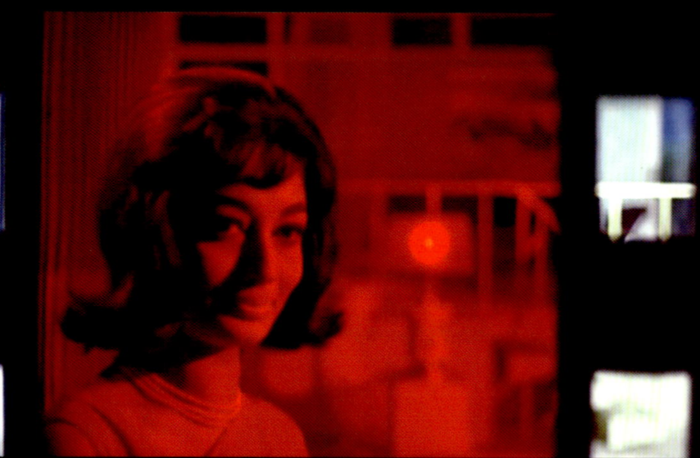

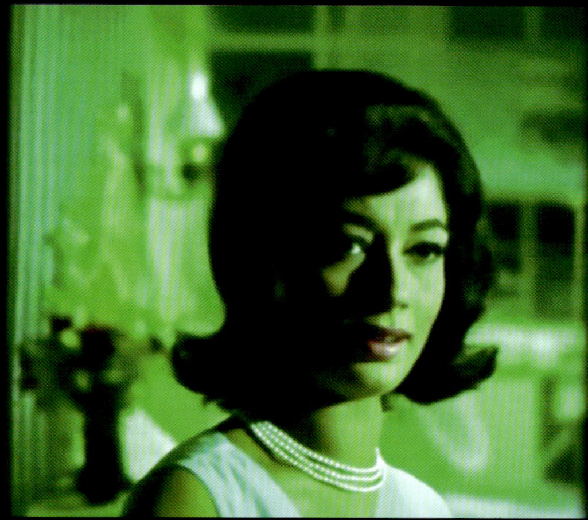

Anita (India, 1967, dir. Raj Khosla)

Desh Mukherjee, the film's art director, was an artist trained at Kolkata's government art college.[7] *Anita*'s opening, like the spectral presence of fashion photography in *Jaal*, exposes the surface tension produced by the mingling of elements from the international circulation of Pop art and psychedelic experimentation with light with the local media of popular magazines and Hindi cinema's musical form. However, there is no attempt to imitate Western styles; instead, these global influences are employed to generate hybrid intermedial events. The most notable feature is the use of glass plates tinted red, green, and blue to frame close-ups of Anita's face. Color is positioned here as a performance, creating "color events" rather than representing events in color. The tinted glass frames foreground a non-narrative, serialized aesthetic, showing Anita walk past them. The frames display a heightened awareness about the new place of color in the expansion of mass-produced visual culture in the 1960s. The influence of Andy Warhol's experiments with color is unmistakable.[8] Warhol experimented with color's plasticity in many of his artworks and films. *Chelsea Girls* (USA, 1966), for instance, is a three-and-a-half-hour two-screen cinematic relay of a series of rooms at the Chelsea Hotel in Manhattan and their goings-on. Occasionally one screen is in black and white while the other is in vivid and somewhat artificial color tones that often render the images almost abstract. Color is used as discrete elements within the larger black-and-white work to comment on the overwhelmingly widespread presence of color in mass consumerism.

When Anita goes missing, the film transitions into a detective film. Neeraj refuses to accept she is dead because he saw her somewhere briefly. His investigations lead him to various people who recall Anita's mysterious persona. One witness is an eccentric man (I. S. Johar), a painter. Neeraj explores this man's home, and the camera scans the wooden interiors of the hillside cottage to reveal walls decorated with framed paintings and drawings that were clearly influenced by popular assumptions about what modern art should look like. The viewer is treated to a brief parodic explanation of modern art as well as a close-up of what appears to be an abstract painting. The painting's abstraction and illegibility serve as catalysts for the man to recall a story about a drunken Anita dressed like a femme fatale in a dazzling red dress, singing a seductive song on a Hong Kong–bound ship.

What is noteworthy here is that the art director, Mukherjee, obviously drew from his knowledge of modernist abstraction to render it in a parodic form for the audience. This is also reminiscent of a similar scene in Michelangelo Antonioni's film *Blow-Up* (UK/Italy/USA, 1966), in which a painter discusses abstraction for the benefit of a fashion photographer, Thomas (David Hemmings). In *Anita*, the sudden move from a discussion about abstract painting to Anita's femme fatale persona, introduced for the first time in the film in a space away from home, provides the audience with a puzzling situation that thrillers rely on to build suspense.[9] While suspense causes anxiety about what to expect next in the narrative, the inclusion of a bizarre discussion about modernist abstraction provides this moment with a quirky playfulness that affectively loops together art with overtly femme fatale attire and style, reinforcing the origin myth of Pop art as a reaction to Abstract Expressionism. Pop artists like Warhol believed it was important to break free from the austere canon of Abstract Expressionism through an engagement with popular culture, in which color played an important role. Did Mukherjee see *Blow-Up*? Was it released in Bombay? I am still not sure. However, in these fragments we can see a transnational context that allows an intermedial occurrence on screen to carry both the art director's embodied knowledge and the signs of a global movement that figured prominently in the 1960s.

The home-movie camera plays a vital role in B. R. Chopra's film *Hamraaz* (India, 1967). Meena (Vimi) falls in love with Captain Rajesh (Raj Kumar), an army officer, and marries him quietly in a temple before he goes to war. Rajesh is killed in battle, and Meena is carrying his child. Her father, concerned about his daughter's reputation, gives up the child to an orphanage but eventually tells his daughter the truth before he dies. Meanwhile, Meena has married Kumar (Sunil Dutt), who knows nothing about her background. Meena discovers her daughter, Sarika, in an orphanage and wishes to adopt her; Kumar, who is not in favor of this, reluctantly agrees to occasional visits.

Kumar is a well-known theater personality, and his home reflects his fortune. Art director Sant Singh evocatively flooded the impressive multilevel residence with a range of colors and expensive fabrics. The presence of the home-movie camera in this opulent residence is not out of place, since only the very wealthy could afford it at the time. We hear it whirring as it records Meena and Sarika during their visits, and Kumar shows Sarika how to operate the camera. Halfway through the narrative, the film morphs into a murder mystery. Rajesh is alive; Meena is brutally murdered by an unknown assailant; and Sarika is missing. After a series of twists and turns, the truth comes to light when Kumar's co-star, Shabnam (Mumtaz), presents footage from the camera. Intending to record moments of play, Sarika had started filming on the terrible day of Meena's murder. When the killer arrived, he was obviously unaware of the camera's presence and its potential.

Home movies are usually performative repositories of the lives of families—rituals and festivities, romantic moments, holidays, and travel.[10] In *Hamraaz*, the home-movie camera records both life and death in color in contrast to the black-and-white family photographs of treasured moments on display. The bereaved Kumar constantly watches footage of romantic moments following Meena's death. The home-movie camera is portrayed as both an apparatus of familial memories available in color and a means for capturing incriminating evidence. As a force within the home, it is carefully managed by people while also possessing the power to act without direct human intervention. Like a major protagonist, the camera offers crucial evidence to nail the killer; it also turns the site of Meena's stabbed body into a spectacle of red blood splashed over a white sari, enough to dismantle any notion of a happy home. (The fascination for blood as a trail of death, along with the use of red vermilion to mark women as married, was played out almost obsessively in several films after the transition to color.) Suspicion of infidelity combined with murder is foregrounded as an intermedial event that plunders any notion of the ideal home in *Hamraaz*.

The staging of intermedial events in *Hamraaz*, as well as the other films discussed in this essay, demonstrates how the introduction of Eastmancolor triggered new approaches to the production of opulent set design and art direction. Color added a new dimension to the spectacle of private property and its expressive appearance on screen through a range of visual techniques. While this is true for most parts of the world, each geographic context generated its own ensemble of aesthetic negotiations. In the case of Bombay cinema, although the proliferation of color and its impact on 1960s set design found diverse expressions, the intermedial use of media objects remains an important element in the creation of interior spaces.

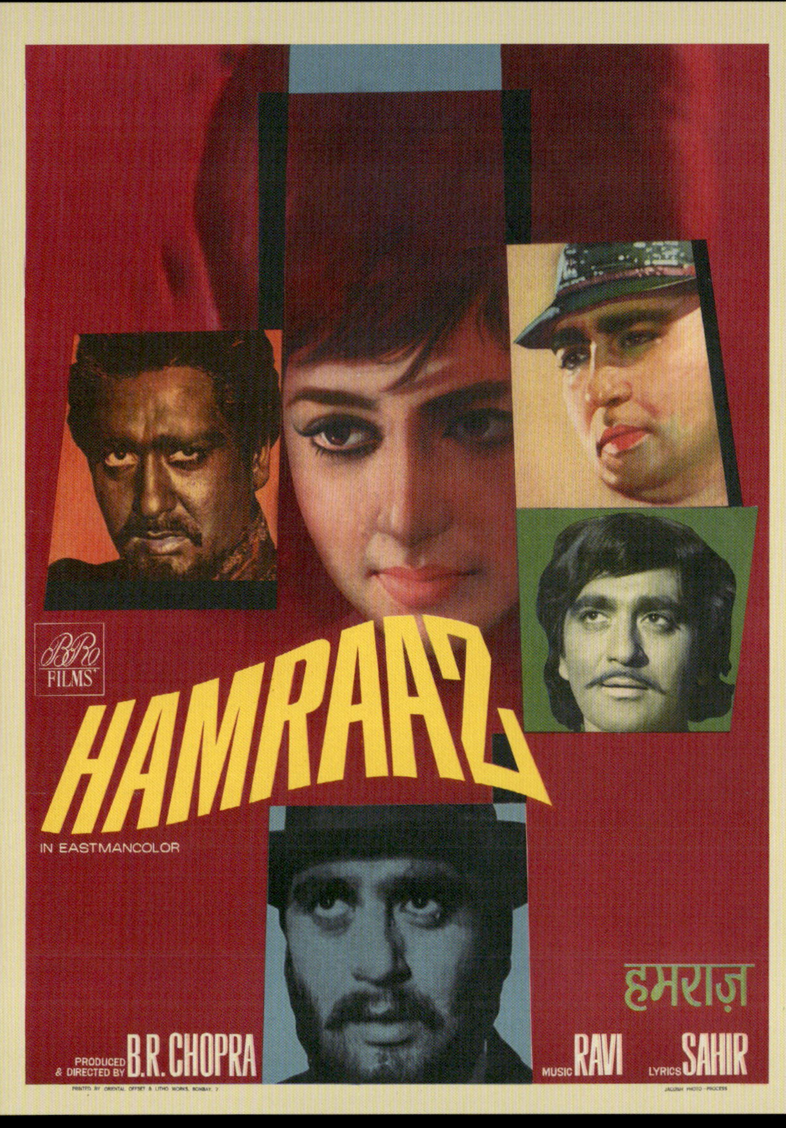

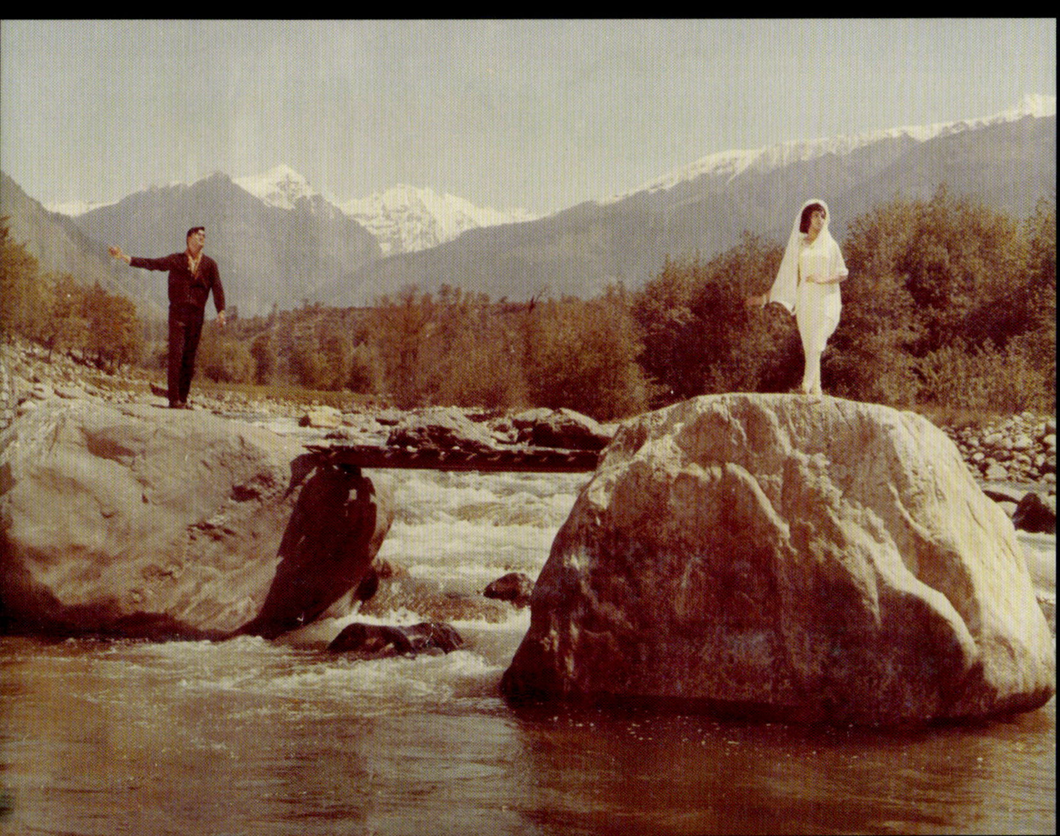

TOP: Theatrical poster for *Hamraaz* (India, 1967, dir. B. R. Chopra)

LEFT: *Hamraaz*, production still

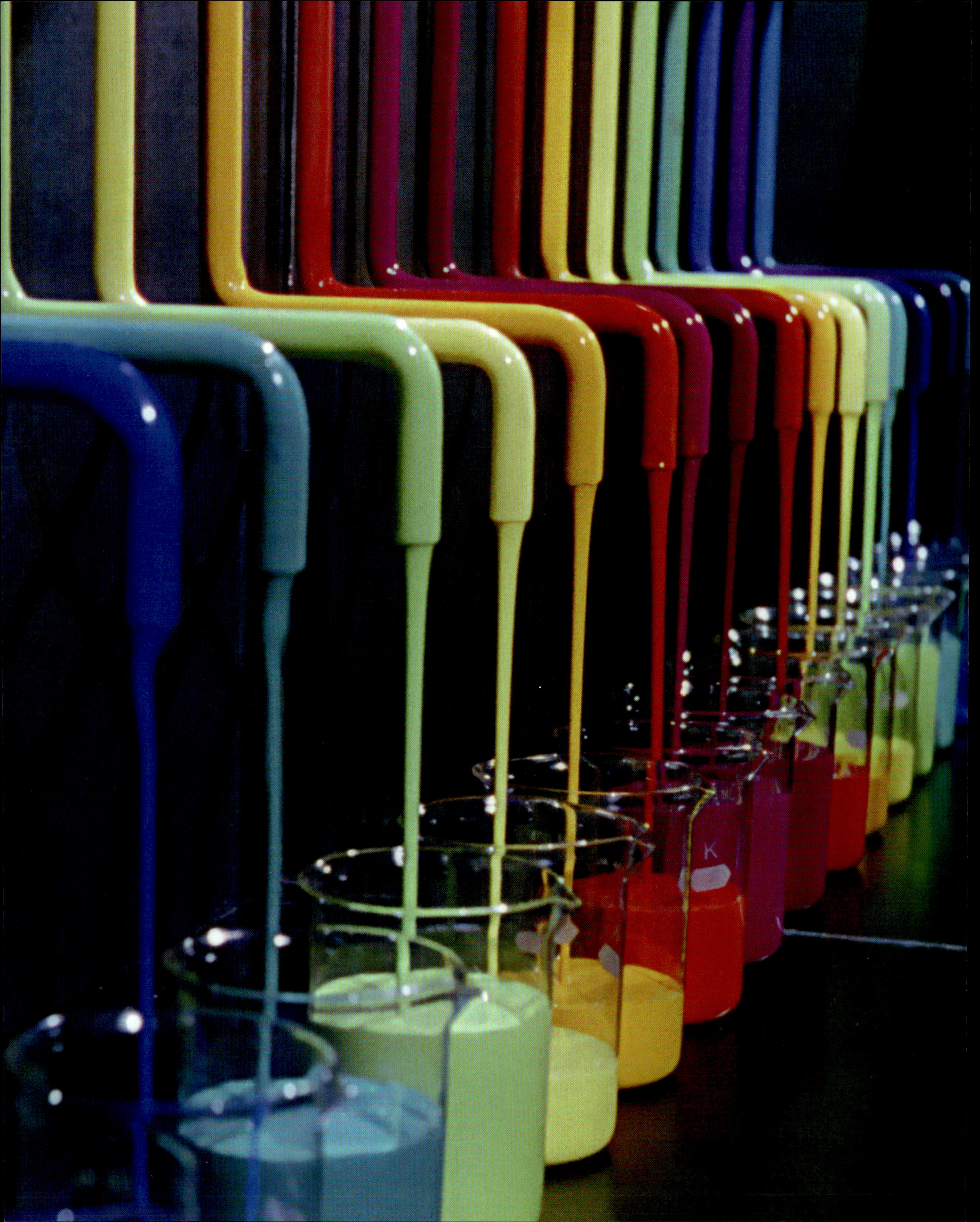
K

KIRSTEN MOANA THOMPSON

AMERICAN ANIMATION IN COLOR

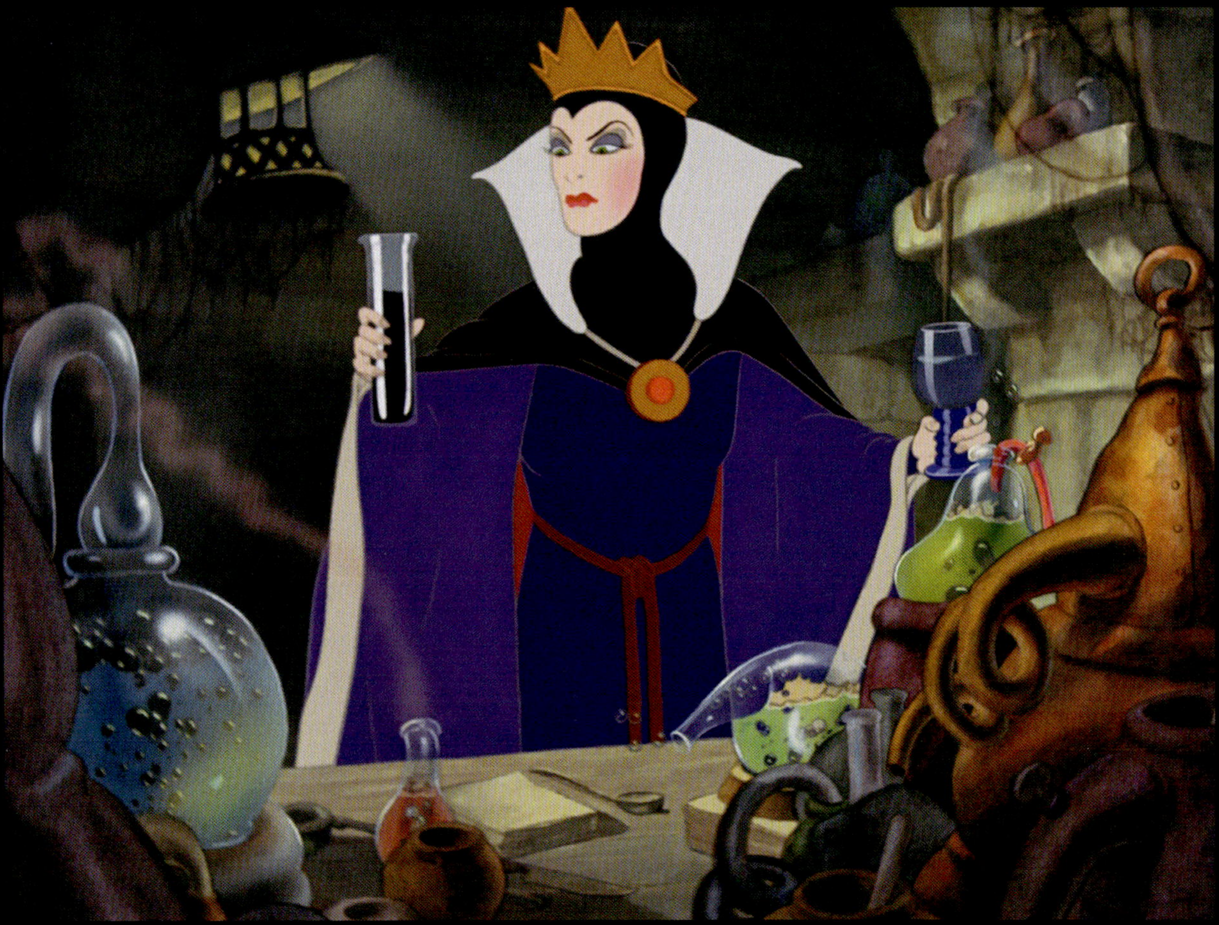

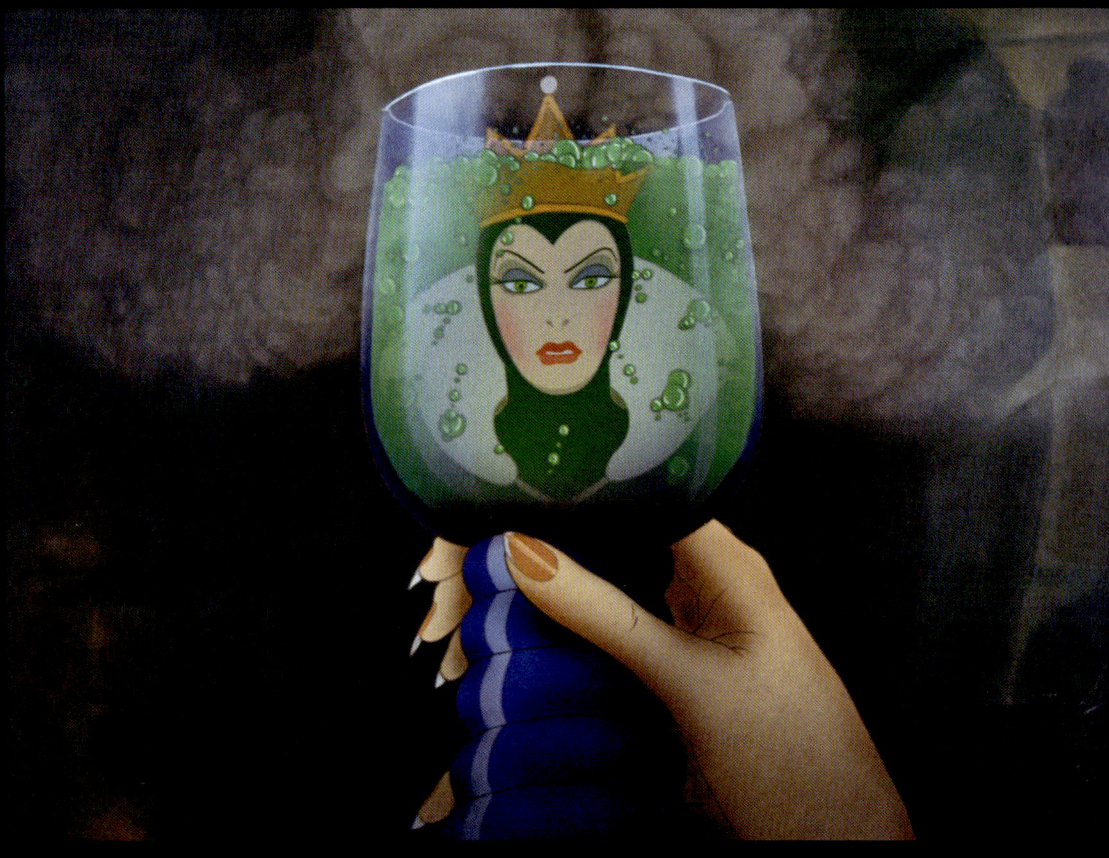

Snow White and the Seven Dwarfs (USA, 1937, dir. David Hand)

> There never was a time in our own work when we were not conscious that we needed color to achieve maximum entertainment in our pictures. For too long it was unavailable to films—and then came TECHNICOLOR.
>
> —Walt Disney[1]

When we think of animation, we might recall the colors of childhood: the bright-green sneer of the Grinch, the rich-red poisoned apple in *Snow White and the Seven Dwarfs* (USA, 1937), the saturated hues of toys and candy. A key device for the expression of mood, personality, and character, color is one of the most emotionally powerful elements in our experience of the motion picture, and its expressivity and vibrancy have long fascinated philosophers, artists, and scientists. Thanks to animation pioneers Walt Disney and Ted Eshbaugh and the chemists and researchers at Technicolor, the magical new process that was Technicolor IV brought a full range of vivid colors into the cinema, transforming the film industry. While color animation had played a role in film's earliest history—with applied color processes like hand-painted, tinted, toned, and stenciled films, as well as in later cinematographic processes—Technicolor IV became the dominant color process in shorts and feature films from 1932 until 1953, offering a vibrant palette with striking hues from rich fuchsias to yellows, purples, greens, and blues.

> I'll go myself to the dwarfs' cottage in a disguise so complete no one will ever suspect. Now, a formula to transform my beauty into ugliness, change my queenly raiment to a peddler's cloak. Mummy dust to make me old. To shroud my clothes, the black of night. To age my voice, an old hag's cackle. To whiten my hair, a scream of fright. A blast of wind to fan my hate! A thunderbolt to mix it well. Now, begin thy magic spell.

So begins the classic scene in *Snow White* in which the wicked Queen concocts a spell to disguise herself as an old peddler, part of her plan to trick Snow White into eating a poisoned apple. Appearing in the first animated feature film released in Technicolor IV, the scene highlights the spectacular expressivity of this new full color process, representing color as dye and as diabolical agent of the black arts.[2] In a series of dissolving close-ups, we see each step in the Queen's chromatic formula. First, she takes a goblet with gray liquid containing mummy dust and adds to it several inky drops of jet black from a test tube, her language drawing attention to the double register of color as both light and dye, while the accompanying shimmering sound and camera movement underscore the magical moment as mummy dust and inky blackness interpenetrate. The third and fourth steps in the chromatic spell invite us to hear color and to see sound. To

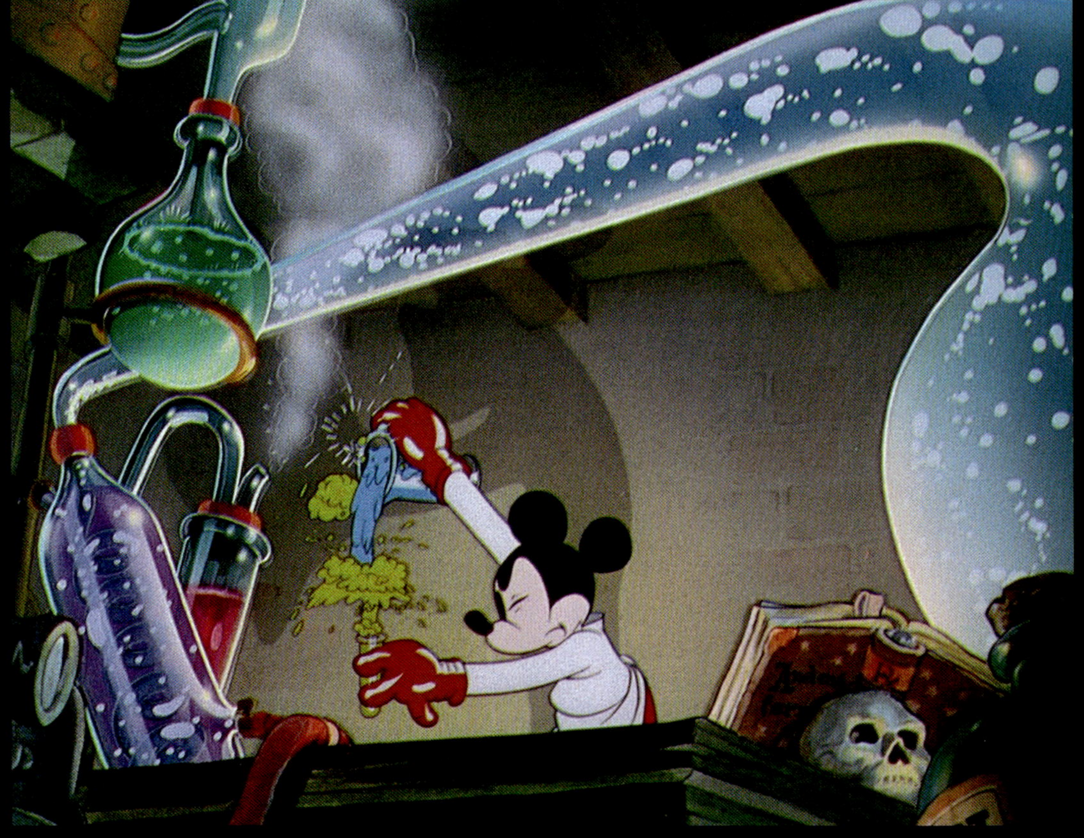

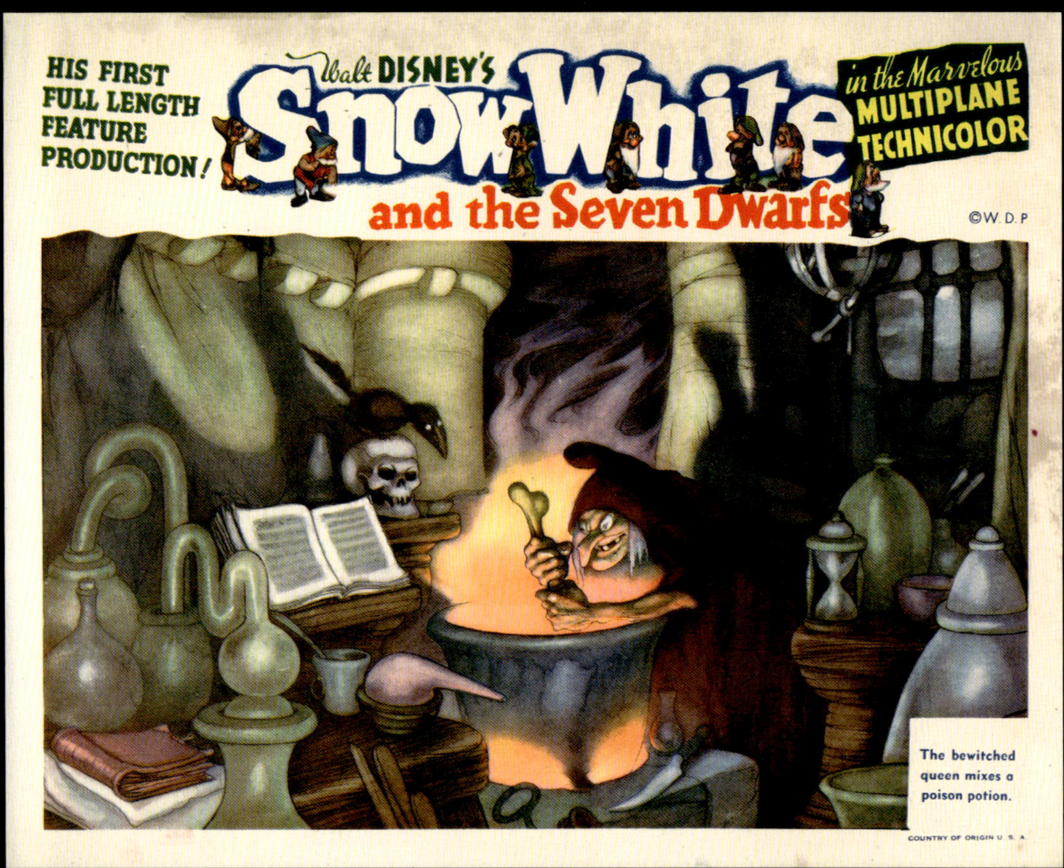

TOP: *The Worm Turns* (USA, 1937, dir. Ben Sharpsteen)

BOTTOM: Lobby card for *Snow White and the Seven Dwarfs* (USA, 1937, dir. David Hand)

"age my voice," an old hag's cackle becomes a beaker of orange bubbling liquid that a purple-blue Bunsen flame heats up, brings to a boil, evaporates, and recondenses into pure red. The saturated contrasts of red against the blue flame are heightened as each drop condenses in rhythm with a cackle as the Queen titrates color and sound together into the inky goblet. Then, to "whiten my hair," a ghostly scream of fright becomes a synesthetic squirt of white, as we see a thick white liquid poured into the Queen's goblet of red, turning it to its complementary color, green. With a flash of thunder and lightning, the image suddenly dissolves into a funnel of color, and the Queen starts to transform. We plummet down color's vortex, inside smears and bubbles of color, as we witness the metamorphosis of her body as youth shifts to old age and from beauty into the ugliness within.

The scene showcases the material and magical qualities of color as transformative agent. The Queen is a master practitioner in the black arts, casting spells for diabolical purpose, but she is also a chemist who measures out mummy dust, the black of night, an old hag's cackle, and a scream of fright. In reality, what we actually see is pure, liquid color: luscious reds, sinister greens, and bubbling oranges, counterpointed by the haughty purple and ominous blacks of the Queen's gown, a cackling red tongue replacing her scarlet lips.

The moment also reminds us of animation's two etymological roots—from the French *animer* and the Latin root *animare* (to breathe or blow). Animation can also mean to endow with life or spirit (anima), to start a chemical reaction, to intensify, or to put into motion, all of which are suggested in Mary Shelley's novel *Frankenstein* (1818), when she used the word "animation" to describe the conversion of lifeless matter in a similar magical laboratory scene.[3] The Queen's transformation can be seen as drawing upon long-standing philosophical ideas in which color was often "the property of some foreign body—usually the feminine, oriental, primitive, infantile, vulgar, queer, or pathological" or, on the other hand, associated with "the superficial, supplementary, inessential, or cosmetic."[4] In these chromophobic traditions, David Batchelor tells us, color is either dangerous, superficial, or both. When viewed through this lens, the concept of diabolical corruption by means of color helps to inform and link the *Snow White* scene to a long philosophical tradition in Renaissance art in which form (*disegno*) was privileged over hue (*colore*).[5] The Queen's cloaking spell brings together these aspects as she uses colored liquids to transform her beautiful surface with magical artifice, to figuratively turn it inside out, as she later does with a potion that bathes a red apple in a cauldron of sickly green color, commanding us, "Look! On the skin! The symbol of what lies within!"

A parallel laboratory scene can be found in Disney's *The Worm Turns* (USA, 1937), released the same year as *Snow White* and clearly alluding to it. Mickey Mouse, in a white lab coat with bright red gloves, is working on a secret formula called the "Courage Builder" (or "The Weak Made Strong"), a potion that gives underdogs like cats and flies super strength against their dog and spider adversaries. Dramatically brought to life by Disney's special effects animators, who created meticulous shadows and light and water effects, Mickey is surrounded by flasks, beakers, and test tubes in highly saturated hues of reds, greens, blues, and purples and whose surfaces gleam with scintillating light and evaporating bubbles. In pursuit of his magic formula, Mickey pours colored liquids from beaker to test tube, each time producing bubbling, sputtering, and sparking puffs of color (with automobile-like sound effects) as the experiment progresses.

While cartoon studios continued to create comedic, musical, and fairy tale shorts as they had since cinema's inception, Technicolor IV transformed the visualization of these and other kinds of stories, foregrounding a rich new spectrum of demonstrative color.[6] This fuller color range replaced earlier, more limited color processes that did not have the capacity to show the yellows, browns, deep blues, and lighter greens that Technicolor IV offered. Color is certainly used to enhance realistic lighting effects in *The Worm Turns*, marking Disney's distinctive attention to the lighting and materiality of liquids and glass, but what is ultimately staged is the spectacular relay of transformative colors, the sensual seduction of Technicolor eye candy ready for us to visually consume. Here the supernatural storyline is a narrative pretext to foreground color *as color*, as transparent as the laboratory glassware. From the sparkling rubies, emeralds, and sapphires that the Seven Dwarfs collect at the mine to the wicked Queen's poisonous red apple in its bubbling cauldron, color was in constant movement in cartoons of the 1930s: from liquid to gas to solid, it was *animated*.

The full color spectrum on display in *Snow White* was the product of several years of experimentation by Technicolor, which had been making so-called natural or photographic color film since its founding in 1915. Of course, cinema had been experimenting with color since its inception with applied color processes such as hand painting, tinting, and toning. Additive color processes like Kinemacolor (1908–15) and Technicolor I (1916–20), in which the black-and-white film carried the color records of the original scene's exposure through the use of colored filters, eventually began to replace applied color. Additive color processes required special projection equipment and had other problems like color fringing and images that were poorly illuminated and in soft focus, and so film manufacturers shifted to a subtractive color system, in which the film negative was a palimpsest of different complementary color matrices that reconstructed the color spectrum.[7] However, other problems remained with subtractive processes like Technicolor II (1922–27).[8] In the late 1920s and early 1930s, competing two- and later three-color processes with such names as Multicolor (1928–32), Cinécolor (1928), and Brewstercolor (1930) were introduced in theatrical features and shorts. Cinécolor was particularly popular with animation studios between 1932 and 1935, as it was much cheaper and faster to process than Technicolor.[9] Unfortunately, it could not reproduce yellows, deep blues, and purples, and Technicolor's third process (1927–32) shared its limitations.

Finally, Technicolor developed a new color process, Technicolor IV (1932–53), that solved the technical problems and provided a rich new array of colors for the first time. Nevertheless, shooting in full color remained a highly expensive proposition for the film industry, requiring special cameras, lighting, makeup, and color consultants provided by Technicolor, as well as more expensive film prints, and the initial industry enthusiasm for color had waned by the early 1930s.[10] It is possible that because the animation industry had led with earlier color experiments in two-color processes, and because of certain inherent technical advantages relating to single frame photography, Technicolor began lobbying the animation industry to try out its new full color process.[11] Independent producers Ted Eshbaugh and Walt Disney would each play a key role in bringing the new process to the screen.

Eshbaugh had been experimenting since 1930 on such two-color processes as Multicolor in cartoons like *Goofy Goat* (USA, 1931) and *The Snowman* (USA, 1932).[12] Invited by Technicolor to create a full color cartoon in the Technicolor IV process in late 1931, he began developing what may have been the first three-color cartoon, *The Wizard of Oz* (USA/Canada, 1933), possibly used by Technicolor to demonstrate the color process to interested studios.[13] Striking and complex in its use of color, *The Wizard of Oz* cartoon short would be released theatrically in the UK and Canada but not in the United States. It featured dazzling shot compositions of peacocks and butterflies in the Emerald City and a rich array of saturated reds, purples, and greens in its tale of Dorothy, the Tin Man, and the Scarecrow (there is no Cowardly Lion). Scenes depicting the Wizard turning rabbits into dancing dolls in a Tiller Girl dance sequence of cool blues and hot pinks offer an inventive surrealism that typified the creative possibilities of the animated art form.

While Eshbaugh was completing the film, Technicolor invited Disney to discuss making a cartoon in color.[14] Overriding the protests of his brother Roy O. Disney, Walt Disney decided to remake his partially completed black-and-white cartoon short *Flowers and Trees* using the Technicolor IV process. *Flowers and Trees* premiered on July 18, 1932, at Sid Grauman's theater and was released on July 30, 1932, as the first cartoon short in Technicolor IV; it would go on to win the Academy Award for Best Short Subject (Cartoon).[15] Because of its undeniable success, United Artists agreed to another three Silly Symphonies in color followed by six more. After the unequivocal success of all these films, Disney was able to sign a three-year contract with Technicolor. On August 30, 1932, Disney was given the exclusive right to make cartoons in the process through the summer of 1935, after which the new three-color process would become open to all studios.[16] (It was likely this contract and a further lawsuit with Frank J. Baum that prevented Eshbaugh from releasing his experimental *Wizard of Oz* in the United States.[17]) The full color process was then rapidly adopted for new animated shorts series like Color Classics (Fleischer Studios / Paramount), Color Rhapsody (Screen Gems / Columbia), Rainbow Parade (Van Beuren / RKO), and Happy Harmonies (MGM); other studios including Walter Lantz, Warner Bros., and Terrytoons also had added full color to their cartoons by the 1940s.[18] British writer Robert Herring remarked on the subtle nuances in the new color palette:

> The color [in Disney's Silly Symphony series] is excellent. Scenes are not limited to one or two colors in varying shades—orange-pink, orange and blood, or ink, watered into faded green—as we have hitherto had to endure. The new Technicolor gives clear full yellow, pale blue that is clean. Light browns as well as dark browns; rich ivy green besides emerald and olive. . . . The lightest of colors are possible, shell-pinks, the strange greens of layers of water, lily-white.[19]

Color enhanced a sense of three-dimensionality and depth, with brightly colored objects appearing larger than darker objects of similar size and shape, and with warm colors (reds, oranges, and yellows) seeming to approach the viewer and cool colors (blues and purples) to recede from the viewer. Technicolor IV enabled a greater naturalism, enabling the blues, browns, and greens of nature in Disney's *The Old Mill*

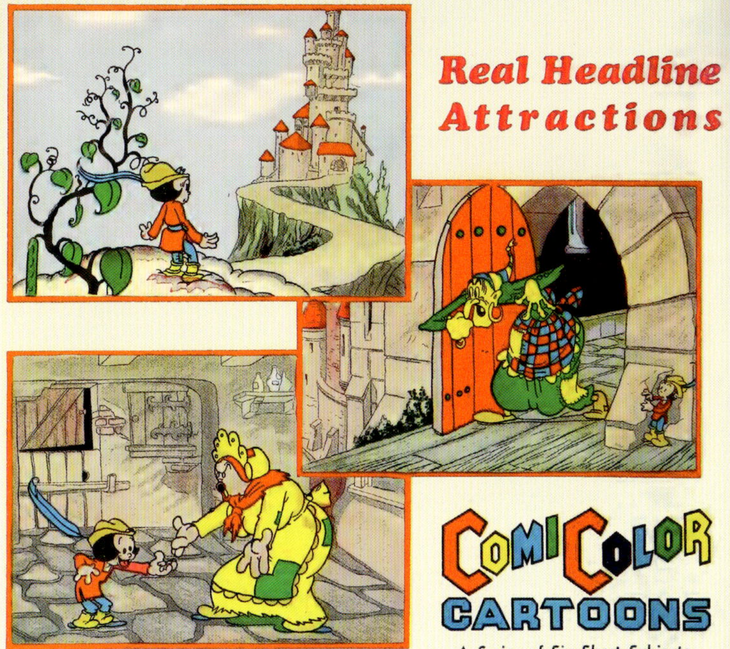
Musical Cartoons in Color
Real Headline Attractions
ComiColor
CARTOONS
A Series of Six Short Subjects
IN CINE-COLOR
Succeeding Subjects to be Selected from The Following Stories Now in Preparation.
"The Brave Tin Soldier", "Sinbad the Sailor", "Puss in Boots", "Cinderella", "The Three Bears," "Jack the Giant Killer", "Tom Thumb", "Aladdin", "Snow White", "Hansel and Gretel", "The Bremen Town Musicians", "The Little Red Hen", "The Snow Queen", "The Ugly Duckling", "The Golden Goose", "Dick Whittington's Cat" and "The Little Mermaid."
World Famous Fantasies Set to Symphonic Music, Rhythmic Lyrics and Presented in Full Color Cartoon Comics — First Subject:
"JACK AND THE BEANSTALK"
by UB IWERKS
Territorial Rights Now Available
CELEBRITY PRODUCTIONS, Inc., 723 Seventh Ave., New York

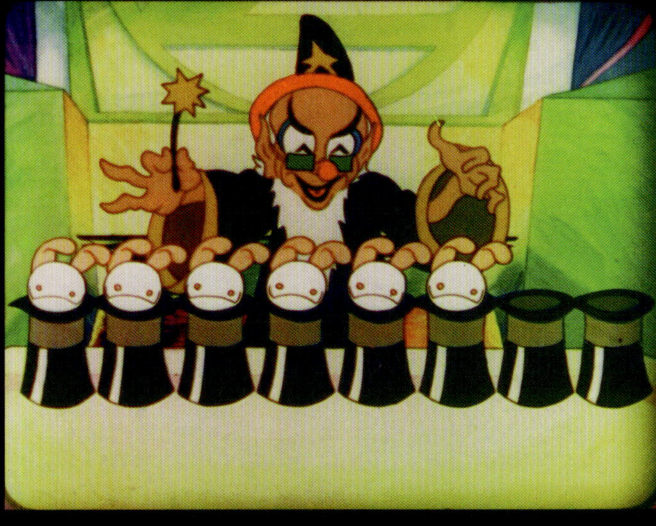

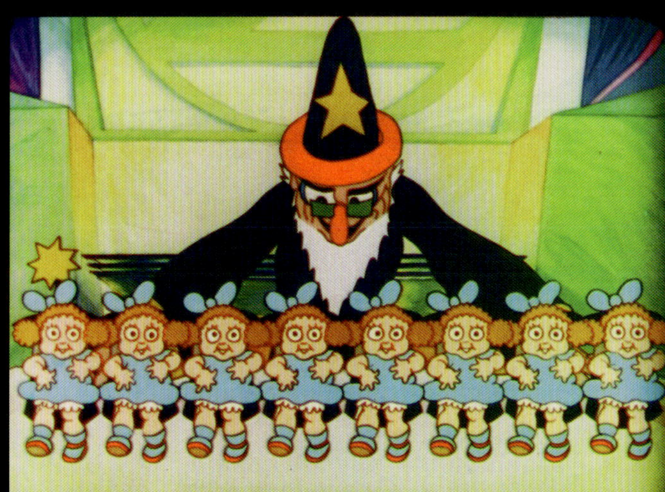

(USA, 1937), the muted pastel browns and greens of the forest in *Snow White*, and the changing seasons in *Bambi* (USA, 1942). Disney believed that color was essential for the animated medium, but it also plays a powerful role in our fantasy and imagination. While color could certainly show a more realistic world, cel animation in the 1930s and 1940s primarily turned to color as a spectacular new attraction. Favoring fairy tales, fables, and musical genres, with colorful subjects from anthropomorphic toys and candy to fantastic jewels, color was a narrative device for product differentiation that foregrounded the spectacular saturation, striking contrast, and affective appeal of the new Technicolor process. In the Fleischer Studios featurette *Aladdin and His Wonderful Lamp* (USA, 1939), Popeye gives Olive Oyl a diamond, an emerald, and a ruby; their luminous glow sequentially blankets the screen in white, green, and red. The radiance requires Olive to don sunglasses, showing the ways in which color stands in for light in animation.

Cel animation could depict fantastic, even hallucinatory worlds, like the "Pink Elephants" sequence in *Dumbo* (USA, 1941), in which the eponymous elephant and Timothy the mouse accidentally drink champagne and start to hallucinate the colorful striped singing elephants, or "technicolor pachyderms," that appear before them.[20] Color was a key component for Disney's newly created special effects artists—those who pioneered fire and water and light effects. From flames and bubbles to fireworks and scintillating stars, these special effects would have been impossible without the hues and contrasts that color offered. Meanwhile, speedsters in the accelerated cartoons of the 1940s—Bugs Bunny, Woody Woodpecker, Woolfy, and the Road Runner—were aided by the colored paint smears that conveyed the zooms and zips of their velocity.

Animated color was also used to celebrate its own production process. In Disney's feature *The Reluctant Dragon* (USA, 1941), we get a seemingly impromptu studio tour with comic writer Robert Benchley from *The New Yorker* through all the different departments of the Walt Disney Studios, from Animation to Storyboarding, including a visit to the "Rainbow Room," or Inking & Painting department. One of the final steps in an assembly-line production, Inking & Painting usually consisted of up to several hundred female workers wearing white gloves and smocks to keep cels free from dust.[21] Colors were affected by how many layers of cels were used; hues had "let downs," which were darker shades used for lower levels in the palimpsest of cels (as many as four could be stacked on top of the background painting and photographed).

With Benchley as our tour guide, the Inking & Painting department sequence introduces us to the pleasurable array of colors that populate the Rainbow Room. As the camera cranes in to one of the portable mills that Disney used to grind pigment, we hear Benchley comment, "That looks very tasty," underscoring color's synesthetic appeal.[22] Benchley's observation is the signal for an extended montage of the Rainbow Room's colored paints and pigments, cut to an upbeat musical track of the Seven Dwarfs' "Heigh-Ho" melody. The musical montage celebrates Disney color's material beauty while underscoring its variety in powdered and liquid forms. Color is staged contrastively, arranged in primary or triadic configurations, ascending analogous sequences of the color spectrum, or juxtaposed in complementary combinations of green and red or blue and yellow as the paint pigment is measured, scooped, and poured. The exuberant sequence celebrates color's materiality and fluidity, hues and saturation.

Cel animation combines both color as pigment, the paint applied to the surface of the cels that is photographed by the camera, and color as light, the optical color of the photographic reproduction of those cels on film. *The Reluctant Dragon*'s Rainbow Room montage theatricalizes the production of color, displaying Technicolor as a dazzling new optical color process through the chromatic pigments of the Inking & Painting department. As Disney painter Susan Ashley, who worked on *Sleeping Beauty* (USA, 1959), once explained, Disney was "known for the best paint in the business.... they had bins, dry color and then they mixed it up from the dry. So, they took us to the lab, and you'd see bins and bins full of this just gorgeous color, you'd go crazy."[23]

From animation's beginnings to more recent films such as Disney / Pixar's *Monsters, Inc.* (USA, 2001), animation has long visualized the assembly-line production process as an occasion for creative play. In the 1930s, the production line, long a popular trope, was also a narrative pretext for playful color, whether it be through the making of a wedding cake in Van Beuren's *Pastrytown Wedding*, pastries in Disney's *The Cookie Carnival* (USA, 1935), or chocolate and candy Easter baskets in Disney's *Funny Little Bunnies* (USA, 1934) and Walter Lantz's *The Egg Cracker Suite* (USA, 1943).[24] Color became a device for liquid play with raspberry, vanilla, and lemon icing squirted by bunnies as red, white, and yellow on the Easter eggs and each other in *Funny Little Bunnies*. In Lantz's *Candyland* (USA, 1935), a child is whisked off by the Sandman to a Candyland factory where red and green beans are squirted full of color to magically turn into jelly beans. In *The Egg Cracker Suite*, more bunnies—those avatars of

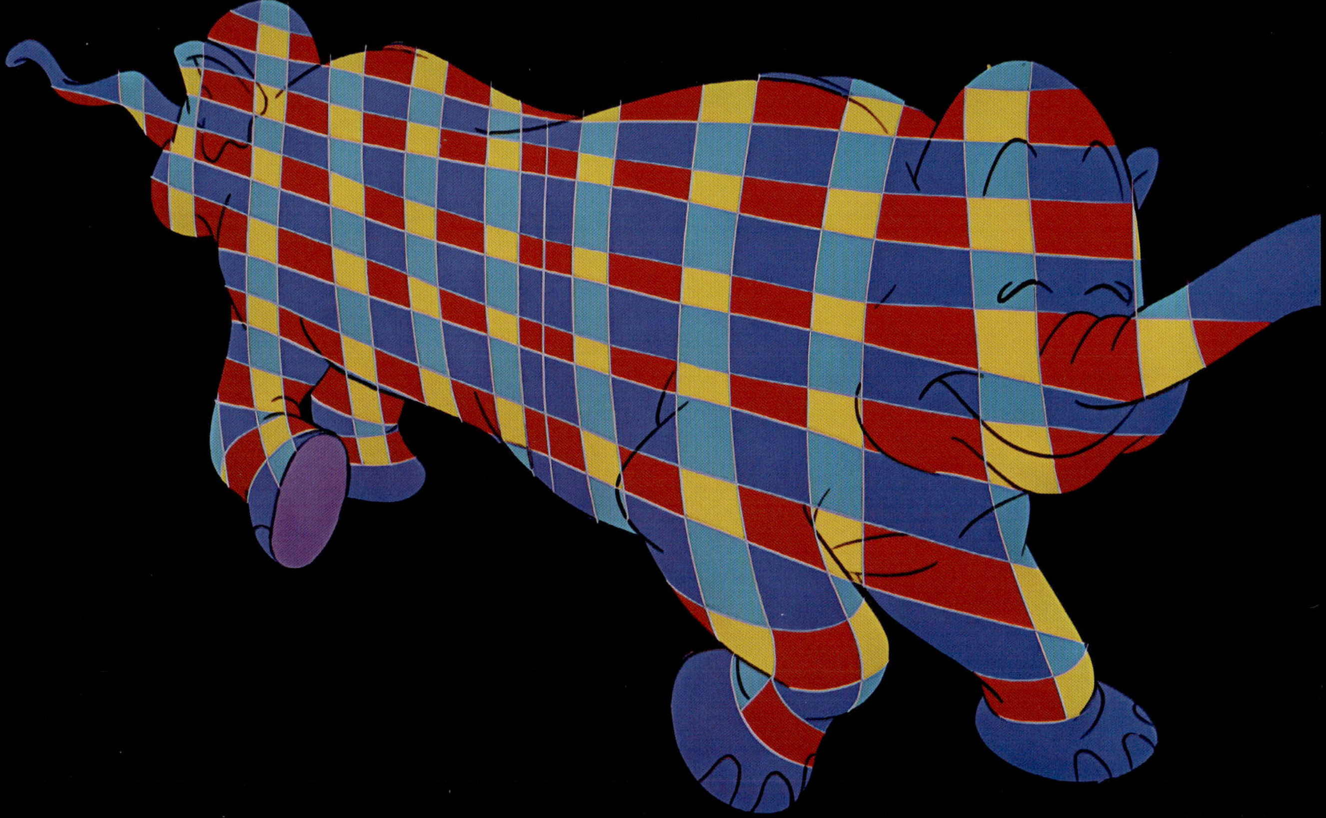

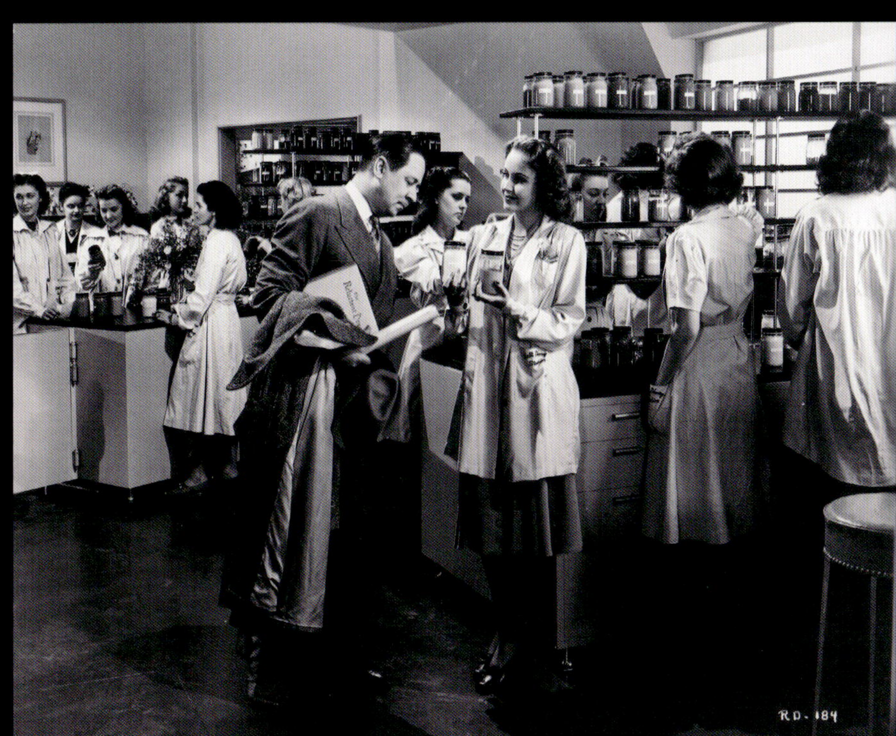

TOP: *Dumbo* (USA, 1941, dir. Ben Sharpsteen)

RIGHT: *The Reluctant Dragon* (USA, 1941, dir. Alfred L. Werker), production still

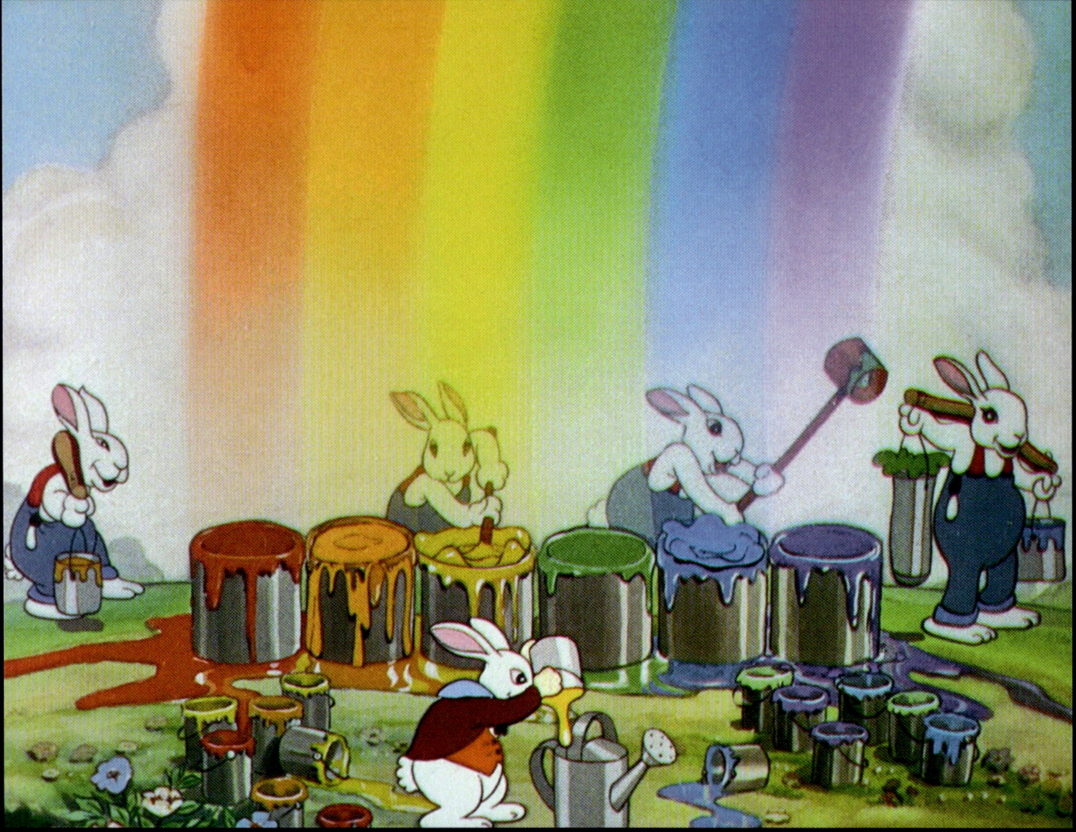

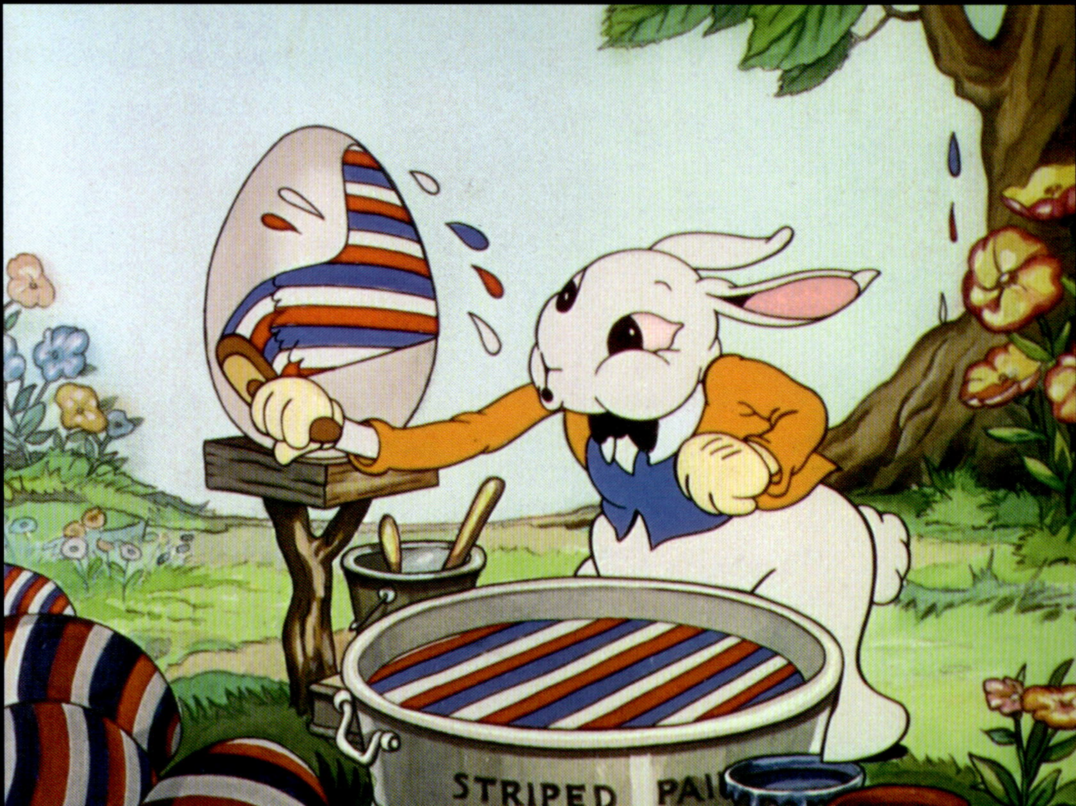

STRIPED

industry and reproduction—milk Technicolor from flowers in order to paint Easter eggs. Technicolor also enabled new possibilities for visual play with colorful patterns and designs: polka dots, stripes, plaid, and checkerboard patterns all became the subject of visual gags in *Funny Little Bunnies*, in which the bunnies draw their paint directly from a waterfall rainbow and magically color these patterns on the eggs, straight from the paint can. In *The Cookie Carnival*, a cookie tramp soothes a weeping cookie girl and, with the assistance of some candy, transforms her into the Queen of the Cookie Carnival by jumping on eclairs that squirt white, light blue, and purple icing to decorate her dress and applying blush and red lipstick from a red candy heart onto her cheeks and mouth. Naturally, the cartoon culminates with a parade in which Hollywood-like spotlights are projected through colored lollipops that filter the communal celebration in red, yellow, orange, purple, and blue.

Cartoon color design emphasized the interrelationship of specific colors, like complementary colors opposite each other on the color wheel: red and green, orange and blue, and yellow and purple. These color strategies could draw upon specific cultural associations with particular combinations, such as the reds and greens of Christmas. In Disney's *Santa's Workshop* (USA, 1932) and its sequel, *The Night before Christmas* (USA, 1933), toys are produced in an assembly line by Santa and his elves and then march in animated parades, offering rich complementary colors of red candy canes and green Christmas trees. Brightly colored tin soldiers, drums, and wrapped presents proliferate in these cartoons to showcase color, as do candy and other objects magically coming to life. Similarly, perfume and medicinal bottles laugh and dance after hours in a pharmacy in a Nutcracker suite of color in MGM's *Bottles* (USA, 1936). Visual gags of anthropomorphized candy also bring with them cultural and racial histories that drew upon stereotypes and imagery from minstrelsy, from brown boys towing "Miss Licorice" to a Polynesian Jell-O dancer and a "Miss Cocoanut" Inuit in *The Cookie Carnival*. Images like these remind us of the ways in which color and its material sources, from indigo to cochineal and cacao, is always inscribed with colonial and racial histories.[25] These and other anthropomorphized Brown and Black characters that appeared in animation for much of the twentieth century reveal the ways that color as material pigment and color as racialized representation continued to be collapsed into each other in visual culture.[26]

Accelerated by the industrial revolution, color has been a ubiquitous element in interior design, media, and visual culture for much of the past century. But in the last decade of the nineteenth century and first decades of the twentieth century, color was still a relative novelty in cinema, conveying luxury and spectacle, the magical and the exotic. By 1932, the film industry was wary of the expense and technical problems that early photographic color processes presented. Through the creative talent of entrepreneurs such as Ted Eshbaugh and Walt Disney, along with Technicolor's commitment to innovation, animation would lead the film industry in demonstrating the enormous appeal of a full color process. Despite the expense of Technicolor, the box office success of Disney's feature film *Snow White and the Seven Dwarfs* affirmed that color could offer far more than novelty; it was able to shape dramatic atmosphere, mood, and emotion as well. Only two years after *Snow White and the Seven Dwarfs*, Victor Fleming's Technicolor live-action feature *The Wizard of Oz* would be released, much of its iconic imagery prefigured in Eshbaugh's 1933 cartoon short, with Dorothy crossing into a wondrous green Emerald City. In magical scenes like these and others in American cartoons of the 1930s, color overwhelms us with its sensual intensity and dramatic appeal, reawakening our childhood memories of holidays and food, beloved toys, and fairy tales. Whether as magic potion, candy cane stripes, or vistas of Emerald City, animated color is ultimately for everyone—for our play and delight, and for our fantasy and imagination.

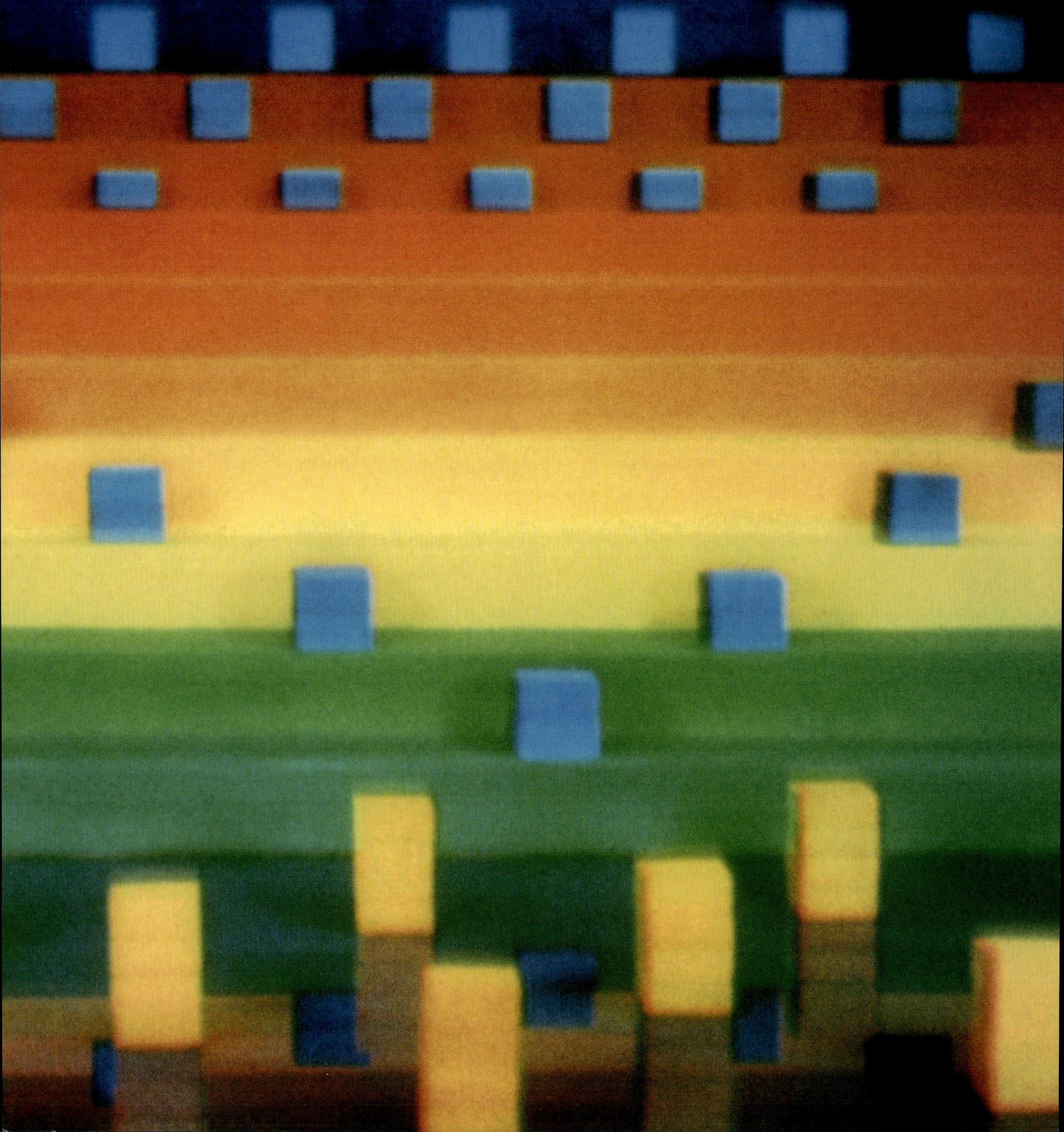

SOPHIA SERRANO

ABSTRACTING COLOR

EXPERIMENTAL CINEMA AND COLOR EFFECTS

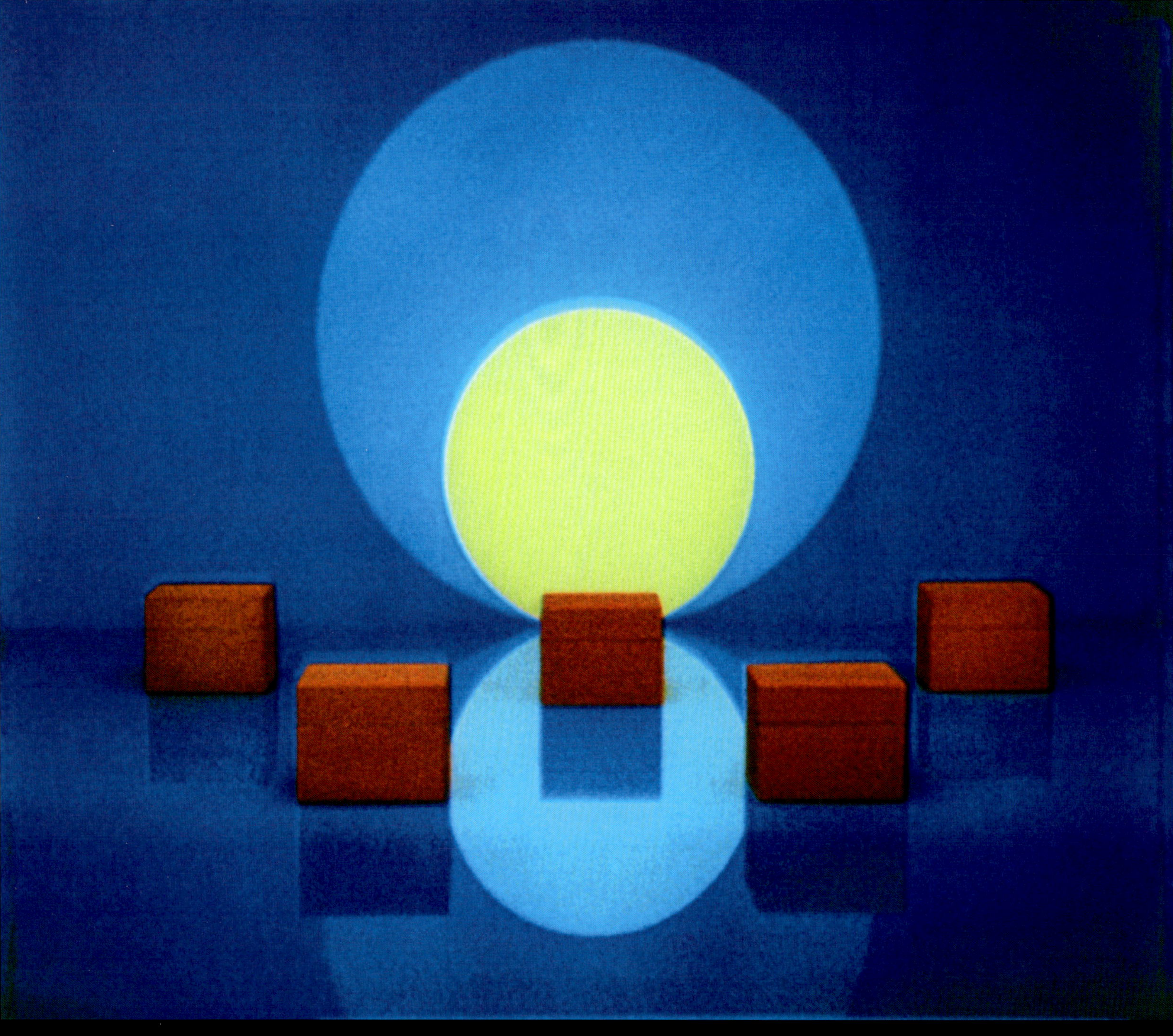

THIS PAGE AND PAGE 220: *Composition in Blue* (*Komposition in Blau*, Germany, 1935, dir. Oskar Fischinger)

The advancing development of color film stocks in the 1930s introduced new ways to experiment with color on the big screen. Building on earlier experimentations that utilized tinting and toning or hand coloring, film artists of the 1930s and 1940s often emphasized the relationship between color and music or sound while relying on innovative effects and animation techniques to dazzle audiences with the unique potentials of film. Such figures as Oskar Fischinger, Mary Ellen Bute, Len Lye, and John and James Whitney explored movement, sound, and color as an alternative to commercial, narrative-bound films.[1] In many cases their works of cinematic color abstraction—exploring color's essence and form once freed from narrative constraints—were an extension of the contemporary abstraction and futurism movements in the art world, with some artists drawing from previous musical training as much as from their visual art practices. While not a comprehensive survey, this essay examines select instances of color experimentation and abstraction, exploring their occasional interactions with and influence on Hollywood filmmaking and commercial industries (though many artists rejected cinema's growing role in the realm of marketing and mainstream entertainment for both financial support and technical practice). Overall, this dialogue between colorized films, experimental techniques, advertisements, and special effects artists in Hollywood contributed to crucial innovations, impacting not only narrative and stylistic trends but also the broader trajectory of visual effects and playing a key role in the success of films.[2]

Even before the innovations of cinema, a variety of color and sound machines demonstrated the appeal of moving color with audiences. Though instances of these devices date back to the seventeenth and eighteenth centuries, in the years preceding and parallel to cinema, artists such as Mary Hallock Greenewalt, Thomas Wilfred, and Oskar Fischinger, among others, continued to invent and use them to explore the synesthetic relationship between color and music, in which the perception of colors is typically synced to specific tones.[3] In many of these cases, the visuals served to *enhance* sound, but regardless these experiments were unified in their reliance on abstracted color and light to evoke emotional responses in viewers.

As a musician, inventor, writer, and activist, Mary Hallock Greenewalt focused especially on the emotional impact of sound and light first by coloring filmstrips (which were ultimately never projected), then by using devices that produced color light projections. She called her greater work in light-color systems Nourathar ("essence of light" in Arabic). Her best-known device, the Sarabet, was refined and redeveloped over decades to play notes and produce colored lights at varying intensities and rhythms. Hallock Greenewalt would file eleven patents for technologies related to her electronic color-light systems starting in 1918, including an advanced

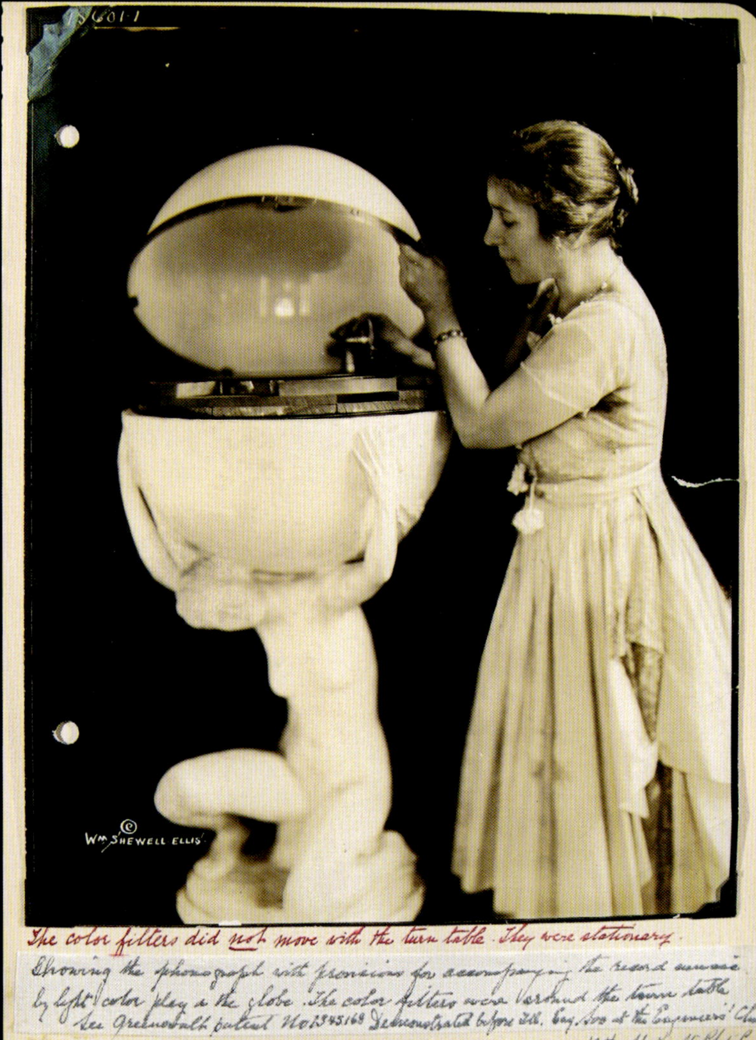

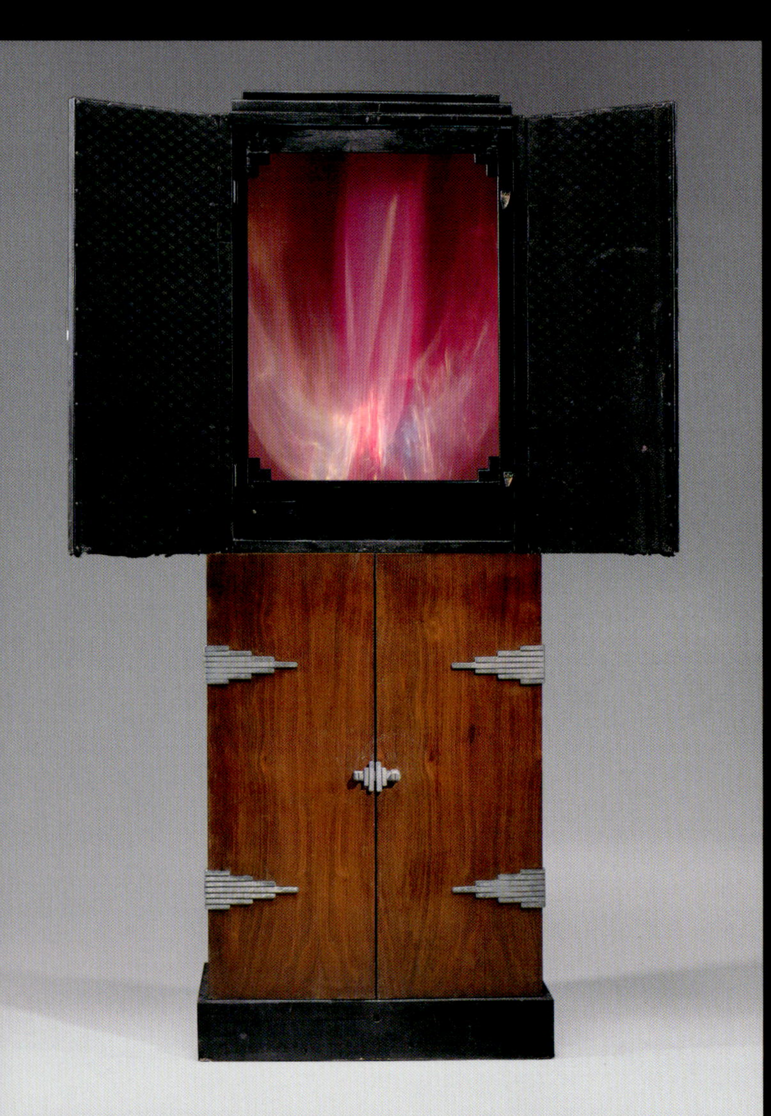

TOP: Mary Hallock Greenewalt with light phonograph, 1920

LEFT: Thomas Wilfred, Unit #86, from the Clavilux Junior (first home Clavilux model) series, 1930

rheostat, which she used in her color-light shows and contracted to major companies. (She was forced to defend her patents in a lawsuit for copyright infringement in 1920.[4]) While she was preoccupied with exploring ways to create an art form, her patented technologies were used by companies including General Electric, which employed them in mobile color-light controls. For example, her innovations enabled color effects and accents on public buildings, fountain lights, and public interiors. Though developed for artistic means, Hallock Greenewalt's inventions monumentally contributed to the increasing presence of colored light in the public arena, something subtle but significant in the greater cultural shift toward color and its saturation of day-to-day life.

Perhaps one of the most notable experimenters with colored light as art was musician and artist Thomas Wilfred, whose career closely paralleled that of Hallock Greenewalt, ultimately leading to litigation over his use of one of her patented technologies. Starting in 1919, Wilfred began experimenting with light as an art medium, calling his light compositions Lumia. While he didn't utilize colored film, he employed projections and screens through devices he made for public and personal use. These Clavilux instruments produced ethereal, slow-moving color reflections created by lenses or tinted screens, ultimately projected together either on the wall, on a large screen, or in the device. In his public performances, these were produced using large switch-boards of controls, keyboards, pedals, and buttons; home devices were more simplified. From the 1930s to the 1960s, Wilfred continued to exhibit his work in New York, including at his own performance hall, producing a few commissions including one for Clairol's headquarters in 1959. Though Wilfred expressed remorse over not having met more success in the art world, today he is one of the most remembered artists to utilize colored light as their main medium.[5] (Of note was the appearance of an excerpt of his work *Opus 161* [1965] as an interlude in Terrence Malick's film *The Tree of Life* [USA, 2011], one example of the many ways filmmakers have drawn from the color experiments of the avant-garde.)

Perhaps the quintessential artist who created technologies that enabled a wider experimentation with color devices as well as color on film was Oskar Fischinger. While Wilfred and Hallock Greenewalt were predominantly focused on devices that produced colored light, Fischinger was a prolific producer of color explorations both on and off film. Born in Germany, he trained as a musician but after working in technical positions such as drafting and engineering was drawn to painting, drawing, film, and animation. His interest in film was sparked by seeing the work of Walter Ruttmann, who made some of the first abstract animations in Germany starting in 1921.[6] Ruttmann offered early examples of colored animations on film, though he worked mainly in additive color methods (tinting and toning or hand painting). Fischinger's abstraction work started with experiments using colored liquids, then moved into tinted and toned films of various wax experiments. In the early 1930s he aided in the development and promotion of Gasparcolor, a subtractive three-color process on a single filmstrip that produced vibrant colors and enabled the creation of phenomenal and widely influential examples of color abstractions and experimentations.[7] *Circles* (*Kreise*, Germany, 1933–34) is believed to be one of the first color films distributed in Europe using the three-color process.[8] A two-minute spectacle of colored circles coordinated with the sounds of Richard Wagner and Edvard Grieg requiring over one thousand drawings, it demonstrated the range and versatility of Gasparcolor. While the short was intended as an experiment in abstraction, Fischinger cleverly turned it into a commercial to evade the Nazi censorship board's ban of abstract art; he added a slogan for Tolirag advertising company at the end of the film to evade the control of authorities.

Fischinger continued his collaboration with Gasparcolor for *Composition in Blue* (*Komposition in Blau*, Germany, 1935). The short featured a spectacular display of vivid geometric shapes brought to life through stop-motion animation set to the music of Otto Nicolai's opera *The Merry Wives of Windsor* (1849). These pieces further established Fischinger's lifelong fascination with using complex, moving shapes and colors to produce a mesmerizing and kinetic experience. His work was widely popular despite Germany's increasing censorship of art. It was also noticed abroad; fortuitously, a scout recruiting technical talent was given two of Fischinger's films to screen in Los Angeles. Looking to escape Germany's Nazi regime, Fischinger seized on the opportunity to move to Hollywood after securing a contract with Paramount starting in 1936. (His tenure there ended abruptly later that year with his resignation, after studio executives refused to produce his commissioned animated sequence in color, which he would later buy back from Paramount, finish, and title *Allegretto* [USA, 1943].) The ensuing years saw Fischinger briefly involved with MGM, but his time in Hollywood is most often associated with his contributions to Walt Disney's *Fantasia* (USA, 1940). Hired to help design the portion of the film set to Bach's Toccata and Fugue in D Minor, his initial concepts were not widely accepted and his contributions ultimately went uncredited at his request—this was partially due to his desire to use even more vivid colors and, by Disney's account, more complex shape patterns than what appear in the final version of the film. However, Fischinger's overall influence on Disney, as well as the concept of a visual symphony and its aesthetic design, was tremendously significant. (His name has since been restored to the *Fantasia* credits by Disney.) As Fischinger biographer William Moritz accounts, "Oskar brought prints of his films, which were screened every week for nine months for the entire Disney staff during lunch and breaks."[9]

One notable nonfilmic invention of Fischinger's is the Lumigraph of the late 1940s (patented in 1955), a "Color-Play Instrument" composed of a two-sided vertical rubber screen that can be played with one's hands to create color patterns on the reverse side.[10] Colored light is emitted through slits in the frame on the side facing the audience, so when the rubber is pressed from behind, it crosses into the field of light to create abstract patterns. One operator's hands can dance behind the screen to a variety of musical tracks, while the colors of the device's lights can be changed by a second player. (Fischinger's son also made variant Lumigraphs in which colors could be controlled with a foot pedal.) Intended as an at-home entertainment and artistic learning device for all ages, it never saw widespread production and distribution, although a very modified version did appear without Fischinger's involvement in *The Time Travelers* (USA, 1964) as a futuristic "love machine." Overall, Fischinger's experimentations in visual music greatly impacted the way artists regarded and approached the medium; his influence and innovations opened the door for artists (such as Harry Smith) to create their own experiments.[11]

New Zealander Len Lye was also gaining notoriety as a visual music artist, using Gasparcolor to make films that explored color and movement.[12] A painter, sculptor, theorist, and filmmaker, Lye created advertisements and short films such as *Rainbow Dance* (UK, 1936), which combined animated colors with the filmed live-action silhouettes of dancer Rupert Doone. Created as an ad for the Post Office Savings Bank, *Rainbow Dance* reflects Lye's fascination with the kinetic: Doone's silhouettes are constantly in motion—dancing with an umbrella, playing a guitar, swinging a tennis racket—while rainbows, the ocean, fish, rain, landscapes, and more move and morph in and out of abstraction around him. *Rainbow Dance*, which followed the success of *A Colour Box* (UK, 1935, made with Dufaycolor), introduced Lye's technique of overlaying live footage with animated color effects. The footage was first shot in black and white, then adjusted. The layered silhouette aesthetic, which made the dancer both readable and abstract, was achieved through an intricate stencil system. Drawn both to the kinetic and abstract, Lye's work was widely influential on abstract cinema.

In New York, Mary Ellen Bute was one of the first filmmakers of animated abstract shorts in the United States. Like Fischinger, her work was critical both in advancing color effects and in introducing broader movie audiences to experimental cinema and abstract animations, as it was often screened as shorts before feature films. Originally from Texas, Bute started as a painter but became interested in stage lighting and, through her use of Wilfred's Clavilux color organ, experimentations with moving light and color with music.[13] The marriage of light and sound as an aesthetic experience would become a prominent theme in much of Bute's work.[14] She was just beginning her film career when she encountered Fischinger's work in New York. As her techniques advanced, Bute directed and produced a number of experiments in color via visual music, with *Color Rhapsodie* (USA, 1948) perhaps her most enthusiastic. Its opening title card describes the film as one of her exercises in "SEEING SOUND; music in addition to pleasing the EAR; brings something to the EYE." Throughout the six minutes of the piece, set to Franz Liszt's Hungarian Rhapsody no. 2, Bute combined a variety of colors and shapes and used circles as a motif, mixing and recycling bold colors on 35mm Technicolor. Her husband and longtime collaborator, Ted Nemeth, was the cinematographer, and at the time of its release roughly thirty-nine feature film theaters were booking Bute's work as openers to movies.[15]

Throughout her career Bute sought out new methods to further her creative visions, including using an oscilloscope, which graphs and tracks electrical voltages. Layering such images with animations, Bute introduced some of the earliest electrically generated images, whose lines and shapes fluctuate and wave, into the realm of experimental film. Unlike many members of the avant-garde, Bute sought out mainstream distribution of her short films through Radio City Music Hall and other commercial theaters.[16] Her black-and-white short film *Rhythm in Light* (USA, 1934) screened before the premiere of the first feature film in full Technicolor, *Becky Sharp* (USA, 1935)—an interesting crossover between the avant-garde and Hollywood's budding relationship with color use.[17] Bute also had an influence on Hollywood filmmaking through her collaborators, working with animator Norman McLaren on *Spook Sport* (USA, 1939) and actor Christopher Walken (in his first screen role) and writer Guy Glover on *The Boy Who Saw Through* (USA, 1956).

While Bute's work was circulating in movie houses, many experimental films were being shared at the Art in Cinema screenings, held at the San Francisco Museum of Art (now the San Francisco Museum of Modern Art) from 1946 to 1954, fostering a vibrant filmmaking community in the Bay Area.

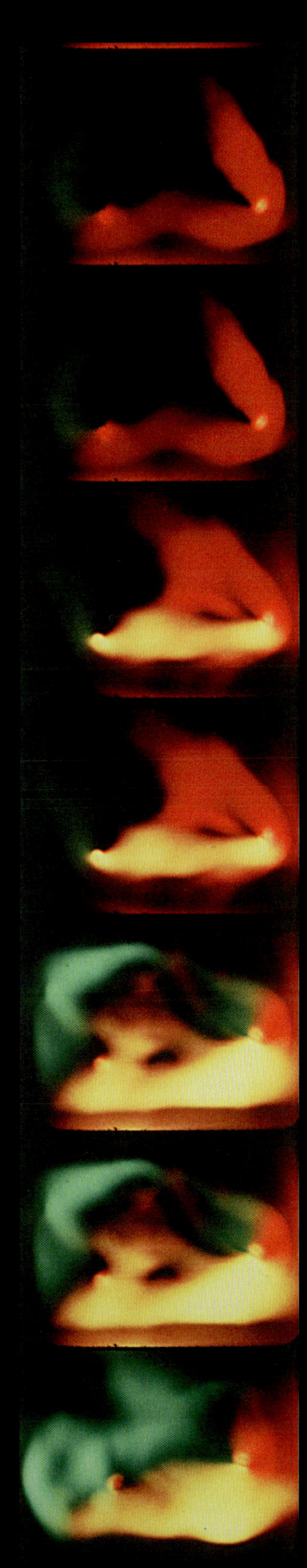

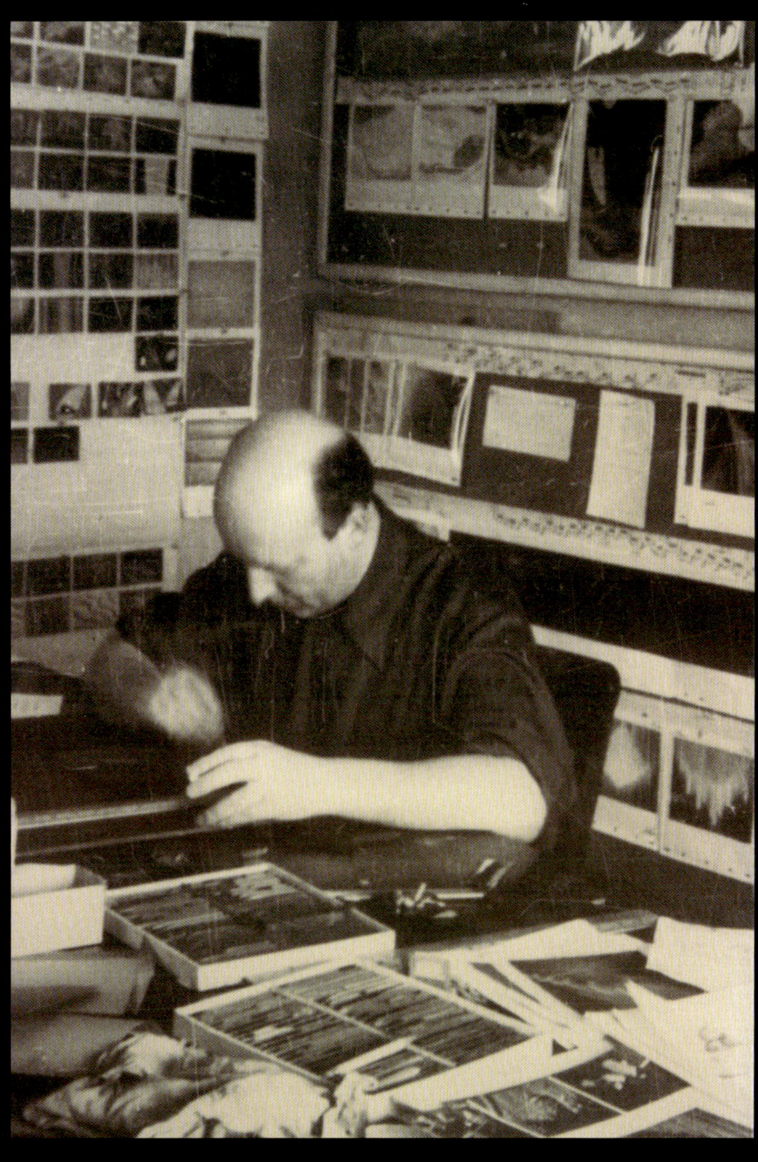

LEFT: Film of a Lumigraph performance by Elfriede Fischinger, 1970

TOP: Oskar Fischinger in his Disney office, ca. 1939

Among its members was artist Jordan Belson, who across his decades of work used various techniques including painting, light projections, and optical printing to produce meditative and colorful "cinematic paintings."[18] He was inspired by the works of Norman McLaren, Oskar Fischinger, and Hans Richter to expand his practice as a painter, developing intricate ethereal visuals on film. As experimental cinema theorist Gene Youngblood described it: "Belson's film is somewhat like slow-motion movies of atomic blasts in Nevada with the desert floor swept across by a tremendous shock wave."[19] Creating nebulous, pulsing images that transition through colorful variants, Belson's prolific filmography overlapped with counterculture practices, drawing from cultural trends within the psychedelic and youth movement of the 1960s and 1970s. His influence can be found in the liquid light shows of the time, such as those by artists Elias Romero and Joshua White and such groups as Single Wing Turquoise Bird, a collective that produced nebulous, transitioning shapes of color for symbolic and representation imagery.

While various artists had used electronic devices in their works, one of the most significant introductions of digital graphics techniques would come in the 1950s with the brothers James and John Whitney. Based in California, home to a booming aviation and aerospace industry, they used an analog computer derived from World War II antiaircraft hardware that John Whitney encountered while working at an aircraft factory.[20] He adapted the technology for mapping graphics and devised a way to film computer animations, producing a series of abstract films showcasing colors and geometric patterns frequently in the shape of a mandala. James Whitney, whose previous works such as *Yantra* (USA, 1957) were the result of extensive hand-drawn animation, featured such visuals in his film *Lapis* (USA, 1966), which he produced using his brother's equipment.

Their contributions would lay the groundwork for later developments in computer-generated imagery (CGI). (Slightly later than the Whitney brothers, New York–based artist Lillian Schwartz created some of the earliest computer graphics in the 1970s. Often overlooked, her vibrantly colored images were developed during her time working at Bell Laboratories.)[21] In addition to his own experimental films, John Whitney contributed animation techniques to a range of commercial, engineering, and feature films through his work at United Productions of America in the 1950s and his own company, Motion Graphics, formed in 1960.[22] A reel promoting his company's capabilities was released in 1961 as *Catalog*. The year after *Yantra*, he collaborated with graphic designer Saul Bass on the iconic opening-title sequence of Alfred Hitchcock's *Vertigo* (USA, 1958), making the colorful and ominous spiraling graphics that foreshadow key themes of the film. In the early 1960s John was especially occupied with his new company; among his numerous projects were graphics for *To the Moon and Beyond* (USA, 1964), shown at the Cinerama Dome during the 1964–65 New York World's Fair.[23] (This would be seen by Stanley Kubrick, who was at the time doing research for his upcoming film *Journey beyond the Stars*, later renamed *2001: A Space Odyssey* [UK/USA, 1968].)

After delving further into the work of John Whitney and seeing his reel of techniques, effects artist Douglas Trumbull (who had also worked on *To the Moon and Beyond*) would ultimately adapt Whitney's slit-scan technique for the famous Star Gate sequence in *2001*.[24] The result was hailed as a major breakthrough for special effects, the fifteen-minute journey often regarded as a masterpiece in visually representing expanded consciousness or another level of cosmic existence. *2001* was released originally on 70mm with stereophonic sound at Cinerama theaters to provide complete immersion in its world. Scholars and visual culture historians have been quick to note the significance of the Star Gate sequence and how it embraced avant-garde art's quest for immersive transcendence on the big screen. Giuliana Bruno places it as a "successor to Oskar Fischinger's three-screen projection piece *Raumlichtkunst* (1926)."[25]

In *Expanded Cinema* (1970), Gene Youngblood compares the work of Belson and the *2001* Star Gate sequence as two examples of Cosmic Cinema, or representations of the sublime. Though Youngblood positions Belson's work as superior, he celebrates Trumbull's incorporation of the avant-garde: "For the first time in commercial cinema we are given the state of the art at its highest point of refinements. *2001* has become the higher ordering principle by which all commercial cinema must be measured."[26] While *2001* was influential on the history of cinema on multiple levels, its impact is especially evident in the scramble of filmmakers to present something "new," putting an emphasis on innovation and effects that could be marketed easily to audiences.[27] At times this meant recruiting outside artists to bring in fresh perspectives, particularly when it came to those in tune with the increasingly prominent youth culture. For example, Belson contributed the special effects for the psychedelic sequences in *Demon Seed* (USA, 1977), as well as scenes of the breaking of the sound barrier and of the eerie, glowing earth in *The Right Stuff* (USA, 1983). Following his groundbreaking work on *2001*, Trumbull

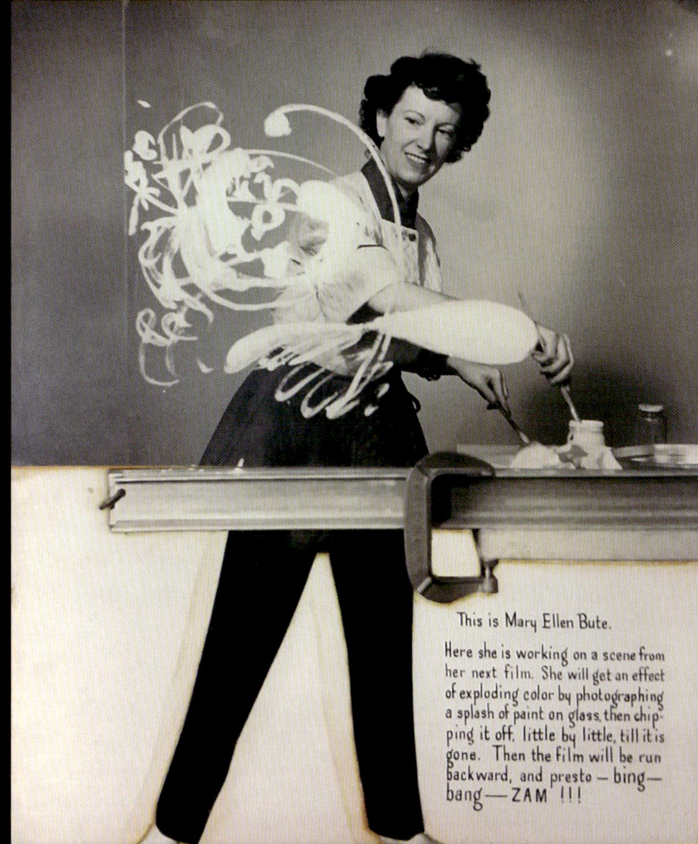

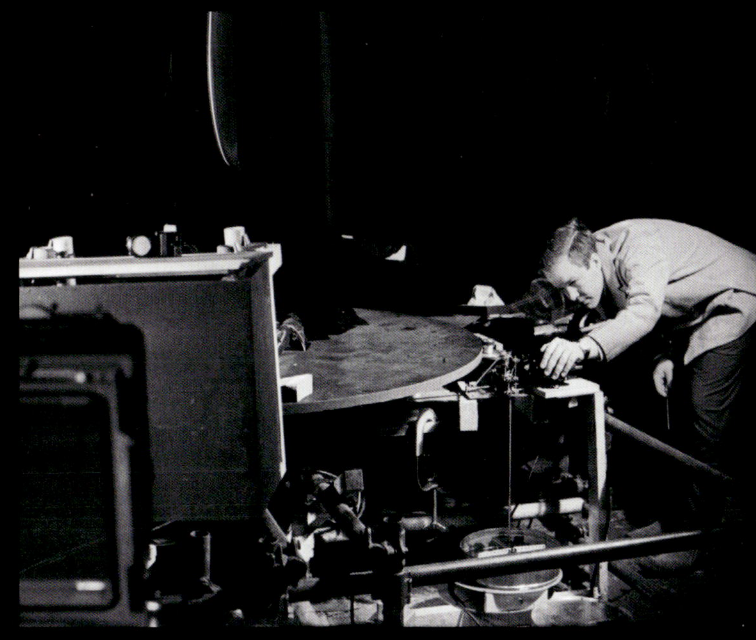

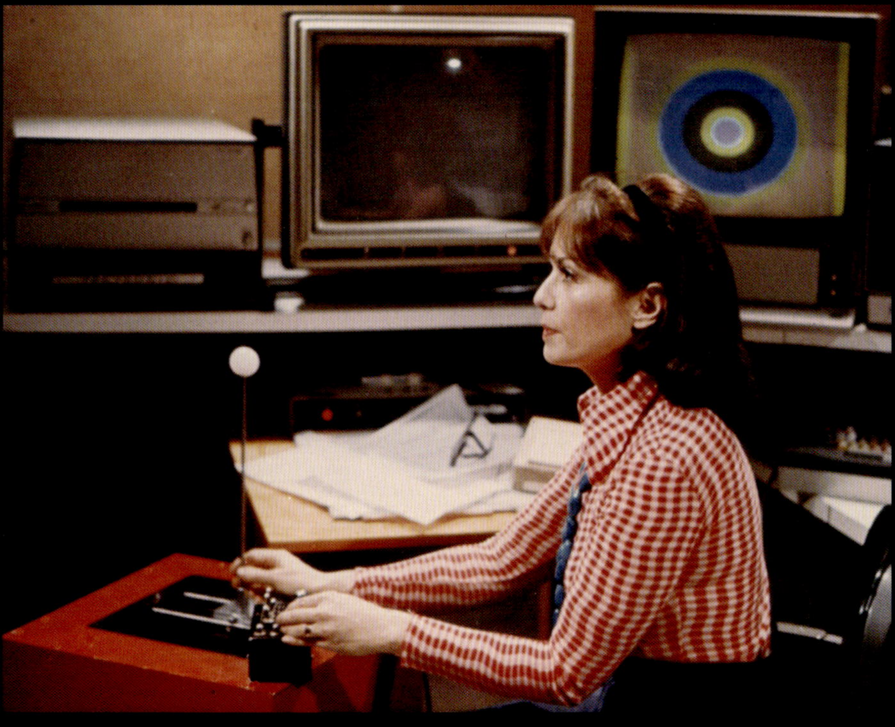

TOP: Mary Ellen Bute in her studio, undated, from a presentation book prepared by Bute

ABOVE: Douglas Trumbull during the production of *2001: A Space Odyssey* (USA/UK, 1968, dir. Stanley Kubrick)

continued to push technical boundaries on several science fiction films, including Steven Spielberg's *Close Encounters of the Third Kind* (USA, 1977).

This drive for "newness" certainly wasn't limited to color effects but involved the field of technical innovation as a whole. The rise of young auteur directors saw an emphasis on seizing on the latest technologies to create the unexpected in their features. However, the shift in color is also evident; *Close Encounters of the Third Kind*, *Star Wars: A New Hope* (USA, 1977), *Blade Runner* (USA, 1982), and *Tron* (USA, 1982) are just a few of the films that increasingly drew upon intense and vivid colors to signify outer space, dystopian futures, and other fantastical realms or characters. Advances in lighting, cinematography, editing, and CGI also allowed a greater emphasis on surreal, unnatural colors.

The electric colors of *Tron* were accomplished with back-lit animation and matte techniques. A leading early example of CGI in Hollywood, the movie famously combined live action and computer animation to build the radiant cyberworld of the Grid. Upon its release, film critic Roger Ebert described *Tron* as "a technological sound-and-light show … a machine to dazzle and delight us."[28] Despite production challenges, *Tron*'s heavy emphasis on color, lighting, and sound effects pushed the film's sequences to the brink of complete abstraction, prioritizing an ethereal and surreal atmosphere over narrative substance. *Blade Runner* also exemplified this turn, using vivid neon lights and colors as part of the mise-en-scène and lighting palette to emphasize the future's extreme urban decay and underscoring the otherwise gray and bleak world that surrounds Harrison Ford's Rick Deckard. The film was hailed for its distinct aesthetic, further reinvigorating the aesthetic neo-noir genre with a neon pulse. In both instances, the visuals are incorporated into the narrative, but their hyperstylized nature at times seems to take priority over the story, echoing early experimental artists' search for different modes of nonnarrative expression through light, color, and music. *Enter the Void* (France/Germany/Italy, 2009) and *The Neon Demon* (France/Denmark/USA, 2016) are notable examples of films with extreme neon color palettes; both feature colorful CGI and LED sequences that provide cohesion to the films' otherwise chaotic, obscured, or surreal realities.

Overall, these connections and collaborations between experimental artists and mainstream industries signify the crucial role such innovators play in the greater trajectory of cinema. As early artists sought to better understand color and its capabilities to evoke certain emotions and reactions from audiences, they brought new and unconventional ideas into Hollywood and commercial industries. From colored light shows and in-home color devices to short experiments and intricate animations, the variety of experimentations advanced our technical capabilities and reframed the public's expectations of color in entertainment as a whole. While both artists and filmmakers in Hollywood showed a fascination with and emphasis on color from the earliest iterations of color techniques in film, these examples show the various ways artists prioritized this approach over narrative constrictions. As Hollywood embraced auteurs such as Hitchcock, Kubrick, and Ridley Scott, these directors often drew directly from the work of experimental artists to incorporate the unexpected and cutting edge into their oeuvre. With these instances celebrated by the general public, the prioritization of color, abstraction, and/or indulgence in hyperrealistic palettes grew increasingly common and relied upon in our entertainment and commercial industries.

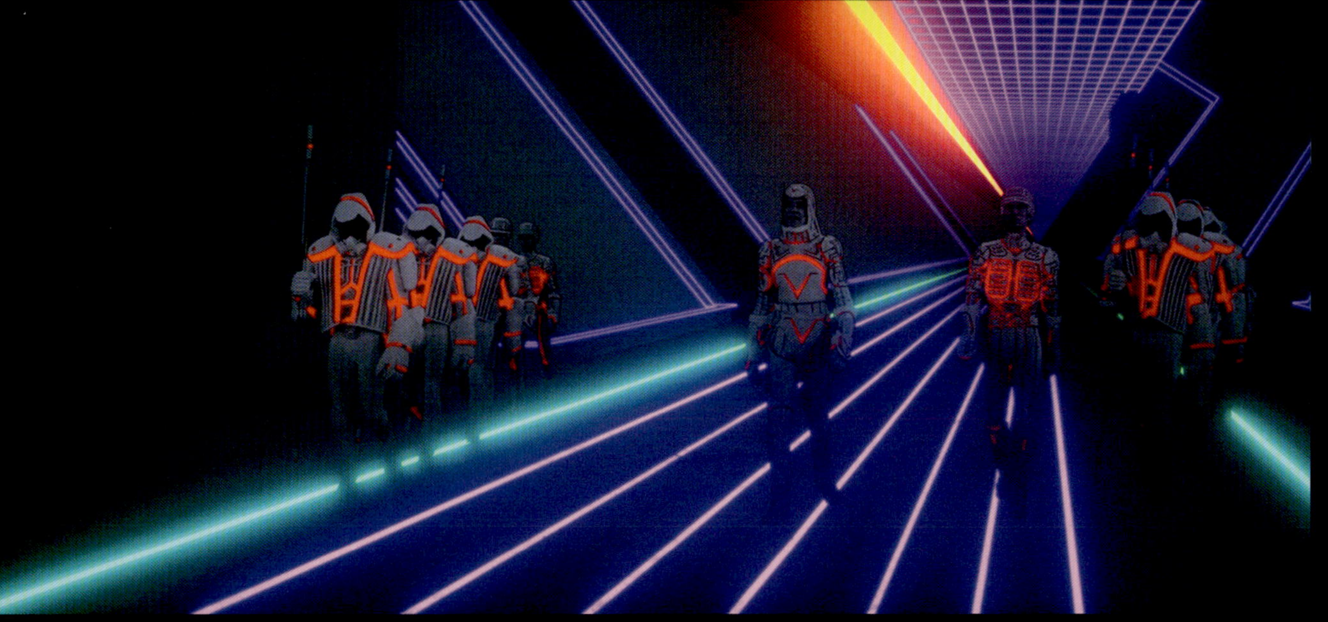

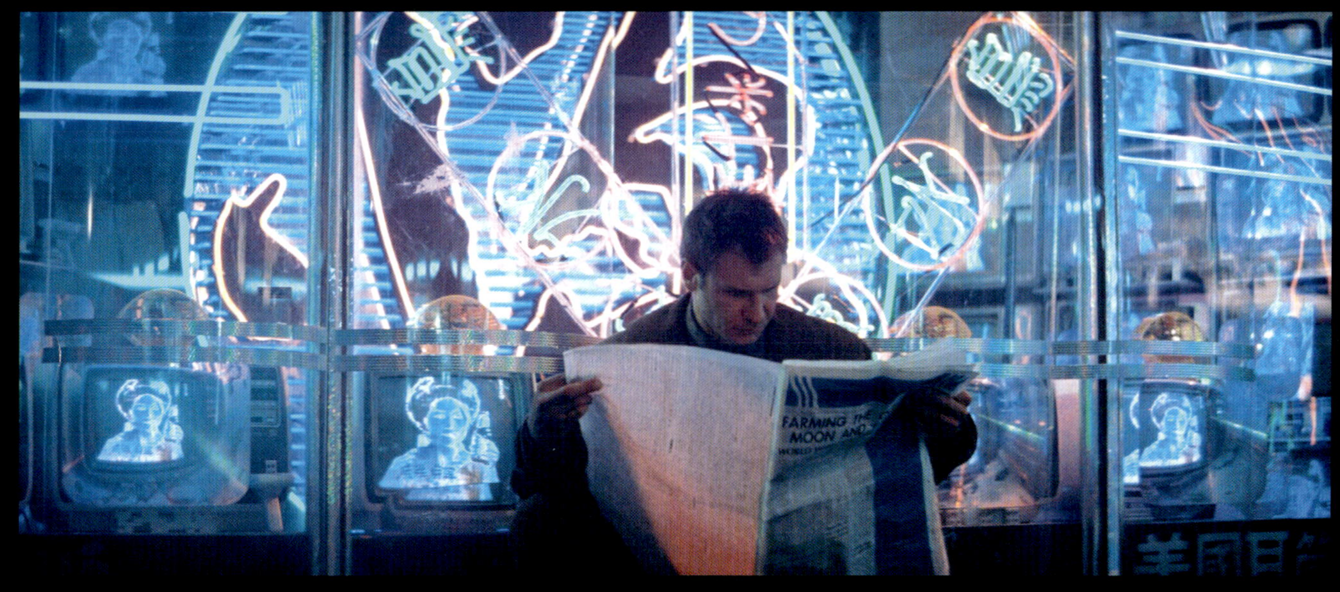

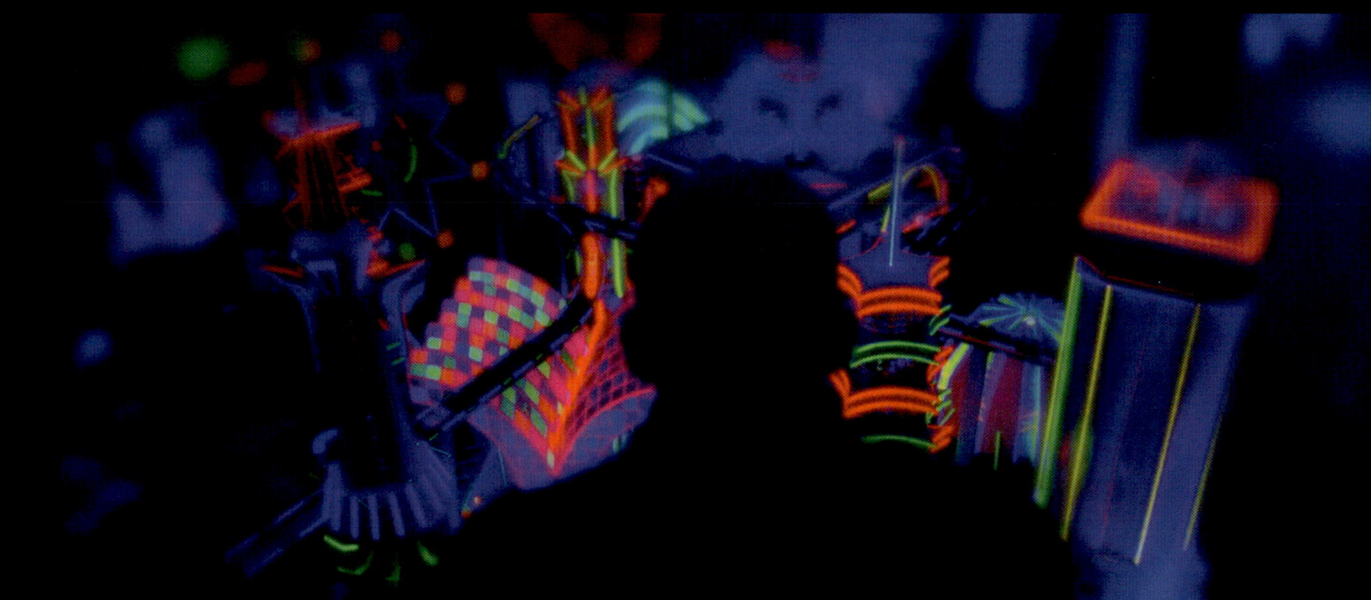

FROM TOP: *Tron* (USA, 1982, dir. Steven Lisberger), *Blade Runner* (USA, 1982, dir. Ridley Scott), and *Enter the Void* (France/Germany/Italy, 2010, dir. Gaspar Noé)

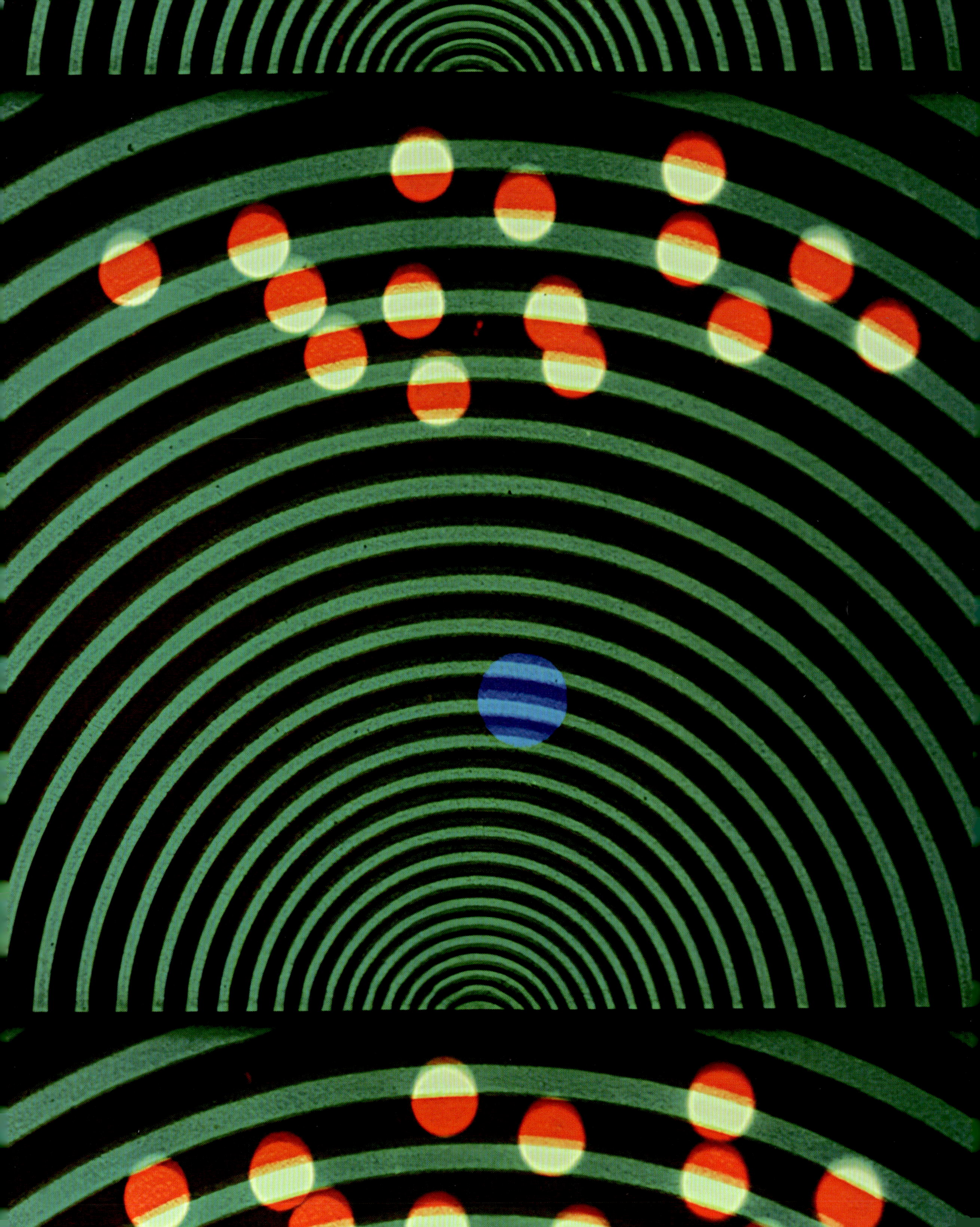

EXPERIMENTAL FILMS

For decades, color has inspired artists to experiment and push the boundaries of the moving image with dazzling abstractions created using a variety of techniques. Inquisitive, trippy, and rebellious, these pieces challenged narrative conventions, influencing popular culture and Hollywood, especially during the 1960s and 1970s. The following images, from Oskar Fischinger's *Circles* (*Kreise*, 1933–34), Mary Ellen Bute's *Color Rhapsodie* (1948), Len Lye's *Rainbow Dance* (1936), Walt Disney's *Fantasia* (1940), James Whitney's *Lapis* (1966), and Jordan Belson's *Samadhi* (1967), represent only a few examples of the wondrous places color abstraction can take us.

Circles (*Kreise*, Germany, 1933–34, dir. Oskar Fischinger)

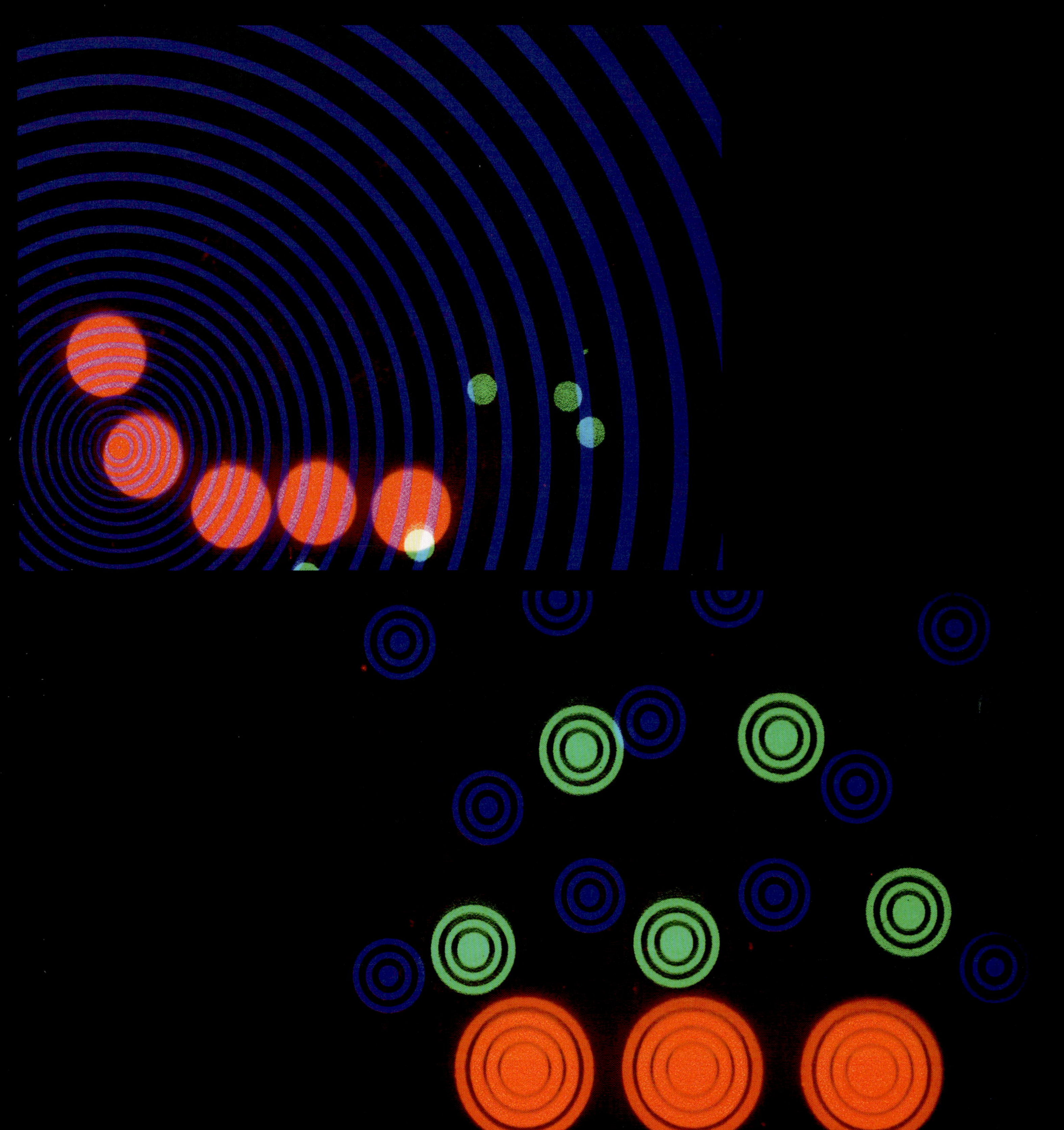

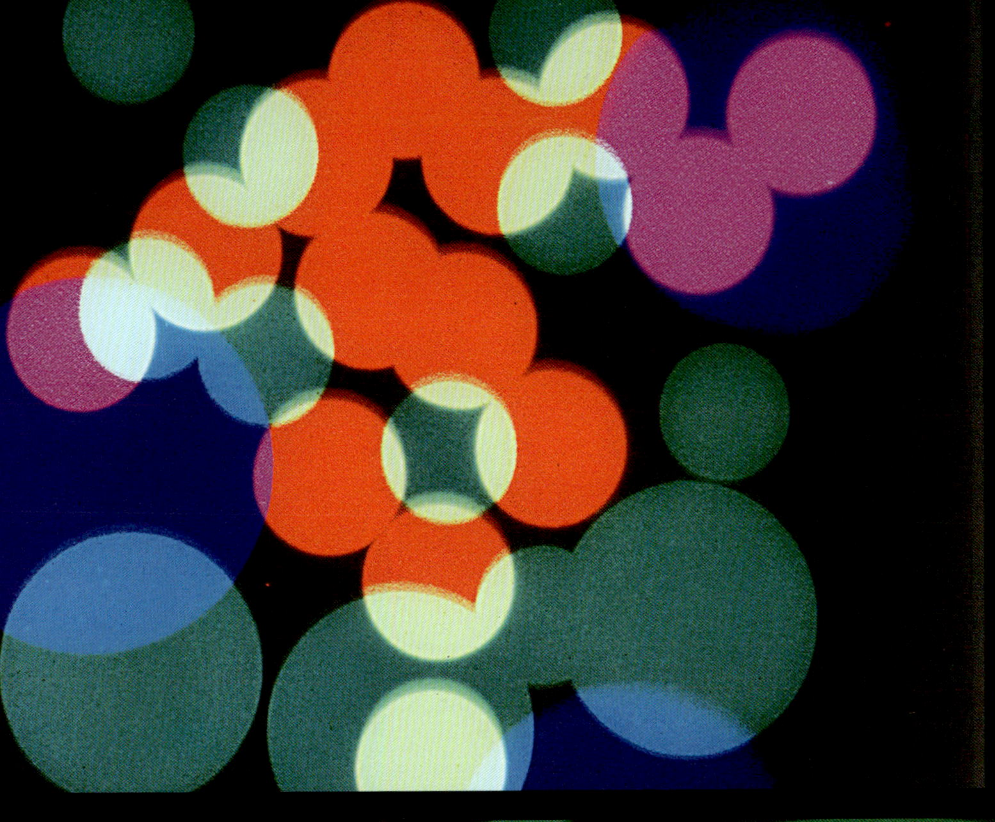

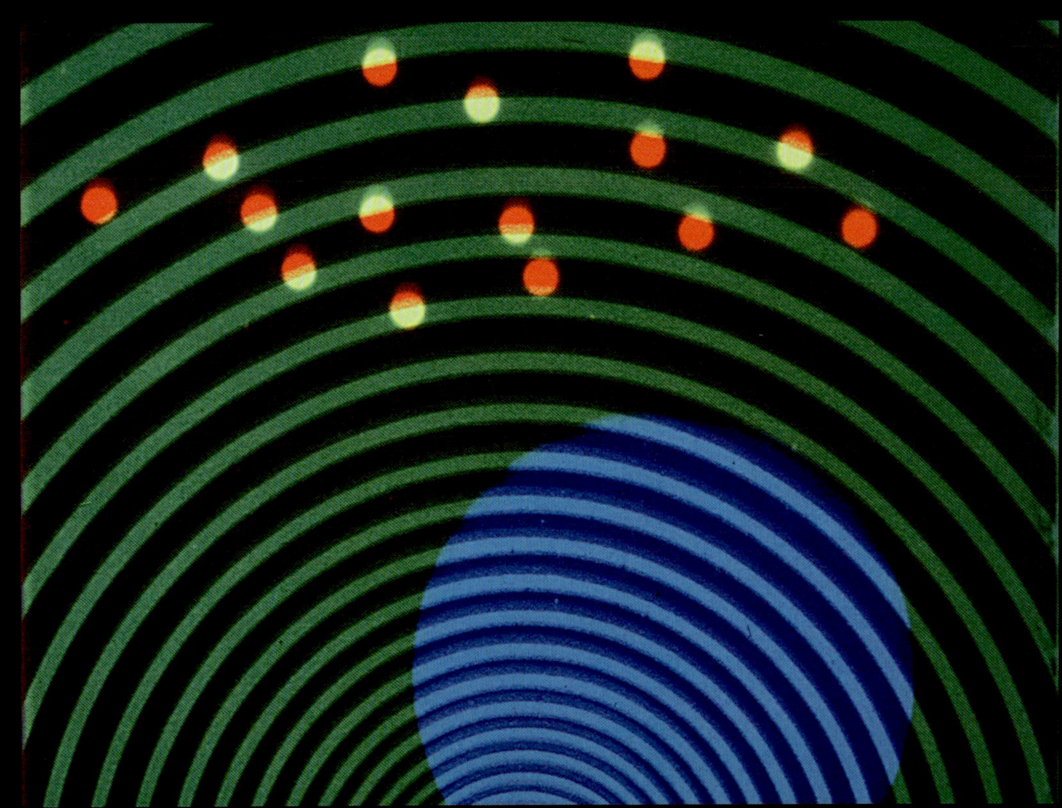

Circles (*Kreise*, Germany, 1933–34, dir. Oskar Fischinger)

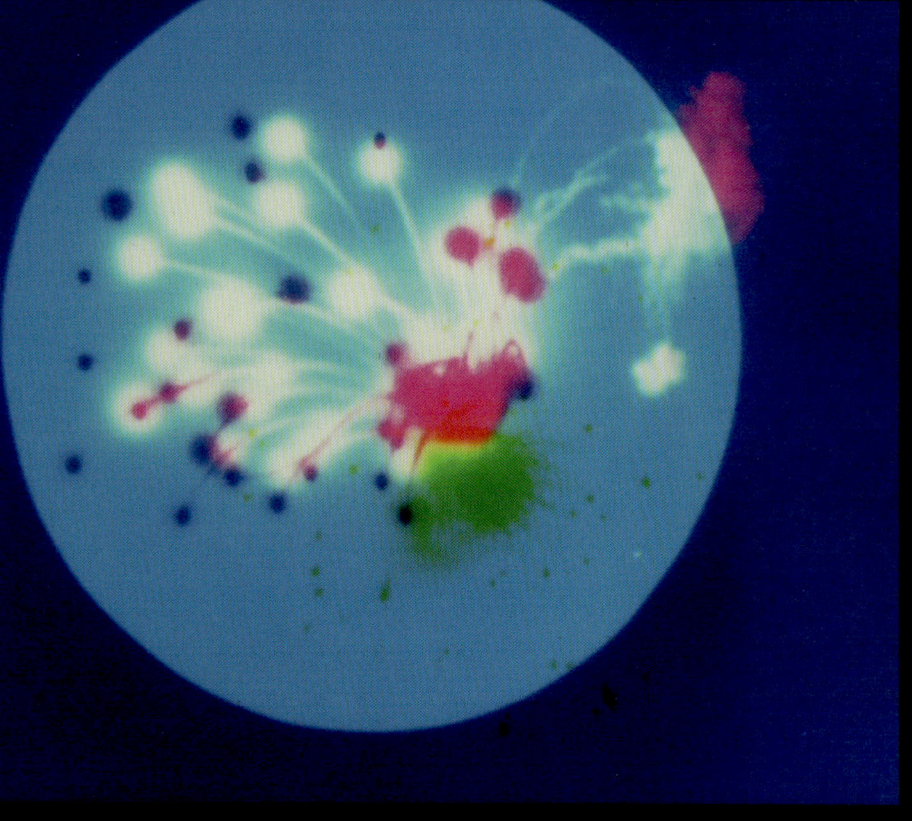

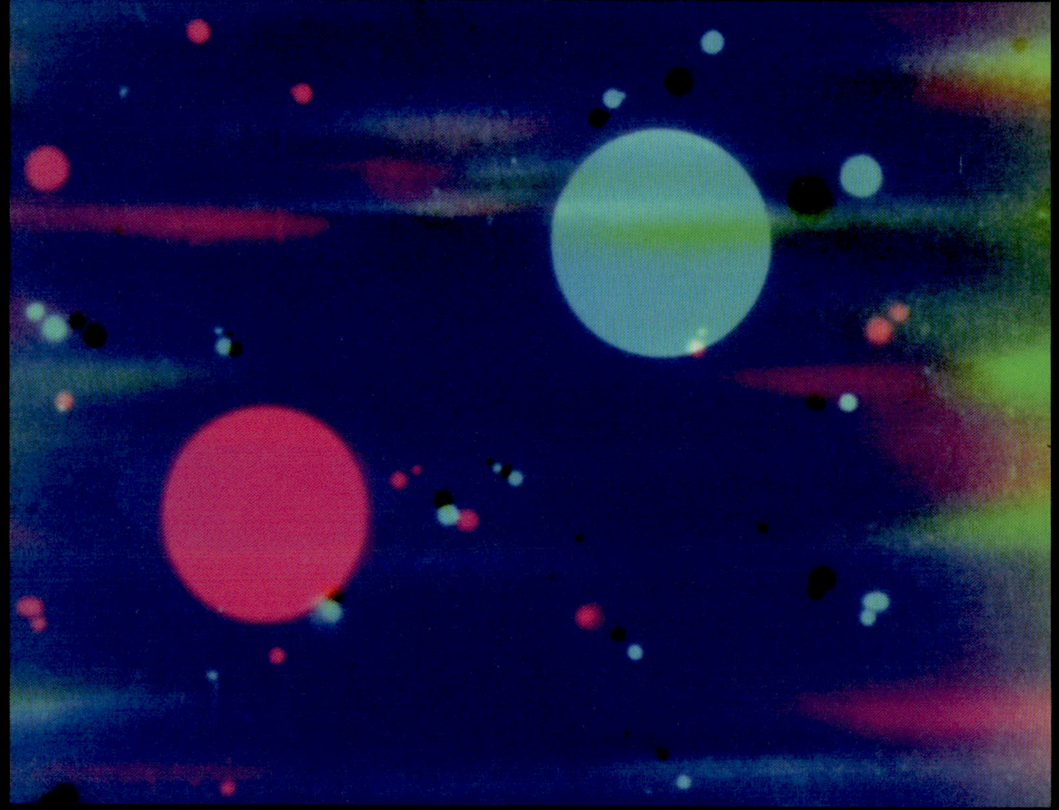

Color Rhapsodie (USA, 1948, dir. Mary Ellen Bute)

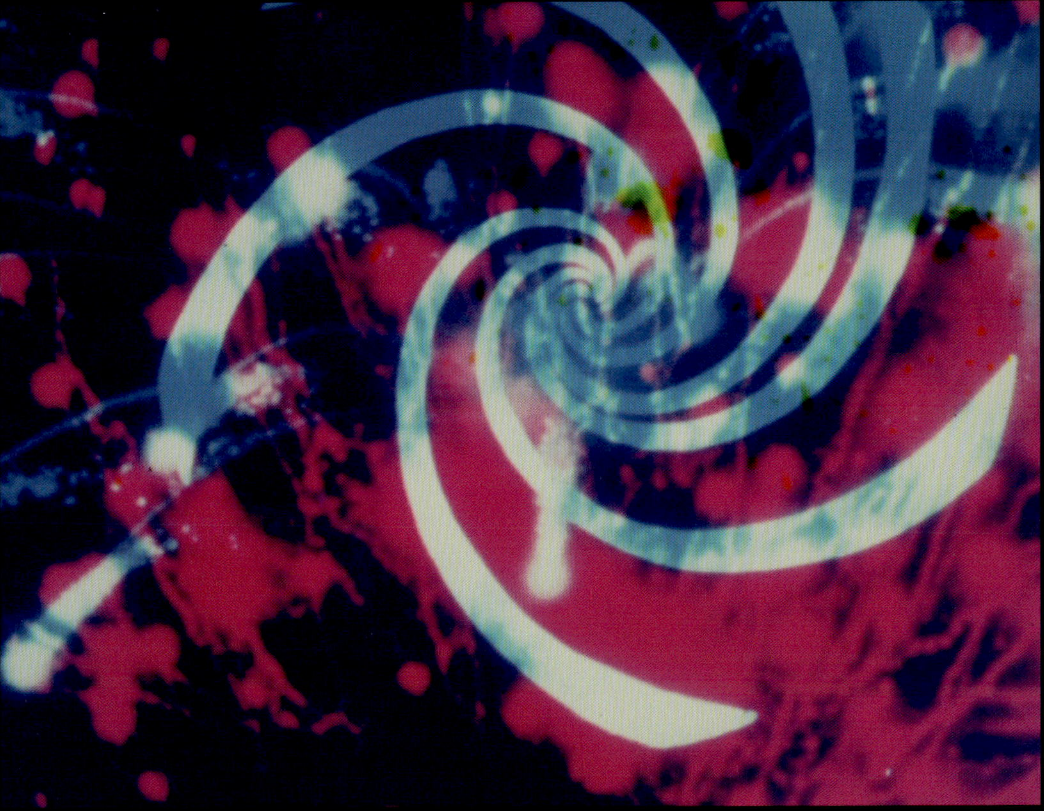

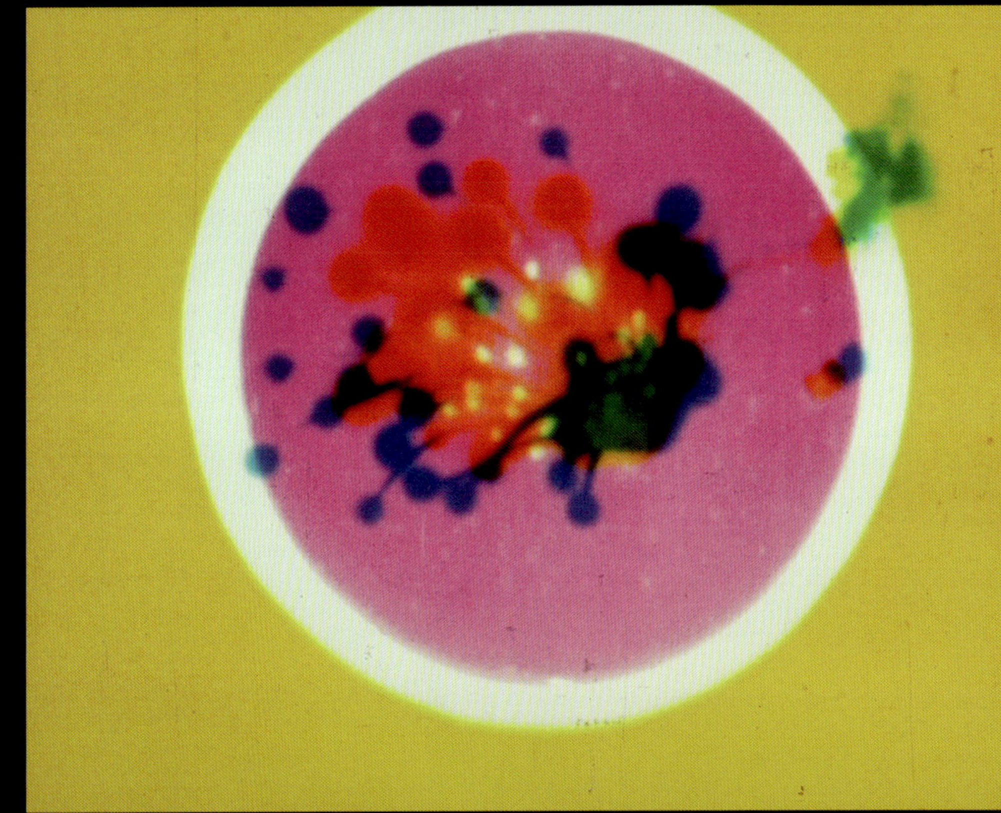

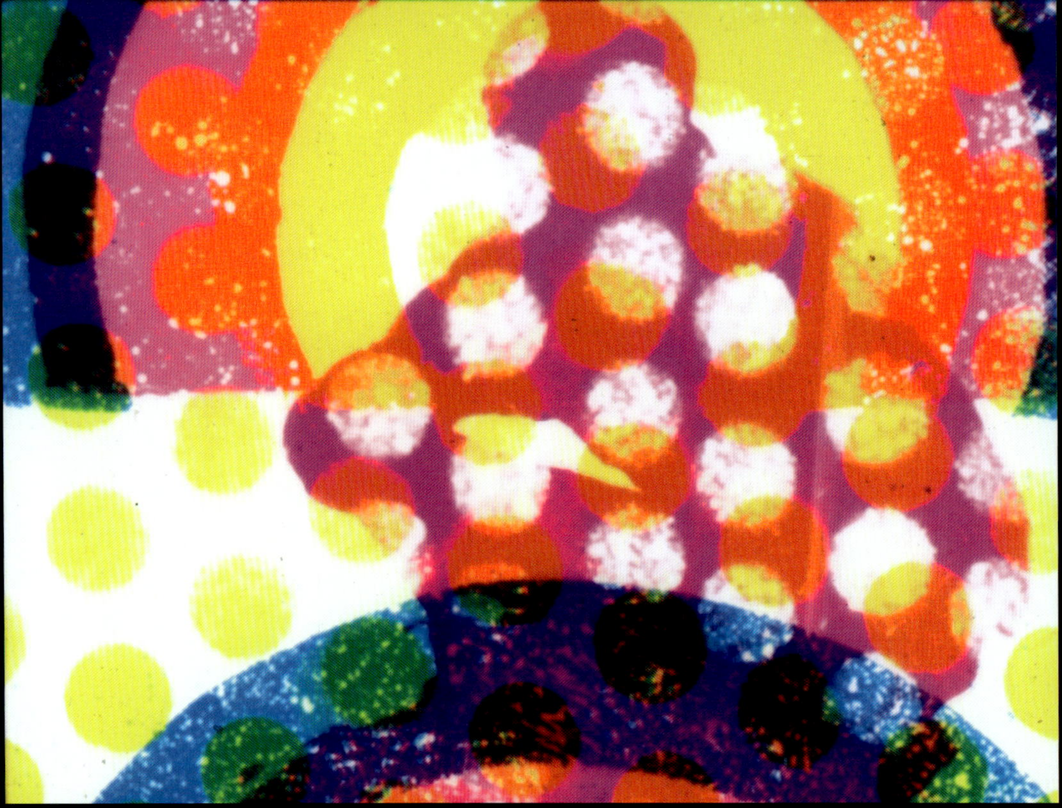

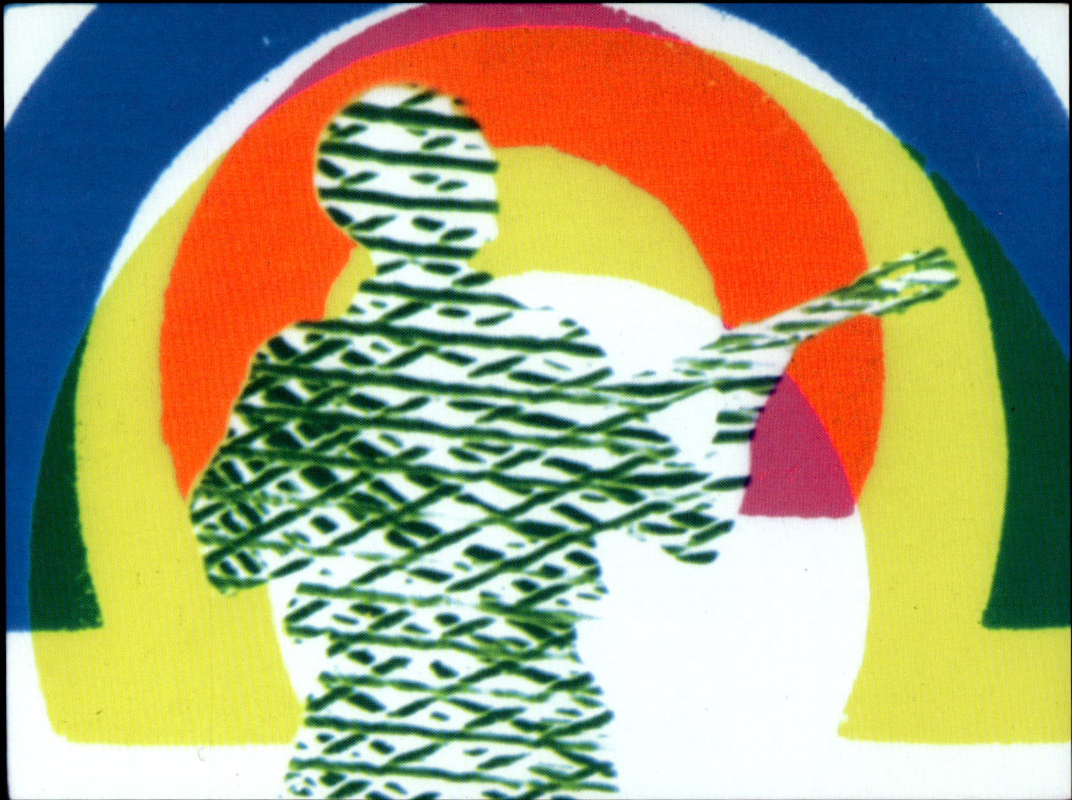

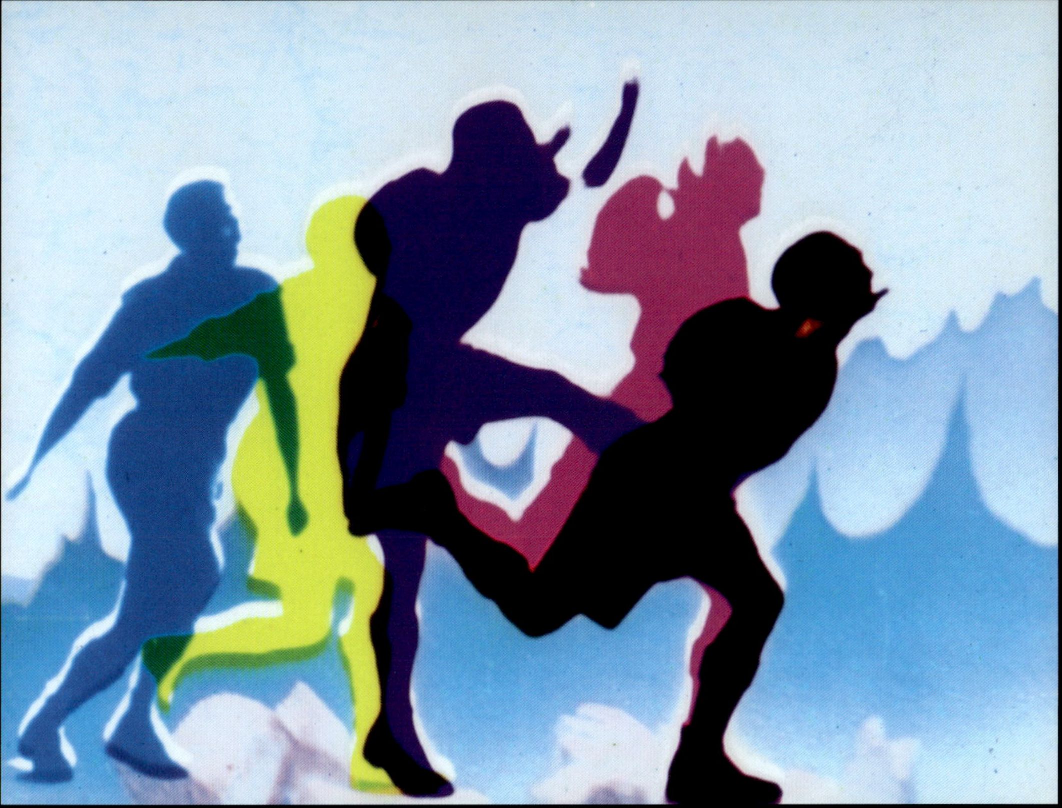

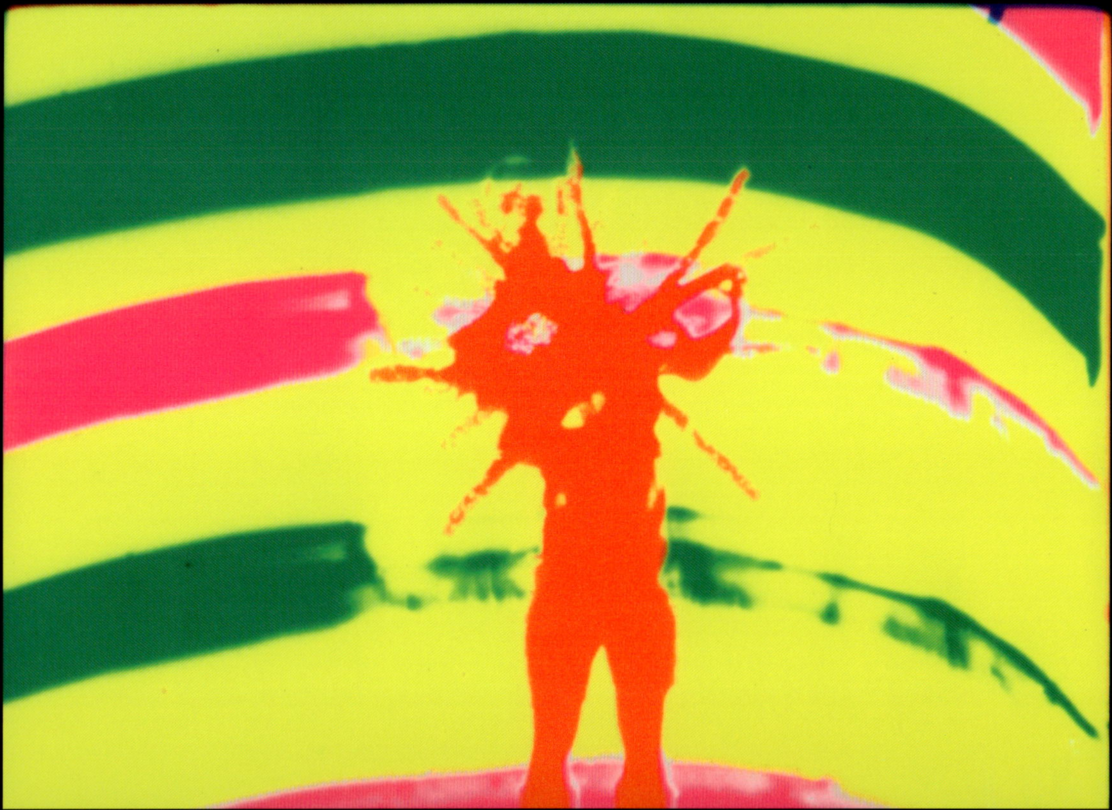

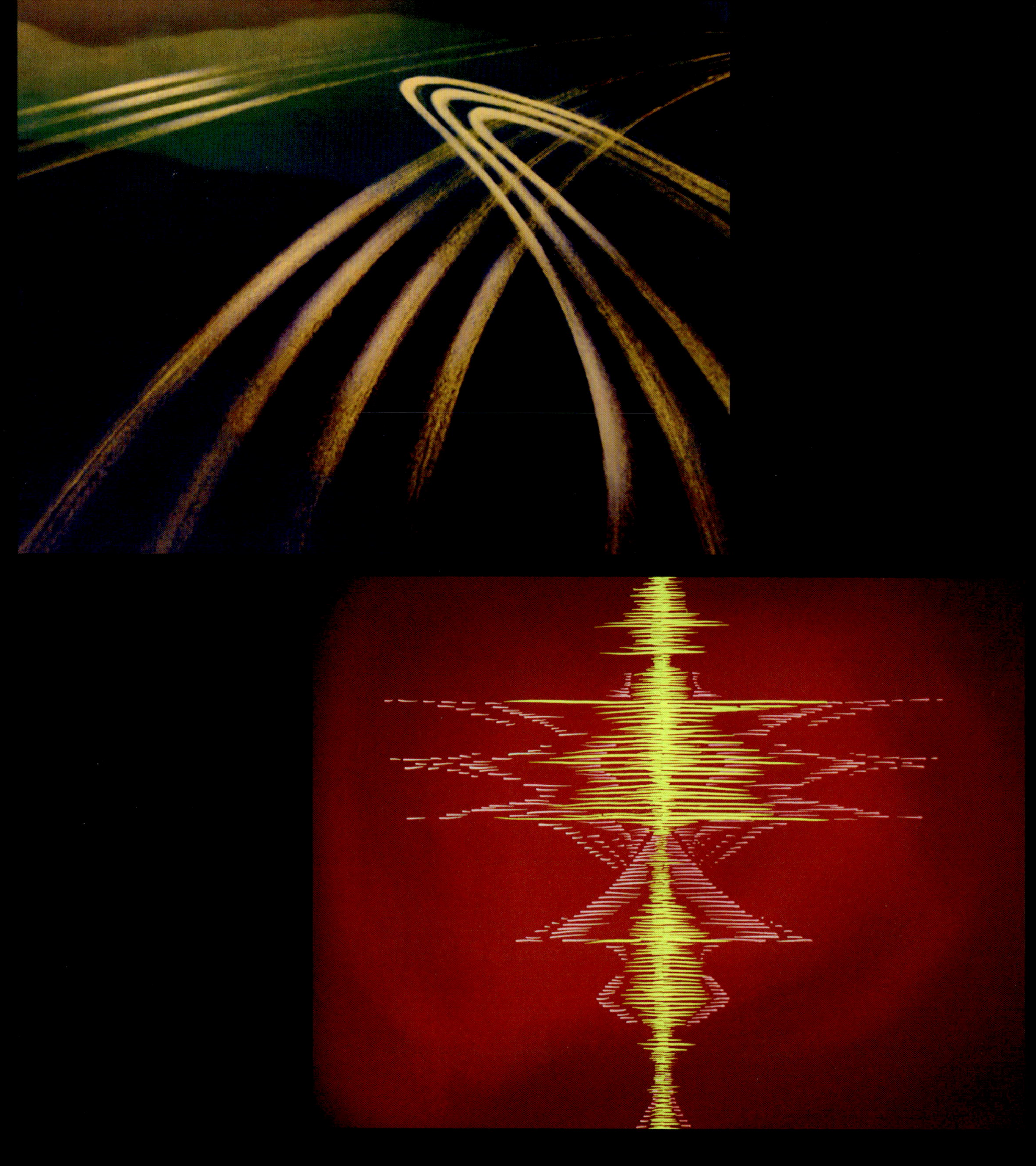

Fantasia (USA, 1940, dirs. Ben Sharpsteen, James Algar, Samuel Armstrong, Ford Beebe, Norman Ferguson, Jim Handley, T. Hee, Wilfred Jackson, Hamilton S. Luske, Bill Roberts, and Paul Satterfield)

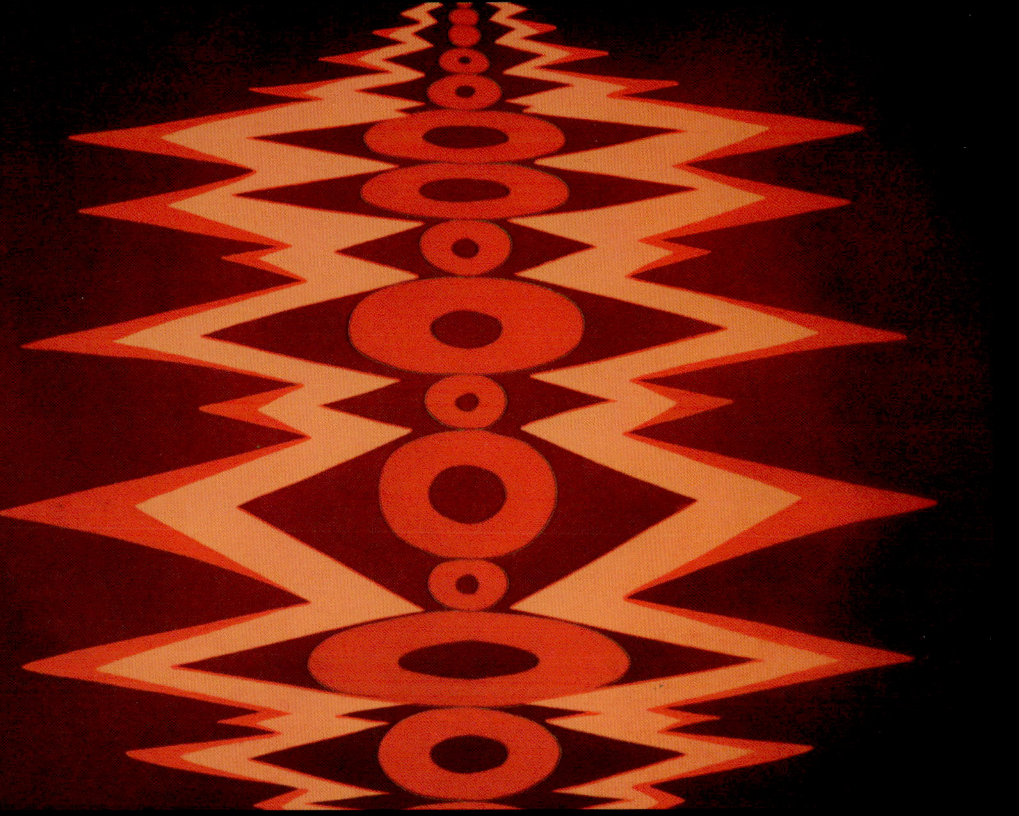

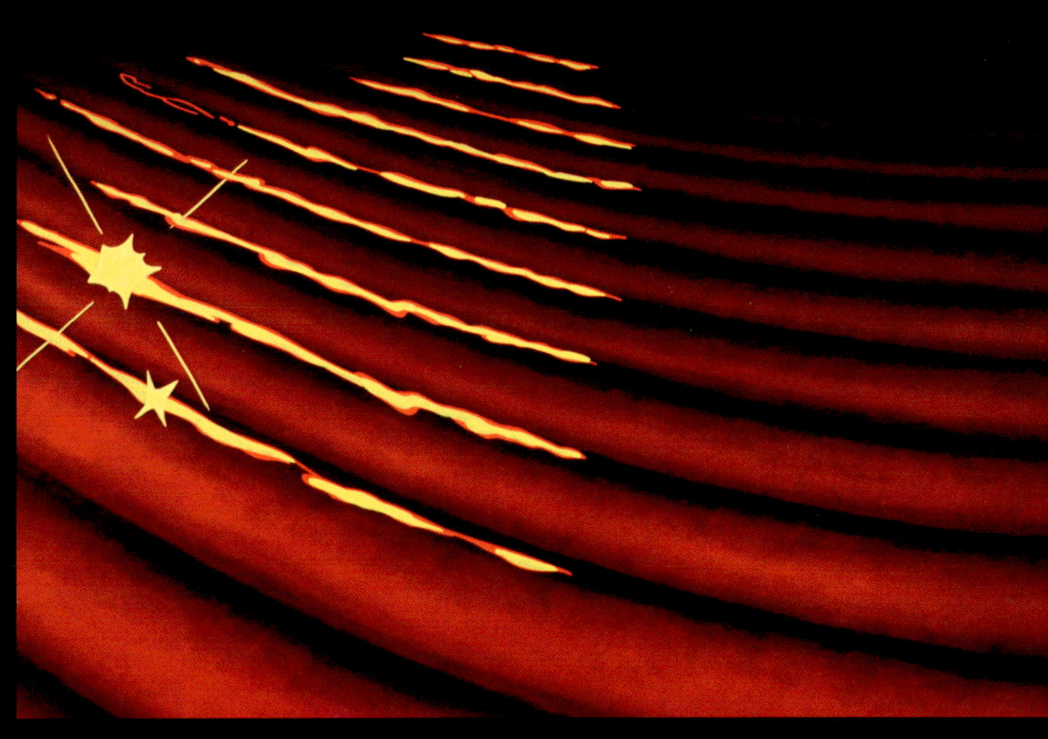

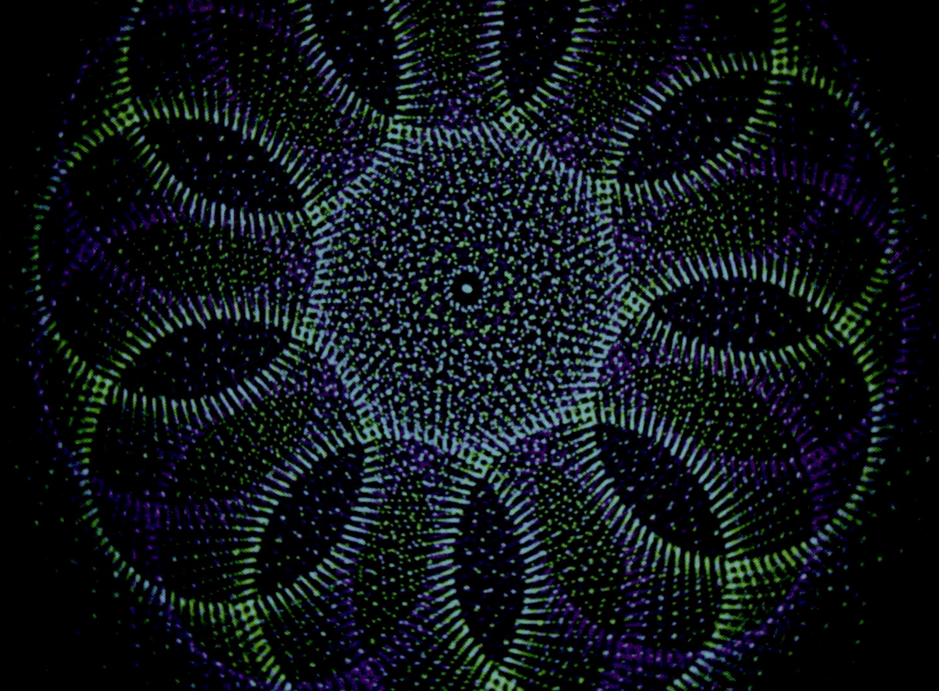

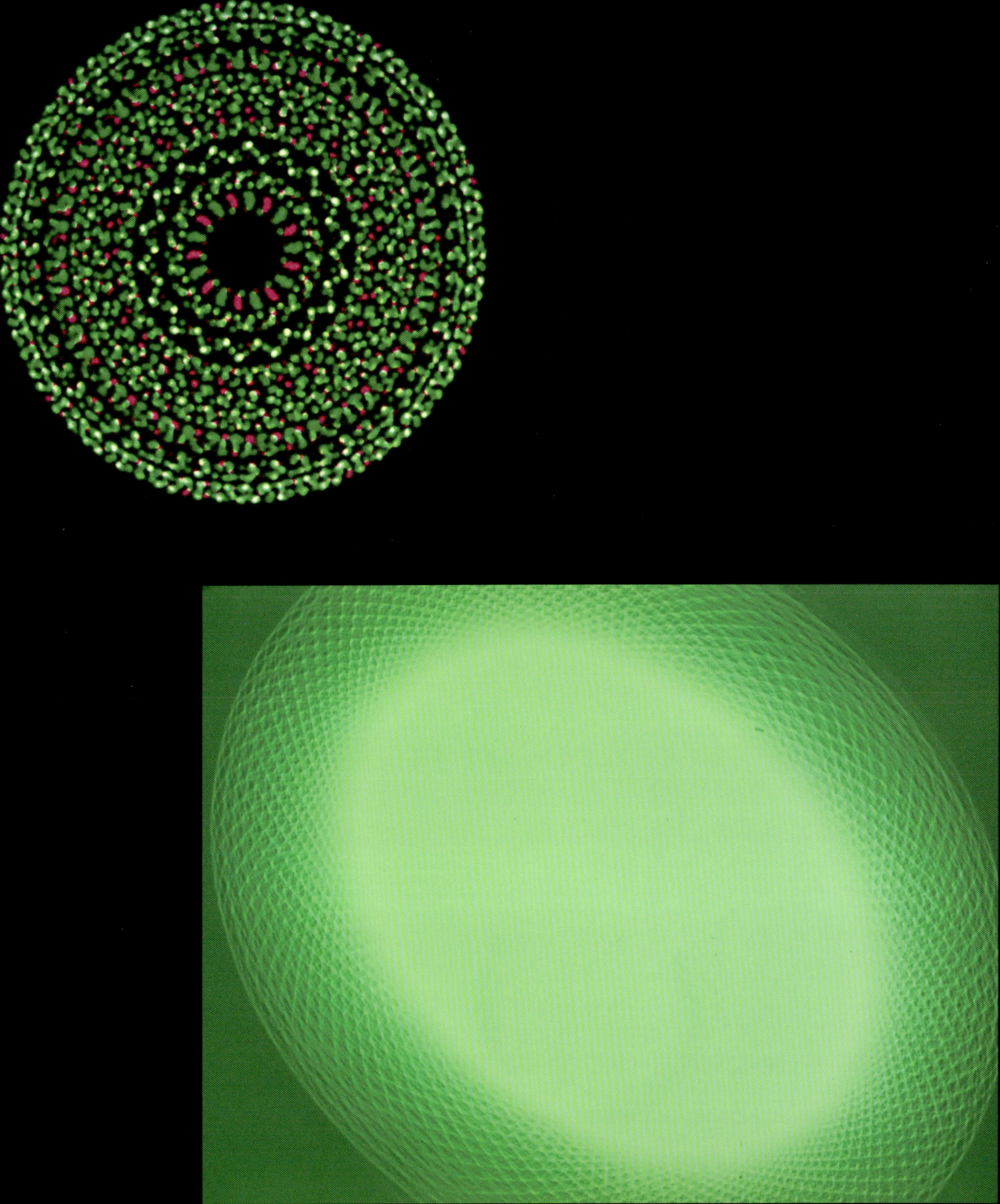

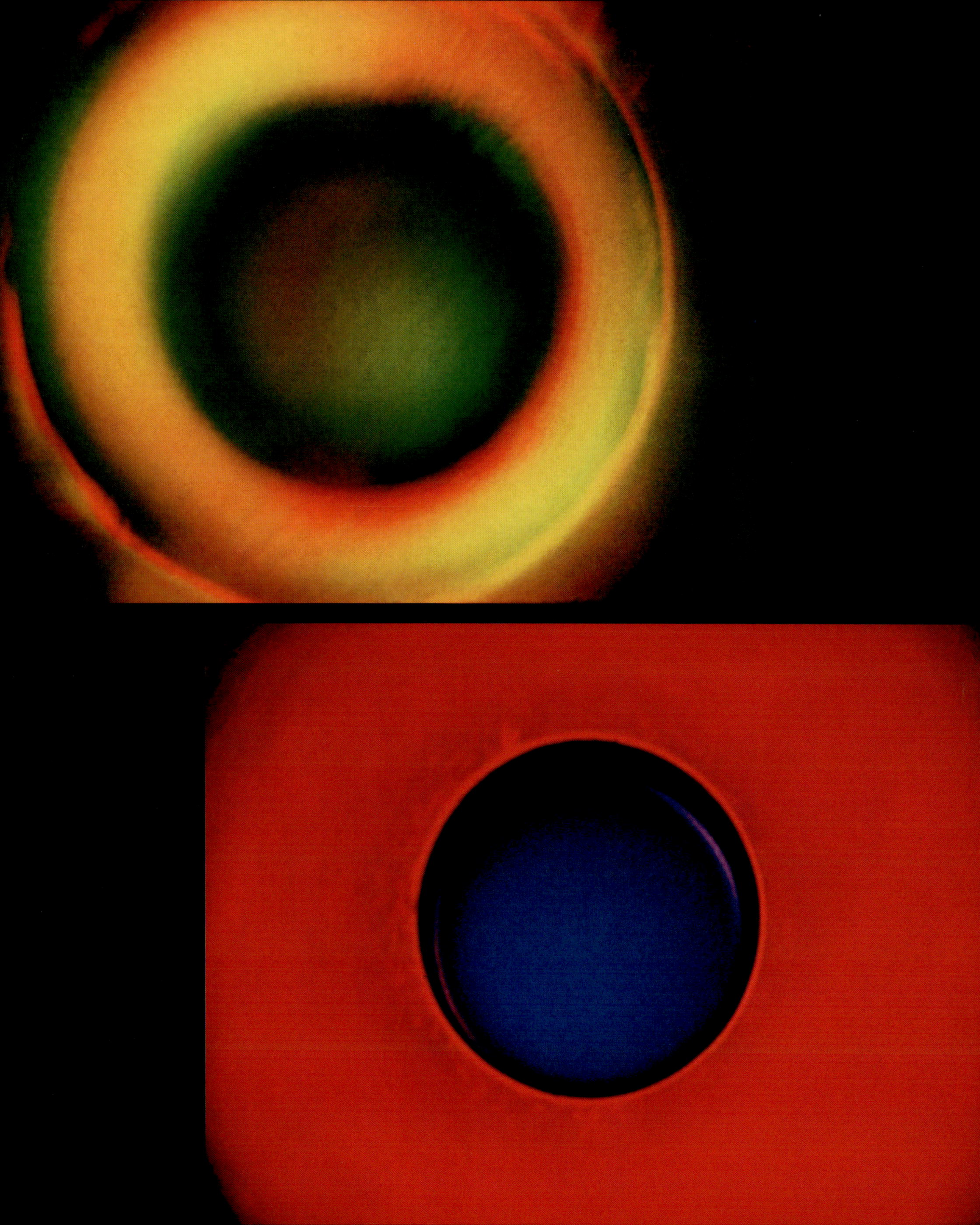

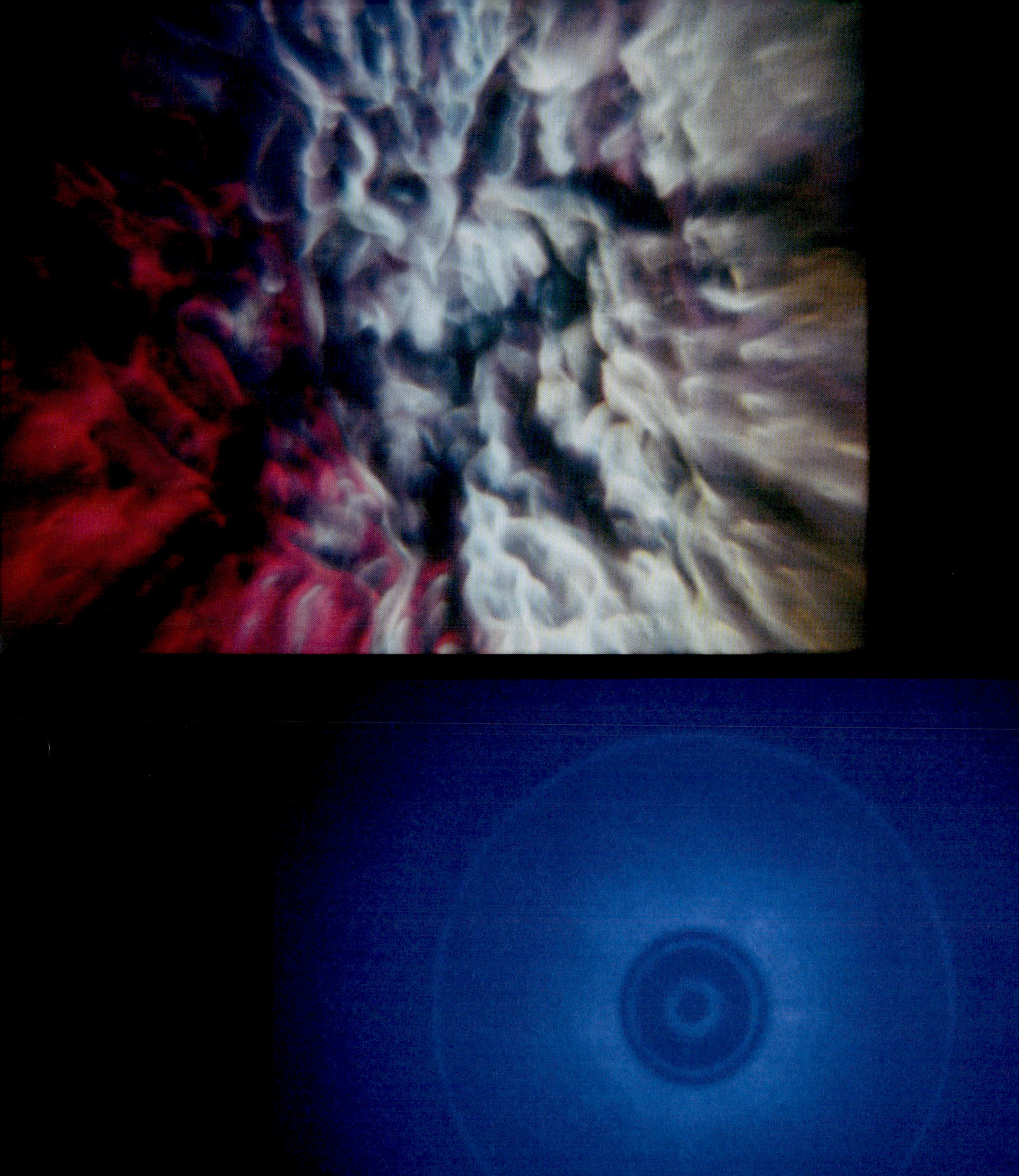

BARBARA FLUECKIGER

A SELECTED TIMELINE OF HISTORICAL FILM COLORS

I developed and first published the Timeline of Historical Film Colors (filmcolors.org) in April 2012. It has grown over the years into a comprehensive resource for the investigation of film color technology and aesthetics, illustrating a broad variety of historical innovations with over twenty thousand photographs of historical films taken at archives in Europe, the United States, and Japan. The following spotlights some of the most relevant techniques for color films, selected either because they laid a foundation for future work or because they were highly original or successful.

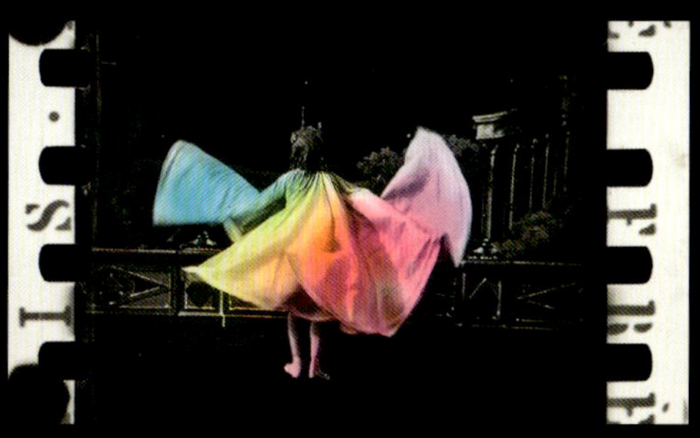

Loïe Fuller (France, 1905)

HAND COLORING
1895

PRINCIPLE: Applied colors, manual application

Previously applied to magic lantern slides, this technique involved the coloring of individual frames by hand with very fine brushes. Any water-based translucent dye was suited to the process, although most often the coloring was done with acid dyes. The process was very time consuming and tedious, given film speeds of sixteen to twenty frames per second. Therefore it was mostly abandoned when stencil coloring was introduced. In contrast to stenciled films, hand-colored ones often have soft outlines, and the application of color varies from frame to frame.

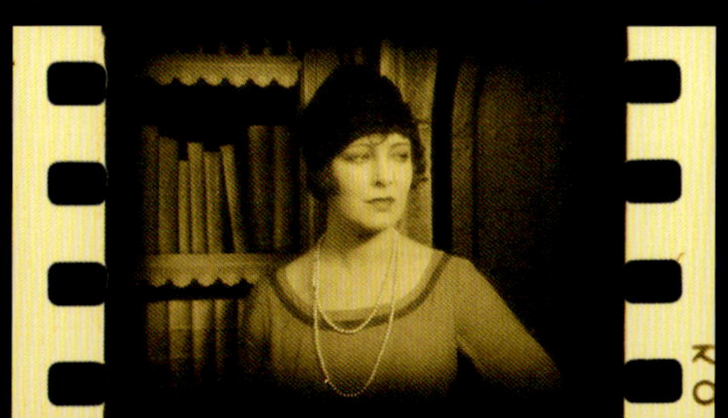

Downhill (UK, 1927, dir. Alfred Hitchcock)

TINTING
1896

PRINCIPLE: Applied colors, dyed gelatin

For tinting, the positive print is immersed in a variety of dye baths, scene by scene. To this end, the print is cut into fragments and reassembled after the dyeing process. The dye homogeneously attaches to the strip's entire gelatinized surface, including the perforation area. Synthetic dyes were usually dissolved in a weak acid solution to form a chemical bond with the gelatin.

Tinting can be identified by brighter image areas that are colored uniformly, while darker parts remain black. Sometimes, however, dyes fade or produce complex color alterations due to their chemical nature; tinting was occasionally combined with toning, which makes identification more difficult.

While there were some conventional metaphorical associations for particular colors, such as blue for night scenes or red for fire, they were neither fixed nor mandatory. It is therefore necessary to analyze the color scheme in each individual film with regard to its narrative structure unfolding in space and time.

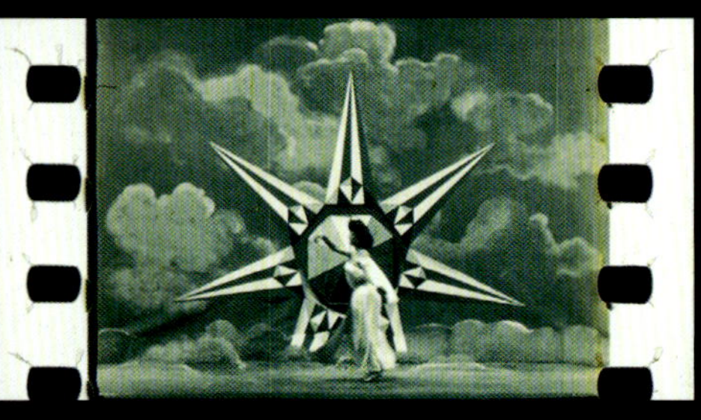

Voyage around a Star (*Voyage autour d'une étoile*, France, 1906, dir. Gaston Velle)

TONING
1896

PRINCIPLE: Applied colors, silver replacement

In contrast to tinting, toning involves a chemical reaction converting the silver image. In this reaction the neutral silver image in the emulsion of a positive film is replaced by one consisting of colored metal compounds. These were usually iron ferrocyanide (Prussian blue) for blue, copper ferrocyanide for red/brown, silver sulfide for sepia, or, rarely, uranium ferrocyanide for reddish brown. Though toning had been used in still photography, film required the introduction of translucent toning compounds to allow for projection. There were two chemical recipes available for toning. In the one-bath process, the silver image is converted to silver ferrocyanide and then combined with a colored ferrocyanide. In the two-bath process, metallic ferrocyanide first bleaches the metal silver into silver ferrocyanide, then the silver ferrocyanide is converted to colored metal ferrocyanide.

In principle, toned images can be identified easily by the transparent bright image parts and perforation areas, while the shadows and dark parts are colored in a specific hue. In practice, however, the brighter parts can also be affected by the diffusion of dyeing compounds or a combination of tinting and toning.

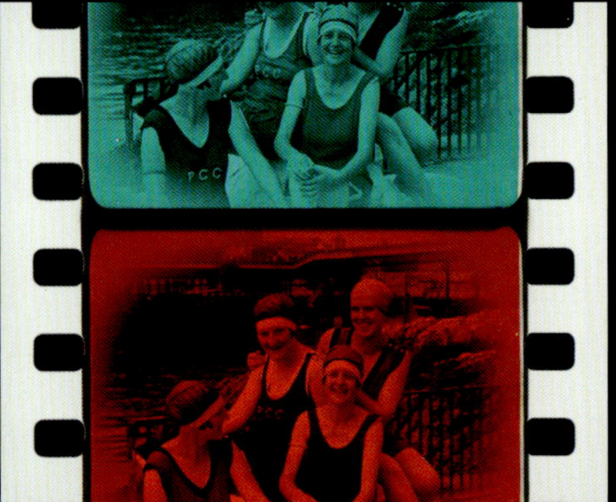

The Open Road (UK, 1925, dir. Claude Friese-Greene)

FRIESE-GREENE
1898

PRINCIPLE: Additive two- or three-color, alternately stained

INVENTOR: William Friese-Greene

"Friese-Greene Natural Colour, which is also sometimes referred to as the Spectrum Colour process after the company formed to promote it, was an adaptation by Claude Friese-Greene of his father William's work with Biocolour. In the earlier process, a rotating disc was placed before the camera lens which exposed the film through alternate red and green filters, the resulting print consisting of alternating red and green records which were then dyed red and green, respectively. Claude Friese-Greene retained the rotating disc and the red filter but replaced the green filter with an open aperture partly filled by a yellow filter. This unusual combination was the result of a number of years of experimentation with alternatives to red and green, which were the standard for two-colour additive processes, and which Claude Friese-Greene felt was partly the cause of headache-inducing flickering which had dogged previous processes.... The completed film was then processed to make a black-and-white negative record which was then put through a machine which tinted red the frames taken through the red filter, and cyan (blue/green) the frames taken through the yellow filter/open aperture. Upon projection, using the principle of persistence of vision, the alternating tinted frames blurred together to produce a full two-colour image, but there is some debate as to whether the print was shown at 24fps or 32fps. It is logical to assume that the speed, as with Kinemacolor, was 30–32fps, which was twice the normal silent speed, but the existing material in the BFI National Archive runs satisfactorily at 24fps."

Simon Brown, "Technical Appendix," in Sarah Street, *Colour Films in Britain: The Negotiation of Innovation, 1900–1955* (London: British Film Institute and Palgrave Macmillan, 2012), 271.

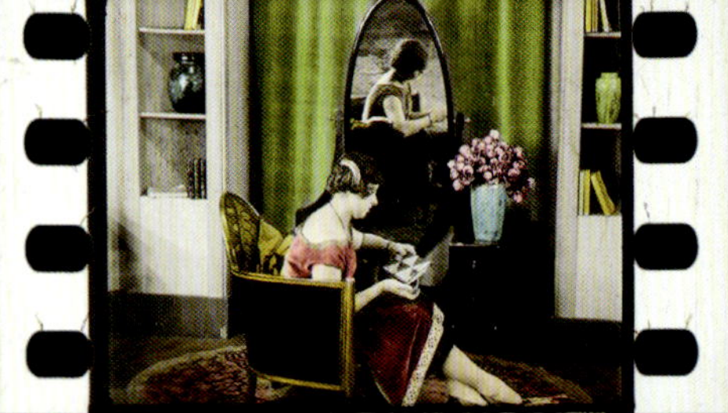

Pathé Revue no. 46: De Mode der taschjes te Parijs (France, 1924)

PATHÉCOLOR / PATHÉCHROME / STENCIL COLORING
1903–28

PRINCIPLE: Applied colors, stencil, dyed gelatin

INVENTORS: Pathé and others

Stencil coloring required the manual cutting, frame by frame, of the area that was to be tinted onto another identical print, one for each color. Usually the number of colors applied ranged from three to six. A stencil print would be made by tracing the outlines of the image areas on a magnified guide print projected onto a ground glass. (A pantograph reduced the enlargement back to frame size.) The process was highly improved by the introduction of a cutting machine that performed the cutting on the stencil print with a needle. When cut out manually, the gelatin had to be removed from the stencil print to form a transparent strip. In the machine-cutting process the stencil was cut into a blank film directly. For every color the stencil print was fed in register with the positive print into a printing machine, where the acid dye was applied by a continuous velvet band soaked with color.

Several hundred women performed the exacting tasks at the Pathé workshop in Vincennes, France. Similar techniques were applied by Gaumont, Oskar Messter, and the Cinemacoloris process invented by Segundo de Chomón. Stencil-colored films can be identified by the sharp outlines that define the colored areas. Color hues were most often soft pastels. Stencil-colored images have a painterly quality but often strive for a reality effect. In contrast, hand-colored films often have soft outlines, and the application of color varies from frame to frame.

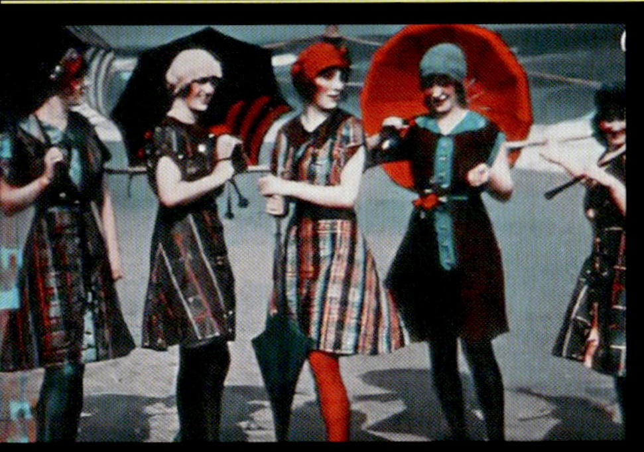

A Visit to the Seaside (UK, 1908, dir. George Albert Smith)

KINEMACOLOR
1908–15

PRINCIPLE: Additive two-color, rotary filter

INVENTORS: George Albert Smith and Charles Urban (The Natural Color Kinematograph Company, Ltd.)

Kinemacolor was an additive process involving alternating red and green filters that were applied to the shutter in front of the camera and in front of the projector. Kinemacolor was the most successful of the so-called natural color processes (now called mimetic) in early cinema, those that translate the scene in front of the camera into a colored depiction by chemical or optical means or a combination of both. Though it flourished between 1908 and 1913, the principle of recording color separations with revolving shutter filters was first proposed by the German Hermann Isensee as early as 1897. It was further developed by Frederick Marshall Lee and Edward Raymond Turner, who patented in 1899 a three-color system (financed by Charles Urban) that proved to be impractical. It was impossible to keep the three records in register, as both the cameras and the projectors were not devised for the necessary high frame rates.

However, a reduction to only two colors failed to reproduce the whole color spectrum, unable to render blue to violet hues and having yellow-tinged whites. To compensate for this problem, George Albert Smith, who applied for his first patent in 1906, proposed to add blue-violet filters to the projection light. Depending on the color temperature of the projection lamp, the green filter had to be adjusted to produce a satisfying result. Also, at a running speed of at least thirty-two frames per second, Kinemacolor required double the minimum frame rate. Time parallax—the slight temporal offset between the red and green records—created small differences that resulted in color fringes when objects or scenes were moving.

Many contemporary witnesses were nevertheless enthusiastic about the rendition of colors. "They are not pictures, but realities" was a PR slogan of the Natural Colour Kinematograph Company that recurred in reviews. Urban, the owner of the company, incessantly postulated the educational benefit of movies in natural colors. As Smith pointed out in 1908, one of the main challenges in developing the process was to sensitize the orthochromatic black-and-white stock, which was naturally sensitive to blue, to the red end of the color spectrum. Basic research on the properties of the filters, the sensitized stock, and the projection lamp with regard to human color perception was crucial to establish the proper balance between the red and green records.

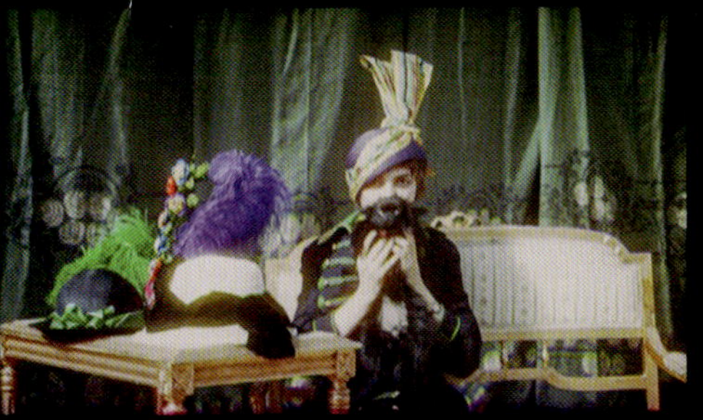

La Mode de Paris (France, 1912)

GAUMONT CHRONOCHROME
1912–20

PRINCIPLE: Additive three-color, sawn-off lenses and filters, simultaneous taking and projection

INVENTOR: Léon Gaumont (Gaumont)

"Gaumont's additive process employed a triple lens fitted with green, red, and blue filters in the camera and the projector, each picture being recorded in three black and white frames of different gradations. When overlapped in projection, each with its respective filter, the three frames with their corresponding latent colours merged into a single trichrome picture.

A unique feature of the Chronochrome system is the height of its 35mm film frame, reduced from the 18mm in standard silent prints to 14mm, equal to a 1:1.71 aspect ratio. The panoramic look was meant to facilitate alignment of the converging projection angles, and to reduce the amount of film stock needed in cameras and projectors: with its narrower frames, a Chronochrome film used 2.25 times the amount of film stock of a conventional 35mm print, rather than three times as much, as would have been required with three frames of standard size for each picture. The central lens with a red colour filter was stationary; above and below it, the lenses with green and blue filters were adjusted vertically and horizontally, either by hand or with an electrical remote device controlled by a technician sitting in the auditorium. When properly in register, Chronochrome films are admired for the variety and brilliance of their colours. Pictures of inanimate objects captured at close range possess a startling three-dimensional look; the exquisite tonal harmony of outdoor scenes is especially striking where there are vast expanses of primary colours, as in the sea against a blue sky. The magic was dissolved in the blurred renditions of fast movements and small objects seen at long distances, exactly as had happened with Kinemacolor.

Gaumont's and Urban's additive colour systems required extra light to compensate for the filters: with its 33 percent rate of light absorption, Kinemacolor used 250 percent more electric power than a normal film projection; Chronochrome was even worse, as its blue filter alone absorbed almost one third of all the available light from the projector's lamphouse. The fatal drawback of Gaumont's otherwise brilliant technique had to do with its mechanical design: Chronochrome films could be screened at the 'standard' speed of 16 frames per second, but were incompatible with conventional 35mm projectors because of Chronochrome's multiple exposure system (three frames projected at the same time) and aspect ratio; moreover, it was not possible to adapt the triple-lens device to any other projection equipment."

Paolo Cherchi Usai, *Silent Cinema: A Guide to Study, Research and Curatorship*, 3rd ed. (London: British Film Institute, 2019), 56–57.

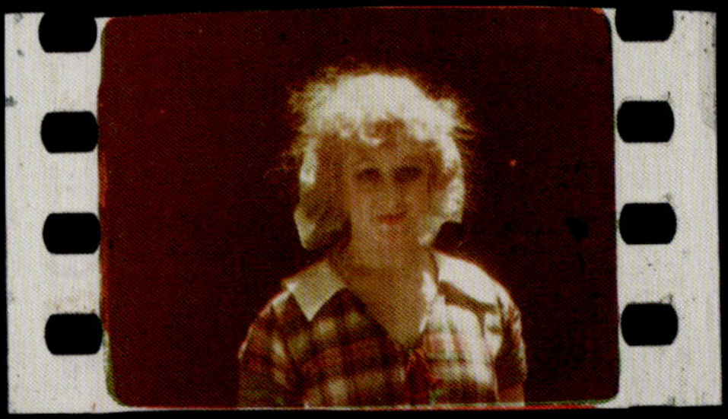

The Gulf Between (USA, 1918, dir. Wray Physioc)

TECHNICOLOR I

1916–20

PRINCIPLE: Additive two-color, beam splitter

INVENTORS: Herbert Kalmus, Daniel Frost Comstock, and William Burton Westcott (Technicolor)

The first Technicolor process was similar to Kinemacolor, the most commercially successful additive process in early film. To avoid Kinemacolor's heavy color fringing due to time parallax, Technicolor introduced a beam splitter. During filming, the beam splitter worked in combination with filters in the camera to divide the incoming light into a red and a green separation negative on black-and-white stock. Thus the red and the green records were taken at the same time from the same point of view. When projected in the cinema the two images were combined by additive mixture through corresponding red and green filters into one picture. The reduction of the whole color range to two colors (and their additive combinations) was necessary because of the complex optical arrangement. In practice, however, it proved to be very difficult to align the two images during projection.

The disappointing experience with this process led to Technicolor's decision to abandon additive processes and to switch to subtractive ones. The beam splitter was the most important invention of Technicolor I, and all successive color processes invented by Technicolor relied on this optical system.

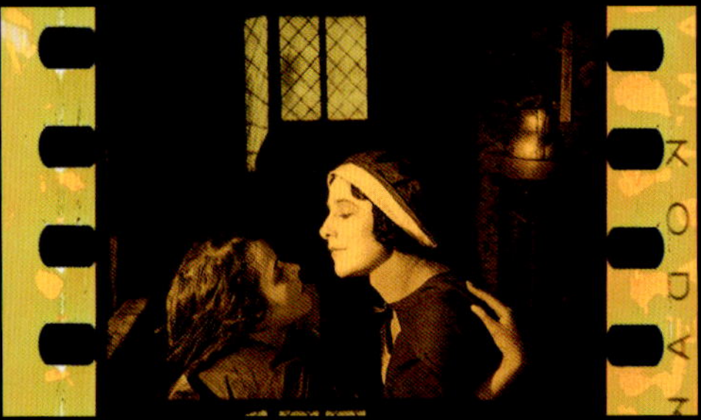

Joan the Woman (USA, 1916, dir. Cecil B. DeMille)

HANDSCHIEGL / DEMILLE-WYCKOFF PROCESS

1916–28

PRINCIPLE: Applied color, imbibition

INVENTORS: Max Handschiegl and Alvin Wyckoff

Similar to stenciling, the Handschiegl process was applied mechanically to manually defined image parts. After the film was shot and edited, a separate print was made for each applied color. In contrast to stenciling, the image parts to be colored were covered with an opaque paint. Subsequently a dupe-negative was made. A tanning developer hardened the gelatin in the exposed areas while leaving the blocked-out areas soft. The softer parts absorbed the acid dyes, which were then transferred onto the positive print during an imbibition process. Usually up to three colors were applied to a film. The process allowed for a subtle blending of different colors.

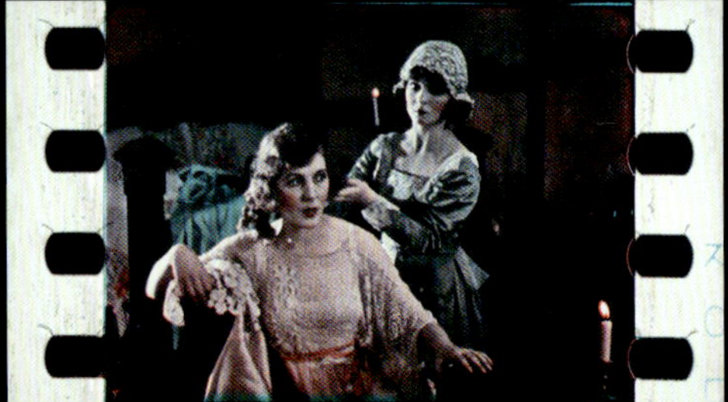

The Glorious Adventure (USA/UK, 1922, dir. J. Stuart Blackton)

PRIZMA II

1919–23

PRINCIPLE: Subtractive two-color, toning on double-coated film

INVENTOR: William van Doren Kelley (Prizma Company)

"In its final form Prizma made use of duplitized positive film. As in previous Prizma systems, the original negatives were alternate frame sequential exposures. The Prizma negative was printed on both sides of the positive film in a special printer. After developing in a normal black and white developer it was bleached in a bath that converted the two images to silver iodide. Two methods appear to have been used for dyeing the duplitized prints:

1. The film was wound tightly on a drum and the exposed side was dyed. When this step was completed, the film was dried and reversed onto a second drum and dyed the other color.

2. The print was coated with a removable resist on the side printed from the blue-green negative. The red-orange negative side was then dyed blue-green. When the dyeing was completed the resist was removed and the film was dried. Next the red-orange side was coated with resist and the other side of the print was dyed red-orange."

Roderick T. Ryan, *A History of Motion Picture Color Technology* (London: Focal Press, 1977), 91–94.

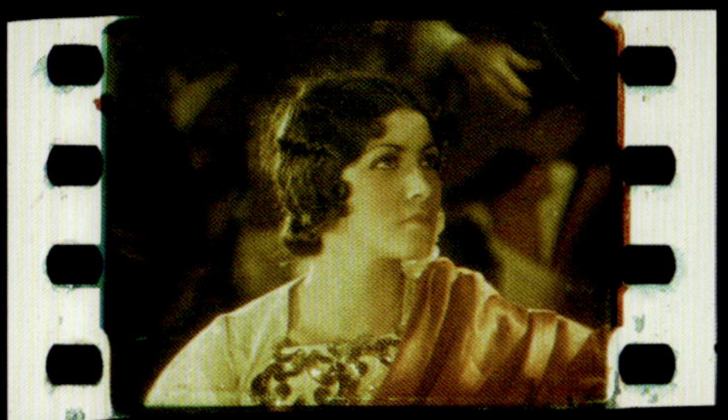

King of Jazz (USA, 1930, dir. John Murray Anderson)

TECHNICOLOR II
1922–27

PRINCIPLE: Subtractive two-color, two-toned films, cemented

INVENTOR: Technicolor

The first subtractive two-color process introduced by Technicolor captured incoming light through a beam splitter with red and green filters. However, in contrast to the first Technicolor process, the two images were recorded on one negative strip. This was achieved by the pull-down of two frames simultaneously, a process that required double speed in the camera. These two frames were arranged in pairs, whereby the green record was inverted upside down.

These two images were then step-printed onto two positives. A tanning process hardened the silver image. In the following step the soft portions were washed away. The relief matrices were then glued together, and the opposite sides of the film were dyed red-orange and blue-green, respectively.

Although the first film shot in this process, *The Toll of the Sea* (1922), was a huge commercial success, the system encountered many practical difficulties. The cemented film tended to scratch more easily and more noticeably; even worse, it curled as a result of irregular shrinking caused by the heat of the projector. In addition, costs were very high, and Technicolor faced difficulties to deliver on time due to its limited capacities. Very few feature films were shot entirely in color. More often, films contained short scenes in Technicolor while the rest of them were dyed by the usual applied processes. Over time Technicolor II prints fade to orange.

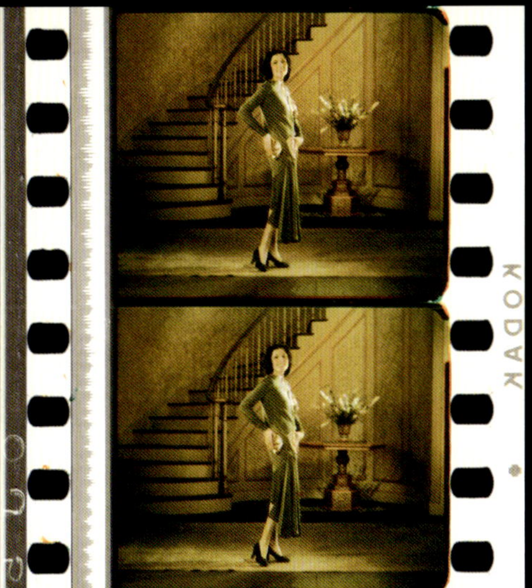

Fashion News (USA, 1927)

TECHNICOLOR III
1927–32

PRINCIPLE: Subtractive two-color, beam splitter, dye transfer

INVENTOR: Technicolor

The third Technicolor process used the same camera as Process II to combine a pair of frames of the red and green records, respectively, on the black-and-white negative. In the new process, however, the two images were printed on one side of the positive by the dye-transfer or imbibition process.

For the dye transfer, again matrices were prepared by hardening the gelatin with a tanning developer and washing away the soft portions of the gelatin. These reliefs were then dyed with the complementary hues in green-blue and red-orange, respectively. In the imbibition process the dyes were transferred by contact onto a blank film that was specially prepared to absorb the color and to prevent it from bleeding.

While this process was very sophisticated in terms of mechanical precision, it was still a two-color process and as such was not able to offer the whole range of colors. Nevertheless it was an economic success when, in the wake of the transition to sound, many producers also started to shoot in color at the end of the 1920s. In addition, the Technicolor company launched a publicity campaign in fan magazines to support the acceptance of color films. However, the company was unable to handle the huge demand without compromising quality. Thus, after a short peak in color production at the turn of the 1930s, the number of Technicolor films declined quickly again.

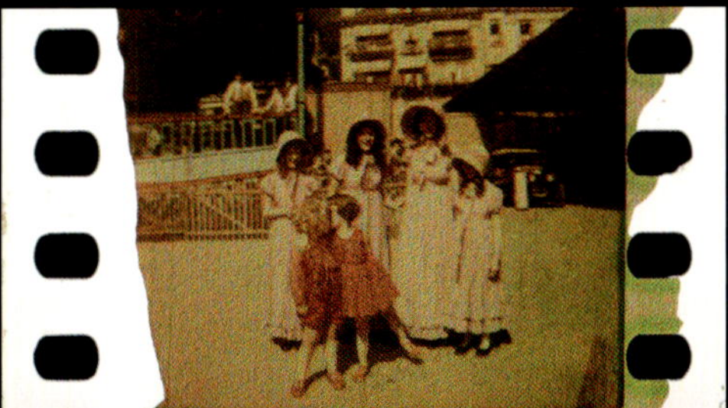

Cinécolor sample, ca. 1929

AUTOCHROME / CINÉCOLOR
1928

PRINCIPLE: Additive three-color, mosaic screen

INVENTORS: Auguste and Louis Lumière

Many attempts were made to apply the Autochrome process invented by the Lumière brothers to motion pictures. Transparent potato-starch grains with a diameter of fifteen to twenty micrometers were colored in the additive primaries red, green, and blue (in fact, blue-purple). The spaces between the grains were blackened by carbon particles. This process created a colored mosaic screen through which the emulsion was exposed. By a reversal process a positive print of the film was created. As in pointillism, the color impression was formed in the eye of the viewer.

Several problems prevented the successful adoption of the process by motion picture production. The starch grains tended to form clusters of the same color, leading to an uneven formation of the pattern. When set in motion this randomized but uneven pattern became highly visible and obtrusive due to the notable changes between individual frames. As in all screen processes, the small filters lowered the speed of the stock considerably and thus necessitated higher illumination and produced darker images.

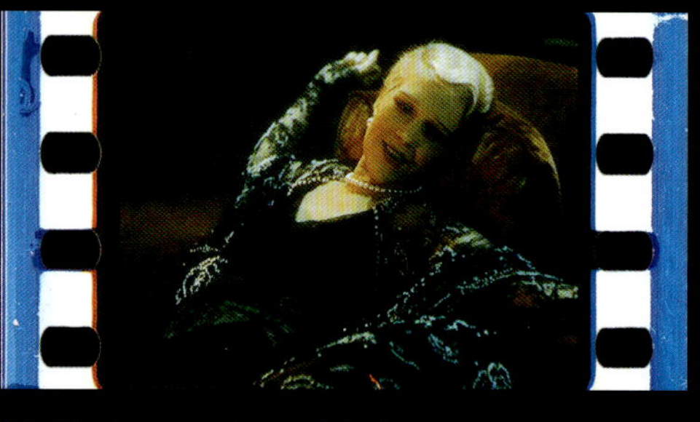

Multicolor sample, undated

MULTICOLOR
1928–32

PRINCIPLE: Subtractive two-color, bipack, duplitized

INVENTOR: Multicolor

"In the Multicolor (two-color) subtractive process, two negative films are run simultaneously through any standard camera with their emulsion surfaces in contact. The front negative is orthochromatic, with the surface layer dyed orange-red to act as a filter for the image recorded on the rear panchromatic film. Double-coated yellow-dyed positive film is used for printing the pair of images in register on opposite sides of the film. The images are colored by a combined dye toning and chemical toning method and are varnished before projection to protect them from scratching."

G. E. Matthews, "Principles and Processes of Photography in Natural Colors," *The American Annals of Photography*, 1930, 222–35; reprinted in *Journal of the Society of Motion Picture Engineers* 16 (1931): 188–219.

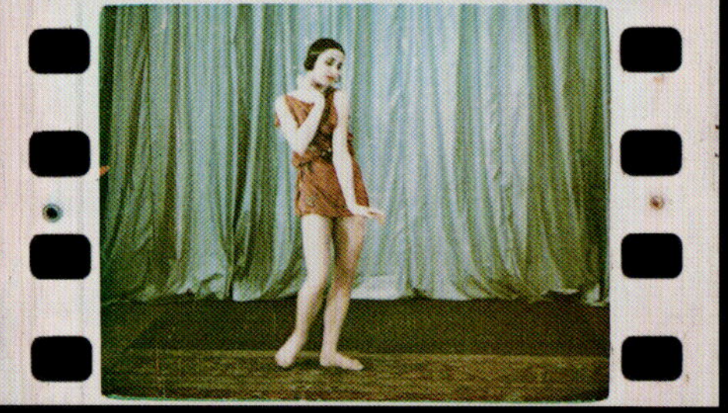

Sirius Farben-Film (Germany, 1929, dirs. Ludwig Horst and Hans Horst)

SIRIUS
1929

PRINCIPLE: Subtractive two-color, beam splitter, double-coated

INVENTOR: Ludwig Horst (Sirius Kleuren Film Maatschappij)

"The Dutch Sirius Color process (1929) used a camera with a beam-splitting system behind the lens to expose a single film, the film passing through two gates at right angles to each other. The double-coated print film was dye-toned. The process was demonstrated in London early in 1930 but was used only for a few shorts and advertising films."

Brian Coe, *The History of Movie Photography* (Westfield, NJ: Eastview, 1981), 129.

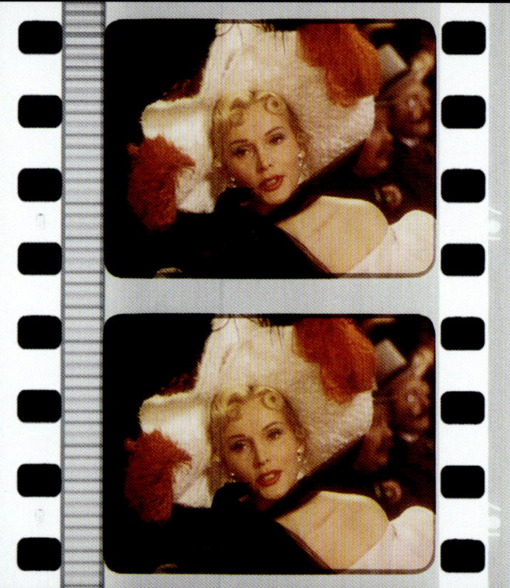

Moulin Rouge (UK, 1952, dir. John Huston)

TECHNICOLOR IV
1932–53

PRINCIPLE: Subtractive three-color, color separation, beam splitter, dye transfer

INVENTOR: Technicolor

Technicolor IV dominated the color film market from the mid-1930s to the 1950s. In a special camera, three black-and-white negative films were exposed through a beam splitter that consisted of two prisms arranged to form a cube. Incoming light passed directly to a frame aperture fitted with a green-transmitting filter to the negative for the green record and was directed by a semitransparent gold- or silver-dusted mirror at a right angle to the bipack film, placed behind a magenta filter. The front film was orthochromatic for the blue record and contained a red-orange dye to block the blue light; the second film was panchromatic (sensitive to the full color spectrum) and captured the red record.

In the early years of the process, before the dye transfer was executed the blank film was exposed with a weak key image in black and white from the green record to improve perceived image sharpness. The blank film also contained the silver image of the black-and-white optical soundtrack and the frameline. For the dye transfer the three records were printed onto the corresponding matrices, one for each color. Similar to Process III, these matrices were developed, bleached, and washed to form reliefs that could absorb the dyes for the imbibition of the projection print. Since this is a subtractive process, the dyes were complementary to the taking colors: magenta for the green record, yellow for the blue record, and cyan for the red separation. These dyes were then transferred onto the blank film containing the key image, one after the other. Pin-registration to align the three records on top of each other was crucial for a sharp image without color fringing.

As a reaction to the problems with Process III, Technicolor took great care in maintaining a high standard of quality control. A cornerstone in this strategy was the Color Advisory Service, directed by Natalie M. Kalmus. The color consultants advised how to develop a color score in accordance with the narrative structure of a film. Set and costume design, props, makeup, and lighting, as well as the camera work, were all overseen by the Technicolor company. The dominant ideology of Technicolor advised a restrained use of colors with an emphasis on "naturalness," strictly subordinate to the story development. Colors should subtly convey dramatic moods and impressions to the audience. Kalmus also suggested the use of conventional color associations, such as red for passion or anger.

Cameramen were specially trained to handle the difficult process, which required many tests before shooting began. Special care had to be given to shadows and highlights, as white image parts tended to produce obtrusive blotches of white while blacks offered unwanted color hues. Also, the emulsion was very slow, requiring high levels of illumination that were adjusted to the color temperature of daylight. Both of these requirements led to the dominant use of carbon-arc lamps.

Later, with the introduction of the chromogenic Eastmancolor negative/positive process, it became possible to shoot with a conventional one-strip camera. For Technicolor V in 1954, three black-and-white color separations were produced from an Eastmancolor negative and printed with Technicolor's dye transfer on blank film.

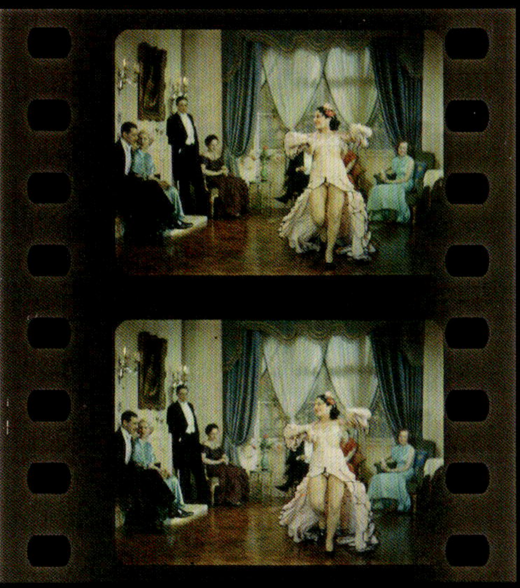

Dufaycolor sample, undated

DUFAYCOLOR
1933–58

PRINCIPLE: Additive three-color, line screen, 35mm and 16mm, reversal and negative-positive stock

INVENTORS: Louis Dufay, Thomas Thorne Baker, and Charles Bonamico (Dufaycolor Ltd., later Dufay-Chromex)

Dufaycolor was a line-screen process whereby incident light was filtered through a pattern of tiny color patches created by diagonal lines in red, green, and blue, the so-called réseau. When viewed from an appropriate distance, the pattern fused in the eye of the observer to form a variety of hues, similar to the dots in pointillism paintings. The Frenchman Louis Dufay invented this pattern for still photography in 1908. Different companies exploited the process and changed the arrangement several times during its evolution, but the principle remained the same.

The application of the réseau onto the film was a very complicated and demanding process. The acetate film base was first coated with a blue layer. This was followed by the application of lines printed in a greasy ink resist so that the intervening lines could be bleached and dyed green. The resist was then removed for a new layer of resist lines applied at a different angle for bleaching and the application of the red dye. As a result of this process a pattern was formed: blue and green rectangles in combination with thinner red lines. (In the different Dufaycolor systems, the order of the colors varied; for instance, Spicer-Dufay stock consisted of red and green rectangles with blue lines.) Finally, a varnish was applied to protect the réseau, and the base was coated with a panchromatic emulsion.

Exposure was done through the réseau on the black-and-white emulsion and the film developed by a black-and-white process, a majority by a reversal process. Although the pattern was very fine, it was still visible on the screen due to the high degree of magnification in projection. More importantly, shooting, development, and screening could be operated with the usual equipment for black-and-white cinematography. Therefore, the process was a viable and cheap alternative to Technicolor. Documentaries, experimental films, and home movies were shot in Dufaycolor.

Since up to 80 percent of light was absorbed by the filters, Dufaycolor required high levels of illumination, both for exposure and projection. To compensate for light absorption, the dyes had flat, overlapping spectral transmission curves that led to the desaturation of the colors. Printing from negatives posed specific problems because interferences occur when two regular patterns are overlaid on top of each other, producing an artifact called moiré. The solution required that the pattern of the negative be destroyed in the printing process, which was done through an aperture mask in combination with diffuse light. Similar problems arise when Dufaycolor film has to be digitized, since the diagonal pattern of the film and the orthogonal pixel structure interfere equally. Therefore scanning requires very high resolution and a light source with three narrow bands for spectral transmission in the primaries, similar to the ones used in the Dufaycolor printing process.

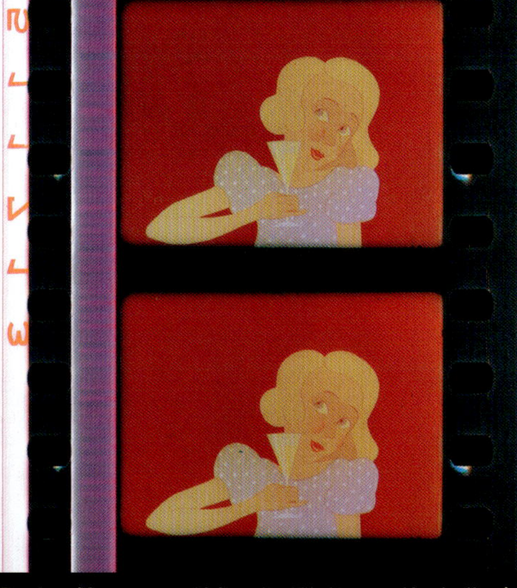

Perlen (Germany, 1936, dir. Wolfgang Kaskeline)

GASPARCOLOR
1933–44

PRINCIPLE: Subtractive three-color, silver dye-bleach, multilayer film

INVENTOR: Béla Gaspar (Gasparcolor Naturwahre Farbenfilm GmbH)

Gasparcolor was the first three-color multilayer monopack film available for practical use. It consisted of a double-coated print film with a cyan layer on one side and two layers, dyed magenta and yellow, on the other side. As a consequence of this arrangement, the process required black-and-white separation records of the red, blue, and green light, produced either by a beam-splitter camera or by successive photographs taken through the corresponding filters. Thus most of the films produced with Gasparcolor were animation films. Gaspar's process was chemically and optically sophisticated and elegant, producing brilliant and very stable colors. Its silver dye-bleach process involved the controlled destruction of dyes in relation to the amount of developed silver present at a specific locus, which makes it a chromolytic process as opposed to the more widespread chromogenic, whereby dyes are added in relation to the silver. Gelatin emulsions were dyed before exposure; after development the dyes were bleached by acid thiourea with the silver serving as a local catalyst. Since the dyes are destroyed in the exposed areas, Gasparcolor is a reversal process.

Although the chromolytic principle was proposed very early, many obstacles had to be resolved for a practical solution. For instance, as Gaspar pointed out, for optical reasons it was not possible to sensitize the layers to the complementary spectrum of the dyes. Therefore Gaspar chose an arbitrary connection between the colored light for exposure and the corresponding dyes; for example, the green separation was exposed by blue filtered light on the magenta dyed layer and the blue separation by the use of red filtered light on the yellow layer.

Due to the rise of the Nazis, Gaspar had to flee Germany before World War II. While he established a plant in London, he could not convince American producers to adopt his process. In the late 1950s, however, the principle was revived by Ciba-Geigy and distributed as Cibachrome (later Ilfochrome) for photographic paper prints. Gasparcolor prints can be identified by the emulsion layers on both sides of the film; the colors of the layers become visible with scratches or cuts. In addition, the soundtrack is printed in color.

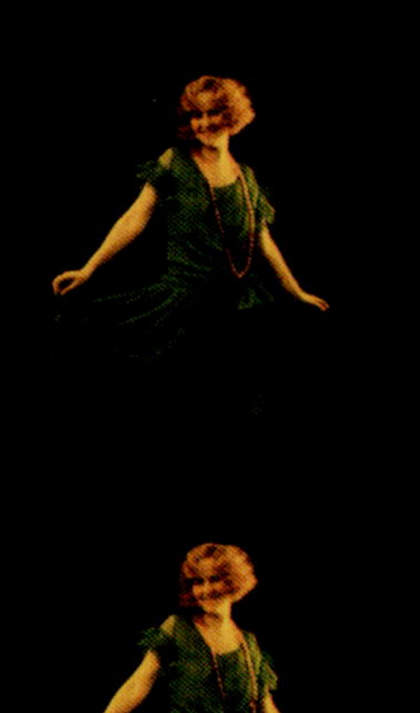

Parisian Modes in Colour (USA, 1926)

KODACHROME
1935

PRINCIPLE: Subtractive three-color, chromogenic monopack, reversal, 8mm to 16mm

INVENTORS: Leopold D. Mannes and Leopold Godowsky (Eastman Kodak)

"In 1930 [Leopold] Mannes and [Leo] Godowsky were invited to join the staff of the Kodak Research Laboratory, where they concentrated on methods of processing multilayer films, while their colleagues worked out ways of manufacturing them. The result was the new Kodachrome film, launched in 1935. Three very thin emulsion layers were coated on a film base, the emulsions being sensitized with non-wandering dyes to red, green and blue light, the red-sensitive layer being at the bottom. To deal with the unwanted blue sensitivity of the red and green layers, a yellow filter layer was provided below the top coating and above the bottom two. A single exposure produced a record of the red, green and blue content of the scene in the three layers....

The new process was released first in the form of 16mm movie film, announced in April 1935. 8mm movie film followed in May 1936, and 35mm and 828 size films for still photography were released in September 1936. Because of the very complex processing involved, the Kodachrome films had to be returned to the manufacturer for processing, and the film was sold with the cost of development included. The new Kodachrome film was sensitive enough to permit exposures of 1/30 second at f/8 in good light. ...the cost of processing compared not unfavorably with the cost of a black and white film together with developing and printing charges. At first the films were returned in an uncut strip, for the customer to mount as slides, or to project in a film strip projector.... The Kodachrome film was the first commercial integral tripack film, and with its great transparency favourably contrasted with the rather dense additive screen plates and films [such as Dufaycolor].

However, the processing cycle was very complex, and the stability of the dyes was not very good. Both problems were resolved with the introduction of an improved process in 1938. The film, of the same construction as before, was first developed to a black and white negative. Then, the film was re-exposed through the back to a red light, which affected only the bottom layer, which was then developed in a cyan dye-forming developer. Then the film was re-exposed from the top to blue light, and the top layer was developed in a yellow dye-forming developer. Finally, a magenta dye-forming developer, containing a chemical fogging agent, was used to develop the middle layer. Now, the film had both negative and positive images in silver in each layer, and positive dye images. It remained only to bleach out the silver images, and the yellow filter layer, and a colour transparency of dye images only was left. The basis of the Kodachrome film process has remained unchanged ever since. The improved process was still complex enough that the processing of the film could only be carried out by the manufacturer, or by a laboratory equipped with the necessary complex machinery. In November 1938 the new process was made available also in sheet film form as Kodachrome Professional film.... Kodachrome Professional film remained on the market until 1951, when it was superseded by Kodak Ektachrome film, introduced in 1946, which could be processed by the professional user."

Brian Coe, *Colour Photography: The First Hundred Years 1840–1940* (London: Ash & Grant, 1978), 128–29.

Kodachrome II, introduced in 1961, was the first film stock since 1936 that was specifically meant for amateur use. Eastman Kodak presented the material as superior to the "regular Kodachrome," with a higher speed of 25 ASA for daylight and 40 ASA for photoflood illumination, heightened sharpness, and improved image quality.

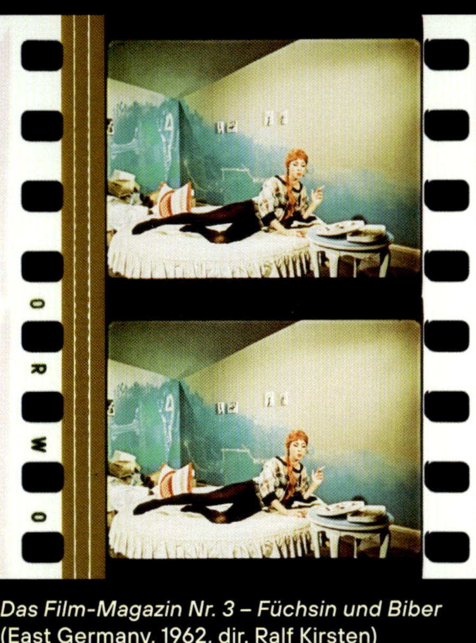

Das Film-Magazin Nr. 3 – Füchsin und Biber (East Germany, 1962, dir. Ralf Kirsten)

AGFACOLOR NEU / AGFACOLOR
1936

PRINCIPLE: Subtractive three-color, chromogenic monopack, reversal (from 1936), negative/positive process (from 1939)

INVENTORS: Wilhelm Schneider and Gustav Wilmanns (IG Farbenindustrie; Agfa; Filmfabrik Wolfen)

"A survey of the history of monopack or multi-layer photographic color processes is given, including the coloring methods of greatest importance at the present time. These are: (a) silver dye-bleaching [or chromolytic] methods and (b) silver dye-coupling [or chromogenic] methods. Silver dye-coupling methods appear to be most promising, and have been successfully applied to monopack films according to two distinct principles. In one method, color-forming compounds are added to the developing solutions. Color separation in this method depends upon control of the speed at which bleaching solutions penetrate superposed emulsion layers.

In the second method, employed in the new Agfacolor process, the different color-forming substances, instead of being added to the developing solution, are incorporated in emulsions that are coated in superposition so that three differently colored images are simultaneously formed in a single development. The metallic silver is subsequently removed by solvents leaving only pure dye images.

This new process is based upon the pioneer work on color-forming methods of R. Fischer who, before the [first] World War, developed the process substantially as it is now being used. The contributions made by Agfa in improving this process are the perfection of dyestuff coupling components better than those available to Fischer, improved methods of preventing diffusion of the color-forming compounds, and methods of precisely controlling the manufacture of multilayer film upon a large scale, so that the present film is the practical expression in commercial form of Fischer's process."

"The New Agfacolor Process," *Journal of the Society of Motion Picture Engineers*, May 1937, 561–62.

After World War II the city of Wolfen, where Agfacolor was produced, became part of East Germany. Agfa operated a second plant in Leverkusen, West Germany, to produce its chromogenic film stock. In 1964 the East German company rebranded their color film stocks as ORWO (an abbreviation of Original Wolfen).

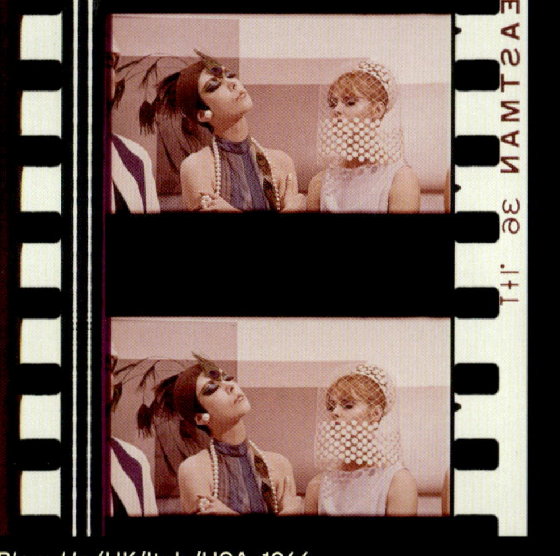

Blow-Up (UK/Italy/USA, 1966, dir. Michelangelo Antonioni)

EASTMANCOLOR
1950

PRINCIPLE: Subtractive three-color, chromogenic monopack

INVENTOR: Eastman Kodak

"The Eastman Colour Films are multilayer films of the type in which the layers are not separated after exposure. Films of this class are known as Multilayer, Monopack or Integral Tripack. 'Multilayer' is descriptive not only of this particular group of films, but also those in which the layers may be separated after exposure, while 'Monopack' is liable to be associated with a particular process which has been quite widely employed by Technicolor. 'Integral Tripack' is therefore adopted as the most convenient term for describing the Eastman Colour Films.

Three types of Eastman Colour Film are manufactured. These are the Colour Negative Film, intended for use as the picture negative material in the camera; the Colour Internegative Film, used for a similar purpose to black-and-white duplicating negative film; and Colour Print Film, which may be employed in preparing prints from either the Colour Negative or Colour Internegative. A special black-and-white Separation Positive Film is also provided and this is intended for use in preparing three separation positives from the Colour Negative. The separation positives form

Integral tripack camera films have the advantage that they may be used in a standard black-and-white camera, and apart from a check on the colour correction and focus of the lens, no special precautions are necessary. It is of interest to note that the colours of integral tripack negatives, as well as the densities, are reversed compared with the original scene.

The coloured images in Eastman Colour Films are produced by a method known as dye-coupling development. For this a special developing agent is used in conjunction with a second compound known as the colour-forming coupler. Photographic development is a process of chemical reduction brought about by the developing agent, which is oxidized in proportion to the amount of silver formed. The oxidized developing agent combines with the colour-forming coupler to create a dye of appropriate colour, the concentration of which is proportional to the amount of silver in the image. The dye thus formed must be insoluble in water so that the reaction shall be quite local and a dye image of high resolution obtained. The silver image is removed at a later stage of

ACKNOWLEDGMENTS

Working on *Color in Motion* has been a wonderful learning experience. In developing and refining our approach to the project, we have been lucky to meet many experts in the field of cinematic color: scholars, filmmakers, collectors, film archivists. They have generously supported the project through their knowledge, research, hands-on experience, and passion and were always ready to share their expertise. A number of them—Barbara Flueckiger, Joshua Yumibe, Kirsten Moana Thompson, and Ranjani Mazumdar—agreed to join the project's advisory board, and we thank them for dedicating many hours to thinking through *Color in Motion* with us, connecting us to other sources, and contributing essays and imagery to this book. Internally, this project would not have succeeded without the hard work, expertise, and support of research assistant Alexandra James Salichs and curatorial assistant Manouchka Kelly Labouba, fellow ringmasters of the rainbow; the many hours spent dreaming and envisioning together were precious. We also extend our gratitude to Academy Gold program intern Frances Wendorf.

A big thank-you goes to the Getty Foundation for including us in their PST ART: *Art & Science Collide* initiative. Through their financial support and, just as importantly, by providing a platform for learning and connecting with other institutions and organizations, they have furthered our awareness and understanding of more sustainable exhibition work, our climate impact, and eco-friendly thinking. The platforms for dialogue and exchange Heather MacDonald and her team have created proved invaluable to our endeavor. A Getty-organized conversation with Jody Deming, professor of oceanography at the University of Washington and one of the leads of the Ocean Memory Project, was especially inspiring. Deming emphasized the intersection of arts and science in her approach, highlighting the role of experimentation and the inevitability of failure as a catalyst for learning and ultimately success. This challenged us as curators to break free from our comfort zones, embrace experimentation, and accept the possibility of failure. As a methodology, it felt resonant with cinema's own history of relentless exploration with color since its inception.

Many clips in the exhibition and images in this book are frames from films that Barbara Flueckiger and her Scan2Screen team (particularly Lutz Garmsen) have scanned specifically for us. We would like to thank the film archives that were willing to open their vaults and pull their most valuable films: Eye Filmmuseum, Amsterdam; Library of Congress, Washington, DC; Bundesarchiv-Filmarchiv, Berlin; and Lichtspiel/Kinemathek, Bern.

Our exhibition does not solely consist of film projections; it features contemporary and historical color technologies, costumes, props, drawings, and interactives, many of which are on view for the very first time. Our gratitude goes to our lenders and colleagues at other film-collecting institutions: Laurent Mannoni, Laure Parchemenko, and La Cinémathèque Française, Paris; Nancy Kauffman, Deborah Stoiber, Sophia Lorent, Beth Rennie, Todd Gustavson, and the George Eastman Museum, Rochester, New York; Cindy Keefer and the Center for Visual Music, Los Angeles; Mary Walsh, Tammy Crosson, and the Inking & Painting department at Walt Disney Animation Studios; Steve Gainer and the American Society of Cinematographers Museum, Los Angeles; Larry McQueen and the Collection of Motion Picture Costume Designs; the Museum of Popular Culture, Seattle; Ryan Lintleman and Shannon Perich at the Smithsonian National Museum of American History, Washington, DC; Eva Hielscher at the Deutsches Filminstitut & Filmmuseum, Frankfurt; Giovanna Fossati at the Eye Filmmuseum, Amsterdam; and Matt Severson, Anne Coco, Warren Sherk, Dawn Jaros, and many other wonderful colleagues at our own Margaret Herrick Library, as well as Joe Lindner at the Academy Film Archive. Studio and production company archives in Los Angeles have also been tremendously helpful in shaping the content in our galleries; many thanks go to Andrea Kalas, Randall Thropp, and Paramount Pictures Archives; Rachel Parham, Natalie Auxier, and NBCUniversal Archives and Collections; Jarrett Hartman and Walt Disney Archives; Jesus Aguirre and Warner Bros. Discovery Archives; Gilbert Emralino and Keith Kutscher at Sony Pictures Entertainment; and Rachel Bernstein and the Amblin Hearth Archive.

Much like filmmaking, realizing an exhibition is a huge team effort that requires the creativity, dedication, and professionalism of many. *Color in Motion* would not have been possible without the support of the Academy Museum's leadership team: Director and President Jacqueline Stewart, Chief Operating Officer and General Counsel Brendan Connell, Jr., and Chief Audience Officer Amy Homma. We also thank our greater museum team for making our dream come true: Executive Vice President of Exhibitions Shraddha Aryal and her team, including Daquian Cao, Phy Cottrell, Kelly Howland, Audra Jacot, Stephen Morrissey, Andrew Mueller, Christopher Richmond, Will Slade, Lindsay Stavros, BJ Thomas, and especially Laura Belevica, who together with Kristy Jennings, Kalani Mah, and Emily Tobias developed an outstanding exhibition design; Vice President of Registration and Collection Management Sonja Wong Leaon and her team, including Lina Candrella, Jillian Griffith, Sophie Hunter, and Rio Lopez; Senior Director of Foundation and Government Relations Dawn Mori, with Sabira Parajuli, and Talha Demir; Vice President of Advancement Matthew Youngner, along with Christine Joyce Rodriguez and Kiara Tinch; Chelsea Bingham, Madeleine Heppermann, and Lars Eckstrom, Publications; Lena Wong and Bria Grant, Museum Legal; Vice President of Touring Exhibitions Susan Jenkins; and Juli Schulz, Impact and Inclusion. Thanks also to Vice President of Curatorial Affairs Doris Berger and the entire curatorial team for their collegial support.

The exhibition catalogue would be inconceivable without the leadership and commitment of Director of Publications Stacey Allan and the team she assembled. Our wonderful editor, Jane Hyun, worked with the authors to hone their texts, and Jessica Fleischmann of Still Room pulled everything together into a truly beautiful book design. Tony Manzella and Echelon did a remarkable job ensuring color accuracy, a vital component of this book, and the support of proofreader Dianne Woo was also invaluable. We thank the members of our advisory board who, along with professor of film Sarah Street, contributed thoughtful essays to the publication. Ivy Donnell, Rebecca Hall, Rebecca Lyon, Laurens Orij, Charles Poynton, Andrew Stockman, Kyle Westphal, and Genevieve Yue generously participated in conversations that also enrich this publication. Scholar Lorna Roth gave us valuable insights into her research on color calibration and race as we shaped the publication's scope.

We hope *Color in Motion* will be an exhibition and catalogue that people can enjoy with all senses, finding it experiential, educational, memorable, and inspiring. There are endless ways to approach and understand color on the big screen, and we hope the stories we have presented both enrich and provoke new revelations about how people perceive it.

Jessica Niebel
Senior Exhibitions Curator

Sophia Serrano
Assistant Curator

ACADEMY MUSEUM OF MOTION PICTURES BOARD OF TRUSTEES

NOTES

THE MATERIALITY AND TECHNOLOGY OF FILM COLORS
Barbara Flueckiger

1. The photos of historical color film prints and negatives were taken with a standardized, custom-tailored camera set up for my project, the Timeline of Historical Film Colors (filmcolors.org), a comprehensive resource for the technology, aesthetics, and restoration of color films. See also the excerpt of the timeline in this publication (pages 246–55).

2. See Thomas Bedding, "Practical Moving-Picture Making. Tinting and Toning," *The Bioscope*, no. 157 (October 1909): 23–25; and the manuals produced by the Eastman Kodak Company (1916, 1918, 1922), Pathé (L. Didiée, *Le film vierge Pathé: Manuel de développement et de tirage* [Paris: Pathé-Cinéma, 1926]), and Agfa (1925).

3. See Léopold Löbel, "Le Coloris," in *La technique cinématographique: Projection, fabrication des films* (Paris: Dunod, 1922), 312–33; Joshua Yumibe, *Moving Color: Early Film, Mass Culture, Modernism* (New Brunswick, NJ: Rutgers University Press, 2012), 78–97; and Céline Ruivo, "Le Livre de fabrication de la compagnie générale des phonographes cinématographes et appareils de précision: À propos d'une source pour l'histoire des recherches sur la couleur chez Pathé Frères entre 1906 et 1908," *1895: Revue d'Histoire du Cinéma*, no. 71 (2013): 47–60.

4. Bregtje Lameris, "Pathécolor: 'Perfect in Their Renditions of the Colours of Nature,'" *Living Pictures: The Journal of the Popular and Projected Image before 1914* 2, no. 2 (2003): 46–58.

5. See, for instance, Nicola Mazzanti, "Colours, Audiences, and (Dis)Continuity in the 'Cinema of the Second Period,'" *Film History* 21, no. 1 (2009): 67–93.

6. Paolo Cherchi Usai, *Silent Cinema: An Introduction* (London: British Film Institute, 2000), 160.

7. See Anke Wilkening, "Die Restaurierung von *Das Cabinet des Dr. Caligari*," *VDR Beiträge zur Erhaltung von Kunst- und Kulturgut* 2 (2014): 27–47; and my "Color Analysis for the Digital Restoration of *Das Cabinet des Dr. Caligari*," *The Moving Image: Journal of the Association of Moving Image Archivists* 15, no. 1 (Spring 2015): 22–43.

8. See Tom Gunning, "Loïe Fuller and the Art of Motion: Body, Light, Electricity, and the Origins of Cinema," in *Camera Obscura, Camera Lucida*, ed. Richard Allen and Malcolm Turvey (Amsterdam: Amsterdam University Press, 2003), 75–90; Lucy Fischer, "Poetry in Motion: Costume, Choreography and the Showgirl Revue in American Cinema in the 1920s–40s," in *Birds of Paradise: Costume as Cinematic Spectacle*, ed. Marketa Uhlirova (London: Koenig Books, 2013), 218–32; Yumibe, *Moving Color*, 39; and Jelena Rakin, *Film Farbe Fläche: Ästhetik des kolorierten Bildes im Kino 1895–1930* (Marburg, Germany: Schüren, 2021).

9. See Eirik Frisvold Hanssen, "Symptoms of Desire: Colour, Costume, and Commodities in Fashion Newsreels of the 1910s and 1920s," *Film History* 21, no. 2 (2009): 107–21; Stella Bruzzi, "Clothes, Power and the Modern Femme Fatale: *The Last Seduction*, *Disclosure*, *Single White Female*," in *Undressing Cinema: Clothing and Identity in the Movies* (London: Routledge, 1997); Olivia Kristina Stutz, "Such (Dye-)Stuff as Dreams Are Made On: Material Interactions between the Photography, Film, and Fashion Industries," in *Color Mania: The Material of Color in Photography and Film*, ed. Barbara Flückiger, Eva Hielscher, and Nadine Wietlisbach (Zurich: Lars Müller; Winterthur, Switzerland: Fotomuseum Winterthur, 2020), 121–31; and Noemi Daugaard, "Colorful Bodies in Motion: Chromatic Corporealities and the Discursive Construction of Color Film Technology, 1895–1940" (PhD diss., University of Zurich, 2023).

10. John Belton, in conversation and private message with the author, November 3, 2023. See also John Belton, "Color: From Novelty to Norm," in *Storia del cinema*, ed. Gian Piero Brunetta (Turin, Italy: Einaudi, 2001); and Belton, "Images as Visual Effects," in *Special Effects on the Screen: Faking the View from Méliès to Motion Capture*, ed. Martin Lefebvre and Marc Furstenau (Amsterdam: Amsterdam University Press, 2022), 89–111.

11. The Lee and Turner process yielded three short test films (UK, 1902), heralded as the first color films some years ago, when the British Film Institute reconstructed their colors digitally from surviving film elements.

12. Sarah Street, *Colour Films in Britain: The Negotiation of Innovation, 1900–55* (London: British Film Institute and Palgrave Macmillan, 2012), 11–14.

13. Gorham Kindem, "The Demise of Kinemacolor: Technological, Legal, Economic, and Aesthetic Problems in Early Color Cinema History," *Cinema Journal* 20, no. 2 (Spring 1981): 8.

14. Kindem, 3.

15. See Noemi Daugaard and Josephine Diecke, "Farbfilmverfahren und Historiografie(n): Ein interdisziplinärer Ansatz," *ffk Journal*, no. 5 (2020): 153–70; Diecke, "Qualitätsfilm aus Wolfen. Die diskursive Konstruktion von Agfacolor und Orwocolor im globalen Spannungsfeld, 1936–1990" (PhD diss., University of Zurich, 2022); and Daugaard, "Colorful Bodies in Motion."

16. Paolo Cherchi Usai, "Le miracle du Chronochrome," *Cinémathèque*, no. 3 (Spring/Summer 1993): 83–91.

17. Laurent Mannoni, "Chronochrome Gaumont," in *Encyclopedia of Early Cinema*, ed. Richard Abel (London: Routledge, 2005), 117.

18. See Daugaard, "Colorful Bodies in Motion," 137–38. This period preceded Hollywood's Production Code, also known as the Hays Code, a set of self-imposed guidelines that took effect in 1934 as a measure to reduce nudity and immoral content in Hollywood films. It was during this pre-code period that Leonard T. Troland, director of research at Technicolor, could explicitly reference female attraction as a promotional vehicle for color films: "Undoubtedly the greatest 'kick' of color, at least for the male members of an audience, consists in the value which it adds to the delineation of feminine beauty. All pretty girls in black and white are pale and consumptive. In the color film they look as we like to see them in every day life or, even better, on the stage. I do not know to what extent it is moral to advocate the cause of colored motion pictures on the ground that color adds to 'sex appeal.'" Leonard T. Troland, "Some Psychological Aspects of Natural Color Motion Pictures," *Transactions of the Society of Motion Picture Engineers* 11, no. 32 (1927): 687–88.

19. For more on the subject, see Richard Dyer, *White: Essays on Race and Culture* (London: Routledge, 1997); Lorna Roth, "The Fade-Out of Shirley, a Once-Ultimate Norm: Colour Balance, Image Technologies, and Cognitive Equity," in *The Melanin Millennium: Skin Color as 21st Century International Discourse*, ed. Ronald E. Hall (Dordrecht: Springer Netherlands, 2013), 273–86; and Daugaard, "Colorful Bodies in Motion," 109.

20. See James Layton and David Pierce, *The Dawn of Technicolor, 1915–1935* (Rochester, NY: George Eastman House, 2015); and John Belton, "'Taking the Color Out of Color': Two-Colour Technicolor, *The Black Pirate*, and Blackened Dyes," in *The Colour Fantastic: Chromatic Worlds of Silent Cinema*, ed. Giovanna Fossati, Victoria Jackson, Bregt Lameris, Elif Rongen-Kaynakçi, and Sarah Street (Amsterdam: Amsterdam University Press, 2018), 97–108.

21. Layton and Pierce, *The Dawn of Technicolor*, 142–45.

22. For Technicolor's guidelines, see Natalie M. Kalmus, "Color Consciousness," *International Projectionist* 8, no. 6 (June 1935): 15–17. See also Christine N. Brinckmann, "Chords of Color," in *Color and Empathy: Essays on Two Aspects of Film* (Amsterdam: Amsterdam University Press, 2015), 34–35.

23. Noemi Daugaard, "Avant-Gardist Colors in a Political Tug-of-War: Gasparcolor between Art and Fascism," in *Color Mania: The Material of Color in Photography and Film*, ed. Barbara Flückiger, Eva Hielscher, and Nadine Wietlisbach (Winterthur, Switzerland: Fotomuseum Winterthur; Zurich: Lars Müller, 2020), 187–95.

24. See Anna Batistová, "Glorious Agfacolor, Breathtaking Totalvision and Monophonic Sound: Colour and 'Scope' in Czechoslovakia," in *Color and the Moving Image: History, Theory, Aesthetics, Archive*, ed. Simon Brown, Sarah Street, and Liz Watkins (New York: Routledge, 2013), 47–55; and Sarah Street, Keith M. Johnston, Paul Frith, and Carolyn Rickards, *Colour Films in Britain; The Eastmancolor Revolution* (London: British Film Institute and Bloomsbury, 2021).

25. See Heather Heckman, "Undervalued Stock: Eastman Color's Innovation and Diffusion, 1900–1957" (PhD diss., University of Wisconsin-Madison, 2014); John Waner, *Hollywood's Conversion of All Production to Color Using Eastman Color Professional Motion Picture Films* (Newcastle, ME: Tobey, 2000); and Joëlle Kost, "Das Spiel von Licht und Farbe: Eine *ästhetische* Analyse des chromogenen Farbfilms von 1955 bis 1995" (PhD diss., University of Zurich, 2023).

26. Josephine Diecke, "'Keeping Your Enemies Closer': Strategies of Knowledge Transfer at the East German Filmfabrik Wolfen," in *Global Color: The Monopack Revolution at Midcentury*, ed. Sarah Street and Joshua Yumibe (New Brunswick, NJ: Rutgers University Press, 2024).

27. Martin Scorsese, letter to the editor, *Film Comment* 16, no. 1 (January–February 1980): 79.

CHOREOGRAPHING COLOR

Jessica Niebel

1. Émile Reynaud was a French inventor who, among others, developed the animation device called the Praxinoscope. His improved version would become the projection apparatus the Théâtre Optique, which he constructed himself. In 1892, Reynaud's hand-painted animated series *Pantomimes lumineuses* was the first exhibition of film projection.

YELLOW AND *TRAFFIC*

1. For more on the "Mexico filter," see Darrell Hope, "The *Traffic* Report with Steven Soderbergh," *DGA Monthly* 25, no. 5 (January 2001), http://www.dga.org/news/v25_5/feat_soderbergh.php3.

2. Howard LaFranchi, "Mexicans Wince at Hollywood's Sepia Portrait," *The Christian Science Monitor*, March 23, 2001, https://www.csmonitor.com/2001/0323/p1s4.html.

3. LaFranchi.

4. Paul Read, "'Unnatural Colours': An Introduction to Colouring Techniques in Silent Era Movies," *Film History* 21, no. 1 (2009): 7–46.

5. Read.

6. Barbara Flueckiger, "Technicolor No. III," Timeline of Historical Film Colors, accessed July 15, 2023, https://filmcolors.org:443/timeline-entry/1300/.

7. Mario T. García, *Memories of Chicano History: The Life and Narrative of Bert Corona*, Latinos in American Society and Culture (Berkeley: University of California Press, 1995), https://doi.org/10.1525/9780520916548.

8. García.

GREEN AND *VERTIGO*

1. Alfred Hitchcock, "Some Thoughts on Color by Alfred Hitchcock," *Advertiser* (Adelaide, Australia), September 4, 1937, 13.

2. Hitchcock.

WOMEN AND COLOR TECHNOLOGIES

Sarah Street

1. John Gage, *Colour and Meaning: Art, Science and Symbolism* (London: Thames and Hudson, 1999), 36. A controversy developed among sixteenth-century Italian art critics on whether a painting's value lay in its design or drawing—which was associated with masculine, rational notions of line—or in its color, associated with superficiality, emotion, and femininity. As David Batchelor notes, generations of philosophers, artists, art historians, and cultural theorists have been prejudiced against color, often associating it with "the feminine, the oriental, the primitive, the infantile, the vulgar, the queer or the pathological." David Batchelor, *Chromophobia* (London: Reaktion Books, 2000), 22–23.

2. Biological females typically have two X chromosomes, whereas men typically have one. The perception of red found on the X chromosome is a standard configuration. The second chromosome, however, receives a slight variation, and the combination that occurs in about 40 percent of women may provide a broader spectrum of color vision in the red-orange range. Color perception is also influenced by other factors, including cultural, linguistic, and societal considerations.

3. Images painted on glass slides were the basis of magic lantern projections that were popular in the mid-19th century and constituted an important pre-cinematic form of visual entertainment. Hand-painting black-and-white photographs was a popular method of colorizing postcards by the end of the 19th century.

4. Joshua Yumibe, *Moving Color: Early Film, Mass Culture, Modernism* (New Brunswick, NJ: Rutgers University Press, 2012), 45.

5. Yumibe, 49.

6. Other producers of hand-colored films at the turn of the century included Robert W. Paul in the UK and the Lubin Company in the USA. The Edison Company became a major producer of silent motion pictures following Thomas Edison's invention of the Projecting Kinetoscope, known as the Vitascope.

7. Stéphanie Salmon and Jacques Malthête, "Élisabeth and Berthe Thuillier," in *Women Film Pioneers Project* ed. Jane Gaines, Radha Vatsal, and Monica Dall'Asta (New York: Columbia University Libraries, 2020), https://doi.org/10.7916/d8-734m-kr16.

8. Paul Read, "'Unnatural Colours': An Introduction to Colouring Techniques in Silent Era Movies," *Film History* 21, no. 1 (2009): 16.

9. Germaine Berger, interview by Jorge Dana, translated by Niki Kolaitis, "Colour by Stencil: Germaine Berger and Pathécolor," *Film History* 21, no. 2 (2009): 182.

10. Trick films included spectacular visual effects such as slow motion, multiple exposure, and illusions of flying or disappearance. Fairy films, derived from the French *féerie* tradition, were typically based on fantasy. They relied less on visual effects and were usually longer and more narrative based.

11. Sarah Street and Joshua Yumibe, *Chromatic Modernity: Color, Cinema, and Media of the 1920s* (New York: Columbia University Press, 2019), 80–85.

12. Delaunay's designs were showcased in Paris at the 1925 Exposition des Arts Décoratifs, and a luxury department store in Amsterdam owned by Metz and Co. sold scarves, fabrics, and accessories that were branded "Sonia."

The Keller-Dorian lenticular process was invented by Rodolphe Berthon in 1908 and supported by industrialist Albert Keller-Dorian. A three-color filter (red, green, and blue) was placed in the camera lens, and "the screen image is formed by microscopic optical elements engraved on the film base." François Ede, "Un épisode de l'histoire de la couleur au cinéma: Le procédé Keller-Dorian et les films lenticulaires," *1895: Revue d'Histoire du Cinéma* 71 (2013): 187–202.

13. Relations between the couple deteriorated in the mid-1940s, when Herbert planned to remarry. Natalie filed a lawsuit in 1948 claiming their divorce was invalid because they had continued to live together, and that she was entitled to a financial settlement. She lost the court case and retired, and for many years her work as a professional was overshadowed by sensationalist newspaper reportage of the case. Sarah Street, "A Suitable Job for a Woman: Color and the Work of Natalie Kalmus," in *Doing Women's Film History: Reframing Cinemas, Past and Future*, ed. Christine Gledhill and Julia Knight (Urbana: University of Illinois Press, 2015), 206–17.

14. Imbibition, also known as dye-transfer printing, was introduced by Technicolor in 1926. It became the company's long-lasting legacy, the technical details of which involved "separate color records imparted onto a blank 1,000-foot strip of gelatin-coated 35mm film. Cyan, yellow, and magenta dyes were added one at a time by pressing a dyed matrix, or relief film, into contact with the blank for a short time." "Dye-Transfer Printing," George Eastman Museum's Technicolor 100 website, accessed September, 20, 2023, https://www.eastman.org/technicolor/technology/dye-transfer-printing.

15. Natalie Kalmus, "Color Consciousness," *Journal of the Society of Motion Picture Engineers* 25, no. 2 (August 1935): 139–47.

16. Natalie Kalmus Papers, Special Collections, Margaret Herrick Library, Academy of Motion Picture Arts and Sciences, Beverly Hills, 1.f-11: Kay Harrison folder, September 24, 1935.

17. Oswald Morris, *Huston, We Have a Problem: A Kaleidoscope of Filmmaking Memories* (Lanham, MD: Scarecrow Press, 2006), 65–75.

18. Morris, for example, commented that she looked like "an explosion in a paint shop." Quoted in Simon Brown, Sarah Street, and Liz Watkins, eds., *British Colour Cinema: Practices and Theories* (London: British Film Institute, 2013), 16.

19. Sarah Street, *Colour Films in Britain: The Negotiation of Innovation, 1900–55* (London: British Film Institute and Palgrave Macmillan, 2012).

20. It seems to be the case that Natalie's expertise was however valued by Kay Harrison, manager of Technicolor Ltd, the British laboratory that opened in 1937, a month before Natalie arrived in London to supervise the use of Technicolor in Harold Schuster's *Wings of the Morning* (UK, 1937), the first British three-strip Technicolor feature film. Harrison arranged for Natalie to be greeted by a brass band wearing red coats after crossing the Atlantic on the *Queen Mary*. Harrison chose the color of the coats deliberately, noting with irony in a cable to Natalie that they were a fitting welcome for an ambassador from Technicolor. Natalie Kalmus Papers, 1.f-11, cable from Kay Harrison to Natalie Kalmus, February 27, 1937.

21. J. H. Hughes, merchandise manager for A. Harris and Company of Dallas, Texas, for example, asked Natalie how Technicolor might be tied in with the colors of his upcoming spring collections. Since use of the word Technicolor was banned for sponsorship outside the corporation, Natalie allowed her name to be used for this purpose, as if she was following in Margaret Hayden Rorke's footsteps. Natalie Kalmus Papers, 2.f-37, House of Westmoreland folder, 1943–44.

22. Ida Zeitlin, "Great Women of Motion Pictures: Natalie Kalmus," *Screenland* 38, no. 4 (February 1939): 75.

23. Street and Yumibe, *Chromatic Modernity*, 120–22.

24. Andrew Robert Johnston, "The Color of Prometheus: Thomas Wilfred's Lumia and the Projection of Transcendence," in *Color and the Moving Image: History, Theory, Aesthetics, Archive*, ed. Simon Brown, Sarah Street, and Liz Watkins (New York: Routledge, 2013), 67–78.

25. As in the films of Walter Ruttmann, Oskar Fischinger, and other exponents of Absolute Film. See Street and Yumibe, *Chromatic Modernity*, 115–28.

26. Kristian Moen, "Expressive Motion in the Early Films of Mary Ellen Bute," *Animation: An Interdisciplinary Journal* 14, no. 2 (2019): 104.

27. Kristian Moen, *New York's Animation Culture: Advertising, Art, Design, and Film, 1939–1940* (Cham, Switzerland: Palgrave Macmillan/Springer Nature, 2019), 152.

28. A retrospective of her work was held at the Museum of Modern Art, New York, just before she died in 1983. William Moritz, "Mary Ellen Bute: Seeing Sound," *Animation World Network* 1, no. 2 (May 1996), accessed September 20, 2023, https://www.awn.com/mag/issue1.2/articles1.2/moritz1.2.html. Her work has increasingly been presented since 2000 at museums and venues including Museum of Fine Arts, Houston; Harvard Film Archive; Gallery of Modern Art, Brisbane; and others in Germany, Italy, and the United Kingdom.
29. William Moritz, "The Absolute Film," presented at WRO 99 Media Art Biennale, Wroclaw, Poland, April 1999, and posted on the Center for Visual Music's online library, http://www.centerforvisualmusic.org/library/WMAbsoluteFilm.htm.
30. Len Lye was a New Zealand artist who moved to London in the 1920s, where he made short, experimental animated films as products of the GPO and Crown Film Units. He is widely regarded as one of the most influential artists working in the medium at the time. See Scott Anthony and James G. Mansell, *The Projection of Britain: A History of the GPO Film Unit* (London: British Film Institute, 2011). Tait was particularly influenced by Lye's film *A Colour Box* (UK, 1935).
31. Sarah Neely, *Between Categories: The Films of Margaret Tait; Portraits, Poetry, Sound and Place* (Oxford, UK: Peter Lang, 2017).

CHROMATIC BLACKNESS

Joshua Yumibe

1. For an extended discussion, see Joshua Yumibe, "On Vivid Colors and Afrotropes in African and Diasporic Cinemas," in *Global Film Color: The Monopack Revolution at Midcentury*, ed. Sarah Street and Joshua Yumibe (New Brunswick, NJ: Rutgers University Press, 2024). Also see Diana Pozo, "Water Color: Radical Color Aesthetics in Julie Dash's *Daughters of the Dust*," *New Review of Film and Television Studies* 11, no. 4 (December 1, 2013): 424–37.
2. Quoted in Karen Alexander, "*Daughters of the Dust*," *Sight and Sound* 3, no. 9 (1993): 20–23.
3. Andrea Davis Kronlund, "Julie Dash on 'Daughters of the Dust' and Speculative Fiction, Part 3," *Krull Magazine*, March 8, 2017, https://krullmag.com/blog/julie-dash-on-daughters-of-the-dust-and-speculative-fiction-part-3/.
4. Tim Lanza, quoted in Mekado Murphy, "'Daughters of the Dust,' a Seeming Inspiration for 'Lemonade,' Is Restored," *The New York Times*, April 27, 2016, https://www.nytimes.com/2016/04/28/movies/daughters-of-the-dust-restoration-beyonce-lemonade.html.
5. John Akomfrah, "Digitopia and the Spectres of Diaspora," *Journal of Media Practice* 11, no. 1 (January 1, 2010): 23. Relatedly, see Kara Keeling's speculative work on technology and race, *Queer Times, Black Futures* (New York: New York University Press, 2019), especially 117–44.
6. See Larry Clark, oral history interview by Jacqueline Stewart and Jan-Christopher Horak, June 2, 2010, L.A. Rebellion Collection, UCLA Film and Television Archive, transcript, 16–18.
7. Clark, oral history interview. Also see Dash's comments on film stock in Julie Dash, oral history interview by Allyson Field, Jacqueline Stewart, and Jan-Christopher Horak, June 8, 2010, L.A. Rebellion Collection, UCLA Film and Television Archive, transcript, 25–27.
8. See Brian Winston, *Technologies of Seeing: Photography, Cinematography and Television* (London: British Film Institute, 1996); Richard Dyer, *White* (London: Routledge, 1997); James A. Snead, *White Screens, Black Images: Hollywood from the Dark Side* (New York: Routledge, 1994); and Lorna Roth, "The Fade-Out of Shirley, a Once-Ultimate Norm: Colour Balance, Image Technologies, and Cognitive Equity," in *The Melanin Millennium: Skin Color as 21st Century International Discourse*, ed. Ronald E. Hall (Dordrecht, The Netherlands: Springer, 2013), 273–86.
9. Kirsty Sinclair Dootson, "The Politics of Colour," *Frames Cinema Journal*, no. 17 (Summer 2020), https://doi.org/10.15664/fcj.v0i17.2073. Also see her expansive study of color and race, *The Rainbow's Gravity: Colour, Materiality and British Modernity* (London: Paul Mellon Centre for Studies of British Art, 2023).
10. See Vinzenz Brinkmann and Renée Dreyfus, eds., *Gods in Color: Polychromy in the Ancient World* (San Francisco: Fine Arts Museums of San Francisco; Munich: DelMonico Books/Prestel, 2017).
11. For discussions of the colonial aesthetics of color, see Michael Taussig, *What Color Is the Sacred?* (Chicago: University of Chicago Press, 2009); and Natasha Eaton, *Colour, Art and Empire: Visual Culture and the Nomadism of Representation* (London: I. B. Tauris, 2013).
12. Calvin Tomkins, "The Epic Style of Kerry James Marshall," *The New Yorker*, August 2, 2021, https://www.newyorker.com/magazine/2021/08/09/the-epic-style-of-kerry-james-marshall.
13. Akomfrah, "Digitopia," 27.
14. Rosalind Galt, "The Spirits of African Cinema: Redemptive Aesthetics in Mati Diop's *Atlantics*," *Movie: A Journal of Film Criticism*, no. 10 (2022): 104.
15. As Dee Rees notes, these effects were created in-camera by Bradford Young, who removed the lens to flash the film magazine, producing optical whiteouts that were superimposed over the final shot. See the discussion on the making of *Pariah* featuring Rees, Young, Inbal Weinberg, Nekisa Cooper, and Mako Kamitsuna, moderated by Jacqueline Stewart, on the Blu-ray edition of *Pariah* by the Criterion Collection, 2021, approx. 30:27.
16. Young, in discussion moderated by Stewart, approx. 27:00.
17. Chris O'Falt, "'Moonlight' Glow: Creating the Bold Color and Contrast of Barry Jenkins' Emotional Landscape," *IndieWire*, October 26, 2016, https://www.indiewire.com/awards/industry/moonlight-cinematography-color-barry-jenkins-james-laxton-alex-bickel-1201740402/.
18. Michael Boyce Gillespie, "One Step Ahead: A Conversation with Barry Jenkins," *Film Quarterly* 70, no. 3 (2017): 57. On the nature of shine within Black aesthetics, also see Krista A. Thompson, *Shine: The Visual Economy of Light in African Diasporic Aesthetic Practice* (Durham, NC: Duke University Press, 2015).
19. "Cannes Prize Winners Get the Look with FilmLight Grading and Finishing," *Digital Media World*, July 10, 2019, https://digitalmediaworld.tv/post/2460-cannes-prize-winners-get-the-look-with-filmlight-grading-and-finishing.
20. Galt, "The Spirits of African Cinema," 100.

BLUE AND *MOONLIGHT*

1. As director Barry Jenkins explained, "Tarell calls Miami a 'beautiful nightmare' and I think what we've done is paint this nightmare in beautiful tones." Chris O'Falt, "'Moonlight' Glow: Creating the Bold Color and Contrast of Barry Jenkins' Emotional Landscape," *IndieWire*, October 26, 2016, https://www.indiewire.com/awards/industry/moonlight-cinematography-color-barry-jenkins-james-laxton-alex-bickel-1201740402/.
2. O'Falt.

PURPLE AND *CABARET*

1. Christopher Isherwood, "Cabaret [Screenplay] Notes," March 29–April 30, 1969, Christopher Isherwood Papers, Huntington Library, Art Museum, and Botanical Gardens, San Marino, CA. All unattributed quotes are from these treatment notes.
2. Ian Johnstone and Jenny Rees, "Bowles Players," *Radio Times*, April 18, 1974.

THE EASTMANCOLOR EFFECT

Ranjani Mazumdar

1. Jawaharlal Nehru, India's first prime minister, initiated large-scale industrialization soon after the country's independence from colonial rule in 1947. The increased importation of industrial technologies required the use of foreign currency, which resulted in the plummeting of foreign exchange reserves and a major economic downturn beginning in 1957.
2. For discussions on the concept of intermediality, see Bernd Herzogenrath, introduction to *Travels in Intermedia[lity]: Reblurring the Boundaries*, ed.Bernd Herzogenrath (Hanover, NH: Dartmouth College Press, 2012); Sudhir Mahadevan, *A Very Old Machine: The Many Origins of the Cinema in India, 1840–1930* (Albany: State University of New York Press, 2015); and Vebhuti Duggal, "Intermediality," *BioScope: South Asian Screen Studies* 12, nos. 1–2 (2021): 113–16. While the antecedents of cinema and its theorization as a hybrid form is testament to its multimedia origins, the rise of newer technologies has instituted shifts that have made the discussion of intermediality important. The accelerated multiplication of the media and its intersections have shown how intermediality can be thought of as a conceptual, historical, and aesthetic drive that leaves its trace on the body of film. Intermediality also allows us to reflect on the past from the vantage point of the contemporary and vice versa.
3. For a longer discussion on the use of photographs in *Mera Saaya*, see Ranjani Mazumdar, "Photographic Events in Hindi Cinema," in *Points of View: Defining Moments of Photography in India*, ed. Gayatri Sinha (New Delhi: Kiran Nadar Museum of Art, 2022), 248–65.
4. John David Rhodes, *Spectacle of Property: The House in American Film* (Minneapolis: University of Minnesota Press, 2017).
5. Steven Jacobs, "Color and Containment: Domestic Spaces and Restrained Palettes in Hitchcock's First Color Films," in *Color and the Moving Image: History, Theory, Aesthetics, Archive*, ed. Simon Brown, Sarah Street, and Liz Watkins (New York: Routledge, 2013), 179–95.
6. Giuliana Bruno, "Surface Tension, Screen Space," in *Screen Space Reconfigured*, ed. Susanne Ø. Sæther and Synne T. Bull (Amsterdam: Amsterdam University Press, 2020), 35–54.

7. Shoma A. Chatterji, "Desh Mukherjee," *Upperstall: A Better View of Cinema* (blog), March 11, 2016, https://upperstall.com/profile/desh-mukherjee/.
8. Stephen Monteiro, "Performing Color: Mechanized Painting, Multimedia Spectacle, and Andy Warhol's 'Chelsea Girls,'" *Grey Room*, no. 49 (Fall 2012): 32–55.
9. For a detailed account of the cinematic devices deployed to enhance and negotiate suspense in the films of Alfred Hitchcock, see Richard Allen, "Hitchcock and Narrative Suspense: Theory and Practice," in *Camera Obscura, Camera Lucida: Essays in Honor of Annette Michelson*, ed. Richard Allen and Malcolm Turvey (Amsterdam: Amsterdam University Press, 2003), 163–82.
10. Patricia Zimmerman, "Morphing History into Histories: From Amateur Film to the Archive of the Future," *The Moving Image: The Journal of the Association of Moving Image Archivists* 1, no. 1 (2001): 108–30.

AMERICAN ANIMATION IN COLOR
Kirsten Moana Thompson

1. "Wonderland—In Color by Technicolor," *Technicolor News and Views* 13, no. 2 (June 1951): 1.
2. Parts of this essay are excerpted and revised from two of my essays: "Colourful Material Histories: The Disney Paint Formulae, the Paint Laboratory and the Ink and Paint Department," *Animation Practice, Process and Production* 4, no. 1 (2014): 45–66; and "'Quick—Like a Bunny!' The Ink and Paint Machine, Female Labor, and Color Production," *Animation Studies* 9 (February 2014), https://journal.animation studies.org/kirsten-thompson-quick-like-a-bunny/.
3. Cited in Donald Crafton, "The Veiled Genealogies of Animation and Cinema," *Animation: An Interdisciplinary Journal* 6, no. 2 (July 2011): 97–98.
4. David Batchelor, *Chromophobia* (London: Reaktion Books, 2000), 23.
5. Batchelor, *Chromophobia*, 28. See also Jacqueline Lichtenstein, *The Eloquence of Color: Rhetoric and Painting in the French Classical Age*, trans. Emily McVarish (Berkeley: University of California Press, 1993), 194.
6. Scott Higgins, in *Harnessing the Technicolor Rainbow* (Austin: University of Texas Press, 2007), has described this as the demonstration mode of color design, although he focuses on the live-action films *La Cucaracha* (USA, 1934) and *Becky Sharp* (USA, 1935), 19, 22–75.
7. Color fringing happens when colors smear between shots, especially with moving elements in the shot, which was a particular problem with Kinemacolor. For example, see the film short *Banks of the Nile* (*Rive del Nilo*, UK, 1911), available at https://filmcolors.org/galleries/kinemacolor-illustrations/#/image/2462.
8. These problems included the cupping and buckling of the thick filmstrip, where the red matrix (with cyan dye), which was cemented to the green-blue matrix (with magenta dye), tended to deteriorate and separate over time as it was exposed to the heat of the projector's lamp. This problem was eliminated in Technicolor III when the cementing of matrices was replaced by optically generated matrices on one film print. See James Layton and David Pierce, *The Dawn of Technicolor, 1915–1935* (Rochester, NY: George Eastman House, 2015); and Martin B. Hart, "Technicolor: System 2, Subtractive Two-Color Cemented Print, 1922–1927," American Widescreen Museum, https://www.widescreenmuseum.com/oldcolor/technicolor2.htm, accessed October 15, 2023.
9. The two-color Brewstercolor was used in the first American animated cartoon in color, J. R. Bray's *Thomas the Cat* (1920). See Jere Guldin, "Photographing Animated Motion Pictures in Early Color Film Processes," *Animatrix* 7, no. 7 (1993): 20–30. For more on these processes, see entries for "Brewster" on Barbara Flueckiger's Timeline of Historical Film Colors, https://filmcolors.org/timeline-entry/1359/; and "Cinecolor," The American Widescreen Museum, https://www.widescreenmuseum.com/oldcolor/cinecolor2.htm. See also the entries on "Multicolor" and "Autochrome film/Cinécolor" on the Timeline of Historical Film Colors, https://filmcolors.org/timeline-entry/1241/ and https://filmcolors.org/timeline-entry/1400/, all accessed October 17, 2023. For more general information on color film, see Martin B. Hart, "Additive and Subtractive Color Systems Explained," The American Widescreen Museum, https://www.widescreenmuseum.com/oldcolor/additive-subtractive.htm, accessed January 2, 2019.
10. Technicolor charged Disney $170 to rent its special cameras, which were modified for single frame exposure (suitable for photographing animation cels), as well as for other equipment and a special consultant. Prints cost 5–6 cents per foot of film. See Layton and Pierce, *The Dawn of Technicolor*, 248–49, 277.
11. Early experiments included J. R. Bray's *Thomas the Cat* in Brewstercolor and the animated Technicolor III insert in *King of Jazz* (1930) by Walter Lantz Studios. The animation industry could film animation cels with a Technicolor camera modified for single frame photography through a successive exposure method, which shot through filters of red, green, and blue onto a single roll of black-and-white film; Layton and Pierce, *The Dawn of Technicolor*, 277.
12. *Goofy Goat* was announced as the first of a series of twelve "all-color sound cartoons," which included *The Snowman*, and was produced "under a secret color mixing process which [Eshbaugh] developed." "Producing Cartoon Series in Color," *The Film Daily* 58, no. 56 (March 8, 1932): 1.
13. The short is not to be confused with Victor Fleming's 1939 live-action feature. Steve Stanchfield gives the 1931 contract date in "An Archivist's Dream: Eshbaugh's Technicolor 'The Wizard of Oz' (1933)," *Cartoon Research* (blog), September 5, 2019, https://cartoonresearch.com/index.php/an-archivists-dream-eshbaughs-technicolor-the-wizard-of-oz1933/. However, according to Layton and Pierce, Eshbaugh signed a contract in 1933 for *The Wizard of Oz*, which may have been a retroactive one like that of Disney's. See Layton and Pierce, *The Dawn of Technicolor*, 485n30. For more on Eshbaugh, see John McElwee, "A Cartoon Master We've Forgotten," October 21, 2014, *Greenbriar Picture Shows* (blog), http://greenbriarpictureshows.blogspot.com/2014/10/a-cartoon-master-weve-forgotten.html, accessed October 14, 2023, and Steve Stanchfield, "A Little Revisit to Ted Eshbaugh's Work," *Cartoon Research* (blog), July 6, 2023, https://cartoonresearch.com/index.php/a-little-revisit-to-ted-eshbaughs-work/. The restored *Wizard of Oz* short is available on the Thunderbean DVD *Technicolor Dreams and Black and White Nightmares* (2014).
14. Disney remembered, "The Technicolor company itself was behind [me] . . . because they were not quite far enough along with the color process to go into heavy production with any big live-action theatrical feature. A cartoon was ideal for their experimentation." Michael Barrier, *The Animated Man: A Life of Walt Disney* (Berkeley: University of California Press, 2007), 89.
15. Barrier, *The Animated Man*, 89, gives this release date, although Layton and Pierce give July 15 as the premiere date, possibly basing it off the date it was shipped, as cited by Russell Merritt and J. B. Kaufman, *Walt Disney's Silly Symphonies: A Companion to the Classic Cartoon Series* (Glendale, CA: Walt Disney Editions, 2016), 112. *Flowers and Trees* appeared with the MGM feature film *Strange Interlude* (USA, 1932).
16. Disney had made *Flowers and Trees* without a contract with Technicolor, but the August 1932 contract retroactively accorded him the Technicolor IV rights for the already completed film, according to Michael Barrier, *Hollywood Cartoons: American Animation in Its Golden Age* (New York: Oxford University Press, 1999), 585n63. David R. Smith, Disney archivist, letter to Barrier, October 3, 1979.
17. L. Frank Baum's son Frank J. Baum enjoined both Technicolor and Ted Eshbaugh from releasing the film, claiming Eshbaugh had failed to finish *The Wizard of Oz* in a timely manner and was therefore reclaiming distribution rights to the film. This lawsuit joined a previous lawsuit filed by investor J. R. Booth against Technicolor for refusing to release the negative of the film. See Jay Scarfone and William Stillman, *The Road to Oz: The Evolution, Creation and Legacy of a Motion Picture Masterpiece* (Guilford, CT: Lyons Press, 2018), 50; see also *Variety*, March 27 and June 26, 1934.
18. Ub Iwerks's ComiColor series remained in two-color Cinécolor, and his company closed in 1936. He later worked for Leon Schlesinger Productions at Warner Bros., then on the Color Rhapsody series at Columbia before returning to work at Disney in 1940; Barrier, *Hollywood Cartoons*, 167.
19. Robert Herring, "The Cartoon Color-Film," *Close Up* 10, no. 1 (March 1933): 86.
20. In the "Pink Elephants" sequence, we see a green elephant with red vertical stripes march toward a yellow elephant with purple horizontal stripes, and as they cross, they form a two-headed, plaid-patterned elephant, as a chorus sings: "I could stand the sight of worms / And look at microscopic germs / But technicolor pachyderms / Is really too much for me."
21. After cleaned-up pencil drawings were received from animators, inkers precisely traced the outlines of these drawings. Painters would then flip the cels and color in the inked outlines, following numbered specifications from a model sheet created by the color key artist, who determined colors for characters and props. On *Snow White*, 158 cel inkers and painters are credited. See the press release for the Disney feature, 1938, Canemaker Collection, Fales Library, New York University. For more on the Inking & Painting department, see my "Colourful Material Histories"; Maureen Furniss, "Color and Line," in *Art in Motion: Animation Aesthetics*, rev. ed. (London: John Libbey, 2007), 71–74; and the studio-approved text by Mindy Johnson, *Ink and Paint: The Women of Walt Disney's Animation* (Los Angeles: Disney Editions, 2017).

22. For more on the portable mills Disney used in its Inking & Painting department to grind the pigment, see my "Colourful Material Histories," 48–51.
23. Susan Ashley, interview by Sylvia Roemer for oral history of twenty-two inkers and painters, 1995, 2, Women in Animation oral history transcripts (Collection 222), UCLA Library Special Collections, Charles E. Young Research Library, UCLA.
24. *Pastrytown Wedding* was animated by Ted Eshbaugh and Burt Gillett. Eshbaugh would make three cartoons for Van Beuren under the Rainbow Parade series.
25. In the early nineteenth century, colors such as blue from indigo plants and scarlet from cochineal insects were harvested to produce color in labor-intensive processes, while chocolate was processed from cacao. Many of these food and dye products came from British, French, Spanish, and Portuguese imperial plantations in Asia, Africa, and the Pacific until they were replaced by synthetic colors derived from aniline coal-tar following the accidental discovery of mauve in 1856 by William Perkin. For more on the material history of color, see John Gage, *Color and Culture: Practice and Meaning from Antiquity to Abstraction* (Berkeley: University of California Press, 1993); and Philip Ball, *Bright Earth: Art and the Invention of Color* (Chicago: University of Chicago Press, 2001).
26. On the long history of racial representation in animation, see Nicholas Sammond, *Birth of an Industry: Blackface Minstrelsy and the Rise of American Animation* (Durham, NC: Duke University Press, 2015). For more on the relationship of color as pigment and color as race, see Carolyn L. Kane and Lida Zeitlin Wu, eds., *Color Protocols: Technologies of Racial Encoding in Chromatic Media* (Cambridge, MA: MIT Press, forthcoming).

ABSTRACTING COLOR

Sophia Serrano

1. Other notable experimenters include Jordan Belson, Bruno Corra and Arnaldo Ginna, Charles Dockum, Hy Hirsh, Norman McLaren, Walter Ruttmann, and Harry Smith.
2. David E. James, in *The Most Typical Avant-Garde: History and Geography of Minor Cinemas in Los Angeles* (Berkeley: University of California Press, 2005), closely examines how the works of experimental filmmakers, particularly those in Los Angeles, were in continuous dialogue and collaboration, not just opposition, with Hollywood cinema.
3. Alexander Wallace Rimington, Charles Dockum, Alexander László, Bainbridge Bishop, William Schooling, James M. Loring, and Charles F. Wilcox also created devices of interest.
4. Mary Elizabeth Hallock Greenewalt Papers, Collection 867, Historical Society of Pennsylvania, Philadelphia, https://hsp.org/sites/default/files/legacy_files/migrated/findingaid0867greenewalt.pdf. She would finally receive a verdict in her favor in 1932, though ultimately was not compensated for the infringements.
5. Carol Snow and Lynda Zycherman, "Conserving Thomas Wilfred's Lumia Suite, Opus 158," in *Keep It Moving? Conserving Kinetic Art*, ed. Rachel Rivenc and Reinhard Bek (Los Angeles: Getty Conservation Institute, 2018).
6. See William Moritz, *Optical Poetry: The Life and Work of Oskar Fischinger* (Bloomington: Indiana University Press, 2004); ed. Cindy Keefer and Jaap Guldemond, *Oskar Fischinger, 1900–1967: Experiments in Cinematic Abstraction* (Los Angeles: Center for Visual Music; and Amsterdam: Eye Filmmuseum, 2012); and "Oskar Fischinger Biography," Center for Visual Music (website), 2021, http://www.centerforvisualmusic.org/Fischinger/OFBio.htm.
7. Gasparcolor's process of either requiring a beam splitter or taking successive images through each color filter made it especially appealing for use in stop-motion animation. However, it was ultimately unable to compete with the increasingly popular Technicolor, which offered a camera system while Gasparcolor did not. See William Moritz, "Gasparcolor: Perfect Hues for Animation," translation of a lecture given at the Musée du Louvre, Paris, October 6, 1995, http://www.centerforvisualmusic.org/Fischinger/Moritz_GasparColor.htm.
8. Keefer and Guldemond, *Oskar Fischinger*; and Moritz, *Optical Poetry*.
9. Moritz, *Optical Poetry*, 84.
10. For in-depth discussions of the Lumigraph, see Keefer and Guldemond, *Oskar Fischinger*, 193–200; and Moritz, *Optical Poetry*, 137.
11. Harry Smith was a notable artist and filmmaker who experimented with painting on filmstrips and using paper cutouts to make patterns for stop motion. He credited Fischinger as the inspiration for his animations.
12. During this time Lye was based in London. Béla Gaspar of Gasparcolor had also relocated to London to evade the Nazi party in Germany.
13. Mary Ellen Bute, "Abstronics: An Experimental Filmmaker Photographs the Esthetics of the Oscillograph," *Films in Review* 5, no. 6 (June–July 1954); and "Mary Ellen Bute: Abstronics," description of a screening at Light Industry, Brooklyn, New York, November 5, 2013, https://www.lightindustry.org/bute.
14. Bute, "Abstronics."
15. Kit Smyth Basquin, *Mary Ellen Bute: Pioneer Animator* (Bloomington: Indiana University Press, 2020), 163.
16. Basquin, 3, 38.
17. Basquin, 40. It is interesting to note that reviews of *Becky Sharp* commented that the movie "is not the coloration of natural life, but a vividly pigmented dream world of the artistic imagination"; though a narrative feature, color was received as otherworldly and surreal.
18. Cindy Keefer, "Jordan Belson: Biography," in *The Third Mind: American Artists Contemplate Asia, 1860–1989*, ed. Alexandra Monroe (New York: Solomon R. Guggenheim Museum, 2009). Also available online at http://www.centerforvisualmusic.org/BelsonbioCK.htm.
19. Gene Youngblood, *Expanded Cinema* (New York: E. P. Dutton, 1970), 167.
20. William Moritz, "Digital Harmony: The Life of John Whitney, Computer Animation Pioneer," *Animation World Magazine* 2, no. 5 (August 1997).
21. Lillian Schwartz's *Pixillation* (1970) was created through both coding and hand-drawn techniques, starting with black-and-white patterns on the computer layered with hand-colored animations to create a saturated and bright palette. (Schwartz, "Films" page on the artist's website, http://lillian.com/films/.) From the 1970s to 1990s, Schwartz continued to develop coding for computer animation and created software for analyzing art conservation treatments.
22. Moritz, "Digital Harmony."
23. Douglas Trumbull, "*2001: A Space Odyssey*: Douglas Trumbull on Stanley Kubrick's Search for 'Ultimate Perfection,'" *The Hollywood Reporter*, May 25, 2018, https://www.hollywoodreporter.com/movies/movie-news/2001-a-space-odyssey-special-effects-pioneer-douglas-trumbull-remembers-stanley-kubrick-1114803/.
24. Trumbull.
25. Giuliana Bruno, "The Screen as Object: Art and the Atmospheres of Project," in *Dreamlands: Immersive Cinema and Art, 1905–2016*, ed. Chrissie Iles (New York: Whitney Museum of American Art, 2016), 179. *Raumlichtkunst* is an intricate experiment with three-screen projection that Fischinger devised in the 1920s using tinting and toning as well as projected light through colored filters. First performed in 1926, it is one of the earliest examples of immersive installation work with projections. It was restored from the original nitrates and reconstructed by the Center for Visual Music in 2012. For more on *Raumlichtkunst*, see Keefer and Guldemond, *Oskar Fischinger*, 216, and http://www.centerforvisualmusic.org/Raumlichtkunst.html.
26. Youngblood, *Expanded Cinema*, 151.
27. James, *The Most Typical Avant-Garde*, 238.
28. Roger Ebert, review of "Tron," *Chicago Sun-Times*, January 1, 1982.

BIBLIOGRAPHY

Agfa. *Agfa Kine-Handbuch*. Berlin: Aktien-Gesellschaft für Anilin-Fabrikation, 1925.

Akomfrah, John. "Digitopia and the Spectres of Diaspora." *Journal of Media Practice* 11, no. 1 (January 1, 2010).

Alexander, Karen. "*Daughters of the Dust*." *Sight and Sound* 3, no. 9 (1993): 20–23.

Allen, Richard. "Hitchcock and Narrative Suspense: Theory and Practice." In *Camera Obscura, Camera Lucida*, edited by Malcolm Turvey and Richard Allen, 163–82. Amsterdam: Amsterdam University Press, 2003. https://www.jstor.org/stable/j.ctt46n2cn.13.

Anthony, Scott, and James G. Mansell. *The Projection of Britain: A History of the GPO Film Unit*. London: British Film Institute, 2011.

Ball, Philip. *Bright Earth: Art and the Invention of Color*. Chicago: University of Chicago Press, 2001.

Barrier, Michael. *The Animated Man: A Life of Walt Disney*. Berkeley: University of California Press, 2007. https://doi.org/10.1525/j.ctt1ppcjs.

——. *Hollywood Cartoons: American Animation in Its Golden Age*. New York: Oxford University Press, 1999.

Basquin, Kit Smyth. *Mary Ellen Bute: Pioneer Animator*. Bloomington: Indiana University Press, 2020.

Batchelor, David. *Chromophobia*. London: Reaktion Books, 2000.

Batistová, Anna. "Glorious Agfacolor, Breathtaking Totalvision and Monophonic Sound: Colour and 'Scope' in Czechoslovakia." In *Color and the Moving Image: History, Theory, Aesthetics, Archive*, edited by Simon Brown, Sarah Street, and Liz Watkins, 47–55. New York: Routledge, 2013.

Bedding, Thomas. "Practical Moving-Picture Making. Tinting and Toning." *The Bioscope*, no. 157 (October 1909): 23–25.

Belton, John. "Color: From Novelty to Norm." Volume 4 of *Storia del cinema*, edited by Gian Piero Brunetta. Turin, Italy: Einaudi, 2001.

——. "Images as Visual Effects." In *Special Effects on the Screen: Faking the View from Méliès to Motion Capture*, edited by Martin Lefebvre and Marc Furstenau, 89–111. Amsterdam: Amsterdam University Press, 2022.

——. "'Taking the Color Out of Color': Two-Colour Technicolor, *The Black Pirate*, and Blackened Dyes." In *The Colour Fantastic: Chromatic Worlds of Silent Cinema*, edited by Giovanna Fossati, Victoria Jackson, Bregt Lameris, Elif Rongen-Kaynakçi, and Sarah Street, 97–108. Amsterdam: Amsterdam University Press, 2018.

Brinckmann, Christine N. "Chords of Color." In *Color and Empathy: Essays on Two Aspects of Film*. Amsterdam: Amsterdam University Press, 2015.

Brinkmann, Vinzenz, and Renée Dreyfus, eds. *Gods in Color: Polychromy in the Ancient World*. San Francisco: Fine Arts Museums of San Francisco; Munich: DelMonico Books/Prestel, 2017.

Brown, Simon, Sarah Street, and Liz Watkins, eds. *British Colour Cinema: Practices and Theories*. London: British Film Institute, 2013.

——. *Color and the Moving Image: History, Theory, Aesthetics, Archive*. New York: Routledge, 2013.

Bruno, Giuliana. "The Screen as Object: Art and the Atmospheres of Project." In *Dreamlands: Immersive Cinema and Art, 1905–2016*, edited by Chrissie Iles, New York: Whitney Museum of American Art, 2016.

——. "Surface Tension, Screen Space." In *Screen Space Reconfigured*, edited by Susanne Ø. Saether and Synne T. Bull, 35–54. Amsterdam: Amsterdam University Press, 2020. https://doi.org/10.1515/9789048529056-003.

Bruzzi, Stella. "Clothes, Power and the Modern Femme Fatale: *The Last Seduction, Disclosure, Single White Female*." In *Undressing Cinema: Clothing and Identity in the Movies*. London: Routledge, 1997.

Bute, Mary Ellen. "Abstronics: An Experimental Filmmaker Photographs the Esthetics of the Oscillograph." *Films in Review* 5, no. 6 (June–July 1954).

"Cannes Prize Winners Get the Look with FilmLight Grading and Finishing," *Digital Media World*, July 10, 2019. https://digitalmediaworld.tv/post/2460-cannes-prize-winners-get-the-look-with-filmlight-grading-and-finishing.

Center for Visual Music. "Oskar Fischinger Biography." Center for Visual Music (website), 2021. http://www.centerforvisualmusic.org/Fischinger/OFBio.htm.

Chatterji, Shoma. "Desh Mukherjee." *Upperstall: A Better View of Cinema* (blog), March 11, 2016. https://upperstall.com/profile/desh-mukherjee/.

Cherchi Usai, Paolo. "Le miracle du Chronochrome." *Cinémathèque*, no. 3 (Spring/Summer 1993): 83–91.

——. *Silent Cinema: A Guide to Study, Research and Curatorship*. 3rd ed. London: British Film Institute, 2019.

——. *Silent Cinema: An Introduction*. London: British Film Institute, 2000.

Clark, Larry. L.A. Rebellion: Larry Clark Oral History Interview. Interview by Jan-Christopher Horak and Jacqueline Stewart, June 2, 2010. L.A. Rebellion Collection, UCLA Film and Television Archive.

Coe, Brian. *Colour Photography: The First Hundred Years 1840–1940*. London: Ash & Grant, 1978.

——. *The History of Movie Photography*. Westfield, NJ: Eastview, 1981.

Crafton, Donald. "The Veiled Genealogies of Animation and Cinema." *Animation: An Interdisciplinary Journal* 6, no. 2 (July 2011).

Craig, G. J. "Eastman Colour Films for Professional Motion Picture Work." *British Kinematography* 22, no. 5 (1953): 146–58.

Dana, Jorge. "Colour by Stencil: Germaine Berger and Pathécolor." Translated by Niki Kolaitis. *Film History* 21, no. 2 (2009): 180–83. https://doi.org/10.2979/FIL.2009.21.2.180.

Dash, Julie. L.A. Rebellion: Julie Dash Oral History Interview. Interview by Allyson Field, Jan-Christopher Horak, and Jacqueline Stewart, June 8, 2010. L.A. Rebellion Collection, UCLA Film and Television Archive.

Daugaard, Noemi. "Avant-Gardist Colors in a Political Tug-of-War: Gasparcolor between Art and Fascism." In *Color Mania: The Material of Color in Photography and Film*, edited by Barbara Flückiger, Eva Hielscher, and Nadine Wietlisbach, 187–95. Winterthur, Switzerland: Fotomuseum Winterthur; Zurich: Lars Müller, 2020.

——. "Colorful Bodies in Motion: Chromatic Corporealities and the Discursive Construction of Color Film Technology, 1895–1940." PhD diss., University of Zurich, 2023.

Daugaard, Noemi and Josephine Diecke. "Farbfilmverfahren und Historiografie(n): Ein interdisziplinärer Ansatz." *ffk Journal*, no. 5 (2020): 153–70.

Didiée, L. *Le film vierge Pathé: Manuel de développement et de tirage*. Paris: Pathé-Cinéma, 1926.

Diecke, Josephine. "'Keeping Your Enemies Closer': Strategies of Knowledge Transfer at the East German Filmfabrik Wolfen." In *Global Color: The Monopack Revolution at Midcentury*, edited by Sarah Street and Joshua Yumibe. New Brunswick, NJ: Rutgers University Press, 2024.

——. "Qualitätsfilm aus Wolfen. Die diskursive Konstruktion von Agfacolor und Orwocolor im globalen Spannungsfeld, 1936–1990." PhD diss., University of Zurich, 2022.

Disney, Walt. "Growing Pains." *Journal of the Society of Motion Picture Engineers* 36, no. 1 (January 1941).

Dootson, Kirsty Sinclair. "The Politics of Colour." *Frames Cinema Journal*, no. 17 (2020). https://doi.org/10.15664/fcj.v0i17.2073.

——. *The Rainbow's Gravity: Colour, Materiality, and British Modernity*. London: Paul Mellon Centre for Studies in British Art, 2023.

Duggal, Vebhuti. "Intermediality." *BioScope: South Asian Screen Studies* 12, nos. 1–2 (2021): 113–16. https://doi.org/10.1177/09749276211026085.

Dyer, Richard. *White: Essays on Race and Culture*. London: Routledge, 1997.

Eastman Kodak Company. *Tinting and Toning of Eastman Positive Motion Picture Film*. Rochester, NY: Eastman Kodak, 1916.

——. *Tinting and Toning of Eastman Positive Motion Picture Film*. Rochester, NY: Eastman Kodak, 1918.

——. *Tinting and Toning of Eastman Positive Motion Picture Film*. Rochester, NY: Eastman Kodak, 1922.

Eaton, Natasha. *Colour, Art and Empire: Visual Culture and the Nomadism of Representation*. International Library of Visual Culture 12. London: I. B. Tauris, 2013.

Ebert, Roger. Review of "Tron." *Chicago Sun-Times*, January 1, 1982.

Ede, François. "Un épisode de l'histoire de la couleur au cinéma: Le procédé Keller-Dorian et les films lenticulaires." *1895: Revue d'Histoire du Cinéma* 71 (2013): 187–202.

Fischer, Lucy. "Poetry in Motion: Costume, Choreography and the Showgirl Revue in American Cinema in the 1920s–40s." In *Birds of Paradise: Costume as Cinematic Spectacle*, edited by Marketa Uhlirova, 218–32. London: Koenig Books, 2013.

Flueckiger, Barbara. "Color Analysis for the Digital Restoration of *Das Cabinet des Dr. Caligari*." *The Moving Image: Journal of the Association of Moving Image Archivists* 15, no. 1 (Spring 2015): 22–43.

——. Timeline of Historical Film Colors (online research database project), 2012–present. filmcolors.org.

Furniss, Maureen. *Art in Motion: Animation Aesthetics*. Rev. ed. London: John Libbey, 2007.

Gage, John. *Color and Culture: Practice and Meaning from Antiquity to Abstraction*. Berkeley: University of California Press, 1993.

——. *Colour and Meaning: Art, Science and Symbolism*. London: Thames and Hudson, 1999.

Galt, Rosalind. "The Spirits of African Cinema: Redemptive Aesthetics in Mati Diop's *Atlantics*." *Movie: A Journal of Film Criticism*, no. 10 (2022): 97–106.

García, Mario T. *Memories of Chicano History: The Life and Narrative of Bert Corona*. Latinos in American Society and Culture 2. Berkeley: University of California Press, 1995. https://doi.org/10.1525/9780520916548.

George Eastman Museum. Technicolor 100 (website). https://www.eastman.org/technicolor.

Gillespie, Michael Boyce. "One Step Ahead: A Conversation with Barry Jenkins." *Film Quarterly* 70, no. 3 (2017): 52–62. https://doi.org/10.1525/FQ.2017.70.3.52.

Guldin, Jere. "Photographing Animated Motion Pictures in Early Color Film Processes." *Animatrix* 7, no. 7 (1993): 20–30.

Gunning, Tom. "Loïe Fuller and the Art of Motion: Body, Light, Electricity, and the Origins of Cinema." In *Camera Obscura, Camera Lucida*, edited by Richard Allen and Malcolm Turvey, 75–90. Amsterdam: Amsterdam University Press, 2003.

Hallock Greenewalt, Mary Elizabeth. Papers. Collection 867, The Historical Society of Pennsylvania, Philadelphia. https://hsp.org/sites/default/files/legacy_files/migrated/findingaid0867greenewalt.pdf.

Hanssen, Eirik Frisvold. "Symptoms of Desire: Colour, Costume, and Commodities in Fashion Newsreels of the 1910s and 1920s." *Film History* 21, no. 2 (2009): 107–21.

Harrison, Kay. Cable to Natalie Kalmus, February 27, 1937. Natalie Kalmus Papers, Special Collections, Margaret Herrick Library, Academy of Motion Picture Arts and Sciences, Los Angeles.

Hart, Martin B. The American Widescreen Museum (website). https://www.widescreenmuseum.com.

Heckman, Heather. "Undervalued Stock: Eastman Color's Innovation and Diffusion, 1900–1957." PhD diss., University of Wisconsin-Madison, 2014.

Herring, Robert. "The Cartoon Color-Film." *Close Up* 10, no. 1 (March 1933).

Herzogenrath, Bernd. Introduction to *Travels in Intermedia[lity]: ReBlurring the Boundaries*, edited by Bernd Herzogenrath. Hanover, NH: Dartmouth College Press, 2012.

Higgins, Scott. *Harnessing the Technicolor Rainbow*. Austin: University of Texas Press, 2007.

Hitchcock, Alfred. "Some Thoughts on Color by Alfred Hitchcock." *Advertiser* (Adelaide, Australia), September 4, 1937, 13.

Hope, Darrell. "The *Traffic* Report with Steven Soderbergh." *DGA Monthly* 25, no. 5 (January 2001). https://www.dga.org/news/v25_5/feat_soderbergh.php3.

Isherwood, Christopher. "Cabaret [Screenplay] Notes," March 29–April 30, 1969. Christopher Isherwood Papers, Huntington Library, Art Museum, and Botanical Gardens, San Marino, CA.

Jacobs, Steven. "Color and Containment: Domestic Spaces and Restrained Palettes in Hitchcock's First Color Films." In *Color and the Moving Image: History, Theory, Aesthetics, Archive*, edited by Simon Brown, Sarah Street, and Liz Watkins. New York: Routledge, 2013.

James, David E. *The Most Typical Avant-Garde: History and Geography of Minor Cinemas in Los Angeles*. Berkeley: University of California Press, 2005.

Johnson, Mindy. *Ink and Paint: The Women of Walt Disney's Animation*. Los Angeles: Disney Editions, 2017.

Johnston, Andrew Robert. "The Color of Prometheus: Thomas Wilfred's Lumia and the Projection of Transcendence." In *Color and the Moving Image: History, Theory, Aesthetics, Archive*, edited by Simon Brown, Sarah Street, and Liz Watkins, 67–78. New York: Routledge, 2013.

Johnstone, Ian, and Jenny Rees. "Bowles Players." *Radio Times*, April 18, 1874.

Kalmus, Natalie. "Color Consciousness." *International Projectionist* 8, no. 6 (June 1935): 15–17.

——. "Color Consciousness." *Journal of the Society of Motion Picture Engineers* 25, no. 2 (August 1935): 139–47. https://doi.org/10.5594/J05386.

——. Papers, Special Collections, Margaret Herrick Library, Academy of Motion Picture Arts and Sciences, Los Angeles.

Kane, Carolyn L., and Lida Zeitlin Wu, eds. *Color Protocols: Technologies of Racial Encoding in Chromatic Media*. Cambridge, MA: MIT Press, forthcoming.

Keefer, Cindy. "Jordan Belson: Biography." In *The Third Mind: American Artists Contemplate Asia, 1860–1989*, edited by Alexandra Munroe. New York: Solomon R. Guggenheim Museum, 2009.

Keefer, Cindy, and Jaap Guldemond, eds. *Oskar Fischinger, 1900–1967: Experiments in Cinematic Abstraction*. Los Angeles: Center for Visual Music; Amsterdam: Eye Filmmuseum, 2012.

Keeling, Kara. *Queer Times, Black Futures*. Sexual Cultures. New York: New York University Press, 2019.

Kindem, Gorham. "The Demise of Kinemacolor. Technological, Legal, Economic, and Aesthetic Problems in Early Color Cinema History." *Cinema Journal* 20, no. 2 (Spring 1981): 3–14.

Kost, Joëlle. "Das Spiel von Licht und Farbe: Eine ästhetische Analyse des chromogenen Farbfilms von 1955 bis 1995." PhD diss., University of Zurich, 2023.

Kronlund, Andrea Davis. "Julie Dash on 'Daughters of the Dust' and Speculative Fiction, Part 3." *Krull Magazine*, March 8, 2017. https://krullmag.com/blog/julie-dash-on-daughters-of-the-dust-and-speculative-fiction-part-3/.

LaFranchi, Howard. "Mexicans Wince at Hollywood's Sepia Portrait." *The Christian Science Monitor*, March 23, 2001. https://www.csmonitor.com/2001/0323/p1s4.html.

Lameris, Bregtje. "Pathécolor: 'Perfect in Their Renditions of the Colours of Nature.'" *Living Pictures: The Journal of the Popular and Projected Image before 1914* 2, no. 2 (2003): 46–58.

Layton, James, and David Pierce. *The Dawn of Technicolor, 1915–1935*. Rochester, NY: George Eastman House, 2015.

Lichtenstein, Jacqueline. *The Eloquence of Color: Rhetoric and Painting in the French Classical Age*. Translated by Emily McVarish. Berkeley: University of California Press, 1993.

Löbel, Léopold. "Le Coloris." In *La technique cinématographique: Projection, fabrication des films*, 312–33. Paris: Dunod, 1922.

Mahadevan, Sudhir. *A Very Old Machine: The Many Origins of the Cinema in India, 1840–1930*. Albany: State University of New York Press, 2015.

Mannoni, Laurent. "Chronochrome Gaumont." In *Encyclopedia of Early Cinema*, edited by Richard Abel. London: Routledge, 2005.

"Mary Ellen Bute: Abstronics." Description of a screening at Light Industry, Brooklyn, New York, November 5, 2013. https://www.lightindustry.org/bute.

Matthews, G. E. "Principles and Processes of Photography in Natural Colors." *The American Annals of Photography*, 1930, 222–35. Reprinted in *Journal of the Society of Motion Picture Engineers* 16 (1931): 188–219.

Mazumdar, Ranjani. "Photographic Events in Hindi Cinema." In *Points of View: Defining Moments of Photography in India*, edited by Gayatri Sinha, 248–65. New Delhi: Kiran Nadar Museum of Art, 2022.

Mazzanti, Nicola. "Colours, Audiences, and (Dis) Continuity in the 'Cinema of the Second Period.'" *Film History* 21, no. 1 (2009): 67–93.

McElwee, John. "A Cartoon Master We've Forgotten." *Greenbriar Picture Shows* (blog), October 21, 2014. https://greenbriarpictureshows.blogspot.com/2014/10/a-cartoon-master-weve-forgotten.html.

Merritt, Russell, and J. B. Kaufman, eds. *Walt Disney's Silly Symphonies: A Companion to the Classic Cartoon Series*. Glendale, CA: Walt Disney Editions, 2016.

Moen, Kristian. "Expressive Motion in the Early Films of Mary Ellen Bute." *Animation: An Interdisciplinary Journal* 14, no. 2 (2019): 102–16. https://doi.org/10.1177/1746847719859194.

——. *New York's Animation Culture: Advertising, Art, Design, and Film, 1939–1940*. Palgrave Animation. Cham, Switzerland: Palgrave Macmillan/Springer Nature, 2019. https://doi.org/10.1007/978-3-030-27931-8.

Monteiro, Stephen. "Performing Color: Mechanized Painting, Multimedia Spectacle, and Andy Warhol's 'Chelsea Girls.'" *Grey Room*, no. 49 (Fall 2012): 32–55. https://doi.org/10.1162/GREY_a_00087.

Moritz, William. "The Absolute Film." Presented at WRO 99 Media Art Biennale, Wroclaw, Poland, April 1999, and posted on the Center for Visual Music's online library, http://www.centerforvisualmusic.org/library/WMAbsoluteFilm.htm.

——. "Digital Harmony: The Life of John Whitney, Computer Animation Pioneer." *Animation World Magazine* 2, no. 5 (August 1997).

——. "Gasparcolor: Perfect Hues for Animation." Translation of a lecture given at the Musée du Louvre, Paris, October 6, 1995. http://www.centerforvisualmusic.org/Fischinger/Moritz_GasparColor.htm.

——. "Mary Ellen Bute: Seeing Sound." *Animation World Network* 1, no. 2 (May 1996). https://www.awn.com/mag/issue1.2/articles1.2/moritz1.2.html.

——. *Optical Poetry: The Life and Work of Oskar Fischinger*. Bloomington: Indiana University Press, 2004.

Morris, Oswald. *Huston, We Have a Problem: A Kaleidoscope of Filmmaking Memories*. Filmmakers Series 124. Lanham, MD: Scarecrow Press, 2006.

Murphy, Mekado. "'Daughters of the Dust,' a Seeming Inspiration for 'Lemonade,' Is Restored." *The New York Times*, April 27, 2016. https://www.nytimes.com/2016/04/28/movies/daughters-of-the-dust-restoration-beyonce-lemonade.html.

Neely, Sarah. *Between Categories: The Films of Margaret Tait; Portraits, Poetry, Sound and Place.* Studies in the History and Culture of Scotland 7. Oxford, UK: Peter Lang, 2017.

"The New Agfacolor Process." *Journal of the Society of Motion Picture Engineers*, May 1937, 561–62.

Nowotny, Robert A. *The Way of All Flesh Tones: A History of Color Motion Picture Processes, 1895–1929.* New York: Garland, 1983.

O'Falt, Chris. "'Moonlight' Glow: Creating the Bold Color and Contrast of Barry Jenkins' Emotional Landscape." *IndieWire*, October 26, 2016. https://www.indiewire.com/awards/industry/moonlight-cinematography-color-barry-jenkins-james-laxton-alex-bickel-1201740402/.

Pozo, Diana. "Water Color: Radical Color Aesthetics in Julie Dash's *Daughters of the Dust.*" *New Review of Film and Television Studies* 11, no. 4 (December 1, 2013): 424–37. https://doi.org/10.1080/17400309.2013.812707.

"Producing Cartoon Series in Color." *The Film Daily* 58, no. 56 (March 8, 1932).

Rakin, Jelena. *Film Farbe Fläche: Ästhetik des kolorierten Bildes im Kino 1895–1930.* Marburg, Germany: Schüren, 2021.

Read, Paul. "'Unnatural Colours': An Introduction to Colouring Techniques in Silent Era Movies." *Film History* 21, no. 1 (2009): 7–46.

Rees, Dee, Bradford Young, Inbal Weinberg, Nekisa Cooper, and Mako Kamitsuna. "Making of *Pariah.*" Interview by Jacqueline Stewart. *Pariah*, Blu-ray disc. New York: Criterion Collection, 2021.

Rhodes, John David. *Spectacle of Property: The House in American Film.* Minneapolis: University of Minnesota Press, 2017. https://doi.org/10.5749/j.ctt1pwt7cf.

Roemer, Sylvia. Transcript of interviews for oral history of twenty-two inkers and painters, 1995. Women in Animation Oral History Transcripts (Collection 222), UCLA Library Special Collections, Charles E. Young Research Library, UCLA.

Roth, Lorna. "The Fade-Out of Shirley, a Once-Ultimate Norm: Colour Balance, Image Technologies, and Cognitive Equity." In *The Melanin Millennium: Skin Color as 21st Century International Discourse*, edited by Ronald E. Hall, 273–86. Dordrecht, The Netherlands: Springer Netherlands, 2013. https://doi.org/10.1007/978-94-007-4608-4_18.

Ruivo, Céline. "Le Livre de fabrication de la compagnie générale des phonographes cinématographes et appareils de précision: À propos d'une source pour l'histoire des recherches sur la couleur chez Pathé Frères entre 1906 et 1908." *1895: Revue d'Histoire du Cinéma*, no. 71 (2013): 47–60.

Ryan, Roderick T. *A History of Motion Picture Color Technology.* London: Focal Press, 1977.

Salmon, Stéphanie, and Jacques Malthête. "Élisabeth and Berthe Thuillier." In *Women Film Pioneers Project*, edited by Jane Gaines, Radha Vatsal, and Monica Dall'Asta. New York: Columbia University Libraries, 2020. https://doi.org/10.7916/d8-734m-kr16.

Sammond, Nicholas. *Birth of an Industry: Blackface Minstrelsy and the Rise of American Animation.* Durham, NC: Duke University Press, 2015.

Scarfone, Jay, and William Stillman. *The Road to Oz: The Evolution, Creation and Legacy of a Motion Picture Masterpiece.* Guilford, CT: Lyons Press, 2018.

Schwartz, Lillian F. "Films." Page on artist's website. http://lillian.com/films/.

Scorsese, Martin. Letter to the editor. *Film Comment* 16, no. 1 (January–February 1980): 79.

Sennwald, Andre. "The Screen: The Radio City Music Hall Presents 'Becky Sharp.'" *The New York Times*, June 14, 1935.

Snead, James A. *White Screens, Black Images: Hollywood from the Dark Side.* New York: Routledge, 1994. https://doi.org/10.4324/9780203700631.

Snow, Carol, and Lynda Zycherman. "Conserving Thomas Wilfred's Lumia Suite, Opus 158." In *Keep It Moving?: Conserving Kinetic Art*, edited by Rachel Rivenc and Reinhard Bek. Los Angeles: Getty Conservation Institute, 2018.

"Snow White Disney Press Release," 1938. Canemaker Collection, Fales Library, New York University.

Sparke, Penny. *The Modern Interior.* London: Reaktion Books, 2008.

Stanchfield, Steve. "An Archivist's Dream: Eshbaugh's Technicolor 'The Wizard of Oz' (1933)." *Cartoon Research* (blog), September 5, 2019. https://cartoonresearch.com/index.php/an-archivists-dream-eshbaughs-technicolor-the-wizard-of-oz1933/.

———. "A Little Revisit to Ted Eshbaugh's Work." *Cartoon Research* (blog), July 6, 2023. https://cartoonresearch.com/index.php/an-archivists-dream-eshbaughs-technicolor-the-wizard-of-oz1933/.

Street, Sarah. *Colour Films in Britain: The Negotiation of Innovation, 1900–55.* London: British Film Institute and Palgrave Macmillan, 2012.

———. "A Suitable Job for a Woman: Color and the Work of Natalie Kalmus." In *Doing Women's Film History: Reframing Cinemas, Past and Future*, edited by Christine Gledhill and Julia Knight. Urbana: University of Illinois Press, 2015.

Street, Sarah, and Joshua Yumibe. *Chromatic Modernity: Color, Cinema, and Media of the 1920s.* Film and Culture. New York: Columbia University Press, 2019. https://doi.org/10.7312/stre17982.

Street, Sarah, Keith M. Johnston, Paul Frith, and Carolyn Rickards. *Colour Films in Britain: The Eastmancolor Revolution.* London: British Film Institute and Bloomsbury, 2021.

Stutz, Olivia Kristina. "Such (Dye-)Stuff as Dreams Are Made On: Material Interactions between the Photography, Film, and Fashion Industries." In *Color Mania: The Material of Color in Photography and Film*, edited by Barbara Flückiger, Eva Hielscher, and Nadine Wietlisbach, 121–31. Zurich: Lars Müller; Winterthur, Switzerland: Fotomuseum Winterthur, 2020.

Taussig, Michael. *What Color Is the Sacred?* Chicago: University of Chicago Press, 2009.

Thompson, Kirsten Moana. "Colourful Material Histories: The Disney Paint Formulae, the Paint Laboratory and the Ink and Paint Department." *Animation Practice, Process and Production* 4, no. 1 (2014): 45–66. https://doi.org/10.1386/ap3.4.1.45_1.

———. "'Quick—Like a Bunny!' The Ink and Paint Machine, Female Labor, and Color Production." *Animation Studies* 9 (February 2014). https://journal.animationstudies.org/kirsten-thompson-quick-like-a-bunny/.

Thompson, Krista A. *Shine: The Visual Economy of Light in African Diasporic Aesthetic Practice.* Durham, NC: Duke University Press, 2015. https://doi.org/10.1515/9780822375982.

Tomkins, Calvin. "The Epic Style of Kerry James Marshall." *The New Yorker*, August 2, 2021. https://www.newyorker.com/magazine/2021/08/09/the-epic-style-of-kerry-james-marshall.

Troland, Leonard T. "Some Psychological Aspects of Natural Color Motion Pictures." *Transactions of the Society of Motion Picture Engineers* 11, no. 32 (1927): 680–98.

Trumbull, Douglas. "*2001: A Space Odyssey*: Douglas Trumbull on Stanley Kubrick's Search for 'Ultimate Perfection.'" *The Hollywood Reporter*, May 25, 2018. https://www.hollywoodreporter.com/movies/movie-news/2001-a-space-odyssey-special-effects-pioneer-douglas-trumbull-remembers-stanley-kubrick-1114803/.

Waner, John. *Hollywood's Conversion of All Production to Color Using Eastman Color Professional Motion Picture Films.* Newcastle, ME: Tobey, 2000.

"Westmore (House Of)." Natalie Kalmus Papers, Margaret Herrick Library, Academy of Motion Picture Arts and Sciences, Los Angeles.

Wilkening, Anke. "Die Restaurierung von *Das Cabinet des Dr. Caligari.*" *VDR Beiträge zur Erhaltung von Kunst- und Kulturgut* 2 (2014): 27–47.

Winston, Brian. *Technologies of Seeing: Photography, Cinematography and Television.* London: British Film Institute, 1996.

"Wonderland—In Color by Technicolor." *Technicolor News and Views* 13, no. 2 (June 1951). http://archive.org/details/technewsviews1951-06.

Youngblood, Gene. *Expanded Cinema.* New York: E. P. Dutton, 1970.

Yumibe, Joshua. *Moving Color: Early Film, Mass Culture, Modernism.* Techniques of the Moving Image. New Brunswick, NJ: Rutgers University Press, 2012.

———. "On Vivid Colors and Afrotropes in African and Diasporic Cinemas." In *Global Color: The Monopack Revolution at Midcentury*, edited by Sarah Street and Joshua Yumibe. New Brunswick, NJ: Rutgers University Press, 2024.

Zeitlin, Ida. "Great Women of Motion Pictures: Natalie Kalmus." *Screenland* 38, no. 4 (February 1939).

Zimmermann, Patricia. "Morphing History into Histories: From Amateur Film to the Archive of the Future." *The Moving Image: The Journal of the Association of Moving Image Archivists*, no. 1 (2001): 108–30.

CONTRIBUTORS

BARBARA FLUECKIGER was a professor of film studies at the University of Zurich from 2007 to 2023. Before her academic career in film theory and history, which focused on the relationship between technology and aesthetics, she worked internationally as a film professional. Since 2012 she has developed and curated the online research database that she founded, the Timeline of Historical Film Colors, and has received several awards from leading societies for her contributions to the technology of the audiovisual archiving field. In 2023 she founded her company Scan2Screen US for the promotion and application of a multispectral film scanning process developed with her interdisciplinary team.

ALEXANDRA JAMES SALICHS is a research assistant at the Academy Museum of Motion Pictures and a PhD candidate in cinema and media studies at the University of California, Los Angeles. Her work explores Latinx and Latin American representation through aesthetic, social, and institutional histories with a particular focus on Puerto Rico. James Salichs holds a master's degree in cinema and media studies from Columbia University, where she worked with the Women Film Pioneers Project, Tribeca Film Festival, and Hamptons International Film Festival. Her work has been published in *Critical Studies in Television*, and she has received numerous awards and fellowships.

RANJANI MAZUMDAR is professor of cinema studies at the School of Arts and Aesthetics, Jawaharlal Nehru University, New Delhi. She is author of *Bombay Cinema: An Archive of the City* (2007), editor of two special issues of *BioScope*: *South Asian Screen Studies on Cinema and Techno-materiality* (2013), and author of a dossier on *Pathaan* (2023). She is also co-editor of *A Companion to Indian Cinema* (2022). Her current research focuses on globalization and film culture, intermedial encounters, and the intersection of technology, travel, design, and color in 1960s Bombay cinema.

JESSICA NIEBEL is senior exhibitions curator at the Academy Museum of Motion Pictures, for which she organized *Shifting Perspectives: Vertical Cinema* (2023), *Director's Inspiration: Agnès Varda* (2022, co-curated with Ana Santiago), and the inaugural exhibitions *Hayao Miyazaki* and *The Path to Cinema: Highlights from the Richard Balzer Collection* (both 2021). She previously organized internationally touring exhibitions including *Anime! High Art–Pop Culture* (2008); *Jim Rakete: The State of Things* (2011); *And the Oscar Goes to… 85 Years of the Best Picture Academy Award* (2012); and *Theaters: Cinema Photography by Yves Marchand and Romain Meffre* (2014) as curator at the Deutsches Filminstitut und Filmmuseum in Frankfurt.

SOPHIA SERRANO is assistant curator at the Academy Museum of Motion Pictures, where she has curated exhibitions including *Significant Movies and Moviemakers: Lourdes Portillo* (2023), *The Art of Moviemaking: The Godfather* (2022), *Significant Movies and Moviemakers: Real Women Have Curves* (2021), and *Identity: Costume Design* (2021). Before joining the Academy Museum, she was a research assistant at the Getty Research Institute and a lecturer at Loyola Marymount University, where her courses focused on global cinema and political filmmaking. She completed her PhD in cinema and media studies at the University of Southern California.

SARAH STREET is professor of film at the University of Bristol, United Kingdom. Her publications include *Colour Films in Britain: The Negotiation of Innovation, 1900–55* (2012) and, co-edited with Simon Brown and Liz Watkins, *Color and the Moving Image: History, Theory, Aesthetics, Archive* and *British Colour Cinema: Practices and Theories* (both 2013). Her latest books are *Deborah Kerr* (2018); *Chromatic Modernity: Color, Cinema, and Media of the 1920s* (2019, co-authored with Joshua Yumibe); and *Colour Films in Britain: The Eastmancolor Revolution* (2021, co-authored with Keith M. Johnston, Paul Frith, and Carolyn Rickards).

KIRSTEN MOANA THOMPSON is professor and chair of the Film and Media Department at Seattle University, where she researches and teaches American, German, and Pacific film, with a particular focus on animation and color studies. She is co-editor of *Animation and Advertising* (2019) and *Perspectives on German Cinema* (1996), and also published *Apocalyptic Dread: American Film at the Turn of the Millennium* (2007) and *Crime Films: Investigating the Scene* (2007). She is currently working on three books: *Color, Visual Culture and American Cel Animation*; *Bubbles*; and *Animated America: Intermedial Promotion*.

JOSHUA YUMIBE is professor of film studies at Michigan State University. He is author of *Moving Color: Early Film, Mass Culture, Modernism* (2012); *Fantasia of Color in Early Cinema* (2015, co-authored with Giovanna Fossati, Tom Gunning, and Jonathon Rosen); and *Chromatic Modernity: Color, Cinema, and Media of the 1920s* (2019, co-authored with Sarah Street), which won the Katherine Singer Kovács Book Award (2020) and the Michael Nelson Prize, International Association for Media and History (2021). Yumibe is an editor of *Screen* and of the Contemporary Film Directors series at University of Illinois Press.

LENDERS TO THE EXHIBITION

20th Century Studios
American Society of Cinematographers
Center for Visual Music, Los Angeles
La Cinémathèque Française, Paris
Deutches Filminstitut and Filmmuseum, Frankfurt, Germany
Edko Films Limited
George Eastman Museum, Rochester, NY
The Len Lye Foundation, New Plymouth, New Zealand
Lilies Films
Los Angeles County Museum of Art
Margaret Herrick Library, Academy of Motion Picture Arts and Sciences, Los Angeles
The Collection of Motion Picture Costume Design: Larry McQueen
Museum of Pop Culture, Seattle, WA
NBCUniversal Archives & Collections
Paramount Pictures Corporation
Picture Shop
Pixar Animation Studios
Martin Scorsese Collection, New York
Sony Pictures Entertainment
Steven Spielberg
United American Costume
Walt Disney Animation Studios and the Walt Disney Animation Library, Burbank, CA
The Walt Disney Company
Warner Bros. Discovery Global Archives and Preservation Services
Western Costume Company

ILLUSTRATION CREDITS

The photographs and film images in this book are reproduced with permission. Every reasonable effort has been made to identify and contact the rights holders or their representatives. The publishers would appreciate notification about errors or omissions so these may be corrected in subsequent editions.

Unless otherwise noted, all photographs of archival film prints are courtesy of Barbara Flueckiger and the *Timeline of Historical Film Colors* (filmcolors.org).

Courtesy of A24 Films: 161 bottom, 164–75

© ABC Pictures Corp. and Warner Bros. Entertainment: 180–85

Courtesy of Academy Film Archive: 54 middle right (photo by Barbara Flueckiger)

© Alcon Entertainment, Warner Bros. Entertainment, and Columbia Pictures Industries: 94–103

Courtesy of Amazon Content Services: 72, 79 right

BFI National Archive: frontispiece, 2, 51 middle, 247, 250 bottom (photos by Olivia Kristina Stutz), 255 bottom (photo by Joëlle Kost)

© Block 2 Pictures and Jet Tone Contents: 82–93

Bundesarchiv-Filmarchiv: 252 middle (photo by Olivia Kristina Stutz)

Bundesarchiv-Filmarchiv © Friedrich Wilhelm Murnau Foundation: 59 top left and middle (photos by Barbara Flueckiger), 59 top right (photo by Michelle Beutler)

Collection-Restoration CNC: 128, 132 bottom

© Center for Visual Music: front endpaper, 136 top, 220–22, 227, 232–37, 244–45

Courtesy of Center for Visual Music: 136 bottom (photo by Ted Nemeth), 229 top

Courtesy of Chicago Film Society: 140–51

La Cinémathèque Française, Paris © Friedrich Wilhelm Murnau Foundation: 51 top right (photo by Barbara Flueckiger)

Courtesy La Cinémathèque Française, Paris: 51 bottom (photo by Barbara Flueckiger), 57 left (photo by Stéphane Dabrowski)

Cineteca di Bologna: 48 bottom, 248 top (photos by Barbara Flueckiger)

Courtesy of Cohen Film Collection and Geechee: 152–56

The Collections of The Henry Ford: 229 bottom

DEFA Foundation: 255 top (photo by Josephine Diecke)

Deutsches Filminstitut: 54 middle left, 253 bottom (photos by Barbara Flueckiger)

© Disney: 201–10, 212 top, 217 top, 218, 231 top, 240–41

Courtesy of The Estate of Barbara Hammer and Electronic Arts Intermix, New York: 139

Eye Filmmuseum: 24, 28–29, 34–37, 40, 44–45 (multispectral scans by Scan2Screen); 48 middle, 59 middle and bottom, 61, 115 top (photos by Barbara Flueckiger); 248 bottom, 254 (photos by Olivia Kristina Stutz)

Courtesy of GP Archives: 249 bottom

© GPO, courtesy of BFI National Archive: 238–39

© General Film Distribution: 76 left

Courtesy of the George Eastman Museum: 22–23, 56, 115 bottom (photos by Barbara Flueckiger); 52 bottom; 54 top, 250 middle (photos by Olivia Kristina Stutz)

Gert Koshofer Collection: 52 top, 251 bottom (photos by Barbara Flueckiger)

Courtesy of IFC Films: 231 bottom

© Les Films du Bal, Cinekap, Frakas Productions, Arte France Cinema, and Canal+ International: 161 middle, 163

Library of Congress: 18–21, 25–27, 30–31, 38–39, 41–43 (multispectral scans by Scan2Screen); 48 top, 54 bottom, back endpaper verso (photos by Barbara Flueckiger); 114 top (photo by Olivia Kristina Stutz)

Courtesy of Library of Congress/ Thunderbean: 215 right

Lichtspiel/Kinemathek Bern: front endpaper verso (photo by Barbara Flueckiger); 32–33 (multispectral scans by Scan2Screen)

Courtesy Lions Gate Films: 186–95

Los Angeles County Museum of Art, Kurt J. Wagner, M.D. and C. Kathleen Wagner Collection (M.87.294.47) © Museum Associates/LACMA: 74

Courtesy of Callum MacDonald: 130

Courtesy of Margaret Herrick Library, Academy of Motion Picture Arts and Sciences: 3–14, 64 top, 135 top, 212 bottom, 217 bottom, 229 middle; 250 top, 251 top (photos by Barbara Flueckiger)

© Kerry James Marshall, courtesy of the artist and Jack Shainman Gallery, New York: 159

Mary Elizabeth Hallock Greenewalt papers (0867), Volume 20, DAMS #11779, Historical Society of Pennsylvania, Collection of the Historical Society of Pennsylvania: 224 top

Courtesy of the Media History Digital Library: 215 left

Courtesy of NFDC-National Film Archive of India: 198, 202, 207

Courtesy of National Science and Media Museum: front cover, 46, 57 right, 252 top, 253 top (photos by Barbara Flueckiger); 248 middle (photo by Josephine Diecke and Joëlle Kost)

Courtesy of Paramount Pictures: 81

SODRE National Archive Museum of Image and Word © Friedrich Wilhelm Murnau Foundation: 16, 51 top left (photos by Barbara Flueckiger)

Shemaroo: 196, 201, 204

Courtesy of Andrew Stockman: 64 (bottom), 67

© Turner Entertainment Company: 76 right

Courtesy of UCLA Film and Television Archive: 114 bottom, 251 middle, 252 bottom (photos by Barbara Flueckiger)

© Universal Pictures and Touchstone Pictures: 71

Courtesy of Universal Studios Licensing: 104–13, 116–27, 161 top, back endpaper

Courtesy of Warner Bros. Discovery: 176

© Warner Bros. Entertainment: 62, 68, 79 left, 135 bottom, 231 middle, back cover

© James Whitney and Whitney Editions, Los Angeles: 242–43

Courtesy of Yale University Art Gallery: 224 bottom

INDEX

Page numbers in *italics* refer to illustrations.

This publication accompanies *Color in Motion: Chromatic Explorations of Cinema*, organized by Jessica Niebel and Sophia Serrano and presented at the Academy Museum of Motion Pictures, Los Angeles, October 6, 2024–July 13, 2025.

Color in Motion: Chromatic Explorations of Cinema is among more than sixty exhibitions and programs presented as part of PST ART. Returning in September 2024 with its latest edition, PST ART: *Art & Science Collide*, this landmark regional event explores the intersections of art and science, both past and present. PST ART is presented by Getty. For more information about PST ART: *Art & Science Collide*, please visit pst.art.

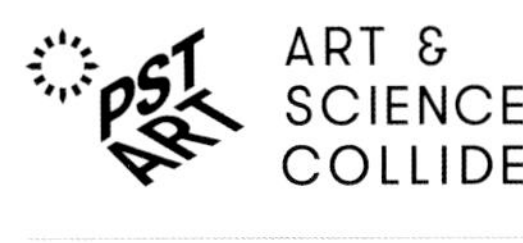

Presented by Getty

Generous support support also provided by the Alfred P. Sloan Foundation Program in Public Understanding of Science and Technology and the Los Angeles County Board of Supervisors through the Los Angeles County Department of Arts and Culture.

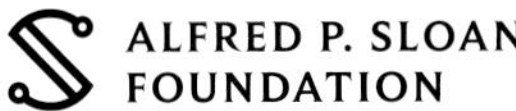

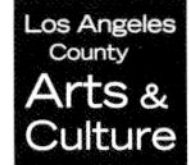

Additional support provided by Emma Koss.

Academy Museum Digital Engagement Platform sponsored by Bloomberg Philanthropies.

Bloomberg Philanthropies

Published in 2024 by the Academy Museum of Motion Pictures and DelMonico Books • D.A.P.

Academy Museum of Motion Pictures
6067 Wilshire Boulevard
Los Angeles, California 90036
academymuseum.org

DelMonico Books available through:
ARTBOOK | D.A.P.
75 Broad Street, Suite 630
New York, NY 10004
artbook.com
delmonicobooks.com

DESIGN BY Jessica Fleischmann / Still Room with assistance from Lauren Leung Cramer
EDITING BY Jane Hyun
PROOFREADING BY Dianne Woo
INDEXING BY Jane Friedman

Academy Museum of Motion Pictures
DIRECTOR OF PUBLICATIONS Stacey Allan
SENIOR EDITOR Chelsea Bingham
EDITORIAL MANAGER Madeleine Heppermann
SENIOR PUBLICATIONS COORDINATOR Lars Eckstrom

DelMonico Books
PUBLISHER Mary DelMonico
DIRECTOR OF PRODUCTION Karen Farquhar

COLOR SEPARATIONS BY Echelon, Los Angeles

PRINTED AND BOUND IN China

ISBN 978-1-63681-130-7
LCCN: 2024937025

FRONT COVER *La Biche au bois* (France, 1896, dir. Georges Demeny)
FRONT ENDPAPER *Allegretto* (USA, 1936–43, dir. Oskar Fischinger)
FRONT ENDPAPER (VERSO) *Gaumont News* (*Gaumont Actualités*, France, 1926)
FRONTISPIECE *Loïe Fuller* (France, 1905)
BACK ENDPAPER (RECTO) *The Serpentine Dance* (USA, ca. 1894, dir. William Kennedy Dickson)
BACK ENDPAPER *Vertigo* (USA, 1958, dir. Alfred Hitchcock)
BACK COVER *2001: A Space Odyssey* (USA/UK, 1968, dir. Stanley Kubrick)

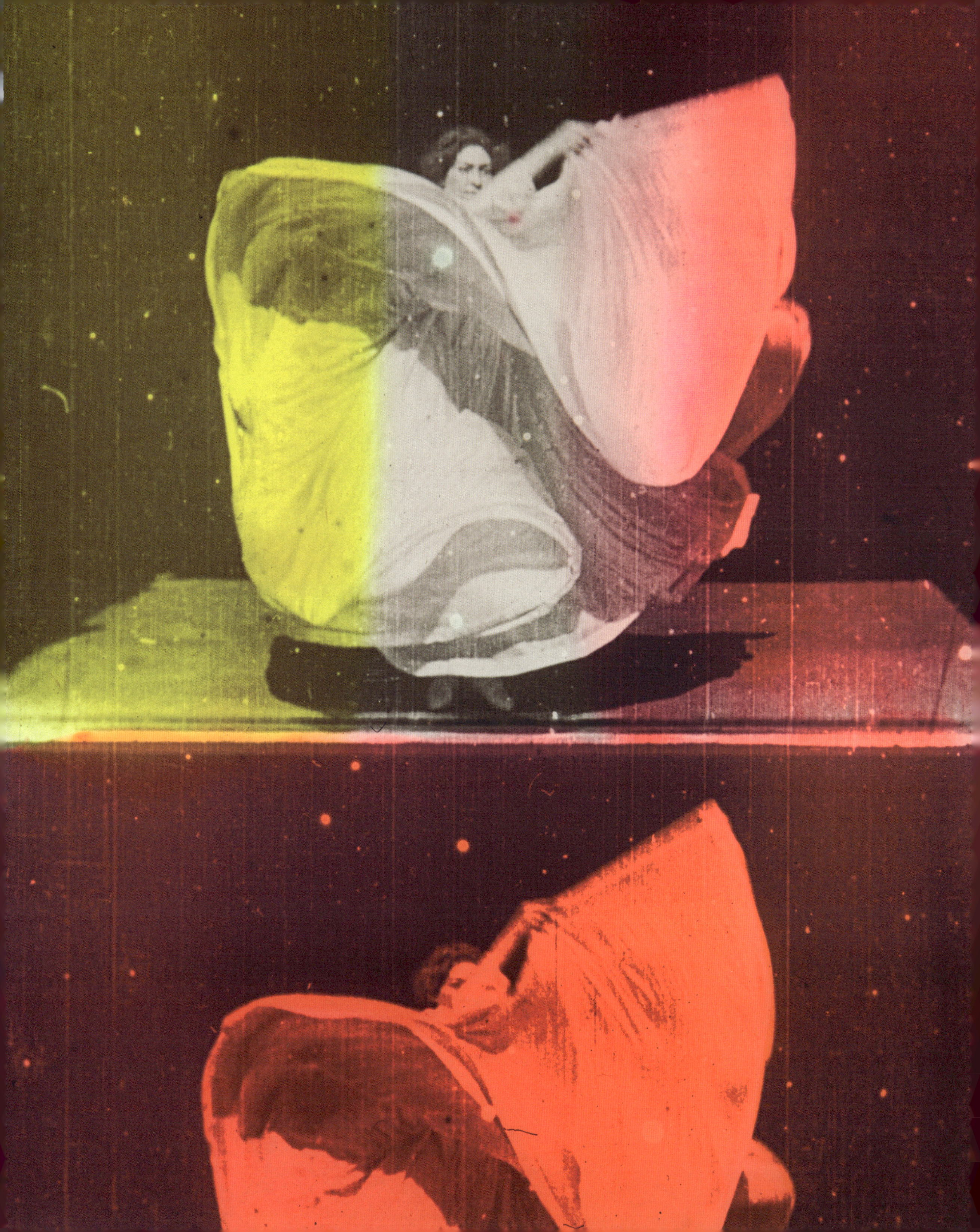

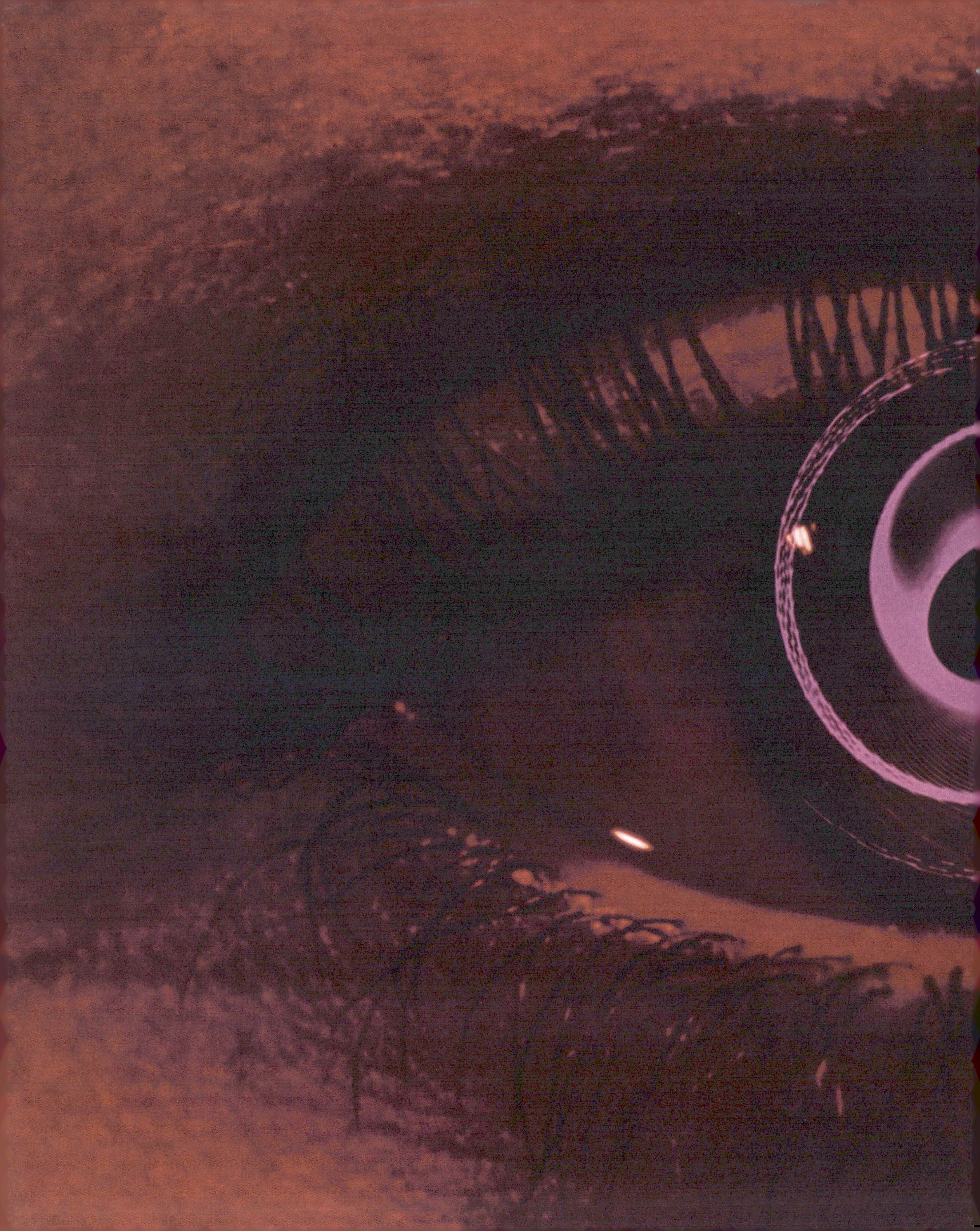